EXPLORING MICROSOFT® OFFICE PROFESSIONAL

Robert T. Grauer

Maryann Barber

University of Miami

Prentice Hall, Englewood Cliffs, New Jersey 07632

Library of Congress Cataloging in Publication Data

Grauer, Robert T., 1945–
    Exploring Microsoft Office Professional / Robert T. Grauer,
  Maryann Barber.
        p.   cm.
    Includes index.
    ISBN 0-13-399676-X
    1. Microsoft Office professional.   2. Microsoft Word (Computer file)
3. Microsoft Excel (Computer file)   4. Microsoft PowerPoint (Computer file)
5. Microsoft Mail.   6. Microsoft Access.   7. Word processing—Computer programs.
8. Business—Computer programs.   9. Electronic spreadsheets.   10. Business
presentations—Graphic methods—Computer programs.   11. Electronic mail systems.
I. Barber, Maryann.   II. Title.
HF5548.4.M525G7 1996
650′.0285′5369—dc20   95-19200
                    CIP

Acquisitions editor: Carolyn Henderson
Editorial / production supervisor: Katherine Evancie
Interior and cover design: Suzanne Behnke
Manufacturing buyer: Paul Smolenski
Developmental editor: Harriet Serenkin
Production coordinator: Renee Pelletier
Editorial assistant: Audrey Regan

©1996 by Prentice Hall, Inc.
A Simon & Schuster Company
Englewood Cliffs, New Jersey 07632

Printed in the United States of America
10   9   8   7   6   5

ISBN 0-13-399676-X

Prentice Hall International (UK) Limited, *London*
Prentice Hall of Australia Pty. Limited, *Sydney*
Prentice Hall of Canada Inc., *Toronto*
Prentice Hall Hispanoamericano, S.A., *Mexico*
Prentice Hall of India Private Limited, *New Delhi*
Prentice Hall of Japan, Inc., *Tokyo*
Simon & Schuster Asia Pte. Ltd., *Singapore*
Editora Prentice Hall do Brasil, Ltda., *Rio de Janeiro*

Contents

Preface   xi

WORD FOR WINDOWS

1

Word for Windows: What Will Word Processing Do for Me?   1

CHAPTER OBJECTIVES   1
OVERVIEW   1
The Windows Desktop   2
    Common User Interface   3
Word for Windows   5
Working in Windows   7
    The Mouse   7   Pull-down Menus   8   Dialog Boxes   9   On-line Help   10
The Basics of Word Processing   13
    Insertion Point   13   Toggle Switches   13   Insertion versus Overtype   13
    Deleting Text   14   Word Wrap   15
Learning by Doing   16
HANDS-ON EXERCISE 1: CREATING A DOCUMENT   17
Troubleshooting   22
HANDS-ON EXERCISE 2: RETRIEVING A DOCUMENT   23
Summary   28
Key Words and Concepts   29
Multiple Choice   29
Exploring Word   32
Case Studies   37

2

Gaining Proficiency: Editing and Formatting   39

CHAPTER OBJECTIVES   39
OVERVIEW   39
Select Then Do   40
Moving and Copying Text   41

Undo and Redo Commands 41

Find and Replace Commands 42

Save Command 43
    Backup Options 43

Scrolling 45

View Menu 46

HANDS-ON EXERCISE 1: EDITING 48

Typography 56
    Typeface 56   Type Size 57   TrueType 58

Format Font Command 59

Page Setup Command 60
    Page Breaks 60

An Exercise in Design 61

HANDS-ON EXERCISE 2: CHARACTER FORMATTING 61

Paragraph Formatting 67
    Alignment 67   Tabs 68   Indents 69

Format Paragraph Command 71
    Borders and Shading 72

HANDS-ON EXERCISE 3: PARAGRAPH FORMATTING 73

Summary 81

Key Words and Concepts 81

Multiple Choice 82

Exploring Word 84

Case Studies 88

3

The Tools: Preparing a Résumé and Cover Letter 91

CHAPTER OBJECTIVES 91

OVERVIEW 91

The Spelling Checker 92
    AutoCorrect 94

Thesaurus 95

Grammar Checker 96

Learning by Doing 98
    The Insert Date Command 101   The Insert Symbol Command 102

Creating an Envelope 102

HANDS-ON EXERCISE 1: PROOFING A DOCUMENT 103

Wizards and Templates 110

HANDS-ON EXERCISE 2: WIZARDS AND TEMPLATES 112

Mail Merge 118
    Implementation in Word 121

HANDS-ON EXERCISE 3: MAIL MERGE 122

Finer Points of Mail Merge   129

Summary   130

Key Words and Concepts   130

Multiple Choice   131

Exploring Word   133

Case Studies   137

MICROSOFT EXCEL

1

Introduction to Microsoft Excel: What Is a Spreadsheet?   1

CHAPTER OBJECTIVES   1
OVERVIEW   1
The Windows Desktop   2
    Common User Interface   3
Working in Windows   5
    The Mouse   5   Pull-down Menus   6   Dialog Boxes   7   On-line Help   9
Introduction to Spreadsheets   11
    The Professor's Grade Book   12   Row and Column Headings   13   Formulas and Constants   14
Microsoft Excel   14
Learning by Doing   16
HANDS-ON EXERCISE 1: INTRODUCTION TO MICROSOFT EXCEL   16
Modifying the Worksheet   20
    Required Commands   22
Toolbars   22
The TipWizard   22
HANDS-ON EXERCISE 2: MODIFYING A WORKSHEET   24
Summary   30
Key Words and Concepts   31
Multiple Choice   31
Exploring Excel   33
Case Studies   39

2

Gaining Proficiency: Copying, Moving, and Formatting   41

CHAPTER OBJECTIVES   41

OVERVIEW 41

A Better Grade Book 42

Cell Ranges 43

Copy Command 43

Move Command 44

Learning by Doing 46

HANDS-ON EXERCISE 1: CREATING A WORKSHEET 46

Formatting 52
    Column Widths 53   Row Heights 54

Format Cells Command 54
    Numeric Formats 54   Alignment 56   Fonts 56   Borders, Patterns, and
    Shading 57

Variations in Printing 57
    Page Setup Command 58   Print Preview Command 59

HANDS-ON EXERCISE 2: FORMATTING A WORKSHEET 62

A Word of Caution 70

Summary 71

Key Words and Concepts 72

Multiple Choice 72

Exploring Excel 74

Case Studies 79

3

Spreadsheets in Decision Making: What If? 81

CHAPTER OBJECTIVES 81
OVERVIEW 81

Analysis of a Car Loan 82
    The PMT Function 84

Home Mortgages 84
    Relative versus Absolute Addresses 86

The Power of Excel 87
    The Fill Handle 87   Pointing 88   The Function Wizard 88

HANDS-ON EXERCISE 1: MORTGAGE ANALYSIS 89

The Grade Book Revisited 95
    Statistical Functions 96   Arithmetic Expressions versus Functions 97
    IF Function 98   Table Lookup Function 100   Date Functions and Date
    Arithmetic 101   Scrolling 102   Freezing Panes 103

The Autofill Capability 104

HANDS-ON EXERCISE 2: EXPANDED GRADE BOOK 105

Summary 112

Key Words and Concepts 113

Multiple Choice 113

Exploring Excel   115
Case Studies   122

4

Graphs and Charts: Delivering a Message   125

CHAPTER OBJECTIVES   125
OVERVIEW   125
Chart Types   126
    Pie Charts   127   Column and Bar Charts   129
Creating a Chart   131
    The ChartWizard   133   Enhancing a Chart   135
HANDS-ON EXERCISE 1: THE CHARTWIZARD   136
Multiple Data Series   145
    Rows versus Columns   146
HANDS-ON EXERCISE 2: MULTIPLE DATA SERIES   148
Object Linking and Embedding   155
HANDS-ON EXERCISE 3: OBJECT LINKING AND EMBEDDING   156
Additional Chart Types   163
    Line Chart   163   Combination Chart   164
Use and Abuse of Charts   164
    Improper (omitted) Labels   165   Adding Dissimilar Quantities   166
Summary   168
Key Words and Concepts   168
Multiple Choice   168
Exploring Excel   170
Case Studies   176

MICROSOFT ACCESS®

1

Introduction to Microsoft Access: What Is a Database?   1

CHAPTER OBJECTIVES   1
OVERVIEW   1
The Windows Desktop   2
Working in Windows   3
    The Mouse   3   Pull-down Menus   5   Dialog Boxes   5   On-line Help   7
Introduction to Access   10
    The Database Window   10
Case Study: The College Bookstore   10
Tables   11

Learning by Doing   13

HANDS-ON EXERCISE 1: INTRODUCTION TO MICROSOFT ACCESS   14

Maintaining the Database   20
    Data Validation   20

Forms, Queries, and Reports   21

HANDS-ON EXERCISE 2: MAINTAINING THE DATABASE   22

Looking Ahead: A Relational Database   29

Summary   31

Key Words and Concepts   32

Multiple Choice   33

Exploring Access   35

Case Studies   40

2

Tables and Forms: Design, Properties, Views, and Wizards   43

CHAPTER OBJECTIVES   43
OVERVIEW   43

Case Study: A Student Database   44
    Include the Necessary Data   45   Store Data in Its Smallest Parts   45
    Avoid Calculated Fields   46

Creating a Table   46
    Data Types   46   Primary Key   47   Views   47   Field Properties   49

HANDS-ON EXERCISE 1: CREATING A TABLE   49

Forms   57
    Form Wizard   58

HANDS-ON EXERCISE 2: CREATING A FORM   59

Command Buttons and Combo Boxes   65

HANDS-ON EXERCISE 3: CUSTOMIZING A FORM   67

Summary   74

Key Words and Concepts   75

Multiple Choice   75

Exploring Access   77

Case Studies   83

3

Information from the Database: Reports and Queries   85

CHAPTER OBJECTIVES   85
OVERVIEW   85

Reports 86
    Anatomy of a Report 86
Apply What You Know 89
    Controls 90
Hands-on Exercise 1: The Report Wizard 90
Introduction to Queries 97
    Query Window 99   Data Type 99   Selection Criteria 100
Hands-on Exercise 2: Creating a Select Query 102
Group/Total Reports 108
Hands-on Exercise 3: Creating a Group/Total Report 110
Summary 117
Key Words and Concepts 118
Multiple Choice 118
Exploring Access 120
Case Studies 126

MICROSOFT® POWERPOINT®

1

Introduction to PowerPoint: Presentations Made Easy 1

CHAPTER OBJECTIVES 1
OVERVIEW 1
Introduction to PowerPoint 2
The Presentation Window 2
    Toolbars 5
Learning by Doing 5
Hands-on Exercise 1: Introduction to PowerPoint 5
Five Different Views 13
    Adding and Deleting Slides 13
Hands-on Exercise 2: PowerPoint Views 16
On-line Help 23
Presentation Hints 24
Hands-on Exercise 3: Rehearsing the Presentation 26
Summary 30
Key Words and Concepts 30
Multiple Choice 30
Exploring PowerPoint 32

2

Creating a Presentation: Wizards, Templates, and Masters 39

CHAPTER OBJECTIVES 39
OVERVIEW 39
Creating a Presentation 40
    The Outline View 40   AutoContent Wizard 42   Pick a Look Wizard 43
HANDS-ON EXERCISE 1: CREATING A PRESENTATION 45
Modifying a Presentation 53
    Color Scheme 53   Changing the Background Shading 55
Creating a Slide Show 57
HANDS-ON EXERCISE 2: SLIDE SHOWS, COLOR SCHEMES, AND BACKGROUNDS 58
PowerPoint Masters 64
HANDS-ON EXERCISE 3: MASTER AND CUE CARDS 65
Summary 69
Key Words and Concepts 70
Multiple Choice 70
Exploring PowerPoint 71

OLE APPENDIX

Appendix A: Object Linking and Embedding 2.0: Sharing Data Among Programs 215

OVERVIEW 215
HANDS-ON EXERCISE 1: EMBEDDING 217
Linking 221
HANDS-ON EXERCISE 2: LINKING 223
Summary 228
Key Words and Concepts 228

Index I-1

Preface

Exploring Microsoft Office is one of several books (modules) in the Prentice Hall *Exploring Windows* series. Other modules include *WordPerfect 6.0, Word 6.0, Microsoft Excel 5.0, Windows 3.1, Access 2.0,* and *PowerPoint.* The books are independent of one another but possess a common design, pedagogy, and writing style intended to serve the application courses in both two- and four-year schools.

Each book in the series is suitable on a stand-alone basis for any course that teaches a specific application; alternatively, several modules can be bound together for a single course that teaches multiple applications. The introductory component, *Exploring Windows 3.1,* assumes no previous knowledge and includes an introductory section for those who have never used a computer.

The *Exploring Windows* series will appeal to students in a variety of disciplines including business, liberal arts, and the sciences. Each module has a consistent presentation that stresses the benefits of the Windows environment, especially the common user interface that performs the same task in identical fashion across applications. Each module emphasizes the benefits of multitasking, demonstrates the ability to share data between applications, and stresses the extensive on-line help facility to facilitate learning. Students are taught concepts, not just keystrokes or mouse clicks, with hands-on exercises in every chapter providing the necessary practice to master the material.

The *Exploring Windows* series is different from other books, both in scope and in the way the material is presented. Students learn by doing. Concepts are stressed and memorization is minimized. Shortcuts and other important Windows information are consistently highlighted in the many boxed tips that appear throughout the series. Every chapter contains an average of two directed exercises at the computer, but equally important are the less structured end-of-chapter problems that not only review the information but extend it as well. The end-of-chapter material is a distinguishing feature of the entire series, an integral part of the learning process, and a powerful motivational tool for students to learn and explore.

FEATURES AND BENEFITS

➤ *Exploring Microsoft Office* presents concepts, as well as keystrokes and mouse clicks, so that students learn the theory behind the applications. They are not just taught what to do but are provided with the rationale for why they are doing it, enabling them to apply the information to additional learning on their own.

➤ No previous knowledge is assumed on the part of the reader. A fast-paced introduction brings the reader or new user up to speed immediately.

➤ Practical information, beyond application-specific material, appears throughout the series. Students are cautioned about computer viruses and taught the importance of adequate backup. The *Exploring Windows* module, for example, teaches students to extend the warranty of a new computer and points out the advantages of a mail-order purchase.

➤ Problem solving and troubleshooting are stressed throughout the series. The authors are constantly anticipating mistakes that students may make and tell the reader how to recover from problems that invariably occur.

- Tips, tips, and more tips present application shortcuts in every chapter. Windows is designed for the mouse, but experienced users gravitate toward keyboard shortcuts once they have mastered basic skills. The series presents different ways to accomplish a given task, but in a logical and relaxed fashion.
- A unique Buying Guide in the introductory module presents a thorough introduction to PC hardware from the viewpoint of purchasing a computer. Students learn the subtleties in selecting a configuration—for example, how the resolution of a monitor affects its size, the advantages of a local bus, and the Intel CPU processor index.

ACKNOWLEDGMENTS

We want to thank the many individuals who helped bring this project to its successful conclusion. We are especially grateful to our editor at Prentice Hall, Carolyn Henderson, without whom the series would not have been possible, and to Harriet Serenkin, the development editor, whose vision helped shape the project. Gretchen Marx of Saint Joseph College produced an outstanding set of *Instructor Manuals*. Greg Hubit, Paul Smolenski, and Katherine Evancie took charge of production. Deborah Emry, our marketing manager at Prentice Hall, developed the innovative campaign that helped make the series a success.

We also want to acknowledge our reviewers, who through their comments and constructive criticism made this a far better book.

Lynne Band, *Middlesex Community College*
Stuart P. Brian, *Holy Family College*
Jerry Chin, *Southwest Missouri State University*
Dean Combellick, *Scottsdale Community College*
Paul E. Daurelle, *Western Piedmont Community College*
David Douglas, *University of Arkansas*
Raymond Frost, *Central Connecticut State University*
James Gips, *Boston College*
Wanda D. Heller, *Seminole Community College*
Ernie Ivey, *Polk Community College*
Jane King, *Everett Community College*
John Lesson, *University of Central Florida*
Alan Moltz, *Naugatuck Valley Technical Community College*
Nancy Monthofen, *Scottsdale Community College*
Delores Pusins, *Hillsborough Community College*
Gale E. Rand, *College Misericordia*
David Rinehard, *Lansing Community College*
Marilyn Salas, *Scottsdale Community College*
Sally Visci, *Lorain County Community College*
David Weiner, *University of San Francisco*
Jack Zeller, *Kirkwood Community College*

A final word of thanks to the unnamed students at the University of Miami who make it all worthwhile. And, most of all, thanks to you, our readers, for choosing this book. Please feel free to contact us with any comments and suggestions. We can be reached most easily on the Internet.

Robert T. Grauer
RGRAUER@UMIAMI.MIAMI.EDU

Maryann Barber
MBARBER@UMIAMI.MIAMI.EDU

Version 6.0

EXPLORING WORD FOR WINDOWS

Word for Windows: What Will Word Processing Do for Me?

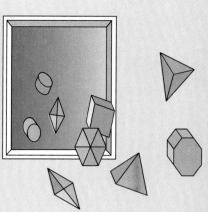

CHAPTER OBJECTIVES

After reading this chapter you will be able to:

1. Explain the concept of a common user interface and its advantage in learning a new application.
2. Describe the basic mouse operations; use a mouse and/or the equivalent keyboard shortcuts to select commands from a pull-down menu.
3. Discuss the function of a dialog box; describe the different types of dialog boxes and the various ways in which information is supplied.
4. Explain the functions of the minimize and maximize or restore buttons; describe the use of the scroll bar and its associated scroll box.
5. Access the on-line help facility and explain its various capabilities.
6. Define word wrap; differentiate between a hard and soft return.
7. Distinguish between the insertion and overtype modes; explain how to switch from one mode to the other.
8. Create, save, retrieve, edit, and print a simple document using Word for Windows.

OVERVIEW

H ave you ever produced what you thought was the perfect term paper only to discover that you omitted a sentence or misspelled a word, or that the paper was three pages too short or one page too long? Wouldn't it be nice to make the necessary changes, and then be able to reprint the entire paper with the touch of a key? Welcome to the world of word processing, where you are no longer stuck with having to retype anything. Instead, you retrieve your work from disk, display it on the monitor and revise it as necessary, then print it at any time, in draft or final form.

This chapter provides a broad-based introduction to word processing and *Word for Windows.* It begins, however, with a discussion of basic Windows concepts, applicable to Windows applications in general, and to Word for Windows in particular. The emphasis is on the common user interface and consistent command structure that facilitates learning within the Windows environment. Indeed, you may already know much of this material, but that is precisely the point; that is, once you know one Windows application, it is that much easier to learn the next.

The second half of the chapter presents (or perhaps reviews) essential concepts of word processing. The hands-on exercises at the conclusion of the chapter allow you to apply all of the material at the computer, and are indispensable to the learn-by-doing philosophy we follow throughout the text.

THE WINDOWS DESKTOP

The *desktop* is the centerpiece of Microsoft Windows and is analogous to the desk on which you work. There are physical objects on your real desk and there are *windows* (framed rectangular areas) and *icons* (pictorial symbols) displayed on the Windows desktop. The components of a window are explained within the context of Figure 1.1, which contains the opening Windows screen on our computer.

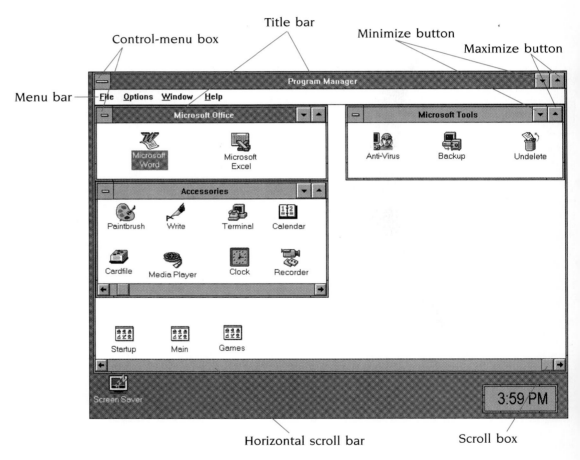

FIGURE 1.1 Program Manager

Your desktop may be different from ours, just as your real desk is arranged differently from that of your friend. You can expect, however, to see a window titled Program Manager. You may or may not see other windows within Program Manager such as the Accessories, Microsoft Tools, and Microsoft Office windows shown in Figure 1.1.

Program Manager is crucial to the operation of Windows. It starts automatically when Windows is loaded and it remains active the entire time you are working in Windows. Closing Program Manager closes Windows. Program Manager is in essence an organizational tool that places applications in groups (e.g., Microsoft Office), then displays those groups as windows or group icons.

Regardless of the windows that are open on your desktop, every window contains the same basic elements: a title bar, control-menu box, and buttons to minimize and to maximize or restore the window. The *title bar* displays the name of the window—for example, Microsoft Office in Figure 1.1. The *control-menu box* accesses a pull-down menu that lets you select operations relevant to the window. The *maximize button* enlarges the window so that it takes the entire desktop. The *minimize button* reduces a window to an icon (but keeps the program open in memory). A *restore button* (a double arrow not shown in Figure 1.1) appears after a window has been maximized and returns the window to its previous size (the size before it was maximized).

Other elements, which may or may not be present, include a horizontal and/or vertical scroll bar and a menu bar. A horizontal (vertical) *scroll bar* will appear at the bottom (right) border of a window when the contents of the window are not completely visible. The *scroll box* appears within the scroll bar to facilitate moving within the window. A *menu bar* is found in the window for Program Manager, but not in the other windows. This is because Program Manager is a different kind of window, an application window rather than a document window.

An *application window* contains a program (application). A *document window* holds data for a program and is contained within an application window. The distinction between application and document windows is made clearer when we realize that Program Manager is a program and requires access to commands contained in pull-down menus located on the menu bar.

MICROSOFT TOOLS

The Microsoft Tools group is created automatically when you install (or upgrade to) MS-DOS 6.0. The name of each icon (Antivirus, Backup, and Undelete) is indicative of its function, and each program is an important tool in safeguarding your data. The Antivirus program allows you to scan disks for known viruses (and remove them when found). The Backup utility copies files from the hard disk to one or more floppy disk(s) in case of hard disk failure. The Undelete program allows you to recover files that you accidentally erased from a disk.

Common User Interface

One of the most significant benefits of the Windows environment is the *common user interface,* which provides a sense of familiarity when you begin to learn a new application. All applications work basically the same way. Hence, once you know one Windows application, even one as simple as the Paintbrush accessory, it will be that much easier for you to learn Word for Windows. In similar fashion, it will take you less time to learn Excel once you know Word, because both applications share a common menu structure with consistent ways to select commands from those menus.

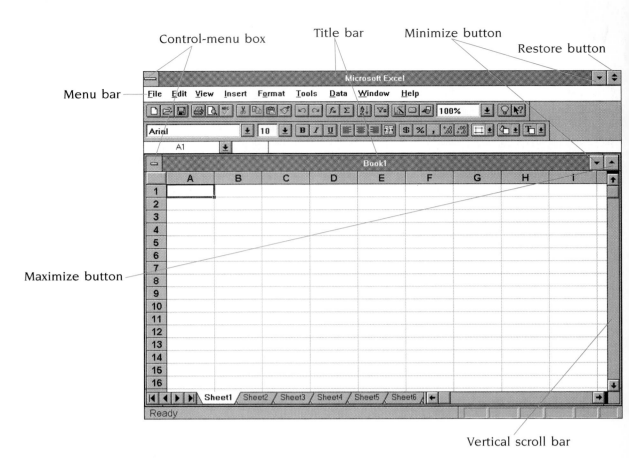

Control-menu box   Title bar   Minimize button

Restore button

Menu bar

Maximize button

Vertical scroll bar

(a) Microsoft Excel Version 5.0

FIGURE 1.2   Common User Interface

Consider, for example, Figures 1.2a and 1.2b, containing windows for Excel and Word, respectively. The applications are very different, yet the windows have many characteristics in common. You might even say that they have more similarities than differences, a remarkable statement considering the programs accomplish very different tasks. A document window (Book1) is contained within the application window for Excel. In similar fashion, a document window (Document1) is present within the application window for Word.

The application windows for Excel and Word contain the same elements as any other application window: a title bar, menu bar, and control-menu box; and minimize and maximize or restore buttons. The menu bars are almost identical; that is, the File, Edit, View, Insert, Format, Tools, Window, and Help menus are present in both applications. (The only difference between the menu bars is that Excel has a Data menu whereas Word has a Table menu.)

The commands within the menus are also consistent in both applications. The File menu contains the commands to open and close a file, the Edit menu has commands to cut, copy, and paste text, and so on. The means for accessing the pull-down menus are also consistent; that is, click the menu name (see mouse basics later in the chapter) or press the Alt key plus the underlined letter of the menu name—for example, Alt+F to pull down the File menu.

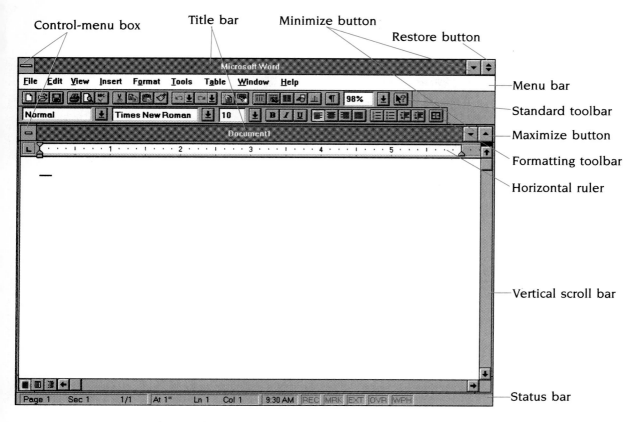

(b) Word for Windows Version 6.0

FIGURE 1.2 Common User Interface (continued)

WORD FOR WINDOWS

We concentrate on the *Word for Windows* screen in Figure 1.2b. Do not be concerned if your screen is different from ours because you can change it to suit your personal preferences. What is important is that you recognize the basic elements in the Word Window, which include toolbars, the ruler, and the status bar.

Toolbars provide immediate access to common commands. Seven built-in toolbars are available, two of which are shown in the figure. The toolbars can be displayed or hidden by using the View menu as described in the hands-on exercises later in the chapter.

The *Standard toolbar* appears immediately below the menu bar and contains buttons for the most basic commands in Word, such as opening and closing a file, printing a document, and so on. The *Formatting toolbar,* under the Standard toolbar, provides access to various formatting operations such as boldface, italics, or underlining. (Toolbars are also present in the Excel window. Many of the buttons are the same in both applications.)

The toolbars may at first appear overwhelming, but there is absolutely no need to memorize what the individual buttons do. That will come with time. We suggest, however, that you will have a better appreciation for the various buttons if you consider them in groups according to their general function as shown in Figure 1.3.

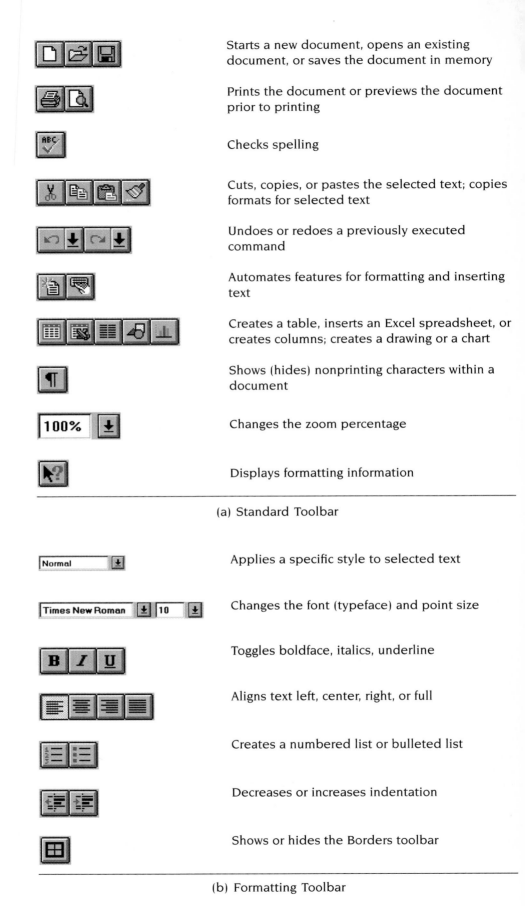

Starts a new document, opens an existing document, or saves the document in memory

Prints the document or previews the document prior to printing

Checks spelling

Cuts, copies, or pastes the selected text; copies formats for selected text

Undoes or redoes a previously executed command

Automates features for formatting and inserting text

Creates a table, inserts an Excel spreadsheet, or creates columns; creates a drawing or a chart

Shows (hides) nonprinting characters within a document

Changes the zoom percentage

Displays formatting information

(a) Standard Toolbar

Applies a specific style to selected text

Changes the font (typeface) and point size

Toggles boldface, italics, underline

Aligns text left, center, right, or full

Creates a numbered list or bulleted list

Decreases or increases indentation

Shows or hides the Borders toolbar

(b) Formatting Toolbar

FIGURE 1.3   Toolbars

The *horizontal ruler* is displayed underneath the toolbars and enables you to change margins, tabs, and indents for all or part of a document. A *vertical ruler* (not shown in the figure) shows the vertical position of text on the page.

The *status bar* at the bottom of the figure displays information about the document. It also shows the status (settings) of various indicators, such as OVR to show that the Word is in the overtype (as opposed to the insertion) mode as explained later in the chapter.

WORKING IN WINDOWS

The next several pages take you through the basic operations common to Windows applications in general, and to Word for Windows in particular. You may already be familiar with much of this material, in which case you are already benefitting from the common user interface. We begin with the mouse and describe how it is used to access pull-down menus and to supply information in dialog boxes. We also emphasize the *on-line help* facility that is present in every Windows application.

The Mouse

The mouse (or track ball) is essential to Word as it is to all Windows applications, and you will need to be comfortable with its four basic actions:

➤ To *point* to an item, move the mouse pointer to the item.
➤ To *click* an item, point to it, then press and release the left mouse button. You can also click the right mouse button to display a shortcut menu with commands applicable to the item you are pointing to.
➤ To *double click* an item, point to it, then click the left mouse button twice in succession.
➤ To *drag* an item, move the pointer to the item, then press and hold the left button while you move the item to a new position.

The mouse is a pointing device—move the mouse on your desk and the *mouse pointer,* typically a small arrowhead, moves on the monitor. The mouse pointer assumes different shapes according to the nature of the current action. You will see a double arrow when you change the size of a window, an I-beam to insert text, a hand to jump from one help topic to the next, or a circle with a line through it to indicate that an attempted action is invalid.

The mouse pointer will also change to an hourglass to indicate Windows is processing your most recent command, and that no further commands may be issued until the action is completed. The more powerful your computer, the less frequently the hourglass will appear. Conversely, the less powerful your system, the more you will see the hourglass.

A right-handed person will hold the mouse in his or her right hand and click the left button. A left-handed person may want to hold the mouse in the left hand and click the right button. If this sounds complicated, it's not, and you can master the mouse with the on-line tutorial provided in Windows (see step 2 in the hands-on exercise on page 17).

Word is designed for a mouse, but it provides keyboard equivalents for almost every command, with toolbars and the ruler offering still other ways to accomplish the most frequent operations. You may at first wonder why there are so many different ways to do the same thing, but you will come to recognize the many options as part of Word's charm. The most appropriate technique depends on personal preference, as well as the specific situation.

If, for example, your hands are already on the keyboard, it is faster to use the keyboard equivalent. Other times, your hand will be on the mouse and that will be the fastest way. It is not necessary to memorize anything, nor should you even try; just be flexible and willing to experiment. The more you do, the easier it will be!

Pull-down Menus

Pull-down menus, such as those in Figure 1.4, are essential to all Windows applications. A pull-down menu is accessed by clicking the menu name (within the menu bar) or by pressing the Alt key plus the underlined letter in the menu name—for example, Alt+H to pull down the Help menu.

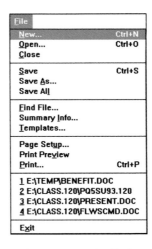
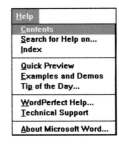

FIGURE 1.4 Pull-down menus

Menu options (commands) are executed by clicking the command once the menu has been pulled down or by pressing the underlined letter (e.g., press C to execute the Close command in the File menu). You can also bypass the menu entirely if you know the equivalent keystrokes shown to the right of the command in the menu (e.g., Ctrl+X, Ctrl+C, or Ctrl+V in the Edit menu to cut, copy, and paste text, respectively). A **dimmed command** (e.g., the Copy command within the Edit menu) indicates that the command is not currently executable; that is, some additional action has to be taken for the command to become available.

Many commands are followed by an **ellipsis** (. . .) to indicate that additional information is required to execute the command. For example, selection of the Find command in the Edit menu requires the user to specify the text to be found. The additional information is entered into a dialog box, which appears immediately after the command has been selected.

Dialog Boxes

A **dialog box** appears whenever additional information is needed to execute a command—that is, whenever a menu option is followed by an ellipsis. The information can be supplied in different ways, which in turn leads to different types of dialog boxes as shown in Figure 1.5.

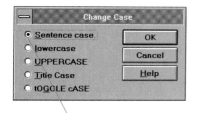

Option buttons indicate
mutually exclusive choices
(only one may be chosen)

(a) Option (radio) Buttons

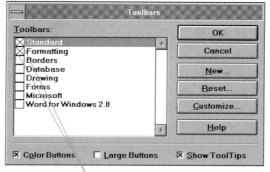

Options are not mutually
exclusive (more than one
may be chosen)

(b) Check Boxes

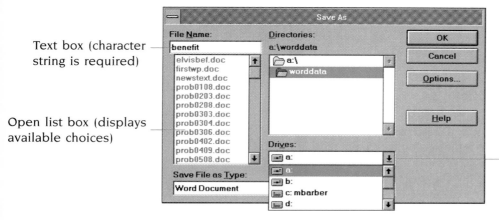

Text box (character
string is required)

Open list box (displays
available choices)

Drop-down list box (click
arrow to see choices)

(c) Text Boxes and List Boxes

FIGURE 1.5   Dialog Boxes

The **option (radio) buttons** in Figure 1.5a indicate mutually exclusive choices, one of which must be chosen; that is, you must choose Sentence case, lowercase, UPPERCASE, Title Case, or tOGGLE cASE. **Check boxes** are used instead of option buttons if the options are not mutually exclusive, that is, if several options can be selected at the same time such as the Standard and Formatting toolbars in Figure 1.5b. The individual options are selected (cleared) by clicking on the appropriate check box.

A **text box** indicates that a character string is required—for example, a file name in the text box of Figure 1.5c. Some text boxes are initially empty and display a flashing vertical bar to indicate the position of the insertion point for the text you will enter. Other text boxes already contain an entry, in which case you can click anywhere in the box to establish the insertion point and edit the entry.

An **open list box,** such as the list of file names or directories in Figure 1.5c, displays the available choices, any one of which is selected by clicking on the desired item. A **drop-down list box,** such as the list of available drives or file types, conserves space by showing only the current selection; click the arrow of a drop-down list box to produce a list of available options.

All three dialog boxes in Figure 1.5 contain one or more **command buttons** to initiate an action. The function of a command button should be apparent from its name. For example, Cancel returns to the previous screen with no action taken, OK accepts the information and closes the dialog box, and Help provides additional explanation.

On-line Help

Word for Windows provides extensive on-line help, which is accessed by pulling down the **Help menu** or by pressing the F1 function key. The Word for Windows Help menu was shown earlier in Figure 1.4 and contains the following choices:

Contents	Displays a list of help topics
Search for Help on . . .	Searches for help on a specific subject
Index	An alphabetical index of all Help topics
Quick Preview	Highlights new features in Word for Windows 6.0 and suggests tips for WordPerfect users coverting to Word
Examples and Demos	Demonstrates major features in Word
Tip of the day . . .	Accesses the Tip of the Day dialog box
WordPerfect Help . . .	Detailed help in converting from WordPerfect to Word
Technical Support	Describes the different types of technical support available
About Microsoft Word . . .	Indicates the specific release of Word you are using

The Contents command displays the window of Figure 1.6a and provides access to all elements within the Help facility. A Help window contains all of the elements found in any other application window: a title bar, minimize and maximize or restore buttons, a control-menu box, and optionally, a vertical and/or horizontal scroll bar. There is also a menu bar with additional commands made available through the indicated pull-down menus.

The **help buttons** near the top of the help window enable you to move around more easily; that is, you can click a button to perform the indicated function. The *Contents button* returns to the screen in Figure 1.6a from elsewhere within Help. The *Search button* produces the screen of Figure 1.6b and allows you to look for information on a specific topic. Type a key word in the text box, and the corresponding term will be selected within the upper list box. Double click the highlighted item to produce a list of available topics on that subject, then double

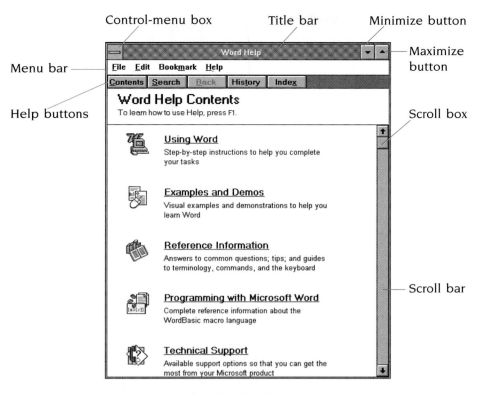

Control-menu box   Title bar   Minimize button

Menu bar

Help buttons

Maximize button

Scroll box

Scroll bar

(a) Opening Screen

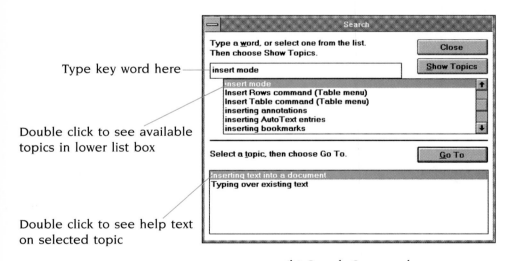

Type key word here

Double click to see available topics in lower list box

Double click to see help text on selected topic

(b) Search Command

FIGURE 1.6 Getting Help

click the topic you want in the lower list box to see the actual help text, such as the screen shown in Figure 1.6c.

The *Back button* returns directly to the previous help topic. The *History button* is more general as it displays a list of all topics selected within the current session and makes it easy to return to any of the previous topics. The *Index button* produces a window containing an alphabetical index of the Help topics.

The ***Tip of the Day*** in Figure 1.6d appears automatically whenever you start Word. The tip can also be accessed on demand by pulling down the Help menu and clicking Tip of the Day. You can see additional tips by clicking the appropriate command button.

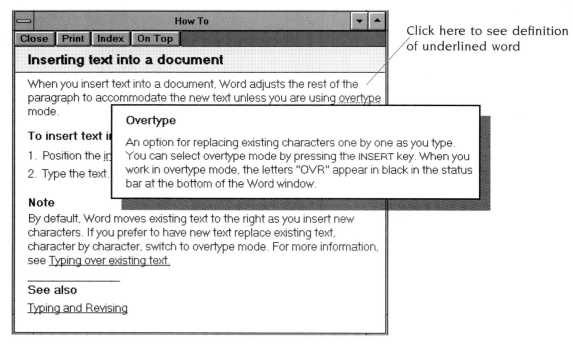

Click here to see definition of underlined word

(c) Help text

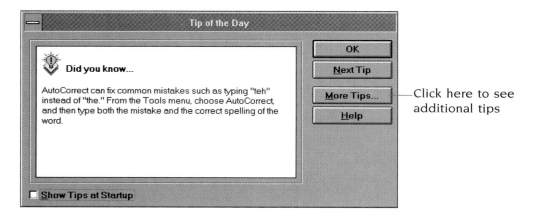

Click here to see additional tips

(d) Tip of the Day

FIGURE 1.6   Getting Help (continued)

ABOUT MICROSOFT WORD

About Microsoft Word on the Help menu displays information about the specific release of Word for Windows including the product serial number. Execution of the command produces a dialog box with a System Information command button; click the button to learn about the hardware installed on your system including the amount of memory and available space on the hard drive.

THE BASICS OF WORD PROCESSING

All word processors, be they DOS- or Windows-based, adhere to certain basic concepts that must be understood if you are to use the program effectively. The next several pages introduce ideas that are applicable to any word processor (and which you may already know). We follow the conceptual material with a hands-on exercise that gives you the opportunity to practice all that you have learned.

Insertion Point

The *insertion point* is a flashing vertical line that marks the place where text will be entered. The insertion point is always at the beginning of a new document, but it can be moved anywhere within an existing document. If, for example, you wanted to add text to the end of a document, you would move the insertion point to the end of the document, then begin typing. The *end-of-file marker* is the horizontal line that indicates the end of the document and beyond which the insertion point cannot be moved.

Toggle Switches

Suppose you sat down at the keyboard and typed an entire sentence without pressing the Shift key. The sentence would be in all lowercase letters. Then you pressed the Caps Lock key and retyped the sentence, again without pressing the Shift key. This time the sentence would be in all uppercase letters. You could repeat the process as often as you like. Each time you pressed the Caps Lock key, the sentence would switch from lowercase to uppercase and vice versa.

The point of this example is to introduce the concept of a *toggle switch,* a device that causes the computer to alternate between two states. The Caps Lock key is an example of a toggle switch; each time you press it, newly typed text will change from uppercase to lowercase and back again. We will see several other examples of toggle switches as we proceed in our discussion of word processing.

Insertion versus Overtype

Word for Windows is always in one of two modes, *insertion* or *overtype,* and uses a toggle switch (the Ins key) to alternate between the two. The status bar displays OVR when the overtype mode is in effect. The indicator is dim when the insertion mode is active, as was shown earlier in Figure 1.2.

Press the Ins key once and you switch from insertion to overtype; press the Ins key a second time and you go from overtype back to insertion. Text that is entered into a document during the insertion mode moves existing text to the right to accommodate the characters being added. Text entered from the overtype mode replaces (overtypes) existing text. Text is always entered or replaced immediately to the right of the insertion point.

The insertion mode is best when you enter text for the first time, but either mode can be used to make corrections. The insertion mode is the better choice when the correction requires you to add new text. The overtype mode is easier when you are substituting one character(s) for another. The difference is illustrated in Figure 1.7.

Figure 1.7a displays the text as it was originally entered, with two misspellings. The letters *se* have been omitted from the word *insertion*, whereas an *x* has been erroneously typed instead of an *r* in the word *overtype*. The insertion mode is used in Figure 1.7b to add the missing letters, which in turn moves the rest of the line to the right. The overtype mode is used in Figure 1.6c to replace the *x* with an *r*.

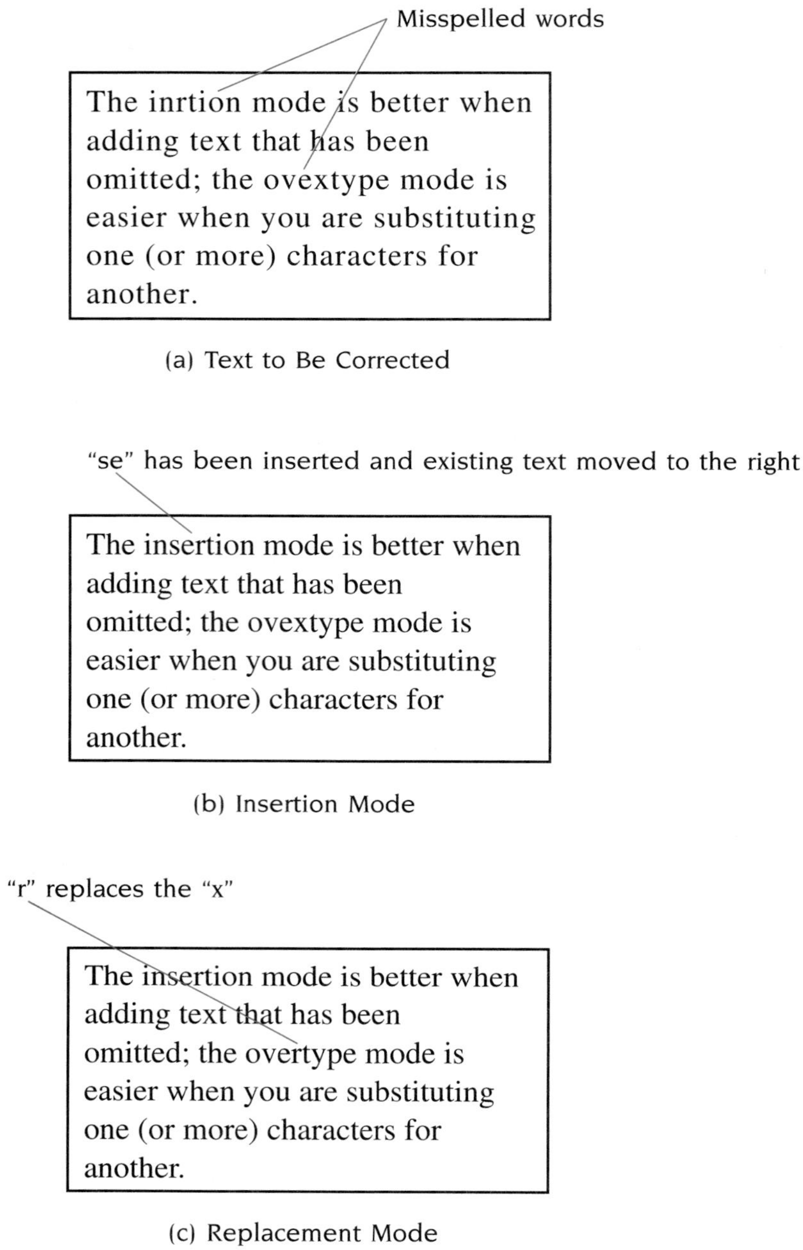

Misspelled words

The inrtion mode is better when
adding text that has been
omitted; the ovextype mode is
easier when you are substituting
one (or more) characters for
another.

(a) Text to Be Corrected

"se" has been inserted and existing text moved to the right

The insertion mode is better when
adding text that has been
omitted; the ovextype mode is
easier when you are substituting
one (or more) characters for
another.

(b) Insertion Mode

"r" replaces the "x"

The insertion mode is better when
adding text that has been
omitted; the overtype mode is
easier when you are substituting
one (or more) characters for
another.

(c) Replacement Mode

FIGURE 1.7   Insertion and Replacement Modes

Deleting Text

The backspace and Del keys delete one character immediately to the left or right
of the insertion point, respectively. The choice between them depends on when
you need to erase a character(s). The backspace key is easier if you want to delete
a character immediately after typing it. The Del key is preferable during subsequent editing.

You can delete a block of text by selecting it (i.e., dragging the mouse over
the text), then pressing the Del key. And finally, you can delete and replace text
in one operation by selecting the text to be replaced and then typing the new text
in its place.

THE UNDO COMMAND

The **Undo command** reverses the effect of the most recent operation and is invaluable at any time, but especially when text is accidentally deleted. Pull down the Edit menu and click Undo (or click the Undo button on the Standard toolbar).

Word Wrap

Newcomers to word processing have one major transition to make from a typewriter, and it is an absolutely critical adjustment. Whereas a typist returns the carriage at the end of every line, just the opposite is true of a word processor; that is, you type continually *without* pressing the enter key because the word processor automatically wraps text from one line to the next. This concept is known as *word wrap* and is illustrated in Figure 1.8.

The word *primitive* does not fit on the current line in Figure 1.8a, and is automatically shifted to the next line, *without* the user having to press the enter key. The user continues to enter the document with additional words being wrapped to subsequent lines as necessary. The only time you use the enter key is at the end of a paragraph, or when you want the cursor to move to the next line, and the end of the current line doesn't reach the right margin.

Word wrap is closely associated with another concept, that of hard and soft carriage returns. A **hard return** is created by the user when he or she presses the enter key at the end of a paragraph. A **soft return** is created by the word processor as it wraps text from one line to the next. The location of the soft returns changes automatically as a document is edited (e.g., as text is inserted or deleted, or as margins or fonts are changed). The location of the hard returns can be changed only by the user, who must intentionally insert or delete each hard return.

There are two hard returns in Figure 1.8b, one at the end of each paragraph. There are also seven soft returns in the first paragraph (one at the end of every line except the last) and four soft returns in the second paragraph. Now suppose the margins in the document are made smaller (that is, the line is made longer) as shown in Figure 1.8c. The number of soft returns drops to four and two (in the first and second paragraphs, respectively) as more text fits on a line and fewer lines are needed. The revised document still contains the two original hard returns, one at the end of each paragraph.

The original IBM PC was extremely pr	The original IBM PC was extremely primitive
primitive cannot fit on current line	primitive is automatically moved to next line

(a) Entering the Document

FIGURE 1.8 Word Wrap

The original IBM PC was extremely primitive (not to mention expensive) by current standards. The basic machine came equipped with only 16Kb RAM and was sold without a monitor or disk (a TV and tape cassette were suggested instead). The price of this powerhouse was $1565.¶

You could, however, purchase an expanded business system with 256Kb RAM, two 160Kb floppy drives, monochrome monitor, and 80-cps printer for $4425.¶

Hard return created by pressing the enter key

(b) Completed Document

The original IBM PC was extremely primitive (not to mention expensive) by current standards. The basic machine came equipped with only 16Kb RAM and was sold without a monitor or disk (a TV and tape cassette were suggested instead). The price of this powerhouse was $1565.¶

You could, however, purchase an expanded business system with 256Kb RAM, two 160Kb floppy drives, monochrome monitor, and 80-cps printer for $4425.¶

Hard returns in same position

(c) Completed Document

FIGURE 1.8   Word Wrap (continued)

LEARNING BY DOING

We believe strongly in learning by doing, and thus there comes a point where you must sit down at the computer if the discussion is to have real meaning. The exercises in this chapter are linked to one another in that you create a simple document in Exercise 1, then retrieve and edit that document in Exercise 2. The ability to save and retrieve a document is critical, and you do not want to spend an inordinate amount of time entering text, unless you are confident in your ability to retrieve it later.

The first exercise also introduces you to the data disk that accompanies this text and that can be used to store the documents you create. (Alternatively, you can store the documents on a hard disk if you have access to your own computer.) The data disk also contains a variety of documents that are used in the hands-on exercises throughout the text.

HANDS-ON EXERCISE 1:

Creating a Document

Objective To load Word for Windows, then create, save, and print a simple document. The exercise introduces you to the data disk that accompanies the text and reviews basic Windows operations: pull-down menus, dialog boxes, on-line help, and the use of a mouse. Use Figure 1.9 as a guide in doing the exercise.

Step 1: Load Windows
➤ Type **WIN** and press **enter** to load Windows if it is not already loaded.
➤ The appearance of your desktop will be different from ours, but it should resemble Figure 1.1 at the beginning of the chapter. You will most likely see a window containing Program Manager, but if not, you should see an icon titled Program Manager near the bottom of the screen; double click this icon to open the Program Manager window.

Step 2: Master the mouse
➤ A mouse is essential to the operation of Word as it is to all other Windows applications, and it is important that you master its operation. The easiest way to practice is with the mouse tutorial found in the Help menu of Windows itself.
➤ Click the **Help menu.** Click **Windows Tutorial.**
➤ Type **M** to begin, then follow the on-screen instructions.
➤ Exit the tutorial when you are finished.

Step 3: Install the data disk
➤ Do this step *only* if you have your own computer and want to copy the files from the data disk to the hard drive.
➤ Place the data disk in drive A (or whatever drive is appropriate).
➤ Pull down the **File menu.** Click **Run.**
➤ Type **A:INSTALL C** in the text box. Click **OK.** (The drive letters in the command, A and C, are both variable. If, for example, the data disk were in drive B and you wanted to copy its files to drive D, you would type the command **B:INSTALL D**)
➤ Follow the on-screen instructions.

Step 4: Load Word for Windows
➤ Double click the icon for the group containing Word for Windows—for example, Microsoft Office, if that group is not already open. Double click the Program icon for **Word** (or Microsoft Word).
➤ Click the **maximize button** (if necessary) so that the application window containing Word takes the entire screen as shown in Figure 1.9a.
➤ Do not be concerned if your screen is different from ours as we include a troubleshooting section immediately following this exercise.

Click here to return to your document

Clear the check box to cancel the tips upon loading Word

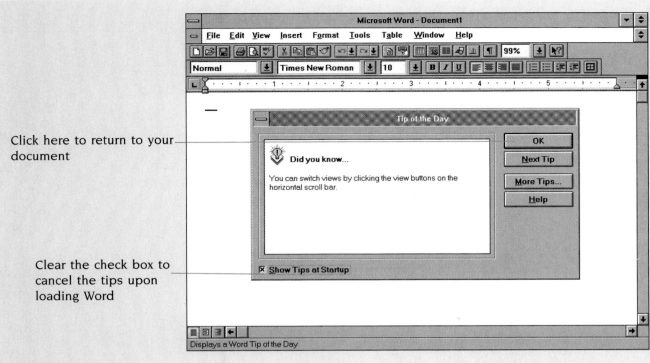

(a) Opening Word Screen with the Tip of the Day (steps 4 and 5)

FIGURE 1.9   Hands-on Exercise 1

DOUBLE CLICKING FOR BEGINNERS

If you are having trouble double clicking, it is because you are not clicking quickly enough, or more likely, because you are moving the mouse (however slightly) between clicks. Relax, hold the mouse firmly in place, and try again.

Step 5: Tip of the Day
➤ Word displays a tip of the day every time it is loaded. If you do not see a tip, pull down the **Help menu** and click **Tip of the Day.**
— To cancel the tips when you start Word, **clear** the box to **Show Tips at Startup.**
— To see a tip when you start Word, **click** the box to **Show Tips at Startup.**
➤ Click **OK** to begin working on your document.

Step 6: Create the document
➤ Create the document in Figure 1.9b by typing just as you would on a typewriter with one exception—do *not* press the enter key at the end of a line because Word will automatically wrap text from one line to the next.
➤ Press the **enter key** at the end of the paragraph.
➤ Proofread the document and correct any errors. Use the **Ins key** to toggle between the insertion and overtype mode as appropriate.

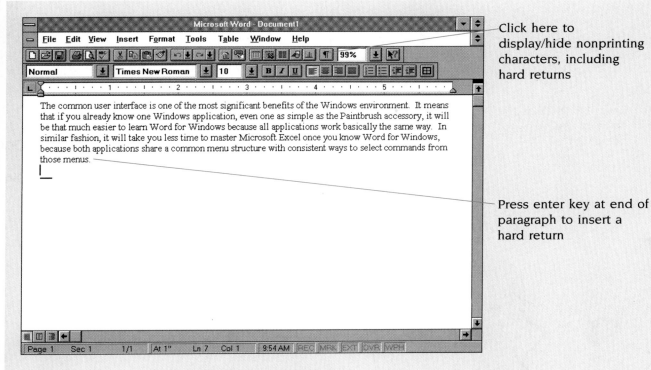

Click here to display/hide nonprinting characters, including hard returns

Press enter key at end of paragraph to insert a hard return

(b) Create the Document (step 6)

FIGURE 1.9 Hands-on Exercise 1 (continued)

DISPLAY THE HARD RETURNS

Click the Show/Hide button on the Standard Toolbar to display the hard returns (paragraph marks) and other nonprinting characters (such as tab characters or blank spaces) contained within a document. The Show/Hide button (denoted by the ¶ symbol indicating a hard return) functions as a toggle switch: the first time you click it, the hard returns are displayed, the second time you press it, the returns are hidden; and so on.

Step 7: Save the document

➤ Pull down the **File menu.** Click **Save.**

➤ Alternatively you can press **Alt+F** to pull down the File menu, then type the letter **S,** or you can click the **save button** on the Standard toolbar. Regardless of the technique you choose you should see the Save As dialog box in Figure 1.9c.

➤ Click the **drop-down list box** in the middle of the screen to specify the appropriate drive, drive C or drive A, depending on whether or not you installed the data disk in step 3.

➤ Scroll through the directory list box until you come to the **WORDDATA** directory. Double click this directory to make it the active directory.

➤ Click in the text box for File Name. Click and drag over DOC1.DOC, then type **BENEFIT** as the name of your document (the DOC extension is added automatically).

➤ Click **OK** or press the **enter key.**

Enter BENEFIT as the name of the document

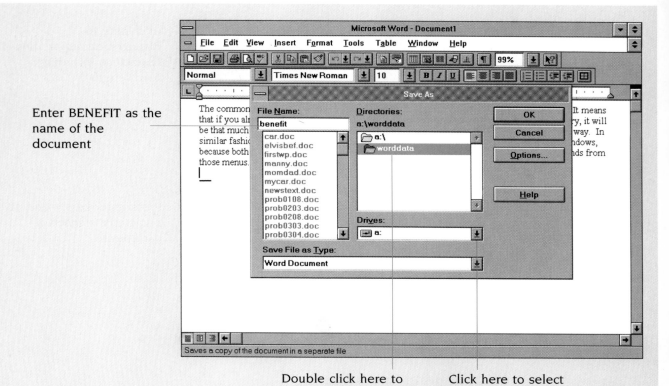

Double click here to select the WORDDATA subdirectory

Click here to select the drive

(c) The Save Command (step 7)

FIGURE 1.9 Hands-on Exercise 1 (continued)

LEARN TO TYPE

The ultimate limitation of any word processor is the speed at which you enter data; hence the ability to type quickly is invaluable. Learning how to type is far from an insurmountable problem, especially with the availability of computer-based typing programs. As little as a half hour a day for a couple of weeks will have you up to speed, and if you do any significant amount of writing at all, the investment will pay off many times.

Step 8: Print the document

➤ Pull down the **File menu.**

➤ Click **Print** to produce the dialog box of Figure 1.9d.

➤ Click the **OK** command button to print the document.

➤ You can also click the **Print icon** on the Standard toolbar to print the document without seeing the dialog box.

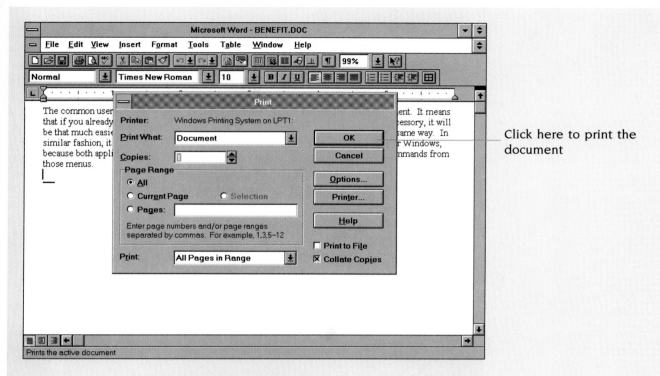

Click here to print the document

(d) The Print Command (step 8)

FIGURE 1.9 Hands-on Exercise 1 (continued)

EXECUTE COMMANDS QUICKLY

The fastest way to select a command from a pull-down menu is to point to the menu name, then drag the pointer (i.e., press and hold the left mouse button) to the desired command and release the mouse. The command is executed when you release the button.

Step 9: Exit Word

➤ The easiest way to exit (close) Word is to double click the **control-menu box** at the left of the title bar. Alternatively, you can pull down the **File menu** and click **Exit,** or you can press **Alt+F4** prior to pulling down the File menu.

➤ Exit Word and return to Program Manager.

Step 10: Exit Windows

➤ The consistent command structure within Windows means that the same operation is accomplished the same way in different applications; that is, you can exit from Program Manager using any of the techniques described in the previous step.

➤ Pull down the **File menu** in Program Manager.

➤ Select the **Exit Windows** command. You will see an informational message indicating that you are leaving Windows, and requiring that you click the **OK** command button to confirm the operation.

TROUBLESHOOTING

We trust that you completed the hands-on exercise without difficulty, and that you were able to create, save, and print the document in Figure 1.9. There is, however, one area of potential confusion in that Word offers different views of the same document depending on the preferences of the individual user. It is very likely that your screen will not match ours and, indeed, there is no requirement that it should. The *contents* of your document, however, should be identical to ours.

Figure 1.9 displayed the document in the ***Normal view.*** Figure 1.10 displays an entirely different view called the ***Page Layout view.*** Each view has its advantages. The Normal view is faster, but the Page Layout view more closely resembles the printed page as it displays the top and bottom margins, a vertical ruler, and other elements not seen in the Normal view. The Normal view is better for entering text and editing. The Page Layout view is used to apply the finishing touches and check a document prior to printing.

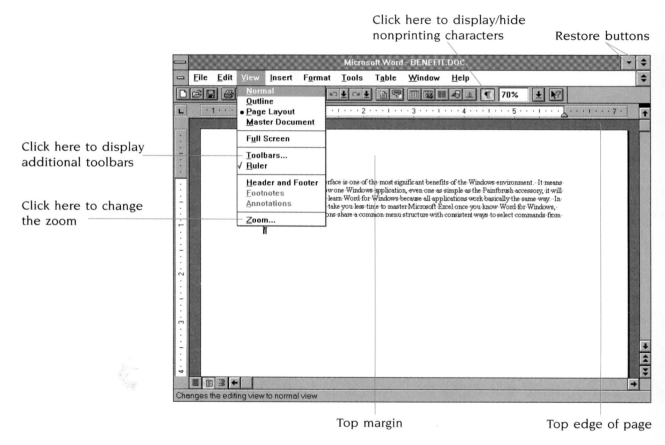

FIGURE 1.10 Troubleshooting

Your screen may or may not match either figure, and you will undoubtedly develop preferences of your own. The following suggestions will help you match the screens of Figure 1.9:

➤ If the application window for Word does not take the entire screen, and/or the document does not take the entire window within Word, click the maximize button in the application and/or the document window. There are two restore buttons in Figure 1.9b to indicate that the application window and its associated document window have been maximized.

➤ If the text does not come up to the top of the screen—that is, you see the top edge of the page (as in Figure 1.10)—it means that you are in the Page Layout view instead of the Normal view. Pull down the View menu and click Normal to match the document in Figure 1.9b.

➤ If the text seems unusually large or small, it means that you or a previous user elected to zoom in or out to get a different perspective on the document. Pull down the View menu, click *Zoom,* then click Page Width so that the text takes the entire line as in Figure 1.9b.

➤ If you see the ¶ and other nonprinting symbols it means that you or a previous user elected to display these characters. Click the Show/Hide button on the Standard Toolbar to make the symbols disappear.

➤ If the Standard or Formatting toolbar is missing and/or a different toolbar is displayed, pull down the View menu, click Toolbars, then click the appropriate toolbars on or off. If the ruler is missing, pull down the View menu and click Ruler.

THE WRONG KEYBOARD

Word for Windows facilitates conversion from WordPerfect by providing an alternative (software-controlled) keyboard that implements WordPerfect conventions. If you are sharing your machine with others, and if various keyboard shortcuts do not work as expected, it could be because someone else has implemented the WordPerfect keyboard. Pull down the Tools menu, click Options, then click the General tab in the dialog box. Clear the check box next to Navigation keys for WordPerfect users to return to the normal Word for Windows keyboard.

HANDS-ON EXERCISE 2:

Retrieving a Document

Objective To retrieve an existing document, revise it, and save the revision; to demonstrate the Undo command and on-line help. Use Figure 1.11 as a guide in the exercise.

Step 1: Retrieve a document

➤ Repeat the necessary steps from the first exercise to load Word.

➤ Pull down the **File menu.** Click **Open.**

➤ Alternatively you can press **Alt+F** to pull down the File menu and type the letter **O,** or you can click the **open button** on the Standard toolbar. Regardless of the technique you choose, you should see a dialog box similar to the one in Figure 1.11a.

➤ Click the appropriate drive, drive C or drive A, as in the first exercise.

➤ Double click the **WORDDATA** directory to make it the active directory.

➤ Double click **BENEFIT.DOC** to retrieve the document from the first exercise.

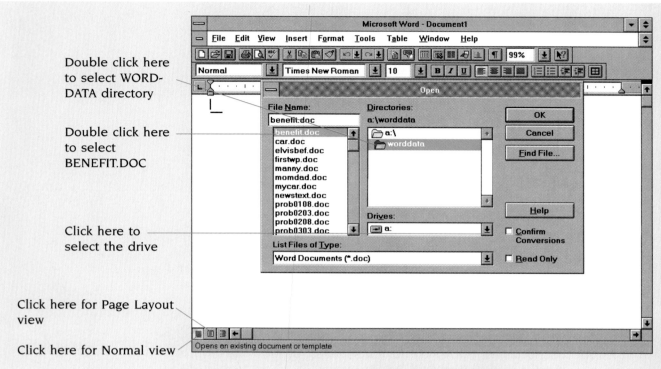

Double click here to select WORD-DATA directory

Double click here to select BENEFIT.DOC

Click here to select the drive

Click here for Page Layout view

Click here for Normal view

(a) The Open Command (step 1)

FIGURE 1.11   Hands-on Exercise 2

Step 2: The view menu (troubleshooting)

➤ To change views in the document, pull down the **View menu** and click **Normal** or **Page Layout.** You can also click the appropriate icon at the bottom of the application window.

➤ To hide or display toolbars, pull down the **View menu,** click **Toolbars,** then click to check or clear the boxes for the individual toolbars.

➤ To change the size and amount of text displayed in the window, pull down the **View menu,** click **Zoom,** then click the desired percentage. (We suggest 100% or Page Width.)

➤ There may still be subtle differences between your screen and ours, depending on the resolution of your monitor. These variations, if any, need not concern you at all as long as you are able to complete the exercise.

CHANGE TOOLBARS WITH THE RIGHT MOUSE BUTTON

You can display (hide) toolbars with the right mouse button provided at least one toolbar is visible. Point to any toolbar, then click the right mouse button to display a shortcut menu listing the available toolbars. Click the individual toolbars on or off as appropriate.

Step 3: Display the hard returns

➤ The **Show/Hide icon** on the Standard toolbar functions as a toggle switch to display (hide) the hard returns (and other nonprinting characters) in a document.

➤ Click the **Show/Hide icon** to display the hard returns as in Figure 1.11b.

➤ Click the **Show/Hide icon** a second time to hide the nonprinting characters.

➤ Display or hide the paragraph markers as you see fit.

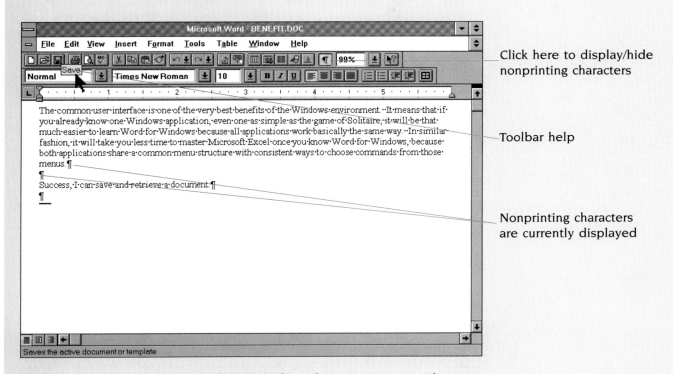

Click here to display/hide nonprinting characters

Toolbar help

Nonprinting characters are currently displayed

(b) Corrected Document with Paragraph Markers (steps 2, 3, and 4)

FIGURE 1.11 Hands-on Exercise 2 (continued)

TOOLBAR HELP

Point to any button on any toolbar and Word displays the name of the toolbar button, which is indicative of its function. If pointing to a button has no effect, pull down the View menu, click Toolbars, and check the box to Show Tool Tips.

Step 4: Modify the document

➤ Press **Ctrl+End** to move to the end of the document.

➤ Press the **enter key** once or twice to add a blank line(s).

➤ Add the sentence, **Success, I can save and retrieve a document!**

➤ Make the following additional modifications to practice editing:
  — Change the phrase, *most significant* to **very best.**
  — Change *Paintbrush accessory* to **game of Solitaire.**
  — Change the word *select* to **choose.**

➤ Switch between the insertion and overtype modes as necessary. Press the **Ins key** or double click the **OVR** indicator on the status bar to toggle between the insertion and overtype modes.

Step 5: Save the changes
➤ It is very, very important to save your work repeatedly during a session.
➤ Pull down the **File menu** and click **Save,** or click the **save button** on the Standard toolbar. This time you will not see a dialog box, because the document is saved automatically under the existing name (BENEFIT.DOC).

THE INSERTION POINT VERSUS THE I-BEAM

The mouse pointer changes to an *I-beam* whenever you move the pointer into the editing area. The I-beam is very different from the insertion point; you must click the mouse to position the insertion point if you scroll using the mouse. The insertion point changes automatically if you use the keyboard to move through the document.

Step 6: Deleting text
➤ Point to the first character in the document. **Press and hold the left mouse button** as you drag the mouse over the first sentence. Release the mouse.
➤ The sentence should remain highlighted (selected) as in Figure 1.11c. The selected text is the text that will be affected by the next command.
➤ Click anywhere else in the document to deselect the text.
➤ Repeat the process to reselect the first sentence.
➤ Press the **De**l key to delete the highlighted text (the first sentence) from the document.

Click and drag to select the first sentence

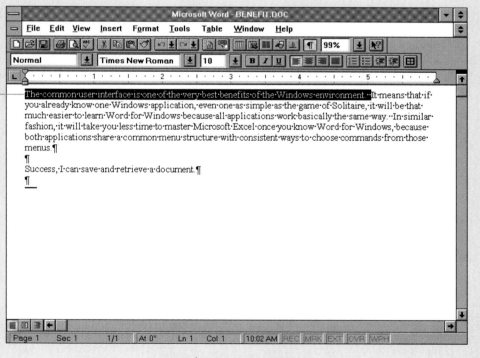

(c) Selecting Text (step 6)

FIGURE 1.11   Hands-on Exercise 2 (continued)

Step 7: The Undo command

➤ Pull down the **Edit menu** as in Figure 1.11d.

➤ Click **Undo** to reverse (undo) the previous command.

➤ The deleted text should be returned to your document. The Undo command is a tremendous safety net and can be used at almost any time.

➤ Click anywhere outside the highlighted text to deselect the sentence.

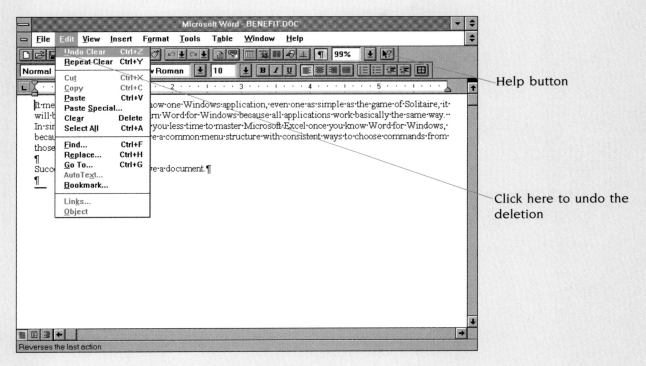

(d) The Undo Command (step 7)

FIGURE 1.11 Hands-on Exercise 2 (continued)

Step 8: On-line help

➤ Pull down the **Help menu.** Click **Search for Help on.** Type **undo** in the text box.

➤ Double click **Undo command (Edit menu)** when you see it appear in the upper list box.

➤ Double click **Undo command (Edit menu)** when it appears in the lower list box to produce a screen similar to Figure 1.11e. Read the help screen.

➤ Double click the **control-menu box** in the help screen to exit Help and return to the document.

HELP TIPS

Click the Help button on the Standard toolbar (the mouse pointer changes to include a large question mark), then click any other toolbar icon to display a help screen with information about that button. Double click the Help button to produce the Search dialog box that is normally accessed through the Help menu.

Double click here to
return to the document

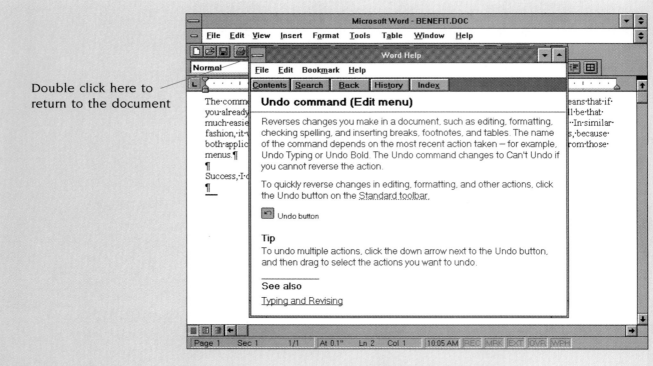

(e) On-line Help (step 8)

FIGURE 1.11   Hands-on Exercise 2 (continued)

Step 9: Print the revised document
- Save the document a final time.
- Print the revised document.
- Exit Word (and Windows) as you did at the end of the previous exercise.

SUMMARY STATISTICS

Pull down the File menu, click Summary Info, then click the Statistics command button. The resulting dialog box displays information about the current document including its approximate size, the date it was created, the date it was last saved, and the total editing time. You can print this information together with the document by setting the appropriate option. Pull down the Tools menu, click Options, click the Print tab, then check the box to print summary information. The summary statistics will appear the next time you print a document.

SUMMARY

The common user interface ensures that all Windows applications are similar in appearance and work basically the same way, with common conventions and a consistent menu structure. It provides you with an intuitive understanding of any application, even before you begin to use it, and means that once you learn one application, it is that much easier to learn the next.

The mouse is essential to Word as it is to all other Windows applications, but keyboard equivalents are provided for virtually all operations. The Standard and Formatting toolbars offer yet another way to execute common commands. On-line help provides detailed information about all aspects of Word.

A word processor is always in one of two modes, insertion or overtype, and uses a toggle switch (the Ins key) to alternate between the two. The insertion point marks the place within a document where text is added or replaced.

The enter key is pressed at the end of a paragraph, not the end of a line, because Word automatically wraps text from one line to the next. A hard return is created by the user when he or she presses the enter key; a soft return is created by Word as it wraps text and begins a new line.

Key Words and Concepts

Application window	Horizontal ruler	Restore button
Check box	I-beam	Scroll bar
Click	Icon	Scroll box
Command button	Index button	Soft return
Common user interface	Insertion mode	Standard toolbar
Control-menu box	Insertion point	Status bar
Desktop	Maximize button	Text box
Dialog box	Menu bar	Tip of the Day
Dimmed command	Minimize button	Title bar
Document window	Mouse pointer	Toggle switch
Double click	Normal view	Toolbar
Drag	On-line help	Undo command
Drop-down list box	Open list box	Vertical ruler
Ellipsis	Option button	View menu
End-of-file marker	Overtype mode	Windows
Formatting toolbar	Page Layout view	Word for Windows
Hard return	Point	Word wrap
Help button	Program Manager	Zoom
Help menu	Pull-down menu	

Multiple Choice

1. When entering text within a document, the enter key is normally pressed at the end of every:
   (a) Line
   (b) Sentence
   (c) Paragraph
   (d) All of the above

2. Which of the following is true regarding scrolling?
   (a) You can scroll a document in a vertical direction
   (b) You can scroll a document in a horizontal direction
   (c) Both (a) and (b)
   (d) Neither (a) nor (b)

to perform

3. Which of the following will execute a command from a pull-down menu?
   (a) Clicking on the command once the menu has been pulled down
   (b) Typing the underlined letter in the command
   (c) Both (a) and (b)
   (d) Neither (a) nor (b)

4. The File Open command:
   (a) Brings a document from disk into memory
   (b) Brings a document from disk into memory, then erases the document on disk
   (c) Stores the document in memory on disk
   (d) Stores the document in memory on disk, then erases it from memory

5. The File Save command:
   (a) Brings a document from disk into memory
   (b) Brings a document from disk into memory, then erases the document on disk
   (c) Stores the document in memory on disk
   (d) Stores the document in memory on disk, then erases the document from memory

6. What is the easiest way to change the phrase, *revenues, profits, gross margin*, to read *revenues, profits, and gross margin*?
   (a) Use the insertion mode, position the insertion point before the *g* in gross, then type the word *and* followed by a space
   (b) Use the insertion mode, position the insertion point after the *g* in gross, then type the word *and* followed by a space
   (c) Use the overtype mode, position the insertion point before the *g* in gross, then type the word *and* followed by a space
   (d) Use the overtype mode, position the insertion point after the *g* in gross, then type the word *and* followed by a space

7. What happens if you press the Ins key *twice in a row* from within Word?
   (a) You will be in the insertion mode
   (b) You will be in the overtype mode
   (c) You will be in the same mode you were in before pressing the key at all
   (d) You will be in the opposite mode you were before pressing the key at all

8. What is the significance of three dots next to a menu option?
   (a) The option is not accessible
   (b) A dialog box will appear if the option is selected
   (c) A help window will appear if the option is selected
   (d) There are no equivalent keystrokes for the particular option

9. What is the significance of a menu option that appears faded (dimmed)?
   (a) The option is not currently accessible
   (b) A dialog box will appear if the option is selected
   (c) A help window will appear if the option is selected
   (d) There are no equivalent keystrokes for the particular option

10. Which of the following elements may be found within a help window?
    (a) Title bar, menu bar, and control-menu box
    (b) Minimize, maximize, and/or a restore button
    (c) Vertical and/or horizontal scroll bars
    (d) All of the above

11. A document has been entered into Word with a given set of margins which are subsequently changed. What can you say about the number of hard and soft returns before and after the change in margins?
    (a) The number of hard returns is the same, but the number and/or position of the soft returns is different
    (b) The number of soft returns is the same, but the number and/or position of the hard returns is different
    (c) The number and position of both hard and soft returns is unchanged
    (d) The number and position of both hard and soft returns is different

12. Which of the following is an example of a toggle switch within Word?
    (a) The Ins key
    (b) The Caps Lock key
    (c) The Show/Hide button on the Standard toolbar
    (d) All of the above

13. Which of the following is true regarding a dialog box?
    (a) Option buttons indicated mutually exclusive choices
    (b) Check boxes imply that multiple options may be selected
    (c) Both (a) and (b)
    (d) Neither (a) nor (b)

14. Which of the following will exit Word and return to Windows?
    (a) Double clicking the control-menu box in the title bar for Word
    (b) Pressing Alt+F4 from anywhere within Word
    (c) Pulling down the File menu and clicking on Exit
    (d) All of the above

15. Which of the following actions will end a Windows session?
    (a) Double clicking on the control-menu box of the Program Manager
    (b) Double clicking on the control-menu box of Word
    (c) Both (a) and (b)
    (d) Neither (a) nor (b)

ANSWERS

1. c
2. c
3. c
4. a
5. c
6. a
7. c
8. b
9. a
10. d
11. a
12. d
13. c
14. d
15. a

1. Use Figure 1.12 to identify the elements of a Word screen by matching each element with the appropriate letter:

_____ Restore button	_____ Minimize button
_____ Control-menu box	_____ Vertical scroll bar
_____ Standard toolbar	_____ Scroll box
_____ Formatting toolbar	_____ Menu bar
_____ Horizontal ruler	_____ Status bar

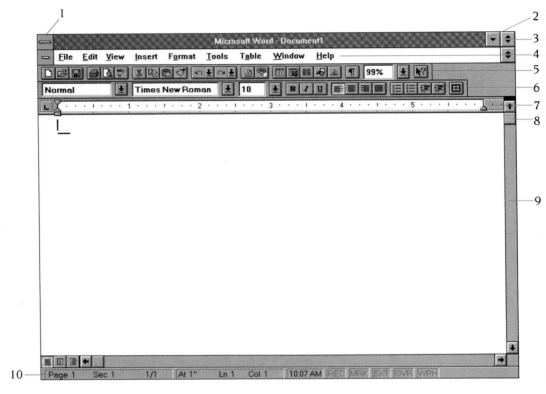

FIGURE 1.12   Screen for Problem 1

2. The common user interface: Answer the following with respect to Figures 1.2a and 1.2b that appeared earlier in the chapter.
   a. Which pull-down menus are common to both Excel and Word?
   b. How do you access the Edit menu in Excel? in Word?
   c. How do you open a file in Word? Do you think the same command will work in Excel as well?
   d. Which icons correspond to the Open and Save commands in the Excel toolbar? Which icons correspond to the Open and Save commands in the Word toolbar?
   e. Which icons will boldface, italicize, and underline selected type? Are the icons descriptive of the tasks they perform?
   f. What do your answers to parts a through e tell you about the advantages of a common user interface?

3. What is the difference between:
   a. The insertion and overtype modes?

b. Deleting a character using the backspace and Del keys?

c. Typing when text is selected versus typing when no text has been selected?

d. The I-beam and the insertion point?

e. The insertion point and the end-of-file marker?

f. The Standard and Formatting toolbars?

g. The normal and page layout views?

h. A hard and soft carriage return?

4. Troubleshooting: The informational messages in Figure 1.13 appeared (or could have appeared) in response to various commands issued during the chapter.

a. Which command produced the message in Figure 1.13a? What action is necessary to correct the indicated problem?

b. Which command produced the message in Figure 1.13b? When would No be an appropriate response to this message?

c. The message in Figure 1.13c appeared in response to a File Open command in conjunction with the file shown earlier in Figure 1.11a. What is the most likely corrective action?

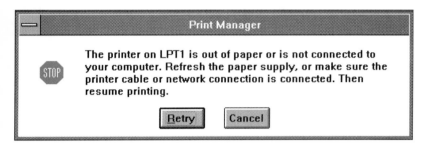

(a) Informational Message 1

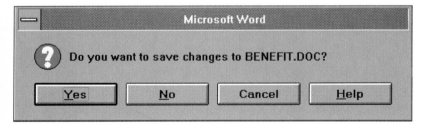

(b) Informational Message 2

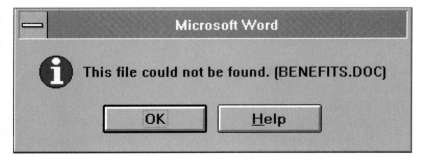

(c) Informational Message 3

FIGURE 1.13 Informational Messages for Problem 4

5. Answer the following with respect to the dialog box in Figure 1.14.
   a. Which command produced the dialog box?
   b. Can the Print to File and Collate Copies boxes be checked at the same time?
   c. What happens if you click the Collate Copies box, given that it is already checked?
   d. Which options (if any) are mutually exclusive?
   e. What do the three dots following the Options command button indicate?
   f. What happens when you click the Cancel command button? Which key has the same effect?
   g. What happens when you click the OK command button? Which key has the same effect as clicking on the OK button when it is highlighted?

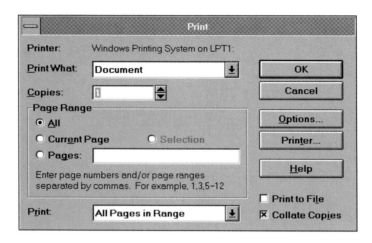

FIGURE 1.14 Dialog Box for Problem 5

6. Exploring help: Answer the following with respect to Figure 1.15:
   a. What is the significance of the scroll box that appears within the scroll bar?
   b. What happens if you click the down (up) arrow within the scroll bar?
   c. What happens if you press the maximize button? Might this action eliminate the need to scroll within the help window?
   d. How do you print the help topic shown in the window?
   e. What keystroke will move you to the beginning of a line? to the end of a line?

7. Answer the following with respect to Figure 1.16:
   a. What is the name of the document currently being edited?
   b. Which view is selected, Page Layout view or Normal?
   c. Is the ruler present? the Formatting toolbar? the Standard toolbar? How do you cause the missing elements to reappear?
   d. Which mode is active, insertion or overtype? How do you switch from one mode to the other?
   e. How do you display (hide) the hard carriage returns? Are the hard returns displayed in the figure?
   f. Has the application window for Word been maximized? Has the document window within Word been maximized?
   g. Add your name at the top of the document, then create and print the entire document. Submit the completed document to your instructor.

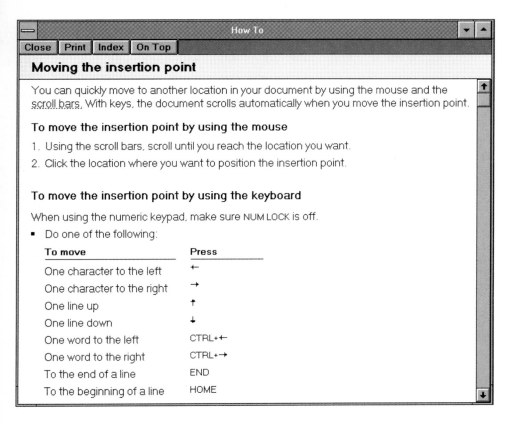

FIGURE 1.15 Screen for Problem 6

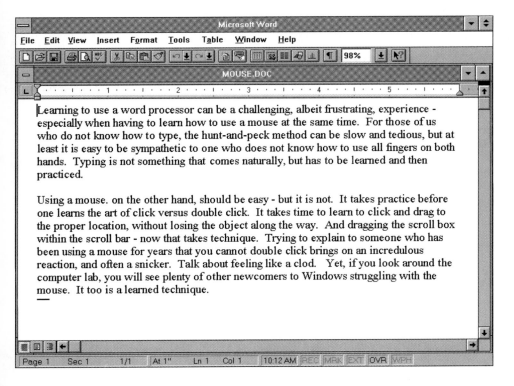

FIGURE 1.16 Screen for Problem 7

8. Retrieve the PROB0108.DOC document in Figure 1.17 from the WORD-DATA subdirectory, then make the following changes:

a. Select the text *Your name* and replace it with your name.

b. Replace *January 1, 1994* with the current date.

c. Insert the phrase *one or* in line 2 so that the text reads . . . *one or more characters than currently exist.*

d. Delete the word *And* from sentence 4 in line 5, then change the *w* in *when* to a capital letter to begin the sentence.

e. Change the phrase *most efficient* to *best*.

f. Place the insertion point at the end of sentence 2, make sure you are in the insertion mode, then add the following sentence: *The insertion mode adds characters at the insertion point while moving existing text to the right in order to make room for the new text.*

g. Place the insertion point at the end of the last sentence, press the enter key twice in a row, then enter the following text: *There are several keys that function as toggle switches of which you should be aware. The Ins key switches between the insertion and overtype modes, the Caps Lock key toggles between upper- and lowercase letters, and the Num Lock key alternates between typing numbers and using the cursor control keys.*

h. Save the revised document, then print it and submit it to your instructor.

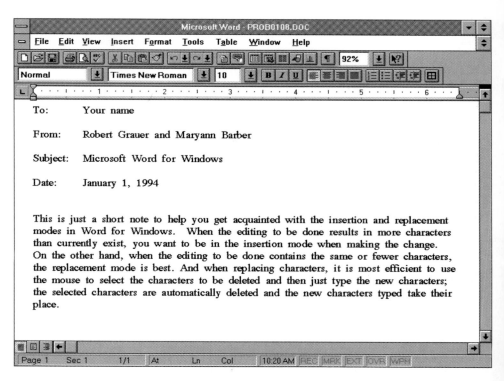

FIGURE 1.17   Screen for Problem 8

9. Prepare a one-page memo (approximately 250 words) from student to instructor detailing your background. Include any previous knowledge of computers you may have, prior computer courses you have taken, your objectives for the course, and so on. Also, indicate whether you own a PC,

whether you have access to one at work, and/or whether you are considering purchase. Include any other information about yourself and/or your computer-related background. Your one page of text should consist of at least two paragraphs. After you have created your memo, print it and submit it to your instructor.

10. Write a short essay (three to four paragraphs) describing your favorite fictional character—whether it be a character from a cherished novel or short story, a classic or recently released movie, or even a mythological tale. Give a brief physical and/or psychological description of the character, an explanation of the role he/she plays in the fictional world in which he/she exists, and the reasons why this character has inspired you to feel as you do. When you have completed the essay, proofread it for errors, make any corrections necessary, then print it and submit it to your instructor for a grade.

Case Studies

It's a Mess

Newcomers to word processing quickly learn the concept of word wrap and the distinction between hard and soft returns. This lesson was lost, however, on your friend who created the document HELPME.DOC on the data disk. The first several sentences were entered without any hard returns at all, whereas the opposite problem exists toward the end of the document. This is a good friend and her paper is due in one hour. Please help.

Planning for Disaster

Do you have a backup strategy? Do you even know what a backup strategy is? You had better learn, because sooner or later you will wish you had one. You will erase a file, be unable to read from a floppy disk, or worse yet suffer a hardware failure in which you are unable to access the hard drive. The problem always seems to occur the night before an assignment is due. The ultimate disaster is the disappearance of your computer, by theft or natural disaster (e.g., Hurricane Andrew or the Los Angeles earthquake). Describe in 250 words or less the backup strategy you plan to implement in conjunction with your work in this class.

A Letter Home

You really like this course and want very much to have your own computer, but you're strapped for cash and have decided to ask your parents for help. Write a one-page letter describing the advantages of having your own system and how it will help you in school. Tell your parents what the system will cost, and that you can save money by buying through the mail. Describe the configuration you intend to buy (don't forget to include the price of software), and then provide prices from at least three different companies. Cut out the advertisements and include them in your letter. Bring your material to class and compare your research with that of your classmates.

Computer Magazines

A subscription to a computer magazine should be given serious consideration if you intend to stay abreast in a rapidly changing field. The reviews on new products are especially helpful and you will appreciate the advertisements should you need to buy. Go to the library or a newsstand and obtain a magazine that appeals to you, then write a brief review of the magazine for class. Describe the features you like and don't like. Devote at least one paragraph to an article or other item you found useful.

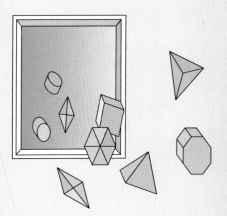

2

Gaining Proficiency: Editing and Formatting

After reading this chapter you will be able to:

1. Define the select-then-do methodology; describe several shortcuts with the mouse and/or the keyboard to select text.

2. Use the clipboard and/or the drag-and-drop capability to move and copy text within a document.

3. Use the Find and Replace commands to substitute one character string for another.

4. Differentiate between the Save and Save As commands; describe various backup options that can be selected.

5. Define scrolling; scroll to the beginning and end of a document.

6. Distinguish between the Normal and Page Layout views; state how to change the view and/or magnification of a document.

7. Explain TrueType; distinguish between a serif and a sans serif typeface; use the Format Font command to change the font and/or type size.

8. Use the Format Paragraph command to change line spacing, alignment, tabs and indents, and to control pagination; use the Borders and Shading command to box and shade text.

9. Describe the Undo and Redo commands and how they are related to one another.

10. Use the Page Setup command to change the margins and/or orientation; differentiate between a soft and hard page break.

OVERVIEW

The previous chapter taught you the basics of Word for Windows and enabled you to create and print a simple document. The present chapter significantly extends your capabilities by offering a variety of commands that let you change the contents and appearance of a document. These operations are known as editing and formatting, respectively.

You will learn how to move and copy text within a document, how to find and replace one character string with another, and how to implement various backup options. You will also learn the basics of typography and be able to switch between the different fonts included within Windows. You will be able to change the justification, indentation, and line spacing. You will learn how to change margins and page orientation, and how to create a page break. All of these commands are used in three hands-on exercises that are the very essence of the chapter.

As you read the chapter, realize that there are many different ways to accomplish the same task and that it would be impossible to cover them all. Our approach is to present the overall concepts and suggest the ways we think are most appropriate at the time we introduce the material. We also offer numerous shortcuts in the form of boxed tips that appear throughout the chapter and urge you to explore further on your own. It is not necessary for you to memorize anything as on-line help is always available. Be flexible and willing to experiment.

WRITE NOW, EDIT LATER

You write a sentence, then change it, and change it again, and one hour later you've produced a single paragraph. It happens to every writer—you stare at a blank screen and flashing cursor and are unable to write. The best solution is to brainstorm and write down anything that pops into your head, and to keep on writing. Don't worry about typos or spelling errors because you can fix them later. Above all, resist the temptation to continually edit the few words you've written because overediting will drain the life out of what you are writing. The important thing is to get your ideas on paper.

SELECT THEN DO

Virtually every operation in Word takes place within the context of a *select-then-do* methodology; that is, you select a block of text, then you execute the command to operate on that text. The most basic way to select text is by dragging the mouse. Click at the beginning of the selection, press and hold the left mouse button as you move to the end of the selection, then release the mouse.

There are, however, a variety of shortcuts to facilitate the process. You can double click anywhere within a word to select the word. You can press the Ctrl key and click the mouse anywhere within a sentence to select the sentence. Additional shortcuts are presented in each of the hands-on exercises, at which point you will have an opportunity to practice.

Selected text is affected by any subsequent operation; for example, clicking the boldface or italics icon changes the selected text to boldface or italics, respectively. You can also drag the selected text to a new location, press the Del key to erase the selected text, or execute any other editing or formatting command. The selected text remains highlighted until you click elsewhere in the document.

SHORTCUT MENUS

Point anywhere within a document, then click the right mouse button to display a *shortcut menu*. Shortcut menus contain commands appropriate to the item you have selected. Click in the menu to execute a command, or click outside the menu to close the menu without executing a command.

MOVING AND COPYING TEXT

The ability to move and/or copy text is essential in order to develop any degree of proficiency in editing. A move operation removes the text from its current location and places it elsewhere in the same (or even a different) document; a copy operation retains the text in its present location and places a duplicate elsewhere. Either operation can be accomplished using the Windows clipboard and a combination of the *Cut, Copy,* and *Paste commands.* (A shortcut, using the mouse to *drag and drop* text from one location to another, is described on page 55.)

The *clipboard* is a temporary storage area available to any Windows application. Selected text is cut or copied from a document and placed into the clipboard from where it can be pasted to a new location(s). A move requires that you select the text and execute a Cut command to remove the text from the document and place it in the clipboard. You then move the insertion point to the new location, and finally you paste the text from the clipboard into the new location. A copy operation necessitates the same steps except that the selected text is copied rather than cut.

The Cut, Copy, and Paste commands are found in the Edit menu, or alternatively, can be executed by clicking the appropriate icons on the toolbar. The contents of the clipboard are replaced by each subsequent Cut or Copy command. They are unaffected by the Paste command; that is, the contents of the clipboard can be pasted into multiple locations in a document.

DELETE WITH CAUTION

You work too hard developing your thoughts to see them disappear in a flash. Hence, instead of deleting large blocks of text, try moving them to the end of your document where they can be recalled later if you change your mind. A related practice is to remain in the insert mode (as opposed to overtype) to prevent the inadvertent deletion of existing text as new ideas are added.

UNDO, REPEAT, AND REDO COMMANDS

The *Undo command* was used in Chapter 1 but is repeated here because it is invaluable at any time, especially when text is accidentally deleted. Pull down the Edit menu and click Undo (or click the Undo button on the Standard toolbar) to reverse the effect of the most recent operation. Use the command whenever something happens to your document that is confusing or different from what you had intended.

The *Repeat command* (also in the Edit menu) repeats the most recent editing or formatting change. Use the command whenever you want to make the same revision several times in a document; for example, when you want to add the same

---

100 LEVELS OF UNDO

Incredible, perhaps, but Word enables you to undo the last 100 changes to a document. Click the arrow next to the Undo button on the Standard toolbar to produce a list of your previous actions, then click the action you want to undo.

---

phrase in multiple places in a long document.

The **Redo command** works in conjunction with the Undo command; that is, every time a command is undone it can be redone at a later time.

FIND AND REPLACE COMMANDS

The **Find command** enables you to locate a specific occurrence of a character string in order to perform a subsequent editing or formatting operation. The **Replace command** incorporates the Find command and allows you to locate and optionally replace (one or more occurrences of) a character string with a different character string.

The two strings are known as the find and replacement strings, respectively. Each may consist of a single letter, a word, a sentence, or any combination of text. The two strings do *not* have to be the same length; for example, you could replace *16* with *sixteen.* The commands are illustrated in Figure 2.1.

The search may or may not be **case sensitive.** A case-sensitive search (where Match Case is selected as in Figure 2.1a) matches not only the characters, but the use of upper- and lowercase letters; that is, *There* is different from *there,* and a search on one will not identify the other. A **case-insensitive** search (where Match Case is *not* selected) is just the opposite and finds both *There* and *there.* The search may also specify a match on the **whole word only,** which will identify *there,* but not *therefore* or *thereby.*

Will not find *There* or *THERE*

Will not find *therefore* or *thereby*

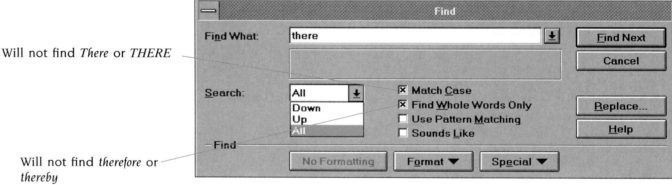

(a) Find Command

FIGURE 2.1   Find and Replace Commands

The Replace command in Figure 2.1b implements either **selective replacement,** which lets you examine the character string in context and decide whether to replace it, or **automatic replacement,** where the substitution is made automatically. The latter often produces unintended consequences and is generally not recommended; for example, if you substitute the word *text* for *book,* the phrase *text book* would become *text text,* which is not what you had in mind.

Selective replacement is implemented in Figure 2.1b by clicking the Find Next command button, then clicking (or not clicking) the Replace button to make the substitution. Automatic or **global replacement** (through the entire document) is implemented by clicking the Replace All button.

The Find and Replace commands can include formatting and/or special characters. You can, for example, change all italicized text to boldface, or you can change five consecutive spaces to a tab character. You can also introduce a wild card into the search string; for example, find all four-letter words that begin with "f" and end with "l" such as "fall", "fill", or "fail." You can even search for a word based on how it sounds; for example, search for Marion, check the Sounds Like check box, and find both Marion and Marian.

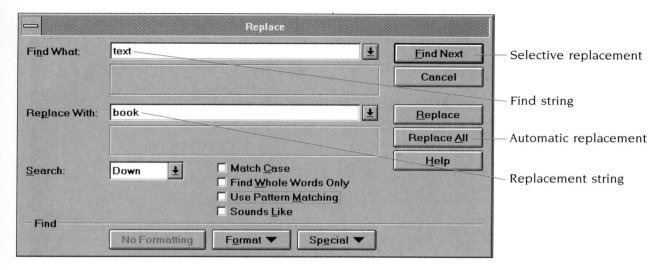

(b) Replace Command

FIGURE 2.1   Find and Replace Commands (continued)

SAVE COMMAND

The **Save command** copies the document currently being edited (the document in memory) to a permanent storage medium, that is, to disk. The initial execution of the command requires you to assign a filename (from one to eight characters) and automatically assigns the extension DOC to the document. All subsequent executions of the Save command will save the document under the name you entered, replacing the previously saved version with the new one. The **Save As command** saves the document under a different name. It is useful when you want to retain a copy of the original document as well as the document on which you are making changes.

We cannot overemphasize the importance of periodically saving a document, so that if something does go wrong, you won't lose all of your work. Nothing is more frustrating than to lose two hours of effort, due to an unexpected problem in Windows or to a temporary loss of power. Save your work frequently, at least once every 15 minutes. Pull down the File menu and click Save, or click the save icon on the Standard toolbar. Do it!

QUIT WITHOUT SAVING

There will be times when you do not want to save the changes to a document—for example, when you have edited it beyond recognition and wish you had never started. Pull down the File menu and click the Close command, then click No in response to the message asking whether you want to save the changes to the document. Pull down the File menu, click Open to reopen the file, then start over from the beginning.

Backup Options

Word offers several different **backup** options. We believe the most important is the option that creates a backup copy in conjunction with every Save command as illustrated in Figure 2.2. (See step 3 in the hands-on exercise for instructions on how to establish this option.)

Step 1 – Create FOX.DOC

```
The fox jumped over the fence
```

Saved to disk →

FOX.DOC

Step 2 – Retrieve FOX.DOC

```
The fox jumped over the fence
```

Retrieve FOX.DOC ←

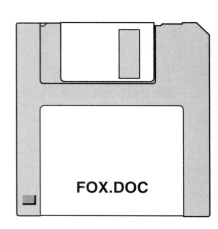

FOX.DOC

Step 3 – Edit and save FOX.DOC

```
The quick brown fox jumped over
the fence
```

Saved to disk →

FOX.DOC (new version)

FOX.BAK (old version)

FIGURE 2.2   Backup Procedures

Assume, for example, that you have created the simple document, *The fox jumped over the fence,* and saved it under the name FOX.DOC. Assume further that you edit the document to read, *The quick brown fox jumped over the fence,* and that you saved it a second time. The second Save command changes the name of the original document from FOX.DOC to FOX.BAK, then saves the current contents of memory as FOX.DOC. In other words, the disk now contains two versions of the document: the current version (FOX.DOC) and the most recent previous version (FOX.BAK), to which the **BAK extension** was automatically assigned.

The cycle goes on indefinitely, with FOX.DOC always containing the current version, and FOX.BAK the most recent previous version. Thus if you revise and save the document a third time, FOX.DOC will contain the latest revision while FOX.BAK would contain the previous version alluding to the quick brown fox. The original (first) version of the document disappears entirely since only two versions are kept.

The contents of FOX.DOC and FOX.BAK are different. The latter enables you to retrieve the previous version if you inadvertently edit beyond repair or accidentally erase the current version of FOX.DOC. Should this occur (and it will), you can always retrieve its predecessor and at least salvage your work prior to the last save operation.

KEEP DUPLICATE COPIES OF IMPORTANT FILES

It is absolutely critical to maintain duplicate copies of important files on a separate disk stored away from the computer. In addition, you should print each new document at the end of every session, saving it before printing (power failures happen when least expected, for example, during the print operation). Hard copy is not as good as a duplicate disk, but it is better than nothing.

SCROLLING

Scrolling is necessary when a document is too large to be viewed in its entirety. Figure 2.3a, for example, displays the top portion of a document as it would appear on the monitor. Figure 2.3b shows the entire (printed) document. To see the complete document in the monitor, you need to scroll, whereby new lines will be brought into view as the old lines disappear.

Scrolling comes about automatically as you reach the bottom of the screen. Entering a new line of text, clicking on the down arrow within the scroll bar, or

---

SCROLLING TIP

Scroll quickly through a document by clicking above or below the scroll box to scroll up or down an entire screen. Move to the top, bottom, or an approximate position within a document by dragging the scroll box to the corresponding position in the scroll bar; for example, dragging the scroll box to the middle of the bar moves the mouse pointer to the middle of the document. Realize, however, that both techniques move the mouse pointer, but *not* the insertion point; that is, you must click the mouse after scrolling to change the position of the insertion point.

Insertion point

Drag the scroll box to scroll quickly through the document (to the beginning, end, or approximate position)

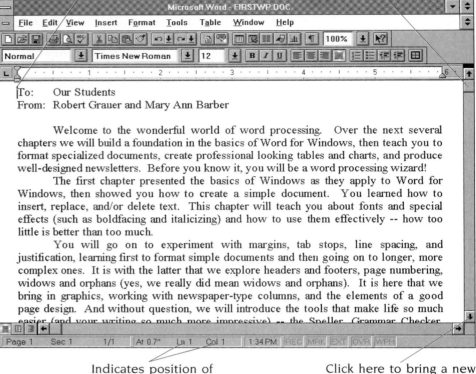

Indicates position of insertion point

Click here to bring a new line into view

(a) Screen Display

FIGURE 2.3   Scrolling

pressing the down arrow key brings a new line into view at the bottom of the screen and simultaneously removes a line at the top. (The process is reversed at the top of the screen.)

Scrolling occurs most often in a vertical direction as shown in Figure 2.3. It can also occur horizontally, when the length of a line in a document exceeds the number of characters that can be displayed horizontally on the screen. Note, too, the position of the insertion point in Figure 2.3a and how this information is communicated on the status bar.

VIEW MENU

The **_View menu_** provides different views of a document. Each view can be displayed at different magnifications, which in turn determine the amount of scrolling necessary to see remote parts of a document.

The **_Normal view_** is the default and the one you use most of the time. The **_Page Layout_** view more closely resembles the printed document and displays the top and bottom margins, headers and footers, and other features that do not appear in the Normal view. The Normal view is faster, however, because Word spends less time formatting the display.

To: Our Students
From: Robert Grauer and Mary Ann Barber

   Welcome to the wonderful world of word processing. Over the next several chapters we will build a foundation in the basics of Word for Windows, then teach you to format specialized documents, create professional looking tables and charts, and produce well-designed newsletters. Before you know it, you will be a word processing wizard!
   The first chapter presented the basics of Windows as they apply to Word for Windows, then showed you how to create a simple document. You learned how to insert, replace, and/or delete text. This chapter will teach you about fonts and special effects (such as boldfacing and italicizing) and how to use them effectively -- how too little is better than too much.
   You will go on to experiment with margins, tab stops, line spacing, and justification, learning first to format simple documents and then advancing to longer, more complex ones. It is with the latter that we explore headers and footers, page numbering, widows and orphans (yes, we really did mean widows and orphans). It is here that we bring in graphics, working with newspaper-type columns, and the elements of a good page design. And without question, we will introduce the tools that make life so much easier (and your writing so much more impressive) -- the Speller, Grammar Checker, Thesaurus, Glossaries, and Styles.
   If you are wondering what all these things are, read on in the text and proceed with the hands-on exercises. Create a simple newsletter, then really knock their socks off by adding graphics, fonts, and Word Art. Create a simple calendar and then create more intricate forms that no one will believe were done by little old you. Create a résumé with your beginner's skills and then make it look like so much more with your intermediate (even advanced) skills. Last, but not least, run a mail merge to produce the cover letters that will accompany your résumé as it is mailed to companies across the United States (and even the world).
   It is up to you to practice, for it is only through working at the computer that you will learn what you need to know. Experiment and don't be afraid to make mistakes. Practice and practice some more.
   Our goal is for you to learn and to enjoy what you are learning. We have great confidence in you, and in our ability to help you discover what you can do. And to prove us right, we'd love to have you mail us copies of documents that you have created.
Write to us at the following address:

       Dr. Robert Grauer/Ms. Mary Ann Barber
       University of Miami
       421 Jenkins Building
       Coral Gables, Florida 33124

   We look forward to hearing from you and hope that you will like our text book. You are about to embark on a wonderful journey toward computer literacy. Be patient, be inquisitive, and enjoy.

(b) Printed Document

FIGURE 2.3   Scrolling (continued)

   The **Zoom command** displays the document on the screen at different magnifications such as 75%, 100%, or 200%. (The Zoom command does not affect the size of the text on the printed page.) A Zoom percentage (magnification) of 100% displays the document in the approximate size of the text on the printed page. You can increase the percentage to 200% to make the characters appear larger. You can also decrease the magnification to 75% to see more of the document at one time.
   You can also let Word determine the magnification for you, by selecting one of three additional Zoom options—Page Width, Whole Page, or Many Pages. Figure 2.4a, for example, displays a two-page document in Page Layout view. Figure 2.4b shows the corresponding settings in the Zoom command. (The 29% magnification is determined automatically once you specify the number of pages as shown in the figure.)

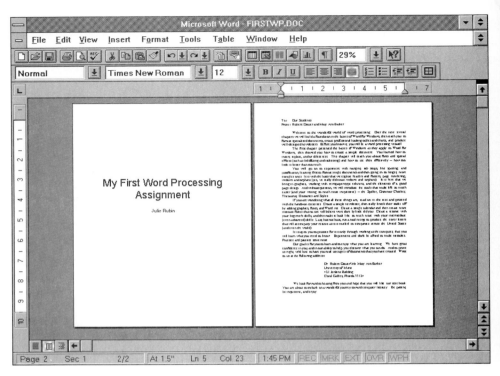

(a) Page Layout View (Zoom to Many Pages)

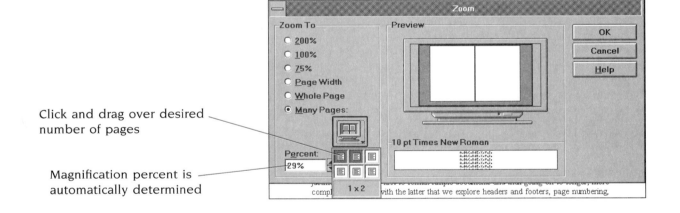

Click and drag over desired number of pages

Magnification percent is automatically determined

(b) Zoom Command

FIGURE 2.4   View Menu and Zoom Command

HANDS-ON EXERCISE 1:

Editing

Objective To edit an existing document; to change the view and magnification of a document; to scroll through a document. To use the Find, Replace, and Save As commands; to move and copy text using the clipboard and the drag-and-drop facility. Use Figure 2.5 as a guide in the exercise.

Step 1: Load the practice document

➤ Load Word as described in the hands-on exercises from Chapter 1.

➤ Pull down the **File menu** and click **Open** (or click the Open icon on the Standard toolbar).

➤ Click drive C or drive A, depending on whether or not you copied the data disk to your hard drive.

➤ Scroll through the directory list box until you come to the **WORDDATA** directory. Double click this directory.

➤ Scroll through the file list box until you come to the **FIRSTWP.DOC.** Double click the file name to open the document as shown in Figure 2.5a.

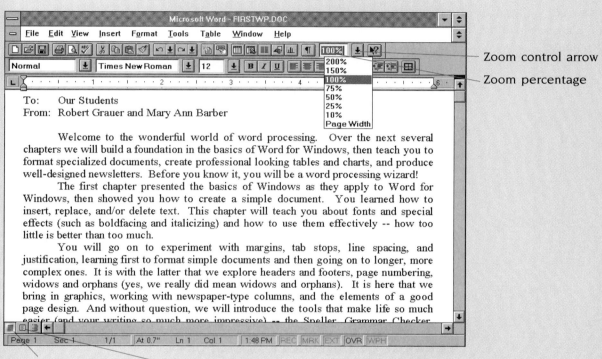

Zoom control arrow

Zoom percentage

Normal view icon   Page layout icon

(a) The View Menu and Zoom Control (steps 1 and 2)

FIGURE 2.5   Hands-on Exercise 1

Step 2: The View menu

➤ Change the view:

— Pull down the **View menu.** Click **Normal.**
or Click the **Normal view icon** on the status bar.

➤ Change the zoom percentage:

— Pull down the **View menu.** Click **Zoom.** Click **100%.** Click **OK.**
or Click the **Zoom control arrow** on the Standard toolbar, drag to 100%, and release the mouse.

Step 3: Establish Automatic Backup (The BAK file)

➤ Pull down the **Tools menu.** Click **Options.**

➤ Click the **Save tab** to produce the dialog box of Figure 2.5b.

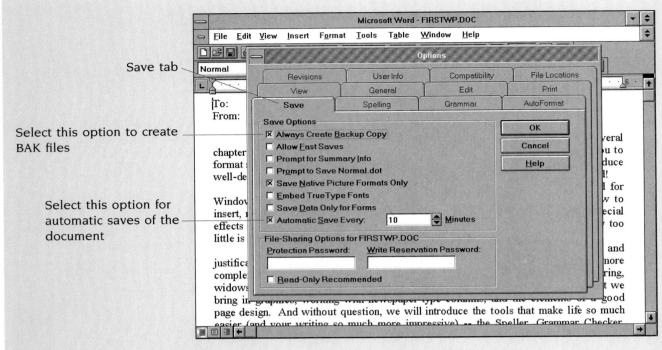

Save tab

Select this option to create BAK files

Select this option for automatic saves of the document

(b) The Options Command

FIGURE 2.5   Hands-on Exercise 1 (continued)

➤ Click the first check box to choose **Always Create Backup Copy** (creation of a BAK file). Adjust the other options as you see fit; for example, you can specify that the document be saved every 10 minutes.

➤ Click **OK.**

CHANGE THE DEFAULT DIRECTORY

The *default directory* is the directory where Word retrieves (saves) documents unless it is otherwise instructed. To change the default directory, pull down the Tools menu, click Options, click the File Locations tab, click Documents, and click the Modify command button. Enter the name of the new directory (for example, C:\WORDDATA), click OK, then click the Close button. The next time you access the File menu the default directory will reflect these changes.

Step 4: The Save As command

➤ Pull down the **File menu.** Click the **Save As** command to produce the dialog box in Figure 2.5c.

➤ Enter a filename from one to eight characters, for example, **PRACTICE** (the DOC extension is added automatically), and press **enter.**

➤ There are now two identical copies of the file on disk—FIRSTWP.DOC, which we supplied, and PRACTICE.DOC, which you just created. The title bar of the document window shows the latter name.

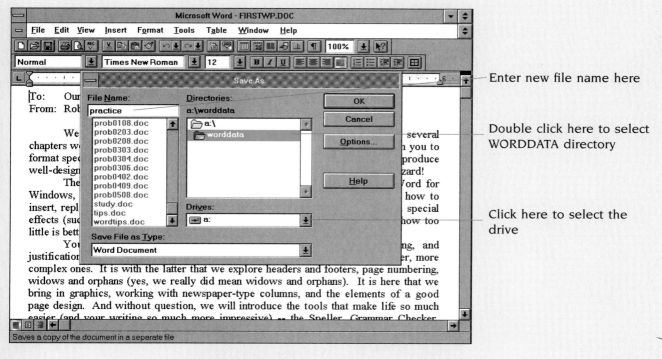

- Enter new file name here

- Double click here to select WORDDATA directory

- Click here to select the drive

(c) Save As Command (step 4)

FIGURE 2.5 Hands-on Exercise 1 (continued)

Step 5: Scrolling

➤ Click the **down arrow** at the bottom of the vertical scroll bar to move down in the document, causing the top line to disappear and be replaced with a new line at the bottom.

➤ Click the **down arrow** several times to move through the document, then click the **up arrow** key to scroll in the other direction.

➤ Drag the **scroll box** to the bottom of the scroll bar, to the top of the scroll bar, then to the middle of the scroll bar, noting that in every instance the insertion point does *not* follow the scrolling; that is, you must **click the mouse** to move the insertion point to the new location after scrolling with the mouse.

KEYBOARD SHORTCUTS: MOVING WITHIN A DOCUMENT

Press **Ctrl+Home** and **Ctrl+End** to move to the beginning and end of a document. Press **Home** and **End** to move to the beginning and end of a line. Press **PgUp** or **PgDn** to scroll one screen in the indicated direction. The advantage to scrolling via the keyboard (instead of the mouse) is that the insertion point moves as you scroll.

Step 6: Insertion versus Overtype

➤ Press the **Ins** key once or twice until you clearly see OVR in one of the status boxes at the bottom of the screen.

- ➤ Press the **Ins** key once more so that OVR becomes dim. You are now in the insert mode.
- ➤ Press **Ctrl+Home** to move to the beginning of the document, click immediately before the period ending the first sentence, press the **space bar,** then add the phrase **and desktop publishing.**
- ➤ Drag the **scroll box** to scroll to the bottom of the document, and click immediately before the M in Ms. Mary Ann Barber.
- ➤ Press the **Ins** key (OVR should appear in the status bar) to toggle to the replacement mode, then type **Dr.** to replace Ms.
- ➤ Press **Ctrl+Home** to move to the beginning of the document. Click and drag the mouse to select the phrase **Our Students.** Type your name to replace the highlighted text.
- ➤ Pull down the **File menu** and click **Save** (or click the **Save icon**) to save the changes.

Step 7: Find and Replace
- ➤ Press **Ctrl+Home** to move to the beginning of the document.
- ➤ Pull down the **Edit menu.** Click **Replace** to produce the dialog box of Figure 2.5d.
- ➤ Type **text** in the Find What text box.
- ➤ Press the **Tab key.** Type **book** in the Replace With text box.
- ➤ Click the **Find Next button** to find the first occurrence of the word "text." The dialog box remains on the screen and the first occurrence of "text" is highlighted. This is *not* an appropriate substitution; that is, you should not substitute "book" for "text" at this point.
- ➤ Click the **Find Next button** to move to the next occurrence. This time the substitution is appropriate.
- ➤ Click **Replace** to make the change and automatically move to the next occurrence where the substitution is again inappropriate.
- ➤ Click **Find Next** a final time. Word will indicate that it has finished searching the document. Click **OK.**
- ➤ Change the Find and Replace strings to **Mary Ann** and **Maryann,** respectively.
- ➤ Click the **Replace All button** to make the substitution globally without confirmation. Word will indicate that it has finished searching and that two replacements were made. Click **OK.**
- ➤ Click the **Close command button** to close the dialog box. Save the document.

Step 8: The clipboard
- ➤ Press **PgDn** to scroll toward the end of the document until you come to the paragraph beginning *It is up to you.*
- ➤ Select the sentence *Practice and practice some more* by dragging the mouse over the sentence. (Be sure to include the period.) The sentence will be highlighted as shown in Figure 2.5e.
- ➤ Pull down the **Edit menu.** Click **Copy** to copy the selected text to the clipboard.
- ➤ Scroll to the end of the document. **Click the mouse** (to move the insertion point). Press the **enter key** twice.
- ➤ Pull down the **Edit menu.** Click **Paste** to copy the selected sentence.

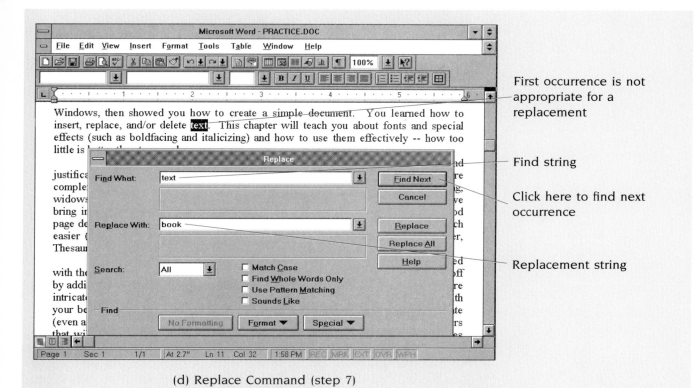

First occurrence is not appropriate for a replacement

Find string

Click here to find next occurrence

Replacement string

(d) Replace Command (step 7)

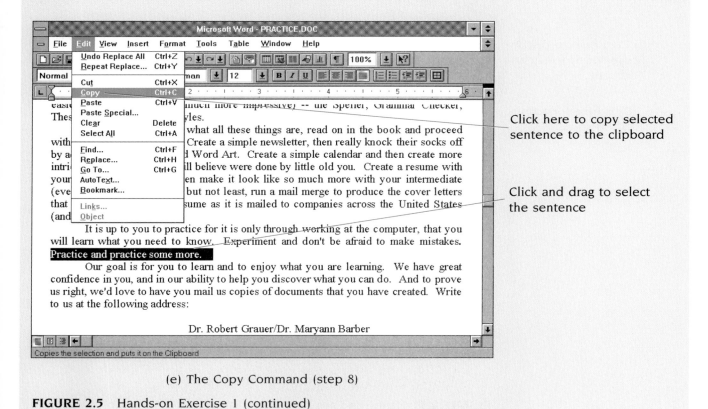

Click here to copy selected sentence to the clipboard

Click and drag to select the sentence

(e) The Copy Command (step 8)

FIGURE 2.5 Hands-on Exercise 1 (continued)

➤ Move the insertion point to the end of the first paragraph (ending with the word "wizard"). Press the **space bar** twice.

➤ Pull down the **Edit menu.** Click **Paste** to copy the sentence a second time.

➤ Save the document.

CUT, COPY, AND PASTE

Ctrl+X, **Ctrl+C**, and **Ctrl+V** are shortcuts to cut, copy, and paste, respectively, and apply to Word for Windows, Excel, and Windows applications in general. (The shortcuts are easier to remember when you realize that the operative letters, X, C, and V are next to each other at the bottom left side of the keyboard.) You can also use the Cut, Copy, and Paste icons on the Standard toolbar, which are also found on the Standard toolbar in Excel.

Step 9: Undo and Redo

➤ Click the **down arrow** next to the Undo tool to display the previously executed actions as in Figure 2.5f.

➤ The list of actions corresponds to the editing commands you have issued since the start of the exercise. (Your list will be different from ours if you deviated from any instructions in the hands-on exercise.)

➤ Click the **down arrow** for the Redo command. You will hear a beep indicating that there are no actions to be redone; that is, the Undo command has not yet been issued and so there is nothing to redo.

Click here to display previously executed actions

Click here for actions to redo

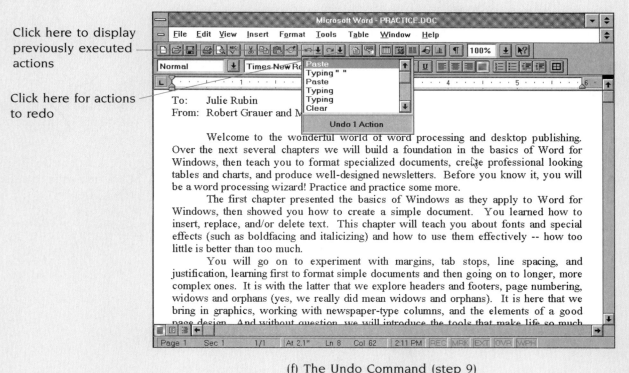

(f) The Undo Command (step 9)

FIGURE 2.5 Hands-on Exercise 1 (continued)

➤ Click the **down arrow** for the Undo command. Click **Paste** (the first command on the list) to undo the most recent editing command; the sentence, *Practice and practice some more,* disappears from the end of the first paragraph.

➤ Click the remaining steps on the undo list to retrace your steps through the exercise. When the list is empty you will have the document as it existed at the start of the exercise.

➤ Click the **down arrow** for the Redo command. This time you will see the list of commands you have undone; click each command in sequence and you will restore the document.

Step 10: Drag and drop

➤ This step takes a little practice, but it is well worth it.

➤ Use the Find command to locate and select the phrase **format specialized documents,** as shown in Figure 2.5g. (Be sure to include the comma and the space after the comma.)

➤ Drag the phrase to its new location immediately before the word "and," then release the mouse button to complete the move. (A dotted vertical bar appears as you drag the text to indicate its new location.)

➤ Click the **drop-down list box** for the **Undo** command; click **Move** to undo the move.

➤ To copy the selected text, press and hold the **Ctrl key** as you drag the text to its new location.

➤ Practice the drag-and-drop procedure several times until you are confident you can move and copy with precision.

➤ Save the document.

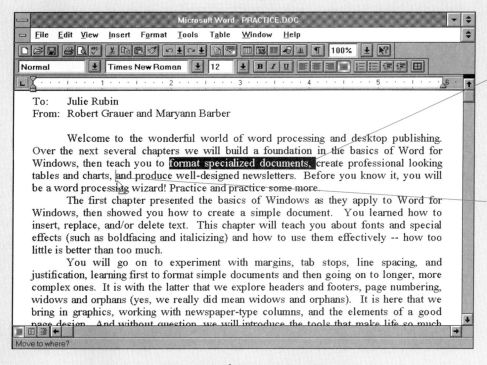

Click and drag to select phrase

Drag to new location (indicated by dotted vertical bar)

(g) Drag and Drop (step 10)

FIGURE 2.5   Hands-on Exercise 1 (continued)

Step 11: Print the completed document

➤ Pull down the **View menu** and select **Page Layout** (or click the **Page Layout button** on the status bar).

➤ Pull down the **View menu,** click **Zoom,** and select **Whole Page** (or use the Zoom control box on the Standard toolbar.)

➤ Your screen should match Figure 2.5h, which shows the completed document.

➤ Pull down the **File menu,** click **Print,** and click **OK** (or click the **Print button** on the Standard toolbar) to print the completed document.

➤ Pull down the **File menu** and click **Exit** (or double click the **control-menu box**) to quit **Word.**

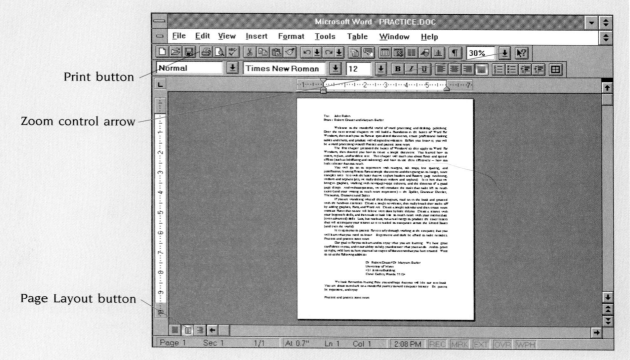

Print button

Zoom control arrow

Page Layout button

(h) The Completed Document (step 11)

FIGURE 2.5   Hands-on Exercise 1 (continued)

TYPOGRAPHY

Typography is the process of selecting typefaces, type styles, and type sizes. The importance of these decisions is obvious, for the ultimate success of any document depends greatly on its appearance. Type should reinforce the message without calling attention to itself and should be consistent with the information you want to convey.

Typeface

A **typeface** is a complete set of characters (upper- and lowercase letters, numbers, punctuation marks, and special symbols). Figure 2.6 illustrates two typefaces, **Times New Roman** and **Arial,** that are supplied with Windows, and which in turn are accessible from Word.

The type you choose should be consistent with the message you want to convey, neither too large nor too small, neither too bold nor too reserved. A serif typeface has tiny cross strokes that end the main strokes of each letter; a sans serif typeface does not.

(a) Times New Roman

The type you choose should be consistent with the message you want to convey, neither too large nor too small, neither too bold nor too reserved. A serif typeface has tiny cross strokes that end the main strokes of each letter; a sans serif typeface does not.

(b) Arial

FIGURE 2.6 Type Faces

One definitive characteristic of any typeface is the presence or absence of tiny cross lines that end the main stroke of each letter. A *serif typeface* has these lines; a *sans serif* (sans from the French for *without*) does not. Times New Roman is an example of a serif typeface. Arial is a sans serif typeface.

Serifs help the eye to connect one letter with the next and are generally used with large amounts of text. This book, for example, is set in a serif typeface. A sans serif typeface is more effective with smaller amounts of text and appears in headlines, corporate logos, airport signs, and so on. Serif typefaces convey a sense of authority; sans serif typefaces produce a more informal result.

Any typeface can be set in different styles (e.g., regular, boldface, or italics). A *font* (as the term is used in Windows) is a specific typeface in a specific style; for example, **Arial bold** or *Times New Roman italic*.

TYPOGRAPHY TIP: USE RESTRAINT

More is not better especially in the case of too many typefaces and styles, which produce cluttered documents that impress no one. Try to limit yourself to a maximum of two typefaces per document, but choose multiple sizes and/or styles within those typefaces. Use boldface or italics for emphasis, but do so in moderation, because if you emphasize too many elements the effect is lost.

Type Size

Type size is a vertical measurement and is specified in points. One *point* is equal to 1/72 of an inch; that is, there are 72 points to the inch. The measurement is made from the top of the tallest letter in a character set (for example, an upper-case T) to the bottom of the lowest letter (for example, a lowercase y). Most documents are set in 10 or 12 point type; newspaper columns may be set as small as 8 point type. Type sizes of 14 points or higher are ineffective for large amounts of text. Figure 2.7 shows the same phrase set in varying type sizes.

Some typefaces appear larger (smaller) than others even though they may be set in the same point size. The type in Figure 2.6a, for example, looks smaller than the corresponding type in Figure 2.6b even though both are set in the same point size. This is because the Arial typeface users longer ascenders (strokes that climb upward from the baseline) and longer descenders (strokes that reach downward) than the Times New Roman design.

This is Arial 8 point type

This is Arial 10 point type

This is Arial 12 point type

This is Arial 18 point type

This is Arial 24 point type

(a) Sans Serif Typeface

This is Times New Roman 8 point type

This is Times New Roman 10 point type

This is Times New Roman 12 point type

This is Times New Roman 18 point type

This is Times New Roman 24 point type

(b) Serif Typeface

FIGURE 2.7   Type Size

TrueType

Windows 3.1 supports a new type of font technology known as ***TrueType,*** which uses the same fonts for the monitor and the printer. This means that your document is truly WYSIWYG, and that the fonts you see on the monitor will be identical to those in the printed document. Equally important, TrueType fonts are scalable, so that you can select any font in any size, from 4 to 127 points. And finally, TrueType fonts are accessible from any Windows application; that is, you can use the same fonts in Excel as in Word.

Windows itself includes 14 TrueType fonts: *Times New Roman* (in regular, bold, italic, and bold italic styles), *Arial* (in regular, bold, italic, and bold italic styles) *Courier New* (in regular, bold, italic, and bold italic styles), and two special fonts: *Symbol* and *Wingdings.* Word for Windows provides several additional fonts, giving you a great deal of flexibility in the documents you create.

All fonts are classified as either monospaced or proportional. A ***monospaced font*** such as Courier New has a fixed pitch (uniform character width). Monospaced fonts are used in tables and financial projections where items must be precisely lined up, one beneath the other. A ***proportional font***—for example, Times New Roman or Arial—allocates a different amount of space for each character according to the width of the character. Proportional fonts create a more professional appearance and are appropriate for most documents.

FORMAT FONT COMMAND

The ***Format Font command*** gives you complete control over the size and style of the text in a document. Execution of the command produces the dialog box in Figure 2.8, in which you specify the font (typeface), style, and point size. You can choose any of the special effects and/or change the underline options (whether or not spaces are to be underlined). You can even change the color of the text on the monitor, but you need a color printer for the printed document. The Character Spacing tab produces a different set of options in which you control the spacing of the characters.

The Preview box shows the text as it will appear in the document. The message at the bottom of the dialog box indicates that Times New Roman is a True-Type font and that the same font will be used on both the screen and the monitor.

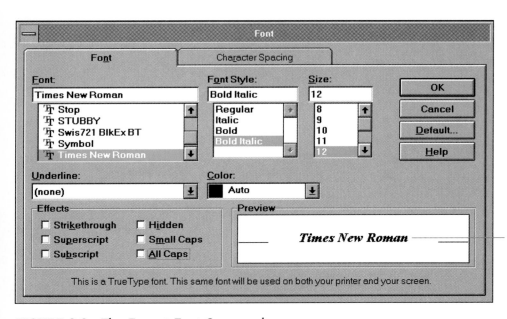

Text as it will appear in the document

FIGURE 2.8 The Format Font Command

FORMAT PAINTER

The ***Format Painter*** copies the formatting of the selected text to other places in a document. Select the text with the formatting you want to copy, then double click the Format Painter button on the Standard Toolbar. The mouse pointer changes to a paintbrush to indicate that you can paint other areas in the document with the current formatting; just drag the paintbrush over the additional text, which will assume the identical formatting characteristics as the original selection. Repeat the painting process as often as necessary, then click the Format Painter button a second time to return to normal editing.

PAGE SETUP COMMAND

The **Page Setup command** in the File menu lets you change margins, paper size (and orientation), paper source, and/or layout. All parameters are accessed from the dialog box in Figure 2.9 by clicking the appropriate tab within the dialog box.

The default margins are indicated in Figure 2.9a and are one inch on the top and bottom of the page, and one-and-a-quarter inches on the left and right. You can change any (or all) of these settings by entering a new value in the appropriate text box, either by typing it explicitly or clicking the up/down arrow. The margins in the figure apply to the whole document regardless of the position of the insertion point. (Different margins can be in effect for different parts of a document by creating sections, a concept discussed in Chapter 5.)

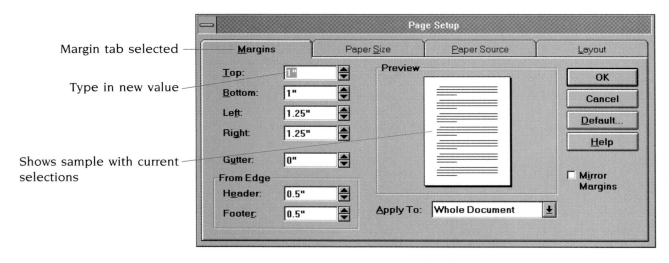

(a) Margins

FIGURE 2.9   Page Setup Command

The Paper Size tab within the Page Setup command enables you to change the orientation of a page as shown in Figure 2.9b. **Portrait orientation** is the default. **Landscape orientation** flips the page 90 degrees so that its dimensions are 11 × 8½ rather than the other way around. Note, too, the Preview box in the figure, which shows how the document will appear with the selected parameters.

The Paper Source tab is used to specify which tray should be used on printers with multiple trays, and is helpful when you want to load different types of paper simultaneously. The Layout tab is used to create headers and footers and is discussed in Chapter 4.

Page Breaks

One of the first concepts you learned was that of word wrap, whereby Word inserts a soft return at the end of a line in order to begin a new line. The number and location of the soft returns change automatically as you add or delete text within a document. Soft returns are very different from the hard returns inserted by the user, whose number and location remain constant.

In much the same way, Word creates a **soft page break** to go to the top of a new page when text no longer fits on the current page. And just as you can insert a hard return to start a new paragraph, you can insert a **hard page break** to force any part of a document to begin on a new page. (Press **Ctrl+Enter** to create a hard page break.)

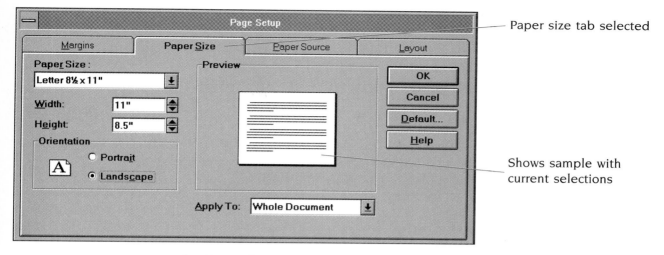

Paper size tab selected

Shows sample with current selections

(b) Size and Orientation

FIGURE 2.9   Page Setup Command (continued)

AN EXERCISE IN DESIGN

The following exercise has you retrieve an existing document from the data disk, then experiment with various typefaces, type styles, and point sizes. The original document uses a monospaced (typewriter style) font, without boldface or italics, and you are asked to improve its appearance. The first step directs you to save the document under a new name so that you can always return to the original if necessary.

There is no right and wrong with respect to design and you are free to choose any combination of fonts that appeal to you. The exercise takes you through various formatting options but lets you make the final decision. It does, however, ask you to print the final document and submit it to your instructor.

IMPOSE A TIME LIMIT

A word processor is supposed to save time and make you more productive. It will do exactly that provided you use the word processor for its primary purpose—writing and editing. It is all too easy, however, to lose sight of that objective and spend too much time formatting the document. Concentrate on the content of your document rather than its appearance. Impose a time limit on the amount of time you will spend on formatting. End the session when the limit is reached.

HANDS-ON EXERCISE 2:

Character Formatting

Objective Experiment with character formatting; to change fonts and to use boldface and italics; to copy formatting with the Format Painter; to insert a page break and see different views of a document. Use Figure 2.10 as a guide in the exercise.

Step 1: Load the practice document.

➤ Pull down the **File menu.** Click **Open** (or click the Open icon on the Standard toolbar).

➤ If you have not yet changed the default directory:
— Click the appropriate drive.
— Scroll through the directory list box until you come to the **WORDDATA** directory.
— Double click the **WORDATA** directory.

➤ Double click **TIPS.DOC** to open the document.

➤ Pull down the **File menu.** Click the **Save As** command to save the file as **MYTIPS.DOC.** The title bar reflects MYTIPS.DOC, but you can always return to the original TIPS.DOC document if you edit the duplicated file beyond repair.

➤ Pull down the **View menu** and click **Normal** (or click the **Normal View button** on the Status Bar).

➤ Set the magnification (zoom) to **Page Width.**

TIP: SELECTING TEXT

The *selection bar,* a blank column at the far left of the document window, makes it easy to select a line, paragraph, or the entire document.

➤ To select a line, move the mouse pointer to the selection bar, point to the line, and click the left mouse button.

➤ To select a paragraph, move the mouse pointer to the selection bar, point to any line in the paragraph, and double click the mouse.

➤ To select the entire document, move the mouse pointer to the selection bar and press the **Ctrl** key while you click the mouse.

Step 2: Shortcut menu

➤ Select the first tip as shown in Figure 2.10a.

➤ Click the **right mouse button** to produce the Shortcut menu shown in the figure. The Shortcut menu contains commands from both the Edit and Format menus.

➤ Click outside the menu to close the menu without executing a command.

➤ Press the **Ctrl key** as you click the selection bar to select the entire document, then click the **right mouse button** to display the Shortcut menu.

➤ Click **Font** to execute the Format Font command.

Step 3: Changing fonts

➤ Click the **down arrow** on the Font list box of Figure 2.10b to scroll through the available fonts. Select a different font—for example, Times New Roman.

➤ Click the **down arrow** in the Font Size list box to choose a point size.

➤ Click **OK** to change the font and point size for the selected text.

➤ Pull down the **Edit menu** and click **Undo** (or click the **Undo button** on the Standard toolbar) to return to the original font.

➤ Experiment with different fonts and/or different point sizes until you are satisfied with the selection; we chose 12 point Times New Roman.

➤ Save the document.

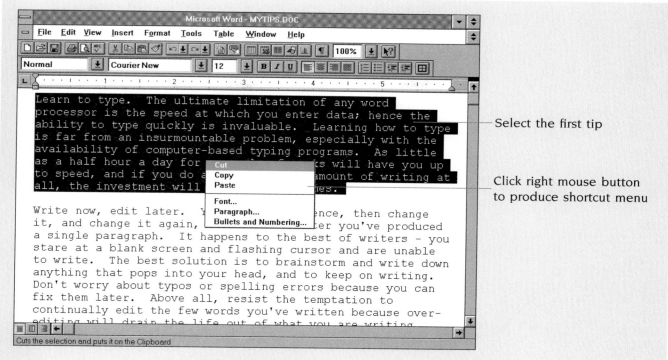

Select the first tip

Click right mouse button
to produce shortcut menu

(a) Shortcut Menu (step 2)

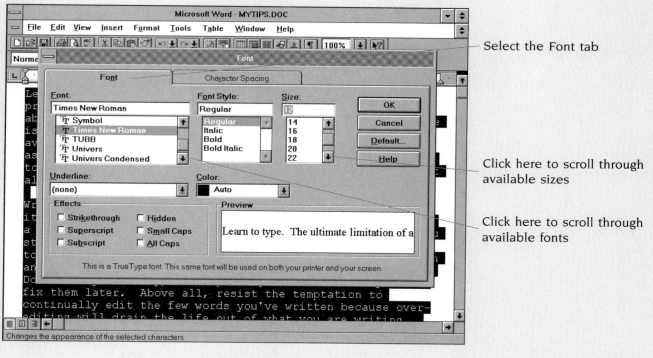

Select the Font tab

Click here to scroll through
available sizes

Click here to scroll through
available fonts

(b) The Format Font Command (step 3)

FIGURE 2.10   Hands-on Exercise 2

Step 4: Boldface and italics

➤ Drag the mouse over the sentence **Learn to Type** at the beginning of the
document.

- Click the **Italics button** on the Formatting toolbar to italicize the selected phrase. The phrase should remain highlighted.
- Click the **Boldface button** to boldface the selected text; the text is now in boldface and italics.
- Experiment with different styles (boldface, italics, underlining, or boldface-italics) until you are satisfied. The italics, boldface, and underline buttons function as toggle switches; that is, clicking the italics button when text is already italicized returns the text to normal.
- Save the document.

DESELECTING TEXT

The effects of a formatting change are often difficult to see when text is highlighted. Thus, it is often necessary to deselect the text in order to see the results of a formatting command.

Step 5: The Format Painter
- Click anywhere within the sentence **Learn to Type.**
- **Double click** the **Format Painter button** on the Standard toolbar. The mouse pointer changes to a paintbrush as shown in Figure 2.10c.
- Drag the mouse pointer over the next title, **Write now, edit later,** and release the mouse. The formatting from the original sentence (boldface italics in Figure 2.10c) has been applied to this sentence as well.
- Drag the mouse pointer (in the shape of a paintbrush) over the remaining titles in the document to copy the formatting.
- Click the **Format Painter button** after you have painted the last tip.
- Save the document.

DIALOG BOX SHORTCUTS

You can use the mouse to click an option button, to mark a check box on or off, or to pull down a drop-down list box and select an option. You can also use a keyboard shortcut for each of these actions.

- Press Tab (Shift+Tab) to move forward (backward) from one field or command button to the next
- Press Alt plus the underlined letter to move directly to a field or command button
- Press Enter to activate the highlighted command button
- Press Esc to exit the dialog box without taking action
- Press the Space Bar to toggle check boxes on or off
- Press the down arrow to open a list box once the list has been accessed; press the up or down arrow to move between options in a list box

Step 6: Change margins
- Press **Ctrl+End** to move to the end of the document as shown in Figure 2.10d.
- You will see a dotted line indicating a soft page break. (If you do not see

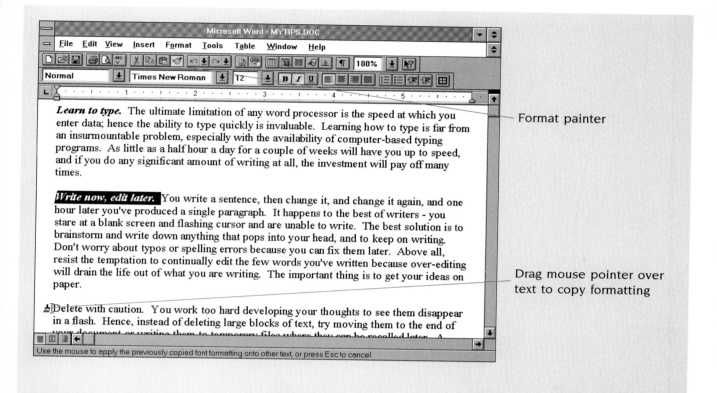

Format painter

Drag mouse pointer over text to copy formatting

(c) The Format Painter (step 5)

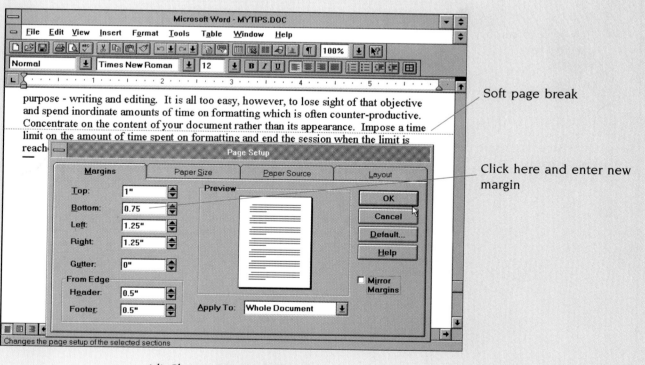

Soft page break

Click here and enter new margin

(d) Change Margins (step 6)

FIGURE 2.10 Hands-on Exercise 2 (continued)

the page break, it means that your document fits on one page because you used a different font and/or a smaller point size; we used 12 point Times New Roman.)

➤ Pull down the **File menu.** Click **Page Setup.**
➤ Change the bottom margin to **.75** inch. Click **OK.** The page break disappears because we can fit more text on the page.
➤ Save the document.

Step 7: Create a title page
➤ Press **Ctrl+Home** to move to the beginning of the document.
➤ Press **enter** three or four times to add a few blank lines.
➤ Press **Ctrl+Enter** to insert a hard page break. You will see the words "Page Break" in the middle of a dotted line as shown in Figure 2.10e.
➤ Press the **up arrow key** two times.
➤ Enter the title **Word Processing Tips.** Select the title and format it in a larger point size, such as 24 points.
➤ Enter your name on the next line in a different point size, such as 14 points.
➤ Select both the title and your name as shown in the figure. Click the **Center justification button** on the Standard toolbar.
➤ Save the document.

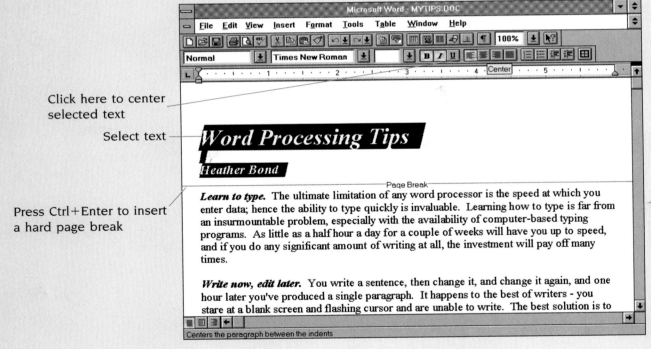

Click here to center selected text

Select text

Press Ctrl+Enter to insert a hard page break

(e) Create the Title Page (step 7)

FIGURE 2.10 Hands-on Exercise 2 (continued)

Step 8: The completed document
➤ Pull down the **View menu** and click **Page Layout** (or click the **Page Layout button** on the status bar).

➤ Click the **Zoom control arrow** on the Standard toolbar and drag to select **Two Pages.** Release the mouse to view the completed document in Figure 2.10f.

➤ Exit Word.

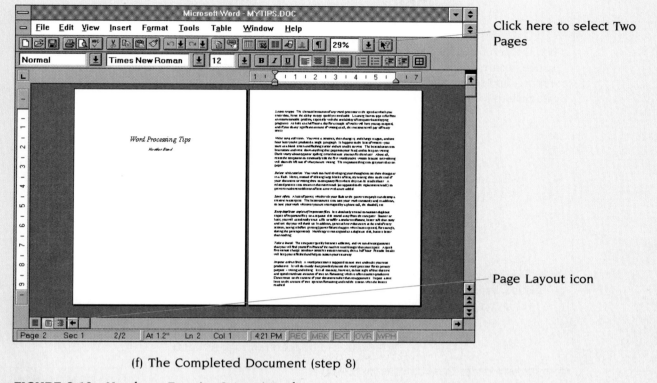

Click here to select Two Pages

Page Layout icon

(f) The Completed Document (step 8)

FIGURE 2.10 Hands-on Exercise 2 (continued)

PARAGRAPH FORMATTING

A change in typography is only one way to alter the appearance of a document. You can also change its indentation, *alignment,* or line spacing, or you can include borders or shading for added emphasis. All of these features are implemented at the paragraph level and affect the entire paragraph, regardless of the position of the insertion point when the command is executed.

Alignment

Text can be aligned in four different ways as shown in Figure 2.11. It may be fully justified (flush left/flush right), left aligned (flush left with a ragged-right margin), right aligned (flush right with a ragged-left margin), or centered within the margins (ragged left and right).

Left-aligned text is perhaps the easiest to read. The first letters of each line align with each other, helping the eye to find the beginning of each line. The lines themselves are of irregular length. There is uniform spacing between words. The ragged margin on the right adds white space to the text, giving it a lighter and more informal look.

Fully justified text produces lines of equal length, with the spacing between words adjusted to align at the margins. It may be more difficult to read than text

We, the people of the United States, in order to form a more perfect Union, establish justice, insure domestic tranquility, provide for the common defense, promote the general welfare, and secure the blessings of liberty to ourselves and our posterity, do ordain and establish this Constitution for the United States of America.

(a) Fully Justified (flush left/flush right)

We, the people of the United States, in order to form a more perfect Union, establish justice, insure domestic tranquility, provide for the common defense, promote the general welfare, and secure the blessings of liberty to ourselves and our posterity, do ordain and establish this Constitution for the United States of America.

(b) Left Aligned (flush left/ragged right)

We, the people of the United States, in order to form a more perfect Union, establish justice, insure domestic tranquility, provide for the common defense, promote the general welfare, and secure the blessings of liberty to ourselves and our posterity, do ordain and establish this Constitution for the United States of America.

(c) Right Aligned (flush right/ragged left)

We, the people of the United States, in order to form a more perfect Union, establish justice, insure domestic tranquility, provide for the common defense, promote the general welfare, and secure the blessings of liberty to ourselves and our posterity, do ordain and establish this Constitution for the United States of America.

(d) Centered (ragged left/ragged right)

FIGURE 2.11   Alignment

that is left aligned because of the uneven (sometimes excessive) word spacing and/or the greater number of hyphenated words needed to justify the lines.

Type that is centered or right justified is restricted to limited amounts of text where the effect is more important than the ease of reading. Centered text, for example, appears frequently on wedding invitations or formal announcements. Right-justified text is used with figure captions and short headlines.

Tabs

Anyone who has used a typewriter is familiar with the function of the Tab key; that is, press Tab and the insertion point moves to the next *tab stop* (a measured position to align text at a specific place.) The Tab key functions identically within Word except it is more powerful because you can choose from four different types of tab stops (left, center, right, and decimal). You can also specify a *leader character,* typically dots or hyphens, to draw the reader's eye across the page. Tabs are often used to create tables within a document.

The default tab stops are set every 1/2 inch and are left aligned. You can change the alignment and/or position with the Format Tabs command in Figure 2.12. Four types of alignment are possible:

➤ Left alignment, where the text *begins* at the tab stop and corresponds exactly to the Tab key on a typewriter

➤ Right alignment, where the text *ends* at the tab stop; right alignment is commonly used to align page numbers in a table of contents

➤ Center alignment, where text centers over the tab stop

➤ Decimal alignment, which lines up numeric values in a column on the decimal point

Figure 2.12 illustrates a dot leader in combination with a right tab to produce a Table of Contents. The default tab stops have been cleared in Figure 2.12a, in favor of a single right tab at 5.5 inches. The option button for a dot leader has also been checked. The resulting document is shown in Figure 2.12b.

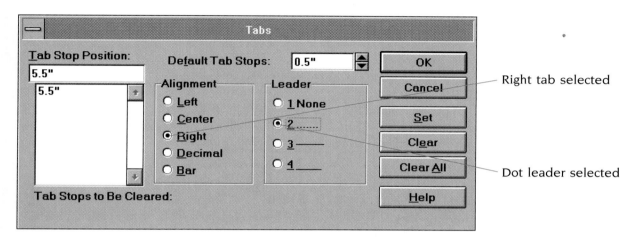

(a) Tab Stops

Right tab selected

Dot leader selected

Right tab with a dot leader

Chapter 1: Introduction...3
Chapter 2: Gaining Proficiency.................................. 32
Chapter 3: The Tools.. 61
Chapter 4: The Professional Document........................... 99
Chapter 5: Desktop Publishing..................................124

(b) Table of Contents

FIGURE 2.12   Tabs

Indents

Individual paragraphs can be indented so that they appear to have different margins from the rest of a document. Indentation is established at the paragraph level; thus different indentation can be in effect for different paragraphs. One paragraph may be indented from the left margin only, another from the right margin only, and a third from both the left and right margins. The first line of any paragraph may be indented differently from the rest of the paragraph. And finally, a paragraph may be set with no indentation at all, so that it aligns on the left and right margins.

The indentation of a paragraph is determined by three settings: the ***first-line indent,*** the ***left indent,*** and the ***right indent.*** The default values for all three parameters are zero, and produce a paragraph with no indentation as shown in Figure 2.13a. Positive values for the left and right indents offset the paragraph from both margins as shown in Figure 2.13b.

The left and right indents are defined as the distance between the text and the left and right margins, respectively. Both parameters are set to zero in this paragraph, and so it aligns on both margins.

(a) No Indents

Positive values for the left and right indents offset a paragraph from the rest of a document and are often used for long quotations. This paragraph has left and right indents of one-half inch each.

(b) Left and Right Indents

In addition to setting left and right indents, you can indent the first line of a paragraph. This paragraph uses a first-line indent, which is equivalent to pressing the Tab key at the beginning of a paragraph.

(c) First Line Indent

A hanging indent sets the first line of a paragraph to left of the remaining lines. Hanging indents are used for added emphasis and often appears with numbered or bulleted lists.

(d) Hanging Indent

FIGURE 2.13 Indents

The first-line indent affects only the first line in the paragraph as shown in Figure 2.13c (and is an alternative to pressing the Tab key). A negative value for the first-line indent creates a *hanging indent* as shown in Figure 2.13d and is often used with bulleted or numbered lists.

Indents affect an entire paragraph and can be set when the insertion point is anywhere within the paragraph. To change the indentation of multiple paragraphs, first select the paragraphs, then set the indentation.

INDENTS VERSUS MARGINS

Indents measure the distance between the text and the margins. Margins mark the distance from the text to the edge of the page. Indents are determined at the paragraph level, whereas margins are established at the section (document) level. The left and right margins are set (by default) to 1.25 inches each; the left and right indents default to zero. The first-line indent is measured from the setting of the left indent and can be either positive or negative.

FORMAT PARAGRAPH COMMAND

The **Format Paragraph command** sets the indentation, tab stops, line spacing, and alignment for the selected paragraph(s). The command also provides a preview that lets you see the options in effect—for example, a hanging indent, line spacing of 1.5 lines, and full justification as shown in Figure 2.14a.

Figure 2.14b illustrates an entirely different set of options in which you control the text flow (pagination) of a document. You are already familiar with the concept of **page breaks,** and the distinction between soft page breaks (inserted by Word) versus hard page breaks (inserted by the user). The check boxes in Figure 2.14b enable you to prevent awkward page breaks that detract from the appearance of a document.

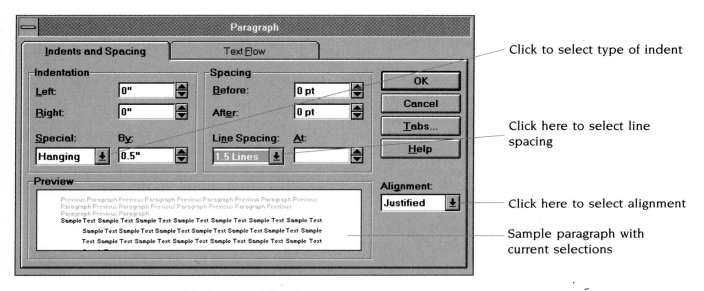

(a) Indents and Spacing

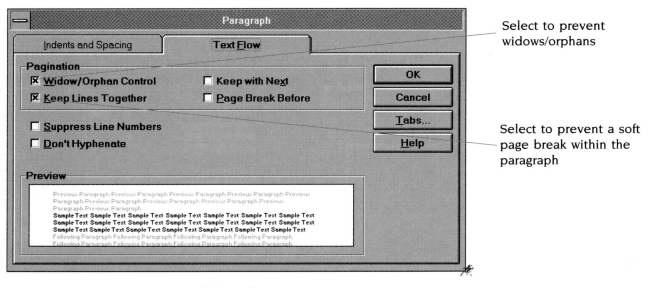

(b) Text Flow

FIGURE 2.14   The Format Paragraph Command

You might, for example, want to prevent **widows and orphans,** terms used to describe isolated lines that seem lost and out of place. A widow refers to the last line of a paragraph appearing by itself at the top of a page; an orphan is the first line of a paragraph appearing by itself at the bottom of a page.

You can also impose additional controls by clicking one or more check boxes. Use the Keep Lines Together option to prevent a break within a paragraph—that is, to ensure that the entire paragraph appears on the same page. Use the Keep with Next option to prevent a page break between the selected paragraph and the following paragraph.

FORMATTING AND THE PARAGRAPH MARK

The **paragraph mark** ¶ at the end of a paragraph does more than just indicate the presence of a hard return. It also stores all of the formatting in effect for the paragraph. Hence in order to preserve the formatting when you move or copy a paragraph, you must include the paragraph mark in the selected text. Click the Show/Hide button on the toolbar to display the paragraph mark and make sure it has been selected.

Borders and Shading

The **Borders and Shading command** in Figure 2.15 puts the finishing touches on a document. It lets you create boxed and/or shaded text as well as place horizontal or vertical lines around a paragraph. You can choose from several different line styles in any color (assuming you have a color printer). You can place a uniform border around a paragraph (choose Box), or you can create a **drop shadow effect** with thicker lines at the right and bottom. You can also apply lines to selected sides of a paragraph(s) by clicking the desired sides within the Border sample box and then selecting a line style.

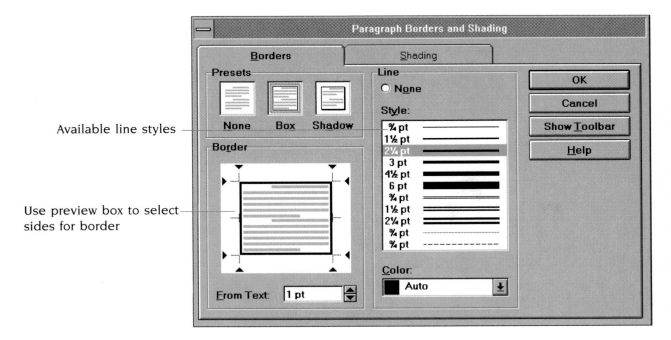

(a) Borders

FIGURE 2.15 Paragraph Borders and Shading

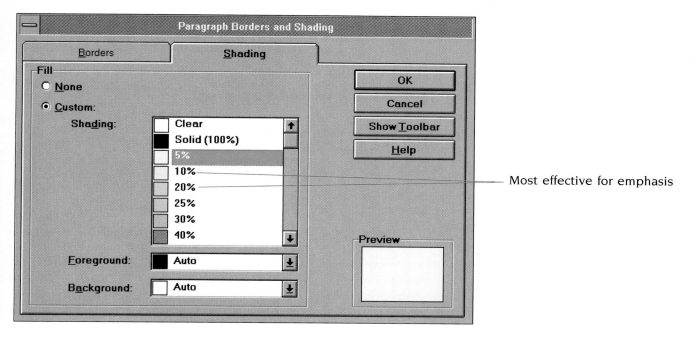

Most effective for emphasis

(b) Shading

FIGURE 2.15 Paragraph Borders and Shading (continued)

Shading is implemented independently of the border. Clear (no shading) is the default. Solid (100%) shading creates a solid box where the text is unreadable. Shading of 10 or 20 percent is generally most effective to add emphasis to the selected paragraph.

HELP WITH FORMATTING

It's all too easy to lose sight of the formatting in effect, so Word provides a Help button on the Standard toolbar. Click the button, and the mouse pointer assumes the shape of a large question mark. Click anywhere in a document to display the formatting in effect at that point. Click the Help button a second time to exit Help.

HANDS-ON EXERCISE 3:

Paragraph Formatting

Objective To practice line spacing, alignment, justification, tabs and indents; to implement widow and orphan protection; to box and shade a selected paragraph. Use Figure 2.16 as a guide in the exercise.

Step 1: Load the practice document.
➤ Open the **MYTIPS** document from the previous exercise.
➤ Pull down the **File menu.** Save the document as **MYTIPS2.DOC.**
➤ If necessary change to the Page Layout view. Pull down the **Zoom control**

button and click **Two Pages** to match the view in Figure 2.16a.

➤ Select the entire second page as shown in the figure.

➤ Press the **right mouse button** to produce the shortcut menu.

➤ Click **Paragraph** to produce the dialog box in Figure 2.16b.

Click here to view Two Pages

Select entire page

Click right mouse button to produce shortcut menu

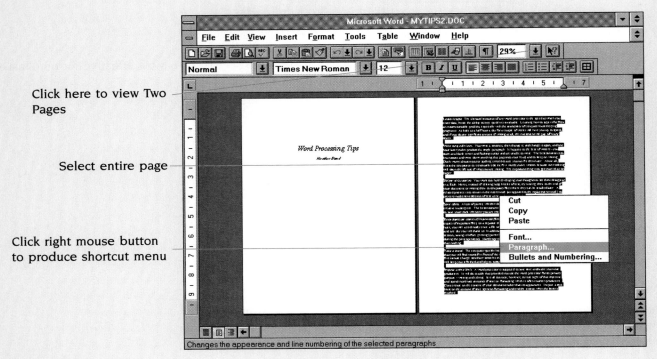

(a) Select Then Do (step 1)

FIGURE 2.16 Hands-on Exercise 3

SELECT TEXT WITH THE F8 EXTEND KEY

Position the insertion point at the beginning of the text you want to select, then press the F8 (extend) key The letters EXT will appear in the status bar. Use the arrow keys to extend the selection in the indicated direction; for example, press the down arrow key to select the line. You can also press any character—for example, a letter, space, or period—to extend the selection to the first occurrence of that character. Press Esc to cancel the selection mode.

Step 2: Line spacing, justification, and text flow

➤ If necessary, click the **Indents and Spacing tab** to view the options in Figure 2.16b.

➤ Click the **down arrow** on the list box for Line Spacing and select **1.5 Lines.**

➤ Click the **down arrow** on the Alignment list box and select **Justified** as shown in Figure 2.16b.

➤ Click the tab for **Text Flow.** Check the box for **Keep Lines Together.** If necessary, check the box for **Widow/Orphan Control.**

➤ Click **OK** to accept all of the settings in the dialog box; that is, you need to

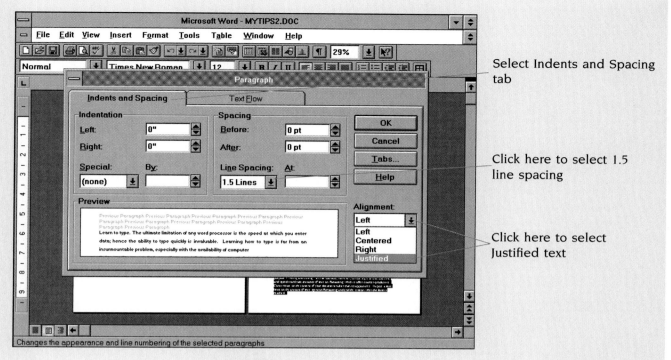

Select Indents and Spacing tab

Click here to select 1.5 line spacing

Click here to select Justified text

(b) Format Paragraph Command (step 2)

FIGURE 2.16 Hands-on Exercise 3 (continued)

click OK only once to accept the settings for Indents and Spacing and Text Flow.

➤ Click anywhere in the document to deselect the text and see the effects of the formatting changes. The document is fully justified and the line spacing has increased.

➤ Save the document.

PARAGRAPH FORMATTING AND THE INSERTION POINT

Indents, tabs, line spacing, justification, and text flow are set at the paragraph level and affect the entire paragraph. The position of the insertion point within the paragraph does not matter; that is, the insertion point can be anywhere within the paragraph when the Format Paragraph command is executed.

Step 3: Tabs

➤ Pull down the **View menu,** click **Zoom,** then select **Page Width** (or use the **Zoom control box** on the Standard toolbar to achieve the same result).

➤ Scroll through the document until you see the first paragraph. Click at the beginning of the first paragraph.

➤ Press the **Tab key** to indent the paragraph as shown in Figure 2.16c. The first line is indented .5 inch corresponding to the first tab stop.

➤ Pull down the **Format menu.** Click **Tabs** to produce the dialog box in Figure 2.16c.

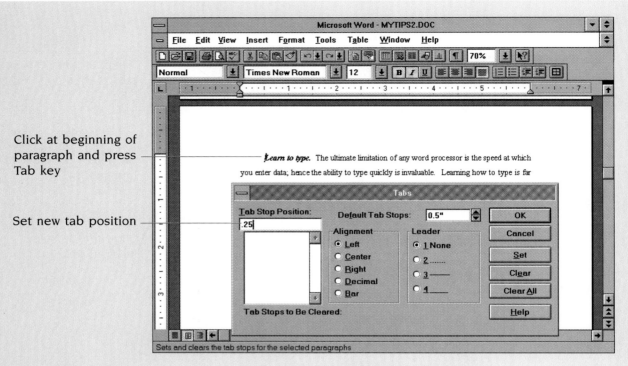

Click at beginning of paragraph and press Tab key

Set new tab position

(c) Format Tabs Command (step 3)

FIGURE 2.16 Hands-on Exercise 3 (continued)

➤ Click the **Tab Stop Position** text box. Type **.25.** Click **OK.** The indentation in the paragraph changes to .25 inch corresponding to the new tab stop.

➤ Decide whether or not to indent the remaining paragraphs. (We opted to remove the Tab by clicking at the beginning of the paragraph and pressing the **backspace key.**)

TABS AND THE RULER

Use the ruler to insert or delete a tab stop and/or change the type of tab. Select the paragraph (or paragraphs) in which you want to change the tab settings. To insert a tab stop, click the Tab Alignment button on the left of the ruler until you see the symbol for the tab stop you want:

∟ *Left tab*
⊥ *Centered tab*
⌐ *Right tab*
⊥̇ *Decimal tab*

then click the position on the ruler where you want the tab stop to be. To delete an existing tab stop, just drag it off the ruler. Use the Format Tabs command for more precise settings.

Step 4: Indents
➤ Select the second paragraph as shown in Figure 2.16d. (The second paragraph will not be indented.)

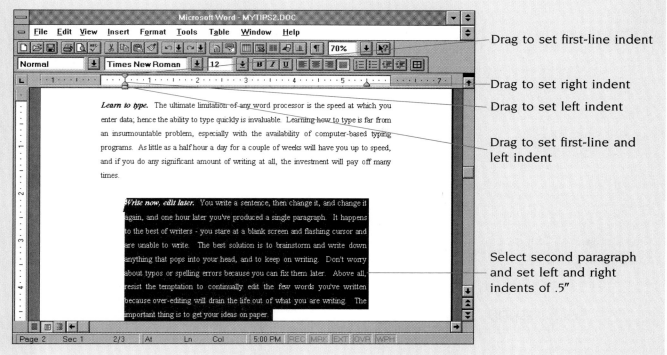

Drag to set first-line indent

Drag to set right indent

Drag to set left indent

Drag to set first-line and left indent

Select second paragraph and set left and right indents of .5"

(d) Indents and the Ruler (step 4)

FIGURE 2.16 Hands-on Exercise 3 (continued)

➤ Pull down the **Format menu** and click **Paragraph** (or press the **right mouse button** to produce the shortcut menu and click **Paragraph**).

➤ If necessary, press the **Indents and Spacing tab** in the Paragraph dialog box.

➤ Click the **up arrow** on the Left Indentation text box to set the **Left Indent** to **.5** inch. Set the **Right indent** to **.5** inch. Click **OK.** Your document should match Figure 2.16d.

➤ Save the document.

INDENTS AND THE RULER

Use the ruler to change the first-line, left, and/or right indents. Select the paragraph (or paragraphs) in which you want to change indents, then drag the appropriate indent markers to the new location.

First-line indent only	drag the top triangle at the left margin
Left indent only	drag the bottom triangle at the left margin (the box will also move)
First-line *and* left indent	drag the box on the bottom at the left margin
Right indent	drag the triangle at the right margin

If the first line indent changes when you wanted to change only the left indent, it means you dragged the box instead of the triangle. Click the Undo button and try again. (You can always use the Format Paragraph command rather than the ruler if you continue to have difficulty.)

Step 5: Borders and Shading

➤ Pull down the **Format menu.** Click **Borders and Shading** to produce the dialog box in Figure 2.16e.

➤ If necessary, click the **Borders tab.** Click the rectangle labeled **Box** under Presets. Click a style for the line around the box.

➤ Click the **Shading Tab.** Click **10%** within the open list box.

➤ Click **OK** to accept the settings for both Borders and Shading.

➤ Save the document.

Click here for all four sides to have a border line

Select line style

Sample border

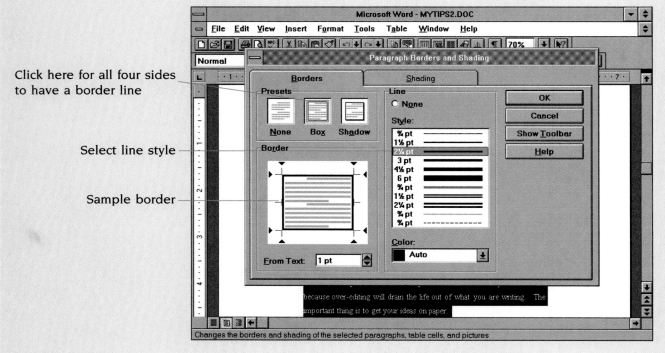

(e) Borders and Shading (step 5)

FIGURE 2.16   Hands-on Exercise 3 (continued)

THE BORDERS BUTTON

Click the Borders button on the Formatting toolbar to display (hide) the Borders toolbar, which contains icons for all capabilities within the Borders and Shading command. The Borders toolbar contains a list box for the line width, icons for the border styles, and a second list box for shadings.

Step 6: Help with Formatting

➤ Click outside the selected text to see the effects of the Borders and Shading command.

➤ Click the **Help button** on the Standard toolbar. The mouse pointer changes to include a large question mark.

➤ Click inside the boxed paragraph to see the formatting in effect for this paragraph as shown in Figure 2.16f.

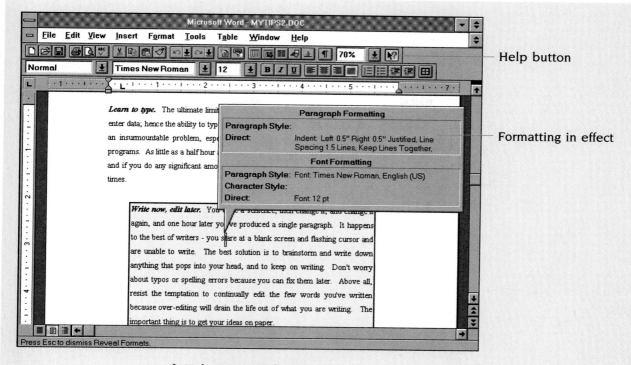

Help button

Formatting in effect

(f) Help Command (step 6)

FIGURE 2.16 Hands-on Exercise 3 (continued)

➤ Click the **Help button** a second time to exit help. The mouse pointer returns to normal.

THE INDENT AND UNINDENT BUTTONS

The Formatting toolbar provides yet another way to indent (unindent) a paragraph(s). The Indent button moves the entire paragraph to the right; that is, it indents the paragraph to the next tab stop and wraps the text to fit the new indentation. The Unindent button moves the paragraph one tab stop back (to the left).

Step 7: The Zoom Command

➤ Pull down the **View menu.** Click **Zoom** to produce the dialog box in Figure 2.16g.

➤ Click the **Many Pages** option button. Click the icon within the monitor and drag to display three pages across as shown in the figure. Release the mouse. Click **OK.**

Step 8: The Completed Document

➤ Your screen should match the one in Figure 2.16h, which displays all three pages of the document.

➤ The Page Layout view displays both a vertical and a horizontal ruler.

➤ The boxed and indented paragraph is clearly shown in the second page.

➤ The soft page break between pages two and three occurs between tips rather than within a tip; that is, the text of each tip is kept together on the same page.

➤ Save the document. Exit Word.

Click and drag over three pages

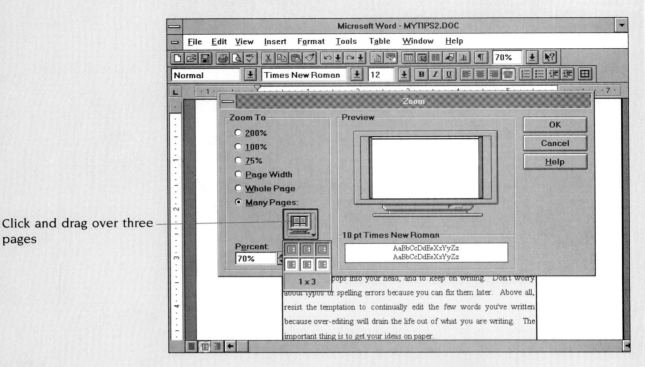

(g) The View Zoom Command (step 7)

Horizontal ruler

Vertical ruler

Page break occurs between tips

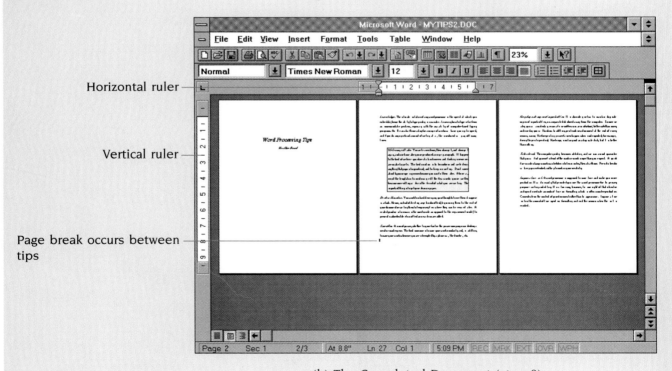

(h) The Completed Document (step 8)

FIGURE 2.16 Hands-on Exercise 3 (continued)

SUMMARY

Virtually every operation in Word is done within the context of select-then-do; that is, select the text, then execute the necessary command. Text may be selected by dragging the mouse, by using the selection bar to the left of the document, or by using the keyboard. Text is deselected by clicking anywhere within the document.

The Find and Replace commands locate a designated character string, then optionally replace one or more occurrences of that string with a different character string. The search may be case sensitive and/or restricted to whole words as necessary.

Text is moved or copied through a combination of the Cut, Copy, and Paste commands and/or the drag-and-drop facility. The contents of the clipboard are replaced by any subsequent Cut or Copy command, but are unaffected by the Paste command; that is, the same text can be pasted into multiple locations.

The Undo command reverses the effect of previous commands. The Undo and Redo commands work in conjunction with one another; that is, every command that is undone can be redone at a later time.

Scrolling occurs when a document is too large to be seen in its entirety. Scrolling with the mouse changes what is displayed on the screen, but does not move the insertion point; that is, you must click the mouse to move the insertion point. Scrolling via the keyboard (for example, PgUp and PgDn) changes what is seen on the screen as well as the location of the insertion point.

The Page Layout view displays top and bottom margins, headers and footers, and other elements not seen in the Normal view. The Normal view is faster because Word spends less time formatting the display. Both views can be seen at different magnifications.

The Save command copies the document in memory to disk under its existing name. The Save As command saves the document under a different name. It is useful when you want to retain a copy of the current document prior to all changes as well as a copy of the revised document.

TrueType fonts are scalable and accessible from any Windows application. The Format Font command enables you to choose the typeface (e.g., Times New Roman or Arial), style (e.g., boldface or italics), and point size.

The Format Paragraph command determines line spacing, justification, tabs and indents, text flow, borders, and shading. All are set at the paragraph level and affect the entire paragraph. Margins are set in the Page Setup command and affect the entire document (or section).

Key Words and Concepts

Alignment
Arial
Automatic replacement
Backup
BAK extension
Borders and Shading
   command
Case-insensitive
   replacement
Case-sensitive
   replacement

Centered tab
Clipboard
Copy command
Cut command
Decimal tab
Default directory
Drag and drop
Drop shadow effect
Find command
First-line indent

Font
Format Font command
Format Painter
Format Paragraph
   command
Global replacement
Hanging indent
Hard page break
Landscape orientation
Leader character

Left indent
Left tab
Monospaced font
Normal view
Page break
Page Layout view
Page Setup command
Paragraph mark
Paste command
Point size
Portrait orientation
Proportional font
Redo command

Replace command
Right indent
Right tab
Ruler
Sans serif typeface
Save As command
Save command
Scrolling
Select-then-do
Selection bar
Selective replacement
Serif typeface
Shortcut menu

Soft page break
Tab stop
Times New Roman
TrueType
Typeface
Type size
Typography
Undo Command
View menu
Whole word
    replacement
Widows and orphans
Zoom command

 Multiple Choice

1. Which of the following commands does *not* place data onto the clipboard?
   (a) Cut
   (b) Copy
   (c) Paste
   (d) All of the above

2. What happens if you select a block of text, copy it, move to the beginning of the document, paste it, move to the end of the document, and paste the text again?
   (a) The selected text will appear in three places: at the original location, and at the beginning and end of the document
   (b) The selected text will appear in two places: at the beginning and end of the document
   (c) The selected text will appear in just the original location
   (d) The situation is not possible; that is, you cannot paste twice in a row without an intervening cut or copy operation

3. What happens if you select a block of text, cut it, move to the beginning of the document, paste it, move to the end of the document, and paste the text again?
   (a) The selected text will appear in three places: at the original location and at the beginning and end of the document
   (b) The selected text will appear in two places: at the beginning and end of the document
   (c) The selected text will appear in just the original location
   (d) The situation is not possible; that is, you cannot paste twice in a row without an intervening cut or copy operation

4. Which of the following are set at the paragraph level?
   (a) Borders and shading
   (b) Tabs and indents
   (c) Line spacing and justification
   (d) All of the above

5. How do you change the font for *existing* text within a document?
   (a) Select the text, then choose the new font
   (b) Choose the new font, then select the text
   (c) Either (a) or (b)
   (d) Neither (a) nor (b)

6. The Page Setup command can be used to change:
   (a) The margins in a document
   (b) The orientation of a document
   (c) Both (a) and (b)
   (d) Neither (a) nor (b)

7. Which of the following is a true statement regarding indents?
   (a) Indents are measured from the edge of the page rather than from the margin
   (b) The left, right, and first-line indents must be set to the same value
   (c) The insertion point can be anywhere in the paragraph when indents are set
   (d) Indents must be set with the Format Paragraph command

8. The spacing in an existing multipage document is changed from single spacing to double spacing. What can you say about the number of hard and soft page breaks before and after the formatting change?
   (a) The number of soft page breaks is the same, but the number and/or position of the hard page breaks is different
   (b) The number of hard page breaks is the same, but the number and/or position of the soft page breaks is different
   (c) The number and position of both hard and soft page breaks are the same
   (d) The number and position of both hard and soft page breaks are different

9. The default tab stops are set to:
   (a) Left indents every ½ inch
   (b) Left indents every ¼ inch
   (c) Right indents every ½ inch
   (d) Right indents every ¼ inch

10. Which of the following describes the Arial and Times New Roman fonts?
    (a) Arial is a sans serif font, Times New Roman is a serif font
    (b) Arial is a serif font, Times New Roman is a sans serif font
    (c) Both are serif fonts
    (d) Both are sans serif fonts

11. The find and replacement strings must be
    (a) The same length
    (b) The same case, either upper or lower
    (c) The same length and the same case
    (d) None of the above

12. Assume that you are in the middle of a multipage document. How do you scroll to the beginning of the document and simultaneously change the insertion point?
    (a) Press Ctrl+Home
    (b) Drag the scroll bar to the top of the scroll box
    (c) Both (a) and (b)
    (d) Neither (a) nor (b)

13. A right-handed person will normally:
   (a) Click the right and left mouse button to access a pull-down menu and shortcut menu, respectively
   (b) Click the left and right mouse button to access a pull-down menu and shortcut menu, respectively
   (c) Click the left mouse button to access either type of menu
   (d) Click the right mouse button to access either type of menu

14. Which of the following deselects a selected block of text?
   (a) Clicking anywhere outside the selected text
   (b) Clicking any alignment icon on the toolbar
   (c) Clicking the boldface, italics, or underline buttons
   (d) All of the above

15. Which command saves the document in memory and creates a backup copy with the BAK extension?
   (a) The Save command, provided the proper backup option has been set
   (b) The Save As command, provided the proper backup option has been set
   (c) The Save command irrespective of the backup options in effect
   (d) The Save As command irrespective of the backup options in effect

ANSWERS

1. c	**6.** c	**11.** d
2. a	**7.** c	**12.** a
3. b	**8.** b	**13.** b
4. d	**9.** a	**14.** a
5. a	**10.** a	**15.** a

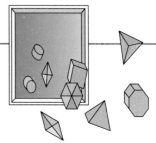

EXPLORING WORD

1. Use Figure 2.17 to match each action with its result; a given action may be used more than once.

Action	**Result**
a. Click at 1	___ Undo the previous two commands
b. Click at 2	___ Cut the selected text from the document
c. Click at 3	___ Change the alignment of the current paragraph to fully justified
d. Click at 4	
e. Click at 5	___ Change the font of the selected text to Arial
f. Click at 6	___ Change the left and right margins to 1.5″
g. Click at 7	___ Change the size of the selected text to 16 point
h. Click at 8	___ Boldface the selected text
i. Click at 9	___ Change to the Page Layout view
j. Click at 10	___ Paint another word with the same format as the currently selected word
	___ Change the magnification to Whole Page

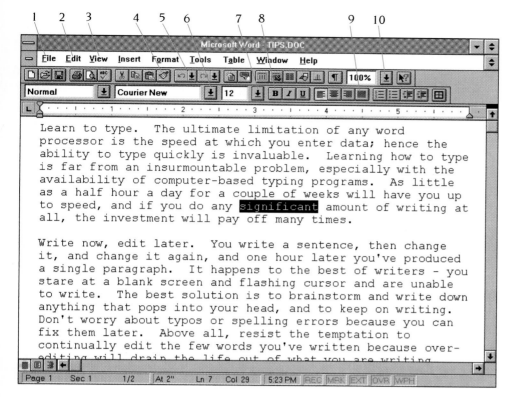

FIGURE 2.17 Screen for Problem 1

2. Use the Preamble to the Constitution as the basis for the following exercise, which you are to complete and submit to your instructor. Enter the text as shown below:

We, the people of the United States, in order to form a more perfect Union, establish justice, insure domestic tranquility, provide for the common defense, promote the general welfare, and secure the blessings of liberty to ourselves and our posterity, do ordain and establish this Constitution for the United States of America.

 a. Choose any typeface you like, but specify italic as the style, and 10 points as the size. Use single spacing and left justification.
 b. Copy the preamble to a new page, then change the specifications for the copied text to double spacing and full justification. Use the same typeface as before, but choose regular rather than italic for the style.
 c. Create a title page for your assignment, containing your name, course name, and appropriate title. Use a different typeface for the title page than for the rest of the document. Set the title in at least 24 points. Submit all three pages to the instructor.
3. Figure 2.18 displays an additional practice document on the data disk.
 a. Open the document PROB0203.DOC on the data disk.
 b. Copy the sentence, *Discretion is the better part of valor,* to the beginning of the first paragraph.
 c. Move the second paragraph to the end of the document.
 d. Change the typeface of the entire document to 12 point Arial.
 e. Change all whole word occurrences of *feel* to *think*.
 f. Change the spacing of the entire document from single spacing to 1.5. Change the justification of the entire document to fully justified.

g. Set the phrases *Format Font Command* and *Format Paragraph Command* in italics.

h. Indent the second paragraph .25 inch on both the left and right.

i. Box and shade the last paragraph.

j. Create a title page that precedes the document. Set the title, *Discretion in Design,* in 24 point Arial bold and center it approximately two inches from the top of the page. Right justify your name toward the bottom of the document in 12 point Arial regular.

k. Save the modified document as SOLUTION.DOC.

l. Print the revised document and submit it to your instructor.

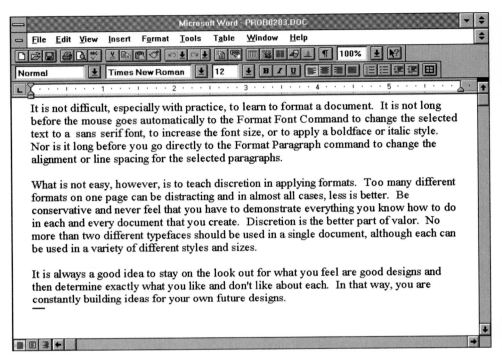

FIGURE 2.18   Screen for Problem 3

4. Prepare a personal ad for placement in a newspaper that could be distributed to the class at large. Any writing style is acceptable, but try to make it creative. A poem or limerick would be fine. The only requirement is to demonstrate proficiency in the use of a word processor, with adherence to the following specifications:

a. Fully justified text

b. A line length of 4 inches

c. Boldface the information for a reply (centered on the last line), which should consist of the last four digits of your social security number and the first two characters of your last name.

d. A sample appears below:

Dynamic professor seeks motivated students for exciting course in Windows applications. Presentation of Windows concepts, Word, Microsoft Excel, and Presentation graphics. Approximately 10 homework assignments, two tests, and a final. No previous knowledge of computers is required.

Respond to 1234GR

5. Describe at least one way, using the mouse or keyboard, to do each of the following. (The answers are found in the boxed tips throughout the chapter. Alternatively, you can access the on-line help facility to find the information.) How do you:

a. Scroll to the beginning or end of a document? Does the action you describe also change the insertion point?

b. Select a sentence? a paragraph? the entire document?

c. Set the left and right indents?

d. Insert an additional tab stop?

e. Copy the formatting in a block of text to multiple places in the same document?

f. Change highlighted text to boldface, italics, or underlining?

g. Change the line spacing and justification for a selected paragraph?

h. Save the document under a different name?

i. Box and shade a selected paragraph?

6. Word for Windows can be used to prepare any kind of document, not only one that is limited to traditional text—for example, the set of dots below. Recreate the figure below consisting of multiple rows of dots. (To make life really interesting, you might try doing this with the fewest number of commands possible. Compare your solution to that of your neighbor.)

The figure represents the children's game of *dots,* in which the players take turns connecting two adjacent dots. Each player is allowed one line per turn, except in the event that the last line drawn completes a box. In that case, the player puts his or her initial in the box and goes again. The player with the most boxes at the end of the game wins. Most of the action takes place at the end of the game, at which time runs of 10, 20, or 30 boxes are possible.

7. The boxed tips that have appeared throughout the chapter have been collected into a single file, PROB0207.DOC, and placed on the data disk. Open the file and format the tips in the most attractive way possible. Add a title page with your name, but indicate that the tips were taken from *Exploring Word for Windows* by Grauer and Barber. Print the formatted document and submit it to your instructor.

8. The document in Figure 2.19 exists on the data disk but with no formatting. Open the file PROB0208.DOC, then implement the changes below so that your file matches the document in the figure.
   a. Set top and bottom margins of 2 inches each.
   b. Set left and right margins of 1 inch each.
   c. Establish 1.5 line spacing for the document. Leave an extra line between the paragraphs.
   d. Change the typeface for the body of the document to 12 point Times New Roman.
   e. Find the word Arial within the document, then change its typeface to 12 point Arial.
   f. Use italics and boldface italics on the highlighted terms as shown in the figure.
   g. Set the title of the document in 18 point Arial bold. Center the title.
   h. Fully justify the document (flush left/flush right).
   i. Place a border around the entire document.

TYPOGRAPHY

The art of formatting a document is more than just knowing definitions, but knowing the definitions is definitely a starting point. A *typeface* is a complete set of characters with the same general appearance, and can be *serif* (cross lines at the end of the main strokes of each letter) or *sans serif* (without the cross lines). A *type size* is a vertical measurement, made from the top of the tallest letter in the character set to the bottom of the lowest letter in the character set. *Type style* refers to variations in the typeface, such as boldface and italics.

Several typefaces are shipped with Windows, including *Times New Roman*, a serif typeface, and *Arial,* a sans serif typeface. Times New Roman should be used for large amounts of text, whereas Arial is best used for titles and subtitles. It is best not to use too many different typefaces in the same document, but rather to use only one or two and then make the document interesting by varying their size and style.

FIGURE 2.19   Document for Problem 8

 Case Studies

Computers Past and Present

The ENIAC was the scientific marvel of its day and the world's first operational electronic computer. It could perform 5,000 additions per second, weighed 30 tons, and took 1,500 square feet of floor space. The price was a modest $486,000 in 1946 dollars. The story of the ENIAC and other influential computers of the authors' choosing is found in the file HISTORY.DOC, which we forgot to format, so we are asking you to do it for us. Be sure to use appropriate emphasis to highlight the names of the various computers.

Your Own Reference Manual

The clipboard is a temporary storage area available to all Windows applications. Selected text is cut or copied from one document into the clipboard, from where it can be pasted into another document altogether. Use on-line help to obtain detailed information on several topics within Word for Windows, then use the Edit Copy command to copy the information to the clipboard, and paste it into a new document, which will become your personal reference manual. To really do an outstanding job, you will have to format the reference manual after the information has been copied from the clipboard. Be sure to include a title page.

Fonts, Fonts, and More Fonts

In the beginning fonts were expensive and Courier was good enough. Then came TrueType and all of a sudden font packages that used to cost hundreds of dollars were sold for almost nothing. The problem is that fonts have gotten out of hand and most of us have many more than we use. Do you really need all of the fonts on your system? Do you have any idea how much disk space the fonts require? Which fonts are your favorites and where did you get them? In what type of documents are they used? Can you suggest some type of strategy for font management and selection? Answer these questions in a nicely formatted report of one to two pages.

Your First Consultant's Job

Go to a real installation—for example, a doctor's or an attorney's office, the company where you work, or the computer lab at school. Determine the backup procedures that are in effect, then write a one-page report indicating whether the policy is adequate and, if necessary, offering suggestions for improvement. Your report should be addressed to the individual in charge of the business and it should cover all aspects of the backup strategy—that is, which files are backed up and how often, and what software is used for the backup operation. Use appropriate emphasis (for example, bold italics) to identify any potential problems. This is a professional document (it is your first consultant's job), and its appearance must be perfect in every way.

3

The Tools: Preparing a Résumé and Cover Letter

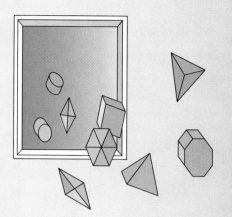

CHAPTER OBJECTIVES

After reading this chapter you will be able to:

1. Describe the AutoCorrect feature.
2. Implement a spell check; describe the function of the custom dictionary.
3. Use the thesaurus to look up synonyms and antonyms.
4. Explain the objectives and limitations of the grammar checker.
5. Insert symbols and a date field into a document.
6. Create an envelope.
7. Use wizards and templates to create a document.
8. Distinguish between the main document and data source used in a mail merge; create and print a set of form letters.

OVERVIEW

Is summer vacation or graduation coming close and the pressure for a job getting to you? Would you like to prepare a professional résumé and associated cover letter, and be able to mail it to multiple potential employers? In this chapter, we tell you how as we present the tools to add the finishing touches to a document and make it as error free as possible. We show you how to use a spelling checker and introduce the thesaurus as a means of adding precision to your writing. We present the grammar checker as a convenient way of finding a variety of errors but remind you that there is no substitute for carefully proofreading the final document.

The chapter is built around a résumé and the associated cover letter to a potential employer. We show you how to add the date to a letter, how to insert special symbols, and how to create and print an envelope. We present the concept of a mail merge, which takes the tedium out of sending form letters, as it creates the same letter many times, changing the addressee's name and address from letter to letter. The chapter also introduces the wizards and templates built into Word to help you create professionally formatted documents quickly and easily.

We believe this to be a very enjoyable chapter that will add significantly to your capability in Word for Windows. As always, learning is best accomplished by doing, and the hands-on exercises are essential to master the material.

THE SPELLING CHECKER

The *spelling checker* is an integral part of any full-featured word processor. You are well advised to use it because spelling errors make your work look sloppy and discourage the reader before he or she has read what you had to say. They can cost you a job, a grade, a lucrative contract, or an award you deserve.

The spelling checker can be used at any time; for example, to check an individual word, a block of selected text, or the document as a whole. Each word is checked against a built-in dictionary, with any mismatch (a word found in the document but not the built-in dictionary) flagged as an error.

The dictionary included with Word is limited to standard English and does not include many proper names, acronyms, abbreviations, or specialized terms, and hence, the use of any such item is considered a misspelling. You can, however, add such words to a *custom dictionary* so that they will not be flagged in the future. You can also purchase specialized dictionaries containing medical or legal terminology, or even a foreign language dictionary. The spelling checker will inform you of repeated words and irregular capitalization. It cannot, however, flag properly spelled words that are used improperly, and thus cannot tell you that *Two bee or knot too be* is not the answer.

The spelling checker is called from the Tools menu or by clicking the Spell Check icon on the Standard toolbar. Its capabilities are illustrated in conjunction with the text in Figure 3.1a. The spelling checker goes through the document and returns the errors one at a time, offering several options for each mistake. You can change the misspelled word to one of the alternatives suggested by Word, leave the word as is, or you can add the word to a custom dictionary.

The first error is *embarassing* with Word's suggestion(s) for correction displayed in the list box in Figure 3.1b. To accept the highlighted suggestion, click the *Change command button* and the substitution will be made automatically in the document. To accept an alternate suggestion, click the desired word, then click the Change command button. You can also click the AutoCorrect button so that in the future, the mistake will be corrected as it is typed, as described in the next section.

The spelling checker detects both irregular capitalization and duplicated words as shown in Figures 3.1c and 3.1d, respectively. The error in Figure 3.1e, *Grauer,* is not a misspelling per se, but a proper noun not found in the standard dictionary. No correction is required, and the appropriate action is to skip the word (taking no further action)—or better yet, add it to the custom dictionary so that it will not be flagged in future sessions. And finally, we could not resist including the example in Figure 3.1f, which shows another use of the spelling checker.

A spelling checker will catch embarassing mistakes, iRregular capitalization, and duplicate words words. It will also flag proper nouns, for example Robert Grauer, but you can add these terms to an auxiliary dictionary so that they will not be flagged in the future. It will not, however, notice properly spelled words that are used incorrectly; for example, Two bee or knot to be is not the answer.

(a) The Text

FIGURE 3.1   The Spelling Checker

Word not found in dictionary

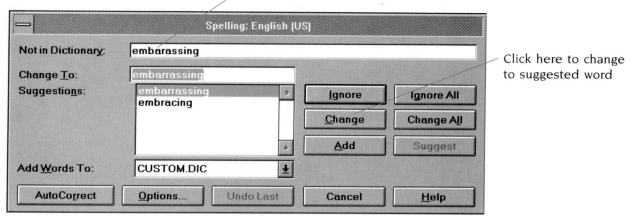

(b) Ordinary Misspelling

Irregular capitalization

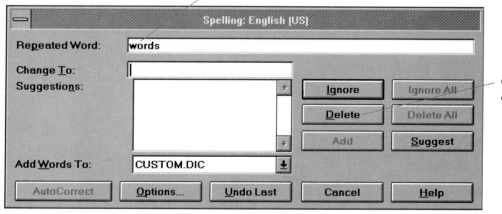

(c) Irregular Capitalization

Repeated word

Click here to delete duplication

(d) Duplicated Word

FIGURE 3.1   The Spelling Checker (continued)

Click here to skip
the word

Click here to add word
to custom dictionary

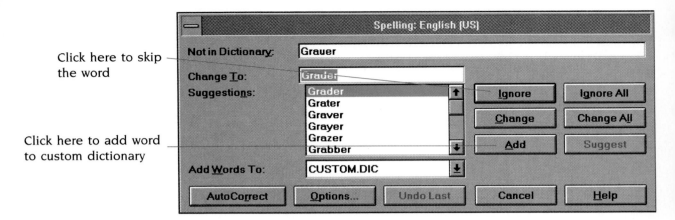

(e) Proper Noun

Wild-card represents
any character

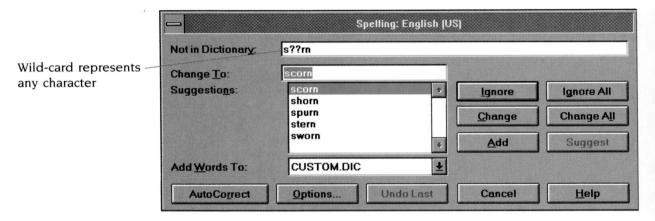

(f) Help with Crosswords

FIGURE 3.1   The Spelling Checker (continued)

HELP IN CROSSWORDS

Quick, what is a five-letter word, meaning severe or firm, with the pattern S _ _ R N? If you answered stern, you don't need our help. But if not, you might want to use the spelling checker to come up with the answer. Type the pattern using a question mark for each unknown character—for example, S??RN—then click the spelling checker icon on the toolbar. Word will return all of the matching words in the dictionary (scorn, shorn, spurn, stern, and sworn). It's then a simple matter to pick out the word that fits.

AutoCorrect

The *AutoCorrect feature* corrects mistakes as they are made without any effort on your part. It makes you a better typist. If, for example, you typed *teh* instead of *the,* Word would change the spelling without even telling you. Word will also change *adn* to *and, i* to *I,* and *occurence* to *occurrence.*

Word includes a predefined table of common mistakes and uses that table to make substitutions whenever it encounters an error it recognizes. You can add additional items to the table to include the frequent errors you make. You can also use the feature to define your own shorthand; for example, *cis* for Computer Information Systems as shown in Figure 3.2.

The AutoCorrect feature will change ordinary quotes (" ") to smart quotes (" "). It will also correct mistakes in capitalization; for example, it will capitalize the first letter in a sentence, recognize that MIami should be Miami, and capitalize the days of the week.

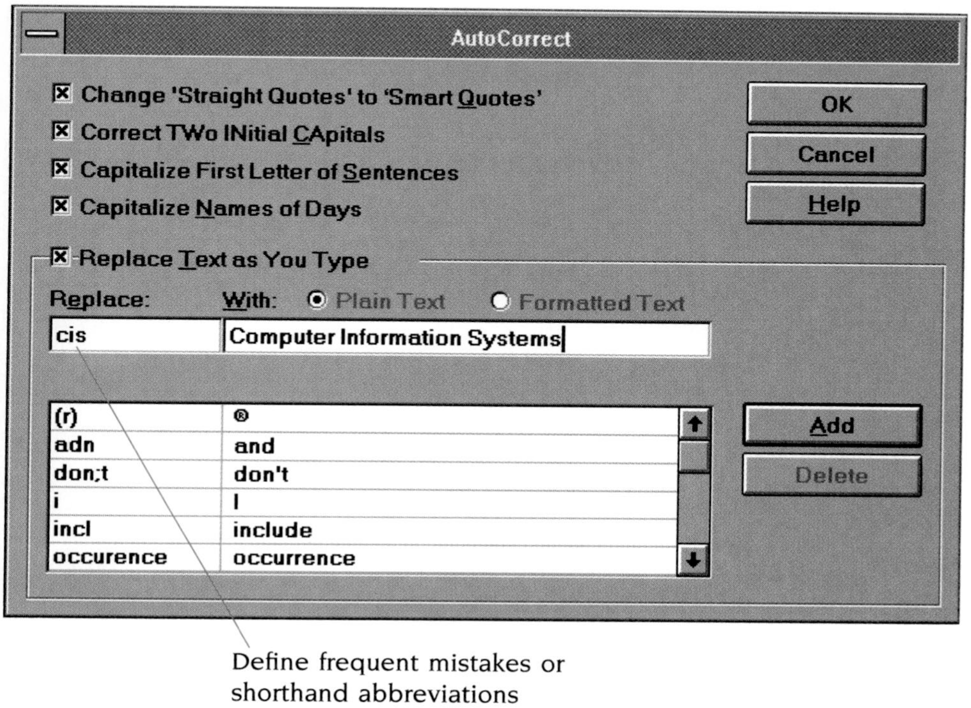

Define frequent mistakes or shorthand abbreviations

FIGURE 3.2 AutoCorrect

THESAURUS

Mark Twain said the difference between the right word and almost the right word is the difference between a lightning bug and lightning. The *thesaurus* is the second major tool in a word processor, and to our way of thinking, is as essential as a spelling checker. The thesaurus is both fun and educational; it helps you to avoid repetition, and it polishes your writing.

The thesaurus is called from the Tools menu (or with the **Shift+F7** keyboard equivalent). You position the cursor at the appropriate word within the document, then invoke the thesaurus and follow your instincts. The thesaurus recognizes multiple meanings and forms of a word (for example, adjective, noun, and verb) as in Figure 3.3a, and (by double clicking) allows you to look up any listed meaning to produce additional choices as in Figure 3.3b.

Substitutions in the document are made automatically by selecting the desired *synonym* and clicking the *Replace button.* You can explore further alternatives by selecting a synonym and clicking on the *Look Up button.* The thesaurus also provides a list of *antonyms* for most entries as in Figure 3.3c.

Synonyms for currently selected meaning

Different meanings for word (Double click to look up and produce additional choices)

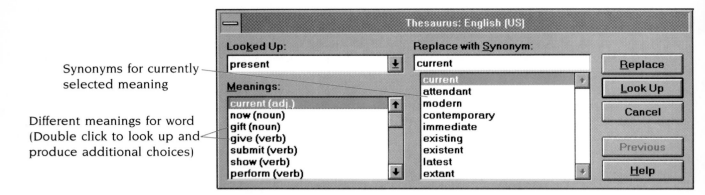

(a) Initial Word

Additional choices shown for selected meaning

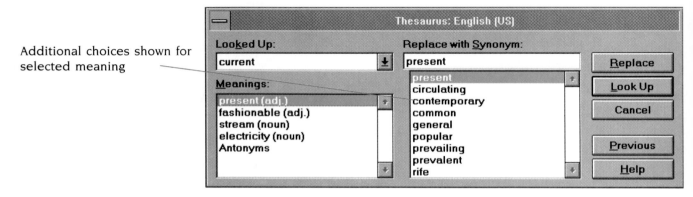

(b) Alternate Forms

Click here to see a list of antonyms

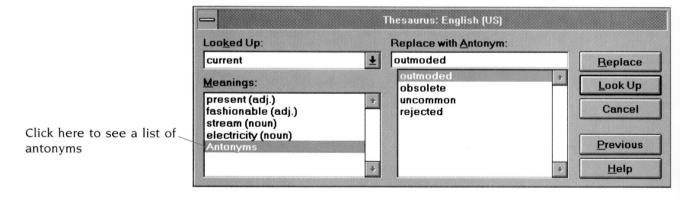

(c) Antonyms

FIGURE 3.3 The Thesaurus

GRAMMAR CHECKER

The **_grammar checker_** attempts to catch mistakes in punctuation, writing style, and word usage by comparing strings of text within a document to a series of predefined rules. As with the spelling checker, errors are brought to the screen where you can accept the suggested correction and make the replacement automatically, or more often, edit the highlighted text and make your own changes.

You can also ask the grammar checker to explain the rule it is attempting to enforce. Unlike a spelling checker the grammar checker is subjective, and what seems appropriate to you may be objectionable to someone else. The English language is also too complex for the grammar checker to detect every error, although it will find many errors.

The grammar checker caught the inconsistent phrase in Figure 3.4a and suggested the appropriate correction (*catch* instead of *catches*). In Figure 3.4b, it suggested the elimination of the superfluous comma. These examples show the grammar checker at its best, but much of the time it is more subjective and less capable. It objects, for example, to the phrase *all men are created equal* in Figure 3.4c, citing excessive use of the passive voice; whether or not you accept the suggestion is entirely up to you. Note, too, that the entire paragraph in Figure 3.4d went through without error, showing that there is simply no substitute for carefully proofreading every document.

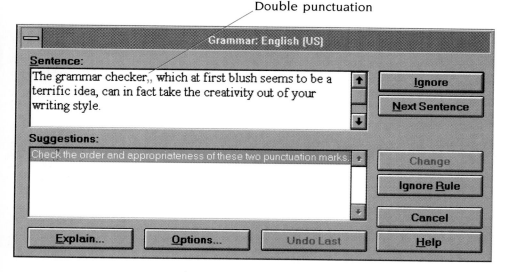

Inconsistent phrase

Grammar: English (US)

Sentence:
A grammar checker may catches obvious mistakes such as an inconsistency between the subject and verb.

Ignore
Next Sentence

Suggestions:
Consider catch instead of catches

Click here to make the suggested change

Change
Ignore Rule
Cancel

Explain...   Options...   Undo Last   Help

(a) Inconsistent Verb

Double punctuation

Grammar: English (US)

Sentence:
The grammar checker,, which at first blush seems to be a terrific idea, can in fact take the creativity out of your writing style.

Ignore
Next Sentence

Suggestions:
Check the order and appropriateness of these two punctuation marks.

Change
Ignore Rule
Cancel

Explain...   Options...   Undo Last   Help

(b) Doubled Punctuation

FIGURE 3.4   The Grammar Checker

Click here to ignore suggestion

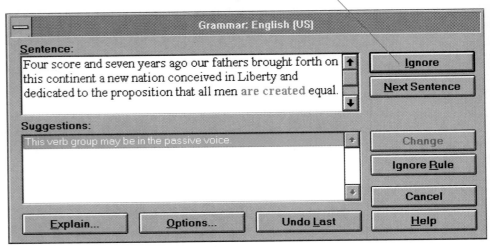

(c) Subjective Rules

Most items are not notice because English is just to complicated and the grammar program will accept this entire paragraph even though it contains many errors and this sentence is very long and the paragraph does not make any cents. It did not find any mistakes in the next sentence that used notice rather than noticed, to instead of too, and cents instead of sense. It does not object to misplaced tenses such as yesterday I will go to the store or tomorrow I went to the store.

(d) Limitations

FIGURE 3.4   The Grammar Checker (continued)

CASUAL OR BUSINESS WRITING

Word enables you to change almost every aspect of its environment to suit your personal preference. One option you may want to change is the rules in effect within the grammar checker—for example, whether Word should check for business or casual writing. Pull down the Tools menu, click Options, then click the Grammar tab. Choose the option(s) you want, then click OK.

LEARNING BY DOING

The hands-on exercise that follows shortly is based on the cover letter and accompanying résumé shown in Figure 3.5. The cover letter includes the date and requires an envelope in which it can be mailed. Both requirements are used to introduce additional capabilities within Word for Windows.

ELVIS AARON PRESLEY
1 Graceland Mansion
Memphis, Tennessee

Professional Objective

To emerge from hiding and perform once more before live audiences at major Las Vegas night clubs

Academic Background

1953 - Graduated from Humes High School, Memphis, Tennessee

Work Experience

1954 - 1977, Featured Singer - Concert Circuit

Traveled extensively on the concert circuit, including 22 club appearances in Las Vegas and Lake Tahoe

1956 - 1977, Recording Artist

Recorded 72 albums, including *Loving You, Elvis' Christmas Album, Elvis Is Back, G.I. Blues, Blue Hawaii, Elvis for Everyone, How Great Thou Art, Worldwide 50 Gold Award Hits, Moody Blues*

1956 - 1972, Recording Artist

Recorded 38 Top Ten hits, 18 of which climbed to #1 on the chart, including *Heartbreak Hotel, Hound Dog, Don't Be Cruel, Love Me Tender, All Shook Up, Teddy Bear, Jailhouse Rock, Hard Headed Woman, Stuck on You, It's Now or Never, Are You Lonesome Tonight, Good Luck Charm,* and *Suspicious Minds.*

1956 - 1972, Movie and Television Star

Performed in 38 feature length movies, including *Love Me Tender, Jailhouse Rock, Blue Hawaii, Viva Las Vegas, The Trouble with Girls,* and *Elvis on Tour.*

Featured on 15 television shows, including *The Milton Berle Show, The Steve Allen Show, Ed Sullivan's Toast of the Town,* and the *Today Show.*

1958 - 1960, Soldier, United States Army

Served in the United States Army as a tank crewman with the Third Armored Division. Stationed in Germany.

Honors

Picture placed on United States Postage Stamp
3 Grammy Awards
Male Entertainer of the Year

References

Colonel Thomas Andrew Parker, Manager
John Q. Public, Elvis Impersonator's Association
Priscilla Presley, Actress

(a) Résumé

FIGURE 3.5   The Presley Comeback

ELVIS PRESLEY

Graceland Mansion
Memphis, TN 38116
(901) 332-3322

November 28, 1993

Mr. David Letterman
1697 Broadway
New York, NY 10019

Dear Mr. Letterman,

I am seeking an engagement as the lead act at a Las Vegas night club. I have extensive experience both in private clubs and road tours throughout the United States, and have enclosed my résumé for your review.

It has been some time since I have been in the public eye, but I have never stopped singing or living my music. I am well aware of current trends and have many new songs that will, without question, catch the public's imagination. Everyone needs a gimmick in today's market and I have several extraordinary ideas in mind.

I would welcome the opportunity to meet you to discuss my ideas and audition my new act. Please contact me at the above address or call me at 1-800-HOUND-DOG. I look forward to hearing from you.

Sincerely,

Elvis

(b) Cover Letter

FIGURE 3.5 The Presley Comeback (continued)

The Insert Date Command

The **Insert Date command** puts the date (and/or time) into a document. The date is not inserted as a specific value, but as a **field** (or code) that is updated automatically when the document is printed. (The date may also be updated manually by the appropriate command from a pull-down or shortcut menu.) Word recognizes the entry in the document as a **date field** and retrieves the date from the computer's internal clock, saving you the work of manually updating the document.

The date may be printed in a variety of formats as shown in Figure 3.6. Note that the Insert as Field box is checked, so that the date is inserted as a field. If the box were not checked, the date would be inserted as **date text** and would remain the same, regardless of when the document is retrieved.

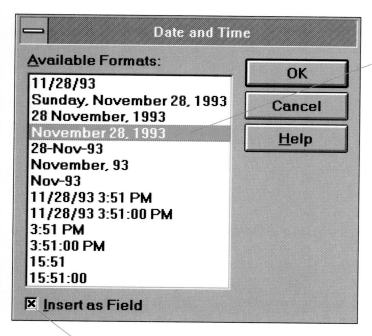

Selected format for date

Check box must be selected to enter date as a field

FIGURE 3.6 Insert Date and Time Command

The Insert Symbol Command

One quality that distinguishes the professional document is the use of typographic characters or foreign language symbols; for example, ^{TM} rather than TM, © rather than (C), or ½ and ¼, rather than 1/2 and 1/4. Many of these symbols are contained within the Wingdings or Symbols fonts that are supplied with Windows.

The ***Insert Symbol command*** provides easy access to all of the fonts installed on your system. Choose the font—for example, Wingdings in Figure 3.7—select the desired symbol, then click the Insert command button to place the character into the document. Remember, too, that TrueType fonts are scalable, from 4 to 127 points, enabling you to create some truly unusual documents.

Click here to insert selected character into document

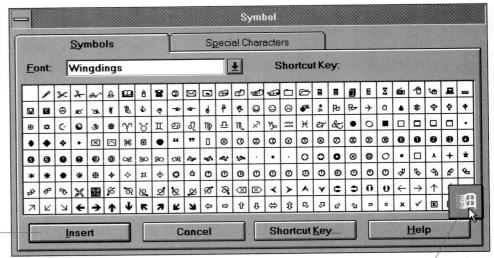

FIGURE 3.7 Insert Symbol Command

Selected character

Creating an Envelope

Anyone who has used a word processor knows that printing an envelope poses potential problems in that the physical document (the envelope) is a different size than the letter it will contain. Word saves you the trouble of having to change margins and orientation by providing the ***Envelopes and Labels command*** in the Tools menu. Execution of the command produces a dialog box where you supply or edit the necessary addresses. Word takes care of the rest.

The addressee's information can be taken directly from the cover letter as described in step 8 of the following exercise. The return address can be entered directly in the dialog box, or it can be selected from a set of previously stored return addresses. Word also lets you choose from different size envelopes; it will even supply the postal bar code if you request that option.

HANDS-ON EXERCISE 1:

Proofing a Document

Objective To use the auto correction, spelling checker, thesaurus, and grammar checker; to insert the date and special symbols into a document; to create (and print) an envelope. Use Figure 3.8 as a guide.

Step 1: Load the practice document
➤ Pull down the **File menu** and click **Open** (or click the **File Open button** on the Standard toolbar).
➤ If you have not yet changed the default directory:
  — Click the appropriate drive.
  — Scroll through the directory list box until you come to the **WORDDATA** directory.
  — Double click the **WORDDATA** directory.
➤ Double click **ELVISBEF.DOC** to open the document.
➤ Pull down the **File menu.** Click the **Save As** command to save the document as **ELVISAFT.DOC.** Click **OK.**
➤ The title bar reflects **ELVISAFT.DOC,** but you can always return to the original document if you edit the duplicated file beyond redemption.
➤ If necessary, change to the **Normal view** at **Page Width.**

Step 2: The date field
➤ Point to the date, click the **right mouse button** to produce the shortcut menu shown in Figure 3.8a, then click **Update Field.** The document displays today's date rather than the date in our letter because the date was inserted into the document as a field rather than text.
➤ Click anywhere in the date; the date is displayed in gray to indicate it is a field and not text.
➤ Press **Shift+F9** and the date is displayed as a date field.
➤ Press **Shift+F9** a second time and the field is replaced by the formatted date.

FIELD CODES VERSUS FIELD RESULTS

All fields are displayed in a document in one of two formats, as a *field code* or as a *field result.* A field code appears in braces and indicates instructions to insert variable data when the document is printed; a field result displays the information as it will appear in the printed document. You can toggle the display between the field code and field result by pressing **Shift+F9** during editing.

Step 3: AutoCorrect
➤ The phrase, *as the lead act,* has been omitted in the first sentence of the letter.
➤ Be sure you are in the insertion mode. Click immediately before the word *at* in the first line of the letter.
➤ Type the *misspelled* phrase **as teh lead act.** Try to look at the monitor as you type the word *teh* to see the AutoCorrect feature in action; Word will correct the misspelling and change *teh* to *the.*

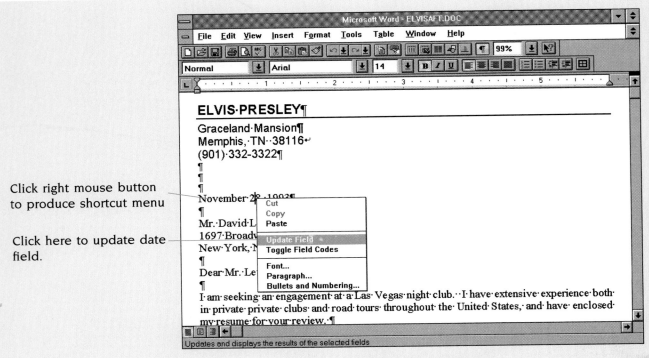

Click right mouse button to produce shortcut menu

Click here to update date field.

(a) The Date Field (step 2)

FIGURE 3.8 Hands-on Exercise 1

➤ If you did not see the correction being made, click the arrow next to the Undo command on the Standard toolbar and undo the last several actions. Click the arrow next to the Redo command and redo the corrections in order to see the typing and auto correction.

➤ Save the file.

CREATE YOUR OWN SHORTHAND

Use AutoCorrect to expand abbreviations such as "usa" for United States of America. Pull down the Tools menu, click AutoCorrect, type the abbreviation and the expanded entry, then click the Add command button. Click OK to exit the dialog box and return to the document. The next time you type usa in a document, it will automatically be expanded to the United States of America.

Step 4: The spelling checker
➤ Press **Ctrl+Home** to move to the beginning of the document.
➤ Pull down the **Tools menu.** Click **Spelling** (or click the **Spelling icon** on the toolbar) to initiate the spelling check. Presley is flagged as the first misspelling as shown in Figure 3.8b.
➤ Click the **Ignore command button** to accept Presley as written (or click the Add command button to add Presley to the custom dictionary). Ignore Graceland as well (or add it to the custom dictionary).

Spell Check icon

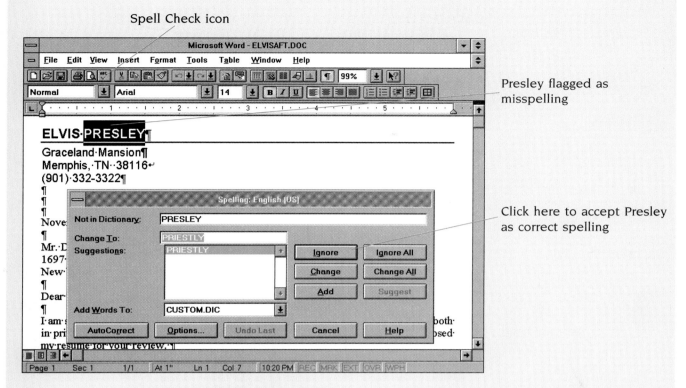

Presley flagged as misspelling

Click here to accept Presley as correct spelling

(b) The Spell Check (step 4)

FIGURE 3.8 Hands-on Exercise 1 (continued)

➤ Continue checking the document, which returns misspellings and other irregularities one at a time. Click the appropriate command button as each mistake is found:
   — Click **Delete** to delete the second occurrence of the repeated word (private).
   — Click **Change** to correct the irregular capitalization in everyone.
   — Click **Change** to accept the correct spelling for gimmick.
   — Click **Change** to accept the correct spelling for Sincerely.
➤ Click **OK** when the spelling check is complete.
➤ Save the document.

THE CUSTOM DICTIONARY

It's easy to add a word to the custom dictionary, but how do you delete a word if you've added it incorrectly? Word anticipates the problem and allows you to edit the custom dictionary as an ordinary Word document. Pull down the Tools menu, click Options, and select the Spelling tab. Click the custom dictionary you want (if there is more than one), click Edit, click Yes, then click OK. Make the necessary changes, save the file as text, then be sure to close the custom dictionary so that it is available the next time you run a spell check.

Step 5: The thesaurus

➤ Click anywhere within a word you wish to change—for example, the word **magnificent** in Figure 3.8c.

➤ Pull down the **Tools menu.** Click **Thesaurus** to display synonyms for the selected word (magnificent) as shown in the figure.

➤ Double click **grand** (in either list box) to display synonyms for this word.

➤ Click the **Previous command button** to return to the original synonyms for magnificent.

➤ Click **extraordinary** in the list of synonyms. Click **Replace.**

➤ Change other words as you see fit; for example, we changed **chance** to **opportunity.**

➤ Save the document.

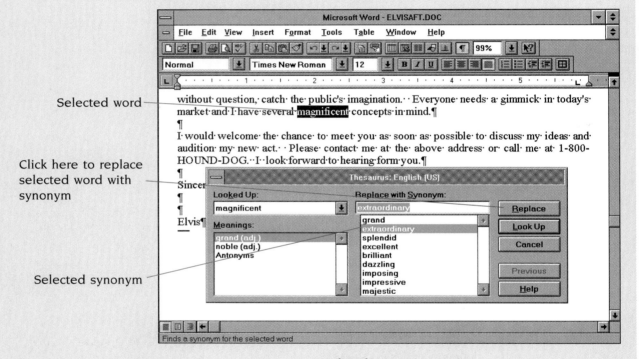

(c) The Thesaurus (step 5)

FIGURE 3.8 Hands-on Exercise I (continued)

TO CLICK OR DOUBLE CLICK

The thesaurus displays the different meanings and forms of the selected word. Click any meaning, and its synonyms appear in the synonym list box in the right of the window. Double click any meaning or synonym, and Word will look up the selected word and provide additional meanings and synonyms.

Step 6: The grammar checker

➤ Pull down the **Tools menu.** Click **Options.** Click the **Grammar tab** to customize the grammar checker.

- ➤ Click **Strictly (all rules).** Clear the box to **Check Spelling.** If necessary, click the box to **Show Readability statistics.**
- ➤ Click **OK.** Your options match ours and your results should match the steps in this exercise.
- ➤ Press **Ctrl+Home** to move to the beginning of the document.
- ➤ Pull down the **Tools menu** a second time. Click **Grammar** to begin checking the document. Suggestions for correction will be returned one at a time; you can accept or reject the suggestions as you see fit.
- ➤ Click the **Explain button** at any time to display an explanation of the rule as shown in Figure 3.8d. (Double click the **control-menu box** to close the explanation window.) We elected to keep the phrase *in the public eye* by clicking the **Ignore button,** but we accepted the next suggestion to change *concepts* to ideas.
- ➤ We deleted the phrase *as soon as possible,* by clicking in the document, selecting the phrase *as soon as possible,* and pressing the **Del key.**
- ➤ The grammar checker is not perfect, but it does detect one very significant error: the incorrect use of *form* rather than *from* in the last sentence.
- ➤ Click **OK** after viewing the readability statistics to return to the document.
- ➤ Save the document.

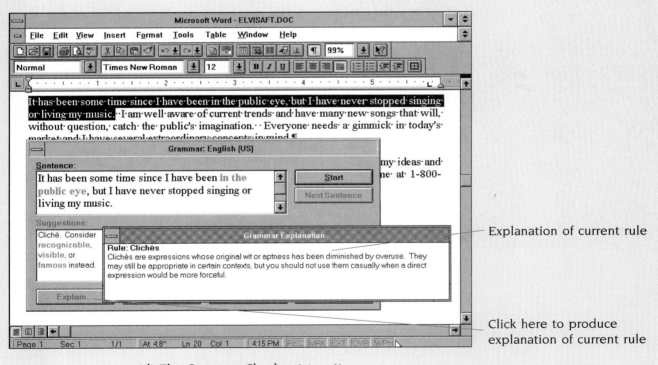

(d) The Grammar Checker (step 6)

FIGURE 3.8   Hands-on Exercise 1 (continued)

Step 7: Special characters
- ➤ The proper spelling of résumé places accents over both e's. Click before the first e in resume (in the first paragraph of the letter).
- ➤ Pull down the **Insert menu,** click **Symbol,** and choose **normal text** from the Font list box.

- ➤ Click the **é** as shown in Figure 3.8e. Click the **Insert button** to insert the character into the document.
- ➤ Click in the document window and delete the unaccented e. Click before the second e. Click **Insert.** Click **Close.** Delete the second unaccented e.
- ➤ Save the document.

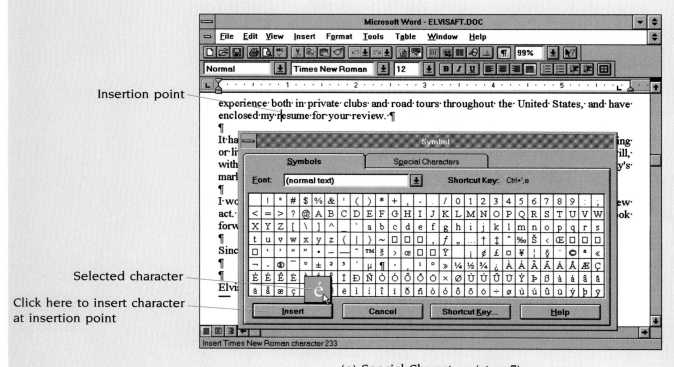

(e) Special Characters (step 7)

FIGURE 3.8   Hands-on Exercise 1 (continued)

Step 8: Create an envelope
- ➤ Pull down the **Tools menu.** Click **Envelopes and Labels** to produce the dialog box in Figure 3.8f.
- ➤ David Letterman's address should already be on the envelope because Word inserts the first address it finds; if this is not the case, just type the address yourself. Enter the return address as well.
- ➤ Click the **Add to document** command button. Click **Yes** or **No** depending on whether you want to change the default return address.

CUSTOMIZE THE TOOLBAR

The envelope button is a perfect addition to the Standard toolbar if you print envelopes frequently. Pull down the Tools menu, click Customize, then click the Toolbars tab in the dialog box. If necessary, click the arrow in the Categories list box, select Tools, then drag the envelope button to the Standard toolbar. Click Close. Click the envelope button the next time you need to create an envelope or label.

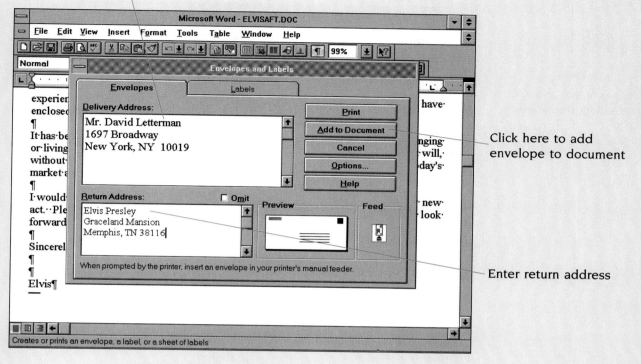

Address automatically
entered

Click here to add
envelope to document

Enter return address

(f) Creating an Envelope (step 8)

FIGURE 3.8 Hands-on Exercise 1 (continued)

Step 9: The Completed Document

➤ Click the **Page Layout icon** on the status bar. Click the **Zoom control arrow** on the Standard toolbar and select **Two Pages.** You should see the completed letter and envelope as shown in Figure 3.8g.

➤ Do *not* print the envelope unless you can manually feed an envelope to the printer.

➤ Click the page containing the letter (page two in our document)

➤ Pull down the **File menu.** Click **Print.** Click the **Current Page command button.** Click **OK** to print only the letter.

➤ Pull down the **File menu.** Click **Close** to close the document, saving it if prompted.

➤ You are still in Word and ready to begin the next exercise.

PRINT SELECTED PAGES

Why print an entire document if you want only a few pages? Pull down the File menu and click Print as you usually do to initiate the printing process. Click the Pages option button, then enter the page numbers and/or page ranges you want; for example, 3, 6-8 will print page three and pages six through eight.

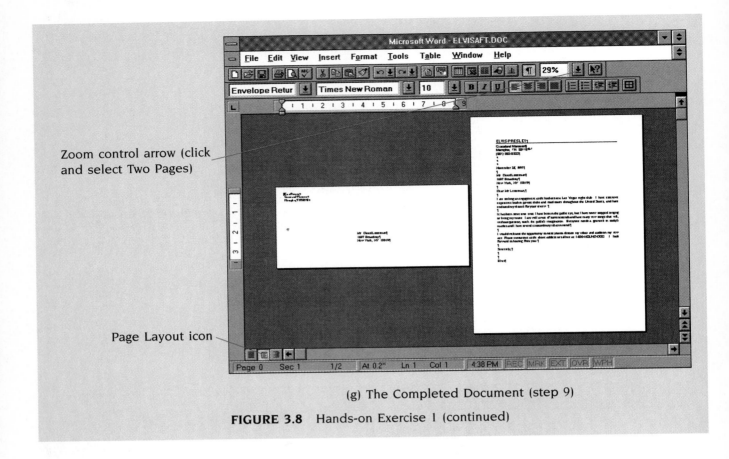

Zoom control arrow (click and select Two Pages)

Page Layout icon

(g) The Completed Document (step 9)

FIGURE 3.8   Hands-on Exercise I (continued)

WIZARDS AND TEMPLATES

The letter to David Letterman and the accompanying résumé were based on designs (templates) provided by Word. Elvis supplied the content but Word took care of the formatting. That left Elvis free to concentrate on the message he wanted to deliver.

A ***template*** is a partially completed document that contains formatting, text, and/or graphics. It may be as simple as a memo or as complex as a résumé or newsletter. Word provides a variety of templates for common documents including a letter, memo, report, or fax cover sheet. You can design your own templates or you can use the ones built into Word. (Every document is in fact based on a general-purpose template known as the Normal Document Template; that is, unless you choose a different template, Word will base each new document on the Normal template.)

A ***wizard*** attempts to make the process even easier, by asking questions, then creating the template for you. Word supplies eight different wizards: Agenda, Award, Calendar, Fax Cover Sheet, Letter, Memo, Newsletter, and Résumé, four of which are illustrated in Figure 3.9.

Wizards and templates help you to create professionally designed documents, but they are only a beginning. The content is still up to you. Some wizards are easier to use than others. The calendar wizard, for example, asks you for the month, year, and type of calendar, then completes the document for you. The Fax Cover Sheet, Agenda, and Award wizards create a template, but require you to enter additional information. The ***Résumé wizard*** is more complex and requires a knowledge of styles in order to be used effectively. (Styles are covered in Chapter 4.)

	Sun	Mon	Tue	Wed	Thu	Fri	Sat
		1	2	3	4	5	6
November	7	8	9	10	11	12	13
	14	15	16	17	18	19	20
	21	22	23	24	25	26	27
1993	28	29	30				

(a) Calendar

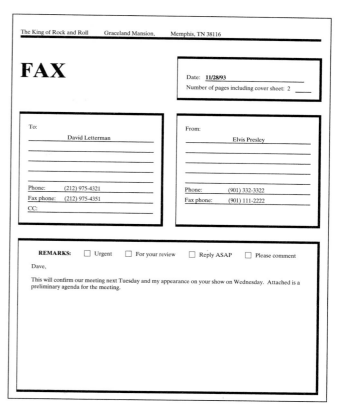

(b) Fax Cover Sheet

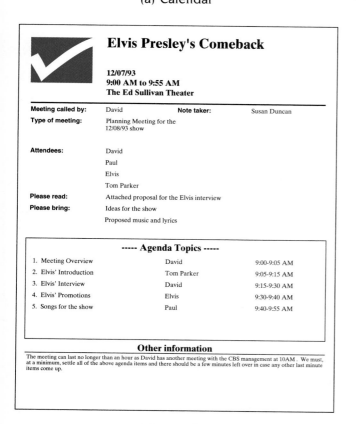

(c) Agenda

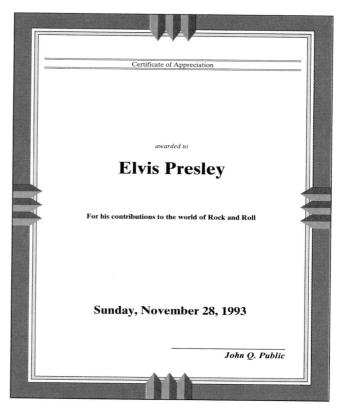

(d) Award

FIGURE 3.9 What You Can Do with Wizards

Any document that is created with a wizard or template can be saved under its own name, then edited like any other document. Wizards and templates are illustrated in the following exercise, which also shows you how to work with multiple documents at the same time.

HANDS-ON EXERCISE 2:

Wizards and Templates

Objective To use wizards and templates to create two documents based on existing templates. To view multiple documents at the same time. Use Figure 3.10 as a guide.

Step 1: The File New command
➤ If necessary, change to the **Page Layout** view at **Page Width.**
➤ Pull down the **File menu.** Click **New** to produce the dialog box in Figure 3.10a.
➤ Double click **Fax Wizard** in the open list box to start the Fax Wizard.

Double click here to select the Fax Wizard

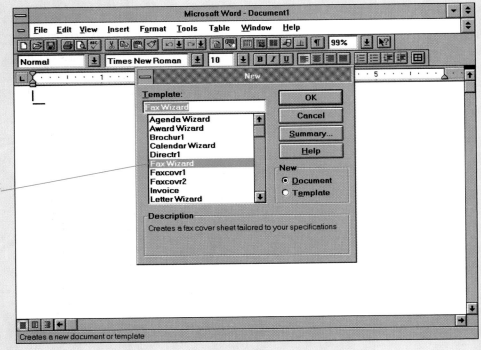

(a) The File New Command (step 1)

FIGURE 3.10   Hands-on Exercise 2

Step 2: The Fax Wizard
➤ The *Fax Wizard* asks a series of questions in order to build a template. Each question is displayed in its own screen.
➤ Click **Portrait** orientation as shown in Figure 3.10b. Click the **Next command button.**

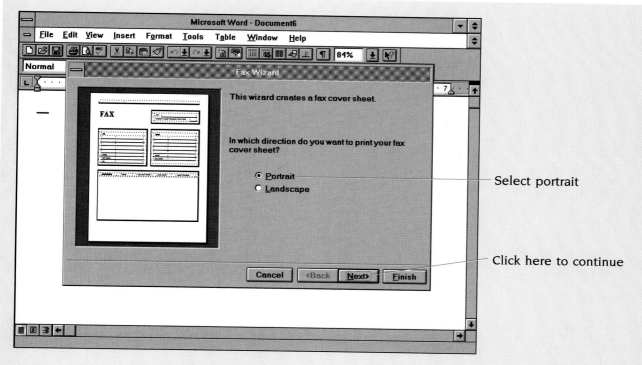

Select portrait

Click here to continue

(b) The Fax Wizard (step 2)

FIGURE 3.10 Hands-on Exercise 2 (continued)

➤ Choose a style for the cover sheet. (We chose Jazzy.) Click **Next.**
➤ Enter your name, your company's name, and your mailing address (or enter the corresponding information for Elvis). Click **Next.**
➤ Click in the text boxes to enter your telephone number and your fax number. Click **Next.**
➤ You will see a message indicating that the Fax Wizard has all the information it needs. Click Yes or No depending on whether or not you want help as you complete the fax.
➤ Click the **Finish command button.**
➤ Save the document as **ELVISFAX.DOC.**

Step 3: Complete the Fax
➤ Figure 3.10c displays the Fax cover sheet created by the Fax Wizard based on the answers you supplied.
➤ Type David Letterman's name and phone number as shown in the figure.
➤ Click in the **Remarks** area. Type the text of the fax as shown in Figure 3.10d.
➤ Click the **Spell check icon** on the Standard toolbar to begin a spell check. Correct any misspellings.
➤ Save the file.

Step 4: The Agenda Wizard
➤ Pull down the **File menu.** Click **New** to produce the dialog box that displays the available wizards.
➤ Double click the **Agenda Wizard** in the open list box to start the Agenda Wizard.

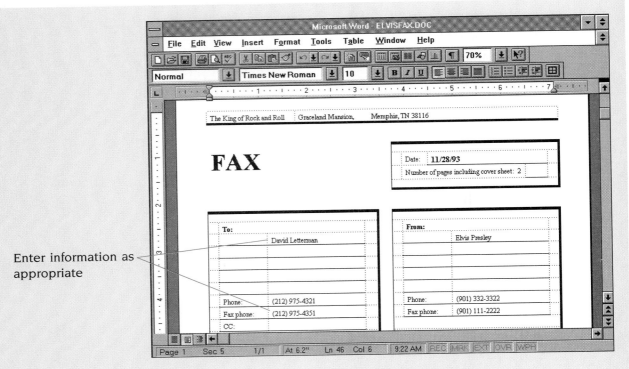

Enter information as appropriate

(c) Complete the Fax (step 3)

Spell check icon

Click here and enter text for fax

Misspelled word

Click here to correct misspelling

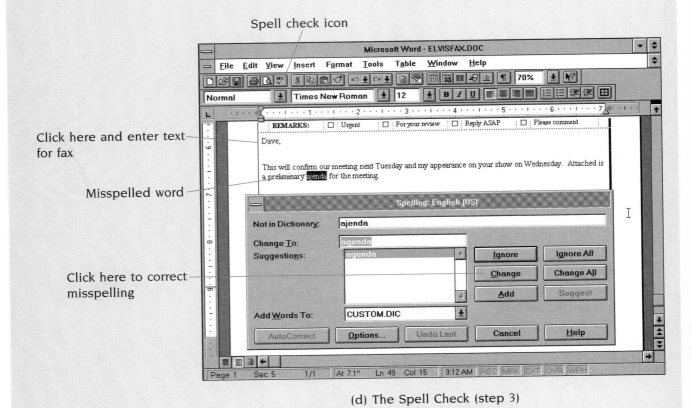

(d) The Spell Check (step 3)

FIGURE 3.10 Hands-on Exercise 2 (continued)

- ➤ The *Agenda Wizard* asks a series of questions in order to build a template. Each question is displayed in its own screen.
- ➤ Click the option button for the style you want—for example, **Boxes** in Figure 3.10e. Click **Next.**
- ➤ Enter the Date and Starting Time of the meeting. Click **Next.**
- ➤ Enter the main topic to be discussed and the location of the meeting. Click **Next.**
- ➤ Check (clear) the boxes corresponding to the items you want (don't want) placed on the agenda; for example, check the boxes for **Please Read** and **Please Bring.** Click **Next.**
- ➤ Check the boxes for the persons you want mentioned on the agenda; for example, check the boxes for attendees and the note taker. Click **Next.**

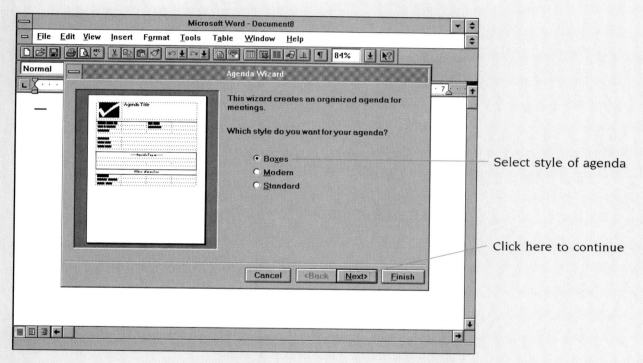

(e) The Agenda Wizard (step 4)

FIGURE 3.10   Hands-on Exercise 2 (continued)

RETRACE YOUR STEPS

Wizards guide you every step of the way but what if you make a mistake? Click the Back command button to return to a previous step and enter a different answer, then continue working with the wizard.

Step 5: The Agenda Wizard (continued)
- ➤ Continue to answer the questions posed by the Agenda Wizard.
- ➤ Enter the Agenda topics as shown in Figure 3.10f; press the **Tab key** to move

Enter agenda topics (press Tab to
move from text box to text box)

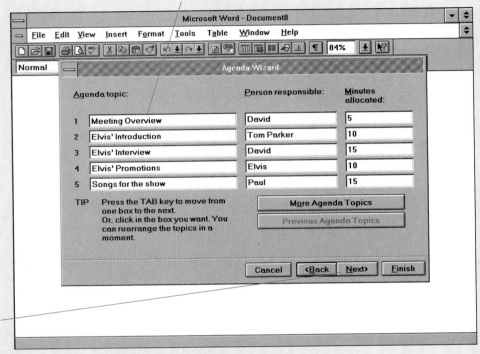

Click here to continue

(f) The Agenda Wizard (step 5)

FIGURE 3.10   Hands-on Exercise 2 (continued)

from one text box to the next. Click the **Next command button** when you
have completed the topics.

➤ If necessary, reorder the topics by clicking the desired topic, then clicking the
Move Up or **Move Down** command button. Click **Next** when you are
satisfied with the agenda.

➤ Click the **Yes** or **No** button depending on whether you want a form to record
the minutes of the meeting. Click **Next.**

➤ You will see a message indicating that the Agenda Wizard has all the information it needs. Click **Yes** or **No** depending on whether or not you want help
as you complete the agenda.

➤ Click the **Finish command button.**

➤ Save the document as **ELVAGNDA.DOC.**

Step 6: Complete the Agenda

➤ Figure 3.10g displays the agenda created by the Agenda Wizard based on the
answers you supplied.

➤ Complete the Agenda by entering the additional information, such as the
names of the attendees and the specifics of what to read or bring, as shown
in the figure.

➤ Change to the **Page Layout** view. Zoom to **Whole Page** to see the document
you have created.

➤ Save the file.

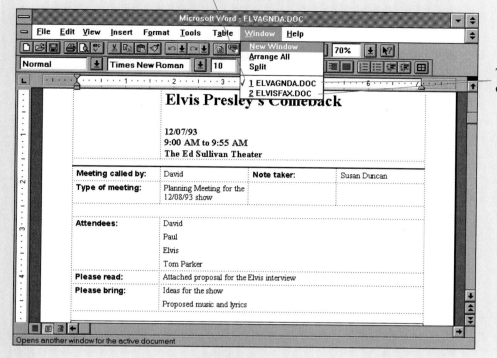

Indicates active document

Two documents are currently open

(g) Complete the Agenda (step 6)

FIGURE 3.10 Hands-on Exercise 2 (continued)

AWARD YOURSELF

Use the *Award Wizard* to create a certificate for yourself citing the outstanding work you have done so far. The Award Wizard lets you choose one of four styles (formal, modern, decorative, or jazzy) in either portrait or landscape orientation. It's fun, it's easy, and you deserve it!

Step 7: View both documents simultaneously

➤ Pull down the **Window menu** to see the names of the open documents: Document1, ELVAGNDA.DOC, and ELVISFAX.DOC.

➤ Click **Document1** to switch to this document. (Document1 is an empty document that is opened when Word is loaded.) Pull down the **File menu.** Click **Close.**

➤ Pull down the **Window menu** a second time as shown in Figure 3.10g. This time, two documents are open, ELVISFAX.DOC and ELVAGNDA.DOC, although only one (ELVAGNDA.DOC) is visible on the screen. The check mark next to ELVAGNDA.DOC indicates that it is the active document.

➤ Click the **Print button** on the Standard toolbar to print ELVAGNDA.DOC.

➤ Pull down the **Window menu.** Click **ELVISFAX.DOC** to switch to this document. Click the **Print button** on the Standard toolbar to print it.

➤ Pull down the **Window menu** a final time. Click **Arrange All** to display open windows simultaneously as shown in Figure 3.10h. Click in either window to change the active document, then scroll or edit the document in that window.

➤ Pull down the **File menu** and exit Word.

Active document —

Click anywhere in window
to make ELVISFAX.DOC
the active document

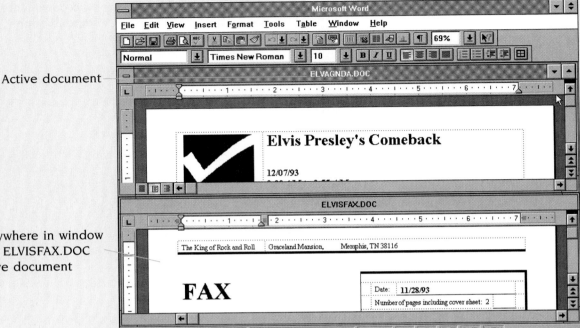

(h) View Both Documents (step 7)

FIGURE 3.10 Hands-on Exercise 2 (continued)

MAIL MERGE

A *mail merge* takes the tedium out of sending form letters, as it creates the same letter many times, changing the name, address, and other information as appropriate from letter to letter. You might use the mail merge capability to look for a job upon graduation, when you send essentially the same letter to many different people. The concept is illustrated in Figure 3.11, where Elvis drafts a form letter describing his comeback, then merges that letter with a set of names and addresses, to produce the individual letters.

A mail merge requires the creation of two separate files: the *main document* in Figure 3.11a and the *data source* in Figure 3.11b. The main document contains standardized text together with one or more merge fields to indicate where variable information is to be inserted in the individual letters. The data source contains the information that varies from letter to letter—for example, an addressee's title, name, and address.

Word organizes the data source as a table. The first row is called the header row and identifies the fields in the remaining rows. Every other row contains the information needed to create one letter and is called a data *record.* Every data record contains the same fields in the same order—for example, Title, FirstName, LastName, and so on.

ELVIS PRESLEY

Graceland Mansion
Memphis, TN 38116
(901) 332-3322

November 28, 1993

≪Title≫ ≪FirstName≫ ≪LastName≫
≪Address1≫
≪City≫, ≪State≫ ≪Zipcode≫

Dear ≪Title≫ ≪LastName≫,

I am seeking an engagement as the lead act at a Las Vegas night club. I have extensive experience both in private clubs and road tours throughout the United States, and have enclosed my résumé for your review.

It has been some time since I have been in the public eye, but I have never stopped singing or living my music. I am well aware of current trends and have many new songs that will, without question, catch the public's imagination. Everyone needs a gimmick in today's market and I have several extraordinary ideas in mind.

I would welcome the opportunity to meet you to discuss my ideas and audition my new act. Please contact me at the above address or call me at 1-800-HOUND-DOG. I look forward to hearing from you.

Sincerely,

Elvis

(a) The Main Document

Title	FirstName	LastName	Address1	City	State	Zipcode
Mr.	David	Letterman	1697 Broadway	New York	NY	10019
Mr.	Arsenio	Hall	5555 Melrose Avenue	Hollywood	CA	90038
Mr.	Jay	Leno	3000 West Alameda Avenue	Burbank	CA	91523

(b) The Data Source

FIGURE 3.11 The Mail Merge

The main document and the data source are created in conjunction with one another, with the *merge codes* in the main document referencing the corresponding fields in the data source. The first line in the address contains three entries in angled brackets, *<<Title>> <<FirstName>> <<LastName>>*; these entries are not typed explicitly but are entered through special commands described in the hands-on exercise.

The merge process examines each record in the data source and substitutes the appropriate field values for the corresponding merge codes as it creates the individual form letters. For example, the first three fields in the first record will produce *Mr. David Letterman*; the same fields in the second record will produce, *Mr. Jay Leno,* and so on.

In similar fashion, the second line in the address of the main document contains the *<<Address1>>* field, and the third line *<<City>>*, *<<State>>*, and *<<Zipcode>>* fields. The salutation repeats the *<<Title>>* and *<<LastName>>* fields. The mail merge prepares the letters one at a time, with one letter created for every record in the data source until the file of names and addresses is exhausted. The individual letters are shown in Figure 3.11c. Each letter begins on a new page.

ELVIS PRESLEY

Graceland Mansion
Memphis, TN 38116
(901) 332-3322

November 28, 1993

Mr. Jay Leno
3000 West Alameda Avenue
Burbank, CA 91523

Dear Mr. Leno,

I am seeking an engagement as the lea
experience both in private clubs and r
enclosed my résumé for your review.

It has been some time since I have been
or living my music. I am well aware of
without question, catch the public's in
market and I have several extraordinar

I would welcome the opportunity to m
act. Please contact me at the above a
forward to hearing from you.

Sincerely,

Elvis

ELVIS PRESLEY

Graceland Mansion
Memphis, TN 38116
(901) 332-3322

November 28, 1993

Mr. Arsenio Hall
5555 Melrose Avenue
Hollywood, CA 90038

Dear Mr. Hall,

I am seeking an engagement as the lea
experience both in private clubs and r
enclosed my résumé for your review.

It has been some time since I have been
or living my music. I am well aware of
without question, catch the public's im
market and I have several extraordinar

I would welcome the opportunity to m
act. Please contact me at the above a
forward to hearing from you.

Sincerely,

Elvis

ELVIS PRESLEY

Graceland Mansion
Memphis, TN 38116
(901) 332-3322

November 28, 1993

Mr. David Letterman
1697 Broadway
New York, NY 10019

Dear Mr. Letterman,

I am seeking an engagement as the lead act at a Las Vegas night club. I have extensive experience both in private clubs and road tours throughout the United States, and have enclosed my résumé for your review.

It has been some time since I have been in the public eye, but I have never stopped singing or living my music. I am well aware of current trends and have many new songs that will, without question, catch the public's imagination. Everyone needs a gimmick in today's market and I have several extraordinary ideas in mind.

I would welcome the opportunity to meet you to discuss my ideas and audition my new act. Please contact me at the above address or call me at 1-800-HOUND-DOG. I look forward to hearing from you.

Sincerely,

Elvis

(c) The Printed Letters

FIGURE 3.11 The Mail Merge (continued)

The zip code should be defined as a separate field in the data source in order to sort on zip code and take advantage of bulk mail. A person's first and last name should also be defined separately, so that you have access to either field, perhaps to create a friendly salutation such as Dear Joe or to sort on last name.

Implementation in Word

The implementation of a mail merge in Word is easy, provided you understand the basic concept. In essence there are three things you must do:

1. Create and save the main document
2. Create and save the data source
3. Merge the main document and data source to create the individual letters

The Mail Merge command is located in the Tools Menu. Execution of the command displays the Mail Merge Helper, which lists the steps in the mail merge process and guides you every step of the way.

The screen in Figure 3.12 shows the Mail Merge Helper as it would appear after steps 1 and 2 have been completed. The main document has been created and saved as FORMLET.DOC. The data source has been created and saved as NAMES.DOC. All that remains is to merge the files and create the individual form letters. The options in effect indicate that the letters will be created in a new document. (The Query Options command button enables you to select and/or sort the records in the data source prior to the merge; these options are discussed after the hands-on exercise.)

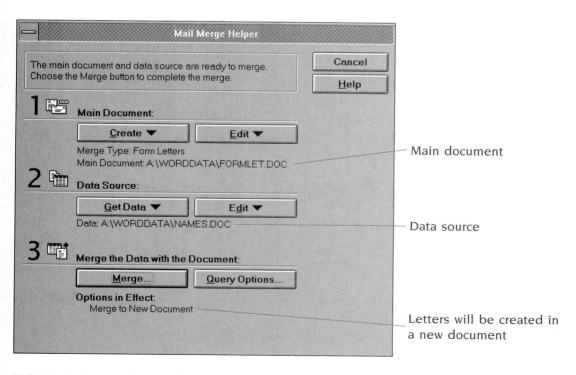

FIGURE 3.12 Mail Merge Helper

```
MAIL MERGE HELP

Pull down the Help menu, search on Mail Merge, then select Mail Merge: Step
by Step. Click the maximize button to maximize the help window and increase
the amount of information displayed on the screen. Press the Tab key to jump
from one highlighted topic to the next, or press the enter key to display the
highlighted topic. Press Alt+Tab to move back and forth between the open
applications, which include Word Help, How To, and Word itself (with the
edited document).
```

HANDS-ON EXERCISE 3:

Mail Merge

Objective To create a main document and associated data source; to implement a mail merge and produce a set of form letters.

Step 1: Retrieve the cover letter
- ➤ Pull down the **File menu.** Click **Open.**
- ➤ Double click **ELVISAFT.DOC** to open the edited version of the cover letter from the first exercise.
- ➤ Pull down the **File menu.** Save the document as **FORMLET.DOC.**
- ➤ Pull down the **View menu** and click **Page Layout** (or click the **Page Layout button** on the status bar).
- ➤ Click the **Zoom control arrow** on the Standard toolbar and select **Two Pages.** Release the mouse to see the envelope and letter as in Figure 3.13a.
- ➤ The merge could be developed to print envelopes in addition to form letters, but we will omit the envelope from the exercise. Click and drag to select the envelope, then press the **Del key** to delete the envelope from the document.

Step 2: Create the Main Document
- ➤ Click the **Zoom control arrow** to change to **Page Width.**
- ➤ Delete David Letterman's address at the beginning of the letter as well as the salutation so that your letter matches Figure 3.13b.
- ➤ Save the letter.
- ➤ Pull down the **Tools menu.** Click **Mail Merge.** Click the **Create command button** to create the main document as shown in Figure 3.13b.
- ➤ Click **Form Letters,** then click **Active Window** to indicate that you will use FORMLET.DOC (in the active window) as the main document.

Step 3: Create the Data Source
- ➤ Click **Get Data,** then click **Create Data Source** to produce the dialog box in Figure 3.13c.
- ➤ Word provides commonly used field names for the data source, but not all of the data fields are necessary.
- ➤ Click **JobTitle,** then click the **Remove Field Name** command button. Delete the Company, Address2, PostalCode, Country, HomePhone, and WorkPhone fields in similar fashion.

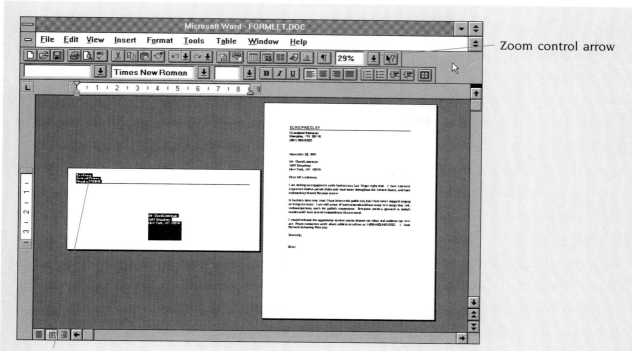

Zoom control arrow

Select all text on envelope
and press Del key

(a) Delete the Envelope (step 1)

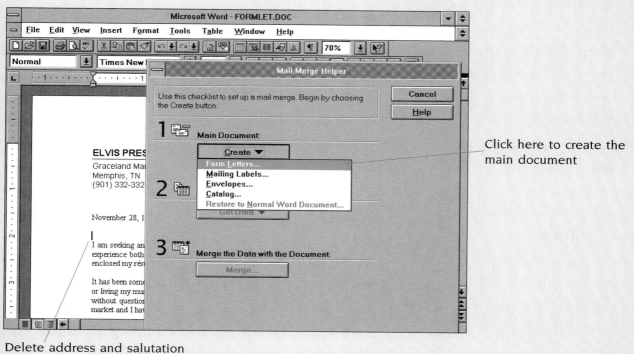

Click here to create the
main document

Delete address and salutation

(b) Create the Form Letter (step 2)

FIGURE 3.13   Hands-on Exercise 3

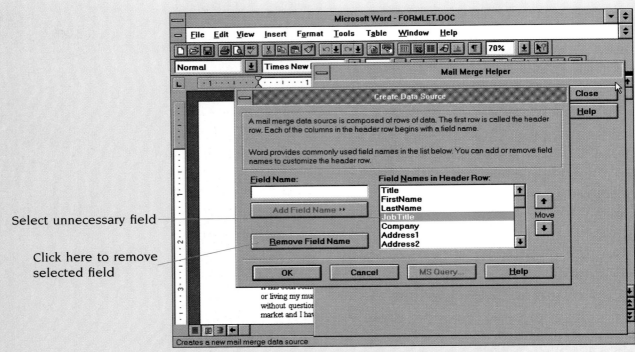

Select unnecessary field

Click here to remove
selected field

(c) Create the Data Source (step 3)

FIGURE 3.13 Hands-on Exercise 3 (continued)

➤ Click in the **Field Name** text box. Type **Zipcode.** Click the **Add Field Name** command button to add this field.

➤ Click **OK** to end the definition of the data source. Type **NAMES** in the File Name text box as the name of the data source. Click **OK** to save the file.

➤ You will see a message indicating that the data source does not contain any records. Click **Edit Data Source.**

Step 4: Add the Data

➤ Enter data for the first record. Type **Mr.** in the Title field. Press **Tab** to move to the next (FirstName) field and type **David.** Continue in this fashion until you have completed the first record as shown in Figure 3.13d.

➤ Click **Add New** to enter the data for Arsenio Hall:
— Mr. Arsenio Hall
— 5555 Melrose Avenue
— Hollywood, CA 90038

➤ Click **Add New** to enter the data for Jay Leno:
— Mr. Jay Leno
— 3000 West Alameda Avenue
— Burbank, CA 91523

➤ Click **OK** to end the data entry and return to the main document.

Step 5: Add the merge fields

➤ Click in the main document immediately below the date. Press **enter** to leave a blank line between the date and the first line of the address.

➤ Click the **Insert Merge Field** button on the Merge toolbar. Click **Title** from the list of fields within the data source. The title field is inserted into the main document and enclosed in angled brackets as shown in Figure 3.13e.

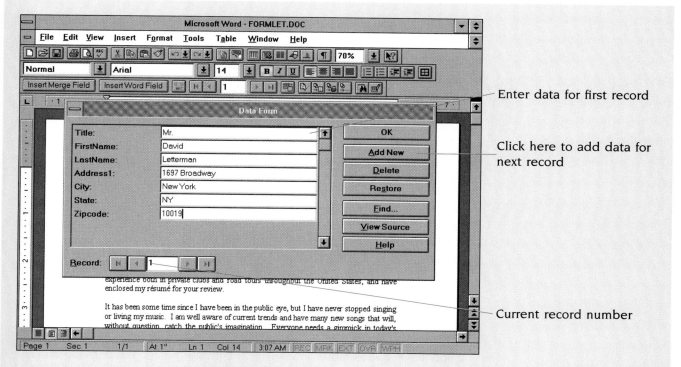

Enter data for first record

Click here to add data for next record

Current record number

(d) Adding Data (step 4)

Click here to insert merge code for Last name at insertion point

Insert Merge field button

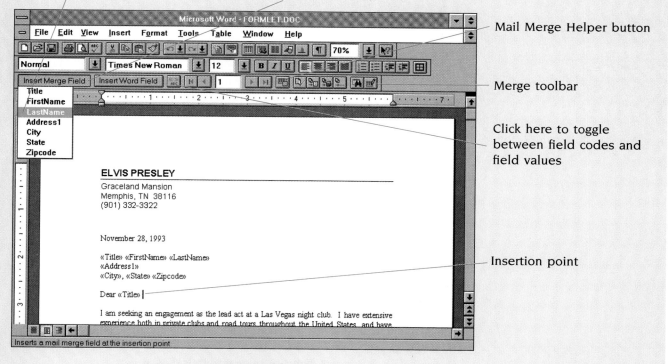

Mail Merge Helper button

Merge toolbar

Click here to toggle between field codes and field values

Insertion point

(e) Inserting Data Fields (step 5)

FIGURE 3.13   Hands-on Exercise 3 (continued)

- Press the **space bar.** Click the **Insert Merge Field** button a second time. Click **FirstName.** Press the **space bar.**
- Click the **Insert Merge Field** button again. Click **LastName.**
- Press **enter** to move to the next line in the address. Enter the remaining fields in the address as shown in Figure 3.13e. Enter the merge fields for the salutation as well. Type a **comma** after the salutation.
- Save the main document.

Step 6: The Mail Merge toolbar
- The Mail Merge toolbar enables you to preview the form letters before they are created.
- Click the **<<abc>> button** on the Merge toolbar to display field values rather than field codes; you will see Mr. David Letterman instead of <<Title>> <<FirstName>> <<LastName>>, etc.
- The **<<abc>> button** functions as a toggle switch; click it once and you switch from field codes to field values; click it a second time and you go from field values back to field codes. Display the field values.
- Look at the text box on the Merge toolbar, which displays the number 1 to indicate the first record. Click the ▶ **button** to display the form letter for the next record (Arsenio Hall).
- Click the ▶ **button** again to display the form letter for the next record (Jay Leno). The toolbar indicates you are on the third record. Click the ◀ **button** to return to the previous (second) record.
- Click the |◀ button to move directly to the first record (David Letterman). Click the ▶| button to display the form letter for the last record (Jay Leno).

Step 7: The Mail Merge Helper
- Click the **Mail Merge Helper button** on the Merge toolbar to display the dialog box in Figure 3.13f.
- The Mail Merge Helper shows your progress thus far:
  — The main document has been created and saved as FORMLET.DOC.
  — The data source has been created and saved as NAMES.DOC.
- Click the Merge command button to produce the dialog box in Figure 3.13g.

EDIT THE DATA SOURCE

Click the Mail Merge Helper button to display a dialog box with information about the mail merge, click the Edit command button under Data Source, then click the file containing the data source. Click the View Source command button to see multiple records in the data source displayed within a table; the first row contains the field names and each succeeding row contains a data record. Edit the data source, then pull down the Window menu and click the name of the file containing the main document to continue working on the mail merge.

Step 8: The merge
- The selected options in Figure 3.13g should already be set:
  — If necessary, click the arrow in the Merge To list box and select New Document.

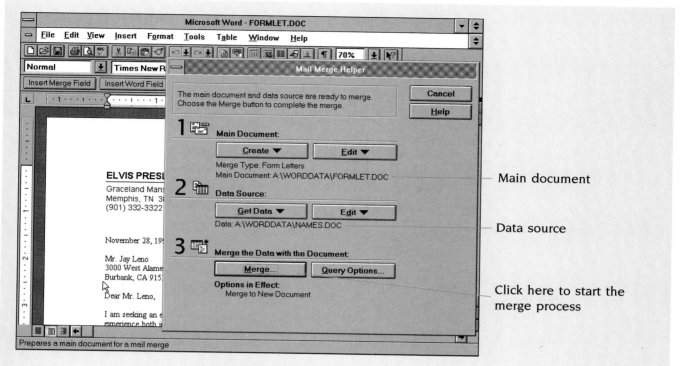

Main document

Data source

Click here to start the
merge process

(f) Mail Merge Toolbar (steps 6 and 7)

Include all records

Suppress blank lines
where no data exists

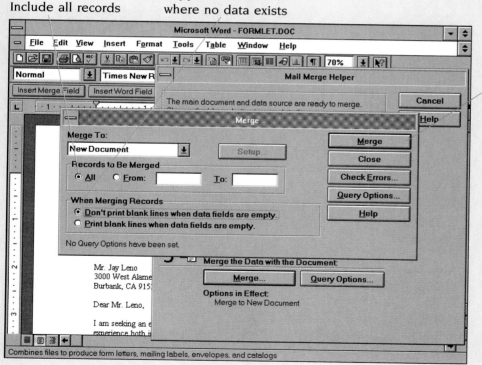

Click here to merge main
document and data source

(g) Merge (step 8)

FIGURE 3.13 Hands-on Exercise 3 (continued)

— If necessary, click the All option button to include all records in the data source.

— If necessary, click the option button to suppress blank lines if data fields are empty.

➤ Click the **Merge command button.** Word pauses momentarily, then generates the three form letters in a new document.

Step 9: The form letters
➤ The title bar of the active window changes to Form Letters1.
➤ Pull down the **View menu.** Click **Zoom.** Click **Many Pages.** Click the monitor icon and drag to display three pages side by side. Click **OK.**
➤ You should see the three form letters as shown in Figure 3.13h.

Step 10: Exit Word
➤ Double click the **control-menu box** in the application window for Word to exit the program.
➤ Pay close attention to the informational messages that ask whether to save the modified file(s). There is no need to save the merged document (Form Letters1) because you can always recreate the merged letters provided you have the main document and data source.
➤ Save the files FORMLET.DOC and NAMES.DOC if you are prompted to do so.

Form Letters1 contains the merged document

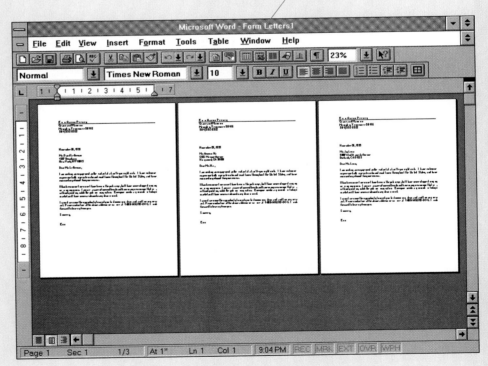

(h) The Individual Form Letters (step 8)

FIGURE 3.13 Hands-on Exercise 3 (continued)

FINER POINTS OF MAIL MERGE

The hands-on exercise just completed acquaints you with the basics of a mail merge, but there is much more that you can do. You can, for example, sort the data source so that the form letters are printed in a different sequence—for example, by zip code to take advantage of bulk mail. You can also select the records that are to be included in the mail merge; that is, a letter need not be sent for every record in the data source.

Figure 3.14 illustrates both options and is accessed through the Query Options command button in the Mail Merge Helper window. The records in the data source may be sorted on as many as three fields, as indicated in Figure 3.14a, which sorts the records by zip code, and by last name within zip code. Both fields are in ascending (low-to-high) sequence.

The dialog box in Figure 3.14b lets you specify which records in the data source will receive an individual letter by establishing selection criteria; for example, letters will be sent only to those persons living in California. The implemen-

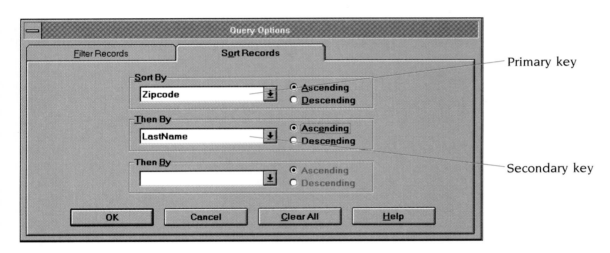

(a) Sorting Records

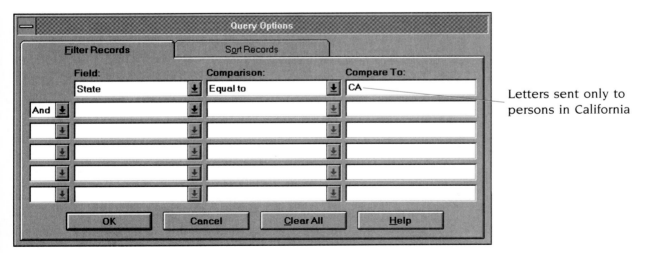

(b) Selecting Records

FIGURE 3.14 Finer Points of Mail Merge

tation is straightforward and you can impose additional rules or clear an existing rule by clicking the appropriate command button.

SUMMARY

The spelling checker compares the words in a document to those in a standard and/or custom dictionary. It will detect misspellings, duplicated phrases, and/or irregular capitalization, but will not flag properly spelled words that are used incorrectly.

The AutoCorrect feature corrects predefined spelling errors and/or mistakes in capitalization automatically as the words are entered. The feature can also be used to create a personal shorthand as it will expand abbreviations as they are typed.

The thesaurus suggests synonyms and/or antonyms. It can also recognize multiple forms of a word (noun, verb, and adjective) and offers suggestions for each.

The grammar checker searches for mistakes in punctuation, writing style, and word usage, by comparing strings of text within a document to a series of predefined rules.

The Insert Date command puts a date code into a document that is updated automatically whenever the document is retrieved. The date can be displayed as either a field code or field result during editing.

The Insert Symbol command provides easy access to special characters, making it easy to place typographic characters into a document. Many special symbols are found in the Normal text, Wingdings, and Symbol fonts. All TrueType fonts are scalable from 4 to 127 points.

Wizards and templates help create professionally designed documents with a minimum of time and effort. A template is a partially completed document that contains formatting and other information. A wizard is an interactive program that creates a template based on the answers you supply.

A mail merge creates the same letter many times, changing only the variable data—for example, the addressee's name and address as appropriate—from letter to letter. It is performed in conjunction with a main document and a data source, both of which exist as separate documents. The mail merge can be used to create a form letter for only selected records. It may print those letters in a sequence different from the way the records are stored in the data source.

 Key Words and Concepts

Agenda wizard	Fax wizard	Record
Antonym	Field	Replace button
AutoCorrect feature	Field code	Résumé Wizard
Award wizard	Field result	Spelling checker
Change command button	Grammar checker	Synonym
Custom dictionary	Insert Date command	Template
Data source	Insert Symbol command	Thesaurus
Date field	Look Up button	Wizard
Date text	Mail merge	
Envelopes and Labels command	Main document	
	Merge code	

1. Which of the following will be detected by the spelling checker?
(a) Duplicate words
(b) Irregular capitalization
(c) Both (a) and (b)
(d) Neither (a) nor (b)

2. Which of the following is true about the thesaurus program?
(a) It recognizes different forms of the same word—for example, a noun and a verb
(b) It generally offers antonyms as well as synonyms
(c) Both (a) and (b)
(d) Neither (a) nor (b)

3. Which of the following are unlikely to be found in a custom dictionary?
(a) Proper names
(b) Words related to the user's particular application
(c) Acronyms created by the user for his or her application
(d) Standard words of English usage

4. Ted and Sally both use Word but on different computers. Both have written a letter to Dr. Joel Stutz and have run a spelling check on their respective documents. Ted's program flags *Stutz* as a misspelling, whereas Sally's accepts it as written. Why?
(a) The situation is impossible; if they use identical word processing programs they should get identical results
(b) Ted has added *Stutz* to his custom dictionary
(c) Sally has added *Stutz* to her custom dictionary
(d) All of the above reasons are equally likely as a cause of the problem

5. The spelling checker will do all of the following *except*:
(a) Flag properly spelled words used incorrectly
(b) Identify misspelled words
(c) Accept (as correctly spelled) words that are in the custom dictionary
(d) Suggest alternatives to misspellings it identifies

6. Assume that your document contains the character string T??T, and that you invoke the spelling checker in Word. The program will:
(a) Return an error message
(b) Display all four-letter words in its dictionary that start and end with T
(c) Locate all occurrences of the character string in the document
(d) Do nothing because you have not typed in a replacement string

7. The names and addresses of the individuals slated to receive a form letter are found in:
(a) The main document and the data source
(b) The main document only
(c) The data source only
(d) Neither the main document nor the data source

8. A person's first name, last name, and street address in a mail merge operation are known as
   (a) Characters
   (b) Fields
   (c) Records
   (d) Files

9. Which of the following is true about the Insert Symbol command?
   (a) It can insert a symbol in any size from 4 to 127 points
   (b) It can access any TrueType font
   (c) Both (a) and (b)
   (d) Neither (a) nor (b)

10. The AutoCorrect feature will:
    (a) Correct errors in capitalization as they occur during typing
    (b) Expand user-defined abbreviations as the entries are typed
    (c) Both (a) and (b)
    (d) Neither (a) nor (b)

11. Which of the following is a *false* statement about the date field?
    (a) It is updated automatically whenever the document is printed
    (b) It may be displayed during editing as either a field code or a field result
    (c) It may be displayed in a variety of different formats
    (d) It is the exact equivalent of manually typing the current date into a document except that it is faster

12. Which of the following is a true statement about wizards?
    (a) They are accessed through the New command in the File menu
    (b) They always produce a completely finished document
    (c) Both (a) and (b)
    (d) Neither (a) nor (b)

13. Which of the following best describes how files are saved and printed within the mail merge operation?
    (a) The main document and data source are printed but not saved
    (b) The individual form letters are saved in a separate file but are not printed
    (c) Both (a) and (b)
    (d) Neither (a) nor (b)

14. Which of the following is true about the mail merge operation?
    (a) A letter must be created for every record in the data source but the letters can be printed in a different sequence
    (b) A letter can be created for only a subset of records but the letters must be printed in the same sequence as the data source
    (c) A letter must be created for every record in the data source and the letters must be printed in the same sequence as the data source
    (d) A letter can be created for only a subset of records and the letters may be printed in a different sequence from the records in the data source

15. Which of the following is true regarding the main document and data source associated with the mail merge operation?
    (a) They are stored in the same document
    (b) They are stored in separate documents, but only one can be open at a time

(c) They are stored in separate documents; both can be open at the same time, but only one document can be visible

(d) They are stored in separate documents, both can be open at the same time, and both can be visible at the same time

ANSWERS

1. c	**6.** b	**11.** d
2. c	**7.** c	**12.** a
3. d	**8.** b	**13.** d
4. c	**9.** c	**14.** d
5. a	**10.** c	**15.** d

EXPLORING WORD

1. Use Figure 3.15 to match each action with its result; a given action may be used more than once.

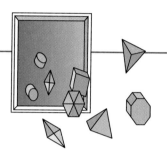

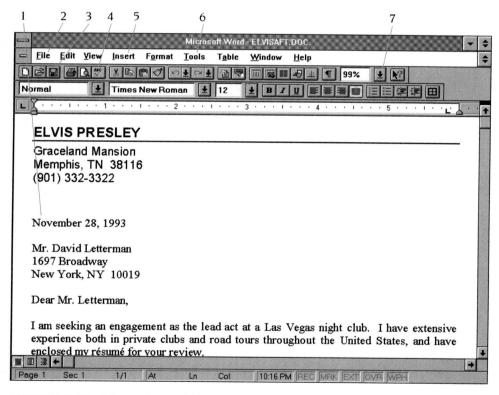

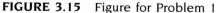

FIGURE 3.15 Figure for Problem 1

Action	Result
a. Click at 1, click at 5	___ Change the format of the date field
b. Click at 2	___ Spell check the current document
c. Click at 3	___ Change the AutoCorrect options in effect
d. Click at 4	___ Save the document
e. Click at 5	___ Use the current document to create a mail merge main document

   f. Click at 6   _____   Insert a ♥ into the document

   g. Click at 7   _____   Change to view two pages side by side

                           _____   Create an envelope

                           _____   Grammar check the current document

                           _____   Create a fax cover sheet

2. Figure 3.16 contains the draft version of the PROB0302.DOC document contained on the data disk.

   a. Proofread the document and circle any mistakes in spelling, grammar, capitalization, or punctuation.

   b. Load the document into Word and run the spelling checker. Did Word catch any mistakes you missed? Did you find any errors that were missed by the program?

   c. Use the thesaurus to come up with alternate words for *document,* which appears entirely too often within the paragraph.

   d. Run the grammar checker on the revised document. Did the program catch any grammatical errors you missed? Did you find any mistakes that were missed by the program?

   e. Add your name to the revised document, save it, print it, and submit the completed document to your instructor.

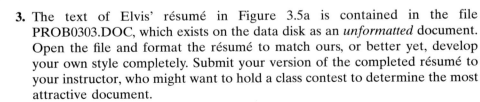

All documents should be thoroughly proofed before they be printed and distributed.This means that documents, at a minimum should be spell cheked,, grammar cheked, and proof read by the author. A documents that has spelling errors and/or grammatical errors makes the Author look unprofessional and illiterate and their is nothing worse than allowing a first impression too be won that makes you appear slopy and disinterested, and a document full or of misteakes will do exactly that. Alot of people do not not realize how damaging a bad first impression could be, and documents full of misteaks has cost people oppurtunities that they trained and prepared many years for.

FIGURE 3.16   Screen for Problem 2

3. The text of Elvis' résumé in Figure 3.5a is contained in the file PROB0303.DOC, which exists on the data disk as an *unformatted* document. Open the file and format the résumé to match ours, or better yet, develop your own style completely. Submit your version of the completed résumé to your instructor, who might want to hold a class contest to determine the most attractive document.

4. The letterhead in the cover letter of Figure 3.5b is simple and open to improvement. Design your own letterhead for Elvis, including an address, telephone, and whatever other information you think appropriate. Use different fonts and/or the Format Border command to introduce horizontal lines to your letterhead. You might also want to decrease the top margin so that your letterhead prints closer to the top of the page. Submit the completed letterhead for entry into a class contest.

5. Exploring mail merge: Create two different letters for members of the ΦΔΓ sorority. The first letter is to be sent to all members, welcoming them for the semester and asking that they be on campus no later than August 25th; the second will be mailed to just the members living in the sorority house, detailing the house rules for the coming year. In addition, modify the data source in Figure 3.17 as follows:

a. Add Anne Green to the file MEMBER.DOC on the data disk, as she has decided to return to school after all. Anne is a junior who will be living in the house, and whose permanent address is 567 West Flagler Street, Tampa, FL 33065.

b. Delete Jackie St. Clair from the file, as she has become inactive.

c. Edit the file to indicate that Jamie Metzger and Francine Blum will be living in the house after all.

Both sets of letters are to be printed in alphabetical order by last name. As previously noted, the welcome back letter is to be sent to everyone, whereas the second letter is only for those members living in the sorority house.

FirstName	LastName	Address1	City	State	Zipcode	Year	House	Dues
Andrea	Lalji	1234 Delaware Avenue	Ft. Lauderdale	FL	33312	Sr	Yes	$350
Francine	Blum	278 West 77 Terrace	Chicago	IL	60620	Jr	No	$200
Lien	Le	9807 S.W. 152 Street	Miami	FL	33157	So	Yes	$350
Sylvia	Gudat	426 Savona Avenue	Minneapolis	MN	55476	Sr	Yes	$350
Debbie	Rowe	8900 W. Jamaica Avenue	New York	NY	10020	So	No	$200
Tiffany	Bost	900 Hurricane Drive	Miami	FL	33124	Jr	No	$200
Kim	Zimmerman	8344 N.W. 74 Street	Gainesville	FL	32601	Sr	Yes	$350
Jackie	St. Clair	456 Ryder Road	Boston	MA	02190	Jr	Yes	$350
Beth Ann	King	900 Mahoney Drive	Buffalo	NY	14203	So	No	$200
Joan	Rhyne	2500 Freshman Way	Miami	FL	33157	Sr	Yes	$200
Carol	Villar	234 Rivo Alto	Miami Beach	FL	33139	Jr	Yes	$350
Lori	Pryor	8976 S.W. 75 Street	San Francisco	CA	94114	So	Yes	$350
Claudia	Moore	3456 Robertson Avenue	Denver	CO	80228	Sr	No	$200
Jessica	Kinzer	7177 Hall Avenue	Atlanta	GA	30316	Jr	Yes	$350
Jennie	Lee	987 Best Street	Charleston	SC	29410	So	Yes	$350
Bianca	Costo	8765 S.W. 79 Court	Miami	FL	33143	Sr	Yes	$350
Jamie	Metzger	5660 N.W. 145 Terrace	Baltimore	MD	21224	So	No	$200
Jennifer	Vedo	8765 Jackson Manor	Santa Rosa	CA	95405	Jr	Yes	$350
Cori	Rice	2980 S.W. 75 Street	Coral Gables	FL	33134	Sr	Yes	$350
Lynda	Black	7500 Reno Road	Houston	TX	77090	So	No	$200

FIGURE 3.17 Data File for Problem 5

6. Answer the following with respect to the screens in Figure 3.18:
   a. What is the name of the file containing the main document? In which subdirectory is it stored?
   b. What is the name of the file containing the data source? In which subdirectory is it stored?
   c. Will every record in the data source be included in the merge?
   d. How would you print the merged letters in zip code order?

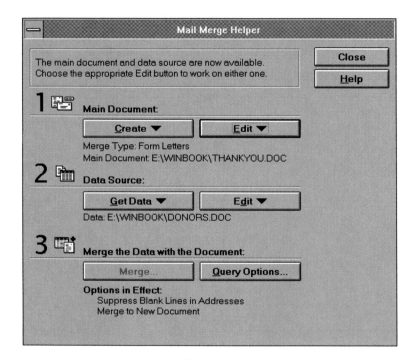

(a) Mail Merge Helper

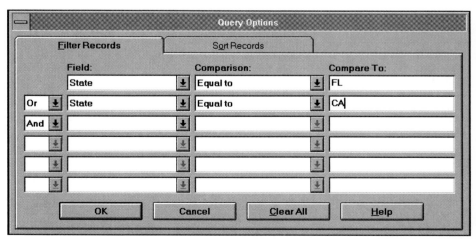

(b) Query Options

FIGURE 3.18 Mail Merge Helper for Problem 6

7. Exploring TrueType: Windows 3.1 includes a total of 14 TrueType fonts, which are accessible from any application. Two of these, Symbols and Wingdings, contain a variety of special characters that can be used to create some unusual documents. Use the Insert Symbol command, your imagination, and the fact that TrueType fonts are scalable from 4 to 127 points, to recreate the documents in Figure 3.19. Better yet, use your imagination to create your own documents.

(a) Using the Symbol Font

(b) Using the Wingding Font

FIGURE 3.19   Insert Symbol Command

 Case Studies

What Else Can Go Wrong?

You don't know how it happened, but your secretary used an old version of both the main document and data source for the most important mail merge of your career. The good news is that it was only a trial effort (only four letters were created) and the real mailing did not go out. There are so many problems that it's hard to describe them all, but there were mistakes in both the main document and data source. You won't even be able to read the main document unless you change the font size. Give this your immediate attention as the mailing is already late; your instructor needs to see the four letters first thing in the morning. Start with the OLDLETER.DOC and OLDDATA.DOC files on the data disk.

A Junior Year Abroad

How lucky can you get? You are spending the second half of your junior year in Paris. The problem is you will have to submit your work in French, and the English version of Word for Windows won't do. Is there a foreign language version available? What about the dictionary and thesaurus? How do you enter the accented characters that occur so frequently? You are leaving in two months so you had better get busy. What are your options? Bon voyage.

A Better Printer

The 200 cps dot matrix printer that has served you (and your brother before you) so well is on its last legs and it's just as well. It's too slow, too noisy, and the output is nowhere as crisp as that of your classmates. You are considering a laser printer and your parents have agreed to help, provided you keep the price down. What are the most important factors in the purchase of a laser printer? How important are speed, resolution, and memory? Are there other types of printers you should consider beside the dot matrix and laser? Summarize your findings in a one-page document to share with your classmates.

Looking for Business

Every business needs customers and one way of finding customers is through the mail. The mechanics of a mail merge are easy. The hard part is obtaining and then maintaining a suitable mailing list. Mailing lists are for sale, however, just like anything else. The hard part is knowing where to look and you are on your own, other than our suggestion to start with the yellow pages. Obtain genuine prices and descriptions for lists that you think will be suitable for your business.

Version 5.0

EXPLORING MICROSOFT EXCEL

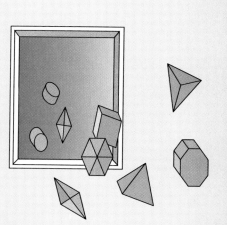

Introduction to Microsoft Excel: What Is a Spreadsheet?

CHAPTER OBJECTIVES

After reading this chapter you will be able to:

1. Explain the concept of a common user interface and its advantage in learning a new application.

2. Describe the basic mouse operations; use a mouse and/or the equivalent keyboard shortcuts to select commands from a pull-down menu.

3. Discuss the function of a dialog box; describe the different types of dialog boxes and the various ways in which information is supplied.

4. Access the on-line help facility and explain its various capabilities.

5. Describe a spreadsheet and suggest several potential applications; explain how the rows and columns of a spreadsheet are identified, and how its cells are labeled.

6. Distinguish between a formula and a constant; explain the use of a predefined function within a formula.

7. Open an Excel workbook; add and delete rows and columns of a worksheet; save and print the modified worksheet.

8. Distinguish between a pull-down menu, a shortcut menu, and a toolbar; describe how the TipWizard is intended to make you more proficient in Excel.

OVERVIEW

This chapter provides a broad-based introduction to spreadsheets and Microsoft Excel. It begins, however, with a discussion of basic Windows concepts, applicable to Windows applications in general, and to Microsoft Excel in particular. The emphasis is on the common user interface and consistent command structure that facilitates learning within the Windows environment. Indeed, you may already know much of this material, but that is precisely the point. Once you know one Windows application, it is that much easier to learn the next.

The second half of the chapter introduces the spreadsheet, the microcomputer application most widely used by managers and executives. Our intent is to show the wide diversity of business and other uses to which the spreadsheet model can be applied. For one example, we draw an analogy between the spreadsheet and the accountant's ledger. For a second example, we create an instructor's grade book.

The chapter covers the fundamentals of spreadsheets as implemented in Excel, which uses the term *worksheet* rather than *spreadsheet*. It discusses how the rows and columns of an Excel worksheet are labeled, the difference between a formula and a constant, and the ability of a worksheet to recalculate itself after a change is made.

The two hands-on exercises in the chapter enable you to apply all of the material at the computer, and are indispensable to the learn-by-doing philosophy we follow throughout the text.

THE WINDOWS DESKTOP

The **desktop** is the centerpiece of Microsoft Windows and is analogous to the desk on which you work. There are physical objects on your real desk and there are **windows** (framed rectangular areas) and **icons** (pictorial symbols) displayed on the Windows desktop. The components of a window are explained within the context of Figure 1.1, which contains the opening Windows screen on our computer.

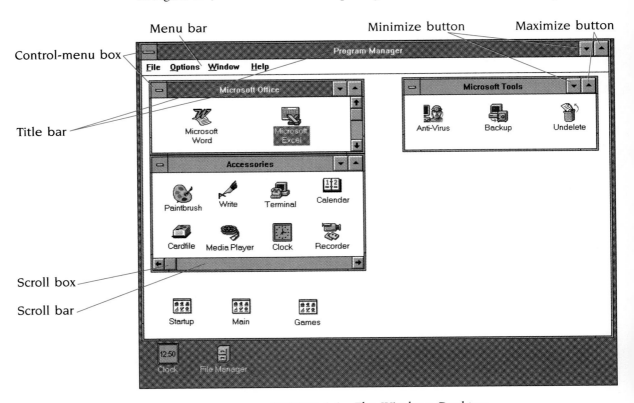

FIGURE 1.1 The Windows Desktop

Your desktop may be different from ours, just as your real desk is arranged differently from those of your friends. You can expect, however, to see a window titled Program Manager. You may or may not see other windows within Program Manager such as the Accessories, Microsoft Tools, and Microsoft Office windows shown in Figure 1.1.

Program Manager is crucial to the operation of Windows. It starts automatically when Windows is loaded and it remains active the entire time you are working in Windows. Closing Program Manager closes Windows. Program Manager is in essence an organizational tool that places applications in groups (e.g., Microsoft Office), then displays those groups as windows or group icons.

Regardless of the windows that are open on your desktop, every window contains the same basic elements: a title bar, control-menu box, and buttons to minimize and to maximize or restore the window. The *title bar* displays the name of the window—for example, Microsoft Office in Figure 1.1. The *control-menu box* accesses a pull-down menu that lets you select operations relevant to the window. The *maximize button* enlarges the window so that it takes the entire desktop. The *minimize button* reduces a window to an icon (but keeps the program active in memory). A *restore button* (a double arrow not shown in Figure 1.1) appears after a window has been maximized and returns the window to its previous size (the size before it was maximized).

Other elements that may or may not be present include a horizontal and/or vertical scroll bar and a menu bar. A horizontal (vertical) *scroll bar* will appear at the bottom (right) border of a window when the contents of the window are not completely visible. The *scroll box* appears within the scroll bar to facilitate moving within the window. A *menu bar* is found in the window for Program Manager, but not in the other windows. This is because Program Manager is a different kind of window, an application window rather than a document window.

An *application window* contains a program (application). A *document window* holds data for a program and is contained within an application window. The distinction between application and document windows is made clearer when we realize that Program Manager is a program and requires access to commands contained in pull-down menus located on the menu bar.

MICROSOFT TOOLS

The Microsoft Tools group is created automatically when you install (or upgrade to) MS-DOS 6.0. The name of each icon (Antivirus, Backup, and Undelete) is indicative of its function, and each program is an important tool in safeguarding your data. The Antivirus program allows you to scan disks for known viruses (and remove them when found). The Backup utility copies files from the hard disk to one or more floppy disk(s) in case of hard disk failure. The Undelete program allows you to recover files that you accidentally erased from a disk.

Common User Interface

One of the most significant benefits of the Windows environment is the *common user interface,* which provides a sense of familiarity when you begin to learn a new application. All applications work basically the same way. Thus, if you already know one Windows application, even one as simple as the Paintbrush accessory, it will be that much easier to learn Microsoft Excel. In similar fashion, it will take you less time to learn Word for Windows once you know Excel, because both applications share a common menu structure with consistent ways to select commands from those menus.

Consider, for example, Figures 1.2a and 1.2b, containing windows for Excel and Word, respectively. The applications are very different, yet the windows have many characteristics in common. You might even say that they have more similarities than differences, a remarkable statement considering the programs accom-

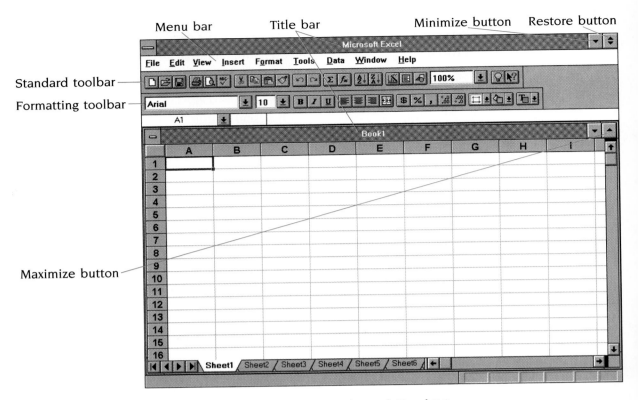

Menu bar   Title bar   Minimize button   Restore button

Standard toolbar

Formatting toolbar

Maximize button

(a) Microsoft Excel 5.0

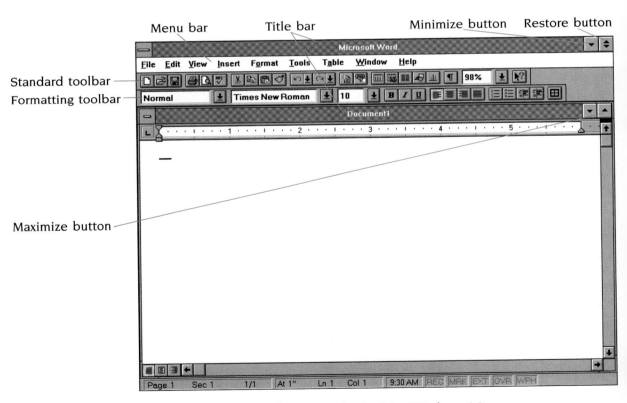

Menu bar   Title bar   Minimize button   Restore button

Standard toolbar

Formatting toolbar

Maximize button

(b) Microsoft Word for Windows 6.0

FIGURE 1.2   The Common User Interface

plish very different tasks. A document window (Book1) is contained in the application window for Excel. In similar fashion, a document window (Document1) is present within the application window for Word.

The application windows for Excel and Word contain the same elements as any other application window: a title bar, menu bar, and control-menu box; and minimize and maximize or restore buttons. The menu bars are almost identical; that is, the File, Edit, View, Insert, Format, Tools, Window, and Help menus are present in both applications. The only difference between the menu bars is that Excel has a Data menu, whereas Word has a Table menu.

The commands within the menus are also consistent in both applications. The File menu contains the commands to open and close a file. The Edit menu contains the commands to cut, copy, and paste text; and so on. The means for accessing the pull-down menus are also consistent; that is, click the menu name (see mouse basics later in the chapter) or press the Alt key plus the underlined letter of the menu name—for example, Alt+F to pull down the File menu.

The application windows for Excel and Word also contain toolbars that provide alternate ways (shortcuts) to execute common commands. The *Standard toolbar* contains buttons (icons) for basic commands such as opening and closing a file or printing a document. The *Formatting toolbar* enables you to change fonts and justification, and to implement boldface, italics, or underlining. *Toolbars* are discussed further on page 22.

THE EXCEL WORKBOOK

An Excel *workbook* is the electronic equivalent of the three-ring binder. A workbook contains one or more worksheets (or chart sheets), each of which is identified by a *tab* at the bottom of the workbook. The worksheets in a workbook are normally related to one another; for example, each worksheet may contain the sales for a specific division within a company. The advantage of a workbook is that all of its worksheets are stored in a single file, which is accessed as a unit.

WORKING IN WINDOWS

The next several pages take you through the basic operations common to Windows applications in general, and to Excel in particular. You may already be familiar with much of this material, in which case you are already benefitting from the common user interface. We begin with the mouse and describe how it is used to access pull-down menus and to supply information in dialog boxes. We also emphasize the on-line help facility, which is present in every Windows application.

The Mouse

The mouse (or trackball) is essential to Microsoft Excel as it is to all other Windows applications, and you must be comfortable with its four basic actions:

➤ To *point* to an item, move the mouse pointer to the item.

➤ To *click* an item, point to it, then press and release the left mouse button. You can also click the right mouse button to display a shortcut menu as described on page 28.

➤ To *double click* an item, point to it, then click the left mouse button twice in succession.

➤ To **drag** an item, move the pointer to the item, then press and hold the left button while you move the item to a new position.

The mouse is a pointing device—move the mouse on your desk and the **mouse pointer,** typically a small arrowhead, moves on the monitor. The mouse pointer assumes different shapes according to the nature of the current action. You will see a double arrow when you change the size of a window, an I-beam to insert text, a hand to jump from one help topic to the next, or a circle with a line through it to indicate that an attempted action is invalid.

The mouse pointer will also change to an hourglass to indicate Excel is processing your most recent command, and that no further commands may be issued until the action is completed. The more powerful your computer, the less frequently the hourglass will appear. Conversely, the less powerful your system, the more you will see the hourglass.

A right-handed person will hold the mouse in his or her right hand and click the left button, whereas a left-handed individual may want to hold the mouse in the left hand and click the right button. If this sounds complicated, it's not, and you can master the mouse with the on-line tutorial provided in Windows (see step 2 in the hands-on exercise on page 16).

MOUSE TIP FOR LEFTIES

Customize the mouse to reverse the actions of the left and right buttons. Double click the Main group icon in Program Manager to open the group, then double click the Control Panel icon. Double click the Mouse icon, click the Swap Left/Right buttons check box, then click OK.

Excel is designed for a mouse, but it provides keyboard equivalents for almost every command, with toolbars offering still other ways to accomplish the most frequent operations. You may (at first) wonder why there are so many different ways to do the same thing, but you will come to recognize the many options as part of Excel's charm. The most appropriate technique depends on personal preference, as well as the specific situation.

If, for example, your hands are already on the keyboard, it is faster to use the keyboard equivalent. Other times, your hand will be on the mouse and that will be the fastest way. It is not necessary to memorize anything, nor should you even try; just be flexible and willing to experiment. The more you do, the easier it will be!

MOUSE TIP: PICK UP THE MOUSE

It seems that you always run out of room on your real desk just when you need to move the mouse a little further. The solution is to pick up the mouse and move it closer to you—the pointer will stay in its present position on the screen, but when you put the mouse down, you will have more room on your desk in which to work.

Pull-down Menus

Pull-down menus, such as those in Figure 1.3, are essential to all Windows applications. A pull-down menu is accessed by clicking the menu name (within the menu bar) or by pressing the Alt key plus the underlined letter in the menu name—for example, Alt+H to pull down the Help menu.

Press C to execute
the Close command

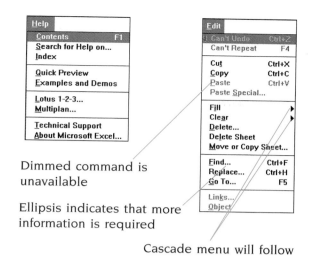

Dimmed command is
unavailable

Ellipsis indicates that more
information is required

Cascade menu will follow

FIGURE 1.3 Pull-down Menus

Menu options (commands) are executed by clicking the command once the menu has been pulled down or by pressing the underlined letter (e.g., press C to execute the Close command in the File menu). You can also bypass the menu entirely if you know the equivalent keystrokes shown to the right of the command in the menu (e.g., Ctrl+X, Ctrl+C, and Ctrl+V in the Edit menu to cut, copy, and paste text, respectively). A ***dimmed command*** (e.g., the Paste command within the Edit menu) indicates that command is not currently executable; that is, some additional action has to be taken for the command to become available.

An arrowhead after a command indicates a ***cascade menu*** will follow with additional menu options. For example, clicking either the Fill or Clear command in the Edit menu produces a secondary menu from which a command must be selected.

Other commands are followed by an ***ellipsis*** (. . .) to indicate that more information is required to execute the command; for example, selection of the Find command in the Edit menu requires the user to specify the text to be found. The additional information is entered into a dialog box, which appears immediately after the command has been selected.

Dialog Boxes

A ***dialog box*** appears when additional information is needed to execute a command—that is, whenever a menu option is followed by an ellipsis. There are many different ways to supply that information, which in turn leads to different types of dialog boxes as shown in Figure 1.4.

Check boxes are used when multiple options can be in effect at the same time. The Toolbars dialog box in Figure 1.4a, for example, uses check boxes to specify the toolbars that are to be displayed. The Standard and Formatting boxes are both checked, and hence both toolbars will be displayed. The check boxes at the bottom of the dialog box indicate that Color Toolbars are to be used and that ToolTips are to be shown. The individual options are selected (or cleared) by clicking on the appropriate check box.

Option buttons indicate mutually exclusive choices, one of which must be chosen. Portrait orientation is selected in the Page Setup dialog box in Figure 1.4b, which automatically deselects Landscape orientation; that is, clicking the Portrait option button automatically clears the Landscape button. The Page Setup dialog box also illustrates the use of a ***tabbed dialog box,*** in which one dialog box provides multiple sets of options, with each set of options on a separate tab. Clicking a tab brings that set of options to the front of the dialog box.

Multiple options can be
in effect at the same time

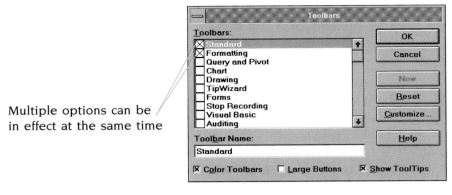

(a) Check Boxes

Tab

Mutually exclusive options

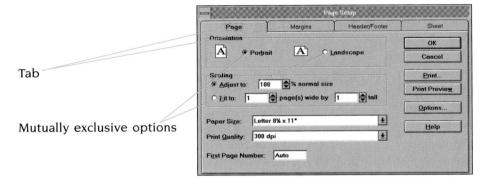

(b) Option Buttons

Text box requires that
specific data be entered

Command buttons

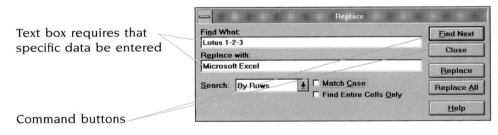

(c) Text Boxes

FIGURE 1.4 Dialog Boxes

A *text box* indicates that specific data is required such as the search and replace character strings in Figure 1.4c. Some text boxes are initially empty and display a flashing vertical bar to mark the insertion point for the text you enter. Other text boxes will already contain an entry, in which case you can click anywhere in the box to establish the insertion point and then edit the entry.

An *open list box,* such as the list of file names in Figure 1.4d, displays the available choices, any of which is selected by clicking the desired item. A *drop-down list box,* such as the list of available drives or file types, conserves space by showing only the current selection; click on the arrow of a drop-down list box to produce a list of available options.

All of the dialog boxes in Figure 1.4 contain one or more *command buttons* to initiate an action. The function of a command button is generally apparent from its name. The Help button produces a context-sensitive help screen. The Cancel button returns to the previous screen with no action taken. The OK command button accepts the information and closes the dialog box.

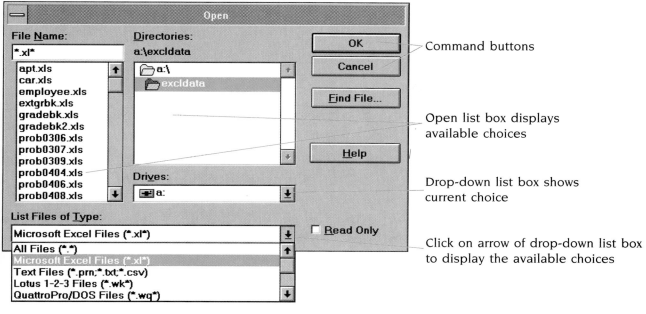

(d) List Boxes

FIGURE 1.4   Dialog Boxes (continued)

On-line Help

Excel provides extensive **on-line help,** which is accessed by pulling down the **Help menu.** The Excel Help menu was shown earlier in Figure 1.3 and contains the following choices:

Contents	Displays a list of help topics
Search for Help on . . .	Searches for help on a specific subject
Index	An alphabetical index of all Help topics
Quick Preview	Highlights new features in Excel 5.0 and suggests tips for Lotus users converting to Microsoft Excel
Examples and Demos	Demonstrates major features in Microsoft Excel
Lotus 1-2-3 . . .	Detailed help in converting from Lotus to Excel
Technical Support	Describes the different types of technical support available
About Microsoft Excel . . .	Indicates the specific release of Excel you are using

The Contents command displays the window of Figure 1.5a and provides access to all elements within the Help Facility. A Help window contains all of the elements found in any other application window: a title bar, minimize and maximize or restore buttons, a control-menu box, and optionally, a vertical or horizontal scroll bar. There is also a menu bar with commands available through the indicated pull-down menus.

The command buttons near the top of the help window enable you to move around more easily; that is, you can click a button to perform the indicated function. The Contents button returns to the screen in Figure 1.5a from elsewhere within Help. The Search button produces the screen of Figure 1.5b and allows you to look for information on a specific topic. Type a key word in the text box and the corresponding term will be selected in the adjacent list box. Double click the highlighted item to produce a list of available topics in the lower list box. Double click the topic you want (or select the topic and click the Go To command button) to see the actual help text, such as the screen shown in Figure 1.5c.

The Back button returns directly to the previous help topic. The History button is more general as it displays a list of all topics selected within the current session and makes it easy to return to any of the previous topics. The Index button produces a window with an alphabetic index of the Help topics.

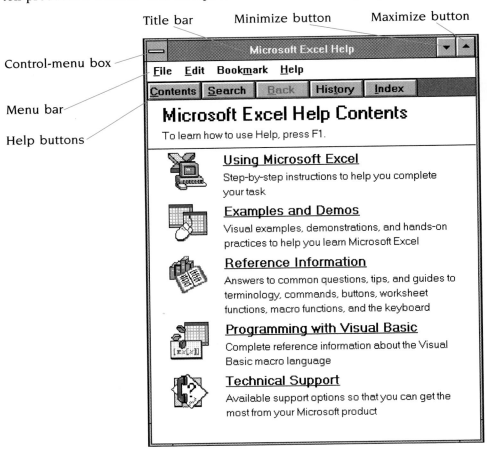

(a) Contents Command

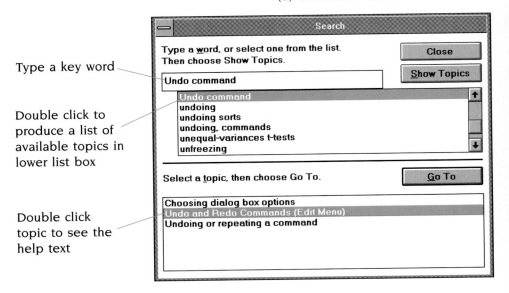

(b) Search Command

FIGURE 1.5 On-line Help

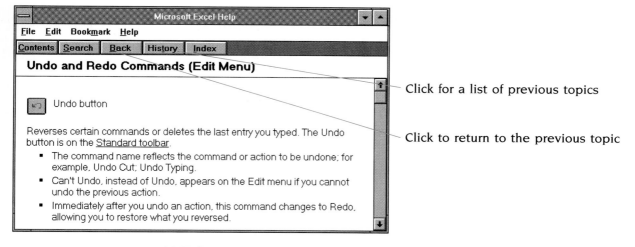

Click for a list of previous topics

Click to return to the previous topic

(c) Help Text

FIGURE 1.5 On-line Help (continued)

INTRODUCTION TO SPREADSHEETS

A *spreadsheet* is the computerized equivalent of an accountant's ledger. As with the ledger, it consists of a grid of rows and columns that enables you to organize data in a readily understandable format. Figures 1.6a and 1.6b show the same information displayed in ledger and spreadsheet format, respectively.

"*What is the big deal?*", you might ask. The big deal is that after you change an entry (or entries), the spreadsheet will, automatically and almost instantly, recompute the entire spreadsheet. Consider, for example, the profit projection spreadsheet shown in Figure 1.6b. As the spreadsheet is presently constructed, the unit price is $20, producing gross sales of $24,000 and a net profit of $4,800. If the unit price is increased to $22 per unit, the spreadsheet recomputes every formula, adjusting the values of gross sales and net profit. The modified spreadsheet of Figure 1.6c appears automatically on your monitor.

								Initials	Date
	Profit Production					Prepared by			
						Approved by			
		1	2	3	4	5	6		
1	Unit Price		20						1
2	Unit Sales		1,200						2
3	Gross Sales		24,000						3
4									4
5	Costs								5
6	Production		10,000						6
7	Distribution		1,200						7
8	Marketing		5,000						8
9	Overhead		3,000						9
10									10
11	Total Cost		19,200						11
12									12
13	Net Profit		4,800						13

(a) The Accountant's Ledger

FIGURE 1.6 The Accountant's Ledger

	A	B
1	Profit Projection	
2		
3	Unit Price	$20
4	Unit Sales	$1,200
5	Gross Sales	$24,000
6		
7	Cost	
8	Production	$10,000
9	Distribution	$1,200
10	Marketing	$5,000
11	Overhead	$3,000
12	Total Costs	$19,200
13		
14	Net Profits	$4,800

(b) Original Spreadsheet

	A	B	
1	Profit Projection		Increase Unit Price
2			
3	Unit Price	$22	
4	Unit Sales	$1,200	
5	Gross Sales	$26,400	
6			Values are automatically adjusted
7	Cost		
8	Production	$10,000	
9	Distribution	$1,200	
10	Marketing	$5,000	
11	Overhead	$3,000	
12	Total Costs	$19,200	
13			
14	Net Profits	$7,200	

(c) Modified Spreadsheet

FIGURE 1.6 The Accountant's Ledger (continued)

With a bottle of white-out or a good eraser the same changes could also be made to the ledger. But imagine for a moment a ledger with hundreds of entries, many of which depend on the entry you wish to change. You can appreciate the time required to make all the necessary changes to the ledger by hand. However, the same spreadsheet, with hundreds of entries, will be recomputed automatically by the computer. And the computer will not make mistakes. Herein lies the advantage of a spreadsheet: the ability to make (or consider making) changes, and to have the computer carry out the recalculation faster and more accurately than could be accomplished manually.

The Professor's Grade Book

A second example of a spreadsheet, one with which you can easily identify, is that of a professor's grade book. The grades are recorded by hand in a notebook, which is nothing more than a different kind of accountant's ledger. Figure 1.7 contains both manual and spreadsheet versions of a grade book.

Figure 1.7a shows a handwritten grade book as it has been done since the days of the little red schoolhouse. For the sake of simplicity, only five students are shown, each with three grades. The professor has computed class averages for each exam, as well as a semester average for every student, in which the final counts *twice* as much as either test; for example, Adams's average is equal to: $(100+90+81+81)/4 = 88$.

Figure 1.7b shows the grade book as it might appear in a spreadsheet, and is essentially unchanged from Figure 1.7a. Walker's grade on the final exam in Figure 1.7b is 90, giving him a semester average of 85 and producing a class average on the final of 75.2. Now consider Figure 1.7c, in which the grade on Walker's final has been changed to 100, causing the class average on the final to go from 75.2 to 77.2, and Walker's semester average to change from 85 to 90. As with the profit projection, a change to any entry within the grade book automatically recalculates all dependent values as well. Hence, when Walker's final exam was regraded, all dependent values (the class average for the final as well as Walker's semester average) were recomputed.

As simple as the idea of a spreadsheet may seem, it provided the first major reason for managers to have a personal computer on their desks. Essentially, anything that can be done with a pencil, a pad of paper, and a calculator can be done faster and far more accurately with a spreadsheet.

(a) The Professor's Grade Book

	A	B	C	D	E
1	Student	Test 1	Test 2	Final	Wgt Avg
2					
3	Adams	100	90	81	88.0
4	Baker	90	76	87	85.0
5	Glassman	90	78	78	81.0
6	Moldof	60	60	40	50.0
7	Walker	80	80	90	85.0
8					
9	Class Avg	84.0	76.8	75.2	

(b) Original Grades

	A	B	C	D	E
1	Student	Test 1	Test 2	Final	Wgt Avg
2					
3	Adams	100	90	81	88.0
4	Baker	90	76	87	85.0
5	Glassman	90	78	78	81.0
6	Moldof	60	60	40	50.0
7	Walker	80	80	100	90.0
8					
9	Class Avg	84.0	76.8	77.2	

Grade changed to 100

Values are automatically adjusted

(c) Modified Spreadsheet

FIGURE 1.7 The Professor's Grade Book

Row and Column Headings

A spreadsheet is divided into rows and columns, with each row and column assigned a heading. Rows are given numeric headings ranging from 1 to a maximum of 16,384. Columns are assigned alphabetic headings from column A to Z, then continue from AA to AZ and then from BA to BZ and so on, until the last of 256 columns is reached.

The intersection of a row and column forms a *cell,* with the number of cells in a spreadsheet equal to the number of rows times the number of columns. The professor's grade book in Figure 1.7, for example, has 5 columns labeled A through E, 9 rows numbered from 1 to 9, and a total of 45 cells. Each cell has a unique *cell reference;* for example, the cell at the intersection of column A and row 9 is known as cell A9. The column heading always precedes the row heading in the cell reference.

Formulas and Constants

Figure 1.8 shows an alternate view of the spreadsheet for the professor's grade book, which displays the *cell contents* rather than the computed values. This figure displays the formulas and constants that were entered into the individual cells that give the spreadsheet its ability to recalculate all values whenever any entry changes.

	A	B	C	D	E
1	Student	Test 1	Test 2	Final	Wgt Avg
2					
3	Adams	100	90	81	=(B3+C3+2*D3)/4
4	Baker	90	76	87	=(B4+C4+2*D4)/4
5	Glassman	90	78	78	=(B5+C5+2*D5)/4
6	Moldof	60	60	40	=(B6+C6+2*D6)/4
7	Walker	80	80	90	=(B7+C7+2*D7)/4
8					
9	Class Avg	=AVERAGE(B3:B7)	=AVERAGE(C3:C7)	=AVERAGE(D3:D7)	

Constant ⟶

Function ⟶

Formula

FIGURE 1.8   The Professor's Grade Book (cell formulas)

A *constant* is an entry that does not change. It may be a number such as a student's grade on an exam, or it may be descriptive text (a label) such as a student's name. A *formula* is a combination of numeric constants, cell references, arithmetic operators, and/or functions, that displays the result of a calculation. Every cell in a spreadsheet contains either a formula or a constant.

A formula always begins with an equal sign; a constant does not. Consider, for example, the formula in cell E3, =(B3+C3+2*D3)/4, which computes Adams's weighted average for the semester. The formula is built in accordance with the professor's rules for computing a student's weighted average, which counts the final twice as much as either exam. (The symbols +, −, *, /, and ^ indicate addition, subtraction, multiplication, division, and exponentiation, respectively. It follows the normal rules for arithmetic precedence. Any expression in parentheses is evaluated first. Exponentiation is done next, then multiplication or division in left to right order, then addition or subtraction also in left-to-right order.)

The formula in cell E3 takes the grade on the first exam (in cell B3), plus the grade on the second exam (in cell C3), plus two times the grade on the final (found in cell D3), and divides the result by four. The fact that we enter a formula for the weighted average rather than a constant means that should any of the individual grades change, all dependent results will also change. This in essence is the basic principle behind the spreadsheet and explains why when one number changes, various other numbers throughout the spreadsheet change as well.

A formula may also include a *function,* or predefined computational task, such as the AVERAGE function in cells B9, C9, and D9. The function in cell B9, for example, =AVERAGE(B3:B7), is interpreted to mean the average of all cells starting at B3 and ending at B7; that is, the average of cells B3, B4, B5, B6, and B7. You can appreciate that functions are often easier to use than the corresponding formulas, especially with larger spreadsheets (and classes with many students).

MICROSOFT EXCEL

Figure 1.9 displays the professor's grade book as it is implemented in Microsoft Excel. Excel shares the common user interface present in all other Windows applications.

You should recognize several familiar elements: the desktop, minimize and restore buttons, a menu bar, horizontal and vertical scroll bars, and a control-menu box.

The desktop in Figure 1.9 contains an application window for Excel. It also contains a document window within Excel for a specific workbook. Both windows have been maximized, with the title bar of the workbook (GRADEBK.XLS) merged into the title bar of the application window. The terminology is important and we distinguish among spreadsheet, worksheet, and workbook. Excel refers to a spreadsheet as a *worksheet.* Spreadsheet is a generic term. Workbook and worksheet are unique to Excel. An Excel workbook contains one or more worksheets. The professor's gradebook is in Sheet1 of the GRADEBK.XLS workbook as indicated by the tabs at the bottom of the workbook.

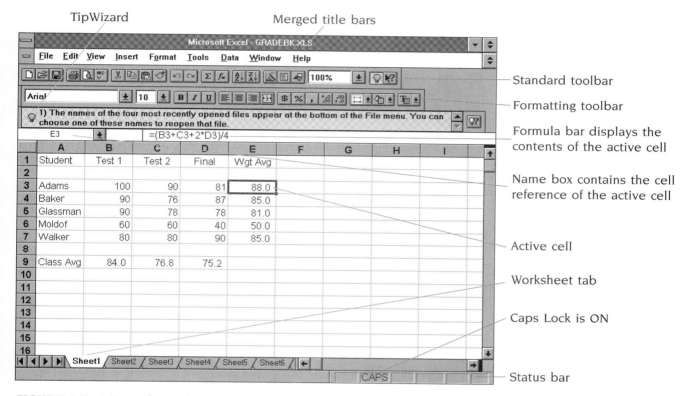

FIGURE 1.9   Microsoft Excel

Figure 1.9 resembles the grade book shown earlier, but it includes several other elements that enable you to create and/or edit the worksheet. The heavy border around cell E3 indicates that it (cell E3) is the *active cell,* and that any actions taken at this point will affect the contents of cell E3. The active cell can be changed by clicking a different cell, or by using the arrow keys to move to a different cell.

The displayed value in cell E3 is 88.0, but as indicated earlier, the cell contains a formula to compute the weighted average rather than containing the number itself. The contents of the active cell, =(B3+C3+2*D3)/4, are displayed in the *formula bar* near the top of the worksheet. The cell reference for the active cell, cell E3 in Figure 1.9, appears in the *Name box* at the left of the formula bar.

Several other elements of Figure 1.9 bear mention. The Standard and Formatting toolbars are displayed below the menu bar and contain icons that provide immediate access to common commands. The TipWizard (see page 22) appears immediately under the toolbars and offers suggestions to make you work more efficiently.

The *status bar* at the bottom of the worksheet keeps you informed of what is happening as you work within Excel. It displays information about a selected command or an operation in progress. It also shows the status of the keyboard toggle switches such as the Caps Lock key, which has been toggled on in the figure.

LEARNING BY DOING

We come now to the first of two hands-on exercises that implement our learn-by-doing philosophy. The initial exercise shows you how to load Windows and practice with the mouse, then directs you to load Microsoft Excel and retrieve the professor's grade book from the data disk that accompanies this text. The data disk expedites the way in which you learn, especially at the beginning, as you can experiment with an existing workbook and its worksheet(s). The exercise has you explore the various elements on the screen, then directs you to change individual student grades and view the resulting recalculation. The exercise also instructs you to print the worksheet and to save the changes you make.

HANDS-ON EXERCISE 1:

Introduction to Microsoft Excel

Objective To load Windows and Microsoft Excel; to retrieve and print an existing worksheet. The exercise introduces you to the data disk that accompanies the text and reviews basic Windows operations: pull-down menus, dialog boxes, and the use of a mouse.

Step 1: Load Windows
➤ Type **WIN,** then press the **enter key** to load Windows if it is not already loaded. The appearance of your desktop will be different from ours, but it should resemble Figure 1.1 at the beginning of the chapter.
➤ You will most likely see a window containing Program Manager, but if not, you should see an icon titled Program Manager near the bottom of the screen; double click on this icon to open the Program Manager window.

DOUBLE CLICKING FOR BEGINNERS

If you are having trouble double clicking, it is because you are not clicking quickly enough, or more likely, because you are moving the mouse (however slightly) between clicks. Relax, hold the mouse firmly in place, and try again.

Step 2: Master the mouse
➤ A mouse is essential to the operation of Microsoft Excel as it is to all other Windows applications. The easiest way to practice is with the mouse tutorial found in the Help menu of Windows itself.
➤ Pull down the **Help menu.** Click **Windows Tutorial.** Type **M** to begin, then follow the on-screen instructions.
➤ Exit the tutorial when you are finished.

Step 3: Install the data disk

➤ Do this step *only* if you have your own computer and want to copy the files from the data disk to the hard drive. Place the data disk in drive A (or whatever drive is appropriate).

➤ Pull down the **File menu.** Click **Run.** Type **A:INSTALL C** in the text box. Click **OK.** (The drive letters in the command, A and C, are both variable. If, for example, the data disk were in drive B and you wanted to copy its files to drive D, you would type the command **B:INSTALL D.**)

➤ Follow the on-screen instructions to install the data disk.

Step 4: Load Microsoft Excel

➤ Double click the icon for the group containing Microsoft Excel if that group is not already open.

➤ Double click the program icon for **Microsoft Excel.**

➤ Click the **maximize button** (if necessary) so that the application window containing Microsoft Excel fills the entire screen.

➤ Click the **maximize button** in the document window (if necessary) to produce a screen similar to Figure 1.10a. (You will not see the Open dialog box until you complete step 5.)

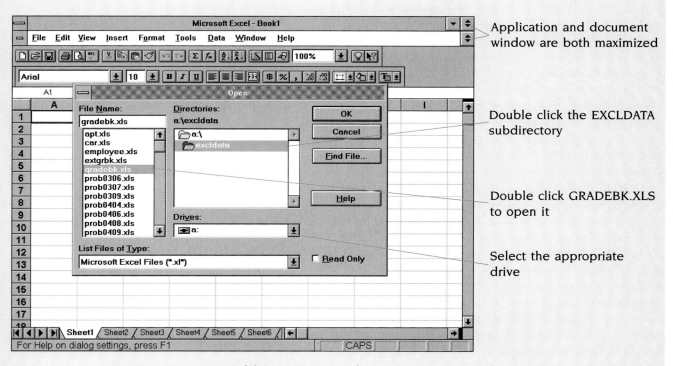

(a) Retrieving a Spreadsheet (steps 4 and 5)

FIGURE 1.10 Hands-on Exercise 1

Step 5: Open the workbook

➤ Pull down the **File menu.** Click **Open** to produce a dialog box similar to the one in Figure 1.10a.

➤ Click the appropriate drive, drive C or drive A.

➤ Double click the root directory (a:\ or c:\) in the Directories list box to display the subdirectories on the selected drive.
➤ Double click the **EXCLDATA** directory to make it the active directory.
➤ Double click **GRADEBK.XLS** to open the workbook for this exercise.

ABOUT MICROSOFT EXCEL

About Microsoft Excel on the Help menu displays information about the specific release of Excel, including the product serial number. Execution of the command produces a dialog box with a System Information command button; click the button to learn about the hardware installed on your system, including the amount of memory and available space on the hard drive.

Step 6: The active cell and formula bar
➤ Click in cell **B3,** the cell containing Adams's grade on the first test.
➤ Cell B3 is now the active cell and is surrounded by a heavy border. The Name box indicates the active cell; the contents of the active cell are displayed in the formula bar.
➤ Click in cell **B4** (or press the **down arrow key**) to make it the active cell. The Name box indicates cell B4, while the formula bar indicates a grade of 90.
➤ Click in cell **E3,** the cell containing the formula to compute Adams's weighted average. The worksheet displays the computed average of 88, but the formula bar displays the formula, =(B3+C3+2*D3)/4, to compute that average.
➤ Continue to change the active cell (with the mouse or arrow keys) and notice how the display in the Name box and formula bar change to reflect the active cell.

THE UNDO COMMAND

The Undo command reverses the effect of the most recent operation and is invaluable at any time, but especially when you are learning. Pull down the Edit menu and click Undo (or click the Undo icon on the Standard toolbar) to cancel the effects of the preceding command. Use the Undo command whenever something happens to your worksheet that is different from what you intended.

Step 7: Experiment (what if?)
➤ Let's assume that an error was made in recording Baker's grade on the second test.
➤ Click in cell **C4,** the cell containing this particular grade.
➤ Enter a corrected value of **86** (instead of the previous entry of 76). Press **enter** (or click in another cell).
➤ The effects of this change ripple through the worksheet, automatically changing the computed value for Baker's average in cell E4 to 87.5. The class average on the second test in cell C9 changes to 78.8.

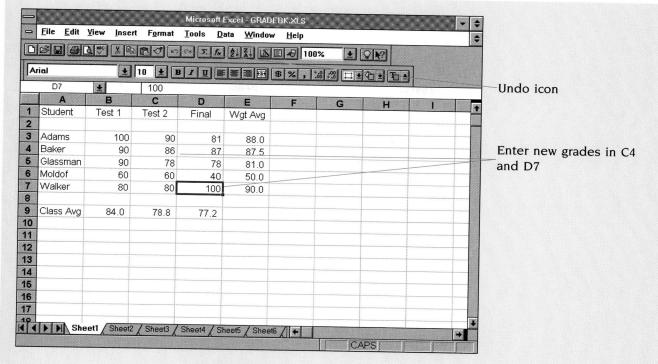

Undo icon

Enter new grades in C4 and D7

(b) What If (step 7)

FIGURE 1.10 Hands-on Exercise 1 (continued)

➤ Change Walker's grade on the final from 90 to **100.** Press **enter** (or click in another cell). Walker's average in cell E7 changes to 90.0, while the class average in cell D9 changes to 77.2.

➤ Your worksheet should match Figure 1.10b.

Step 8: Save the modified worksheet

➤ It is very, very important to save your work periodically during a session.

➤ Pull down the **File menu.** Click **Save** to save the changes (or, alternatively, click the **Save icon,** the third icon from the left, on the Standard toolbar).

Step 9: Print the worksheet

➤ Pull down the **File menu.** Click **Print** to produce a dialog box requesting information about the Print command as shown in Figure 1.10c.

➤ Click the **OK** command button to accept the default options and print the worksheet. You can also click the **printer icon** on the Standard toolbar to print the worksheet immediately and bypass the associated dialog box.

SAVE YOUR WORK

We cannot overemphasize the importance of periodically saving a worksheet, so if something goes wrong, you won't lose everything. Nothing is more frustrating than to lose two hours of effort, due to an unexpected problem in Windows or to a temporary loss of power. Save your work frequently, at least once every 15 minutes. Click the Save icon on the Standard toolbar or pull down the File menu and click Save. Do it!

Save icon

Printer icon

Click here to print the
worksheet

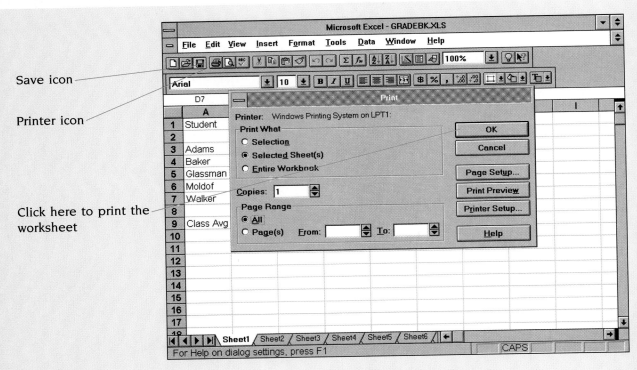

(c) Print the Spreadsheet (step 9)

FIGURE 1.10   Hands-on Exercise 1 (continued)

EXECUTE COMMANDS QUICKLY

The quickest way to select a command from a pull-down menu is to point
to the menu name, then drag the pointer (i.e., press and hold the left
mouse button) to the desired command, and release the mouse. The command is executed when you release the button.

Step 10: Exit Excel and Windows

➤ Pull down the **File menu.** Click **Exit** to close Excel and return to Program
Manager.

➤ Pull down the **File menu** in Program Manager. Click **Exit Windows.** You will
see an informational message indicating that you are leaving Windows. Click
the **OK** command button to exit.

MODIFYING THE WORKSHEET

We trust that you completed the hands-on exercise without difficulty and that you
are more confident in your ability than when you first began. The exercise was
not complicated, but it did accomplish several objectives and set the stage for a
second exercise, which follows shortly.

Consider now Figure 1.11, which contains a modified version of the professor's grade book. Figure 1.11a shows the grade book at the end of the first hands-
on exercise and reflects the changes made to the grades for Baker and Walker.

	A	B	C	D	E
1	Student	Test 1	Test 2	Final	Wgt Avg
2					
3	Adams	100	90	81	88.0
4	Baker	90	86	87	87.5
5	Glassman	90	78	78	81.0
6	Moldof	60	60	40	50.0
7	Walker	80	80	100	90.0
8					
9	Class Avg	84.0	78.8	77.2	

Formula references cells B3, C3, and D3

Function references rows 3–7

(a) After Hands-on Exercise 1

New column added for the student's major

	A	B	C	D	E	F
1	Student	Major	Test 1	Test 2	Final	Wgt Avg
2						
3	Adams	CIS	100	90	81	88.0
4	Baker	MKT	90	86	87	87.5
5	Coulter	ACC	85	95	100	95.0
6	Davis	FIN	75	75	85	80.0
7	Glassman	CIS	90	78	78	81.0
8	Walker	CIS	80	80	100	90.0
9						
10	Class Avg		86.7	84.0	88.5	

New students added to the class; Moldof deleted from the class

Formula now references cells C3, D3, and E3 as a result of inserted column

Function now averages grades in rows 3–8 as a result of inserted rows

(b) After Hands-on Exercise 2

FIGURE 1.11 The Modified Grade Book

Figure 1.11b shows the worksheet as it will appear at the end of the second exercise. Several changes bear mention:

1. One student has dropped the class and two other students have been added. Moldof appeared in the original worksheet in Figure 1.11a, but has somehow managed to withdraw; Coulter and Davis did not appear in the original grade book but have been added to the worksheet in Figure 1.11b.
2. A new column, containing the student's major, has been added for every student.

The implementation of these changes is accomplished through a combination of the Insert and Delete commands that enable you to add and/or remove rows or columns as necessary. The important thing to realize is that cell references in existing formulas are adjusted *automatically* to account for the changes brought about by the addition (deletion) of rows and columns.

Consider, once again, the formula to compute Adams's weighted average, which is contained in cell E3 of the original grade book, but in cell F3 in the modified grade book. The original formula in Figure 1.11a referenced cells B3, C3, and D3 to obtain the grades on test 1, test 2, and the final. The revised formula in Figure 1.11b reflects the fact that a new column has been inserted, and references cells C3, D3, and E3. The change in the formula is made automatically by Excel without any action on the part of the user (other than to insert the new column).

In similar fashion, the formulas to compute the class averages appear in row 9 of the original worksheet and reflect the entries in rows 3 through 7. The revised worksheet has a net increase of one student, which automatically moves the formulas containing the AVERAGE function to row 10. It also adjusts the AVERAGE function to use values from rows 3 through 8 to accommodate the additional student.

Required Commands

The *Row* and *Column commands* in the *Insert menu* add new row(s) and column(s) to an existing worksheet. Excel automatically adjusts any cell reference in existing formulas to account for the additional rows or columns. If, for example, cell B6 contained the formula =B2+B3 and a new row were inserted between rows 2 and 3, the formula in cell B6 would move to B7 and become =B2+B4.

The *Delete command* in the Edit menu removes existing row(s) or column(s) from a worksheet. Cell references are adjusted automatically to account for the deleted elements. If, for example, cell B6 contained the formula =B2+B3 and row 1 were deleted, the formula in cell B6 would move to cell B5 and become =B1+B2.

The hands-on exercise that follows requires the Open and Save commands found in the File menu. The *Open command* brings a workbook (containing one or more worksheets) from disk into memory. The *Save command* copies the workbook in memory to disk. The *Save As command* saves the workbook under a different name, and is useful when you want to retain a copy of the original workbook (and its worksheets) prior to making changes. The initial execution of the Save command (as well as every execution of the Save As command) requires you to enter a file name from one to eight characters; the extension XLS is assigned automatically.

TOOLBARS

As we have already indicated, Excel provides several different ways to accomplish the same task. Commands may be accessed from a pull-down menu, from a short-cut menu, and/or through keyboard equivalents. Commands can also be executed from one of several toolbars, and since toolbars remain visible throughout a session, this is a technique worth pursuing.

The Standard and Formatting toolbars appear by default and contain most of the basic commands you will need. The icons may at first appear overwhelming, but you will be surprised at how quickly you learn to use them. The easiest way to master the toolbars is to view the icons in groups according to their general function, as shown in Figure 1.12.

Remember, too, there is absolutely no need to memorize the function of the individual buttons (nor should you even try). That will come with time. Indeed, if you use another Microsoft application such as Word for Windows, you already recognize many of the icons on the Standard and Formatting toolbars. Most individuals start by using the pull-down menus, then look for shortcuts along the way. The following exercise describes both techniques and lets you choose the one you prefer. Additional information on customizing toolbars is presented in Chapter 2.

THE TIPWIZARD

The *TipWizard* greets you with a *tip-of-the-day* every time you start Excel but that is only one of its capabilities. The true purpose of the TipWizard is to introduce you to new features by suggesting more efficient ways to accomplish the tasks you are doing.

The TipWizard monitors your work and offers advice throughout a session. The TipWizard button on the Standard toolbar "lights up" whenever there is a suggestion. (Click the button to display the TipWizard; click the button a second time to close it.) You can read the suggestions as they occur and/or review them at the end of a session. You needn't always follow the advice of the TipWizard (at

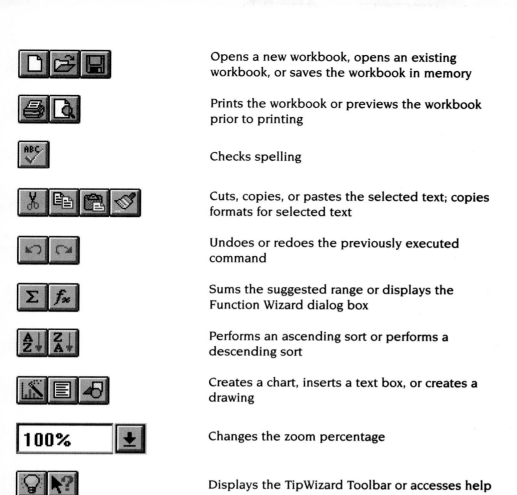

Opens a new workbook, opens an existing workbook, or saves the workbook in memory

Prints the workbook or previews the workbook prior to printing

Checks spelling

Cuts, copies, or pastes the selected text; copies formats for selected text

Undoes or redoes the previously executed command

Sums the suggested range or displays the Function Wizard dialog box

Performs an ascending sort or performs a descending sort

Creates a chart, inserts a text box, or creates a drawing

Changes the zoom percentage

Displays the TipWizard Toolbar or accesses help

(a) The Standard Toolbar

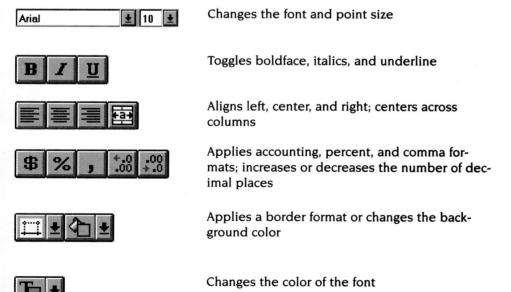

Changes the font and point size

Toggles boldface, italics, and underline

Aligns left, center, and right; centers across columns

Applies accounting, percent, and comma formats; increases or decreases the number of decimal places

Applies a border format or changes the background color

Changes the color of the font

(b) The Formatting Toolbar

FIGURE 1.12 Toolbars

first you may not even understand all of its suggestions), but over time it will make you much more proficient.

The TipWizard will not repeat a tip from one session to the next unless it is specifically reset as described in step 1 of the following exercise. This is especially important in a laboratory situation when you are sharing the same computer with other students.

HANDS-ON EXERCISE 2:

Modifying a Worksheet

Objective To open an existing workbook, to insert and delete rows and columns of a worksheet; to save the revised workbook; to use the TipWizard, Undo command, and on-line help. Use Figure 1.13 as a guide in doing the exercise.

Step 1: Tip of the day

➤ Load Microsoft Excel as described in the previous exercise.

➤ If necessary, click the **TipWizard button** on the Standard toolbar to display the tip of the day as shown in Figure 1.13a. Do not be concerned if your tip is different from ours.

➤ Pull down the **Tools menu,** click **Options,** then click the **General tab** to display the dialog box in Figure 1.13a.

➤ Click the check box to Reset TipWizard. Click **OK.** The contents of the Tip-Wizard box change to indicate that you have reset the TipWizard and that the tips may repeat.

➤ Click the **TipWizard button** a second time to close the TipWizard box.

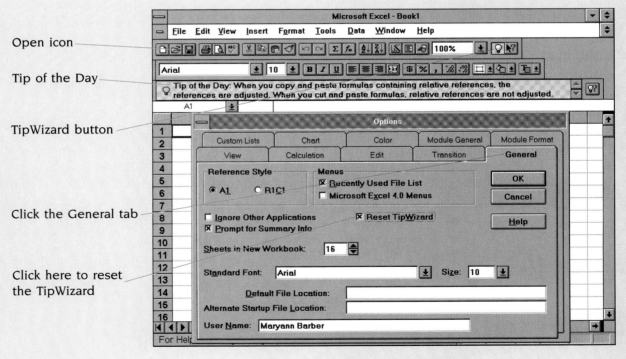

(a) The TipWizard (step 1)

FIGURE 1.13   Hands-on Exercise 2

CHANGING TOOLBARS

You can display (or hide) a toolbar with a shortcut menu provided at least one toolbar is visible. Point to any toolbar, click the right mouse button to display the Toolbar shortcut menu, then click the individual toolbars on or off as appropriate. If you do not see any toolbars, pull down the View menu, click Toolbars to display a dialog box listing the available toolbars, check the toolbars you want displayed, and click OK.

Step 2: Open the workbook
➤ Pull down the **File menu** and click **Open** (or click the **open icon** on the Standard toolbar) to produce a dialog box in which you specify the name of a file to open.
➤ Click the arrow for the Drives drop-down list box. Click the appropriate drive, drive C or drive A, depending on whether you installed the data disk. Double click the root directory (a:\ or c:\) in the Directories list box to display the subdirectories on the selected drive.
➤ Double click the **EXCLDATA** directory to make it the active directory. Double click **GRADEBK.XLS** to open the workbook from the first exercise.

Step 3: The Save As command
➤ Pull down the **File menu.** Click **Save As** to produce the dialog box of Figure 1.13b, which requests the name of the file.
➤ Type **GRADEBK2** as the name of the file (the XLS extension is added automatically). Press the **enter key.** Click the **Cancel command button** (or press the **Esc key**) if you are prompted for summary information.
➤ There are now two identical copies of the file on disk—GRADEBK.XLS, which we supplied, and GRADEBK2.XLS, which you just created. The title bar of the document window reflects the latter name.

SUMMARY INFORMATION

Excel maintains summary information on each workbook that is intended to help you find files more quickly. This is indeed a powerful capability, but it is typically not used by beginners. To suppress the prompt for summary information, pull down the Tools menu, click Options, click the General tab, then clear the box to Prompt for Summary Info.

Step 4: Delete a row
➤ Click any cell in **row 6** (the row you will delete). Pull down the **Edit menu.** Click **Delete** to produce the dialog box in Figure 1.13c. Click **Entire Row.** Click **OK** to delete row 6.
➤ Moldof has disappeared from the grade book, and the class averages (now in row 8) have been updated automatically.

Step 5: The Undo command
➤ Pull down the **Edit menu** and click **Undo Delete** (or click the Undo icon on the Standard toolbar) to reverse the preceding command and put Moldof back in the worksheet.
➤ Click any cell in row 6, and this time delete Moldof for good.

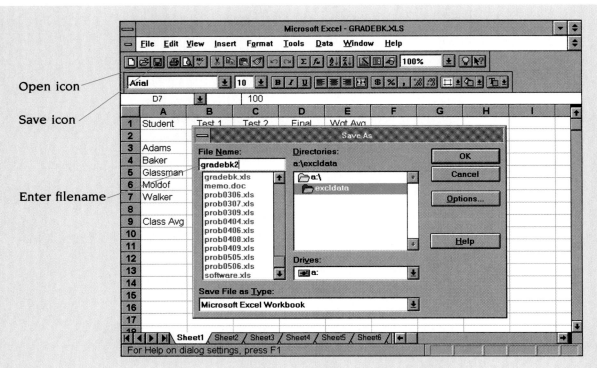

Open icon

Save icon

Enter filename

(b) The Save As command (step 3)

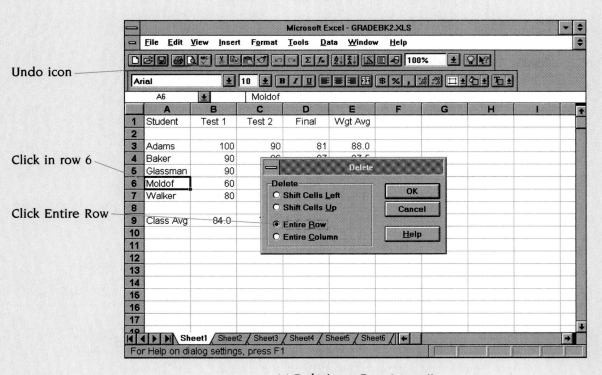

Undo icon

Click in row 6

Click Entire Row

(c) Deleting a Row (step 4)

FIGURE 1.13 Hands-on Exercise 2 (continued)

Step 6: Insert a row

➤ Click any cell in **row 5** (the row containing Glassman's grades).

➤ Pull down the **Insert menu.** Click **Rows** to add a new row above the current row. Row 5 is now blank (it is the newly inserted row) and Glassman (who was in row 5) is now in row 6.

➤ Enter the data for the new student in row 5 as shown in Figure 1.13d:
  —Click in cell **A5.** Type **Coulter.** Press the **right arrow key** or click in cell B5.
  —Type **85.** Press the **right arrow key** or click in cell C5.
  —Type **95.** Press the **right arrow key** or click in cell D5.
  —Type **100.** Press the **right arrow key** or click in cell E5.
  —Enter the formula to compute the weighted average, **=(B5+C5+2*D5)/4;** be sure to begin the formula with an equal sign. Press **enter.**

➤ Click the **Save icon** on the Standard toolbar or pull down the **File menu** and click **Save** to save the changes made to this point.

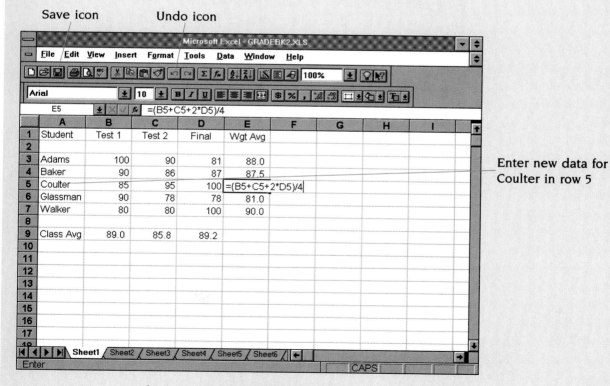

Save icon   Undo icon

Enter new data for Coulter in row 5

(d) Inserting a New Student (step 6)

FIGURE 1.13   Hands-on Exercise 2 (continued)

ERASING VERSUS DELETING

The Edit Delete command deletes the selected cell, row, or column from the worksheet. It is very different from the Edit Clear command, which erases the contents (and/or formatting) of the selected cells, but does not delete the cells from the worksheet. The Edit Delete command causes Excel to adjust cell references throughout the worksheet. The Edit Clear command does not adjust cell references.

Step 7: Use a shortcut menu
- Point to the **row heading** for row 6 (which now contains Glassman's grades). Click the **right mouse button** to produce the shortcut menu in Figure 1.13e.
- Click **Insert** to add a new row 6, which causes Glassman to move to row 7.
- Click in cell **A6.** Type **Davis.** Enter Davis's grades in the appropriate cells (75, 75, and 85 in cells B6, C6, and D6, respectively).
- Click in cell **E6.** Enter the formula to compute the weighted average, **=(B6+C6+2*D6)/4.** Press **enter.**
- Save the workbook.

Step 8: Add a column
- Click any cell in **column B.** Pull down the **Insert menu.** Click **Columns** to insert a new column.
- Column B is now blank (it is the new column) and all existing columns have been moved to the right; that is, the grades for Test 1 are now in column C, the grades for Test 2 in column D, and so on.
- The formulas for the weighted averages have been adjusted to accommodate the additional column; for example, the entry in cell F3 is now =(C3+D3+2*E3)/4.
- Click in cell **B1.** Type **Major.** Click in cell **B3.** Enter the students' majors as shown in Figure 1.13f.

SHORTCUT MENUS

Shortcut menus provide an alternate way to execute commands. Point to any cell, or to any row or column heading, then click the right mouse button to display a shortcut menu with commands appropriate to the item you are pointing to. Point to a command, then click the left mouse button to execute the command from the shortcut menu. Press the Esc key or click outside the menu to close the menu without executing a command.

THE HELP BUTTON

Click the Help button on the Standard toolbar (the mouse pointer changes to include a large question mark), then click any other toolbar icon to display a help screen with information about that button. Double click the Help button to produce the Search dialog box normally accessed through the Help menu.

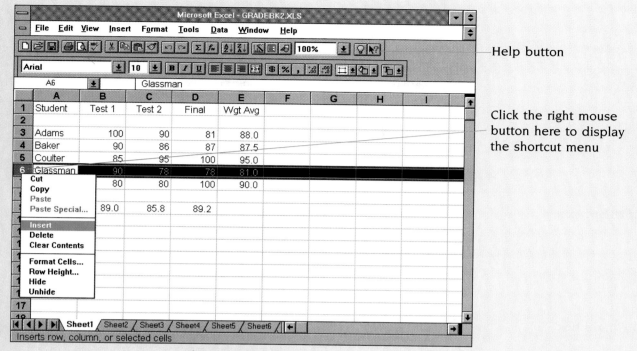

Help button

Click the right mouse button here to display the shortcut menu

(e) Shortcut Menu (step 7)

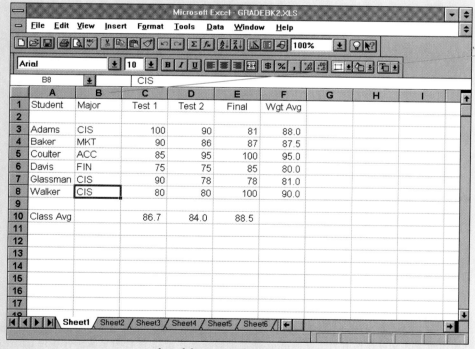

Inserted column

(f) Adding a Column (step 8)

FIGURE 1.13   Hands-on Exercise 2 (continued)

Step 10: The Standard toolbar

➤ Click the **Save icon** on the Standard toolbar to save the workbook.
➤ Click the **Print icon** on the Standard toolbar to print the worksheet.
➤ Click the **TipWizard icon** to open the TipWizard box.

Step 11: On-line help

➤ Pull down the **Help menu.** Click **Search for Help on.** Type **TipWizard** in the text box as shown in Figure 1.13g.

➤ Double click **TipWizard** in the upper list box.

➤ Double click **Using the TipWizard** in the lower list box. Read the How To help screen with information on the TipWizard. Click the **Close command button** when you are finished.

➤ Double click the **control-menu box** in the help screen to exit Help and return to the worksheet.

➤ Pull down the **File menu.** Click **Exit** to leave Excel.

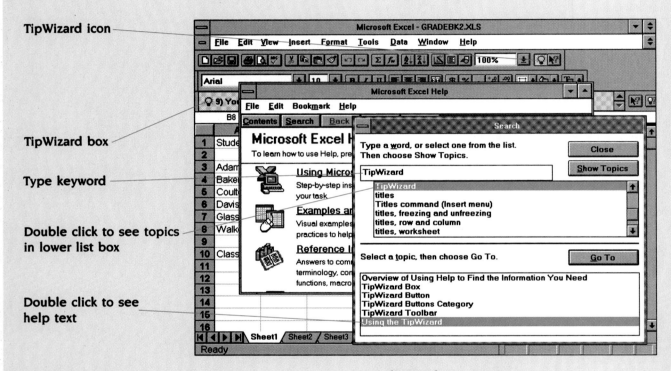

(g) On-line Help (step 11)

FIGURE 1.13 Hands-on Exercise 2 (continued)

SUMMARY

The common user interface ensures that all Windows applications are similar in appearance and work basically the same way, with common conventions and a consistent menu structure. It provides you with an intuitive understanding of any application, even before you begin to use it, and means that once you learn one application, it is that much easier to learn the next.

The mouse is essential to Microsoft Excel as it is to all other Windows applications, but keyboard equivalents are provided for virtually all operations. Toolbars and shortcut menus provide other ways to execute common commands. On-line help provides detailed information about all aspects of Microsoft Excel.

A spreadsheet is the computerized equivalent of an accountant's ledger. It is divided into rows and columns, with each row and column assigned a heading. The intersection of a row and column forms a cell.

Spreadsheet is a generic term. Workbook and worksheet are Excel specific. An Excel workbook contains one or more worksheets.

Every cell in a worksheet (spreadsheet) contains either a formula or a constant. A formula begins with an equal sign, a constant does not. A constant is an entry that does not change and may be numeric or descriptive text. A formula is a combination of numeric constants, cell references, arithmetic operators, and/or functions that produce a new value from existing values.

The Insert and Delete commands add or remove rows or columns as necessary. The Open command brings a workbook from disk into memory; the Save command copies the workbook in memory to disk.

 ## Key Words and Concepts

Active cell	Ellipsis	Restore button
Application window	File Menu	Row command
Cascade menu	Formatting toolbar	Save command
Cell	Formula	Save As command
Cell contents	Formula bar	Scroll bar
Cell reference	Function	Scroll box
Check box	Help menu	Shortcut menu
Click	Icon	Spreadsheet
Column command	Insert menu	Standard toolbar
Command button	Maximize button	Status bar
Common user interface	Menu bar	Tab
Constant	Minimize button	Tabbed dialog box
Control-menu box	Mouse pointer	Text box
Delete command	Name box	TipWizard
Desktop	On-line help	Title bar
Dialog box	Open command	Toolbar
Dimmed command	Open list box	Undo command
Document window	Option button	Value
Double click	Point	Window
Drag	Print command	Workbook
Drop-down list box	Program Manager	Worksheet
Edit menu	Pull-down menu	

 ## Multiple Choice

1. Which of the following will execute a command from a pull-down menu?
  (a) Clicking on the command once the menu has been pulled down
  (b) Typing the underlined letter in the command
  (c) Both (a) and (b)
  (d) Neither (a) nor (b)

2. The File Open command:
  (a) Brings a workbook from disk into memory
  (b) Brings a workbook from disk into memory, then erases the workbook on disk

(c) Stores the workbook in memory on disk

(d) Stores the workbook in memory on disk, then erases the workbook from memory

3. The File Save command:

(a) Brings a workbook from disk into memory

(b) Brings a workbook from disk into memory, then erases the workbook on disk

(c) Stores the workbook in memory on disk

(d) Stores the workbook in memory on disk, then erases the workbook from memory

4. What is the significance of three dots next to a menu option?

(a) The option is not accessible

(b) A dialog box will appear if the option is selected

(c) A help window will appear if the option is selected

(d) There are no equivalent keystrokes for the particular option

5. What is the significance of a menu option that appears faded (dimmed)?

(a) The option is not currently accessible

(b) A dialog box will appear if the option is selected

(c) A help window will appear if the option is selected

(d) There are no equivalent keystrokes for the particular option

6. Which of the following elements may be found within a help window?

(a) Title bar, menu bar, and control-menu box

(b) Minimize, maximize, and/or a restore button

(c) Vertical and/or horizontal scroll bars

(d) All of the above

7. Which of the following is true regarding a dialog box?

(a) Option buttons indicate mutually exclusive choices

(b) Check boxes imply that multiple options may be selected

(c) Both (a) and (b)

(d) Neither (a) nor (b)

8. Which of the following are found in the application windows for both Excel and Word for Windows?

(a) The Standard and Formatting toolbars

(b) The File, Edit, and Help menus

(c) Both (a) and (b) above

(d) Neither (a) nor (b)

9. In the absence of parentheses, the order of operation is:

(a) Exponentiation, addition or subtraction, multiplication or division

(b) Addition or subtraction, multiplication or division, exponentiation

(c) Multiplication or division, exponentiation, addition or subtraction

(d) Exponentiation, multiplication or division, addition or subtraction

10. The entry =AVERAGE(A4:A6):

(a) Is invalid because the cells are not contiguous

(b) Computes the average of cells A4 and A6

(c) Computes the average of cells A4, A5, and A6

(d) None of the above

11. A right-handed person will normally:

(a) Click the right and left mouse buttons to access a pull-down menu and shortcut menu, respectively

(b) Click the left and right mouse buttons to access a pull-down menu and shortcut menu, respectively

(c) Click the left mouse button to access both a pull-down menu and a short-cut menu

(d) Click the right mouse button to access both a pull-down menu and a shortcut menu

12. What is the effect of typing F5+F6 into a cell *without* a beginning equal sign?

(a) The entry is equivalent to the formula =F5+F6

(b) The cell will display the contents of cell F5 plus cell F6

(c) The entry will be treated as a constant and display the literal value F5+F6

(d) The entry will be rejected by Excel, which will signal an error message

13. A worksheet is superior to manual calculation because:

(a) The worksheet computes its entries faster

(b) The worksheet computes its results more accurately

(c) The worksheet recalculates its results whenever cell contents are changed

(d) All the above

14. The cell at the intersection of the second column and third row has the cell reference:

(a) B3

(b) 3B

(c) C2

(d) 2C

15. Which of the following is true?

(a) A worksheet contains one or more workbooks

(b) A workbook contains one or more worksheets

(c) A spreadsheet contains one or more worksheets

(d) A worksheet contains one or more spreadsheets

ANSWERS

1. c	**6.** d.	**11.** b
2. a	**7.** c.	**12.** c
3. c	**8.** c.	**13.** d
4. b	**9.** d.	**14.** a
5. a	**10.** c.	**15.** b

EXPLORING EXCEL

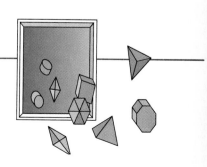

1. Use Figure 1.14 to identify the elements of a Microsoft Excel screen by matching each element with the appropriate letter.

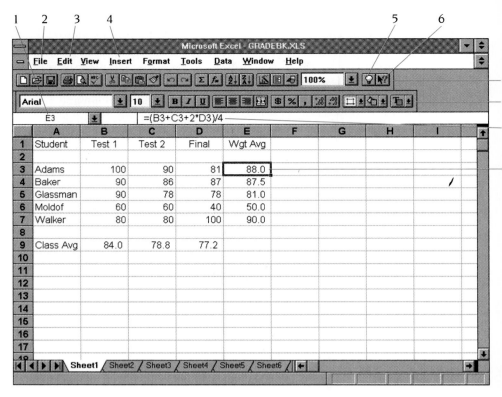

FIGURE 1.14   Screen for Problem 1

___ Formatting toolbar

___ Active cell

___ Contains the Delete command to remove rows from the worksheet

___ Help button

___ TipWizard icon

___ Standard toolbar

___ Contains the Open and Save commands

___ Name box

___ Formula bar

___ Contains the commands to add rows and columns to the worksheet

2. The common user interface: Answer the following with respect to Figures 1.2a and 1.2b that appeared earlier in the chapter.

   a. Which pull-down menus are common to both Excel and Word?

   b. How do you access the Edit menu in Excel? in Word?

   c. How do you open a file in Microsoft Excel? Do you think the same command will work in Microsoft Word as well?

   d. Which icons correspond to the Open and Save commands in the Excel toolbar? Which icons correspond to the Open and Save commands in the Microsoft Word toolbar?

   e. Which icons will boldface, italicize, and underline a selected item in Excel and Word? Are these icons descriptive of the tasks they perform?

   f. What do your answers to parts a through e tell you about the advantages of a common user interface?

3. Troubleshooting: The informational messages in Figure 1.15 appeared (or could have appeared) in response to various commands issued during the chapter.

   a. The message in Figure 1.15a is produced when the user exits Excel, but only under a specific circumstance. When will that message be produced? When would No be an appropriate response to this message?

   b. The message in Figure 1.15b appeared in response to a File Open command in conjunction with the files shown earlier in Figure 1.10a. What is the most likely corrective action?

   c. The message in Figure 1.15c also appears in response to a File Open command. What corrective action needs to be taken?

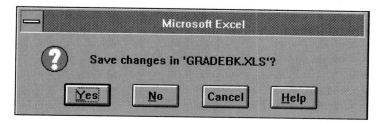

(a) Informational Message 1

(b) Informational Message 2

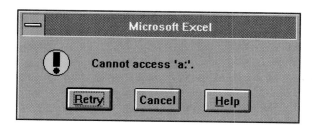

(c) Informational Message 3

FIGURE 1.15 Informational Messages for Problem 3

4. Exploring help: Answer the following with respect to Figure 1.16:

   a. What is the significance of the scroll box that appears within the scroll bar?

   b. What happens if you click on the down (up) arrow within the scroll bar?

   c. What happens if you press the maximize button? Might this action eliminate the need to scroll within the help window?

   d. How do you print the help topic shown in the window?

   e. Which entries in the help screen are underlined? Is there a difference between a dotted and a solid underline?

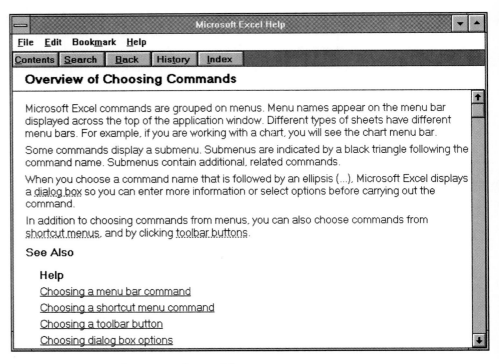

FIGURE 1.16　Help Screen for Problem 4

5. Design a worksheet that would be useful to you. You might want to consider applications such as an annual budget, the cost of a stereo or computer system, the number of calories you consume (burn) in a day, calculation of federal income tax, and so on. The applications are limited only by your imagination.

6. Figure 1.17 contains a simple worksheet showing the earnings for Widgets of America, before and after taxes. The cell values in cells B6, B7, and B9 may be produced in several ways, two of which are shown below. For example:

	Method 1	Method 2
Cell B6	$10000-4000$	$=B3-B4$
Cell B7	$.30*6000$	$=.30*B6$
Cell B9	$6000-1800$	$=B6-B7$

Which is the better method, and why?

	A	B
1	Widgets of America	
2		
3	Revenue	10000
4	Expenses	4000
5		
6	Earnings before taxes	6000
7	Taxes	1800
8		
9	Earnings after taxes	4200

FIGURE 1.17　Spreadsheet for Problem 6

7. Answer the following with respect to the screen in Figure 1.18, which depicts the use of a worksheet in a simplified calculation for income tax.

a. Is the application window for Excel maximized?

b. Is the document window containing the worksheet maximized?

c. What is the active cell?

d. What are the contents of the active cell?

e. Assume that the income in cell B2 changes to $125,000. What other numbers will change automatically?

f. Assume that an additional deduction for local income taxes of $3,000 is entered between rows 9 and 10. Which formula (if any) has to be explicitly changed to accommodate the new deduction?

g. Which formula(s) will change automatically after the row containing the additional deduction has been added to the worksheet?

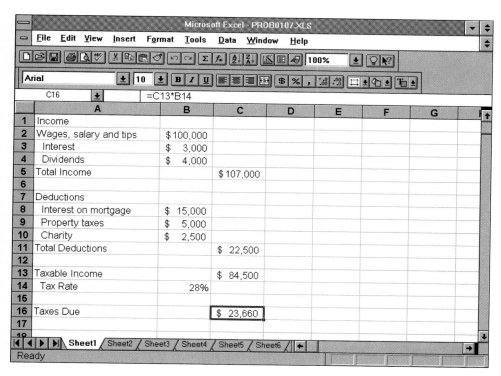

FIGURE 1.18   Spreadsheet for Problem 7

8. Return to the grade book at the end of the second hands-on exercise and implement the following changes:

a. The professor has decided to weigh test 1, test 2, and the final equally, rather than counting the final as two exams.

b. A new student, Milgrom, must be entered on the roster with grades of 88, 80, and 84, respectively.

c. Baker is to be dropped from the class roll.

d. Enter the label, *Grading Assistant,* followed by your name somewhere in the worksheet.

e. Print the worksheet after all modifications have been made and submit it to your instructor.

9. Figure 1.19 contains a simple profit projection in the form of a worksheet that you are to implement in Microsoft Excel. *Be sure to enter formulas* *rather than numbers where appropriate—for example, in the cells containing gross income, total material cost, total labor cost, total cost, and gross profit.*

a. Add your name somewhere in the worksheet and identify yourself as a financial planner. Print the worksheet as it appears in Figure 1.19, then implement the following modifications.

b. Change the selling price in cell B4 to 6, which should automatically change several other numbers in the worksheet—for example, the gross income in cell B5.

c. Add an overhead expense in cell B12 of $1000 (enter an appropriate label in cell A12), then change the formula in cell B13 to accommodate the additional expense.

d. Assume a tax rate of 30 percent. Enter the formula to compute the anticipated tax in row 16 and the after-tax profit in row 17.

e. Assume that the numbers in column B are for 1994. Create a corresponding forecast for 1995 in column C. Assume the number of units sold will be 10 percent higher, and that the selling price and all other costs increase by 8 percent.

f. Add column D for 1996, using the same anticipated rates of change.

g. Print the worksheet a second time after completing the modifications in parts b through f. Submit both versions of the printed worksheet (in part a and part g) to your instructor.

	A	B
1		
2	Income	
3	Number of units	1,500
4	Selling price	$ 8
5	Gross Income	$12,000
6		
7	Expenses	
8	Material cost per unit	$ 4
9	Total material cost	$ 6,000
10	Labor cost per unit	$ 1
11	Total labor cost	$ 1,500
12		
13	Total cost	$ 7,500
14		
15	Gross Profit	$ 4,500

FIGURE 1.19 Spreadsheet for Problem 9

10. Create a worksheet that shows your income and expenses for a typical month according to the format in Figure 1.20. Enter your budget rather than ours.

a. Enter your name in cell A1.

b. Enter the text Monthly Income in cell A3 and the corresponding amount in cell B3.

c. Enter the text Monthly Expenses in A5.

d. Enter at least 5 different expenses in consecutive rows, beginning in A6, and enter the corresponding amounts in column B.

e. Enter the text Total Expenses in the row immediately below your last expense item. Enter the formula to compute the total in the corresponding cell in column B.

	A	B
1	Maryann Barber's Budget	
2		
3	Monthly Income	1000
4		
5	Monthly Expenses	
6	Food	250
7	Rent	350
8	Utilities	100
9	Phone	20
10	Gas	40
11	Total expenses:	760
12		
13	What's left for fun	240

FIGURE 1.20 Spreadsheet for Problem 10

f. Skip one blank row and then enter the text What's left for fun in column A. Enter the formula to compute how much money you have left at the end of the month in column B.

g. Insert a new row eight. Add an additional expense that you left out, entering the text in A8 and the amount in B8. Does the formula for total expenses reflect the additional expense? If not, change the formula so that it does.

h. Change the amount of your monthly income to reflect the fact that you now have a part-time work/study position. Do you now have more money left at the end of the month? Did the formula indicating the amount left recompute automatically to reflect the increased income in cell A3?

i. Why did the formula in step g not reflect the change made, while the formula in step h did reflect the change made?

Case Studies

Buying a Computer

You have decided to buy a PC and have settled on a minimum configuration consisting of an entry-level 80486, with 4MB of RAM, and a 100MB hard disk. You would like a modem if it fits into the budget, and you need a printer. You also need software: DOS, Windows, a Windows-based word processor, and a Windows-based spreadsheet. You can spend up to $2,500 and hope that, at today's prices, you can find a system that goes beyond your minimum requirements—for example, a system with a faster processor, 8MB of RAM, and a 200MB hard disk. We suggest you shop around and look for educational discounts on software and/or a suite of applications to save money.

Create a spreadsheet based on real data that presents several alternatives. Show different configurations from the same vendor and/or comparable systems from different vendors. Include the vendor's telephone number with their estimate. Bring the spreadsheet to class together with the supporting documentation in the form of printed advertisements.

Portfolio Management

A spreadsheet is an ideal vehicle to track the progress of your investments. You need to maintain the name of the company, the number of shares purchased, the date of the purchase, and the purchase price. You can then enter the current price and see immediately the potential gain or loss on each investment as well as the current value of the portfolio. Retrieve the STOCKS.XLS workbook from the data disk, enter the closing prices of the listed investments, and compute the current value of the portfolio.

Accuracy Counts

The UNDERBID.XLS workbook on the data disk was the last assignment completed by your predecessor prior to his unfortunate dismissal. The worksheet contains a significant error, which caused your company to underbid a contract and assume a subsequent loss of $100,000. As you look for the error, don't be distracted by the attractive formatting. The shading, lines, and other touches are nice, but accuracy is more important than anything else. Write a memo to your instructor describing the nature of the error. Include suggestions in the memo on how to avoid mistakes of this nature in the future.

Planning for Disaster

This case has nothing to do with spreadsheets per se, but it is perhaps the most important case of all, as it deals with the question of backup. Do you have a backup strategy? Do you even know what a backup strategy is? You had better learn, because sooner or later you will wish you had one. You will erase a file, be unable to read from a floppy disk, or worse yet suffer a hardware failure in which you are unable to access the hard drive. The problem always seems to occur the night before an assignment is due. The ultimate disaster is the disappearance of your computer, by theft or natural disaster (e.g., Hurricane Andrew, the floods in the Midwest, or the Los Angeles earthquake). Describe in 250 words or fewer the backup strategy you plan to implement in conjunction with your work in this class.

2

Gaining Proficiency: Copying, Moving, and Formatting

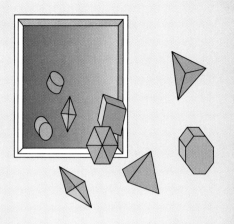

CHAPTER OBJECTIVES

After reading this chapter you will be able to:

1. Explain the importance of isolating assumptions within a worksheet.
2. Define a cell range; select and deselect ranges within a worksheet.
3. Copy and/or move cells within a worksheet; differentiate among relative, absolute, and mixed addresses.
4. Format a worksheet to include boldface, italics, shading, and borders; change the font and/or alignment of a selected entry.
5. Change the width of a column; explain what happens if a column is too narrow to display the computed result.
6. Print a worksheet two ways: to show the computed values or cell formulas.
7. Use the Page Setup command to print a worksheet with or without gridlines and/or row and column headings; preview a worksheet before printing.
8. Use the Formatting toolbar.

OVERVIEW

This chapter continues the grade book example of Chapter 1. It is perhaps the most important chapter in the entire text as it describes the basic commands to create a worksheet. We begin with the definition of a cell range and the commands to build a worksheet without regard to its appearance. We focus on the Copy command and the difference between relative and absolute addresses. We stress the importance of isolating the assumptions within a worksheet so that alternative strategies may be easily evaluated.

The second half of the chapter presents formatting commands to improve the appearance of a worksheet after it has been created. You will be pleased with the dramatic impact you can achieve with a few simple commands, but we emphasize that *accuracy in a worksheet is much more important than appearance.*

The two hands-on exercises are absolutely critical if you are to master the material. As you do the exercises, you will realize that there are many different ways to accomplish the same task. Our approach is to present the most basic way first and the shortcuts later. You will like the shortcuts better, but you may not remember them and hence you need to understand the underlying concepts. You can always find the necessary command from the appropriate menu, and if you don't know which menu, you can always look to on-line help.

A BETTER GRADE BOOK

Figure 2.1 contains a much improved version of the professor's grade book. The most obvious difference is in the appearance of the worksheet, as a variety of formatting commands have been used to make it more attractive. The exam scores and weighted averages are centered under the appropriate headings. Boldface and italics are used for emphasis. Shading is used to highlight different areas of the worksheet. The title has been centered over the worksheet.

Title added

Shading, bold, and italics used for emphasis

Values are centered

Exam weights are indicated

	A	B	C	D	E
1	CIS 120 - Spring 1994				
2					
3	Student	Test 1	Test 2	Final	Average
4	Costa, Frank	70	80	90	82.5
5	Ford, Judd	70	65	80	73.8
6	Grauer, Jessica	90	80	98	91.5
7	Kinzer, Jessica	80	78	98	88.5
8	Krein, Darren	85	70	95	86.3
9	Moldof, Adam	75	75	80	77.5
10					
11	Class Averages	78.3	74.7	90.2	
12					
13	Exam Weights	25%	25%	50%	

FIGURE 2.1   A Better Grade Book

The most *significant* difference, however, is that the weight of each exam is indicated within the worksheet, and the formulas to compute the student averages are based on these values. In other words the professor can change the contents of the cells containing the exam weights, and see immediately the effect on the student averages.

This is one of the most important concepts in the development of a worksheet and enables the professor to explore alternative grading strategies. The professor may notice, for example, that the class did significantly better on the final than on either of the first two exams. He or she may decide to give the class a break and increase the weight of the final relative to the other tests. What if the professor increases the weight of the final to 60% and decreases the weight of the other tests? What if he or she decides that the final should count 70%? The effect of these changes can be seen immediately by entering the new exam weights in the appropriate cells at the bottom of the worksheet.

CELL FORMULAS

A worksheet should always be printed twice, once to show the computed results, and once to show the cell formulas. To display cell formulas, pull down the Tools menu, click Options, click the View tab, then check the box for formulas. Use the Page Setup command to specify cell gridlines and row and column headings, then click the Print command button to print.

CELL RANGES

Every command in Excel operates on a rectangular group of cells known as a *range*. A range may be as small as a single cell or as large as the entire worksheet. It may consist of a row or part of a row, a column or part of a column, or multiple rows and columns. The cells within a range are specified by indicating the diagonally opposite corners, typically the upper-left and lower-right corners of the rectangle. For example, cells A1 through E13 (A1:E13) indicate the active area of the worksheet in Figure 2.1.

The easiest way to select a range is by dragging the mouse; that is, click at the beginning of the range, press and hold the left mouse button as you move to the end of the range, then release the mouse. Once selected, the range is highlighted and its cells are affected by any subsequent command. The range remains selected until another range is defined or until you click another cell anywhere on the worksheet.

COPY COMMAND

The *Copy command* duplicates the contents of a cell, or range of cells, and saves you from having to enter the contents of every cell individually. It is much easier, for example, to enter the formula to compute the test average once, and copy it to obtain the average for the remaining tests, rather than explicitly entering the formula for every test.

Figure 2.2 illustrates how the copy command can be used to duplicate the formula to compute the class average. The cell that you are copying from, cell B11, is called the *source range.* The cells that you are copying to, cells C11 to D11, are the *destination* (or target) *range.* The formula is not copied exactly, but is adjusted as it is copied, to compute the average for the respective test.

	A	B	C	D	E
1			*CIS 120 - Spring 1994*		
2					
3	*Student*	*Test 1*	*Test 2*	*Test 3*	*Average*
4	Costa, Frank	70	80	90	=$B13*B4+$C$13*C4+$D$13*D4
5	Ford, Judd	70	65	80	=$B13*B5+$C$13*C5+$D$13*D5
6	Grauer, Jessica	90	80	98	=$B13*B6+$C$13*C6+$D$13*D6
7	Kinzer, Jessica	80	78	98	=$B13*B7+$C$13*C7+$D$13*D7
8	Krein, Darren	85	70	95	=$B13*B8+$C$13*C8+$D$13*D8
9	Moldof, Adam	75	75	80	=$B13*B9+$C$13*C9+$D$13*D9
10					
11	*Class Averages*	=AVERAGE(B4:B9)	=AVERAGE(C4:C9)	=AVERAGE(D4:D9)	
12					
13	*Exam Weights*	25%	25%	50%	

Absolute reference

Relative reference

Source range (B11)

Destination range (C11:D11)

FIGURE 2.2 A Copy Command

The formula (function) to compute the average on the first test was entered into cell B11 as =AVERAGE(B4:B9). This formula references the cell seven rows above the cell containing the formula (i.e., cell B4 is seven rows above cell B11) as well as cell B9, which is two rows above the formula. When the formula in cell B11 is copied to C11, it is adjusted so that the cells referenced in cell C11 are in the same relative position as those referenced by the formula in cell B11—that is, seven and two rows above the formula itself. Thus the formula in cell C11 becomes =AVERAGE(C4:C9), and in similar fashion, the formula in cell D11 becomes =AVERAGE(D4:D9).

Figure 2.2 also illustrates how the Copy command is used to copy the formula for a student's weighted average, from cell E4 (the source range) to cells E5 through E9 (the destination range). This is slightly more complicated than the previous example, because the formula is based on a student's grades, which vary from one student to the next, and on the exam weights, which do not. The cells referring to the student's grades should adjust as the formula is copied, but the addresses referencing the weights should not.

The distinction between cell references that remain constant versus cell addresses that change is made through a dollar sign. An **absolute reference** remains constant throughout the copy operation and is specified with a dollar sign in front of the column and row designation—for example, $B$13. A **relative reference,** on the other hand, changes during a copy operation and is specified without dollar signs—for example, B4. (A **mixed reference** uses a single dollar sign to make the row relative and the column absolute—for example, $A5—or vice versa, to make the row absolute and the column relative as in A$5. Mixed references are not discussed further.)

Consider, for example, the formula to compute a student's weighted average as it appears in cell E4 of Figure 2.2:

=$B$13*B4+$C$13*C4+$D$13*D4

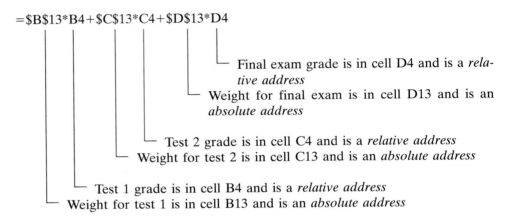

Final exam grade is in cell D4 and is a *relative address*

Weight for final exam is in cell D13 and is an *absolute address*

Test 2 grade is in cell C4 and is a *relative address*
Weight for test 2 is in cell C13 and is an *absolute address*

Test 1 grade is in cell B4 and is a *relative address*
Weight for test 1 is in cell B13 and is an *absolute address*

The formula in cell E4 uses a combination of relative and absolute addresses to compute the student's weighted average. Relative addresses are used for the exam grades (found in cells B4, C4, and D4) and change automatically when the formula is copied to the other rows. Absolute addresses are used for the exam weights (found in cells B13, C13, and D13) and remain constant from student to student.

The copy operation is implemented by using the Windows clipboard and a combination of the **Copy** and **Paste commands** from the Edit menu. The contents of the source range are copied to the **clipboard,** from where they are pasted to the destination range. The contents of the clipboard are replaced with each subsequent Copy command, but are unaffected by the Paste command. Thus you can execute the Paste command several times in succession, to paste the contents of the clipboard to multiple locations.

MOVE COMMAND

The **Move command** is not used in the grade book, but its presentation is essential for the sake of completeness. The Move command transfers the contents of a cell (or range of cells) from one location to another. After the move is completed, the cells where the move originated (that is, the source range) are empty. This is in contrast to the Copy command, by which the entries remain in the source range and are duplicated in the destination range.

A simple move operation is depicted in Figure 2.3a, in which the contents of cell A3 are moved to cell C3, with the formula in cell C3 unchanged after the move. In other words, the Move command simply picks up the contents of cell

A3 (to add the values in cells A1 and A2), and puts it down in cell C3. The source range, cell A3, is empty after the Move command has been executed.

	A	B	C
1	5		
2	2		
3	=A1+A2		

	A	B	C
1	5		
2	2		
3			=A1+A2

— Source range is empty

— Formula is unchanged

(a) Example 1 (only cell A3 is moved)

FIGURE 2.3   The Move Command

Figure 2.3b depicts a situation wherein the formula itself remains in the same cell, but one of the values it references is moved to a new location; that is, the entry in A1 is moved to C1. The formula in cell A3 is adjusted to follow the moved entry to its new location; that is, the formula is now =C1+A2.

	A	B	C
1	5		
2	2		
3	=A1+A2		

	A	B	C
1			5
2	2		
3	=C1+A2		

— Cell reference adjusted to follow moved entry

(b) Example 2 (only cell A1 is moved)

FIGURE 2.3   The Move Command (continued)

The situation is different in Figure 2.3c as the contents of all three cells—A1, A2, and A3—are moved. After the move has taken place, cells C1 and C2 contain the 5 and the 2, respectively, with the formula in cell C3 adjusted to reflect the movement of the contents of cells A1 and A2. Once again the source range (column A) is empty after the move is completed.

	A	B	C
1	5		
2	2		
3	=A1+A2		

	A	B	C
1			5
2			2
3			=C1+C2

— Source range is empty

— Cell references adjusted to follow moved entries

(c) Example 3 (all three cells in column A are moved)

FIGURE 2.3   The Move Command (continued)

Figure 2.3d contains an additional formula in cell B1, which is *dependent* on cell A3, which in turn is moved to cell C3. The formula in cell C3 is unchanged after the move because *only* the formula was moved, *not* the values it referenced. The formula in cell B1 changes (even though the contents of cell B1 were not moved) because cell B1 refers to an entry (A3) that was transferred to a new location (C3).

— Formula references value in A3

	A	B	C
1	5	=A3*4	
2	2		
3	=A1+A2		

	A	B	C
1	5	=C3*4	
2	2		
3			=A1+A2

— Cell reference adjusted to follow moved entry

— Formula is unchanged

(d) Example 4 (dependent cells)

FIGURE 2.3   The Move Command (continued)

Figure 2.3e shows that the specification of an absolute address has no meaning in a Move command. Absolute addresses are treated exactly the same as relative addresses and are adjusted as necessary to reflect the move operation. The example combines Figures 2.3b and 2.3c and shows that all of the absolute references were changed to reflect the entries that moved.

	A	B	C
1	5	=$A$3*4	
2	2		
3	=$A$1+$A$2		

	A	B	C
1		=$C$3*4	5
2			2
3			=$C$1+$C$2

Cell reference adjusted to follow moved entry

Cell references adjusted to follow moved entries

(e) Example 5 (absolute cell addresses)

FIGURE 2.3   The Move Command (continued)

The Move command is a convenient way to improve the appearance of a worksheet after it has been developed. It is subtle in its operation, and we suggest you think twice before moving cell entries because of the complexities involved.

The move operation is implemented by using the Windows clipboard and a combination of the **Cut** and **Paste** commands from the Edit menu. The contents of the source range are transferred to the clipboard, from where they are pasted to the destination range. (The contents of the clipboard are erased by the Paste command when the Paste command follows a Cut command.)

LEARNING BY DOING

As we have already indicated, there are many different ways to accomplish the same task. You can execute commands by using a pull-down menu, a shortcut menu, a toolbar, or the keyboard. In the following exercise we emphasize pull-down menus (the most basic technique) but suggest various shortcuts as appropriate. We also direct you to reset the TipWizard so that Excel can monitor your actions and offer additional suggestions.

Realize, however, that while the shortcuts are interesting, it is far more important to focus on the underlying concepts in the exercise, rather than specific key strokes or mouse clicks. The professor's grade book was developed to emphasize the difference between relative and absolute cell references. The grade book also illustrates the importance of isolating assumptions so that alternative strategies (e.g., different exam weights) can be considered.

HANDS-ON EXERCISE 1:

Creating a Worksheet

Objective To build the worksheet of Figure 2.1 without regard to its appearance; to create a formula containing relative and absolute references; to use the Copy command within a worksheet. Use Figure 2.4 as a guide in doing the exercise.

Step 1: Load Excel

➤ Load Excel as you did in the previous chapter.

➤ If necessary, click the **TipWizard icon** on the Standard toolbar to open the TipWizard box and display the tip of the day.

➤ Pull down the **Tools menu,** click **Options,** and click the **General tab.** Click the check box to **Reset TipWizard,** then click **OK.** The contents of the Tip-Wizard box change to indicate that you have reset the TipWizard and that the tips may repeat.

Step 2: Enter the column headings

➤ Click in cell **A1.** Enter the title of the worksheet, **CIS120 - Spring 1994** as in Figure 2.4a.

➤ Press the **down arrow key** twice to move to cell **A3.** Type **Student.**

➤ Press the **right arrow key** to move to cell **B3.** Type **Test 1.**

➤ Press the **right arrow key** to move to cell **C3.** Type **Test 2.** Type **Final** in cell **D3** and **Average** in cell **D4.**

Step 3: Save the workbook

➤ Pull down the **File menu** and click **Save** (or click the **Save icon** on the Standard toolbar).

➤ If you have not changed the default directory:
— Click drive A or drive C as appropriate.
— Double click the **EXCLDATA** directory to make it the active directory.

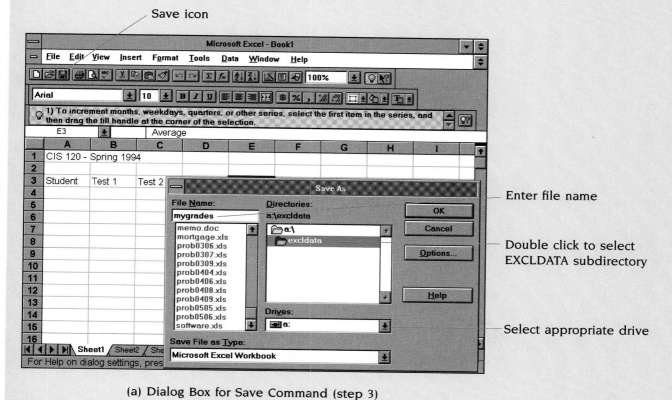

(a) Dialog Box for Save Command (step 3)

FIGURE 2.4   Hands-on Exercise 1

➤ Click in the File Name text box. Type **MYGRADES** as the name of the workbook as shown in Figure 2.4a. Click **OK** (or press **enter**). Click the **Cancel command button** (or press the **Esc key**) if you are prompted for summary information.

CHANGE THE DEFAULT DIRECTORY

The *default directory* is the directory Excel uses to retrieve (save) a workbook unless it is otherwise instructed. To change the default directory, pull down the Tools menu, click Options, and click the General tab. Type the name of the new directory (e.g., C:\EXCLDATA) in the Default File Location text box, then click OK. The next time you access the File menu, the default directory will reflect the change.

Step 4: Enter the student data and literal information
➤ Click in cell **A4** and type **Costa, Frank.**
➤ Move across row 4 and enter Frank's grades on the two tests and the final. Use Figure 2.4b as a guide. Do *not* enter Frank's average in cell E4 as that will be entered as a formula in step 4.
➤ Do *not* be concerned that you cannot see Frank's entire name because the default width of column A is not yet wide enough to display the entire name.

Do not enter the average ———

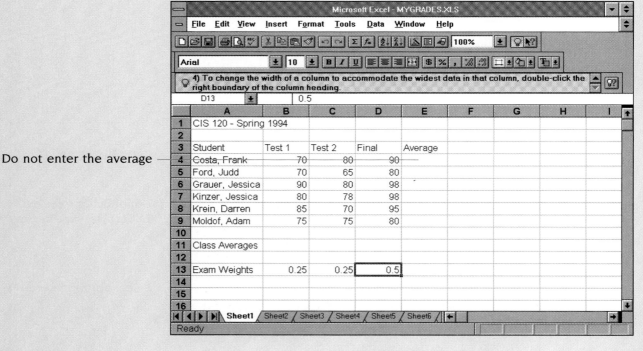

(b) Grade Book after Step 5

FIGURE 2.4   Hands-on Exercise 1 (continued)

➤ Enter the names and grades for the other students in rows 5 through 9. Do *not* enter their averages.

➤ Complete the entries in column A by typing **Class Averages** and **Exam Weights** in cells **A11** and **A13,** respectively.

➤ Save the workbook.

Step 5: Enter the exam weights

➤ Click in cell **B13** and enter **.25,** the weight for the first exam.

➤ Press the **right arrow key** to move to cell **C13** and enter **.25,** the weight for the second exam.

➤ Press the **right arrow key** to move to cell **D13** and enter **.5,** the weight for the final. Do *not* be concerned that the exam weights do not appear as percentages; they will be formatted in the second exercise later in the chapter.

➤ The worksheet should match Figure 2.4b except that column A is too narrow to display the entire name of each student.

Step 6: Compute the weighted average for the first student

➤ Click in cell **E4** and type the formula **=$B$13*B4+$C$13*C4+$D$13*D4** to compute the weighted average for the first student. Press the **enter key** when you have completed the formula.

➤ Check that the displayed value in cell E4 is 82.5, which indicates you entered the formula correctly.

➤ Save the workbook.

CORRECTING MISTAKES

The fastest way to change the contents of an existing cell is to double click in the cell and then make the changes directly in the cell rather than on the formula bar. Use the mouse or arrow keys to position yourself at the point of correction. Press the Ins key to toggle between insertion and replacement and/or use the Del key to delete a character. Press the Home and End keys to move to the first and last characters, respectively.

Step 7: Copy the weighted average

➤ Check that cell **E4,** the source range for the Copy command, is still selected.

➤ Pull down the **Edit menu** as in Figure 2.4c.

➤ Click **Copy**; a flashing border (the *marquee*) will surround cell E4, indicating that its contents have been copied to the clipboard.

➤ Click cell **E5.** Drag the mouse over cells **E5** through **E9** to select the destination range as in Figure 2.4d.

➤ Pull down the **Edit menu** and click **Paste** to copy the contents of the clipboard to the destination range. You should see the weighted averages for the other students in cells E5 through E9.

➤ Press **Esc** to remove the marquee surrounding cell E4.

➤ Click anywhere in the worksheet to deselect cells E5 through E9.

➤ Save the workbook.

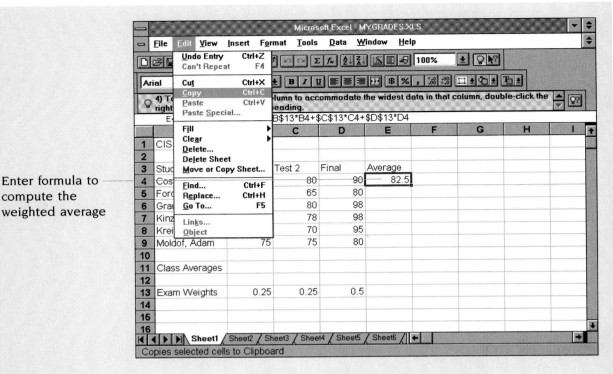

Enter formula to
compute the
weighted average

(c) The Copy Command (steps 6 and 7)

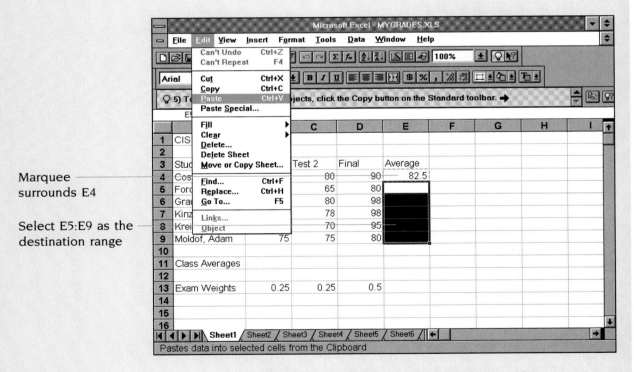

Marquee
surrounds E4

Select E5:E9 as the
destination range

(d) The Marquee and Destination Range (step 7)

FIGURE 2.4 Hands-on Exercise 1 (continued)

CUT, COPY, AND PASTE

Ctrl+X, Ctrl+C, and Ctrl+V are keyboard equivalents to cut, copy, and paste, respectively, and apply to Excel, Word for Windows, and Windows applications in general. (The keystrokes are easier to remember when you realize that the operative letters X, C, and V are next to each other at the bottom left side of the keyboard.) Alternatively, you can use the Cut, Copy, and Paste icons on the Standard toolbar, which are also found on the Standard toolbar in Word for Windows.

Step 8: Compute the class averages

➤ Click in cell **B11** and type the formula **=AVERAGE(B4:B9)** to compute the class average on the first test. Press the **enter key** when you have completed the formula.

➤ Click in cell B11, then click the **right mouse button** to produce the shortcut menu in Figure 2.4e. Click **Copy,** which produces the marquee around cell B11.

➤ Click cell **C11.** Drag the mouse over cells **C11** and **D11,** the destination range for the Copy command.

➤ Click the **Paste icon** on the Standard toolbar to copy the contents of the clipboard to the destination range.

➤ Press **Esc** to remove the marquee. Click anywhere in the worksheet to deselect cells C11 through D11.

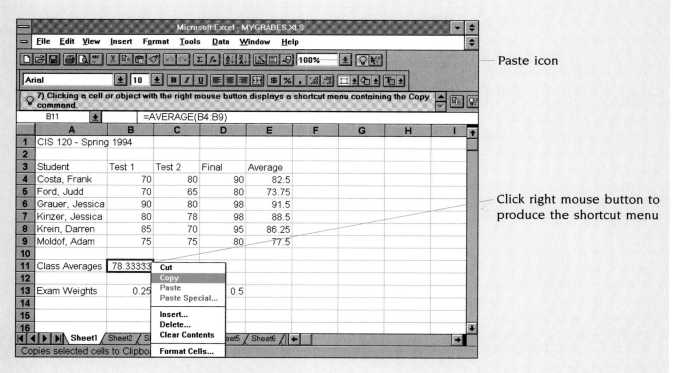

(e) Shortcut Menu (step 8)

FIGURE 2.4 Hands-on Exercise 1 (continued)

Step 9: What if? Change the exam weights

➤ Change the entries in cells **B13** and **C13** to **.20** and the entry in cell **D13** to **.60.** The weighted average for every student changes automatically; for example, Costa and Moldof change to 84 and 78, respectively.

➤ The professor decides this does not make a significant difference and goes back to the original weights; reenter .25, .25, and .50 in cells B13, C13, and D13, respectively.

Step 10: Save the completed workbook

➤ Click the **Save icon** on the Standard toolbar to save the workbook.

➤ Exit Excel if you are not ready to begin the next exercise.

FORMATTING

The professor's grade book is developed in two stages as in Figure 2.5. The exercise just completed created the grade book, but paid no attention to its appearance. It had you enter the data for every student, develop the formulas to compute the semester average for every student based on exam weights at the bottom of the worksheet, and finally, develop the formulas to compute the class averages for each exam.

Figure 2.5a shows the grade book as it exists at the end of the first hands-on exercise. Figure 2.5b shows the grade book at the end of the second exercise after it has been formatted. The differences between the two are due entirely to formatting. Consider:

➤ The exam weights are formatted as percentages in Figure 2.5b as opposed to decimals in Figure 2.5a.

➤ The class and student averages are displayed with a single decimal point in Figure 2.5b as opposed to a variable number of decimal places in Figure 2.5a.

➤ Boldface and italics are used for emphasis as are shading and borders.

➤ Exam grades and computed averages are centered under their respective headings.

➤ The worksheet title is centered across all five columns.

➤ The width of column A has been increased so that the students' names are completely visible.

The next several pages describe how to format the gradebook and make it more attractive. You should not, however, lose sight of accuracy. Be sure a worksheet is correct before you focus on its appearance.

	A	B	C	D	E
1	CIS 120 - Spring 1994				
2					
3	Student	Test 1	Test 2	Final	Average
4	Costa, Fra	70	80	90	82.5
5	Ford, Judd	70	65	80	73.75
6	Grauer, Je	90	80	98	91.5
7	Kinzer, Je	80	78	98	88.5
8	Krein, Dar	85	70	95	86.25
9	Moldof, Ad	75	75	80	77.5
10					
11	Class Ave	78.333	74.667	90.167	
12					
13	Exam Wei	0.25	.025	0.5	

(a) At the End of Exercise 1

	A	B	C	D	E
1	*CIS 120 - Spring 1994*				
2					
3	*Student*	*Test 1*	*Test 2*	*Final*	*Average*
4	Costa, Frank	70	80	90	82.5
5	Ford, Judd	70	65	80	73.8
6	Grauer, Jessica	90	80	98	91.5
7	Kinzer, Jessica	80	78	98	88.5
8	Krein, Darren	85	70	95	86.3
9	Moldof, Adam	75	75	80	77.5
10					
11	*Class Averages*	*78.3*	*74.7*	*90.2*	
12					
13	*Exam Weights*	*25%*	*25%*	*50%*	

Column A is wider

Title is centered over spreadsheet

Shading, bold, and italics are used for emphasis

Averages are displayed with one decimal place

Exam weights are formatted as percentages

(b) At the End of Exercise 2

FIGURE 2.5   Developing the Grade Book

THE FORMATTING TOOLBAR

The Formatting toolbar is the fastest way to implement most formatting operations. There are buttons for boldface, italics, and underlining; justification (including centering across columns); accounting, percent, and comma formats; as well as icons to increase or decrease the number of decimal places. There are also several list boxes that enable you to choose the font, point size, and font color, as well as the type of border and shading.

Column Widths

A column is often too narrow to display the contents of one or more cells in that column. The action taken by Excel depends on whether the cell contains a text or numeric entry, and if it is a text entry, on whether or not the adjacent cell is empty.

The student names in Figure 2.5a, for example, are partially hidden because column A is too narrow to display the entire name. Cells A4 through A9 contain the complete names of each student, but because the adjacent cells in column B contain data, the entries in column A are truncated (cut off) at the cell width. The situation is different for the worksheet title in cell A1. This time the adjacent cell (cell B1) is empty, so that the contents of cell A1 overflow into that cell and are completely visible.

Numbers are treated differently from text and do not depend on the contents of the adjacent cell. Excel displays a series of number signs (######) when a cell containing a numeric entry is too narrow to display the entry in its current format. You can correct the problem by changing the format of the number (e.g., display the number with fewer decimal places). You can also increase the cell width by using the **Column command** in the **Format menu.**

Row Heights

The row height changes automatically as the **font** size is increased. Row 1 in Figure 2.5b, for example, has a greater height than the other rows to accommodate the larger font size in the title of the worksheet. The row height can also be changed manually through the **Row command** in the Format menu.

FORMAT CELLS COMMAND

The **Format Cells command** controls the formatting for Numbers, Alignment, Fonts, Borders, and Patterns (color). Execution of the command produces a tabbed dialog box in which you choose the particular formatting category, then enter the desired options. (Almost every formatting option can also be specified from the **Formatting toolbar.**)

All formatting is done within the context of select-then-do. You select the cells to which the formatting is to apply, then you execute the Format Cells command or click the appropriate icon.

FORMATS VERSUS VALUES

Changing the format of a number changes the way the number is displayed but does *not* change its value. If, for example, you entered 1.2345 into a cell but displayed the number as 1.23, the actual value (1.2345) would be used in all calculations involving that cell.

Numeric Formats

General format is the default format for numeric entries and displays a number according to the way it was originally entered. Numbers are shown as integers (e.g., 123), decimal fractions (e.g, 1.23), or in scientific notation (e.g., 1.23E+10) if the number is larger than the width of the cell or if it exceeds 11 digits. You can also display any number in one of several built-in formats as shown in Figure 2.6a:

➤ **Number format** displays a number with or without commas, and with any number of decimal places.
➤ **Accounting format** displays negative values in parentheses, displays zero values as hyphens, and positions the dollar sign at the left of the cell.
➤ **Date format** applies to any value entered as a date as described in Chapter 3. The date may be displayed in many different formats, such as 3/16/94 or 16-Mar-94.
➤ **Time format** applies to any value entered as a time as described in Chapter 3. The time may be displayed in a variety of formats—for example, 10:50 PM or the equivalent 22:50 (military time).

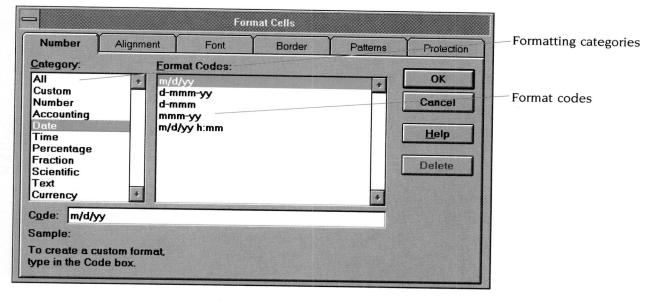

 Formatting categories

Format codes

(a) The Number Tab

FIGURE 2.6 The Format Cells Command

➤ *Percentage format* causes the number to be multiplied by 100 for display purposes only; a percent sign is included, and any number of decimal places can be specified.

➤ *Fraction format* displays a number as a fraction and is appropriate when there is no exact decimal equivalent—for example, 1/3.

➤ *Scientific format* displays a number as a decimal fraction followed by a whole-number exponent of 10; for example, the number 12345 would appear as 1.2345E+04. The exponent, +04 in the example, is the number of places the decimal point is moved to the right or left (if the exponent is negative). Very small numbers have negative exponents; for example, the entry .0000012 would be displayed as 1.2E−06. Scientific notation is used only with very large or very small numbers and is generally not used in a business environment.

➤ *Text format* left justifies the entry and is useful for numerical values that are treated as text, such as zip codes or phone numbers.

➤ *Currency format* displays the value with a $, with commas as appropriate, and with any number of decimal places.

Each formatting category contains its own set of format codes (e.g., five codes in the Date category in Figure 2.6a) that provide additional flexibility within the category. Additional information on formatting codes can be obtained by using on-line help.

DATES VERSUS FRACTIONS

A fraction may be entered directly into a cell by preceding the fraction with an equal sign—for example, =1/3. Omission of the equal sign causes Excel to treat the entry as a date; that is, 1/3 will be stored as January 3 (of the current year).

Alignment

The contents of a cell may be aligned horizontally and/or vertically as indicated by the dialog box of Figure 2.6b. The options for horizontal alignment include left (the default for text), center, right (the default for numbers), and full justification. You can also center an entry across a range of selected cells as in the grade book of Figure 2.5b, which centered the title in cell A1 across columns A through E. The Fill option duplicates the characters in the cell across the entire width of that cell.

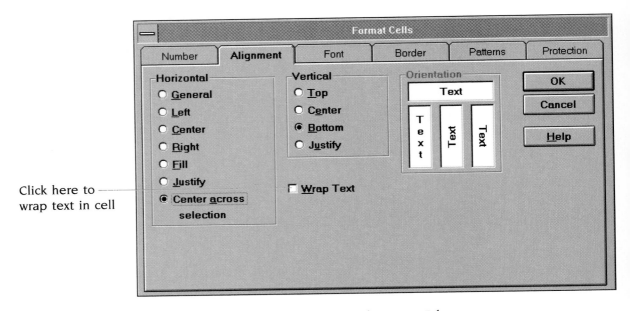

(b) The Alignment Tab

FIGURE 2.6   The Format Cells Command (continued)

Vertical alignment is important only if the row height is changed and the characters are smaller than the height of the row. Entries may be vertically aligned at the top, center, or bottom (the default) of a cell.

It is also possible to wrap the text within a cell to emulate the word wrap capability of a word processor. And finally, you can achieve some very interesting effects by choosing from one of the four orientations within the alignment window.

Fonts

Windows 3.1 supports a font technology known as *TrueType.* TrueType fonts are installed automatically with Windows and are available from any application. You can use the same fonts in Excel as you do in Word for Windows. In addition, True-Type fonts are scalable, allowing you to select any *point size* from 4 to 127 points (there are 72 points to the inch). And finally, TrueType fonts are truly WYSIWYG (What You See Is What You Get), meaning that the worksheet you see on the monitor will match the worksheet produced by the printer.

Windows includes a limited number of TrueType fonts—Arial, Times New Roman, Courier New, Symbol, and Wingdings—which offer sufficient variety to produce some truly impressive worksheets. (Additional fonts are available from Microsoft and/or other vendors.)

Any entry in a worksheet may be displayed in any font, style, or point size as indicated by the dialog box of Figure 2.6c. The example shows Arial, Bold Italic, and 14 points, and corresponds to the selection for the worksheet title in the improved grade book. You can even select a different color, but you will need a color monitor and/or color printer to see the effect.

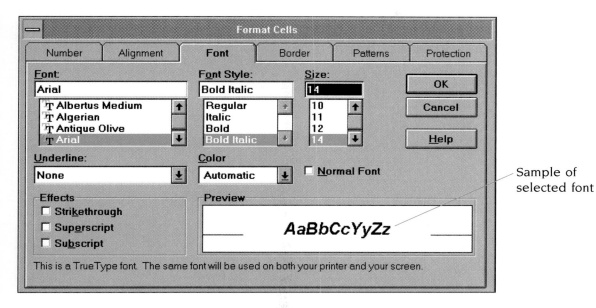

(c) The Font Tab

FIGURE 2.6   The Format Cells Command (continued)

Borders, Patterns, and Shading

The **Border tab** in Figure 2.6d enables you to create a border around a cell (or cells) for additional emphasis. You can outline the entire selection, or you can choose the specific side or sides as indicated in the figure; for example, thicker lines on the bottom and right sides produce a drop shadow, which is very effective. You can also specify a different color for the border, but you will need a color monitor (and printer) to see the effect.

The **Patterns tab** in Figure 2.6e lets you choose a different color to shade the cell and further emphasize its contents. The Pattern list box lets you select an alternate pattern such as dots or slanted lines.

VARIATIONS IN PRINTING

The final way to control the appearance of a worksheet is through printing. You can print a worksheet with or without row and column headings, and with or without the cell **gridlines.** These and other options are controlled by the Page Setup command. You can also view a worksheet prior to printing through the Print Preview command. Both commands are executed from the File menu.

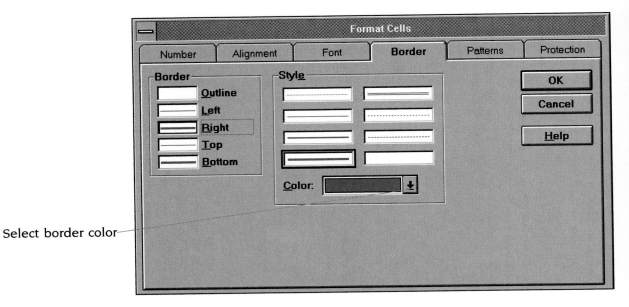

Select border color

(d) The Border Tab

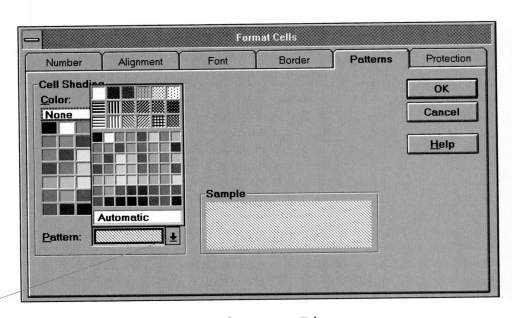

Click here to produce
display of sample
patterns and colors

(e) The Patterns Tab

FIGURE 2.6 The Format Cells Command (continued)

The Page Setup Command

The *Page Setup command* gives you complete control of the printed worksheet. Many of its options may not appear important now, but you will appreciate them as you develop larger and more complicated worksheets later in the text.

The Page tab in Figure 2.7a determines the orientation and scaling of the printed page. *Portrait orientation* (8½ × 11) prints vertically down the page. *Landscape orientation* (11 × 8½) prints horizontally across the page. The option buttons imply mutually exclusive items, one of which *must* be selected; that is, a worksheet must be printed in either portrait *or* landscape orientation. Option buttons are also used to choose the scaling factor. You can reduce (enlarge) the output by a designated scaling factor *or* you can force the output to fit on a specified number of pages.

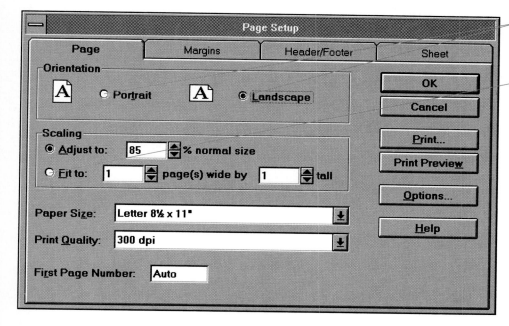

Choose either Landscape or Portrait

Force printout to one page

(a) The Page Tab

FIGURE 2.7   The Page Setup Command

The Margins tab in Figure 2.7b not only controls the margins, but will also center the worksheet horizontally and/or vertically. Check boxes are associated with the centering options and imply that multiple options can be chosen; for example, horizontally and vertically are both selected. The Margin tab also determines the distance of the header and footer from the edge of the page.

The Header/Footer tab in Figure 2.7c lets you create a **header** (and/or **footer**) that appears at the top (and/or bottom) of every page. The pull-down list boxes let you choose from several preformatted entries, or alternatively, you can click the appropriate command button to customize either entry.

The Sheet tab in Figure 2.7d offers several additional options, the most important of which are Gridlines and Row and Column Headings. Information about the additional entries can be obtained by clicking the Help command button.

The Print Preview Command

The **Print Preview command** in the File menu (or the Print Preview command button in Figures 2.7a, 2.7b, and 2.7c) displays the worksheet as it will appear when printed. The command is invaluable and will save you considerable time as you don't have to rely on trial and error to obtain the perfect printout. The Print Preview command is illustrated in Figure 2.7e, which corresponds to the various settings in Figures 2.7a through 2.7d.

Set distance of header/footer from edge of page

Center spreadsheet on printed page

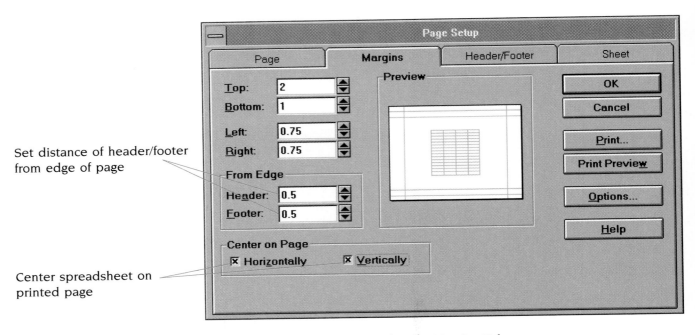

(b) The Margins Tab

Click to choose a preformatted header/footer

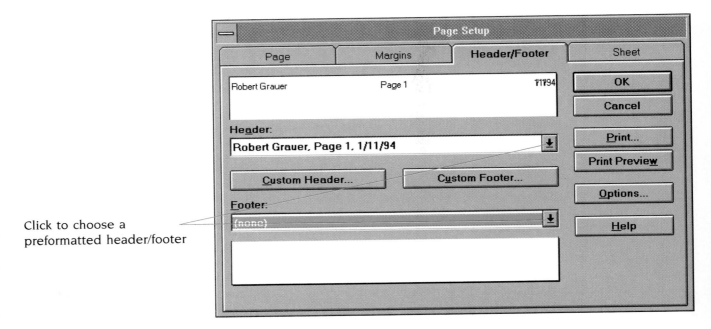

(c) The Header/Footer Tab

FIGURE 2.7 The Page Setup Command (continued)

The worksheet is printed horizontally across the page (landscape orientation in Figure 2.7a). It has been centered horizontally and vertically within the specified margins (Figure 2.7b). A custom header has been chosen and there is no footer (Figure 2.7c). Gridlines and row and column headings both appear (Figure 2.7d).

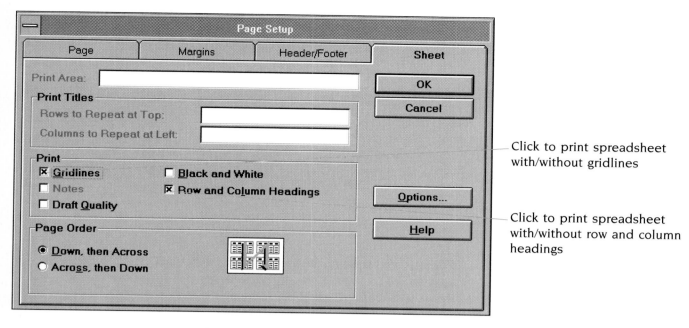

Click to print spreadsheet with/without gridlines

Click to print spreadsheet with/without row and column headings

(d) The Sheet Tab

Click here to return to worksheet

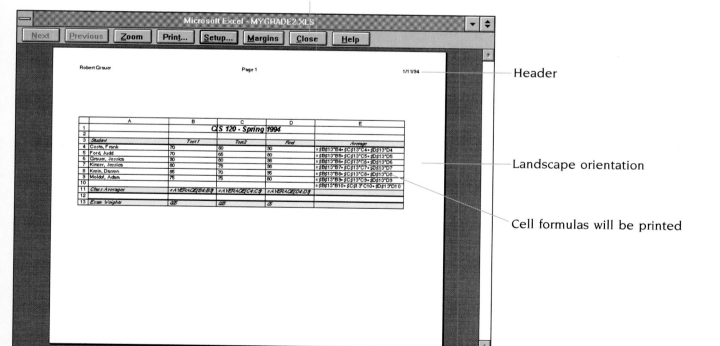

Header

Landscape orientation

Cell formulas will be printed

(e) Print Preview Command

FIGURE 2.7 The Page Setup Command (continued)

Formatting a Worksheet

Objective To format a worksheet using both pull-down menus and the Formatting toolbar; to use boldface, italics, shading, and borders; to change the font and/or alignment of a selected entry; to change the width of a column; to print the cell contents as well as the computed values. Use Figure 2.8 as a guide in doing the exercise.

Step 1: Fonts
➤ Open the MYGRADES.XLS workbook from the first exercise.
➤ Click in cell **A1** to select the cell containing the title of the worksheet.
➤ Pull down the **Format** menu. Click **Cells.** If necessary, click the **Font tab.**
➤ Click **Arial** from the Font list box, **Bold Italic** from the Font Style box, and **14** from the Size box. Click the **OK** command button.

QUIT WITHOUT SAVING

There are times when you will edit a workbook beyond recognition and wish you had never started. The Undo command, useful as it is, reverses only the most recent operation and is of no use if you need to cancel all changes. Pull down the File menu and click on the Close command, then click No in response to the message asking whether to save the changes. Pull down the File menu, click Open to reopen the file, then begin all over.

Step 2: Alignment
➤ Click in cell **A1.** Drag the mouse over cells **A1** through **E1,** which represents the width of the entire worksheet.
➤ Pull down the **Format menu** a second time. Click **Cells.** Click the **Alignment tab.** Click the **Center across selection** option button as in Figure 2.8a. Click **OK** to center the entry in cell A1 over the selected range (cells A1 through E1).
➤ If necessary, click the TipWizard icon to open the TipWizard box; the Tip-Wizard suggests that you click the Center Across Selection button on the Formatting toolbar as a more efficient way to center text.
➤ Click in cell **B3.** Drag the mouse over cells **B3** through **E13.** Click the **Centering icon** on the Formatting toolbar.

Step 3: Increase the width of column A
➤ Click in cell **A4.** Drag the mouse over cells **A4** through **A13.**
➤ Pull down the **Format menu,** click **Column,** then click **AutoFit Selection** as shown in Figure 2.8b. The width of the selected cells increases to accommodate the longest entry in the selected range.
➤ Click the **Save icon** on the Standard toolbar to save the workbook.

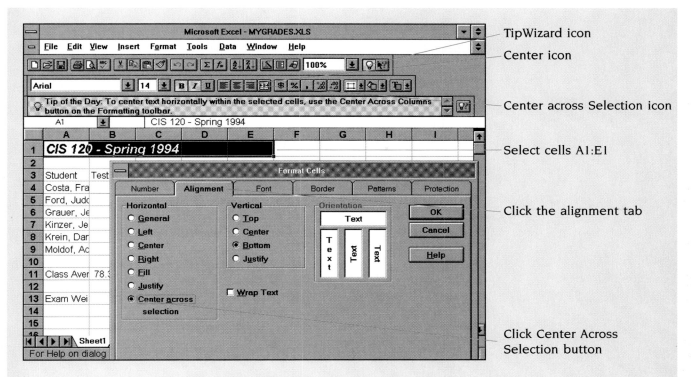

TipWizard icon

Center icon

Center across Selection icon

Select cells A1:E1

Click the alignment tab

Click Center Across Selection button

(a) Center across Columns (step 2)

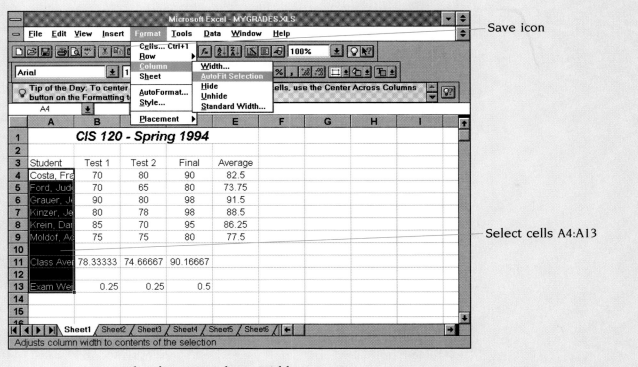

Save icon

Select cells A4:A13

(b) Changing Column Widths (step 3)

FIGURE 2.8 Hands-on Exercise 2 (continued)

COLUMN WIDTHS AND ROW HEIGHTS

Drag the border between column labels to change the column width; for example, to increase (decrease) the width of column A, drag the border between column labels A and B to the right (left). Double click the right boundary of a column heading to change the column width to accommodate the widest entry in that column. Use the same technique to change the row heights.

Step 4: Format the exam weights (shortcut menu versus Formatting toolbar)
➤ Click in cell **B13**. Drag the mouse over cells **B13** through **D13**.
➤ Click the **right mouse button** to produce the shortcut menu in Figure 2.8c. Click **Format Cells** to produce the Format Cells dialog box.
➤ If necessary, click the **Number tab.** Click **Percentage** in the Category list box. Click **0%** in the Format Codes list box. Click the **OK** command button. The exam weights are now displayed with percent signs.
➤ Click the **Undo icon** on the Standard toolbar to cancel the formatting command.
➤ Click the **% icon** on the Formatting toolbar to reformat the exam weights as percentages.

Step 5: Noncontiguous ranges
➤ Select cells **B11** through **D11,** the cells that contain the class averages for the three exams.
➤ Press *and* hold the **Ctrl key** and click cell **E4.** Continue to press the Ctrl key and drag the mouse over cells **E4** through **E9.** Release the **Ctrl key.**
➤ You will see two noncontiguous (nonadjacent) ranges highlighted, cells B11:D11 and cells E4:E9 as in Figure 2.8d.
➤ Format the selected cells using either the Formatting toolbar or the Format menu.
  —To use the Formatting toolbar, click the icon on the toolbar to increase or reduce the number of decimal places as necessary.
  —To use the Format menu, pull down the **Format menu,** click **Cells,** click the **Number tab,** then click **Number** in the category list box. Click in the Code list box. Type **0.0** to display the numbers with a single decimal point. Click the **OK** command button.

AUTOMATIC FORMATTING

Excel converts any number entered with a dollar sign to currency format and any number entered with a percent sign to percentage format. The automatic formatting enables you to save a step by typing $100,000 or 7.5% directly into a cell, rather than entering 100000 or .075, and subsequently having to format the number

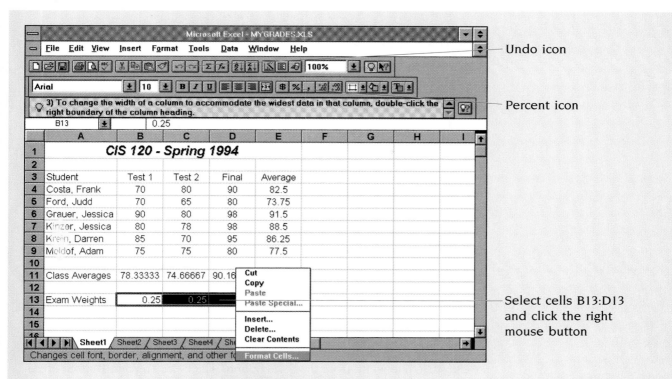

Undo icon

Percent icon

Select cells B13:D13 and click the right mouse button

(c) Format Exam Weights (step 4)

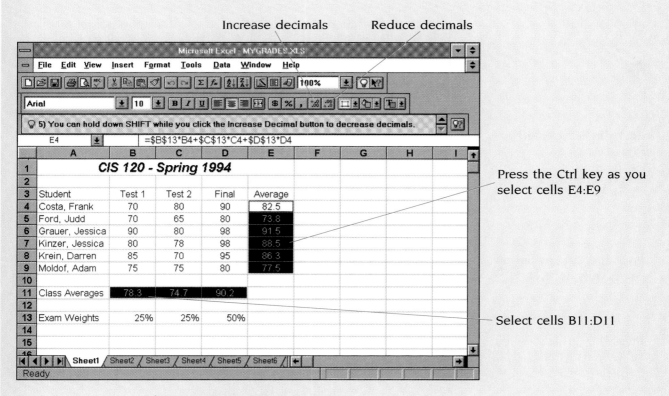

Increase decimals   Reduce decimals

Press the Ctrl key as you select cells E4:E9

Select cells B11:D11

(d) Noncontiguous Ranges (step 5)

FIGURE 2.8 Hands-on Exercise 2 (continued)

THE FORMAT PAINTER

The *Format Painter* copies the formatting of the selected cell to other cells in the worksheet. Click the cell whose formatting you want to copy, then double click the Format Painter button on the Standard toolbar. The mouse pointer changes to a paintbrush to indicate that you can copy the current formatting; just drag the paintbrush over the additional cells, which will assume the identical formatting as the original cell. Repeat the painting process as often as necessary, then click the Format Painter icon a second time to return to normal editing.

Step 6: Borders

➤ Drag the mouse over cells **A3** through **E3.** Press *and* hold the **Ctrl key.** Drag the mouse over the range **A11:E11.** Continue to press the **Ctrl key.** Drag the mouse over the range **A13:E13.**

➤ Pull down the **Format menu** and click **Cells** (or click the **right mouse button** to produce a shortcut menu, then click **Format Cells**). Click the **Border tab** to access the dialog box in Figure 2.8e.

➤ Choose a line width from the Style options. Click the **Top** and **Bottom** boxes in the Border options. Click **OK** to exit the dialog box and return to the worksheet.

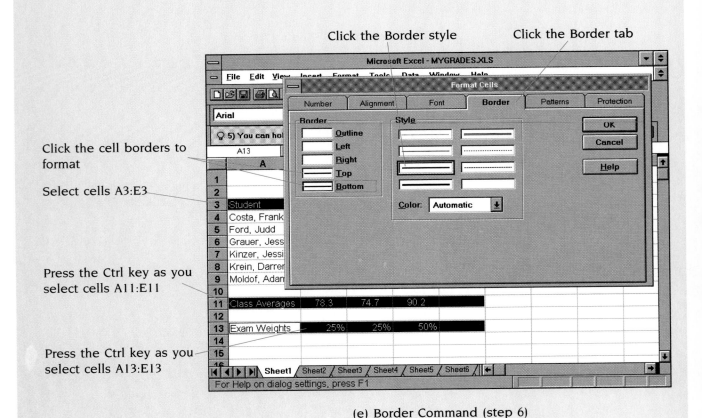

(e) Border Command (step 6)

FIGURE 2.8 Hands-on Exercise 2 (continued)

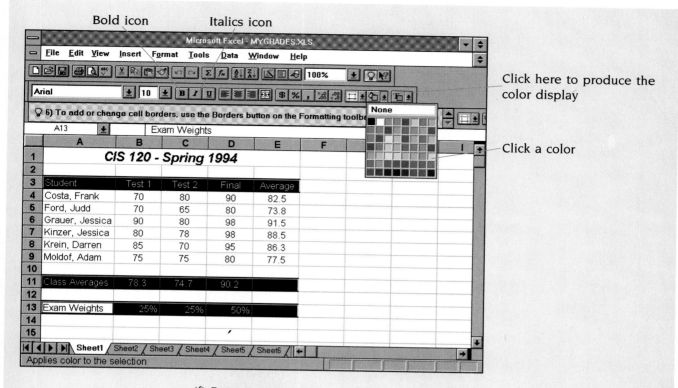

Bold icon   Italics icon

Click here to produce the color display

Click a color

(f) Patterns (step 7)

FIGURE 2.8   Hands-on Exercise 2 (continued)

Step 7: Color

➤ Check that all three ranges are still selected (A3:E3, A11:E11, *and* A13:E13).

➤ Click the **down arrow** on the **Color button** on the Formatting toolbar. Click light grey (or whatever color appeals to you) as shown in Figure 2.8f.

➤ Click the **boldface** and **italics icons** on the Formatting toolbar. Click outside the selected cells to see the effects of the formatting change.

➤ Save the workbook.

SELECTING NONCONTIGUOUS RANGES

Dragging the mouse to select a range always produces some type of rectangle; it may be a single cell, a row or column, or a group of rows and columns. You can, however, select noncontiguous (nonadjacent) ranges by selecting the first range in the normal fashion, then pressing and holding the Ctrl key as you select the additional range(s). This is especially useful when the same command is to be applied to multiple ranges within a worksheet.

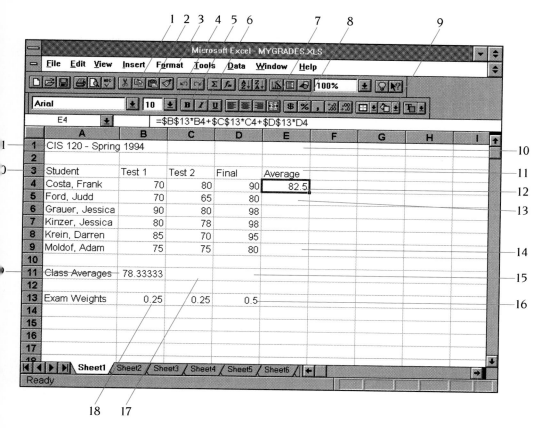

FIGURE 2.10   Screen for Problem 1

Action	Result
i. Click at 12, drag to 14, click at 9	___ Apply boldface and italic formatting to the worksheet title
j. Click at 21, click at 5, click at 6	___ Paste the formula to calculate the test average for test 2 and the final
	___ Shade the student averages a light grey
	___ Center the worksheet title over the width of the worksheet

2. Figure 2.11 contains a worksheet in which the same number (1.2345) has been entered into every cell. The differences in appearance between the various cell entries are produced by different formats in the individual cells. Indicate the precise formatting for every cell.

	A	B	C	D
1	1	$1	123%	1E+00
2	1.23	$1.23	123.45%	1.23E+00
3	1.2345	$1.2345	123.4500%	1.2345E+00

FIGURE 2.11   Spreadsheet for Problem 2

3. Figure 2.12 contains a worksheet depicting simplified payroll calculations for gross pay, withholding tax, social security tax (FICA), and net pay.

	A	B	C	D	E	F	G	H
1	Employee	Hourly	Regular	Overtime	Gross	Withldg	Soc Sec	Net
2	Name	Wage	Hours	Hours	Pay	Tax	Tax	Pay
3	Adams	$ 8.00	40	3	$ 356.00	$ 99.68	$ 23.14	$ 233.18
4	Hall	$ 6.25	40	0	$ 250.00	$ 70.00	$ 16.25	$ 163.75
5	Costo	$ 9.50	25	0	$ 237.50	$ 66.50	$ 15.44	$ 155.56
6	Lee	$ 4.50	40	5	$ 213.75	$ 59.85	$ 13.89	$ 140.01
7	Arnold	$ 6.25	35	0	$ 218.75	$ 61.25	$ 14.22	$ 143.28
8	Vedo	$ 5.50	40	2	$ 236.50	$ 66.22	$ 15.37	$ 154.91
9								
10			Totals:		$1,512.50	$423.50	$98.31	$990.69
11								
12	Assumptions:							
13	Withholding Tax:		28.00%					
14	Social Security Tax:		6.50%					

FIGURE 2.12 Spreadsheet for Problem 3

a. What formula should be entered into cell E3 to compute an individual's gross pay? (An individual receives time and a half for overtime.)

b. What formula should be entered into cell F3 to compute the withholding tax?

c. What formula should be entered into cell G3 to compute the social security tax?

d. What formula should be entered into cell H3 to compute the net pay?

e. What formula should be entered into cell E10 to compute the total gross pay for the company? What formulas should be entered into cells F10 through H10 to compute the remaining totals?

4. Figure 2.13 contains two versions of a worksheet in which sales, costs, and profits are to be projected over a five-year horizon. The worksheets are only partially completed, and the intent in both is to copy the entries from year 2 (cells C2 through C4) to the remainder of the worksheet. As you can see, the first worksheet uses only relative references and the second uses only absolute references. Both worksheets are in error.

a. Show the erroneous entries that will result when column C is copied to columns D, E, and F for both worksheets.

b. What are the correct entries for column C so that the formulas will copy correctly?

	A	B	C	D	E	F
1		Year 1	Year 2	Year 3	Year 4	Year 5
2	Sales	1000	=B2+B2*C7			
3	Cost	800	=B3+B3*C8			
4	Profit	200	=C2-C3			
5						
6	Assumptions:					
7	Annual Sales Increase:		10%			
8	Annual Cost Increase:		8%			

(a) Error 1 (relative cell addresses)

FIGURE 2.13 Spreadsheet for Problem 4

	A	B	C	D	E	F
1		Year 1	Year 2	Year 3	Year 4	Year 5
2	Sales	1000	=$B$2+$B$2*$C$7			
3	Cost	800	=$B$3+$B$3*$C$8			
4	Profit	200	=$C$2-$C$3			
5						
6	Assumptions:					
7	Annual Sales Increase:		10%			
8	Annual Cost Increase:		8%			

(b) Error 2 (absolute cell addresses)

FIGURE 2.13   Spreadsheet for Problem 4 (continued)

5. Figure 2.14 shows how a worksheet can be used to prepare a sales invoice. What is your general impression of the worksheet? Is it formatted attractively? Is it accurate? Is the store receiving the correct amount; that is, is the subtotal shown on the invoice correct? Is Cori paying more or less than she should? Is the state getting the correct sales tax?

	A	B	C	D	E
1			**Kidlets Clothes**		
2			**Customer Invoice**		
3					
4	**Customer Name:**		Cori Rice		
5	**Address:**		7722 S.W. 142 Street		
6			Miami, Florida 33157		
7	**Phone:**		(305) 254-7111		
8					
9	**Item**		**Quantity**	**Cost**	**Total**
10	Reebok sneakers		1	$45.95	$45.95
11	Summer T-shirts		3	$19.99	$59.97
12	Barrettes		2	$6.00	$12.00
13	Shorts		3	$24.99	$74.97
14	**Subtotal**				$117.92
15	**Sales Tax**				$76.65
16	**Total**				$194.57

FIGURE 2.14   Spreadsheet for Problem 5

6. The worksheet in Figure 2.15 exists on the data disk as PROB0206.XLS. Complete the worksheet, following the steps below:

   a. Click cell D6 and enter the formula to calculate the balance due on Kim Mallery's loan.

   b. Copy the formula entered into D6 to the range D7:D11 to calculate the balance due for the other student loans.

   c. Click cell B13 and enter the formula to calculate the total due for all student loans.

   d. Copy the formula entered into B13 to the range C13:D13 to calculate the total amount paid and the total balance due.

   e. Select the cells B6:D13 and format the numbers so that they display with dollar signs and commas, and no decimal places (e.g., $2,500).

f. Select the cells A1:D2 and center the titles across the width of the worksheet. With those cells still selected, change the font to 14 point Arial bold.

g. Select cells A5:D5 and create a bottom border to separate the headings from the data.

h. Save the workbook. Print the worksheet.

	A	B	C	D
1	UNCLE SAM'S LOANS, INC.			
2	College Loans for Good Students			
3				
4				
5	Customer	Amount Due	Amount Paid	Balance Due
6	Mallery, Kim	2500	31.66	
7	Camejo, Oscar	10000	126.67	
8	Rowe, Debbie-Ann	5000	63.33	
9	Bost, Tiffany	3500	44.33	
10	King, Beth Anne	12000	152.01	
11	Lali, Andrea	6000	76	
12				
13	Totals:			

FIGURE 2.15 Spreadsheet for Problem 6

7. Figure 2.16 contains a worksheet that was used to calculate the difference between the Asking Price and Selling Price on various real estate listings that were sold during June. It also contains the commission paid to the real estate agency as a result of selling those listings. Retrieve PROB0207.XLS from the data disk, then complete the worksheet following the steps outlined below:

	A	B	C	D	E	F
1	Coaches Realty - Sales for June					
2						
3			Asking	Selling		
4	Customer	Address	Price	Price	Difference	Commission
5	Landry	122 West 75 Terr.	450000	350000		
6	Spurrier	4567 S.W. 95 Street	750000	648500		
7	Shula	123 Alamo Road	350000	275000		
8	Lombardi	9000 Brickell Place	275000	250000		
9	Johnson	5596 Powerline Road	189000	189000		
10	Erickson	8900 N.W. 89 Street	456000	390000		
11	Bowden	75 Maynada Blvd	300000	265000		
12						
13		Totals:				
14						
15	Commission %:	0.035				

FIGURE 2.16 Spreadsheet for Problem 7

a. Click cell E5 and enter the formula to calculate the difference between the asking price and the selling price for the property belonging to Mr. Landry.

b. Click cell F5 and enter the formula to calculate the commission paid to the agency as a result of selling the property. (You will need to pay close attention to the difference between relative and absolute cell references so that the calculations will be correct when the formulas are copied to the other rows in the next step.)

c. Select cells E5:F5 and copy the formulas to E6:F11 to calculate the difference and commission for the rest of the properties.

d. Click cell C13 and enter the formula to calculate the total asking price, which is the sum of the asking prices for the individual listings in cells C5:C11.

e. Copy the formula in C13 to the range D13:F13 to calculate the other totals.

f. Select the range C5:F13 and format the numbers so that they display with dollar signs and commas, and no decimal places (e.g., $450,000).

g. Click cell B15 and format the number as a percentage.

h. Click cell A1 and center the title across the width of the worksheet. With the cell still selected, select cells A3:F4 as well and change the font to 12 point Arial bold italic.

i. Select cells A4:F4 and create a bottom border to separate the headings from the data.

j. Select cells F5:F11 and shade the commissions.

k. Save the workbook. Print the worksheet.

 Case Studies

Make an Impression

You do excellent work, but somehow you never get noticed. All of your worksheets are completely accurate and meet or exceed the requirements imposed by your supervisor. Something is still lacking, however, and the HELPME.XLS workbook on the data disk is typical of your work. A colleague took a look and said the problem is in formatting or the lack thereof. Let's see what you can do.

Establishing a Budget

You want to join a sorority and you really would like a car. Convince your parents that you can afford both by developing a detailed budget for your four years at school. Your worksheet should include all sources of income (scholarships, loans, summer jobs, work-study, etc.) as well as all expenses (tuition, books, room and board, and entertainment). Make the budget as realistic as possible by building in projected increases over the four-year period.

Your First Million

You have developed the perfect product and are seeking venture capital to go into immediate production. You have a firm order for 100,000 units in the first year at a selling price of $6.00 per unit. Both numbers are expected to increase 20 percent annually. You are able to rent a production facility for $50,000 a year for five years. The variable manufacturing cost is $1.50 per unit and is projected to increase at 10 percent a year. Administration and insurance costs another $25,000 a year and will increase at 5 percent annually. Develop a five-year financial forecast showing profits before and after taxes (assuming a tax rate of 36 percent).

Your worksheet should be completely flexible and capable of accommodating a change in any of the initial conditions or projected rates of increase, *without* having to edit or recopy any of the formulas. This will require you to isolate all of the assumptions (i.e., the initial conditions and rates of increase) in one area of the worksheet, and then reference these cells as absolute references when building the formulas. It's a challenging assignment, but then again you are going to make a lot of money.

Break-even Analysis

Widgets of America has developed the perfect product and is ready to go into production pending a review of a five-year break-even analysis. The manufacturing cost in the first year is $1.00 per unit and is estimated to increase at 5% annually. The projected selling price is $2.00 per unit and can increase at 10% annually. Overhead expenses are fixed at $100,000 per year over the life of the project. The advertising budget is $50,000 in the first year but will decrease 15% a year as the product gains acceptance. How many units have to be sold each year for the company to break even, given the current cost estimates and projected rates of increase?

As in the previous case, your worksheet should be completely flexible and capable of accommodating a change in any of the initial conditions or projected rates of increase. Be sure to isolate all of the assumptions (i.e., the initial conditions and rates of increase) in one area of the worksheet, and then reference these cells as absolute references when building the formulas.

Your Own Reference Manual

The clipboard is a temporary storage area available to all Windows applications. Selected text is cut or copied from one document into the clipboard, from where it can be pasted into another document altogether. Use on-line help to obtain detailed information on several topics in Excel, copy the information to the clipboard, then paste it into a new document, which will become your personal reference manual. To really do an outstanding job, you will have to format the reference manual after the information has been copied from the clipboard. Be sure to include a title page.

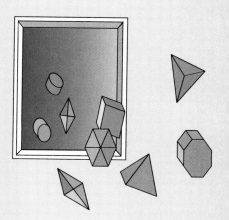

3

Spreadsheets in Decision Making: What If?

CHAPTER OBJECTIVES

After reading this chapter you will be able to:

1. List the arguments of the PMT function and describe its use in financial decisions.

2. Use the Function Wizard to select a function, identify the function arguments, then enter the function into a worksheet.

3. Use the fill handle to copy a cell range to a range of adjacent cells.

4. Use pointing to create a cell formula; explain the advantage of pointing over typing in explicit cell references.

5. Use the AVERAGE, MAX, MIN, and COUNT functions in a worksheet.

6. Use the IF function to implement a decision; explain the table lookup function and how it is used in a worksheet.

7. Describe the DATE and TODAY functions; explain the use of date arithmetic.

8. Describe the additional measures needed to print large worksheets; explain how freezing panes may help in the development of a large worksheet.

9. Use the autofill capability to enter a series into a worksheet.

OVERVIEW

Excel is a truly fascinating program, but it is only a means to an end. A spreadsheet or worksheet is first and foremost a tool for decision making, and the objective of this chapter is to show you just how valuable that tool can be. We begin by presenting two worksheets that we think will be truly useful to you. The first evaluates the purchase of a car and helps you determine just how much car you can afford. The second will be of interest when you are looking for a mortgage to buy a home.

The chapter continues to develop your knowledge of Excel with emphasis on the predefined functions that are built into the program. We consider financial functions such as the PMT function to determine the monthly payment on a loan.

We introduce statistical functions (MAX, MIN, COUNT, and COUNTA), date functions (TODAY and DATE), and the IF and VLOOKUP functions to provide decision making within a worksheet.

The examples in the chapter review the important concept of relative and absolute cell references that was presented in the previous chapter. The hands-on exercises also introduce powerful shortcuts intended to make you more proficient in Excel; these are the fill handle to copy cells within a worksheet, pointing as a more accurate way to enter a formula, and autofill to enter a data series.

ANALYSIS OF A CAR LOAN

Figure 3.1 shows how a worksheet might be applied to the purchase of a car. In essence you need to know the monthly payment, which depends on the price of the car, the down payment, and the terms of the loan. In other words:

➤ Can you afford the monthly payment on the car of your choice?
➤ What if you settle for a less expensive car and receive a manufacturer's rebate?
➤ What if you work next summer to earn money for a down payment?
➤ What if you extend the life of the loan and receive a more favorable interest rate?

The answers to these and other questions determine whether you can afford a car, and if so, which car you will buy, and how you will pay for it. The decision is made easier by developing the worksheet in Figure 3.1, and then by changing the various parameters as indicated.

Figure 3.1a contains a *template* with text entries and cell formulas with formatting already applied, but *without* specific data. The template requires that you enter the price of the car, the manufacturer's rebate, the down payment, the interest rate, and the length of the loan. The worksheet uses these parameters to compute the monthly payment. (Implicit in this discussion is the existence of a PMT function within the worksheet program, which will be explained shortly.)

The availability of the worksheet lets you consider several alternatives, and therein lies its true value. You quickly realize that the purchase of a $14,999 car as shown in Figure 3.1b is prohibitive because the monthly payment is almost $500. Settling for a less expensive car and getting the manufacturer's rebate in Figure 3.1c helps somewhat, but the $413 payment is still too steep. Working next summer to earn an additional $3,000 for the down payment is a necessity (Figure 3.1d), and extending the loan to a fourth year at a lower interest rate makes the purchase possible (Figure 3.1e).

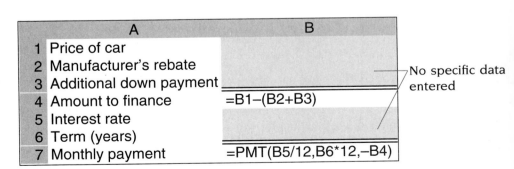

(a) The Template

FIGURE 3.1 "What If" Analysis on Car Loan

	A	B	
1	Price of car	$14,999	Data entered
2	Manufacturer's rebate		
3	Additional down payment		
4	Amount to finance	$14,999	
5	Interest rate	9%	
6	Term (years)	3	
7	Monthly payment	$476.96	

(b) Initial Parameters

	A	B	
1	Price of car	$13,999	Less expensive car
2	Manufacturer's rebate	$1,000	Rebate
3	Additional down payment	$0	
4	Amount to finance	$12,999	
5	Interest rate	9%	
6	Term (years)	3	
7	Monthly payment	$413.36	

(c) Less Expensive Car with Manufacturer's Rebate

	A	B	
1	Price of car	$13,999	
2	Manufacturer's rebate	$1,000	
3	Additional down payment	$3,000	Summer job
4	Amount to finance	$9,999	
5	Interest rate	9%	
6	Term (years)	3	
7	Monthly payment	$317.97	

(d) Summer Job

	A	B	
1	Price of car	$13,999	
2	Manufacturer's rebate	$1,000	
3	Additional down payment	$3,000	
4	Amount to finance	$9,999	
5	Interest rate	8%	Lower interest rate
6	Term (years)	4	More years
7	Monthly payment	$244.10	

(e) Longer Term and Better Rate

FIGURE 3.1   "What If" Analysis on Car Loan (continued)

PMT Function

A function is a predefined formula that accepts one or more **arguments** as input, performs the indicated calculation, then returns another value as output. The **PMT function** requires three arguments (the interest rate per period, the number of periods, and the amount of the loan), from which it computes the associated payment. Consider, for example, the PMT function as it might apply to Figure 3.1b:

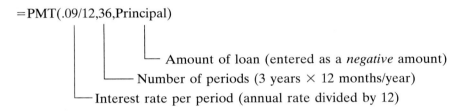

=PMT(.09/12,36,Principal)

                   Amount of loan (entered as a *negative* amount)
            Number of periods (3 years × 12 months/year)
      Interest rate per period (annual rate divided by 12)

Instead of using specific values, however, the arguments in the PMT function are supplied as cell references, so that the computed payment can be based on values supplied by the user elsewhere in the worksheet. Thus, the PMT function is entered as =PMT(B5/12,B6*12,−B4) to reflect the terms of a specific loan whose arguments are in cells B4, B5, and B6. (The principal is entered as a negative amount because the money is lent to you.)

    The analysis associated with Figure 3.1 shows how a worksheet is used in the decision-making process. A person defines a problem, then develops a worksheet that includes all of the associated parameters. He or she can then plug in specific numbers, changing one or more of the variables until a decision can be reached.

HOME MORTGAGES

The PMT function is incorporated into a second example using home mortgages, as shown in Figure 3.2. The worksheet lets you vary the amount of the loan and

	A	B	C	D
1	Amount Borrowed		$100,000	
2	Starting Interest		7.50%	
3				
4		Monthly Payment		
5	Interest	30 Years	15 Years	Difference
6	7.50%	$699.21	$927.01	$227.80
7	8.50%	$768.91	$984.74	$215.83
8	9.50%	$840.85	$1,044.22	$203.37
9	10.50%	$914.74	$1,105.40	$190.66
10	11.50%	$990.29	$1,168.19	$177.90
11	12.50%	$1,067.26	$1,232.52	$165.26

Difference in monthly payment between a 30-year and a 15-year loan

FIGURE 3.2   Variable Rate Mortgages

initial interest rate, then displays the associated monthly payment for a 30- and a 15-year mortgage, respectively.

The information provided by the worksheet is very different from what you might expect initially, but very informative in helping you decide which mortgage to take. Note, for example, that the difference in monthly payments for a $100,000 mortgage at 7.5% is only $227.80. Yes, this is a significant amount of money, but when viewed as a percentage of the total cost of a home (property taxes, maintenance, and so on), it becomes less significant.

Not convinced? Then consider the additional information presented in the worksheets of Figure 3.3. Figure 3.3a indicates the total interest over the life of a $100,000 loan at 7.5% is $151,717 for the 30-year mortgage. In other words, you will pay back the $100,000 in principal plus another $151,717 in interest if you select the longer term. The total interest for the 15-year loan is $66,862, which is less than half as much as for the 30-year loan.

If, like most people, you move before you pay off the mortgage, you will discover that almost all of the early payments in the 30-year loan go to interest rather than principal. The amortization schedule in Figure 3.3b shows that moving at the end of five years (60 months) pays off less than $6,000 of the principal versus almost $22,000 with the 15-year loan. (The latter number is not shown; that is, you have to change the term of the loan in cell C5 to see the amortization for the 15-year loan.)

	A	B	C	D	E
1	Amount Borrowed		$100,000		
2	Starting Interest		7.50%		
3					
4			30 Years		15 Years
5	Interest	Monthly Payment	Total Interest	Monthly Payment	Total Interest
6	7.50%	$699.21	$151,717	$927.01	$66,862
7	8.50%	$768.91	$176,809	$984.74	$77,253
8	9.50%	$840.85	$202,708	$1,044.22	$87,960
9	10.50%	$914.74	$229,306	$1,105.40	$98,972
10	11.50%	$990.29	$256,505	$1,168.19	$110,274
11	12.50%	$1,067.26	$284,213	$1,232.52	$121,854

Less interest is paid on a 15-year loan

(a) Total Interest

FIGURE 3.3   15- vs 30-year Mortgage

	A	B	C	D
1	Amortization Schedule			
2				
3	Principal		$100,000	
4	Annual Interest		7.50%	
5	Term (in years)		30	
6	Payment)		$699.21	
7				
8	Month	Toward Interest	Toward Principal	Balance
9				$100,000
10	1	$625.00	$74.21	$99,925.79
11	2	$624.54	$74.68	$99,851.11
12	3	$624.07	$75.15	$99,775.96
13	4	$623.60	$75.61	$99,700.35
14	5	$623.13	$76.09	$99,624.26
15	6	$622.65	$76.56	$99,547.70
	.	.	.	.
.	.	.	.	.
.	.	.	.	.
65	56	$594.67	$104.55	$95,042.20
66	57	$594.01	$105.20	$94,937.00
67	58	$593.36	$105.86	$94,831.14
68	59	$592.69	$106.52	$94,724.62
69	60	$592.03	$107.19	$94,617.44

5 years (60 months)

Less than $6,000 of the principal has been paid

(b) Amortization Schedule

FIGURE 3.3   15- vs 30-year Mortgage (continued)

Our objective is not to convince you of the merits of one loan over another, but to show you how useful a worksheet can be in the decision-making process. If you do eventually buy a home, and you select a 15-year mortgage, think of us.

Relative versus Absolute Addresses

Figure 3.4 displays the cell formulas for the mortgage analysis. All of the formulas are based on the amount borrowed and the starting interest, in cells C1 and C2, respectively. You can vary either or both of these parameters, and the worksheet will automatically recalculate the monthly payments.

The similarity in the formulas from one row to the next implies that the copy operation will be essential to the development of the worksheet. You must, however, remember the distinction between a *relative* and an ***absolute reference;*** that is, a cell reference that changes during a copy operation (relative) versus one that does not (absolute). Consider, for example, the PMT function as it appears in cell B6:

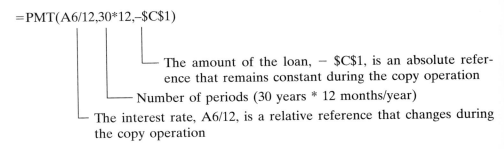

=PMT(A6/12,30*12,–$C$1)

The amount of the loan, – $C$1, is an absolute reference that remains constant during the copy operation

Number of periods (30 years * 12 months/year)

The interest rate, A6/12, is a relative reference that changes during the copy operation

Relative address adjusts during copy operation

Absolute address does not adjust during copy operation

	A	B	C	D
1	Amount Borrowed		$100,000	
2	Starting Interest		7.50%	
3				
4		Monthly Payment		
5	Interest	30 Years	15 Years	Difference
6	=C2	=PMT(A6/12,30*12,–$C$1)	=PMT(A6/12,15*12,–$C$1)	=C6–B6
7	=A6+0.01	=PMT(A7/12,30*12,–$C$1)	=PMT(A7/12,15*12,–$C$1)	=C7–B7
8	=A7+0.01	=PMT(A8/12,30*12,–$C$1)	=PMT(A8/12,15*12,–$C$1)	=C8–B8
9	=A8+0.01	=PMT(A9/12,30*12,–$C$1)	=PMT(A9/12,15*12,–$C$1)	=C9–B9
10	=A9+0.01	=PMT(A10/12,30*12,–$C$1)	=PMT(A10/12,15*12,–$C$1)	=C10–B10
11	=A10+0.01	=PMT(A11/12,30*12,–$C$1)	=PMT(A11/12,15*12,–$C$1)	=C11–B11

FIGURE 3.4 Cell Formulas

The entry A6/12 (which is the first argument in the formula in cell B6) is interpreted to mean "divide the contents of the cell one column to the left by 12." Thus, when the PMT function in cell B6 is copied to cell B7, it (the copied formula) is adjusted to maintain this relationship and will contain the entry A7/12. The Copy command does not duplicate a relative address exactly, but adjusts it from row to row (or column to column) to maintain the relative relationship. The cell reference for the amount of the loan should not change, however, and is specified as an absolute address.

THE POWER OF EXCEL

You already know enough about Excel to develop the worksheet for the mortgage analysis. Excel is so powerful, however, and offers so many shortcuts, that we would be remiss not to show you alternative techniques. This section introduces the fill handle as a shortcut for copying cells, and pointing as a more accurate way to enter cell formulas. It also presents the Function Wizard, which helps you to enter the arguments in a function correctly. Don't overlook the boxed tip on the spell check, a feature we use all the time.

THE SPELL CHECK

Anyone familiar with a word processor takes the spell check for granted, but did you know the same capability exists within Excel? Pull down the Tools menu and click Spelling (or click the Spelling icon on the Standard toolbar), and let Excel do the rest.

The Fill Handle

The *fill handle* is a tiny black square that appears in the lower-right corner of the selected cells. It is the fastest way to copy a cell (or range of cells) to an *adjacent* cell (or range of cells). The process is quite easy and you get to practice in the exercise that follows shortly. In essence you:

➤ Select the cell or cells to be copied.
➤ Point to the fill handle for the selected cell(s), which changes the mouse pointer to a thin cross.
➤ Click and drag the fill handle over the destination range. A border appears to outline the destination range.
➤ Release the mouse to complete the copy operation.

Pointing

A cell address is entered into a formula by typing the reference explicitly (as we have done throughout the text) or by pointing. If you type the address, it is all too easy to make a mistake, such as typing A40 when you really mean A41. ***Pointing*** is more accurate as you use the mouse or cursor keys to reference the cell directly. The process is much easier than it sounds, and you get to practice in the hands-on exercise. In essence you:

➤ Select (click) the cell to contain the formula.
➤ Type an equal sign to begin entering the formula. The status bar indicates the ***Enter mode,*** which means that the formula bar is active as the formula is entered.
➤ Click the cell you want to reference in the formula (or use the cursor keys to move to the cell). A flashing box known as the ***marquee*** appears around the cell, the formula bar includes the cell reference, and the status bar indicates the ***Point mode.***
➤ Type any arithmetic operator to place the cell reference in the formula and return to the Enter mode.
➤ Continue pointing to additional cells until you complete the formula.
➤ Press the enter key to complete the formula.

As with everything else, the more you practice, the easier it is. The hands-on exercise gives you ample opportunity to use what you have learned.

The Function Wizard

The ***Function Wizard*** helps you to select the appropriate function, then helps you to enter the correct arguments for that function into the worksheet. The functions in Excel are grouped into categories as shown in the open list box in the left of Figure 3.5a. Select the function category you want, then choose the function name from within that category. Click the Next command button to produce the dialog box in Figure 3.5b, in which you specify the arguments for the function.

The Function Wizard displays a text box for each argument, a description of each argument (as the text box is selected), and an indication of whether or not the argument is required. (Only the first three arguments are required in the PMT function.) Enter the value, cell reference, or formula for each argument by clicking in the text box and typing the entry, or by clicking the appropriate cell(s) in the worksheet.

Excel displays the calculated value for each argument immediately to the right of the argument. It also shows the computed value for the function as a whole at the top of the dialog box. All you need to do is click the Finish button to insert the function into the worksheet. The Function Wizard is illustrated in step 6 of the following exercise.

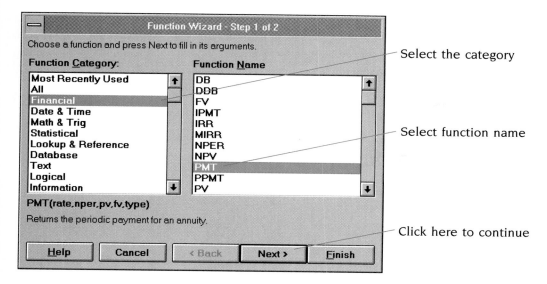

Select the category

Select function name

Click here to continue

(a) Step 1

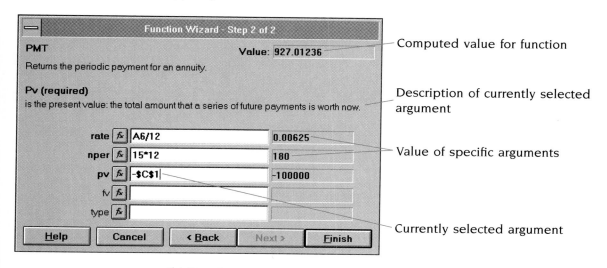

Computed value for function

Description of currently selected argument

Value of specific arguments

Currently selected argument

(b) Step 2

FIGURE 3.5 The Function Wizard

HANDS-ON EXERCISE 1:

Mortgage Analysis

Objective To develop the worksheet for the mortgage analysis; to use pointing to enter a formula and the fill handle to copy a formula. Use Figure 3.6 as a guide.

Step 1: Enter the descriptive labels

➤ Load Excel. Click in cell **A1.** Type **Amount Borrowed.** Click in cell **A2** (or press the **down arrow key**). Type **Starting Interest.**

➤ Click in cell **A4.** Type **Montly Payment.** (We deliberately misspelled "monthly" to illustrate the spell check in step 2.)

➤ Enter the remaining labels in cells A5 through D5 as shown in Figures 3.6a and 3.6b. Do not worry about formatting at this time as all formatting will be done at the end of the exercise.

➤ Save the workbook under the name **MORTGAGE.XLS.** Press **Esc** (or click the **Cancel command button**) if prompted for summary information.

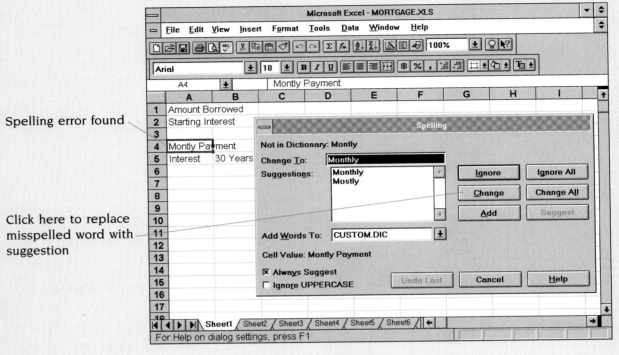

(a) The Spell Check (step 2)

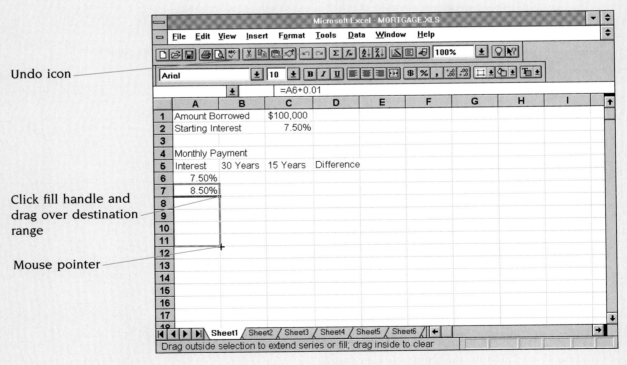

(b) The Fill Handle (step 4)

FIGURE 3.6 Hands-on Exercise 1

Step 2: The Spell Check
➤ Click in cell **A1** to begin the spell check at the beginning of the worksheet. Pull down the **Tools menu** and click **Spelling** (or click the Spelling icon on the Standard toolbar).
➤ Make corrections as necessary; for example, click the **Change command button** in the dialog box of Figure 3.6a to substitute the correct spelling.
➤ Continue checking the worksheet until you see the message indicating that the spell check is complete. Click **OK** when Excel indicates it has finished checking the entire worksheet.

Step 3: Enter the initial conditions
➤ Click in cell **C1.** Type **$100,000** (include the dollar sign and comma).
➤ Click in cell **C2.** Type **7.5%** (include the percent sign). Press **enter.**
➤ Save the workbook.

Step 4: Copy the column of interest rates (the fill handle)
➤ Click in cell **A6.** Type **=C2** to reference the starting interest rate in cell C2.
➤ Click in cell **A7.** Type the formula **=A6+.01** to increment the interest rate by one percent. Press **enter.**
➤ Click in cell **A7.** Point to the **fill handle** in the lower corner of cell A7. The mouse pointer changes to a thin cross.
➤ Drag the **fill handle** over cells **A8 through A11.** A border appears to indicate the destination range as in Figure 3.6b. Release the mouse to complete the copy operation. The formula and associated percentage format in cell A7 have been copied to cells A8 through A11.
➤ Click in Cell **C2.** Type **5%.** The entries in cells A6 through A11 change automatically. Click the **Undo icon** on the Standard toolbar to return to the original interest rate.
➤ Save the workbook.

Step 5: Determine the 30-year payments
➤ Click in cell **B6.** Type the formula **=PMT(A6/12,30*12,−$C$1).** Press the **enter key.** Cell B6 should display $699.21.
➤ Click in cell **B6.** Point to the **fill handle** in the bottom-right corner of cell B6. The mouse pointer changes to a thin cross.
➤ Drag the **fill handle** over cells B7 through B11. A border appears to indicate the destination range. Release the mouse to complete the copy operation. The PMT function in cell B6 has been copied to cells B7 through B11; if you have done this step correctly, cell B11 will display $1,067.26.
➤ If you see a series of pound signs instead of numbers, it means that the cell (column) is too narrow to display the computed results in the selected format. Select the cell(s) containing the pound signs, pull down the **Format menu,** click **Column,** then click **AutoFit Selection** from the cascaded menu.
➤ Save the workbook.

MORE ABOUT THE FILL HANDLE

Use the fill handle as a shortcut for the Edit Clear command. To clear a cell, drag the fill handle to the top of the cell. To clear the contents *and* format, press and hold the Ctrl key as you drag the fill handle to the top of the cell. You can apply the same technique to a cell range by selecting the range, then dragging the fill handle to the top (or left) of the range.

Step 6: The Function Wizard
➤ Click in cell **C6.** Pull down the **Insert menu** and click **Function** (or click the **Function Wizard button** on the Standard toolbar) to display step 1 of the Function Wizard.
➤ Click **Financial** in the Function Category list box. Click **PMT** in the Function Name list box. Click the **Next command button** to display the dialog box in Figure 3.6c.
➤ Click the text box for the rate. Type **A6/12.**
➤ Click the text box for the number of periods (nper). Type **15*12** (indicating 15 years and 12 months per year).
➤ Click the text box for the present value (pv). Type **−$C$1.** (Be sure to include the minus sign.)
➤ Check that the computed values on your monitor match those in Figure 3.6c. Make corrections as necessary.
➤ Click the **Finish command button** to insert the function into the worksheet. Cell C6 should display $927.01.

Step 7: Copy the 15-year payments
➤ Check that cell **C6** is still selected. Point to the **fill handle** in the lower-right corner of cell C6. The mouse pointer changes to a thin cross.
➤ Drag the **fill handle** to copy the PMT function to cells C7 through C11; if you have done the step correctly, cell C11 will display $1,232.52. Adjust the width of the cell if you see a series of pound signs.
➤ Save the workbook.

Step 8: Compute the monthly difference (pointing)
➤ Click in cell **D6.** Type = to begin the formula.

➤ Press the **left arrow key** (or click in cell **C6**), which produces the marquee (flashing box) around the entry in cell C6. The status bar indicates the point mode as shown in Figure 3.6d.

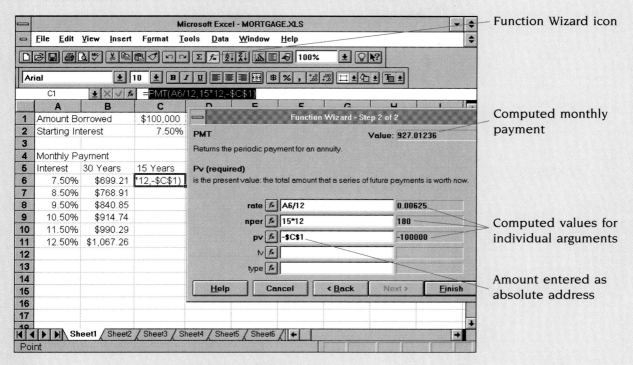

(c) The Function Wizard (step 6)

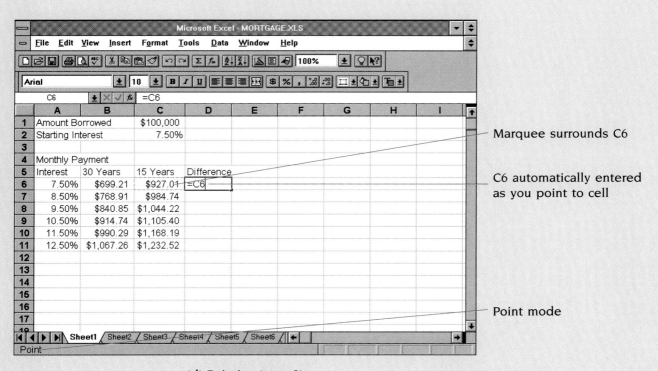

(d) Pointing (step 8)

FIGURE 3.6 Hands-on Exercise 1 (continued)

➤ Press the **minus sign,** then press the **left arrow key** twice (or click in cell B6).
➤ Press **enter** to complete the formula. Cell D6 should display $227.80.
➤ Use the fill handle to copy the contents of cell D6 to cells D7 through D11. If you have done the step correctly, cell D11 will display $165.26 as shown in Figure 3.6e.
➤ Save the workbook.

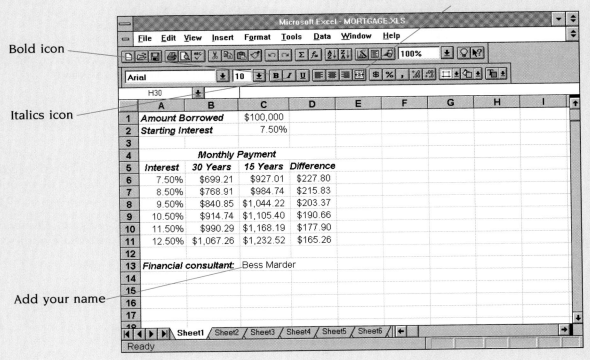

(e) The Completed Spreadsheet (step 9)

FIGURE 3.6   Hands-on Exercise 1 (continued)

THE OPTIMAL (BEST FIT) COLUMN WIDTH

The appearance of pound signs within a cell indicates that the cell width (column width) is insufficient to display the computed results in the selected format. Double click the right border of the column heading to change the column width to accommodate the widest entry in that column. For example, to increase the width of column B, double click the border between the column headings for columns B and C.

Step 9: The finishing touches
➤ Add formatting as necessary, using Figure 3.6e as a guide.
➤ Click cell **A4.** Drag the mouse over cells A4 through D4. Click the **Center Across Columns button** on the Formatting toolbar to center the entry over columns A through D.
➤ Add boldface and/or italics to the text and/or numbers as you see fit.
➤ Type **Financial Consultant** in cell A13. Enter **your name** in cell C13.
➤ Save the workbook.

Step 10: Print the worksheet

➤ Pull down the **File menu** and click **Print Preview** (or click the **Print Preview icon** on the Standard toolbar).

➤ Click the **Setup command button** to display the Page Setup dialog box.
 — Click the **Margins tab.** Check the box to center the worksheet horizontally.
 — Click the **Sheet tab.** Check the boxes to include Row and Column headings and Gridlines.
 — Click **OK** to exit the Page Setup dialog box.

➤ Click the **Print command button** to display the Print dialog box, then click **OK** to print the worksheet.

➤ Press **Ctrl+`** to display the cell formulas. (The left quotation mark is on the same key as the ~.) Widen the cells as necessary to see the complete cell formulas.

➤ Click the **Print icon** on the Standard toolbar to print the cell formulas.

➤ Exit Excel.

THE GRADE BOOK REVISITED

Figure 3.7 contains an expanded version of the professor's grade book that includes more students, an additional test, a potential homework bonus, and the automatic determination of a student's letter grade. The worksheet was built by using several additional capabilities, each of which is explained shortly. Consider:

Date entered with TODAY function   IF function   Table Lookup function

	A	B	C	D	E	F	G	H	I	J
1	6/13/94						Professor's Grade Book			
2										
3	Name	Soc Sec Num	Test 1	Test 2	Test 3	Test 4	Test Avg	Homework	Final Avg	Grade
4	Adams, John	111-22-3333	80	71	70	84	77.8	Poor	77.8	C
5	Barber, Maryann	444-55-6666	96	98	97	90	94.2	OK	97.2	A
6	Boone, Dan	777-88-9999	78	81	70	78	77.0	OK	80.0	B
7	Borow, Jeff	123-45-6789	65	65	65	60	63.0	OK	66.0	D
8	Brown, James	999-99-9999	92	95	79	80	85.2	OK	88.2	B
9	Carson, Kit	888-88-8888	90	90	90	70	82.0	OK	85.0	B
10	Coulter, Sara	100-00-0000	60	50	40	79	61.6	OK	64.6	D
11	Fegin, Richard	222-22-2222	75	70	65	95	80.0	OK	83.0	B
12	Ford, Judd	200-00-0000	90	90	80	90	88.0	Poor	88.0	B
13	Glassman, Kris	444-44-4444	82	78	62	77	75.2	OK	78.2	C
14	Goodman, Neil	555-55-5555	92	88	65	78	80.2	OK	83.2	B
15	Milgrom, Marion	666-66-6666	94	92	86	84	88.0	OK	91.0	A
16	Moldof, Adam	300-00-0000	92	78	65	84	80.6	OK	83.6	B
17	Smith, Adam	777-77-7777	60	50	65	80	67.0	Poor	67.0	D
18										
19	Average		82	78	71	81	HW Bonus	3	Grading Criteria	
20	High		96	98	97	95			(Minimum Req'd)	
21	Low		60	50	40	60				F
22	Range		36	48	57	35			60	D
23									70	C
24	Exam Weights		20%	20%	20%	40%			80	B
25									90	A

Statistical functions

FIGURE 3.7 Extended Grade Book

Statistical functions: The AVERAGE, MAX, and MIN functions are used to compute statistics for the class as a whole. The range of grades is computed by subtracting the minimum value from the maximum value.

IF function: The IF function is used to conditionally add a homework bonus to the student's test average and potentially raise the final average prior to determining the grade. The bonus is awarded to those students whose homework is "OK". Students whose homework grade is poor do not receive a bonus.

Table lookup function: The expanded grade book converts a student's final average to a letter grade, in accordance with the table shown in the lower-right portion of the worksheet. A student needs an average of 60 or higher to earn a D, 70 or higher for a C, and so on.

Date function: The current date appears in the upper-left corner of the worksheet. Date arithmetic (that is, the elapsed time between two dates) is also possible, although it is not illustrated explicitly in the figure.

Large worksheets: The expanded grade book is larger than the applications considered so far, and requires additional commands for viewing on the monitor and for printing.

Statistical Functions

The **MAX, MIN,** and **AVERAGE** functions return the highest, lowest, and average values, respectively, from an argument list. The list may include individual cell references, ranges, numeric values, functions, or mathematical expressions (formulas). The functions are illustrated in the worksheet of Figure 3.8.

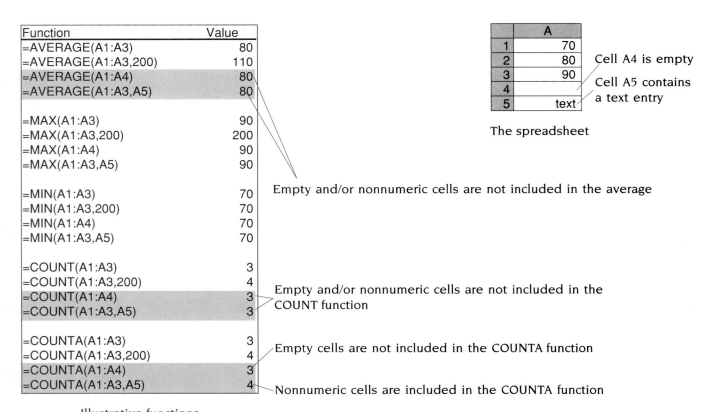

Illustrative functions

FIGURE 3.8 Statistical Functions with a Text Entry

The first example, =AVERAGE(A1:A3), computes the average for cells A1 through A3 by adding the values in the indicated range (70, 80, and 90), then dividing the result by three, to obtain an average of 80. Additional arguments in the form of values and/or cell addresses can be specified within the parentheses; for example, the function =AVERAGE(A1:A3,200) computes the average of cells A1, A2, and A3, and the number 200.

Empty and nonnumeric cells are *not* included in the computation. Thus, since cell A4 is empty, the function =AVERAGE(A1:A4) also returns an average of 80 (240/3), which is the same result as the function =AVERAGE(A1:A3). In similar fashion, the function =AVERAGE(A1:A3,A5) includes only three values in its computation (cells A1, A2, and A3), because the nonnumeric entry in cell A5 is excluded. The results of the MIN and MAX functions are obtained in a comparable way as indicated in Figure 3.8.

The COUNT and COUNTA functions each tally the number of entries in the argument list with a subtle difference. The **COUNT function** returns the number of nonempty cells with numeric entries, including formulas that evaluate to numeric results. The **COUNTA function** returns the number of nonempty cells, including both nonnumeric and numeric values. In Figure 3.8 the functions =COUNT(A1:A3) and =COUNTA(A1:A3) both return a value of 3. The functions =COUNT(A1:A4) and =COUNTA(A1:A4) also return a value of 3 because cell A4 is empty and thus is excluded from both functions. The function =COUNTA(A1:A3,A5) returns a value of 4 because it includes the nonnumeric entry in cell A5.

FIND AND REPLACE

Anyone familiar with a word processor knows the advantages of the Find and Replace commands. The identical capability is available in Excel. Pull down the Edit menu and click Replace, then supply the necessary information in the appropriate text boxes. You may not use the command often, but it is invaluable should the need arise.

Arithmetic Expressions versus Functions

Many worksheet calculations, such as an average or a sum, can be performed in two ways. You can enter a formula such as =(B1+B2+B3)/3, or you can use the equivalent function =AVERAGE(B1:B3). *The use of functions is generally preferable* as shown in Figure 3.9.

The two worksheets in Figure 3.9a may appear equivalent, but the SUM function in the worksheet on the left is superior to the arithmetic expression in the worksheet on the right. The entries in cell A5 of both worksheets return a value of 100.

Now consider what happens if a new row is inserted between existing rows 2 and 3, with the entry in the new cell equal to 25. The SUM function adjusts automatically to include the new value (returning a sum of 125 in the worksheet on the left) because the SUM function was defined originally for the cell range *A1 through A4*. The new row is inserted within these cells, moving the entry in cell A4 to cell A5, and changing the range to include cell A5.

No such accommodation is made in the worksheet on the right because the arithmetic expression was defined to include four *specific* cells, rather than a range of cells. The addition of the new row modifies the cell references (since the values in cells A3 and A4 have been moved to cells A4 and A5), but does not include the new row in the adjusted expression.

Function ——

	A
1	10
2	20
3	30
4	40
5	=SUM(A1:A4)

	A
1	10
2	20
3	30
4	40
5	=A1+A2+A3+A4

—— Formula

(a) Spreadsheets as Initially Entered

Range is adjusted automatically, returning a sum of 125

	A
1	10
2	20
3	25
4	30
5	40
6	=SUM(A1:A5)

	A
1	10
2	20
3	25
4	30
5	40
6	=A1+A2+A4+A5

Addresses for old cells A3 and A4 are changed; the new entry in cell A3 is not included in the sum

(b) Spreadsheets after the Addition of a New Row

Range is adjusted automatically, returning a sum of 80

	A
1	10
2	30
3	40
4	=SUM(A1:A3)

	A
1	10
2	30
3	40
4	=A1+#REF!+A2+A3

#REF! displayed since entry in A2 has been deleted; addresses for cells A3 and A4 are changed to A2 and A3

(c) Spreadsheets after the Deletion of a Row

FIGURE 3.9   Arithmetic Expressions versus Functions

Similar reasoning holds for deleting a row. Figure 3.9c deletes row 2 from the *original* worksheets, which moves the entry in cell A4 to cell A3. The SUM function in the worksheet on the left adjusts automatically to =SUM(A1:A3) and returns the value 80. The formula in the worksheet on the right, however, returns an error (to indicate an illegal cell reference) because it is still attempting to add the entries in four cells, one of which no longer exists. In summary, a function expands and contracts to adjust for insertions or deletions, and should be used wherever possible.

#REF!—ILLEGAL CELL REFERENCE

The #REF! error value is displayed if Excel is unable to evaluate a formula because of an illegal cell reference. The most common cause of the error is deleting the row or column that contained the original cell reference.

IF function

The **IF function** enables decision making to be implemented within a worksheet—for example, a conditional bonus for students whose homework is satisfactory. Students with inferior homework do not get this break.

The IF function has three arguments: a condition that is evaluated as true or false, a value if the condition is true, and a value if the condition is false. Consider:

=IF(condition,value-if-true,value-if-false)

— Displayed value for a false condition
— Displayed value for a true condition
— Condition is either true or false

The IF function returns either the second or third argument, depending on the result of the *logical test* of the condition. If the condition is true, the function returns the second argument, whereas if the condition is false, the function returns the third argument.

The condition uses one of the six *relational operators* in Figure 3.10a. The IF function is illustrated in the worksheet in Figure 3.10b, which produced the examples in Figure 3.10c. In every instance the condition is evaluated, then the second or third argument is displayed, depending on whether the condition is true or false. The arguments may be numeric (1000 or 2000), a cell reference to display the contents of the specific cell (B1 or B2), a formula (B1+10 or B1–10), a function (MAX(B1:B2) or MIN(B1:B2)), or a text entry enclosed in quotation marks ("Go" or "Hold").

Operator	Description
=	Equal to
<>	Not equal to
<	Less than
>	Greater than
<=	Less than or equal to
>=	Greater than or equal to

(a) Relational Operators

	A	B	C
1	10	15	April
2	10	30	May

(b) The Spreadsheet

IF function	Evaluation
=IF(A1=A2,1000,2000)	1000
=IF(A1<>A2,1000,2000)	2000
=IF(A1<>A2,B1,B2)	30
=IF(A1<B1,MAX(B1:B2),MIN(B1:B2))	30
=IF(A1<A2,B1+10,B1–10)	5
=IF(A1=A2,C1,C2)	April
=IF(SUM(A1:A2)>20,"Go","Hold")	Hold

(c) Examples

FIGURE 3.10 The IF Function

The IF function is used in the grade book of Figure 3.7 to award a bonus for homework. Students whose homework is "OK" receive the bonus, whereas other students do not. The IF function to implement this logic for the first student is entered in cell H4 as follows:

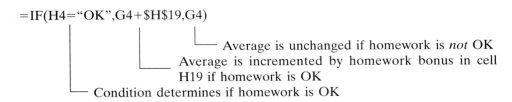

=IF(H4="OK",G4+$H$19,G4)

Average is unchanged if homework is *not* OK

Average is incremented by homework bonus in cell H19 if homework is OK

Condition determines if homework is OK

The IF function compares the value in cell H4 (the homework grade) to the literal "OK." If the condition is true (the homework is OK), the bonus in cell H19 is added to the student's test average in cell G4. If, however, the condition is false (the homework is not OK), the average is unchanged.

The bonus is specified as a cell address rather than a specific value so that the number of bonus points can be easily changed; that is, the professor can make a single change to the worksheet by increasing (decreasing) the bonus in cell H19 and see immediately the effect on every student without having to edit or retype any other formula. An absolute (rather than a relative) reference is used to reference the homework bonus, so that when the IF function is copied to the other rows in the column, the address will remain constant. A relative reference, however, was used for the student's homework and semester averages in cells H4 and G4, because these addresses change from one student to the next.

Table Lookup Function

Consider for a moment how the professor assigns letter grades to students at the end of the semester. He or she computes a test average for each student and conditionally awards the bonus for homework. The professor then determines a letter grade according to a predetermined scale; for example, 90 or above is an A, 80 to 89 is a B, and so on.

The *table lookup function* duplicates this process within a worksheet, by assigning an entry to a cell based on a numeric value contained in another cell. In other words, just as the professor knows where on the grading scale a student's numerical average will fall, the table lookup function determines where within a specified table a numeric value (a student's average) is found, and retrieves the corresponding entry (the letter grade).

The table lookup function requires three arguments: the numeric value to look up, the range of cells containing the table, and the column number within the table that contains the result. These concepts are illustrated in Figure 3.11, which was taken from the expanded grade book in Figure 3.7. The table in Figure 3.11 extends over two columns (I and J) and five rows (21 through 25); that is, the table is located in the range I21:J25. The *break points,* or comparison values (the lowest numeric value for each grade), are contained in column I (the first column in the table) and are in ascending order. The corresponding letter grades are found in column J.

The table lookup function in cell J4 determines the letter grade (for John Adams) based on the computed average in cell I4. Consider:

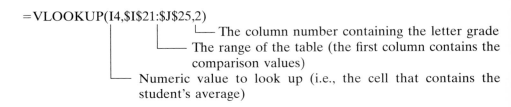

=VLOOKUP(I4,$I$21:$J$25,2)

The column number containing the letter grade

The range of the table (the first column contains the comparison values)

Numeric value to look up (i.e., the cell that contains the student's average)

	A	...	G	H	I	J	
1							
2							
3	**Name**	...	**Test Avg**	**Homework**	**Final Avg**	**Grade**	Cell J4 contains
4	Adams, John	...	77.8	Poor	77.8	C	=VLOOKUP(I4,$I$21: $J$25,2)
	.	.	.	.	.	.	
	.	.	.	.	.	.	
	.	.	.	.	.	.	
18							
19	**Average**		**HW Bonus**	3	**Grading Criteria**		
20	**High**				**(Minimum Req'd)**		Grades are in column J
21	**Low**					F	
22	**Range**				60	D	
23					70	C	Cells I22 through I25
24	**Exam Weights**				80	B	contain the break points
25					90	A	in ascending order

FIGURE 3.11 Table Lookup Function

The first argument is the value to look up, which in this example is Adams's computed average, found in cell I4. A relative reference is used so that the address will adjust when the formula is copied to the other rows in the worksheet.

The second argument is the range of the table, found in cells I21 through J25, as explained earlier. Absolute references are specified so that the addresses will not change when the function is copied to determine the letter grades for the other students. The first column in the table (column I in this example) contains the break points, which must be in ascending order.

The third argument indicates the column where the letter grades are found. To determine the letter grade for Adams (whose computed average is 77.8), the table lookup function searches cells I21 through I25 for the first value greater than 77.8 (the computed average in cell I4). The lookup function finds the number 80 in cell I24. It then backs up one row and retrieves the corresponding letter grade from the second column of the table in that row (cell J23). Adams, with an average of 77.8, is assigned a grade of C.

Date Functions and Date Arithmetic

Excel provides several functions that enable you to work with dates, two of which are illustrated in Figure 3.12. The **TODAY() function** returns the current date, which is the date a worksheet is created or retrieved. The **DATE(yy,mm,dd)** function displays a specific date, such as May 13, 1994. The TODAY() function will display May 13, 1994 only on that specific date. The DATE(94,5,13) function will display May 13, 1994 regardless of the current date.

In actuality, both functions store the date as a **serial date** corresponding to the number of days in this century. January 1, 1900 is stored as the number 1, January 2, 1900 as the number 2, etc. May 13, 1994 corresponds to the number 34467 as can be seen in Figure 3.12.

The fact that dates are stored as serial numbers enables you to compute the number of days between two dates by subtraction. Age, for example, can be computed by subtracting the date of birth from the current date, and dividing the result by 365. Realize, too, that while the subtraction provides the exact number of elapsed days, the subsequent division is only approximate, in that leap years (with 366 days) are not accounted for. Note, too, the IF function in Figure 3.12a, which examines the computed age, then displays an appropriate message indicating whether the individual is legal or still under the age of 21.

Another example of **date arithmetic** is shown in Figure 3.12b, in which a constant is added to the date of purchase in order to obtain the due date. In this example the formula in cell D4 adds the date in cell C4 to the number of days in cell

Displays current date (date spreadsheet is retrieved)

Always displays same date

Serial number stored by Excel

	A	B	C	D
1		Cell Formulas	Date Format	Numeric Format
2	Today's Date	=TODAY()	13-May-94	34467
3	Birthdate	=DATE(73,10,31)	31-Oct-73	26968
4				
5	Elapsed Time (days)	=B1−B2		7499
6	Age (years)	=B3/365		20.5
7				
8		=IF(D6>=21,"LEGAL","Minor")		Minor

(a) Date Functions and Date Arithmetic
(current date: May 13, 1994)

Formula entered: =C4+$C$10

	A	B	C	D
1		Accounts Receivable		
2				
3	Customer	Account Number	Date of Purchase	Date Due
4	Ruce, Doug	R23456	15-Dec-93	14-Jan-94
5	Dembrow, Harriet	D34987	22-Jan-94	21-Feb-94
6	Center, Sol	C12987	31-Jan-94	2-Mar-94
7	Morris, Gail	M87698	3-Feb-94	5-Mar-94
8	Black, Chuck	B09875	26-Feb-94	28-Mar-94
9				
10		Number of days until due:	30	

(b) Date Arithmetic

FIGURE 3.12   Date Functions and Date Arithmetic

C10. The formula is not displayed in the figure but is entered into the worksheet as =C4+$C$10. The combination of a relative and an absolute reference enables the entry in cell D4 to be copied to the remaining cells in that column. A relative reference is used for the purchase date because the cell address changes from row to row. An absolute reference is used for the number of days because that cell address remains constant.

All dates can be formatted to display the month, day, and year as shown in Figure 3.12. You can also enter a date directly (without having to use the DATE function) by typing 5/13/94 or May 13, 1994 in the appropriate cell.

DAYLIGHT SAVINGS TIME

The TODAY function uses the computer's internal clock and calendar to obtain the current time and date. But what if your computer has the wrong information? Open the Main group in Program Manager, double click the Control Panel icon, then double click the Date/Time icon to open a dialog box. Enter the correct time and date, click OK to accept the new settings, then close the Control Panel application.

Scrolling

A large worksheet, such as the extended grade book, can seldom be seen on the monitor in its entirety; that is, only a portion of the worksheet is in view at any given time. The specific rows and columns that are displayed are determined by an operation called *scrolling*, which shows different parts of a worksheet at different times. Scrolling enables you to see any portion of the worksheet at the expense of not seeing another portion. The worksheet in Figure 3.13a, for example, displays column J containing the students' grades, but not columns A and B, which contain the students' names. In similar fashion you can see rows 21 through 25 that display the grading criteria, but you cannot see the column headings.

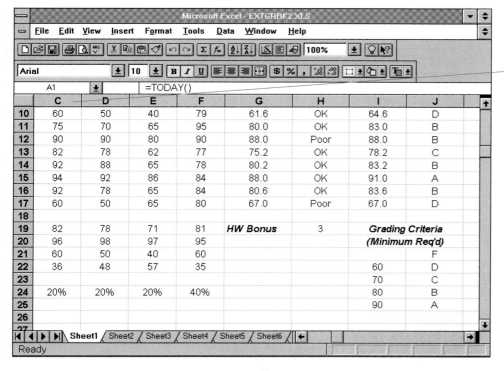

(a) Scrolling

FIGURE 3.13   Large Spreadsheets

Scrolling comes about automatically as the active cell changes and may take place in both a horizontal and a vertical direction. Clicking the right arrow on the horizontal scroll bar (or pressing the right arrow key when the active cell is already in the rightmost column of the screen) causes the entire screen to move one column to the right. In similar fashion, clicking the down arrow in the vertical scroll bar (or pressing the down arrow key when the active cell is in the bottom row of the screen) causes the entire screen to move down one row.

SCROLLING: THE MOUSE VERSUS THE KEYBOARD

You can use either the mouse or the keyboard to scroll within the worksheet, but there is one critical difference. Scrolling with the keyboard also changes the active cell. Scrolling with the mouse does not.

Freezing Panes

Scrolling brings distant portions of a large worksheet into view, but moves the text headings for existing rows and/or columns off the screen. You can, however, retain the row and/or column headings by *freezing panes* as shown in Figure 3.13b. The grades and grading criteria are visible as in the previous figure, but so too are the students' names and column headings.

Look closely at this figure and you will see that columns B through D (social security number, test 1, and test 2) are missing as are rows 4, 5, and 6 (the first three students). You will also notice a horizontal line under row 3, and a vertical line after column A, to indicate that these rows and columns have been frozen. Scrolling still takes place as you move beyond the rightmost column or below the bottom row, but you will always see column A and rows 1, 2, and 3 displayed on the monitor.

The Freeze (Unfreeze) Panes command is found in the pull-down Window menu. It offers the advantage of providing permanent labels for the rows and columns displayed in the monitor regardless of the scrolling in effect. It is especially helpful when viewing or entering data in a large worksheet.

Column A remains on screen; columns B, C, and D are missing

Rows 4, 5, and 6 are missing

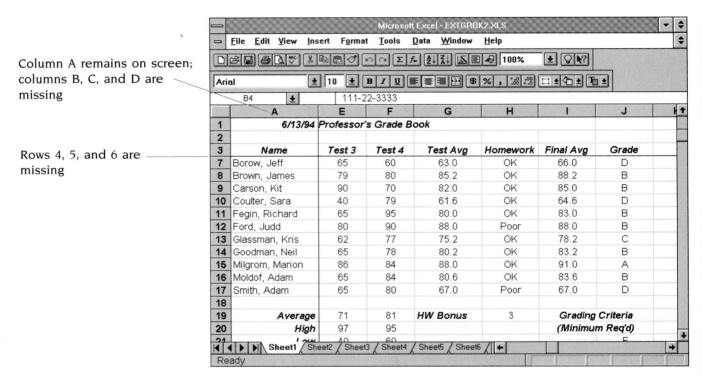

(b) Freezing Panes

FIGURE 3.13   Large Spreadsheets (continued)

THE AUTOFILL CAPABILITY

The last shortcut we will introduce is the *autofill capability,* which creates a series based on the initial value(s) you supply. It is a wonderful shortcut and the quickest way to enter certain types of data. If, for example, you needed the months of the year in 12 successive cells, you would enter January (or Jan) in the first cell, then drag the fill handle over the next 11 cells in the direction you want to fill. Excel will enter the remaining months of the year in those cells.

Excel guesses at the type of series you want and fills the cells accordingly. You can type Monday (rather than January) and Excel will return the days of the week. You can enter a text and numeric combination, such as Quarter 1 or 1st Quarter, and Excel will extend the series appropriately. You can also create a numeric series by entering the first two numbers in that series; for example, to enter the years 1990 through 1999, type 1990 and 1991 in the first two cells, select both of these cells, and drag the fill handle in the appropriate direction over the destination range.

HANDS-ON EXERCISE 2:

Extended Grade Book

Objective To develop the extended grade book; to use statistical (AVERAGE, MAX, and MIN), logical (IF and VLOOKUP), and date functions (TODAY); to demonstrate scrolling and the Freeze Panes command. Use Figure 3.14 as a guide.

Step 1: Open the extended grade book

➤ Pull down the **File menu** and click **Open** (or click the **Open icon** on the Standard toolbar). Double click the **EXTGRBK.XLS** workbook to open a partially completed version of the extended grade book discussed in the chapter.

➤ Pull down the **File menu.** Click **Save As.** Save the workbook as **EXTGRBK2** so that you can return to the original workbook if necessary.

MISSING SCROLL BARS

The horizontal and vertical scroll bars are essential, especially with larger worksheets that cannot be seen in their entirety. If either scroll bar is missing, it is because a previous user elected to hide it. Pull down the Tools menu, click Options, and click the View tab. Click the check boxes to display the Horizontal and Vertical scroll bars, then click the OK command button to exit the dialog box and return to the worksheet.

Step 2: Enter today's date

➤ Click in cell **A1,** the cell that is to contain today's date.

➤ Click the **Function Wizard icon** on the Standard toolbar. Click **Date & Time** in the Function Category list box in step 1 of the Function Wizard.

➤ Click the **down arrow** on the Function Name list box to see the additional Date and Time functions. Click **TODAY** as shown in Figure 3.14a. Click the **Next command button** to move to step 2 of the Function Wizard.

➤ The dialog box on your screen shows there are no arguments for the TODAY function. (The indication of a volatile value means that the date will change every time you open the workbook.) Click the **Finish command button** to insert the date into your worksheet.

➤ Save the workbook.

Step 3: The autofill feature

➤ Click in cell **C3,** the cell containing the label Test 1.

➤ Point to the **fill handle** in the lower-right corner. The mouse pointer changes to a thin cross.

➤ Drag the fill handle over cells **D3, E3,** and **F3.** A border appears to indicate the destination range.

➤ Release the mouse. Cells D3, E3, and F3 now contain the labels Test 2, Test 3, and Test 4, respectively.

CREATE A CUSTOM SERIES

A custom series is very helpful if you repeatedly enter the same lists of data. Pull down the Tools menu, click Options, then click the Custom Lists tab. Click New List in the Custom Lists box, click the Add command button, then enter the items in the series (e.g., Tom, Dick, and Harry) using the enter key to separate one item from the next. The next time you type Tom in a cell and drag the fill handle, you will see the series Tom, Dick, and Harry repeated through the entire range.

Function appears in formula bar

Select category

Select TODAY function

Click here to move to next step

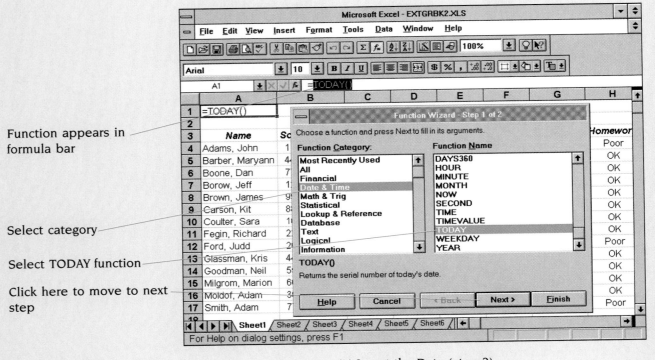

(a) Insert the Date (step 2)

FIGURE 3.14 Hands-on Exercise 2

NOW VERSUS TODAY

The NOW and TODAY functions both return a serial value for the current date. The difference is that the NOW function includes a decimal portion, which reflects the time of day, but the TODAY function does not. The distinction is important only with date arithmetic when the day is half over (after 12PM) because the serial value in the NOW function will be rounded up to the next day. The results of a calculation using the NOW function will differ by one day from the "identical" calculation using the TODAY function.

Step 4: Scrolling and freezing panes

➤ Press **Ctrl+Home** to move to cell A1. Click the **right arrow** on the horizontal scroll bar until column A scrolls off the screen. Cell A1 is still the active cell because scrolling with the mouse does not change the active cell.

➤ Press **Ctrl+Home.** Press the **right arrow key** until column A scrolls off the screen. The active cell changes as you scroll with the keyboard.

➤ Press **Ctrl+Home** to return to cell A1. Click the **down arrow** on the vertical scroll bar (or press the **down arrow key** until row 1 scrolls off the screen). Note whether the active cell changes or not.

➤ Press **Ctrl+Home** again, then click in cell **B4.** Pull down the **Window menu.** Click **Freeze Panes** as shown in Figure 3.14b. You will see a line to the right of column A and below row 3; that is, column A and rows 1 through 3 will always be visible regardless of scrolling.

➤ Click the **right arrow** on the horizontal scroll bar (or press the **right arrow key**) repeatedly until column J is visible. Note that column A is visible (frozen), but that one or more columns are not shown.

➤ Click the **down arrow** on the vertical scroll bar (or press the **down arrow key**) repeatedly until row 25 is visible. Note that rows 1 through 3 are visible (frozen), but that one or more rows are not shown.

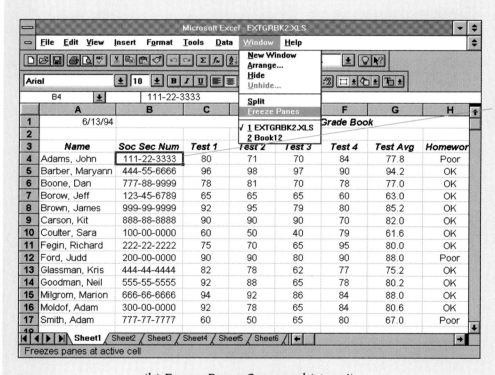

Select B4 to freeze rows above (1–3) and column to the left (A)

(b) Freeze Panes Command (step 4)

FIGURE 3.14 Hands-on Exercise 2 (continued)

Step 5: The IF function

➤ Pull down the **View Menu.** Click **Unfreeze Panes.**

➤ Scroll to the top of the worksheet, then scroll until Column I is visible on the screen. Click in cell **I4.**

➤ Click the **Function Wizard icon** on the Standard toolbar. Click **Logical** in the Function Category list box in step 1 of the Function Wizard. Click **IF** in the Function Name list box, then click the **Next command button** to move to

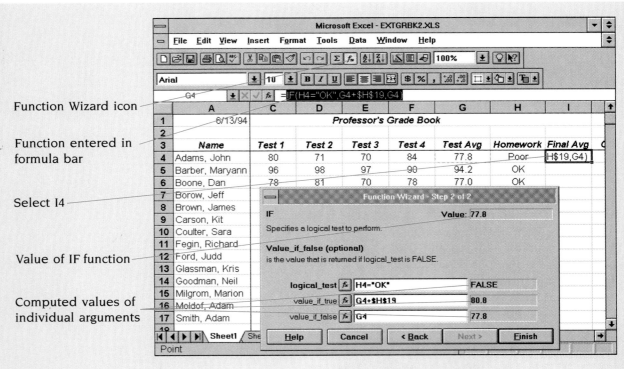

Function Wizard icon

Function entered in formula bar

Select I4

Value of IF function

Computed values of individual arguments

(c) The IF Function (step 5)

FIGURE 3.14 Hands-on Exercise 2 (continued)

step 2 of the Function Wizard and display the dialog box in Figure 3.14c.

➤ Enter the arguments for the IF function as shown in the figure. You can enter the arguments directly or you can use pointing as follows:

— Click the **logical_test** text box. Click cell **H4** in the worksheet. (You may need to move the dialog box to access cell H4. Click and drag the title bar to move the dialog box out of the way.) Type **="OK"** to complete the logical test.

— Click the **value_if_true** text box. Click cell **G4** in the worksheet, type a **plus sign,** click cell **H19** in the worksheet (scrolling if necessary), and finally press the **F4 key** (see tip below) to convert the reference to cell H19 to an absolute reference.

— Click the **value_if_false** text box. Click cell **G4** in the worksheet, scrolling if necessary.

➤ Check that the computed values on your worksheet match those in the figure and make corrections as necessary. Click the **Finish command button** to insert the function into your worksheet.

THE F4 KEY

The F4 key cycles through relative, absolute, and mixed addresses. Click on any reference within the formula bar; for example, click on A1 in the formula =A1+A2. Press the F4 key once and it changes to an absolute reference. Press the F4 key a second time and it becomes a mixed reference, A$1; press it again and it is a different mixed reference, $A1. Press the F4 key a fourth time and it returns to the original relative address, A1.

KEYBOARD SHORTCUTS: MOVING WITHIN A WORKSHEET

Press PgUp or PgDn to scroll an entire screen in the indicated direction. Press Ctrl+Home or Ctrl+End to move to the beginning or end of a worksheet—that is, to cell A1 and to the cell in the lower-right corner, respectively. If these keys do not work, it is because the transition navigation keys (i.e., Lotus conventions) are in effect. Pull down the Tools menu, click Options, and click the Transition tab. Clear the check in the Transition Navigation Keys check box, then click OK.

Step 6: The VLOOKUP function

➤ Click in cell **J4.**

➤ Click the **Function Wizard icon** on the Standard toolbar.

➤ Click **Lookup & Reference** in the Function Category list box in step 1 of the Function Wizard.

➤ Scroll in the Function Name list box until you can select **VLOOKUP.**

➤ Click the **Next command button** to move to step 2 of the Function Wizard and display the dialog box in Figure 3.14d.

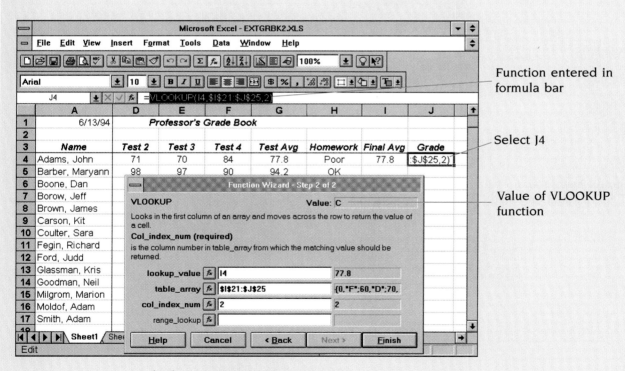

(d) The VLOOKUP Function (step 6)

FIGURE 3.14   Hands-on Exercise 2 (continued)

➤ Enter the arguments for the VLOOKUP function as shown in the figure. You can enter the arguments directly or you can use pointing as follows:
— Click the **lookup_value** text box. Click cell **I4** in the worksheet.

— Click the **table_array** text box. Click cell **I21** and **drag to cell J25** (scrolling if necessary). Press the **F4 key** (see tip on page 108) to convert to an absolute reference.

— Click the **col_index_num** text box. Type **2.**

➤ Check that the computed values on your worksheet match those in the figure and make corrections as necessary. Click the **Finish command button** to insert the function into your worksheet.

➤ Save the workbook.

Step 7: Copy the IF and VLOOKUP functions (the fill handle)

➤ Scroll to the top of the worksheet. Select cells **I4** and **J4** as in Figure 3.14e.

➤ Point to the **fill handle** in the lower-right corner of the selected range. The mouse pointer changes to a thin cross.

➤ Drag the fill handle over cells **I5 through J17.** A border appears to indicate the destination range as shown in Figure 3.14e. Release the mouse to complete the copy operation. If you have done everything correctly, Adam Smith should have a grade of D based on a final average of 67.0.

➤ Save the workbook.

Select I4:J4

Point to fill handle and drag over destination range

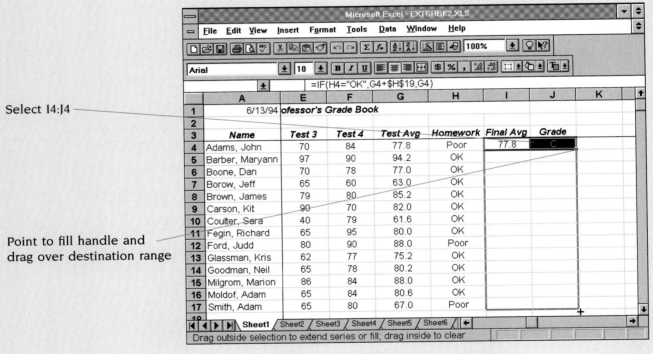

(e) The Fill Handle (step 7)

FIGURE 3.14 Hands-on Exercise 2 (continued)

Step 8: Statistical functions

➤ Click in cell **C19.** Type **=AVERAGE(C4:C17).** Press **enter.** Cell C19 should display 82.

➤ Click in cell **C20.** Type **=MAX(C4:C17).** Press **enter.** Cell C20 should display 96.

➤ Click in cell **C21.** Type **=MIN(C4:C17).** Press **enter.** Cell C21 should display 60.

➤ Click in cell **C22.** Type **=C20:C21.** Press **enter.** Cell C22 should display 36.

#NAME? AND OTHER ERRORS

Excel displays an error value when it is unable to calculate the formula in a cell. Misspelling a function name (e.g., using AVG instead of AVER-AGE) results in #NAME?, which is perplexing at first, but easily corrected once you know the meaning of the error. All error values begin with a number sign (#); pull down the Help menu, click Search, then enter # for a listing and explanation of the error values.

Step 9: Copy the statistical functions (shortcut menu)
➤ Select cells **C19 through C22** as shown in Figure 3.14f. Click the **right mouse button** to display the shortcut menu shown in the figure. Click **Copy.** A marquee appears around the selected cells.
➤ Drag the mouse over cells **D19 through F19.** Click the **Paste icon** on the Standard toolbar to complete the copy operation. If you have done everything correctly, cells F19, F20, F21, and F22 will display 81, 95, 60, and 35, respectively.
➤ Save the workbook.

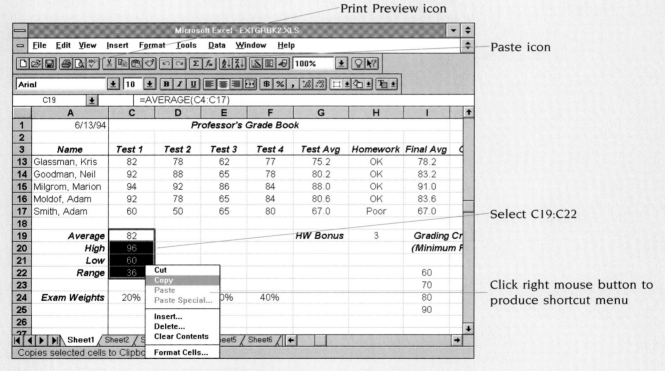

(f) Shortcut Menus (step 9)

FIGURE 3.14   Hands-on Exercise 2 (continued)

Step 10: Print the worksheet
➤ Click the **Print Preview** icon on the Standard toolbar. Click the **Setup command button** to display the Page Setup dialog box.
  — Click the **Page tab.** Click the **Landscape option button.** Click the option button to Fit to one page.

- — Click the **Sheet tab.** Check the boxes for Row and Column Headings and for Gridlines.
- — Click **OK** to exit the Page Setup dialog box.
- — Click the **Print command button,** then click **OK** to print the worksheet.
- ➤ Press **Ctrl+`** to display the cell formulas. (The left quotation mark is on the same key as the ~.)
- ➤ Click the **Print Preview** icon. Adjust the margins and column widths as necessary, click the **Print command button,** then click **OK** to print the worksheet with cell formulas.
- ➤ Exit Excel.

SEE THE WHOLE WORKSHEET

Press Ctrl+Home to move to the beginning of the worksheet. Press the F8 key to enter the extended selection mode (EXT will appear on the status bar), then press Ctrl+End to move to the end of the worksheet and simultaneously select the entire worksheet. Pull down the View menu, click Zoom, then click the Fit Selection option button. Click OK to close the dialog box. The magnification shrinks to display the entire worksheet; how well you can read the display depends on the size of your monitor and the size of the worksheet.

MAKE IT FIT

The Page Setup command offers different ways to make a large worksheet fit on one page. Click the Print Preview icon on the Standard toolbar to view the worksheet prior to printing, click the Margins command button to display (hide) sizing handles for the page margins and column widths, then drag any handle to adjust the margin or column width. You can also click the Setup command button from the Print Preview screen to display the Page Setup dialog box. Use the Page tab to change to *landscape* printing and/or to select the scaling option to Fit to one page.

SUMMARY

The PMT function requires three arguments (the interest rate per period, the number of periods, and the amount of the loan), from which it computes the associated payment.

The fill handle is used to copy a cell or group of cells to a range of adjacent cells. Pointing is a more accurate way to enter a cell reference into a formula as it uses the mouse or cursor keys to reference the cell directly. The Function Wizard helps you choose the appropriate function, then enter the arguments in the proper sequence. The autofill capability creates a series based on the value(s) you supply.

The AVERAGE, MAX, and MIN functions return the average, highest, and lowest values for the designated entries. The COUNT function indicates the number of cells with numeric entries; the COUNTA function displays the number of cells with numeric and/or nonnumeric entries.

The IF function has three arguments: a logical test that is evaluated as true or false, a value if the test is true, and a value if the test is false. The VLOOKUP (table lookup) function also has three arguments: the numeric value to look up, the range of cells containing the table, and the column number within the table that contains the result.

The TODAY() function returns the current date, while the DATE(yy,mm,dd) function returns a specific date. Both functions store the date as a serial number corresponding to the number of days in this century, thus enabling date arithmetic.

Scrolling enables you to view any portion of a large worksheet but moves the headings for existing rows and/or columns off the screen. The Freeze Panes command keeps the row and/or column headings on the screen while scrolling in a large worksheet.

Key Words and Concepts

=AVERAGE	Arguments	Marquee
=COUNT	Assumptions	Point mode
=COUNTA	Autofill capability	Pointing
=DATE	Break point	Portrait
=IF	Custom series	Relational operator
=MAX	Date arithmetic	Relative reference
=MIN	Edit Clear command	Scaling
=NOW	Enter mode	Scrolling
=PMT	Fill handle	Serial date
=SUM	Freezing panes	Spell check
=TODAY	Function Wizard	Table lookup
=VLOOKUP	Landscape	Template
Absolute reference	Logical test	

Multiple Choice

1. Which of the following options may be used to print a large worksheet?
(a) Landscape orientation
(b) Scaling
(c) Reduced margins
(d) All of the above

2. If the results of a formula contain more characters than can be displayed according to the present format and cell width,
(a) The extra characters will be truncated under all circumstances
(b) All of the characters will be displayed if the cell to the right is empty
(c) A series of asterisks will be displayed
(d) A series of pound signs will be displayed

3. Which cell—A1, A2, or A3—will contain the amount of the loan, given the function =PMT(A1,A2,A3)?
    (a) A1
    (b) A2
    (c) A3
    (d) Impossible to determine

4. Which of the following will compute the average of the values in cells D2, D3, and D4?
    (a) The function =AVERAGE(D2:D4)
    (b) The function =AVERAGE(D2,D4)
    (c) Both (a) and (b)
    (d) Neither (a) nor (b)

5. The function =IF(A1>A2,A1+A2,A1*A2) returns
    (a) The product of cells A1 and A2 if cell A1 is greater than A2
    (b) The sum of cells A1 and A2 if cell A1 is less than A2
    (c) Both (a) and (b)
    (d) Neither (a) nor (b)

6. Which of the following is the preferred way to sum the values in cells A1 to A4?
    (a) =SUM(A1:A4)
    (b) =A1+A2+A3+A4
    (c) Either (a) or (b) is equally good
    (d) Neither (a) nor (b) is correct

7. Which of the following will return the highest and lowest arguments from a list?
    (a) HIGH/LOW
    (b) LARGEST/SMALLEST
    (c) MAX/MIN
    (d) All of the above

8. Which of the following is a *required* technique to develop the worksheet for the mortgage analysis?
    (a) Pointing
    (b) Copying with the fill handle
    (c) Both (a) and (b)
    (d) Neither (a) nor (b)

9. Given that cells B6, C6, and D6 contain the numbers 10, 20, and 30, respectively, what value will be returned by the function =IF(B6>10,C6*2,D6*3)?
    (a) 10
    (b) 40
    (c) 60
    (d) 90

10. Which formula will compute the age of a person born on March 16, 1977?
    (a) =TODAY() − DATE(77,3,16)
    (b) =TODAY() − DATE(77,3,16)/365
    (c) =(TODAY() − DATE(77,3,16))/365
    (d) =AGE(77,3,16)

11. What is the best way to enter January 21, 1994 into a worksheet, given that you create the worksheet on that date, and further, given that you always want to display that specific date?

   (a) =TODAY()

   (b) 1/21/94

   (c) Both (b) and (b) are equally acceptable

   (d) Neither (a) nor (b)

12. Which function returns the number of *numeric entries* in the range A2:A6?

   (a) =COUNT(A2:A6)

   (b) =COUNTA(A2:A6)

   (c) =COUNT(A2,A6)

   (d) =COUNTA(A2,A6)

13. What happens if you select a range, then press the right mouse button?

   (a) The range will be deselected

   (b) Nothing; that is, the button has no effect

   (c) The Edit and Format menus will be displayed in their entirety

   (d) A shortcut menu with commands from both the Edit and Format menus will be displayed

14. The worksheet displayed in the monitor shows columns A and B, skips columns D, E, and F, then displays columns G, H, I, J, and K. What is the most likely explanation for the missing columns?

   (a) The columns were previously deleted

   (b) The columns are empty and thus are automatically hidden from view

   (c) Either (a) or (b) is a satisfactory explanation

   (d) Neither (a) nor (b) is a likely reason

15. Given the function =VLOOKUP(C6,D12:F18,3)

   (a) The entries in cells D12 through D18 are in ascending order

   (b) The entries in cells D12 through D18 are in descending order

   (c) The entries in cells F12 through F18 are in ascending order

   (d) The entries in cells F12 through F18 are in descending order

ANSWERS

1. d	**4.** a	**7.** c	**10.** c	**13.** d
2. d	**5.** d	**8.** d	**11.** b	**14.** d
3. c	**6.** a	**9.** d	**12.** a	**15.** a

EXPLORING EXCEL

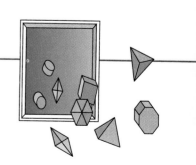

1. Use Figure 3.15 to match each action with its result; a given action may be used more than once, or not at all.

Action

a. Click at 12, type =AVERAGE(, then click at 8, drag to 11, and press enter

Result

___ Freeze column A and rows 1, 2, and 3 on the screen for scrolling

b. Click at 6, then click at 5

c. Click at 1

d. Click at 2

e. Click at 3

f. Click in the lower-right corner of 7, then drag to 10

g. Click at 17, then click at 4

h. Click at 12, drag to 13, then click at 9

i. Click the right mouse button at 17

j. Click at 14, type =, click at 16, type −, click at 15, then press enter

___ Use the autofill feature to enter the column titles for Test 2, Test 3, and Test 4

___ Increase the number of decimal places for the test averages

___ Use the Function Wizard to enter the current date in cell A1

___ Preview the worksheet prior to printing

___ Save the worksheet

___ Enter the formula to compute the range for the scores on Test 1

___ Display a shortcut menu in order to format the date that will be entered in cell A1

___ Enter the function to compute the test average for John Adams

___ Spell check the worksheet

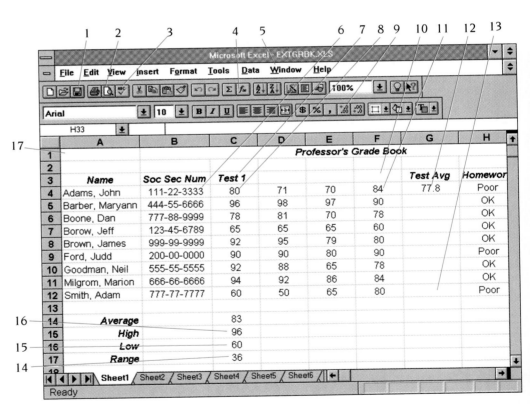

FIGURE 3.15 Screen for Problem 1

2. Consider the two worksheets shown in Figure 3.16 and the entries, =AVERAGE(A1:A4) versus =(A1+A2+A3+A4)/4, both of which calculate the average of cells A1 through A4. Assume that a new row is inserted in the worksheet between existing rows 2 and 3, with the entry in the new cell equal to 100.

a. What value will be returned by the AVERAGE function in worksheet 1 after the new row has been inserted?

b. What value will be returned by the formula in worksheet 2 after the new row has been inserted?

c. In which cell will the AVERAGE function itself be located after the new row has been inserted?

Return to the original problem, but this time delete row 2.

d. What value will be returned by the AVERAGE function in worksheet 1 after the row has been deleted?

e. What will be returned by the formula in worksheet 2 after the row has been deleted?

	A
1	10
2	20
3	30
4	40
5	=AVERAGE(A1:A4)

(a) Worksheet 1

	A
1	10
2	20
3	30
4	40
5	=(A1+A2+A3+A4)/4

(b) Worksheet 2

FIGURE 3.16 Worksheet for Problem 2

3. Answer the following with respect to Figure 3.17. (Cell B5 is empty.) What value will be returned by the worksheet functions?

a. =IF(A1=0,A2,A3)

b. =SUM(A1:A5)

c. =MAX(A1:A5,B1:B5)

d. =MIN(A1:A3,5,A5)

e. =AVERAGE(B1:B4)

f. =AVERAGE(B1:B5)

g. =MIN(10,MAX(A2:A4))

h. =MAX(10,MIN(A2:A4))

i. =COUNTA(A1:A5)

j. =COUNTA(B1:B5)

k. =COUNT(A1:A5)

l. =COUNT(B1:B5)

m. =VLOOKUP(15,A1:B5,2)

n. =VLOOKUP(20,A1:B5,2)

	A	B
1	10	60
2	20	70
3	30	80
4	40	90
5	50	

FIGURE 3.17 Worksheet for Problem 3

4. Refer to the worksheet in Figure 3.3b, which used the PMT function to compute the amortization schedule for a loan.

a. What formula (function) should be entered into cell C6?

b. What formula (function) should be entered into cell D9?

c. What formula should be entered into cell B10? (The amount of each payment that goes toward interest is the interest rate per period times the unpaid balance of the loan.)

d. What formula should be entered into cell C10? (The amount of each payment that goes toward the principal is the payment amount minus the amount that goes toward interest.)

e. What formula should be entered into cell D10?

f. Implement the worksheet in Excel, but supply your own parameters for the principal, interest, and length of the loan. Add your name somewhere in the worksheet, then print the worksheet as well as the cell formulas. Prepare a cover page and submit both printouts to your instructor.

5. The Autofill command: Create the worksheet in Figure 3.18, then select the cells in the range A1 through G1. Point to the fill handle and drag it to row 12.

a. What are the contents of cells A2 through A12? of cells B2 through B12? What can you conclude about the fill handle and the months of the year?

b. What are the contents of cells C2 through C12? of cells D2 through D12? What can you conclude about a repeating series?

c. What are the contents of cells E2 through E12? of cells F2 through F12? Are these results consistent with those of part b?

d. What are the contents of cells G2 through G12? How would you use the autofill feature to enter the years 1993, 1994, and so on in cells G2 through G12?

	A	B	C	D	E	F	G
1	January	Jan	1st Quarter	Quarter 1	Monday	Mon	1992
2							
3							
4							
5							
6							
7							
8							
9							
10							
11							
12							

FIGURE 3.18 The Autofill Command

6. Figure 3.19 contains a worksheet used to determine information about Certificates of Deposit purchased at First National Bank of Miami. Retrieve PROB0306.XLS from the data disk, then complete the worksheet following the steps below:

➤ Enter the function to display the current date in B1.

➤ Enter the formula to calculate the Maturity Date in cell E9. (To determine the Maturity Date, add the duration of the certificate to the date purchased.) Copy the formula to the remaining entries in the column.

➤ Move to cell F9 and enter the formula to calculate the number of days remaining until the certificate matures, or if the certificate has already matured, the text *Matured* should appear in the cell. The determination of whether or not the CD has matured can be made by comparing the Maturity Date to the current date; that is, if the Maturity Date is greater than the current date, the CD has not yet matured.

- Format all of the dates so that they are displayed in the dd-mm-yy format (e.g., 15-May-94 rather than 5/15/94).
- Format the Amount of CD with dollar signs and commas, but no decimal places.
- Center the entries in A3 and A4 over the width of the worksheet. Change the font to 14 point Arial bold italic.
- Boldface the column headings.
- Save and print the worksheet.

	A	B	C	D	E	F
1	Date:					
2						
3	Certificates of Deposit					
4	First National Bank of Miami					
5						
6						# of Days
7			Date		Maturity	Remaining
8	Customer	Amount of CD	Purchased	Duration	Date	Till Mature
9	Harris	500000	12/1/93	180		
10	Bodden	50000	1/30/94	180		
11	Dorsey	25000	2/3/94	180		
12	Rosell	10000	3/30/94	365		
13	Klinger	10000	4/1/94	365		

FIGURE 3.19 Spreadsheet for Problem 6

7. Figure 3.20 contains a worksheet used to determine information about software purchases for HOT SPOT Software Sales. Figure 3.20a shows the worksheet as it exists on disk, while Figure 3.20b shows the completed worksheet. Retrieve PROB0307.XLS from the data disk and complete it so that it is identical to the worksheet in Figure 3.20b. In doing so, you will need the following facts:

- The total sale is determined by multiplying the current price by the number of units sold.
- A discount is given if the total sale is equal to or greater than the discount threshold. (The amount of discount is determined by multiplying the total sale by the discount percentage. The exact percentage to be used is indicated in the assumption area at the bottom of the worksheet.) If the total sale is less than the discount threshold, no discount is given.
- The discounted total is determined by subtracting the amount of discount from the total sale.
- The sales tax is determined by multiplying the discounted total by the sales tax percentage (as indicated in the assumption area).
- The amount due is determined by adding the sales tax to the discounted total.
- The number of customers, highest current price, fewest units sold, average discount, and total amount due are determined by entering the appropriate functions in the indicated cells.

Would it be a good idea to lower the discount threshold to $500 and lower the discount percentage to 10%? Why or why not? Why should the discount threshold, discount percentage, and sales tax percentage be isolated from the main body of the worksheet? What advantages does this give you in working with the worksheet?

(a) Spreadsheet on Disk

	A	B	C	D	E	F	G	H	I
1	HOT SPOT Software Sales								
2	Miami, Florida								
3									
4	Customer		Current	Units	Total	Amount of	Discounted	Sales	Amount
5	Name	Program	Price	Sold	Sale	Discount	Total	Tax	Due
6	Macy's	Windows	59.99	2					
7	Kings Bay Athletics	Word for Windows	295	5					
8	Bloomingdale's	After Dark	29.95	10					
9	Service Merchandise	Excel	495	3					
10	Lord & Taylor	Lotus for Windows	595	3					
11	Burdine's	WordPerfect	245	2					
12	Sports Authority	Word for Windows	295	3					
13	The Gap	Excel	495	7					
14	Home Depot	Windows	59.99	12					
15	Brookstone	Lotus for Windows	595	8					
16	Coconuts	WordPerfect	245	10					
17	Express	Windows	59.99	3					
18									
19									
20	Discount Threshold:		1000				Number of Customers:		
21	Discount Percentage:		0.15				Highest Current Price:		
22	Sales Tax:		0.065				Fewest Units Sold:		
23							Average Discount:		
24							Total Amount Due:		

(a) Spreadsheet on Disk

(b) Completed Spreadsheet

	A	B	C	D	E	F	G	H	I
1	HOT SPOT Software Sales								
2	Miami, Florida								
3									
4	Customer		Current	Units	Total	Amount of	Discounted	Sales	Amount
5	Name	Program	Price	Sold	Sale	Discount	Total	Tax	Due
6	Macy's	Windows	$59.99	2	$119.98	$0.00	$119.98	$7.80	$127.78
7	Kings Bay Athletics	Word for Windows	$295.00	5	$1,475.00	$221.25	$1,253.75	$81.49	$1,335.24
8	Bloomingdale's	After Dark	$29.95	10	$299.50	$0.00	$299.50	$19.47	$318.97
9	Service Merchandise	Excel	$495.00	3	$1,485.00	$222.75	$1,262.25	$82.05	$1,344.30
10	Lord & Taylor	Lotus for Windows	$595.00	3	$1,785.00	$267.75	$1,517.25	$98.62	$1,615.87
11	Burdine's	WordPerfect	$245.00	2	$490.00	$0.00	$490.00	$31.85	$521.85
12	Sports Authority	Word for Windows	$295.00	3	$885.00	$0.00	$885.00	$57.53	$942.53
13	The Gap	Excel	$495.00	7	$3,465.00	$519.75	$2,945.25	$191.44	$3,136.69
14	Home Depot	Windows	$59.99	12	$719.88	$0.00	$719.88	$46.79	$766.67
15	Brookstone	Lotus for Windows	$595.00	8	$4,760.00	$714.00	$4,046.00	$262.99	$4,308.99
16	Coconuts	WordPerfect	$245.00	10	$2,450.00	$367.50	$2,082.50	$135.36	$2,217.86
17	Express	Windows	$59.99	3	$179.97	$0.00	$179.97	$11.70	$191.67
18									
19									
20	Discount Threshold:		$1,000				Number of Customers:		12
21	Discount Percentage:		15.0%				Highest Current Price:		$595.00
22	Sales Tax:		6.5%				Fewest Units Sold:		2
23							Average Discount:		$192.75
24							Total Amount Due:		$16,828.42

(b) Completed Spreadsheet

FIGURE 3.20   Spreadsheet for Problem 7

8. Figure 3.21 suggests how a worksheet can be extended to the preparation of sales invoices. The figure assumes the existence of a template that the user retrieves for each new order. All entries in the shaded area are made after the template is retrieved, depending on the particular order.

   a. What formula should you enter in cell D9 to compute the amount due for the first item?

   b. What entry should you use in cell D14 to compute the subtotal? Your answer should accommodate the potential insertion of additional rows (after row 12) should the customer order more than four items.

	A	B	C	D
1	*INVOICE*			16-Mar-94
2				
3	Customer:	Mr. John Doe		
4		10000 Sample Road		
5		Coral Springs, FL 33065		
6	Tax Status:	Exempt		
7				
8	Quantity	Item	Unit Price	Amount
9	15	Widgets (small)	$14.00	$210.00
10	6	Widgets (medium)	$20.00	$120.00
11	2	Widgets (large)	$25.00	$50.00
12	14	Widgets (extra large)	$30.00	$420.00
13				
14		Subtotal		$800.00
15		Discount	10%	$80.00
16		Sales Tax		$0.00
17			Total	$720.00
18				
19				
20				
21				
22				
23	Sales Tax		Discount	
24	6%		$200	2%
25			$400	5%
26			$750	10%

FIGURE 3.21 Spreadsheet for Problem 8

c. What entry should you use in cell C15 to determine the discount percentage (based on the table shown in the lower-right portion of the worksheet)?

d. What entry should you use in cell D15 to compute the discount?

e. What formula should you use to compute the sales tax? (Customers with a tax status of "Exempt" pay no tax; all other customers pay the tax rate shown in cell A24 for the discounted order.)

f. What formula should you use in cell D17 for the total due?

g. Implement the worksheet in the figure, add your name as the customer, and submit the assignment to your instructor.

9. Use Figure 3.1 at the beginning of the chapter as the basis for this exercise.

a. Open the PROB0309.XLS on the data disk.

b. Enter the parameters for your specific car in cells B1, B2, and B3 as in Figure 3.1. Enter the terms of the loan in cells B5 and B6 to determine the projected monthly payment.

c. The monthly payment is only one expense; that is, a realistic estimate requires insurance, gas, and maintenance. Enter these labels in cells A8, A9, and A10, then put the projected expenses in cells B8, B9, and B10.

d. Add the label *Total* in cell A11, and the formula to compute this amount in cell B11.

e. Insert two rows at the top of the worksheet to accommodate the title of the worksheet. Click in cell A1 and type the title of the worksheet, *Can I Afford It?,* followed by your name.

f. Format the title in boldface, italics, and/or a larger typeface. Leave row 2 blank to offset the title from the remainder of the worksheet.

g. The worksheet can make the decision for you. Click in cell A13 and enter the label, *The Decision. . :* Enter an IF function in cell B13 that will display Yes if the total expenses are $500 or less, and No otherwise.

h. Save the updated workbook.

i. Print the entire worksheet two ways, once with computed values and once with cell formulas. Submit both worksheets to your instructor.

10. Inserting an object: This exercises requires the availability of the ClipArt subdirectory in Word for Windows (or any other clip art collection). Use Figure 3.22 as a guide in the exercise.

a. Open the MORTGAGE.XLS workbook from the first hands-on exercise.

b. Click anywhere in column E, the place where you want the picture to go.

c. Pull down the Insert menu. Click Picture.

d. Click on drive C (or whichever drive contains the WINWORD subdirectory).

e. Double click on the WINWORD subdirectory. Double click the CLIPART subdirectory within the WINWORD directory.

f. If necessary, check the Preview Picture box so that you can see the picture prior to inserting it into the worksheet. Click the picture you want—for example, HOUSES.WMF—then click OK.

g. The picture is now in the worksheet where you can use the normal Windows commands to size and/or move the object.

h Pull down the File menu to save the workbook with the embedded graphic.

i. Print the completed worksheet, graphic and all.

	A	B	C	D	E	F	G	H
1	Amount Borrowed		$100,000					
2	Starting Interest		7.50%					
3								
4		Monthly Payment						
5	Interest	30 Years	15 Years	Difference				
6	7.50%	$699.21	$927.01	$227.80				
7	8.50%	$768.91	$984.74	$215.83				
8	9.50%	$840.85	$1,044.22	$203.37				
9	10.50%	$914.74	$1,105.40	$190.66				
10	11.50%	$990.29	$1,168.19	$177.90				
11	12.50%	$1,067.26	$1,232.52	$165.26				
12								
13	Financial consultant:		Bess Marder					

FIGURE 3.22 Inserting an Object (problem 10)

Case Studies

Startup Airlines

You have been hired as the spreadsheet expert for a small start-up airline that needs to calculate the fuel requirements and associated cost for its available flights. The airline currently has two types of aircraft, a Boeing-727 and a DC-9, which consume 10,000 and 8,000 gallons of fuel, respectively, for each hour in the air. The fuel needed for any given flight depends on the aircraft and number of flying hours; for example, a five-hour flight in a DC-9 can be expected to use 40,000 gallons. In addition, the plane must carry an additional 10% of the required fuel to maintain a holding pattern (4,000 gallons in this example) and an additional 20% as reserve (8,000 gallons in this example). Use the data in AIRLINES.XLS to compute the fuel necessary for the listed flights as well as the estimated cost based on a fuel price of $1.00 per gallon. Your worksheet should be completely flexible and amenable to change; that is, the hourly fuel requirements, price per gallon, and holding and reserve percentages are all subject to change at a moment's notice.

The Financial Consultant

A friend of yours is in the process of buying a home and has asked you to compare the payments and total interest on a 15- and a 30-year loan. You want to do as professional a job as possible and have decided to analyze the loans in Excel, then incorporate the results into a memo written in Word for Windows. As of now the principal is $150,000, but it is very likely that your friend will change his mind several times, and so you want to use the OLE capability within Windows to dynamically link the worksheet to the word processing document. Your memo should include a letterhead that takes advantage of the formatting capabilities within Word; a graphic logo would be a nice touch.

Compensation Analysis

A corporation typically uses several different measures of compensation in an effort to pay its employees fairly. Most organizations closely monitor an employee's salary history, keeping both the present and previous salary in order to compute various statistics, including:

➤ The percent salary increase, which is computed by taking the difference between the present and previous salary, and dividing by the previous salary.
➤ The months between increase, which is the elapsed time between the date the present salary took effect and the date of the previous salary. (Assume 30 days per month for ease of calculation.)
➤ The annualized rate of increase, which is the percent salary increase divided by the months between increase (expressed as a fraction of a year); for example, a 5% raise after 6 months is equivalent to an annualized increase of 10%; a 5% raise after two years is equivalent to an annual increase of 2.5%.

Use the data in SALARIES.XLS to compute salary statistics for the employees who have had a salary increase; employees who have not received an increase should have a suitable indication in the cell. Compute the average, minimum, and maximum value for each measure of compensation for those employees who have received an increase.

The Automobile Dealership

The purchase of a car usually entails extensive bargaining between the dealer and the consumer. The dealer has an asking price but typically settles for less. The commission paid to a salesperson depends on how close the selling price is to the asking price. Exotic Motors has the following compensation policy for its sales staff:

➤ A 3% commission on the actual selling price for cars sold at 95% or more of the asking price.
➤ A 2% commission on the actual selling price for cars sold at 90% or more (but less than 95%) of the asking price.
➤ A 1% commission on the actual selling price for cars sold at less than 90% of the asking price. The dealer will not go below 85% of his asking price.

The dealer's asking price is based on the dealer's cost plus a 20% markup; for example, the asking price on a car that cost the dealer $20,000 would be $24,000.

Develop a worksheet to be used by the dealer, which shows his profit (the selling price minus the salesperson's commission) on every sale. The worksheet should be completely flexible and allow the dealer to vary the markup or commission percentages without having to edit or recopy any of the formulas. Use the data in EXOTIC.XLS to test your worksheet.

The Birthday Problem

How much would you bet *against* two people in your class having the same birthday? Don't be too hasty, for the odds of two classmates sharing the same birthday (month and day) are much higher than you would expect; for example, there is a 50% chance in a class of 23 students that two people will have been born on the same day. The probability jumps to 70% in a class of 30, and to 90% in a class of 41.

You need a basic knowledge of probability to prove these statements, but the solution is readily amenable to a spreadsheet. In essence, you calculate the probability of individuals *not* having the same birthday, then subtract this number from 1, to obtain the probability of the event coming true. In a group of two people, for example, the probability of *not* being born on the same day is 365/366; that is, the second person can be born on any of 365 days and still have a different birthday. The probability of two people having the same birthday becomes $1 - 365/366$.

The probability for *different* birthdays in a group of three people is $(365/366)*(364/366)$; the probability of *not* having different birthdays; that is, of two people having the same birthday, is 1 minus this number. In similar fashion the probability for different birthdays in a group of four people is $(365/366)*(364/366)*(363/366)$, and so on. Can you develop a worksheet that shows the probability of two people being born on the same day in classes of up to 50 students?

4

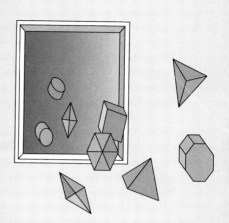

Graphs and Charts: Delivering a Message

After reading this chapter you will be able to:

1. Distinguish between different types of charts, stating the advantages and disadvantages of each.
2. Distinguish between a chart embedded in a worksheet versus one in a separate chart sheet; explain how many charts can be associated with the same worksheet.
3. Use the ChartWizard to create and/or modify a chart.
4. Enhance a chart by using arrows and text.
5. Differentiate between data series specified in rows versus data series specified in columns.
6. Describe how a chart can be statistically accurate, yet totally misleading.
7. Create a compound document consisting of a word processing memo, a worksheet, and a chart.

OVERVIEW

Business has always known that the graphic representation of data is an attractive, easy-to-understand way to convey information. Indeed, business graphics has become one of the most exciting Windows applications, enabling charts (graphs) to be easily created from a worksheet, with just a few simple keystrokes or mouse clicks.

The chapter begins by emphasizing the importance of determining the message to be conveyed by a chart. It describes the different types of charts available within Excel and how to choose among them. It explains how to create a chart by using the ChartWizard, how to embed a chart within a worksheet, and how to create a chart in a separate chart sheet. It also describes how to enhance a chart with arrows and additional text.

The second half of the chapter explains how one chart can plot multiple sets of data, and how several charts can be based on the same worksheet. It describes

125

how to create a compound document, in which a chart and its associated worksheet are dynamically linked to a memo created by a word processor. All told, we think you will find this to be one of the most enjoyable chapters in the text.

CHART TYPES

A *chart* is a graphic representation of data in a worksheet. The chart is created from values in the worksheet known as *data points*. The data points are grouped into one or more *data series*. Each data series appears as a row or column in the worksheet.

The worksheet in Figure 4.1 will be used throughout the chapter as the basis for the charts we will create. Your manager believes that the sales data can be understood more easily from charts than from the strict numerical presentation of a worksheet. You have been given the assignment of analyzing the data in the worksheet and are developing a series of charts to convey that information.

	A	B	C	D	E	F
1	Superior Software Monthly Sales					
2						
3		*Miami*	*Denver*	*New York*	*Boston*	*Total*
4	Word Processing	$50,000	$67,500	$9,500	$141,000	$268,000
5	Spreadsheets	$44,000	$18,000	$11,500	$105,000	$178,500
6	Database	$12,000	$7,500	$6,000	$30,000	$55,500
7	Total	$106,000	$93,000	$27,000	$276,000	$502,000

FIGURE 4.1 Superior Software

The sales data in the worksheet can be presented several ways—for example, by city, by product, or by a combination of the two. Ask yourself which type of chart is best suited to answer the following questions:

➤ What percentage of total revenue comes from each city? from each product?
➤ What is the dollar revenue produced by each city? by each product?
➤ What is the rank of each city with respect to sales?
➤ How much revenue does each product contribute in each city?

In every instance realize that a chart exists only to deliver a message, and that you cannot create an effective chart unless you are sure of what that message is. The next several pages discuss the different types of business charts, each of which is best suited to a particular type of message.

KEEP IT SIMPLE

Keep it simple. This rule applies to both your message and the means of conveying that message. Excel makes it almost too easy to change fonts, styles, type sizes, and colors, and such changes often detract from a chart rather than enhance it. More is not necessarily better, and just because the features are there, does not mean you have to use them. Remember that a chart must ultimately succeed on the basis of content and content alone.

Pie Charts

A *pie chart* is the most effective way to display proportional relationships. It is the type of chart to select whenever words like *percentage* or *market share* appear in the message to be delivered. The pie, or complete circle, denotes the total amount. Each slice of the pie corresponds to the appropriate percentage of the total.

The pie chart in Figure 4.2a divides the pie representing total sales into four slices, one for each city. The size of each slice is proportional to the percentage of total sales in that city. The chart depicts a single data series, which appears in cells B7 through E7 on the associated worksheet. The data series has four data points corresponding to the total sales in each city.

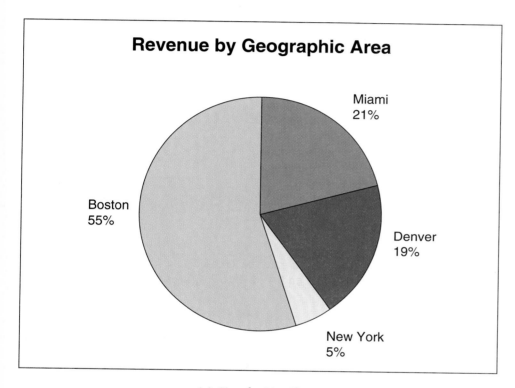

Revenue by Geographic Area

Miami 21%
Denver 19%
New York 5%
Boston 55%

(a) Simple Pie Chart

FIGURE 4.2 Pie Charts

To create the pie chart, Excel computes the total sales ($502,000 in our example), calculates the percentage contributed by each city, and draws each slice of the pie in proportion to its computed percentage. Boston's sales of $276,000 account for 55 percent of the total, and so this slice of the pie is allotted 55 percent of the area of the circle.

An *exploded pie chart,* as shown in Figure 4.2b, separates one or more slices of the pie for emphasis. Another way to achieve emphasis in a chart is to choose a title that reflects the message you are trying to deliver. The title in Figure 4.2a, for example, *Revenue by Geographic Area,* is neutral and leaves the reader to develop his or her own conclusion about the relative contribution of each area. By contrast, the title in Figure 4.2b, *New York Accounts for only 5% of Revenue,* is more suggestive and emphasizes the problems in this office. Alternatively, the chart could be retitled to *Boston Exceeds 50% of Total Revenue* if the intent were to emphasize the contribution of Boston.

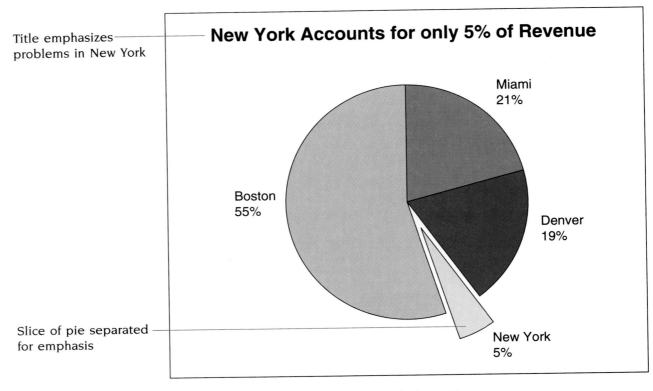

Title emphasizes problems in New York

New York Accounts for only 5% of Revenue

Miami
21%

Denver
19%

New York
5%

Boston
55%

Slice of pie separated for emphasis

(b) Exploded Pie Chart

FIGURE 4.2 Pie Charts (continued)

Three-dimensional pie charts may be created in exploded or nonexploded format as shown in Figures 4.2c and 4.2d. Excel also enables you to add arrows and text for emphasis.

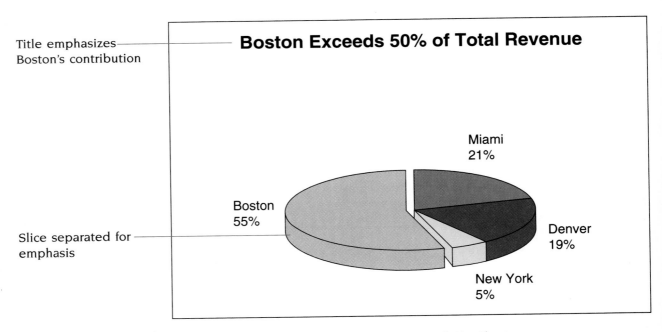

Title emphasizes Boston's contribution

Boston Exceeds 50% of Total Revenue

Miami
21%

Denver
19%

New York
5%

Boston
55%

Slice separated for emphasis

(c) Three-Dimensional Pie Chart

FIGURE 4.2 Pie Charts (continued)

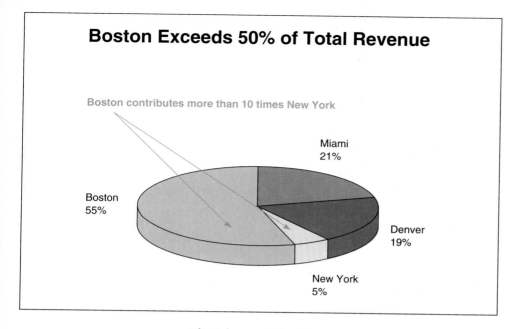

Boston Exceeds 50% of Total Revenue

Boston contributes more than 10 times New York

Miami
21%

Boston
55%

Denver
19%

New York
5%

(d) Enhanced Pie Chart

FIGURE 4.2 Pie Charts (continued)

A pie chart is easiest to read when the number of slices is limited (not more than six or seven), and when small categories (percentages less than five) are not plotted individually. The latter may be avoided by grouping small categories into a single class labeled *Other*.

EXPLODED PIE CHARTS

Click and drag wedges in and out of a pie chart to convert an ordinary pie chart to an exploded pie chart. For best results, pull the wedge out only slightly from the main body of the pie.

Column and Bar Charts

A *column chart* is used when there is a need to show actual numbers rather than percentages. The column chart in Figure 4.3a plots the same data series as the earlier pie chart, but displays it differently. The values for the descriptive category (Miami, Denver, New York, and Boston) are shown along the *X* (horizontal) *axis.* The values of the quantitative variable (monthly sales) are plotted along the *Y* (vertical) *axis.* The height of each column reflects the value of the quantitative variable.

A column chart can be given a horizontal orientation and converted to a *bar chart* as in Figure 4.3b. Some individuals prefer the bar chart over the corresponding column chart because the longer horizontal bars accentuate the difference between the cities. Bar charts are also preferable when the descriptive labels are long and you want to eliminate the crowding that can occur along the horizontal axis of a column chart. As with the pie chart, a title can be developed to lead the reader and further emphasize the message—for example, *Boston Leads All Cities,* in Figure 4.3b.

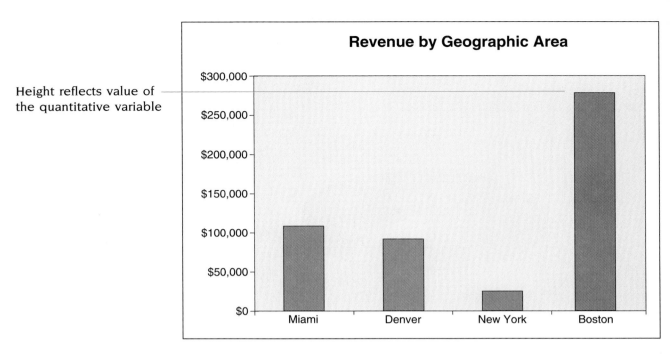

Height reflects value of the quantitative variable

(a) Column Chart

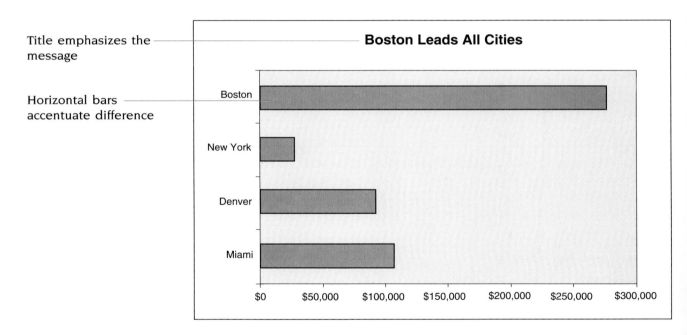

Title emphasizes the message

Horizontal bars accentuate difference

(b) Horizontal Bar Chart

FIGURE 4.3 Column/Bar Charts

A three-dimensional column chart can produce added interest as shown in Figures 4.3c and 4.3d. Figure 4.3d plots a different set of numbers than we have seen so far (the sales for each application, rather than the sales for each city). And again, arrows and text can be added to any chart to enhance the message.

As with a pie chart, column and bar charts are easiest to read when the number of categories is relatively small (seven or less). Otherwise the columns (bars) are plotted so close together that labeling becomes impossible.

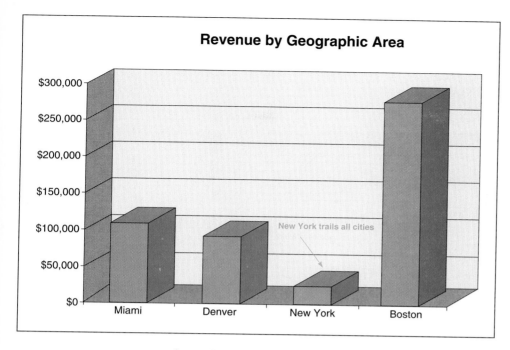

(c) Three-dimensional Column Chart

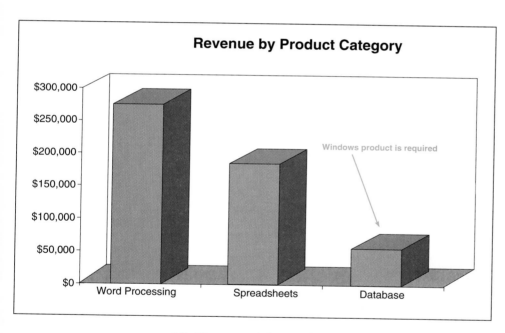

(d) Alternate Column Chart

FIGURE 4.3 Column/Bar Charts (continued)

CREATING A CHART

There are two ways to create a chart in Excel. You can *embed* the chart in a worksheet, or you can create the chart in a separate *chart sheet.* Figure 4.4a displays an embedded column chart. Figure 4.4b shows a pie chart in its own chart sheet. Both techniques are equally valid. The choice between the two depends on personal preference.

Regardless of where it is kept (embedded in a worksheet or in its own chart sheet), a chart is linked to the worksheet on which it is based. The charts in Figure 4.4 plot the same data series (the total sales for each city). Change any of these data points on the worksheet, and both charts will be updated automatically to reflect the new data.

Workbook name ————

Embedded chart ————

Quantitative variables match total sales in B7:E7 ————

Sizing handle ————

Category labels match entries in B3:E3 ————

Renamed tabs indicate contents of associated sheet ————

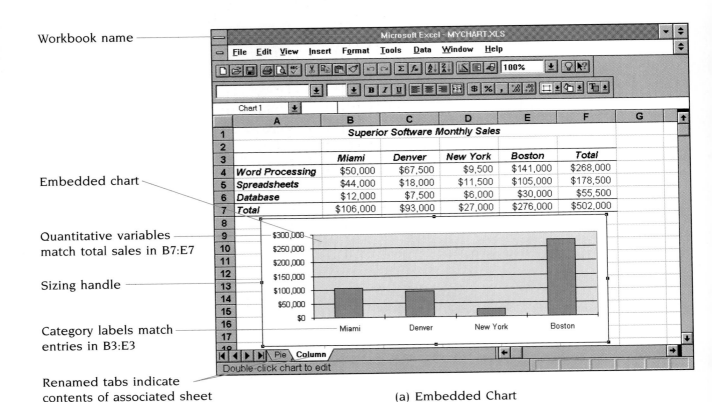

(a) Embedded Chart

FIGURE 4.4 Creating a Chart

Both charts are part of the same workbook (MYCHART.XLS as indicated in the title bar of each figure). The tabs within the workbook have been renamed to indicate the contents of the associated sheet. Additional charts may be created and embedded in the worksheet and/or created in additional chart sheets. And, as previously stated, if you change the worksheet, the chart (or charts) based upon it will also change.

Study the column chart in Figure 4.4a to see how it corresponds to the worksheet on which it is based. The descriptive names on the X axis are known as *category labels* and match the entries in cells B3 through E3. The quantitative values (data points) plotted on the Y axis match the total sales in cells B7 through E7. Even the numeric format matches; that is, the currency format used in the worksheet appears automatically on the scale of the Y axis.

The *sizing handles* on the embedded chart indicate it is currently selected and can be sized, moved, or deleted the same way as any Windows object:

➤ To size the selected chart, point to a sizing handle (the mouse pointer changes to a double arrow), then drag the handle in the desired direction.

➤ To move the selected chart, point to its border (the mouse pointer is a single arrow), then drag the chart to its new location.

➤ To delete the selected chart, press the Del key.

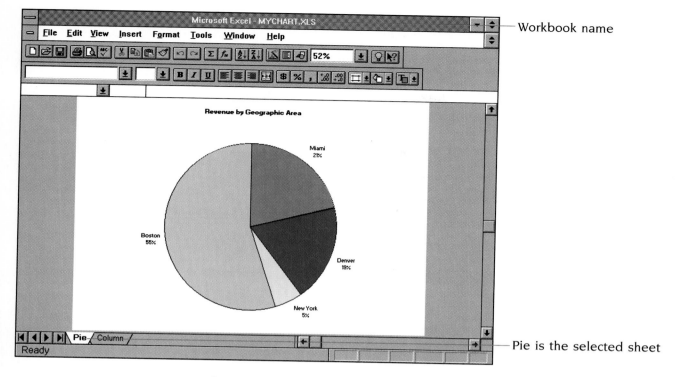

Workbook name

Pie is the selected sheet

(b) Chart Sheet

FIGURE 4.4   Creating a Chart (continued)

The same operations apply to any of the objects within the chart (e.g., its title) as will be discussed in the section on enhancing a chart.

The ChartWizard

The *ChartWizard* is the easiest way to create a chart. Just select the cells that contain the data, click the ChartWizard icon on the Standard toolbar, and let the Wizard do the rest. The process is illustrated in Figure 4.5, which shows how the Wizard creates a column chart to plot total sales by geographic area.

The steps in Figure 4.5 appear automatically, one after the other, as you click the Next command button to move from one step to the next. You can retrace

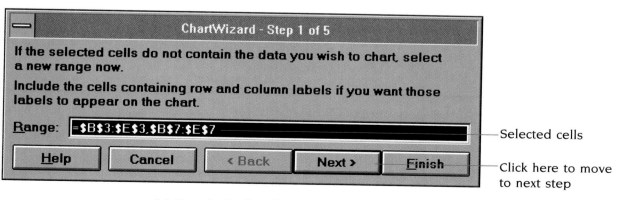

Selected cells

Click here to move to next step

(a) Step 1—Define the Range

FIGURE 4.5   The ChartWizard

Selected chart type

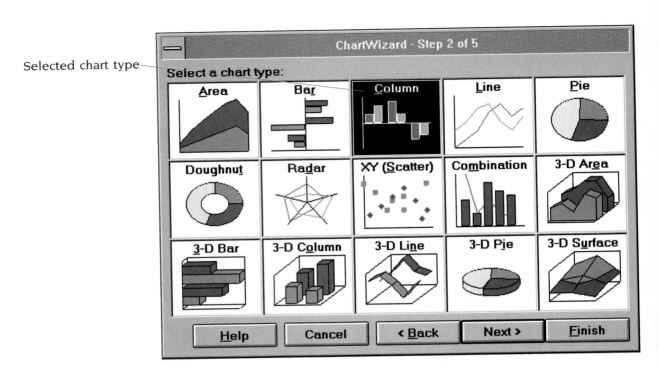

(b) Step 2—Select the Chart Type

Selected format

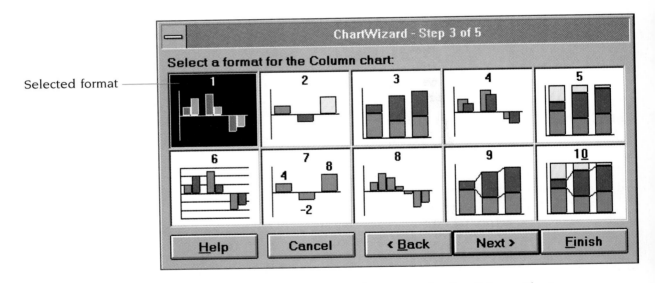

(c) Step 3—Select the Format for the Column Chart

FIGURE 4.5 The ChartWizard (continued)

your steps at any time by pressing the Back command button, access the on-line help facility with the Help command button, or negate the process with the Cancel command button.

Step 1, shown in Figure 4.5a, confirms the range of selected cells, $B$3:$E$3 (containing the city names) and $B$7:$E$7 (containing the total sales for each city). Step 2 asks you to choose one of the available chart types, and step 3 has you choose the specific format for the type of chart you selected. Step 4 shows you a preview of the completed chart. (The distinction between data series in rows

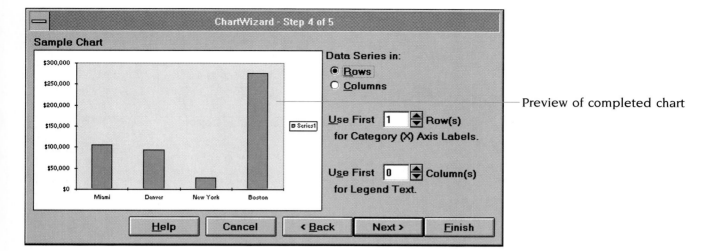

Preview of completed chart

(d) Step 4—Preview the Chart

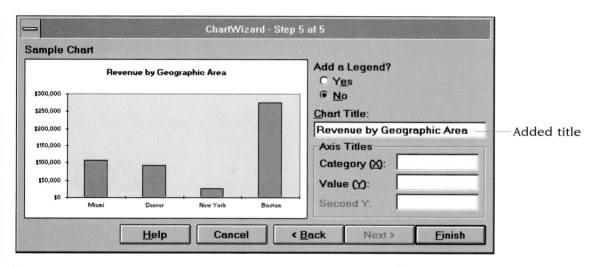

Added title

(e) Step 5—Add Legends and Titles

FIGURE 4.5   The ChartWizard (continued)

versus columns is explained after the hands-on exercise.) Step 5 enables you to add a title and a legend. It's that simple and the entire process takes but a few minutes.

Enhancing a Chart

After you create a chart, you can enhance it in several ways. You can change the chart type, add (remove) a legend, and/or add (remove) gridlines. You can select any part of the chart (e.g., the title) and change its formatting. You can also add arrows and text.

Figure 4.6 displays an enhanced version of the column chart that was created by using the ChartWizard in Figure 4.5. The chart type has been changed to a three-dimensional column chart, and gridlines have been added. Both changes were accomplished by using icons on the ***Chart toolbar.***

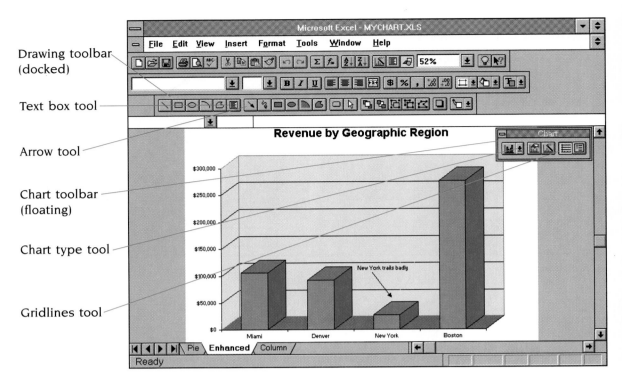

Drawing toolbar (docked)

Text box tool

Arrow tool

Chart toolbar (floating)

Chart type tool

Gridlines tool

FIGURE 4.6 Enhancing a Chart

A text box and an arrow have been added by using the corresponding tools on the ***Drawing toolbar***. A ***text box*** is a block of text that is added to a chart (or worksheet) for emphasis. You can format all or part of the text by selecting it and choosing a different font or point size. You can also apply boldface or italics. Text wraps within the box as it is entered. The text box and ***arrow tool*** are not part of the chart per se, but are inserted as objects that can be moved and sized independently of the chart.

FLOATING TOOLBARS

Any toolbar can be docked along the edge of the application window, or it can be displayed as a floating toolbar within the application window. To move a ***docked toolbar,*** drag the toolbar background. To move a ***floating toolbar*** drag its title bar. To size a floating toolbar, drag any border in the direction you want to go. Double click the background of any toolbar to toggle between a floating toolbar and a docked (fixed) toolbar.

HANDS-ON EXERCISE 1:

The ChartWizard

Objective To create and modify a chart by using ChartWizard; to embed a chart within a worksheet; to create a chart in its own sheet; to enhance a chart to include arrows and text.

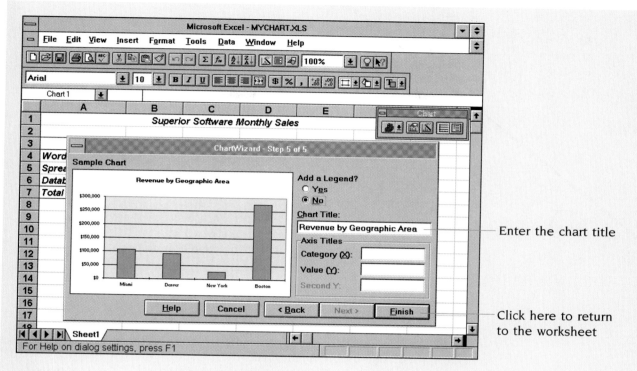

Enter the chart title

Click here to return
to the worksheet

(c) The ChartWizard (step 3)

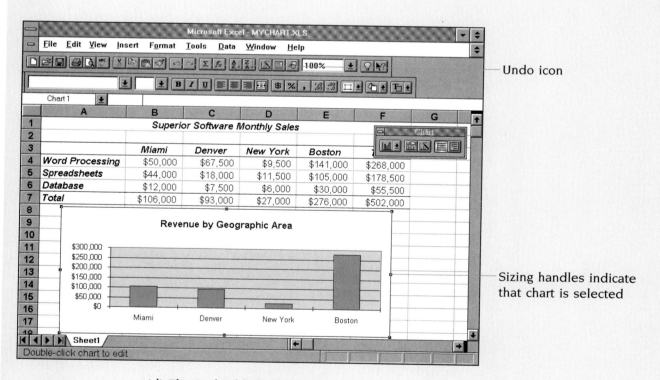

Undo icon

Sizing handles indicate
that chart is selected

(d) The Embedded Chart (step 4)

FIGURE 4.7 Hands-on Exercise 1 (continued)

Step 4: Delete the chart

➤ The chart should be selected from the previous step; if not, click just above the top gridline to select it.

➤ Press the **Del key.** The chart disappears from the worksheet. Click the **Undo icon** on the Standard toolbar to cancel the last command. The chart is back in the worksheet.

➤ Click anywhere outside the chart to deselect it.

MOVING AND SIZING THE EMBEDDED CHART

To move the embedded chart within a worksheet, click anywhere in the chart to select the chart, then drag it to a new location. To size the chart, select it, then drag any of the eight sizing handles in the desired direction.

Step 5: Change the worksheet

➤ Click in cell **B4.** Change the entry to **$300,000.** Press the **enter key.** The totals in cells F4, B7, and F7 change automatically to reflect the increased sales for word processing in the Miami office.

➤ The column for Miami also changes in the chart and is now larger than the column for Boston.

➤ Click the **Undo** button on the Standard toolbar to return to the initial value of $50,000.

➤ The worksheet and chart are restored to their values as shown in Figure 4.7d.

THE FORMAT OBJECT COMMAND

Dress up an embedded chart by changing its border. Select the chart, pull down Format menu, then click Object to produce the Format Object dialog box. Click the Patterns tab, which displays check boxes to choose a shadow effect and rounded corners. You can also specify a different border style, thickness, or color as well as a background color and/or pattern for the entire chart. Click OK to exit the dialog box.

Step 6: Modify the chart

➤ Double click anywhere in the chart to select it for editing. The chart is enclosed in a hashed line as shown in Figure 4.7e.

➤ Pull down the **Format menu.** Click **Chart Type** to display the dialog box in Figure 4.7e.

➤ Click the box containing a **Pie chart.** Click the **3-D option button.** Click **OK.** You will see a three-dimensional pie chart, but the slices are not yet labeled.

➤ Pull down the **Format menu** a second time. Click **AutoFormat** to display a dialog box with various types of pie charts. Click format **number 7,** which will label the slices of the pie with percentages and the city names. Click **OK.** The completed pie chart is shown in Figure 4.7f.

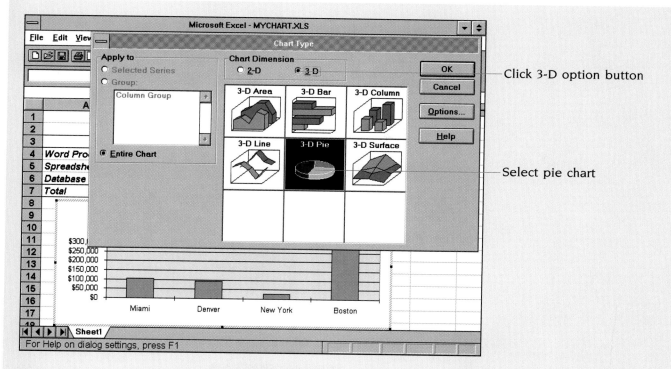

Click 3-D option button

Select pie chart

(e) Change the Chart Type (step 6)

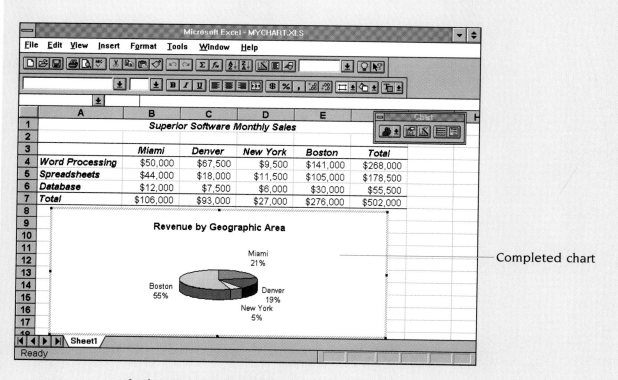

Completed chart

(f) The Completed 3-D Pie Chart (step 6)

FIGURE 4.7 Hands-on Exercise 1 (continued)

Step 7: Create a second chart

➤ Drag the mouse over cells **A4 through A6** to select the category labels (the software categories) as shown in Figure 4.7g.

➤ Press and hold the **Ctrl key** as you drag the mouse over cells **F4 through F6** to select the data series (the cells containing the total sales for the product categories).

➤ Pull down the **Insert menu.** Click **Chart.** Click **As New Sheet** as shown in Figure 4.7g.

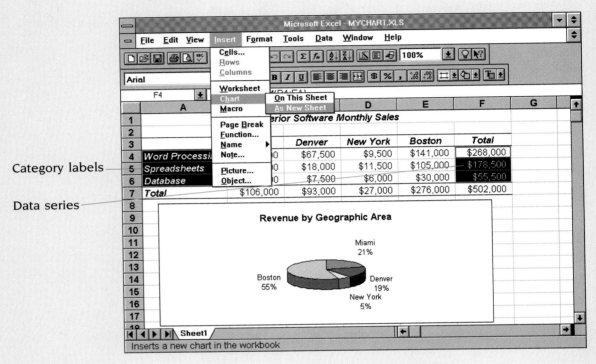

(g) Insert Chart Command (step 7)

FIGURE 4.7   Hands-on Exercise 1 (continued)

Step 8: The ChartWizard

➤ You should see step 1 of the ChartWizard with cells A4:A6 and F4:F6 selected. Click the **Next command button** if the range is correct; click the **Cancel command button** if the range is incorrect and begin again.

➤ Click the icon for a **3-D Column chart.** Click the **Next command button.**

➤ Click the column chart format in **box number 1** (the default). Click the **Next command button.**

➤ View the sample chart shown in step 4 of the ChartWizard:
   — If you are satisfied, click the **Next command button.**
   — If you are not satisfied, click the **Back command button** to return to the previous step, where you can change the chart format.

➤ Complete the chart in step 5 of the ChartWizard:
   — Click the **No option button** to suppress the legend.
   — Click in the text box. Type **Revenue by Product Category.**
   — Click the **Finish command button.**

➤ You should see the chart in Figure 4.7h, but without the text box and arrow.

➤ Save the workbook.

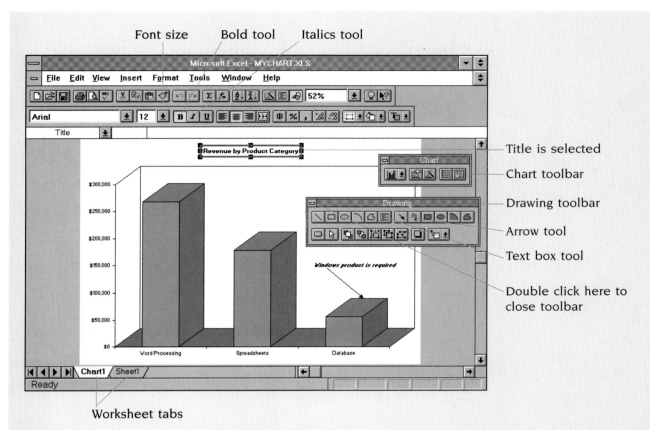

Font size   Bold tool   Italics tool

Title is selected

Chart toolbar

Drawing toolbar

Arrow tool

Text box tool

Double click here to close toolbar

Worksheet tabs

(h) Enhance the Chart (step 9)

FIGURE 4.7   Hands-on Exercise 1 (continued)

Step 9: Workbook tabs

➤ The 3-D column chart has been created in the chart sheet labeled Chart1. Click the **Sheet1 tab** to return to the worksheet and embedded chart from the first part of the exercise.

➤ Click the **Chart1 tab** to return to the chart sheet containing the 3-D column chart.

THE SHORTCUT MENU

Point to a cell (or group of selected cells), a worksheet tab, a toolbar, or chart (or a selected part of the chart), then click the **right mouse button** to display a shortcut menu. All shortcut menus are context sensitive and display commands appropriate for the selected item.

Step 10: Enhance the chart

➤ Point to any visible toolbar. Click the **right mouse button** to display the Toolbar shortcut menu. Click **Drawing** to display the Drawing toolbar, which will be used to enhance the chart.

➤ Click the **black arrow button** on the Drawing toolbar. The mouse pointer changes to a thin cross.

➤ Click in the chart where you want the arrow to begin, drag the mouse to extend the arrow, then release the mouse to complete the arrow as shown in Figure 4.7h.

➤ Click the **text box button** on the Drawing toolbar. The mouse pointer changes to a thin cross. Click in the chart where you want the text box to begin, drag the mouse to extend the box, then release the mouse.

➤ Click the **Boldface** and **Italics icons** on the Formatting toolbar. Type **Windows product is required** as shown in Figure 4.7h. Click outside the text box to complete the entry.

➤ Click the title of the Chart. You will see sizing handles around the title to indicate it has been selected.

➤ Click the arrow on the Font Size box on the Formatting toolbar. Click **18** to increase the size of the title.

➤ Double click the control-menu box on the Drawing toolbar to close it.

➤ Save the workbook.

Step 11: Print the worksheet
➤ Pull down the **File menu** and click **Print** to display the dialog box in Figure 4.7i.

➤ Click the appropriate option button according to the item(s) you wish to print; for example, click **Selected Sheet(s)** to print just the column chart. Click **OK** to print the selection.

Click here to display TipWizard box

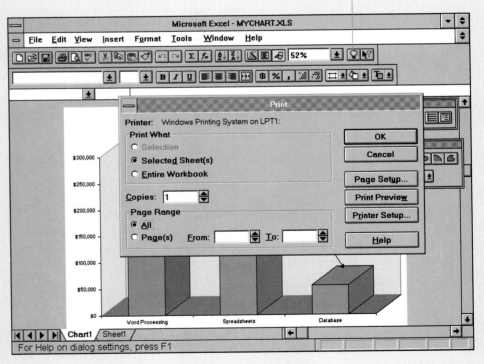

(i) Print the Chart (step 10)

FIGURE 4.7 Hands-on Exercise 1 (continued)

➤ Click the **TipWizard icon** to open the TipWizard box. Click the **up arrow** on
the tip box to review the suggestions made by the TipWizard during the exercise.

➤ Pull down the **File menu.** Click **Exit** to quit Excel.

MULTIPLE DATA SERIES

The charts presented so far displayed only a single data series—for example, the
total sales by location or the total sales by product category. Although such charts
are useful, it is often necessary to view *multiple data series* on the same chart.

Figure 4.8a displays the sales in each location according to product category.
We see the rankings within each city, and further, that word processing is the leading application in three of the four cities. Figure 4.8b plots the identical data but
in stacked columns rather than side-by-side.

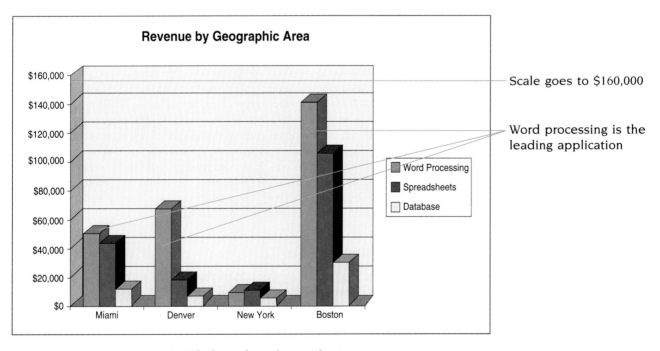

(a) Side-by-side Column Chart

FIGURE 4.8   Column Charts

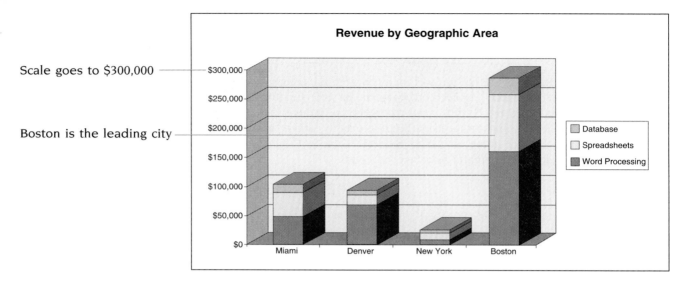

Scale goes to $300,000 ———

Boston is the leading city ———

(b) Stacked Column Chart

FIGURE 4.8 Column Charts (continued)

The choice between the two types of charts depends on your message. If, for example, you want your audience to see the individual sales in each product category, the *side-by-side columns* are more appropriate. If, on the other hand, you want to emphasize the total sales for each city, the *stacked columns* are preferable. Note, too, the different scale on the Y axis in the two charts. The side-by-side columns in Figure 4.8a show the sales of each product category and so the Y axis goes only to $160,000. The stacked columns in Figure 4.8b, however, reflect the total sales for each city and thus the scale goes to $300,000.

The biggest difference is that the stacked column explicitly totals the sales for each city while the side-by-side column does not. The advantage of the stacked column is that the city totals are clearly shown and can be easily compared, and further, the relative contributions of each product category within each city are apparent. The disadvantage is that the segments within each column do not start at the same point, making it difficult to determine the actual sales for the individual product categories or to compare the product categories between cities.

Realize too, that for a stacked column chart to make sense, its numbers must be additive. This is true in Figure 4.8b, where the stacked columns consist of three components, each of which is measured in dollars, and which can be logically added together to produce a total. You shouldn't, however, automatically convert a side-by-side column chart to its stacked column equivalent. It would not make sense, for example, to convert a column chart that plots unit sales and dollar sales side by side, to a stacked column chart that adds the two. Units and dollars represent different physical concepts, and are not additive.

Rows versus Columns

Figure 4.9 illustrates a critical concept associated with multiple data series—whether the data series are in rows or columns. Figure 4.9a displays the worksheet we have been using throughout the chapter with multiple data series selected. Figure 4.9b contains the resultant chart when the data series are in rows (B4:E4, B5:E5, and B6:E6). Figure 4.9c displays the chart based on data series in columns (B4:B6, C4:C6, D4:D6, and E4:E6).

Both charts plot a total of twelve data points (three product categories for each of four locations) but group the data differently. Figure 4.9b displays the data

	A	B	C	D	E	F
1		*Superior Software Monthly Sales*				
2						
3		*Miami*	*Denver*	*New York*	*Boston*	*Total*
4	Word Processing	$50,000	$67,500	$9,500	$141,000	$268,000
5	Spreadsheets	$44,000	$18,000	$11,500	$105,000	$178,500
6	Database	$12,000	$7,500	$6,000	$30,000	$55,500
7	Total	$106,000	$93,000	$27,000	$276,000	$502,000

(a) The Worksheet

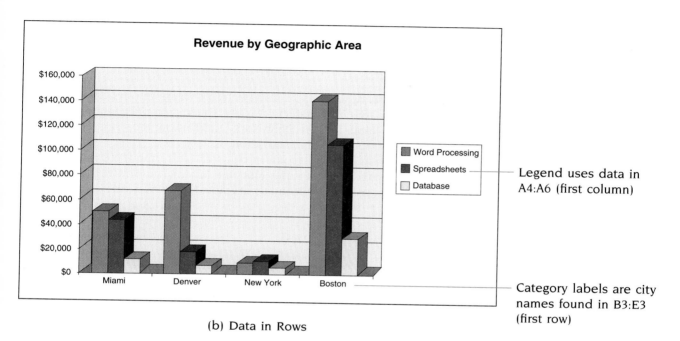

(b) Data in Rows

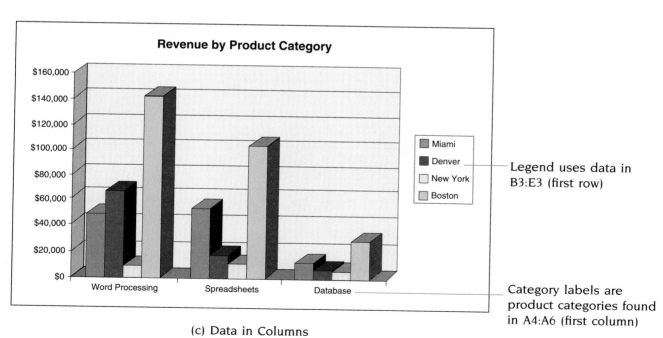

(c) Data in Columns

FIGURE 4.9 Multiple Data Series

by city; that is, the sales of three product categories are shown for each of four cities. Figure 4.9c is the reverse and groups the data by product category; this time the sales of the four cities are shown for each of three product categories. The choice between the two depends on your message and whether you want to emphasize revenue by city or by product category. It sounds complicated, but it's not and Excel will create either chart for you according to your specifications.

➤ If you specify that the data are in rows (Figure 4.9b), the Wizard will
  — Use the first row (cells B3 through E3) in the selected range for the category labels on the X axis
  — Use the first column (cells A4 through A6) for the legend text
➤ If you specify that the data are in columns (Figure 4.9c), the Wizard will
  — Use the first column (cells A4 through A6) in the selected range for the category labels on the X axis
  — Use the first row (cells B3 through E3) for the legend text

Stated another way, the data series in Figure 4.9b are in rows. Thus there are three data series, one for each product category. The first data series plots the word processing sales in Miami, Denver, New York, and Boston; the second series plots the spreadsheet sales for each city, and so on.

The data series in Figure 4.9c are in columns. This time there are four data series, one for each city. The first series plots the Miami sales for word processing, spreadsheets, and database; the second series plots the Denver sales for each software category, and so on.

DEFAULT SELECTIONS

Excel makes a default determination as to whether the data are in rows or columns by assuming that you want fewer data series than categories. Thus, if the selected cells contain more rows than columns, it will assume that the data series are in columns. If, on the other hand, there are more columns than rows, it will assume the data series are in rows. You can override the default selection by editing the chart with the ChartWizard.

HANDS-ON EXERCISE 2:

Multiple Data Series

Objective To plot multiple data series in the same chart; to differentiate between data series in rows and columns; to create and save multiple charts associated with the same worksheet.

Step 1: Open the Software workbook
➤ Load Excel. Pull down the **File menu** and click **Open** (or click the **Open icon** on the Standard toolbar).
➤ Open the **SOFTWARE.XLS** workbook from the first exercise. Save this workbook as **MYCHART2.XLS** so that you can return to the original workbook if necessary.

➤ Reset the TipWizard as you have been doing throughout the text.
➤ Drag the mouse over cells **A3 through E6** as shown in Figure 4.10a.

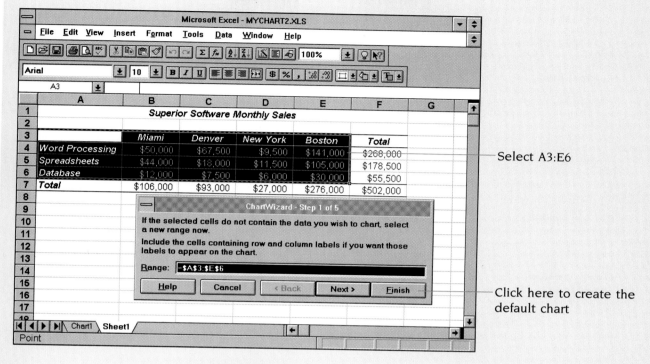

(a) Multiple Data Ranges (step 2)

FIGURE 4.10 Hands-on Exercise 2

THE F11 KEY

The F11 key is the fastest way to create a chart in its own worksheet. Select the data, including the legends and category labels, then press the F11 key to create the chart according to the default format built into Excel. After the *default chart* has been created, you can use the chart toolbar or shortcut menus to choose a different chart type and/or customize the formatting.

Step 2: Create the default chart

➤ Be sure that cells A3 through E6 are still selected. Pull down the **Insert menu.** Click **Chart.** Click **As New Sheet** to bring up step 1 of the ChartWizard as shown in Figure 4.10a.

➤ Click the **Finish command button** to skip the remaining steps in the ChartWizard and create the default chart in Figure 4.10b.

➤ The workbook now has two worksheets. The newly created chart is in the chart sheet labeled Chart1. The data on which the chart is based is in the worksheet labeled Sheet1.

➤ Save the workbook.

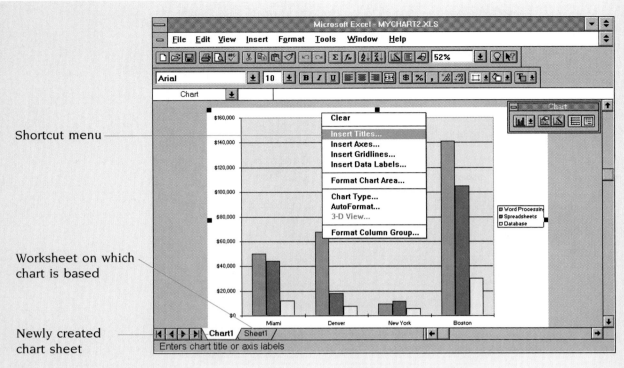

Shortcut menu

Worksheet on which chart is based

Newly created chart sheet

(b) The Default Chart (step 3)

FIGURE 4.10   Hands-on Exercise 2 (continued)

MOVING BETWEEN WORKSHEETS

Press Ctrl+PgDn to move to the next sheet (worksheet or chart sheet) in a workbook. Press Ctrl+PgUp to return to the previous sheet.

Step 3: Add the title

➤ Point just above the top gridline and click the **right mouse button** to produce the shortcut menu in Figure 4.10b. (If you see a different shortcut menu, press Esc, point elsewhere in the chart, and click the right mouse button a second time.)

➤ Click **Insert Titles** on the shortcut menu to bring up the Titles dialog box. Click the **check box** next to Chart Title. Click **OK.**

➤ Type the title of the chart, **Revenue by Geographic Area.** Press the **enter key.** The title should still be selected.

➤ Click the arrow on the Font Size box on the Formatting toolbar as shown in Figure 4.10c. Click **18** to increase the size of the title. Click outside the title to deselect it.

Step 4: Change the chart type

➤ Pull down the **Format menu** and click **AutoFormat.** (You can also point to the chart and click the **right mouse button,** then select **AutoFormat** from the shortcut menu.)

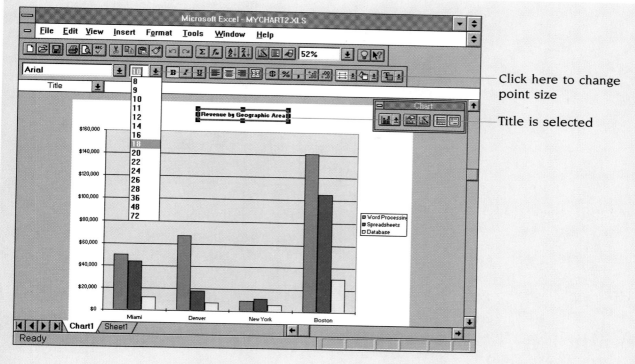

(c) Add the Title (step 3)

FIGURE 4.10 Hands-on Exercise 2 (continued)

➤ Click the **down arrow** on the Galleries list box to scroll through the chart types. Click **3-D Column** to produce the dialog box in Figure 4.10d.

➤ Click format number **1.** Click **OK.** The chart changes to a 3-D column chart.

Step 5: Renaming and copying sheets

➤ Point to the workbook tab labeled **Chart1.** Click the **right mouse button** to produce a shortcut menu pertaining to worksheet tabs. Click **Rename** to display the Rename Sheet dialog box. Type **Area.** Click **OK.**

➤ Point to the workbook tab labeled **Sheet1.** Click the **right mouse button** to produce a shortcut menu. Click **Rename** to display the Rename Sheet dialog box. Type **Sales Data.** Click **OK.**

➤ Point to the workbook tab named **Area** (that was previously Chart1). Click the **right mouse button.** Click **Move or Copy** to display the dialog box in Figure 4.10e.

➤ Click **Sales Data** in the Before Sheet list box. Click the check box to **Create a Copy.** Click **OK.**

➤ Excel pauses, then creates a duplicate chart sheet called Area (2).

COPYING A WORKSHEET

The fastest way to copy a worksheet (chart sheet) is to press and hold the Ctrl key as you drag the workbook tab to a second location in the workbook. Rename the copied tab (or any tab for that matter) by pointing to the tab and clicking the right mouse button to produce a shortcut menu. Click Rename, then enter the new name in the resulting dialog box.

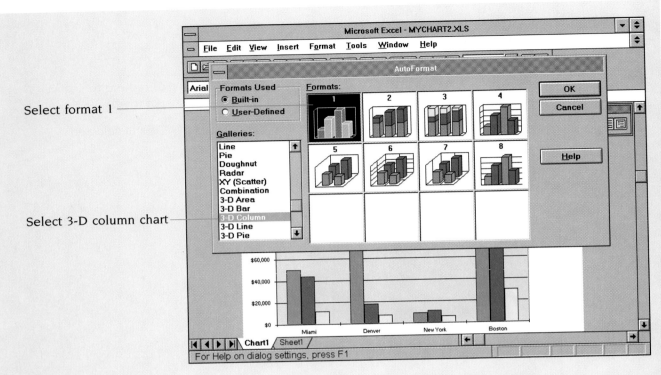

Select format 1

Select 3-D column chart

(d) The AutoFormat Command (step 4)

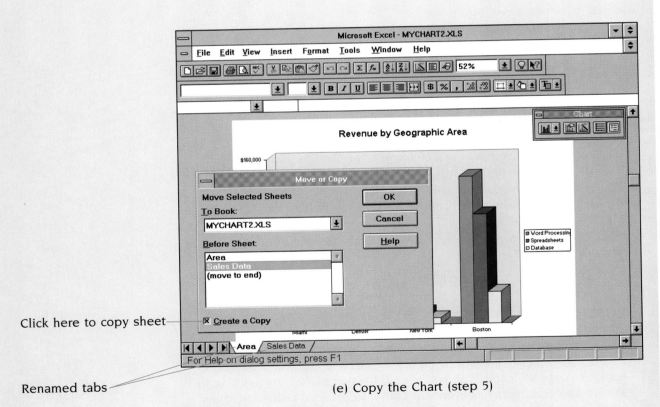

Click here to copy sheet

Renamed tabs

(e) Copy the Chart (step 5)

FIGURE 4.10 Hands-on Exercise 2 (continued)

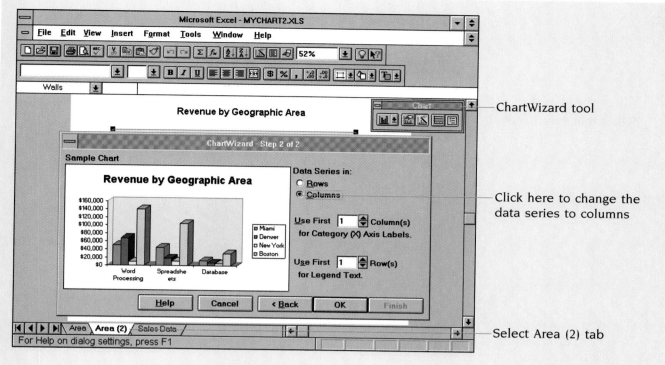

ChartWizard tool

Click here to change the data series to columns

Select Area (2) tab

(f) Change the Data Series (Step 6)

FIGURE 4.10   Hands-on Exercise 2 (continued)

Step 6: Change the data series

➤ Click the **Area (2) tab** to make it the active sheet. Click anywhere in the chart to select the chart.

➤ Click the **ChartWizard icon** on the Chart toolbar. You will see a dialog box indicating step 1 of 2 in ChartWizard. Click the **Next command button** to produce the dialog box in Figure 4.10f.

➤ Click the **Columns option button** to change the data series to columns, which will display the data by product category rather than location. Click **OK** to produce the chart in Figure 4.10g.

➤ Click anywhere in the title of the chart to select the title. Drag the mouse over **Geographic Area** to select this text. Type **Product Category.**

➤ Point to the workbook tab labeled **Area (2).** Click the **right mouse button** to produce a shortcut menu. Click **Rename** to produce the Rename Sheet dialog box. Type **Product.** Click **OK.** The workbook tabs are labeled Area, Product, and Sales Data, respectively.

Step 7: The stacked column chart

➤ Pull down the **Format menu** and click **AutoFormat.** (You can also point to the chart and click the **right mouse button,** then select **AutoFormat** from the shortcut menu.)

➤ Click format **2** in the Formats area. Click **OK.** The chart changes to a stacked bar chart as shown in Figure 4.10h.

➤ Double click the **control-menu box** or pull down the **File menu** and click **Exit** to quit Excel. Save the workbook if you are prompted to do so.

Chart title was changed ——

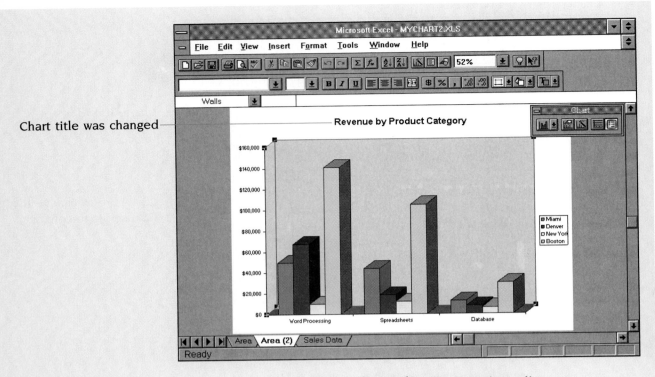

(g) Revenue by Product Category (step 6)

Stacked columns ——

Renamed tab ——

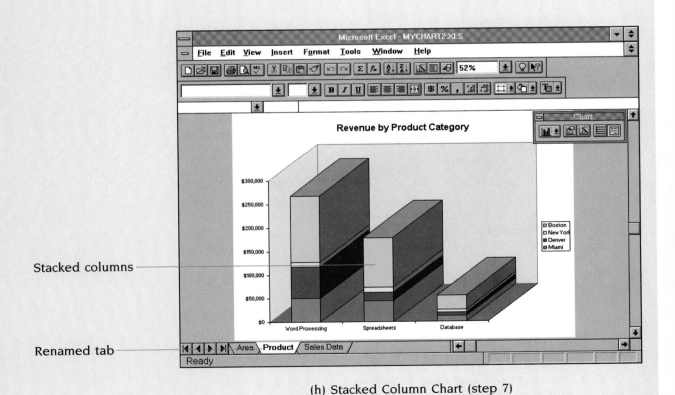

(h) Stacked Column Chart (step 7)

FIGURE 4.10   Hands-on Exercise 2 (continued)

OBJECT LINKING AND EMBEDDING

One of the primary advantages of Windows is the ability to produce a **compound document**—that is, a document with data from multiple applications. The memo in Figure 4.11 was created in Word for Windows and contains a worksheet and a chart that were created in Excel.

Pasting is the simplest way to develop a compound document and is done with the cut, copy, and paste commands present in all Windows applications. You cut or copy data onto the clipboard, then paste it into a different application to produce a compound document. There are, however, two disadvantages to the simple paste operation. First, it is *static,* meaning that if the data is subsequently changed in the original document, the change is not reflected in the compound document. Second, once data has been pasted into a compound document, it can no longer be edited using the original application.

Object Linking and Embedding *(OLE)* offers a superior way to share data. In actuality, there are two distinct techniques, linking and embedding. Our discussion focuses on linking. (See Appendix A in Grauer and Barber, *Exploring Word for Windows 6.0,* Prentice Hall, 1994, for an example of embedding.) The following terminology is essential:

➤ An **object** is any piece of data created by a Windows application—for example, a worksheet or a chart created in Excel.

➤ The **source document** is the place where the object originates. The source document—for example, an Excel worksheet—is created by the **server application,** Excel 5.0.

➤ The **destination document** is the file into which the object is placed. The destination document—for example, a Word document—is created by the **client application,** Word for Windows.

Linking provides a *dynamic* connection between the source and destination documents; that is, change the object in the source document and the object automatically changes in the destination document. The destination document does not contain the object per se, but a representation of the object, as well as a pointer (that is, a link) to the file containing the object. Linking requires that the object be saved prior to establishing the link.

The exercise that follows links two objects, a worksheet and a chart, to a Word document. As you do the exercise, both applications (Word and Excel) will be open, and it will be necessary to switch back and forth between the two. Thus the exercise also demonstrates the **multitasking** capability within Windows and the use of the **task list** to display the open applications. (See pages 53–77 in Grauer and Barber, *Exploring Windows,* Prentice Hall, 1994, for additional information on object linking and embedding, multitasking, and the common user interface.)

IN-PLACE EDITING

The in-place editing capability in Object Linking and Embedding 2.0 enables you to edit an embedded object by double clicking the object. The title bar continues to reflect the client application (e.g., Word for Windows), but the toolbar and pulldown menus will reflect the server application (e.g., Excel). There are two exceptions. The File and Window menus are those of the client application (Word) so that you can save the compound document and/or arrange multiple documents within the client application.

To: Mr. White
                             Chairman, Superior Software

From: Heather Bond
                             Vice President, Marketing

Subject: May Sales Data

The May sales data clearly indicate that Boston is outperforming our other geographic areas. It is my feeling that Ms. Bost, the office supervisor, is directly responsible for its success and that she should be rewarded accordingly. In addition, we may want to think about transferring her to New York, as they are in desperate need of new ideas and direction. I will be awaiting your response after you have time to digest the information presented.

Superior Software Monthly Sales

	Miami	Denver	New York	Boston	Total
Word Processing	$50,000	$67,500	$9,500	$141,000	$268,000
Spreadsheets	$44,000	$18,000	$11,500	$105,000	$178,500
Database	$12,000	$7,500	$6,000	$30,000	$55,500
Total	$106,000	$93,000	$27,000	$276,000	$502,000

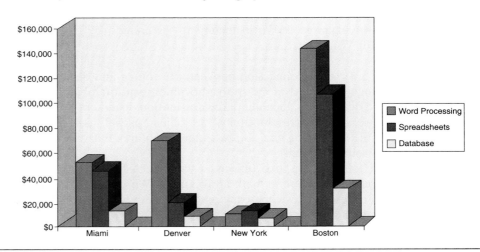

Revenue by Geographic Area

FIGURE 4.11   A Compound Document

HANDS-ON EXERCISE 3:

Object Linking and Embedding

Objective To create a compound document consisting of a memo, worksheet, and chart. The exercise is written for Word for Windows but will work with any Windows word processor that supports Object Linking and Embedding.

Step 1: Copy the worksheet to the clipboard

➤ Load Excel. Open the **MYCHART2.XLS** workbook that was used in the second exercise.

➤ Click the tab for **Sales Data.** Click cell **A1.** Drag the mouse over cells **A1 through F7** so that the entire worksheet is selected as shown in Figure 4.12a.

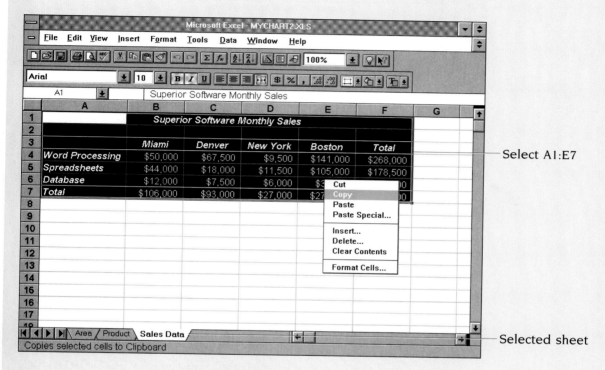

Select A1:E7

Selected sheet

(a) Copy the Worksheet (step 1)

FIGURE 4.12   Hands-on Exercise 3 (continued)

➤ Press the **right mouse button** to display the shortcut menu. Click **Copy.** A flashing dashed line (the marquee) appears around the entire worksheet, indicating that it has been copied to the clipboard.

Step 2: Load Word

➤ Press **Ctrl+Esc** to display the task list as in Figure 4.12b. The contents of the task list depend on the applications open on your system. You should see Microsoft Excel - MYCHART2.XLS and Program Manager. You may also see other open applications.

➤ Double click **Program Manager** to switch to Program Manager.

➤ If necessary, open the group window that contains Word 6.0 (for example, Microsoft Office), then double click the **Microsoft Word 6.0 program icon** to load the word processor.

Step 3: Open the Word document

➤ Pull down the **File menu** and click **Open** (or click the **Open icon** on the standard toolbar).

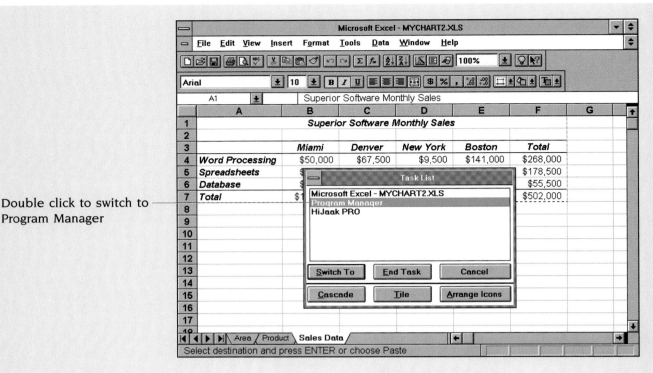

Double click to switch to Program Manager

(b) The Task List (step 2)

FIGURE 4.12 Hands-on Exercise 3 (continued)

➤ Click the **drop-down list box** to specify the appropriate drive (which is the same drive you have been using throughout the text).
➤ Scroll through the directory list box until you come to the **WORDDATA** directory. Double click this directory to make it the active directory.
➤ Double click **MEMO.DOC** to open this document. Type your name in the memo in place of Mr. White.
➤ Pull down the **View menu.** Click **Page Layout.** Pull down the **View menu** a second time. Click **Zoom.** Click the **Page Width** option button. Click **OK.** You should see the document in Figure 4.12c.

THE COMMON USER INTERFACE

The common user interface provides a sense of familiarity from one Windows application to the next. Even if you have never used Word for Windows, you will recognize many of the elements present in Excel. Both applications share a common menu structure with consistent ways to execute commands from those menus. The Standard and Formatting toolbars are present in both applications. Many keyboard shortcuts are also common—for example, Ctrl+Home and Ctrl+End to move to the beginning and end of a document or worksheet.

Step 4: Create the Link
➤ Press **Ctrl+End** to move to the end of the memo.

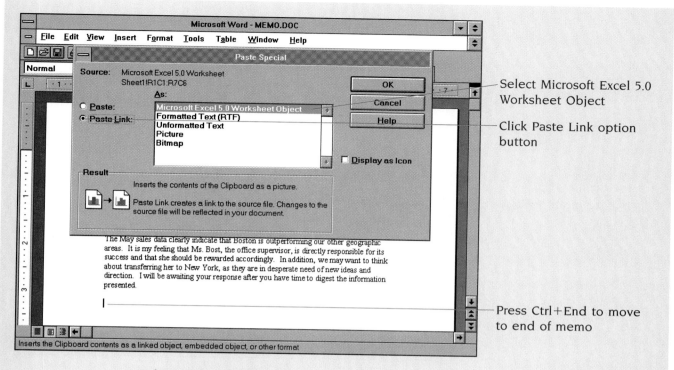

Select Microsoft Excel 5.0 Worksheet Object

Click Paste Link option button

Press Ctrl+End to move to end of memo

(c) The Word Document (steps 3 and 4)

FIGURE 4.12 Hands-on Exercise 3 (continued)

➤ Pull down the **Edit menu.** Click **Paste Special** to produce the dialog box in Figure 4.12c.

➤ Click **Microsoft Excel 5.0 Worksheet Object.** Click the **Paste Link** option button. Click **OK** to insert the worksheet into the document.

➤ Press the **enter key** twice (to allow for space between the worksheet and the chart that will be added in step 6).

➤ Pull down the **File menu** and click **Save** (or click the **Save button** on the Standard toolbar) to save the document.

Step 5: Return to Excel

➤ Press **Ctrl+Esc** to display the task list as in Figure 4.12d. Microsoft Excel and Word 6.0 are both on the task list because both applications are currently open. Microsoft Word - MEMO.DOC is currently highlighted because that is the active application and document.

➤ Double click **Microsoft Excel - MYCHART2.XLS** to return to the worksheet.

USE ALT+TAB TO SWITCH BETWEEN APPLICATIONS

Press and hold the Alt key while you press and release the Tab key repeatedly to cycle through the open applications. Release the Alt key when you see the title bar of the application you want.

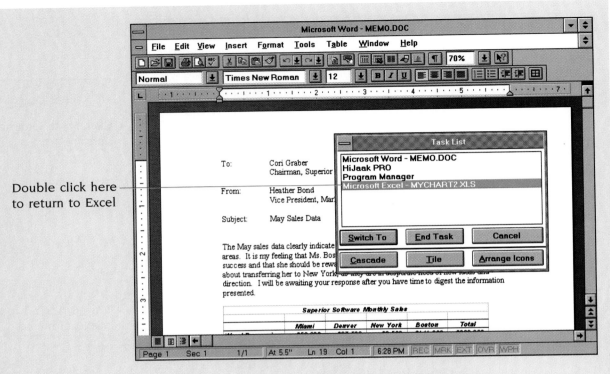

Double click here
to return to Excel

(d) Return to Excel (step 5)

FIGURE 4.12   Hands-on Exercise 3 (continued)

Step 6: Copy the chart to the clipboard

➤ Click outside the selected area to deselect the cells from step 1.

➤ Click the **Area tab** at the bottom of the worksheet window to activate the chart sheet.

➤ Point just inside the border of the chart. Click the left mouse button to select the chart. Be sure you have selected the entire chart and that you see the same sizing handles as in Figure 4.12e.

➤ Pull down the **Edit menu** and click **Copy** (or click the **Copy button** on the Standard toolbar). The marquee will appear around the chart to indicate it has been copied to the clipboard.

➤ Press and hold the **Alt key** while you press and release the **Tab key** repeatedly to cycle through the open applications. Release the Alt key when you see **Microsoft Word - MEMO.DOC** in a box in the middle of the screen as in Figure 4.12e.

Step 7: Add the chart to the document

➤ Press **Ctrl+End** to move to the end of the Word document.

➤ Pull down the **Edit menu.** Click **Paste Special.** Click the **Paste Link** option button. If necessary, click **Microsoft Excel 5.0 Chart Object.** Click **OK** to insert the chart into the document.

➤ Click the **up** or **down arrow** on the vertical scroll bar so that you will be able to see the worksheet and the chart as shown in Figure 4.12f. (Do not be concerned if you do not see all of the chart.)

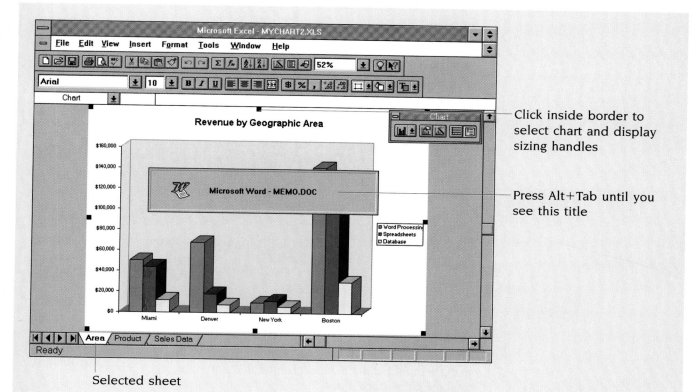

Click inside border to select chart and display sizing handles

Press Alt+Tab until you see this title

Selected sheet

(e) Copy the Chart (step 6)

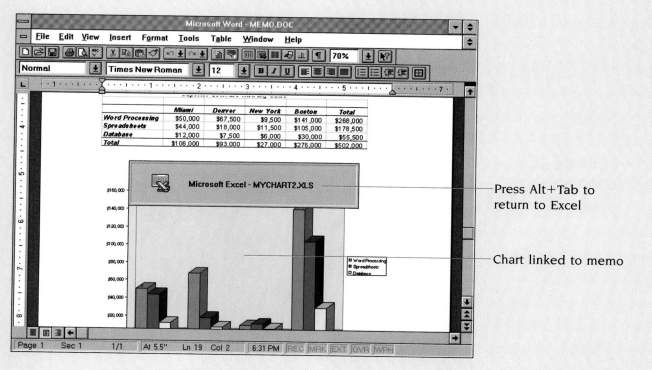

Press Alt+Tab to return to Excel

Chart linked to memo

(f) Add the Chart to the Document (step 7)

FIGURE 4.12 Hands-on Exercise 3 (continued)

➤ Look carefully at the worksheet and chart in the document. The sales for word processing in New York are currently $9,500 and the chart reflects this amount.

➤ Save the document.

Step 8: Modify the worksheet

➤ Press and hold the **Alt key** while you press and release the **Tab key** repeatedly to cycle through the open applications. Release the Alt key when you see **Microsoft Excel - MYCHART2.XLS** in a box in the middle of the screen as shown in Figure 4.12f.

➤ Click the **Sales Data tab** to return to the worksheet.

➤ Click in cell **D4.** Type **$200,000.** Press **enter.** You may need to widen the column to see the change.

➤ Click the **Area tab.** The chart has been modified automatically and reflects the increased sales for New York.

Step 9: The modified document.

➤ Press and hold the **Alt key** while you press and release the **Tab key** repeatedly to cycle through the open applications. Release the Alt key when you see **Microsoft Word - MEMO.DOC.**

➤ The active application changes back to Word as shown in Figure 4.12g. The worksheet and chart have been modified automatically because of the links established in steps 4 and 7.

➤ Click the **Print preview icon** on the Standard toolbar to view the entire document as shown in Figure 4.12h.

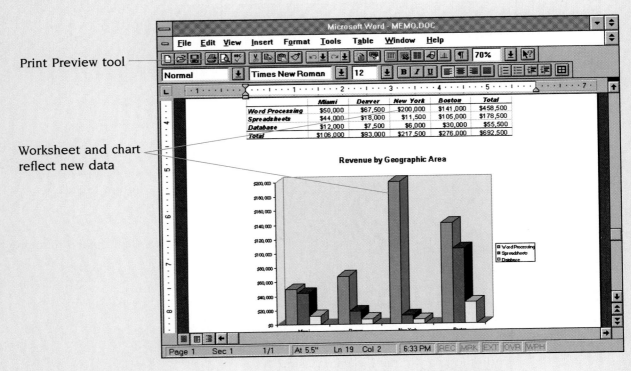

Print Preview tool

Worksheet and chart reflect new data

(g) The Modified Document (step 9)

FIGURE 4.12   Hands-on Exercise 3 (continued)

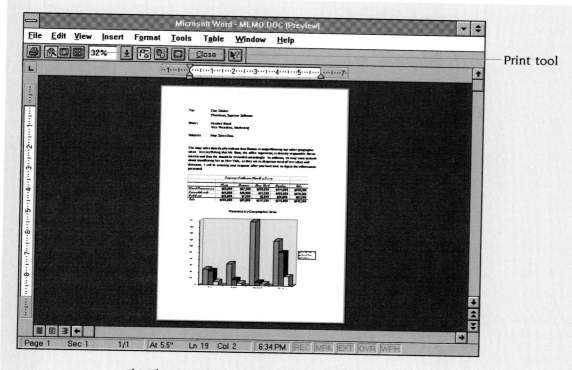

Print tool

(h) The Print Preview Command (step 9)

FIGURE 4.12 Hands-on Exercise 3 (continued)

➤ Click the **Print icon** to print the document. Click the **Close command button** to return to the document.
➤ Exit Word. Exit Excel. Exit Windows.

ADDITIONAL CHART TYPES

Excel offers a total of 15 chart types, each with several formats. The chart types are displayed in the ChartWizard (see Figure 4.5b) and are listed here for convenience. The chart types are: Area, Bar, Column, Line, Pie, Doughnut, Radar, XY (scatter), Combination, 3-D Area, 3-D Bar, 3-D Column, 3-D Line, 3-D Pie, and 3-D Surface.

It is not possible to cover every type of chart and so we concentrate on the most common. We have already presented the bar, column, and pie charts and continue with the line and combination charts. We use a different example, the worksheet in Figure 4.13a, which plots financial data for the National Widgets Corporation.

Line Chart

A *line chart* is appropriate for any message associated with time-related information—for example, the five-year trend of revenue and income in Figure 4.13b. A line chart plots one or more data series (e.g., revenue and income) against a descriptive category (e.g, year). As with a column chart, the quantitative values are plotted along the vertical scale (Y axis) and the descriptive category along the horizontal scale (X axis). The individual data points are connected by a straight line, and a legend is used to distinguish one data series from another.

	A	B	C	D	E	F
1	National Widgets Financial Data					
2		*1989*	*1990*	*1991*	*1992*	*1993*
3	Revenue	$50,000,000	$60,000,000	$70,000,000	$80,000,000	$90,000,000
4	Income	$10,000,000	$8,000,000	$6,000,000	$4,000,000	$2,000,000
5	Stock Price	$40	$35	$36	$31	$24

(a) The Worksheet

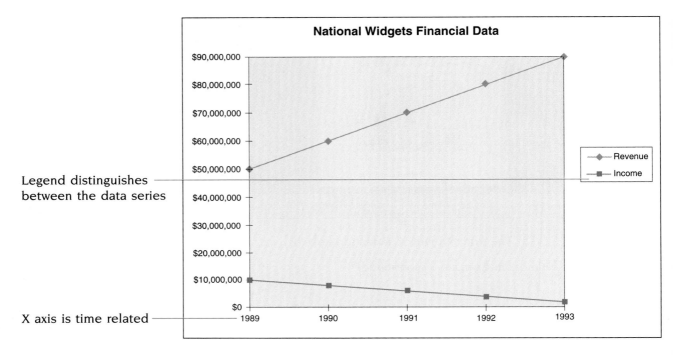

(b) Line Chart

FIGURE 4.13   National Widgets Financial Data

Combination Chart

A **combination chart** is used when different scales are required for multiple data series that are plotted against the same descriptive variable. The chart in Figure 4.13c plots revenue, income, and stock price over the five-year period. The same scale can be used for revenue and income (both are in millions of dollars), but an entirely different scale is needed for the stock price. Note, too, how a line graph showing the declining price of the stock is imposed on the column chart showing the increased revenue. A picture is indeed worth a thousand words, and investors in National Widgets can see at a glance the true status of their company.

USE AND ABUSE OF CHARTS

The hands-on exercises in the chapter demonstrate how easily numbers in a work-sheet can be converted to their graphic equivalent. *The numbers can, however, just as easily be converted into erroneous or misleading charts, a fact that is often over-looked.* Indeed, some individuals are so delighted just to obtain the charts, that they accept the data without question. Accordingly, we present two examples of

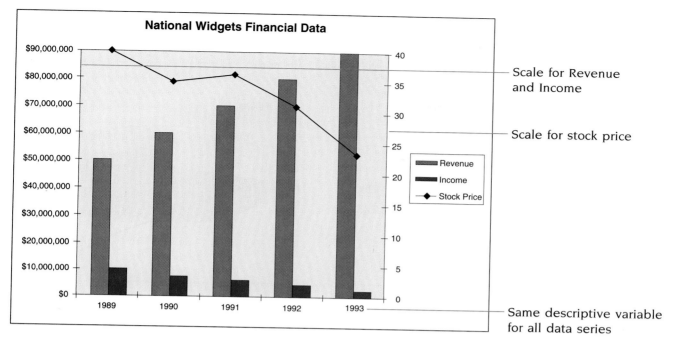

National Widgets Financial Data

Scale for Revenue and Income

Scale for stock price

Same descriptive variable for all data series

(c) Combination Chart

FIGURE 4.13   National Widgets Financial Data (continued)

statistically accurate, yet entirely misleading, graphical data, drawn from charts submitted by our students in response to homework assignments.

> Lying graphics cheapen the graphical art everywhere . . . When a chart on television lies, it lies millions of times over; when a *New York Times* chart lies, it lies 900,000 times over to a great many important and influential readers. The lies are told about the major issues of public policy—the government budget, medical care, prices, and fuel economy standards, for example. The lies are systematic and quite predictable, nearly always exaggerating the rate of recent change.
>
> **Edward Tufte**

Improper (omitted) Labels

The difference between *unit sales* and *dollar sales* is a concept of great importance, yet one that is often missed. Consider, for example, the two pie charts in Figures 4.14a and 4.14b, both of which are intended to identify the leading salesperson based on the underlying worksheet in Figure 4.14c. The charts yield two different answers, Jones and Smith, respectively, depending on which chart you use.

As you can see, the two charts reflect different percentages and would appear therefore to contradict each other. Both charts, however, are technically correct as the percentages depend on whether they express unit sales or dollar sales. *Jones is the leader in terms of units, whereas Smith is the leader in terms of dollars.* The latter is generally more significant, and hence the measure that is probably most important to the reader. Neither chart, however, was properly labeled (there is no

Omitted titles can lead to
erroneous conclusions

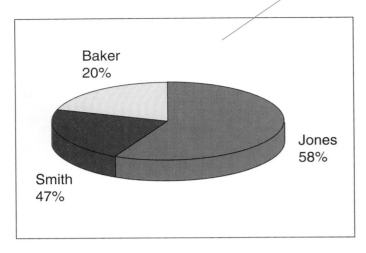

(a) Units

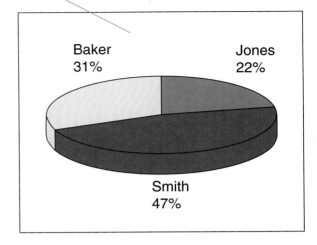

(b) Dollars

Sales Data - First Quarter							
		Jones		Smith		Baker	
		Units	Dollars	Units	Dollars	Units	Dollars
Product 1	$1	200	$200	20	$20	30	$30
Product 2	$5	50	$250	30	$150	30	$150
Product 3	$20	5	$100	50	$1,000	30	$600
	Totals:	255	$550	100	$1,170	90	$780

(c) Underlying Spreadsheet

FIGURE 4.14   Omitted Labels

indication of whether units or dollars are plotted), which in turn may lead to erroneous conclusions on the part of the reader.

Adding Dissimilar Quantities

The conversion of a side-by-side column chart to a stacked column chart is a simple matter, requiring only a few mouse clicks. Because the procedure is so easy, however, it can be done without thought, and in situations where the stacked column chart is inappropriate.

Figures 4.15a and 4.15b display a side-by-side and a stacked column chart, respectively. One chart is appropriate and one chart is not. The side-by-side columns in Figure 4.15a indicate increasing sales in conjunction with decreasing profits. This is a realistic portrayal of the company, which is becoming less efficient because profits are decreasing as sales are increasing.

The stacked column chart in Figure 4.15b plots the identical numbers. It is deceptive, however, as it implies an optimistic trend whose stacked columns reflect a nonsensical addition. The problem is that although sales and profits are both measured in dollars, they should not be added together because the sum does not represent a meaningful concept.

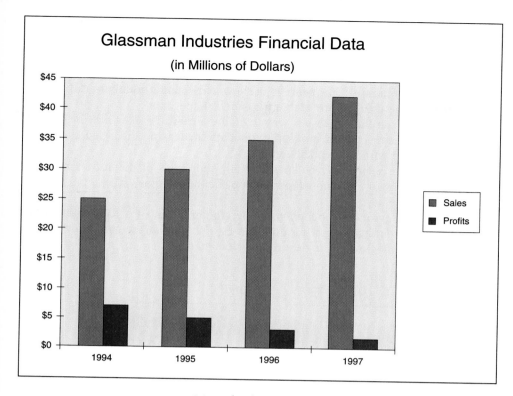

(a) Multiple Bar Chart

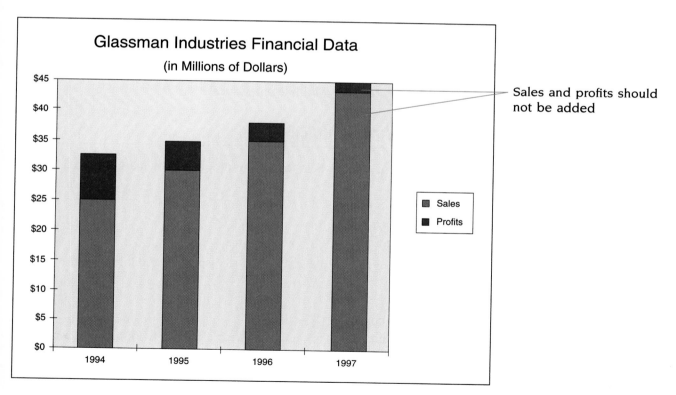

(b) Stacked Bar Chart

FIGURE 4.15 Adding Dissimilar Quantities

SUMMARY

A chart is a graphic representation of data in a worksheet. The type of chart chosen depends on the message to be conveyed. A pie chart is best for proportional relationships. A column or bar chart is used to show actual numbers rather than percentages. A line chart is preferable for time-related data.

The ChartWizard is the easiest way to create a chart. A chart may be embedded in a worksheet or created in a separate chart sheet. An embedded chart may be moved or sized within a worksheet.

Multiple data series may be specified in either rows or columns. Excel will choose the first row or column as appropriate for the category labels and legends to differentiate the series.

Object Linking and Embedding enables the creation of a compound document. The linking is dynamic in nature; that is, a change in the source document is automatically reflected in the destination document.

 Key Words and Concepts

3-D column chart	Data point	Multitasking
3-D pie chart	Data series	Object
Arrow tool	Default chart	Object Linking and
Bar chart	Destination document	Embedding (OLE)
Category label	Docked toolbar	Pie chart
Chart	Drawing toolbar	Server application
Chart sheet	Embedded chart	Side-by-side columns
Chart toolbar	Exploded pie chart	Sizing handles
ChartWizard	Floating toolbar	Source document
Client application	Legend	Stacked columns
Column chart	Line chart	Task list
Combination chart	Linking	Text box
Compound document	Multiple data series	

 Multiple Choice

1. Which type of chart is best to portray proportion or market share?
   (a) Pie chart
   (b) Line
   (c) Column chart
   (d) Combination chart

2. Which type of chart is typically used to display time-related data?
   (a) Pie chart
   (b) Line chart
   (c) Column chart
   (d) Combination chart

3. Which chart type is *not* suitable to display multiple data series?
   (a) Pie chart
   (b) Column chart
   (c) Both (a) and (b)
   (d) Neither (a) nor (b)

4. Which of the following is best to display *additive information* from multiple data series?
  (a) A column chart with the series stacked one on top of another
  (b) A column chart with the data series side by side
  (c) Both (a) and (b) are equally appropriate
  (d) Neither (a) nor (b) is appropriate

5. A workbook must contain:
  (a) A separate chart sheet for every worksheet
  (b) A separate worksheet for every chart sheet
  (c) Both (a) and (b)
  (d) Neither (a) nor (b)

6. Which of the following is true regarding an embedded chart?
  (a) It can be moved elsewhere within the worksheet
  (b) It can be made larger or smaller
  (c) Both (a) and (b)
  (d) Neither (a) nor (b)

7. Which of the following will produce a shortcut menu?
  (a) Pointing to a workbook tab and clicking the right mouse button
  (b) Pointing to an embedded chart and clicking the right mouse button
  (c) Pointing to a selected cell range and clicking the right mouse button
  (d) All of the above

8. Which of the following is done *prior* to invoking the ChartWizard?
  (a) The data series are selected
  (b) The location of the embedded chart within the worksheet is specified
  (c) Both (a) and (b)
  (d) Neither (a) nor (b)

9. Which of the following will display sizing handles when selected?
  (a) An embedded chart
  (b) The title of a chart
  (c) A text box or arrow
  (d) All of the above

10. Which of the following is true?
  (a) Ctrl+Esc displays the task list
  (b) Alt+Tab switches between open applications
  (c) Both a and b
  (d) Neither a nor b

11. Which of the following is true regarding the compound document (the memo containing the worksheet and chart) that was created in the chapter?
  (a) The worksheet is the source document and the memo is the destination document
  (b) Excel is the server application and Word for Windows is the client application
  (c) Both (a) and (b) above
  (d) Neither (a) nor (b)

12. In order to represent multiple data series on the same chart:
- (a) The data series must be in rows and the rows must be adjacent to one another on the worksheet
- (b) The data series must be in columns and the columns must be adjacent to one another on the worksheet
- (c) The data series may be in rows or columns so long as they are adjacent to one another
- (d) The data series may be in rows or columns with no requirement to be next to one another

13. If multiple data series are selected and rows are specified,
- (a) The first row will be used for the category (X axis) labels
- (b) The first column will be used for the legend
- (c) Both (a) and (b)
- (d) Neither (a) nor (b)

14. If multiple data series are selected and columns are specified,
- (a) The first column will be used for the category (X axis) labels
- (b) The first row will be used for the legend
- (c) Both (a) and (b)
- (d) Neither (a) nor (b)

15. Which of the following is true about the scale on the Y axis in a column chart that plots multiple data series side by side, versus one that stacks the values one on top of another?
- (a) The scale for the stacked columns will contain larger values than if the columns are plotted side by side
- (b) The scale for the side-by-side columns will contain larger values than if the columns are stacked
- (c) The values on the scale will be the same regardless of whether the columns are stacked or side by side
- (d) The values on the scale will be different, but it is not possible to tell which chart will contain the higher values

ANSWERS

1. a	**6.** c	**11.** c
2. b	**7.** d	**12.** d
3. a	**8.** a	**13.** c
4. a	**9.** d	**14.** c
5. d	**10.** c	**15.** a

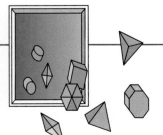

EXPLORING EXCEL

1. Use Figure 4.16a to match each action with its result; a given action may be used more than once or not at all.

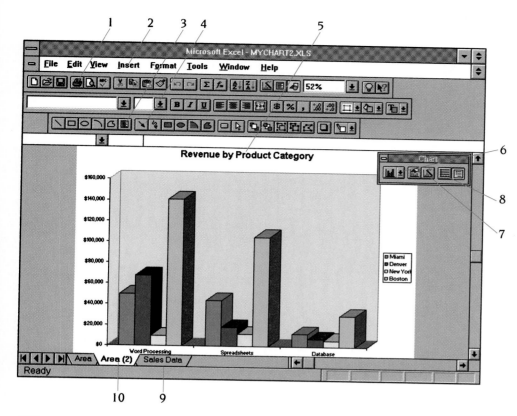

FIGURE 4.16 Screen for Problem 1

Action	Result
a. Click at 1	___ Activate the Sales Data sheet
b. Click at 2	___ Create gridlines on the chart
c. Click at 3	___ Change the font used for the chart title
d. Click at 4	
e. Double click at 5	___ Rename the current sheet
f. Click at 6	___ Place an arrow on the chart
g. Click at 7	___ Change the chart type
h. Click at 8	___ Create a new chart on its own sheet
i. Click at 9	___ Print the chart
j. Click the right mouse button at 10	___ Place a text box on the chart
	___ Change the data series from columns to rows

2. The value of a chart is aptly demonstrated by writing a verbal equivalent to a graphic analysis. Accordingly, write the corresponding written description of the information contained in Figure 4.8a. Can you better appreciate the effectiveness of the graphic presentation?

3. The worksheet of Figure 4.17c is the basis for the two charts of Figures 4.17a and 4.17b. Although the charts may at first glance appear to be satisfactory, each reflects a fundamental error. Discuss the problems associated with each.

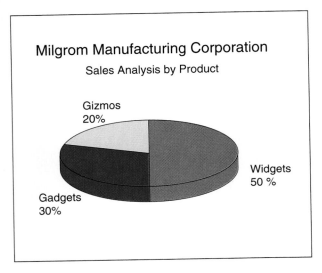

Milgrom Manufacturing Corporation

Sales Analysis by Product

(a) Error 1

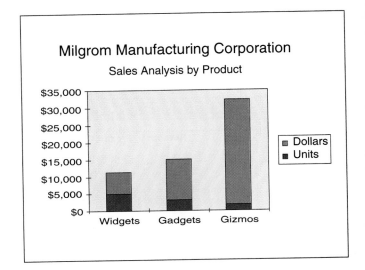

Milgrom Manufacturing Corporation

Sales Analysis by Product

(b) Error 2

Milgrom Manufacturing Corporation
Sales Analysis by Product

	Unit Price	Units Sold	Revenue
Widgets	$1.25	5,000	$6,250
Gadgets	$4.00	3,000	$12,000
Gizmos	$14.99	2,000	$29,980

(c) The Worksheet

FIGURE 4.17 Worksheet for Problem 3

4. Using the data disk: Answer the following with respect to the worksheet and embedded chart in Figure 4.18, which are found on the data disk in the file PROB0404.XLS.

   a. Retrieve the worksheet from the data disk.

   b. Change the number in cell B8 to 6,000,000. What corresponding changes take place in the chart?

   c. Change the format for cells B5 to F9 to comma with no decimals. What corresponding changes take place in the chart?

   d. Change the entry in cell A5 to Madrid. What corresponding changes take place in the chart?

   e. Change the chart to a three-dimensional pie chart.

   f. Use the text box and arrow tools to add an appropriate callout.

   g. Type your name in cell A11 of the worksheet.

   h. Print the worksheet and embedded chart and submit it to your instructor.

   i. What would happen if you press the Del key when the chart is selected? Is there anyway to retrieve the chart after it has been deleted?

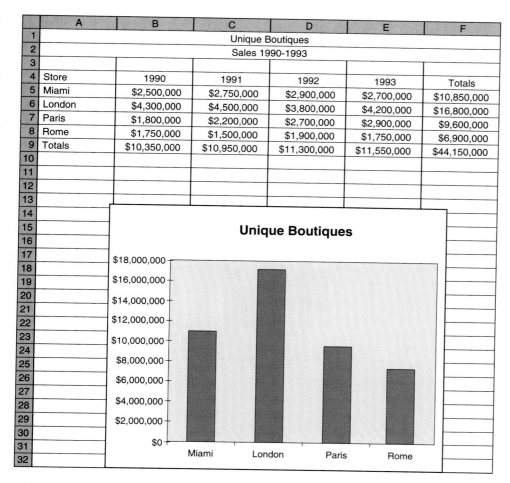

	A	B	C	D	E	F
1			Unique Boutiques			
2			Sales 1990-1993			
3						
4	Store	1990	1991	1992	1993	Totals
5	Miami	$2,500,000	$2,750,000	$2,900,000	$2,700,000	$10,850,000
6	London	$4,300,000	$4,500,000	$3,800,000	$4,200,000	$16,800,000
7	Paris	$1,800,000	$2,200,000	$2,700,000	$2,900,000	$9,600,000
8	Rome	$1,750,000	$1,500,000	$1,900,000	$1,750,000	$6,900,000
9	Totals	$10,350,000	$10,950,000	$11,300,000	$11,550,000	$44,150,000
10						
11						
12						
13						
14						
15						
16						
17						
18						
19						
20						
21						
22						
23						
24						
25						
26						
27						
28						
29						
30						
31						
32						

FIGURE 4.18   Spreadsheet and Graph for Problem 4

5. Answer the following with respect to the worksheet and embedded chart of Figure 4.19.

   a. Are the data series in rows or columns?
   b. How many data series are there?
   c. Which cells contain the category labels?
   d. Which cells contain the legends?
   e. Create the worksheet and embedded chart as shown in Figure 4.19.
   f. Create a second chart in its own chart sheet, which reverses the data series by switching rows and columns.
   g. Add your name to the worksheet, then print the entire workbook and submit it to your instructor.

6. The worksheet in Figure 4.20 is to be used as the basis for several charts depicting information on hotel capacities.

   a. What type of chart is best to show the proportion of total capacity for each hotel?
   b. Which data range(s) should be selected prior to invoking the ChartWizard in order to produce the chart of part a?
   c. What type of chart is best to compare the capacities of the individual hotels to one another?

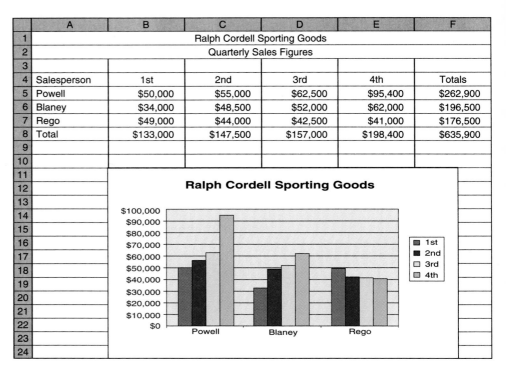

	A	B	C	D	E	F
1	Ralph Cordell Sporting Goods					
2	Quarterly Sales Figures					
3						
4	Salesperson	1st	2nd	3rd	4th	Totals
5	Powell	$50,000	$55,000	$62,500	$95,400	$262,900
6	Blaney	$34,000	$48,500	$52,000	$62,000	$196,500
7	Rego	$49,000	$44,000	$42,500	$41,000	$176,500
8	Total	$133,000	$147,500	$157,000	$198,400	$635,900

FIGURE 4.19 Spreadsheet and Graph for Problem 5

	A	B	C	D
1	Hotel Capacities and Room Rates			
2				
3		Total	Standard	Deluxe
4	Hotel	Rooms	Rate	Rate
5	Holiday Inn	250	$100	$150
6	Hyatt	450	$120	$175
7	Ramada Inn	300	$115	$190
8	Sheraton	750	$95	$150
9	Marriott	575	$100	$175
10	Hilton	600	$80	$120
11	Best Western	350	$75	$125
12	Days Inn	750	$50	$100

FIGURE 4.20 Spreadsheet for Problem 6

    d. Which data range(s) should be selected prior to invoking the ChartWizard in order to produce the chart of part c?

    e. What type of chart is best to show the comparison of the standard and deluxe room rates for all of the hotels, with the two different rates side-by-side for each hotel?

    f. Which data range(s) should be selected prior to invoking the ChartWizard in order to produce the chart of part e?

    g. Could the information in part f be conveyed in a stacked column chart?

    h. The worksheet in Figure 4.20 exists on the data disk as PROB0406.XLS. Create the three charts in parts a, c, and e in separate sheets, then print each chart sheet and submit all three pages to your instructor.

7. Figure 4.21 contains a worksheet with sales data for the chain of four Michael Moldof clothing boutiques. Use the worksheet to develop the following charts:

a. A pie chart showing the percentage of total sales attributed to each store.

b. Redo part a as a column chart.

c. A stacked column chart showing total dollars for each store, broken down by clothing category.

d. A stacked column chart showing total dollars for each clothing category, broken down by store.

e. The worksheet in Figure 4.21 exists on the data disk as PROB0407.XLS. Create the charts in parts a, b, c, and d in separate sheets, then print each chart and submit all four pages to your instructor.

	A	B	C	D	E	F
1		Michael Moldof Men's Boutique - January Sales				
2						
3		Store 1	Store 2	Store 3	Store 4	Total
4	Slacks	$25,000	$28,750	$21,500	$9,400	$84,650
5	Shirts	$43,000	$49,450	$36,900	$46,000	$175,350
6	Underwear	$18,000	$20,700	$15,500	$21,000	$75,200
7	Accessories	$7,000	$8,050	$8,000	$4,000	$27,050
8						
9	Total	$93,000	$106,950	$81,900	$80,400	$362,250

FIGURE 4.21   Spreadsheet for Problem 7

8. The compound document in Figure 4.22 contains a memo and combination chart and is an excellent way to review the entire chapter.

a. Create the combination chart:
   ➤ Retrieve the PROB0408.XLS workbook from the data disk.
   ➤ Select cells A2 through F5.
   ➤ Click the ChartWizard icon and create the combination chart of Figure 4.13c, which appeared earlier in the chapter. (Select combination chart in step 2 and format 2 in step 3.)

b. Create the memo:
   ➤ Use Alt+Tab to switch to Program Manager. Open the program group that contains Word for Windows. Double click on the program icon to open the word processor.
   ➤ Enter the text of the memo as shown in Figure 4.22. Add your name as the financial consultant.
   ➤ Save the word processing document as PROB0408.DOC.

c. Create the compound document:
   ➤ Use Alt+Tab to return to Excel.
   ➤ Click the chart to select it. The sizing handles should appear to indicate that the chart has been selected. Pull down the Edit menu. Click Copy.
   ➤ Use Alt+Tab to return to Word for Windows.
   ➤ Pull down the Edit menu. Click Paste Special. Select Microsoft Excel 5.0 Chart Object as the data type from the list box. Click Paste Link to bring the chart into the memo.
   ➤ Save the memo. Print the memo and submit it to your instructor.

Steven Stocks
Financial Investments
100 Century Towers
New York, New York 10020

To: Carlos Rosell

From: Steven Stocks

Subject: Status Report on National Widgets Corporation

I have uncovered some information that I feel is important to the overall health of your investment portfolio. The graph below clearly shows that while revenues for National Widgets have steadily increased since 1989, income (profits) have steadily decreased. In addition, the stock price is continuing to decline. Although at one time I felt that a turnaround was imminent, I am no longer so optimistic and am advising you to cut your losses and sell your National Widgets stock as soon as possible.

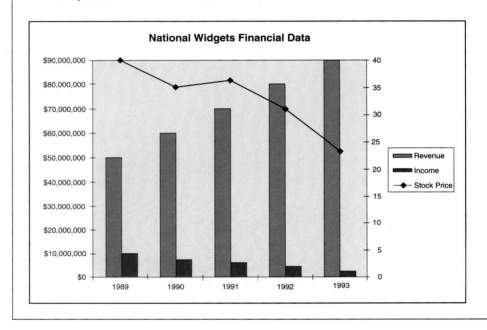

FIGURE 4.22   Compound Document for Problem 8

 Case Studies

University Enrollments

Your assistantship next semester has placed you in the Provost's office, where you are to help create a presentation for the Board of Trustees. The Provost is expected to make recommendations to the Board regarding the expansion of some programs and the reduction of others. You are expected to help the Provost by developing a series of charts to illustrate enrollment trends. The Provost has provided you with an Excel workbook (ENROLMNT.XLS, which is found on the data disk) with summary data over the last several years.

The Budget

Deficit reduction or not, the Federal government spends billions more than it takes in; for example, in fiscal year 1992, government expenditures totaled $1,380 billion versus income of only $1,090, leaving a deficit of $290 billion. Thirty percent of the income came from social security and Medicare taxes, 35% from personal income taxes, 7% from corporate income taxes, and 7% from excise, estate, and other miscellaneous taxes. The remaining 21% was borrowed.

Social security and Medicare accounted for 33% of the expenditures, and the defense budget another 24%. Social programs, including Medicare and Aid to Families with Dependent Children, totalled 17%. Community development (consisting of agricultural, educational, environmental, economic, and space programs) totalled 10% of the budget. Interest on the national debt amounted to 14%. The cost of law enforcement and government itself accounted for the final 2%.

Use the information contained within this problem to create the appropriate charts to reflect the distribution of income and expenditures. Do some independent research and obtain data on the budget, the deficit, and the national debt for the years 1945, 1967, and 1980. The numbers may surprise you; for example, how does the interest expense for the current year compare to the total budget in 1967 (at the height of the Viet Nam war) to the total budget in 1945 (at the end of World War II)? Create charts to reflect your findings, then write your representative in Congress. We are in trouble!

The Annual Report

Corporate America spends a small fortune to produce its annual reports, which are readily available to the public at large. Choose any company and obtain a copy of its most recent annual report. Consolidate the information in the company's report to produce a two-page document of your own. Your report should include a description of the company's progress in the last year, a worksheet with any data you deem relevant, and at least two charts in support of the worksheet or written material. Formatting is important, and you are expected to use a word processor in addition to the worksheet to present the information in an attractive manner.

One Step Beyond

What exactly is a macro? More important, how can macros help you be more productive in using Excel? How do you create a macro? What is the difference between playing and recording a macro? How can you assign a macro to a button that appears on the worksheet? Use the on-line help facility and/or the reference manual to teach yourself the basics of macros, then create three macros in conjunction with creating, displaying, and/or modifying a chart.

Version 2.0

EXPLORING MICROSOFT ACCESS®

Introduction to Microsoft Access: What Is a Database?

CHAPTER OBJECTIVES

After reading this chapter you will be able to:

1. Describe the basic mouse operations; use a mouse and/or the equivalent keyboard shortcuts to select commands from a pull-down menu.
2. Discuss the function of a dialog box; describe the different types of dialog boxes and the various ways in which information is supplied.
3. Access the on-line help facility and explain its capabilities.
4. Define the terms field, record, table, and database.
5. Load Microsoft Access; describe the Database window and the objects in an Access database.
6. Add, edit, and delete records to a table within a database; use the Find command to move to a specific record.
7. Describe the record selector; explain when changes are saved to a database.
8. Explain the importance of data validation in table maintenance.
9. Describe a relational database; distinguish between a one-to-many and a many-to-many relationship.

OVERVIEW

This chapter reviews basic Windows concepts, applicable to Windows applications in general, and to Microsoft Access in particular. The emphasis is on the common user interface and consistent command structure that facilitate learning within the Windows environment. Indeed, you may already know much of this material, but that is precisely the point. Once you know one Windows application, it is that much easier to learn the next.

The chapter also provides a broad-based introduction to database processing and Microsoft Access. We begin by showing how the principles of manual record keeping can be extended to a computerized system. We discuss the basic operations in table maintenance and stress the importance of data validation. We define basic terms such as field, record, table, and database. We describe the objects within an Access database—which, in addition to tables, include forms, queries, and reports. Most significantly, we show how the real power of Access is derived from a database with multiple tables and from the relationships between those tables.

The entire chapter is built around the example of a database for a college bookstore. The two hands-on exercises in the chapter enable you to apply all of the material at the computer, and are indispensable to the learn-by-doing philosophy we follow throughout the text.

THE WINDOWS DESKTOP

The *desktop* is the centerpiece of Microsoft Windows and is analogous to the desk on which you work. There are physical objects on your real desk and there are *windows* (framed rectangular areas) and *icons* (pictorial symbols) displayed on the Windows desktop. The components of a window are explained within the context of Figure 1.1, which contains the opening Windows screen on our computer.

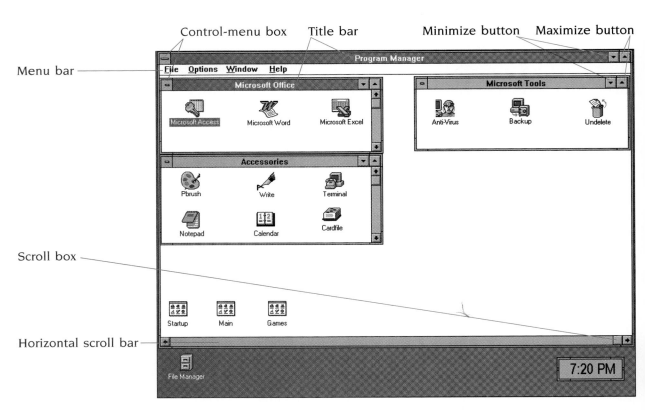

FIGURE 1.1   Program Manager

Your desktop may be different from ours, just as your real desk is arranged differently from those of your friends. You can expect, however, to see a window titled Program Manager. You may or may not see other windows within Program Manager such as the Microsoft Tools and Microsoft Office windows shown in Figure 1.1.

Program Manager is crucial to the operation of Windows. It starts automatically when Windows is loaded and it remains active the entire time you are working in Windows. Closing Program Manager closes Windows. Program Manager is in essence an organizational tool that places applications in groups (e.g., Microsoft Office), then displays those groups as windows or group icons.

Regardless of the windows that are open on your desktop, every window contains the same basic elements: a title bar, control-menu box, and buttons to minimize and to maximize or restore the window. The *title bar* displays the name of the window—for example, Microsoft Office in Figure 1.1. The *control-menu box* accesses a pull-down menu that lets you select operations relevant to the window. The *maximize button* enlarges the window so that it takes up the entire desktop. The *minimize button* reduces a window to an icon (but keeps the program active in memory). A *restore button* (a double arrow not shown in Figure 1.1) appears after a window has been maximized and returns the window to its previous size (the size before it was maximized).

Other elements, which may or may not be present, include a horizontal and/or vertical scroll bar and a menu bar. A horizontal (vertical) *scroll bar* will appear at the bottom (right) border of a window when the contents of the window are not completely visible. The *scroll box* appears within the scroll bar to facilitate moving within the window. A *menu bar* is found in the window for Program Manager, but not in the other windows. This is because Program Manager is a different kind of window, an application window rather than a document window.

An *application window* contains a program (application). A *document window* holds data for a program and is contained within an application window. (The document windows within Program Manager are known as group windows.) The distinction between application and document windows is clearer when we realize that Program Manager is a program and uses commands contained in pull-down menus to manipulate its document (group) windows.

MICROSOFT TOOLS

The Microsoft Tools group is created automatically when you install (or upgrade to) MS-DOS 6.0 or higher. The name of each icon (Antivirus, Backup, and Undelete) is indicative of its function, and each program is an important tool in safeguarding your data. The Antivirus program allows you to scan disks for known viruses (and remove them when found). The Backup utility copies files from the hard disk to one or more floppy disk(s) in case of hard disk failure. The Undelete program allows you to recover files that you accidentally erased from a disk.

WORKING IN WINDOWS

The next several pages take you through the basic operations common to Windows applications in general, and to Access in particular. You may already be familiar with much of this material, in which case you are already benefiting from the *common user interface.* We begin with the mouse and describe how it is used to access pull-down menus and to supply information in dialog boxes. We also emphasize the on-line help facility, which is present in every Windows application.

The Mouse

The mouse (or trackball) is essential to Microsoft Access as it is to all other Windows applications, and you must be comfortable with its four basic actions:

➤ To *point* to an item, move the mouse pointer to the item.

➤ To *click* an item, point to it, then press and release the left mouse button. You can also click the right mouse button to display a shortcut menu.

➤ To *double click* an item, point to it, then click the left mouse button twice in succession.

➤ To *drag* an item, move the pointer to the item, then press and hold the left button while you move the item to a new position.

The mouse is a pointing device—move the mouse on your desk and the *mouse pointer,* typically a small arrowhead, moves on the monitor. The mouse pointer assumes different shapes according to the nature of the current action. You will see a double arrow when you change the size of a window, an I-beam to insert text, a hand to jump from one help topic to the next, or a circle with a line through it to indicate that an attempted action is invalid.

The mouse pointer will also change to an hourglass to indicate that Access is processing your last command, and that no further commands may be issued until the action is completed. The more powerful your computer, the less frequently the hourglass will appear. Conversely, the less powerful your system, the more you will see the hourglass.

A right-handed person will hold the mouse in his or her right hand and click the left button. A left-handed person may want to hold the mouse in the left hand and click the right button. If this sounds complicated, it's not, and you can master the mouse with the on-line tutorial provided in Windows (see step 2 in the hands-on exercise on page 14).

MOUSE TIP FOR LEFTIES
_____

Customize the mouse to reverse the actions of the left and right buttons. Double click the Main group icon in Program Manager to open the group, then double click the Control Panel icon. Double click the Mouse icon, click the Swap Left/Right Buttons check box, then click OK.

Access is designed for a mouse, but it provides keyboard equivalents for almost every command. Toolbars offer still other ways to accomplish the most frequent operations. You may (at first) wonder why there are so many different ways to do the same thing, but you will come to recognize the many options as part of Access's charm. The most appropriate technique depends on personal preference, as well as the specific situation.

If, for example, your hands are already on the keyboard, it is faster to use the keyboard equivalent. Other times, your hand will be on the mouse and that will be the fastest way. It is not necessary to memorize anything, nor should you even try; just be flexible and willing to experiment. The more you do, the easier it will be!

MOUSE TIP: PICK UP THE MOUSE
_____

It seems that you always run out of room on your real desk just when you need to move the mouse a little further. The solution is to pick up the mouse and move it closer to you—the pointer will stay in its present position on the screen, but when you put the mouse down, you will have more room on your desk in which to work.

Field names

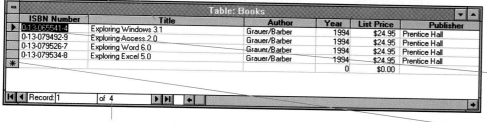

Triangle indicates the record
has not been changed

Indicates the blank record
present at the end of the
table

(a) All Data Has Been Saved

Insertion point indicates where text is entered

Pencil indicates the data has
not been saved

Indicates the blank record at
the end of the table

Five records in the table (one record has been added)

(b) Current Record Has Not Been Saved

FIGURE I.6   Tables

LEARNING BY DOING

We come now to the first of two hands-on exercises that implement our learn-by-doing philosophy. The exercise shows you how to load Windows and practice with the mouse, then directs you to load Microsoft Access and retrieve the Bookstore database from the **data disk** that is available from your instructor.

Remember that Access provides different ways to accomplish the same task. Commands may be accessed from a pull-down menu, from a shortcut menu, through keyboard equivalents, and/or from a toolbar. The various techniques may at first appear overwhelming, but you will be surprised at how quickly you learn them. There is no need to memorize anything nor is there a requirement to use every single technique. Just be flexible and willing to experiment.

CREATE A WORKING DISK

The data disk is almost full and should not be used to add or modify data files referenced in the hands-on exercises. There is no problem if you install the data disk onto your hard drive. If you do not install the data disk to the hard drive, then you must copy the files needed for each exercise from the data disk to a second floppy disk known as a working disk.

HANDS-ON EXERCISE 1:

Introduction to Microsoft Access

Objective To load Windows and Microsoft Access; to open an existing database; to add a record to a table within the database. The exercise introduces you to the data disk that accompanies the text. It also reviews basic Windows operations: pull-down menus, dialog boxes, and the use of a mouse.

Step 1: Load Windows
➤ Type **WIN,** then press the **enter** key to load Windows if it is not already loaded. The appearance of your desktop will be different from ours, but it should resemble Figure 1.1 at the beginning of the chapter.
➤ You will most likely see a window containing Program Manager, but if not, you should see an icon titled Program Manager near the bottom of the screen; double click on this icon to open the Program Manager window.

DOUBLE CLICKING FOR BEGINNERS

If you are having trouble double clicking, it is because you are not clicking quickly enough, or more likely, because you are moving the mouse (however slightly) between clicks. Relax, hold the mouse firmly in place, and try again.

Step 2: Master the mouse
➤ A mouse is essential to the operation of Microsoft Access as it is to all other Windows applications. The easiest way to practice is with the mouse tutorial found in the Help menu of Windows itself.
➤ Pull down the **Help menu.** Click **Windows Tutorial.** Type **M** to begin, then follow the on-screen instructions.
➤ Exit the tutorial when you are finished.

Step 3a: Install the data disk
➤ Do this step *only* if you have your own computer and want to copy the files from the data disk to the hard drive. Place the data disk in drive A (or whatever drive is appropriate).
➤ Pull down the **File menu.** Click **Run.** Type **A:INSTALL C** in the text box. Click **OK.** (The drive letters in the command, A and C, are both variable. If, for example, the data disk were in drive B and you wanted to copy its files to drive D, you would type the command **B:INSTALL D**)
➤ Follow the on-screen instructions to install the data disk.

Step 3b: Create a working disk
➤ Do this step *only* if you are not going to use the hard drive to store the files created in this exercise. Use the Windows File Manager to copy the files **BKSTORE.MDB** and **BKSTORE.LDB** from the data disk to a formatted floppy disk known as the working disk.

Step 4: Load Microsoft Access

➤ Double click the icon for the group containing Microsoft Access if that group is not already open.

➤ Double click the program icon for **Microsoft Access.**

➤ You may or may not see the screen in Figure 1.7a, depending on the options within your system. If the screen is present, **double click** the control-menu box to close the Cue Cards window and begin working on the Bookstore database.

➤ Click the **maximize button** (if necessary) so that the window containing Microsoft Access fills the entire screen.

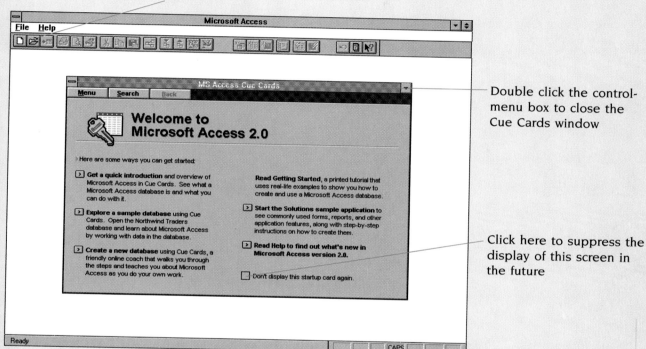

Open Database icon

Double click the control-menu box to close the Cue Cards window

Click here to suppress the display of this screen in the future

(a) Opening Screen (step 1)

FIGURE 1.7 Hands-on Exercise 1

ABOUT MICROSOFT ACCESS

About Microsoft Access on the Help menu displays information about the specific release of Access together with a System Information command button. Click the button to learn about the hardware installed on your system, including the amount of memory and available space on the hard drive.

Step 5: Open the Bookstore database

➤ Pull down the **File menu** and click the **Open Database** command (or click the **Open Database icon** on the toolbar). You will see a dialog box similar to the one in Figure 1.7b.

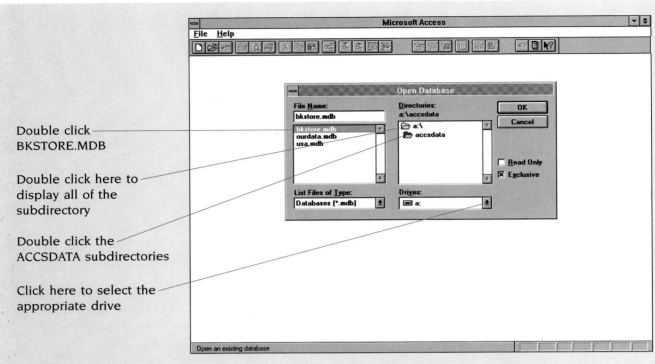

Double click
BKSTORE.MDB

Double click here to
display all of the
subdirectory

Double click the
ACCSDATA subdirectories

Click here to select the
appropriate drive

(b) Opening a Database (step 5)

FIGURE 1.7   Hands-on Exercise 1 (continued)

➤ Click the arrow on the Drives list box to select the appropriate drive—for
  example, drive C or drive A, depending on whether you installed the data
  disk.
➤ Double click the root directory (a:\ or c:\) in the Directories list box to display the subdirectories on the selected drive. Use the working disk if you
  are using drive A.
➤ Double click the **ACCSDATA** directory to make it the active directory.
➤ Double click **BKSTORE.MDB** to open the database for this exercise. The
  Open Database command has loaded the database from disk into memory,
  enabling you to work with the database.

ONE FILE HOLDS ALL

All of the objects in a database (tables, forms, queries, reports, macros,
and modules) are stored in a single file with the *MDB extension.* Execution of the Open Database command in the File menu provides access to
all of the objects via the Database window.

Step 6: Open the Books table
➤ The Table button is already selected. Double click the icon next to **Books** to
  open the table, as shown in Figure 1.7c.
➤ Move and size the window containing the Books table as follows:
  — To move the window, point to the title bar, drag the window to its new
     position, and release the mouse.

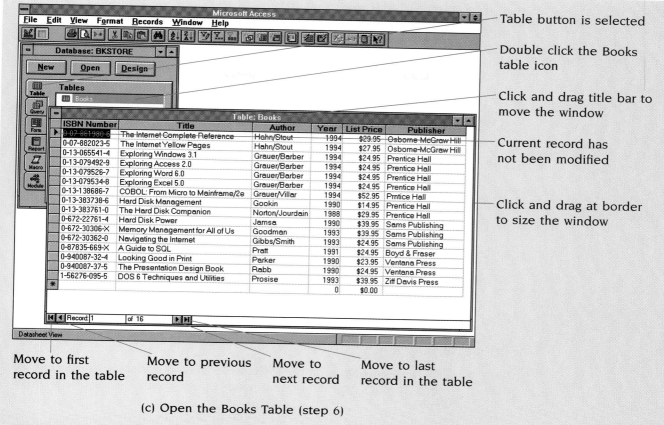

Table button is selected

Double click the Books table icon

Click and drag title bar to move the window

Current record has not been modified

Click and drag at border to size the window

Move to first record in the table

Move to previous record

Move to next record

Move to last record in the table

(c) Open the Books Table (step 6)

FIGURE 1.7 Hands-on Exercise 1 (continued)

— To size the window, point to any border or corner of the window (the pointer changes to a two-headed arrow), then drag until the window is the size you want. Dragging a border changes only one dimension. Dragging a corner changes the length and width simultaneously.

THE WRONG VIEW

If you do not see the records in the table, it is most likely because you are in the wrong view—the Design view rather than the Datasheet view. Pull down the View menu and click Datasheet, or click the Datasheet icon on the toolbar.

Step 7: Moving within a table

➤ Click anywhere in the window containing the Books table. Click the **maximize button** to reduce the clutter on the screen.

➤ Click in any field in the first record, and the status bar indicates record 1 of 16. The triangle symbol in the record selector indicates that the record has not been modified since the last time the table was saved.

➤ You can move from record to record (or field to field) by using either the mouse or the arrow keys.

— Click in any field in the second record. The status bar indicates record 2 of 16.

— Press the **down arrow key** to move to the third record. The status bar indicates record 3 of 16. Press the **left and right arrow keys** to move from field to field within the third record.

➤ You can also use the *navigation buttons* to move from one record to the next.
— Click | ◄ to move to the first record in the table.
— Click ► to move forward in the table to the next record.
— Click ◄ to move back in the table to the previous record.
— Click ► | to move to the last record in the table.

THE COMMON USER INTERFACE

Ctrl+Home and Ctrl+End are keyboard shortcuts that apply universally to every Windows application and move to the beginning and end of a document, respectively. Microsoft Access is no exception. Press Ctrl+Home to move to the first field in the first record of a table. Press Ctrl+End to move to the last field in the last record. Press Home and End to move to the first and last fields in the current record, respectively.

Step 8: Add a record
➤ Click the **New button** on the toolbar. The record selector moves to the last record (record 17). The insertion point is positioned in the first field (ISBN Number).
➤ Enter data for the new record as shown in Figure 1.7d. The record selec-

New button

Current record has not yet been saved

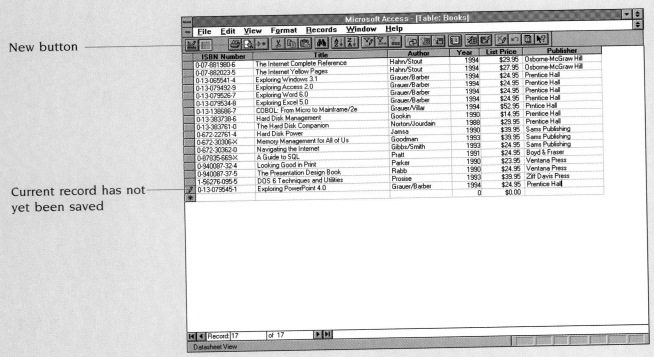

(d) Add a Record (step 8)

FIGURE 1.7 Hands-on Exercise 1 (continued)

tor changes to a pencil as soon as you enter the first character in the new record.

➤ Press the **enter key** when you have entered the last field for the record. The new record is saved, and the record selector changes to a triangle and moves automatically to the next record.

MOVING FROM FIELD TO FIELD

Press the Tab key, the right arrow key, or the enter key to move to the next field in the current record (or the first field in the next record if you are already in the last field of the current record). Press Shift+Tab or the left arrow key to return to the previous field in the current record (or the last field in the previous record if you are already in the first field of the current record).

Step 9: Print the table

➤ Pull down the **File menu** and click **Print** (or click the **Printer icon** on the toolbar). You will see the Print dialog box on your monitor as shown in Figure 1.7e.

➤ Check that the All option button has been selected under Print Range. Click the **OK** command button to accept the default options and print the table.

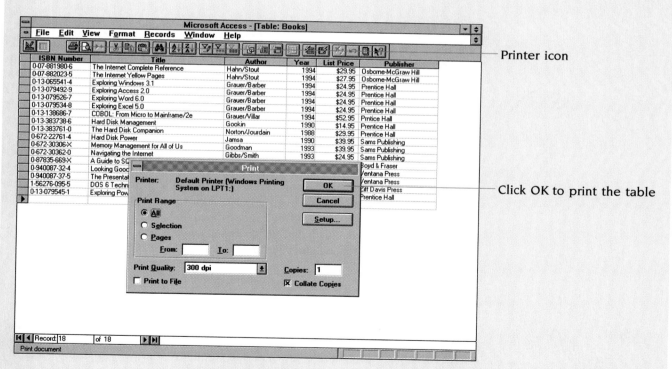

(e) Print the Table (step 9)

FIGURE 1.7   Hands-on Exercise 1 (continued)

Step 10: Exit Access and Windows
➤ Pull down the **File menu.** Click **Exit** to close Access.
➤ Pull down the **File menu** in Program Manager. Click **Exit Windows.** You will see an informational message indicating that you are leaving Windows. Click the **OK** command button to exit.

MAINTAINING THE DATABASE

The exercise just completed showed you how to open an existing table and add records to that table. You will also need to edit and/or delete existing records in order to maintain the database as changes occur. These operations require you to search a table for a specific record in order to make the change. This is best accomplished through the *Find command* in the Edit menu. If, for example, you wanted to change the price of a particular book, you could use the Find command to move directly to that book rather than manually search the table.

As previously indicated, Access automatically saves changes in the current record as soon as you move to the next record. It also remembers the last change you made and allows you to undo that change. The Edit menu contains different Undo commands, depending on the nature of that change. The *Undo Typing command* lets you cancel your most recent change. The *Undo Current Field command* and *Undo Current Record command* cancel all changes to the current field or record, respectively. Even after the changes have been saved (i.e., when you move to the next record), the *Undo Saved Record command* undoes the changes to the previously edited record. Once you begin editing another record, however, changes to the previous record can no longer be undone.

Data Validation

Nor is it sufficient to simply add (edit or delete) a record without adequate checks on the validity of the data. Look carefully at the data in Figure 1.7 and ask yourself if a computer-generated report for Prentice Hall will include *COBOL: From Micro to Mainframe?* The answer is *no* because the publisher field for this book was entered incorrectly. Prentice Hall is misspelled (the first "e" was omitted). You know who the publisher is, but the computer does not because it is searching for the correct spelling.

Data validation is a crucial part of any system. Good systems will anticipate errors you might make and reject those errors prior to accepting data. Access automatically implements certain types of data validation. It will not, for example, let you enter letters where a numeric value is expected (e.g., the Year and Price fields in our example). Other types of validation are implemented by the user. You may decide, for example, to reject any record that omits the title or author. Data validation is described more completely in Chapter 2.

GARBAGE IN, GARBAGE OUT

A computer does exactly what you tell it to do, which is not necessarily what you want it to do. It is absolutely critical, therefore, that you validate the data that goes into a system, or else the associated information will not be correct. No system, no matter how sophisticated, can produce valid output from invalid input. In other words, **garbage in, garbage out (GIGO).**

FORMS, QUERIES, AND REPORTS

We said earlier that an Access database consists of different types of objects such as tables, forms, queries, and reports. Figure 1.8 contains an example of each object as it appears in the Bookstore database.

A table stores data and is the basis for all of the other objects in a database. Figure 1.8a contains the Books table. There are 17 records and six fields for each record.

Figure 1.8b shows the result of a query to select books by a particular publisher (Prentice Hall in this example). A query resembles a table except that it contains selected records, selected fields for those records, and further may list the records in a different order.

Figure 1.8c illustrates a form that can be used to add a new book or edit data for an existing book. You enter data into a form, and Access stores the data in the corresponding table in the database. A form provides a much friendlier interface than does a table and is used for that reason.

Figure 1.8d illustrates a report that prints the books by Prentice Hall. A report may display the results of a query, as in this example, or it may produce entirely different information. All reports provide presentation quality output.

Later chapters discuss forms, queries, and reports in depth. The following exercise is intended as an introduction to what can be accomplished in Access.

ISBN Number	Title	Author	Year	List Price	Publisher
0-07-881980-5	The Internet Complete Reference	Hahn/Stout	1994	$29.95	Osborne-McGraw Hill
0-07-882023-5	The Internet Yellow Pages	Hahn/Stout	1994	$27.95	Osborne-McGraw Hill
0-13-065541-4	Exploring Windows 3.1	Grauer/Barber	1994	$24.95	Prentice Hall
0-13-079492-9	Exploring Access 2.0	Grauer/Barber	1994	$24.95	Prentice Hall
0-13-079526-7	Exploring Word 6.0	Grauer/Barber	1994	$24.95	Prentice Hall
0-13-079534-8	Exploring Excel 5.0	Grauer/Barber	1994	$24.95	Prentice Hall
0-13-079545-1	Exploring PowerPoint 4.0	Grauer/Barber	1994	$24.95	Prentice Hall
0-13-079548-3	Exploring Windows 4.0	Grauer/Barber	1994	$24.95	Prentice Hall
0-13-138686-7	COBOL: From Micro to Mainframe/2e	Grauer/Villar	1994	$52.95	Prentice Hall
0-13-383738-6	Hard Disk Management	Gookin	1990	$14.95	
0-672-22761-4	Hard Disk Power	Jamsa	1990	$39.95	Sams Publishing
0-672-30306-X	Memory Management for All of Us	Goodman	1993	$39.95	Sams Publishing
0-672-30362-0	Navigating the Internet	Gibbs/Smith	1993	$24.95	Sams Publishing
0-87835-669-X	A Guide to SQL	Pratt	1991	$24.95	Boyd & Fraser
0-940087-32-4	Looking Good in Print	Parker	1990	$23.95	Ventana Press
0-940087-37-5	The Presentation Design Book	Rabb	1990	$24.95	Ventana Press
1-56276-095-5	DOS 6 Techniques and Utilities	Prosise	1993	$39.95	Ziff Davis Press
			0	$0.00	

Record: 1   of 17

(a) Books Table

Publisher	Author	Title	ISBN Number	Year	List Price
Prentice Hall	Gookin	Hard Disk Management	0-13-383738-6	1990	$14.95
Prentice Hall	Grauer/Barber	Exploring Access 2.0	0-13-079492-9	1994	$24.95
Prentice Hall	Grauer/Barber	Exploring Excel 5.0	0-13-079534-8	1994	$24.95
Prentice Hall	Grauer/Barber	Exploring PowerPoint 4.0	0-13-079545-1	1994	$24.95
Prentice Hall	Grauer/Barber	Exploring Windows 3.1	0-13-065541-4	1994	$24.95
Prentice Hall	Grauer/Barber	Exploring Windows 4.0	0-13-079548-3	1994	$24.95
Prentice Hall	Grauer/Barber	Exploring Word 6.0	0-13-079526-7	1994	$24.95
Prentice Hall	Grauer/Villar	COBOL: From Micro to Mainframe/2e	0-13-138686-7	1994	$52.95
				0	$0.00

Record: 1   of 8

(b) Publisher Query

FIGURE 1.8   Database Objects

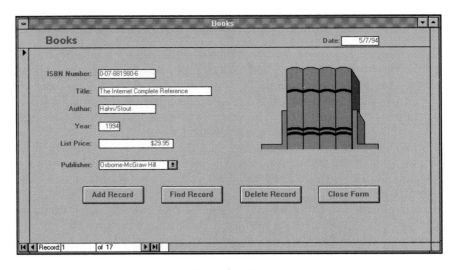

(c) Books Form

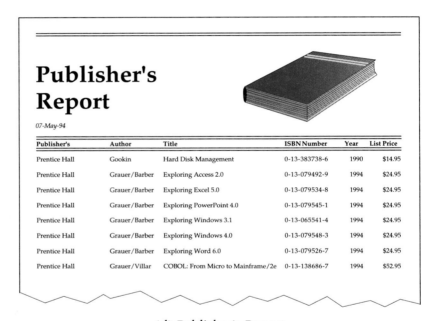

(d) Publisher's Report

FIGURE 1.8   Database Objects (continued)

HANDS-ON EXERCISE 2:

Maintaining the Database

Objective To use the Find command to locate a specific record within a table; to change and delete existing records; to demonstrate data validation; to select and print a report. Use Figure 1.9 as a guide in doing the exercise.

Step 1: Open the Bookstore database

➤ Load Access as you did in the previous exercise.

➤ Pull down the **File menu** and click **Open Database** (or click the *Open Data-base icon* on the toolbar) to display the Open Database dialog box.

➤ Click the arrow on the Drives list box and select the appropriate drive—for example, drive C or drive A, depending on whether you installed the data disk.

➤ Double click the root directory (a:\ or c:\) in the Directories list box to display the subdirectories on the selected drive.

➤ Double click the **ACCSDATA** directory to make it the active directory.

➤ Double click **BKSTORE.MDB** to open the database and display the database window.

➤ The Table Button is already selected. Double click the icon for the **Books table** to open the table from the previous exercise.

➤ Click the **maximize button** to see and access all fields in all records.

➤ *Exploring Powerpoint 4.0,* the book you added in the first exercise, appears in the middle of the table in sequence according to the ISBN field. (This is because the ISBN field has been designated as the primary key, a concept explained in Chapter 2.)

KEYBOARD SHORTCUTS: THE DIALOG BOX

Press Tab or Shift+Tab to move forward (backward) between fields in a dialog box, or press the Alt key plus the underlined letter to move directly to an option. Use the space bar to toggle check boxes on or off and the up and down arrow keys to move between options in a list box. Press enter to activate the highlighted command button and Esc to exit the dialog box without accepting the changes.

Step 2: The Find command

➤ Click anywhere in the Publisher field for the first record.

➤ Pull down the **Edit menu.** Click **Find** to display the dialog box in Figure 1.9a.

➤ Type **Prntice Hall** (omit the first "e"). Check that the other parameters for the Find command match the dialog box in Figure 1.9a.

➤ Click the **Find First command button.** Access moves to record 8, the record containing the designated character string, and selects the Publisher field for that record. You may need to move the dialog box (by dragging its title bar) to see the selected field.

➤ Click the **Close command button** to exit the Find dialog box and continue working in the table.

Step 3: Change an existing record

➤ You should be positioned in the Publisher field of record 8. (The status bar indicates record 8 of 17.) The record selector is a triangle indicating that no changes have yet been made to this record.

➤ Click immediately after the *r* in Prntice to deselect *Prntice Hall* and simultaneously set the insertion point. Type an **e** to correct the publisher's name for this record. The record selector changes to a pencil, indicating that a

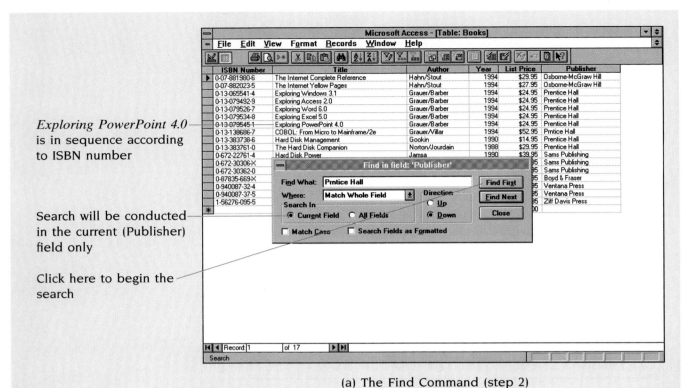

Exploring PowerPoint 4.0 is in sequence according to ISBN number

Search will be conducted in the current (Publisher) field only

Click here to begin the search

(a) The Find Command (step 2)

FIGURE 1.9 Hands-on Exercise 2

change has been made to this record, but that the change has not yet been saved.

➤ Press the **down arrow** to move to the next record and simultaneously save the change you just made. The record selector is again a triangle, indicating that all changes have been saved.

TO SELECT OR NOT SELECT

The fastest way to replace the value in an existing field is to select the field, then type the new value. Access automatically selects the field for you when you use the keyboard (Tab, enter, or arrow keys) to move from one field to the next. Click the mouse to deselect the field if you are replacing only one or two characters rather than the entire field.

Step 4: The Undo command
➤ Pull down the **Edit menu.** Click **Undo Saved Record.** The Publisher field for *COBOL: From Micro to Mainframe* reverts back to the incorrect spelling.
➤ Pull down the **Edit menu** a second time. The Undo command is dim, indicating that you can no longer undo any changes. Press the **Esc** key twice to continue working.
➤ Correct the Publisher field a second time and move to the next record to save your change.

Step 5: The Delete command

➤ Click any field in the row containing the book titled *The Hard Disk Companion.* You can use the Find command as in the previous step, or you can click anywhere in record 10.

➤ Pull down the **Edit menu.** Click **Select Record** to highlight the entire record.

➤ Press the **Del key** to delete the record. You will see a dialog box as shown in Figure 1.9b, indicating that you have just deleted a record and asking you to confirm the deletion. Click **OK.**

➤ Pull down the **Edit menu.** The Undo command is dim, indicating that you cannot undelete a record. Press **Esc** to continue working.

THE ROW SELECTOR

Click the row selector (the box immediately to the left of the first field in a record) to select the record without having to use a pull-down menu. Click and drag the mouse over multiple rows to select several records at the same time.

Step 6: Data validation

➤ Click the **New button** on the toolbar as shown in Figure 1.9c. The record selector moves to the last record (record 17).

➤ Add data as shown in Figure 1.9c, being sure to enter an invalid price by typing **XXX** in the List Price field. Press the **Tab key** to move to the Publisher field.

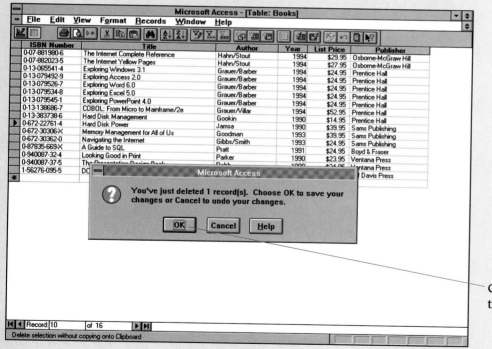

Click here to confirm the deletion

(b) The Delete Command (step 5)

FIGURE 1.9 Hands-on Exercise 2 (continued)

New button

Current record has not yet been saved

Enter XXX to enter an invalid list price

Click OK, then edit the entry

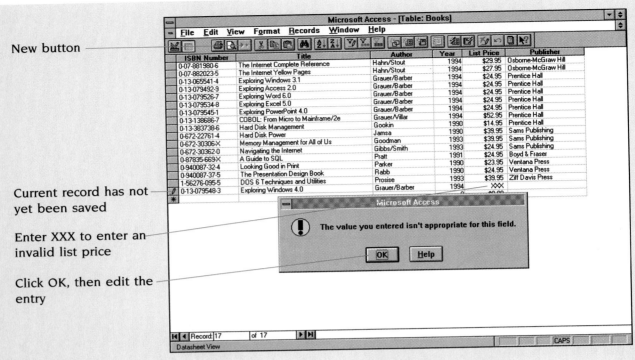

(c) Data Validation (step 6)

FIGURE 1.9 Hands-on Exercise 2 (continued)

> Access displays the dialog box in Figure 1.9c, indicating that the value you entered (XXX) is inappropriate for the List Price field; in other words, you cannot enter letters when Access is expecting a numeric entry.

> Click the **OK** command button to close the dialog box and return to the table. Drag the mouse to select XXX, then enter the correct price ($24.95).

> Press the **Tab key** to move to the Publisher field. Type **Prentice Hall.** Press the **Tab key, right arrow key,** or **enter key** to complete the record and move to the blank record at the end of the table.

> Double click the **control-menu box** to close the Books table and return to the database window.

Step 7: Open the Books form

> Click the **Form button** in the Database window. Double click the **Books form** to open the form as shown in Figure 1.9d.

> Click the **Add Record command button** to move to a new record. The status bar shows record 18 of 18.

> Enter data for the new book as shown in the figure. Click the **Close Form command button** when you are finished.

Step 8: Run a query

> Click the **Query button** in the Database window. Double click the **Publisher query** to run the query.

> You will see the dialog box in Figure 1.9e. Type **Prentice Hall** and press **enter** and you will see the books for the publisher you entered.

> Double click the **control-menu box** to close the query and return to the Database window.

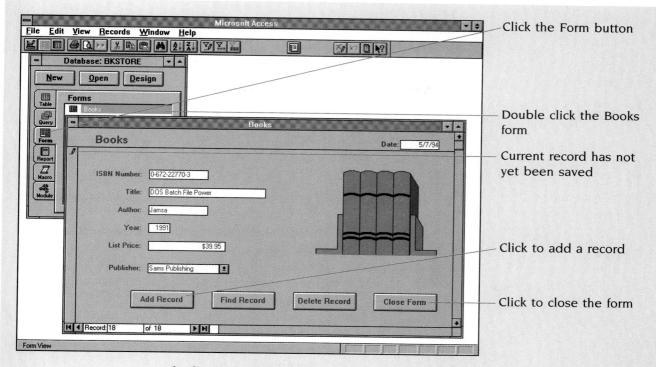

Click the Form button

Double click the Books form

Current record has not yet been saved

Click to add a record

Click to close the form

(d) The Books Form (step 7)

Click the Query object button

Double click to run the query

Enter Prentice Hall to select the corresponding records

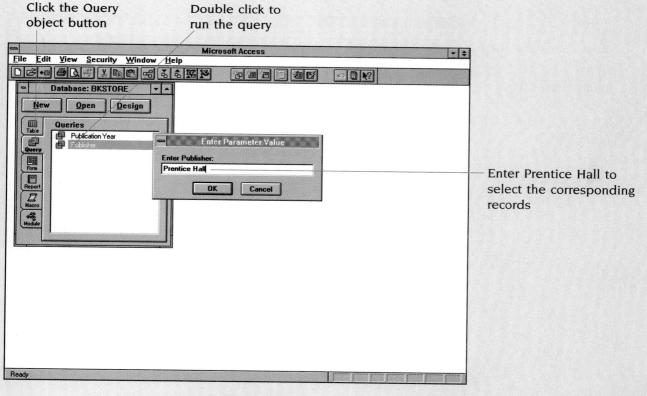

(e) Run a Query (step 8)

FIGURE 1.9 Hands-on Exercise 2 (continued)

THE REPLACE COMMAND

Individuals familiar with a word processor know the advantages of the Replace command. The same capability is available in Access. Pull down the Edit menu and click Replace, then supply the necessary information in the dialog box.

Step 9: Print a report
➤ Click the **Report button** in the Database window to display the available reports.
➤ Double click the icon for the **Publishers report.** Type **Prentice Hall** (or the name of any other publisher) in the Parameter dialog box. Press **enter** to create the report.
➤ Click the **Maximize button** in the Report window so that the report takes the entire screen as shown in Figure 1.9f.
➤ Click the **Zoom button** on the Report toolbar so that you can see the entire page.
➤ Click the **Print button** on the Report toolbar to produce the Print dialog box. Click OK to print the report.
➤ Click the **Close Window button** to close the Report window.

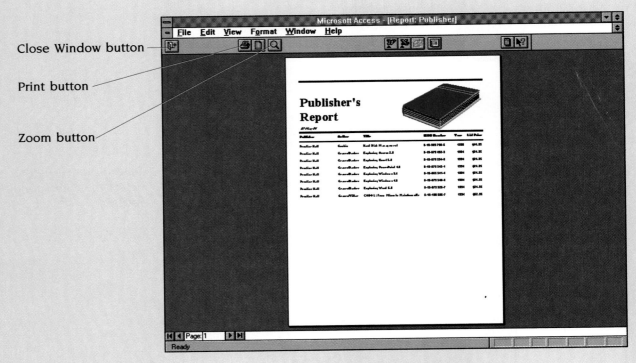

(f) Print a Report (step 9)

FIGURE 1.9   Hands-on Exercise 2 (continued)

Step 10: Exit Access

➤ Pull down the **File menu.** Click **Exit** to leave Access and return to Windows.

LOOKING AHEAD: A RELATIONAL DATABASE

The database we have been using is a simple database in that it contains only one table. The real power of Access, however, is derived from multiple tables and the relationships between those tables. This type of database is known as a *relational database.*

In this section we extend the Bookstore example by including additional tables. We will ask you to look at the data in those tables in order to answer questions about the database. You will need to consider several tables at the same time, but that is precisely what Access does. Once you see how the tables are related to one another, you will be well on your way to designing your own applications.

Pretend again that you are the manager of the bookstore and think about how you would actually use the database. You want information about the individual books, but you also need information about the publishers of those books. At the very least you need the publishers' addresses and phone numbers so that you can order the books. And once you order the books, you need to be able to track the orders, to know when each order was placed, which books were ordered, and how many. These requirements give rise to a database with several additional tables as shown in Figure 1.10.

The Books table in Figure 1.10a is the table we have been using throughout the chapter with one modification. This is the substitution of a PublisherID field instead of the publisher's name. The Books table contains only fields that pertain to a specific book such as the book's ISBN Number, Title, Author, Year (of publication), List Price, and PublisherID. The Publishers table has fields that pertain to the publisher: PublisherID, PublisherName, Address, City, State, Zipcode, and Phone. The PublisherID appears in both tables, which enables us to obtain the publisher's address and phone number for a particular book. Consider:

Query: What are the address and telephone number for the publisher of the book, *Exploring Windows 3.1?*

Answer: *Exploring Windows 3.1* is published by Prentice Hall, which is located at 113 Sylvan Avenue, Englewood Cliffs, NJ, 07632. The telephone number is (800) 526-0485.

To determine the answer, Access would search the Books table for *Exploring Windows 3.1* to obtain the PublisherID (P4 in this example). It would then search the Publishers table for the publisher with this PublisherID and read the address and phone number. The relationship between the publishers and books is an example of a *one-to-many relationship.* One publisher can have many books, but a book can have only one publisher.

(a) Books Table

ISBN	Title	Author	Year	List Price	PublisherID
0-07-881980-6	The Internet Complete Reference	Hahn/Stout	1994	$29.95	P5
0-07-882023-5	The Internet Yellow Pages	Hahn/Stout	1994	$27.95	P5
0-13-065541-4	Exploring Windows 3.1	Grauer/Barber	1994	$24.95	P4
0-13-079492-9	Exploring Access 2.0	Grauer/Barber	1994	$24.95	P4
0-13-079526-7	Exploring Word 6.0	Grauer/Barber	1994	$24.95	P4
0-13-079534-8	Exploring Excel 5.0	Grauer/Barber	1994	$24.95	P4
0-13-138686-7	COBOL: From Micro to Mainframe/2e	Grauer/Villar	1994	$52.95	P4
0-13-383738-6	Hard Disk Management	Gookin	1990	$14.95	P4
0-13-383761-0	The Hard Disk Companion	Norton/Jourdain	1988	$29.95	P4
0-672-22761-4	Hard Disk Power	Jamsa	1990	$39.95	P3
0-672-30306-X	Memory Management for All of Us	Goodman	1993	$39.95	P3
0-672-30362-0	Navigating the Internet	Gibbs/Smith	1993	$24.95	P3
0-87835-669-X	A Guide to SQL	Pratt	1991	$24.95	P1
0-940087-32-4	Looking Good in Print	Parker	1990	$23.95	P2
0-940087-37-5	The Presentation Design Book	Rabb	1990	$24.95	P2
1-56276-095-5	DOS 6 Techniques and Utilities	Prosise	1993	$39.95	P6

(a) Books Table

(b) Publishers Table

PublisherID	Publisher Name	Address	City	State	Zipcode	Phone
P1	Boyd & Fraser	20 Park Paza	Boston	MA	02116	(800)543-8444
P2	Ventana Press	P.O. Box 2468	Chapel Hill	NC	27515	(800)743-5369
P3	Sams Publishing	11711 North College Avenue	Carmel	IN	46032	(800)526-0465
P4	Prentice Hall	113 Sylvan Avenue	Englewood Cliffs	NJ	07632	(800)526-0485
P5	Osborne McGraw-Hill	2600 Tenth Street	Berkeley	CA	94710	(800)338-3987
P6	Ziff Davis Press	5903 Christie Avenue	Emeryville	CA	94608	(800)688-0448

(b) Publishers Table

(c) Orders Table

OrderID	Date	PublisherID
O1	6/12/94	P4
O2	5/31/94	P5
O3	7/01/94	P4
O4	4/30/94	P3
O5	6/18/94	P5
O6	5/22/94	P2
O7	4/18/94	P4
O8	5/01/94	P1

(c) Orders Table

(d) Order Details Table

OrderID	ISBN	Quantity
O1	0-13-065541-4	200
O1	0-13-079492-9	200
O1	0-13-079526-7	200
O1	0-13-079534-8	200
O2	0-07-881980-6	35
O3	0-13-065541-4	200
O3	0-13-079526-7	50
O3	0-13-079534-8	50
O4	0-672-22761-4	25
O4	0-672-30306-X	45
O5	0-07-881980-6	50
O5	0-07-882023-5	75
O6	0-940087-32-4	25
O7	0-13-138686-7	100
O7	0-13-065541-4	50
O8	0-87835-669-X	20

(d) Order Details Table

FIGURE 1.10 The Bookstore Database

Query: Which books are published by Ventana Press?

Answer: Two books, *Looking Good in Print* and *The Presentation Design Book*, are published by Ventana Press.

To answer this query, Access would begin in the Publishers table and search for Ventana Press to determine the PublisherID. It would then select all records in the Books table with a PublisherID of P2. It's easy once you recognize the relationship between the tables.

The Bookstore database in Figure 1.10 has a second one-to-many relationship—between publishers and orders. One publisher can receive many orders, but a given order goes to only one publisher. Use this relationship to answer the following queries:

Query: Which publisher received Order number O2?

Answer: Osborne McGraw-Hill received Order number O2.

To determine the publisher for a specific order, Access would search the Orders table (Figure 1.10c) for the specific order (order number O2 in this example) and obtain the corresponding PublisherID (P5). It would then search the Publishers table for the matching PublisherID and return the publisher's name.

You probably have no trouble recognizing the need for the Books, Publishers, and Orders tables in Figure 1.10. You may be confused, however, by the presence of the Order Details table, which is made necessary by the ***many-to-many relationship*** between orders and books. One order can specify several books, and at the same time, one book can appear in many orders. Consider:

Query: Which books were included in Order number O1?

Answer: *Exploring Windows 3.1, Exploring Excel 5.0, Exploring Word 6.0,* and *Exploring Access 2.0.*

To answer the query, Access would search the Order Details table for all records with an Order-ID of O1. Access would then take the ISBN number for each of these records into the Books table to obtain the title. Can you answer the next query, which is also based on the many-to-many relationship between books and orders?

Query: How many copies of *Exploring Windows 3.1* were ordered in all?

Answer: A total of 450 copies.

This time, Access searches the Books table to obtain the ISBN number for *Exploring Windows 3.1*. It then searches the Order Details table for all records with this ISBN number (0-13-065541-4) to add the individual quantities.

We trust that you were able to answer our queries by intuitively relating the tables to one another. You will also learn how to do this in Microsoft Access when we address this topic in Chapters 4 and 5 and Appendix A. You must first, however, develop a solid understanding of how to work with one table at a time, which is the focus of Chapters 2 and 3.

SUMMARY

The common user interface ensures that all Windows applications are similar in appearance and work basically the same way, with common conventions and a consistent menu structure. It provides you with an intuitive understanding of any application, even before you begin to use it, and means that once you learn one application, it is that much easier to learn the next.

The mouse is essential to Microsoft Access as it is to all other Windows applications, but keyboard equivalents are provided for virtually all operations. Toolbars provide other ways to execute common commands. On-line help provides detailed information about all aspects of Microsoft Access.

The database window displays the objects in a database, which include tables, forms, queries, reports, macros, and modules. The database window enables you to create a new object or to open an existing object.

A table is displayed in one of two views—the design view or the datasheet view. The design view is used to define the table initially and to specify the fields it will contain. The datasheet view is the view you use to add, edit, or delete records.

Each column represents a field. The first row in the table contains the field names. Each additional row contains a record. Every record contains the same fields in the same order.

A record selector symbol is displayed next to the current record and signifies the status of that record. A triangle indicates that you have not changed the data in the current record. A pencil indicates that you are in the process of entering (or changing) the data but that the changes have not yet been saved. An asterisk appears next to the blank record present at the end of every table where you add new records to the table.

A computer does exactly what you tell it to do, which is not necessarily what you want it to do. It is absolutely critical, therefore, that you validate the data that goes into a system, or else the associated information will not be correct.

Access automatically saves any changes in the current record as soon as you move to the next record or when you close the table. The Undo Saved Record command cancels (undoes) the changes to the previously saved record so long as no editing has been done to yet another record.

The real power of Access is derived from multiple tables and the relationships between those tables. This type of database is known as a relational database and is covered later in the text after you have mastered a single table.

Key Words and Concepts

Application window	Datasheet view	Help menu
Asterisk (record selector)	Design view	Icon
	Desktop	Insertion point
Cascade menu	Dialog box	Macro
Check box	Dimmed command	Many-to-many relationship
Click	Document window	
Command button	Double click	Maximize button
Common user interface	Drag	MDB extension
Control-menu box	Drop-down list box	Menu bar
Cue Card	Ellipsis	Microsoft Access
Current record	Field	Minimize button
Data validation	Field name	Module
Database	Find command	Mouse pointer
Database Management System (DBMS)	Form	Navigation button
	GIGO (garbage in, garbage out)	Object
Database window		Object button

One-to-many
  relationship
Open list box
Option button
Pencil (record selector)
Point
Program Manager
Pull-down menu
Query
Record
Record selector symbol
Relational database

Report
Restore button
Scroll bar
Scroll box
Table
Text box
Title bar
Triangle (record
  selector)
Undo Current Field
  command

Undo Current Record
  command
Undo Saved Record
  command
Undo Typing command
Window

 ## Multiple Choice

1. Which of the following will execute a command from a pull-down menu?
  (a) Clicking on the command once the menu has been pulled down
  (b) Typing the underlined letter in the command
  (c) Both (a) and (b)
  (d) Neither (a) nor (b)

2. Which program is always active during a Windows session?
  (a) Program Manager
  (b) Microsoft Access
  (c) Both (a) and (b)
  (d) Neither (a) nor (b)

3. What is the significance of three dots next to a menu option?
  (a) The option is not accessible
  (b) A dialog box will appear if the option is selected
  (c) A help window will appear if the option is selected
  (d) There are no equivalent keystrokes for the particular option

4. What is the significance of a menu option that appears faded (dimmed)?
  (a) The option is not currently accessible
  (b) A dialog box will appear if the option is selected
  (c) A help window will appear if the option is selected
  (d) There are no equivalent keystrokes for the particular option

5. Which of the following elements may be found within a help window?
  (a) Title bar, menu bar, and control-menu box
  (b) Minimize and maximize or restore buttons
  (c) Vertical and/or horizontal scroll bars
  (d) All of the above

6. Which of the following is true regarding a dialog box?
  (a) Option buttons indicate mutually exclusive choices
  (b) Check boxes imply that multiple options may be selected
  (c) Both (a) and (b)
  (d) Neither (a) nor (b)

7. Which of the following is true about moving and sizing a window?
   (a) The title bar is used to size a window
   (b) A border or corner is used to move a window
   (c) Both (a) and (b)
   (d) Neither (a) nor (b)

8. Which of the following objects are contained within an Access database?
   (a) Tables and forms
   (b) Queries and reports
   (c) Both (a) and (b)
   (d) Neither (a) nor (b)

9. The Open Database command:
   (a) Loads a database from disk into memory
   (b) Loads a database from disk into memory, then erases the database on disk
   (c) Stores the database in memory on disk
   (d) Stores the database in memory on disk, then erases the database from memory

10. Which of the following is true regarding the record-selector symbol?
   (a) A pencil indicates that the current record has already been saved
   (b) A triangle indicates that the current record has not changed
   (c) An asterisk indicates the first record in the table
   (d) All of the above

11. Which view is used to add, edit, and delete records in a table?
   (a) The Design view
   (b) The Datasheet view
   (c) Either (a) and (b)
   (d) Neither (a) nor (b)

12. Which of the following is true with respect to a table within an Access Database?
   (a) Ctrl+Home moves to the last field in the last record of a table
   (b) Ctrl+End moves to the first field in the first record of a table
   (c) Both (a) and (b)
   (d) Neither (a) nor (b)

13. Which of the following is true of an Access database?
   (a) Every record in a table contains the same fields as every other record
   (b) Every table contains the same number of records as every other table
   (c) Both (a) and (b)
   (d) Neither (a) nor (b)

14. Which of the following best describes the relationship between publishers and books as implemented in the Bookstore database within the chapter?
   (a) One to one
   (b) One to many
   (c) Many to many
   (d) Impossible to determine

15. Which of the following best describes the relationship between books and orders as implemented in the Bookstore database within the chapter?

(a) One to one
(b) One to many
(c) Many to many
(d) Impossible to determine

ANSWERS

1. c	**9.** a
2. a	**10.** b
3. b	**11.** b
4. a	**12.** d
5. d	**13.** a
6. c	**14.** b
7. d	**15.** c
8. c	

EXPLORING ACCESS

1. Use Figure 1.11 to match each action with its result. A given action may be used more than once or not at all.

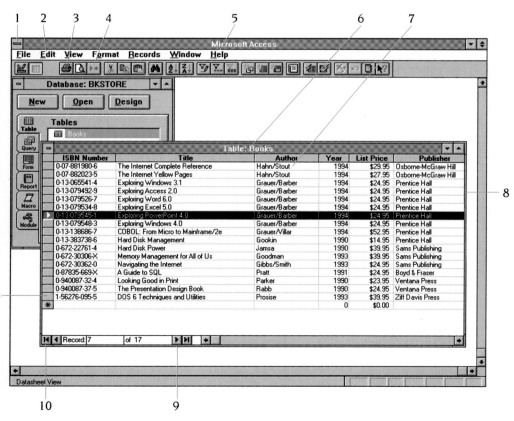
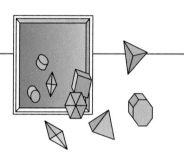

FIGURE 1.11 Screen for Problem 1

Action	Result
a. Double click at 1	___ Go to the first record in the table
b. Click at 3	___ Size the window
c. Click at 4	___ Exit Access
d. Click at 5	___ Add a new record to the table
e. Click and drag at 6	___ Move the window
f. Click at 7, click at 2	___ Go to the next record in the table
g. Click and drag at 8	___ Print the table
h. Click at 9	___ Delete *DOS 6 Techniques and Utilities* from the table
i. Click at 10	___ Find the book written by Jamsa
j. Click at 11, then press the Del key	___ Search for help on adding records

2 Exploring help: Answer the following with respect to Figure 1.12:
   a. What is the significance of the scroll box that appears within the scroll bar?
   b. What happens if you click on the down (up) arrow within the scroll bar?
   c. What happens if you click the maximize button? Might this action eliminate the need to scroll within the help window?
   d. How do you print the help topic shown in the window?
   e. Which entries in the help screen are underlined? What happens if you click an underlined entry?

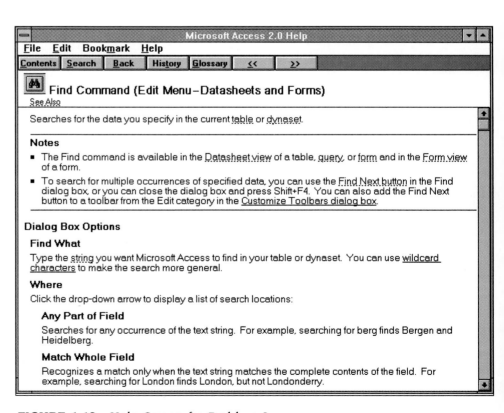

FIGURE 1.12 Help Screen for Problem 2

3. The error messages in Figure 1.13 appeared or could have appeared in conjunction with the hands-on exercises in the chapter. Indicate a potential cause of each error and a suggested course of action to correct the problem.

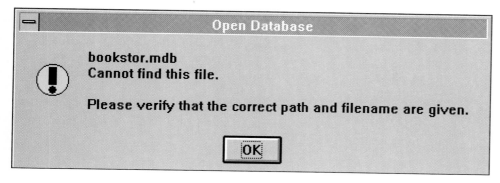

(a) Informational Message 1

(b) Informational Message 2

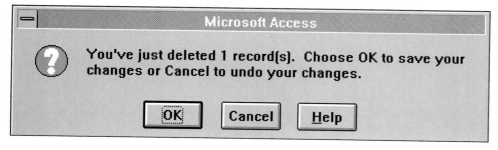

(c) Informational Message 3

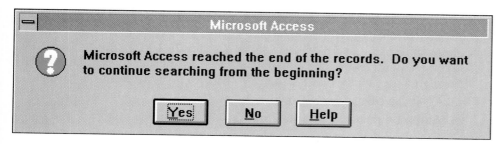

(d) Informational Message 4

FIGURE 1.13 Error Messages for Problem 3

4. The Replace command: The table in Figure 1.14 is a modified version of the Books table used in the chapter.

  a. Can the Current Field and All Fields option buttons in the Replace dialog box be checked simultaneously?

  b. Can the Match Case and Match Whole Field boxes in the Replace dialog box be checked simultaneously?

  c. Assume that the user clicks the All Fields option button, but makes no other changes to the dialog box. Which record will be returned when the user clicks the Find Next command button? Will you need to continue the search from the beginning of the table?

  d. Assume that the user clicks the Replace All command button. Will the replacement be made for the character string, *Prentice Hall Publishers*? for the character string, *prentice hall*?

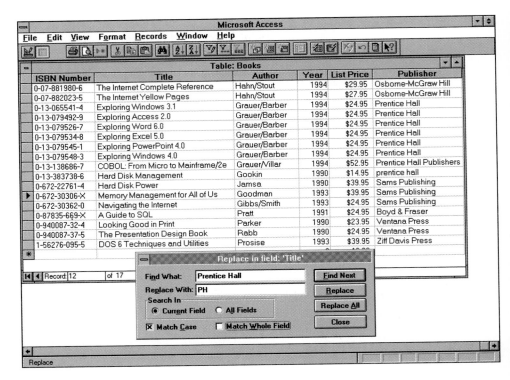

FIGURE 1.14   Screen for Problem 4

5. Data validation: Open the Bookstore database that was used in the chapter to add the book *Excel 4 for Windows,* by Hergert, published by Sybex in 1992, and priced at $14.95. The ISBN number is 0-7821-1016-9. First, however, we want you to enter the data *incorrectly* in order to evaluate the data validation capability that is built into the system. What happens if you:

  a. Omit the title or author field?

  b. Enter a duplicate value for ISBN?

  c. Enter a nonnumeric value for the year or price?

  d. Enter an inappropriate year (e.g., a year in the future)?

  Do you think that additional data validation should be built into the system?

6. Answer the following with respect to the Bookstore database in Figure 1.10:

  a. Which publisher received order number O8?

  b. How many orders have been placed by the bookstore?

c. How many orders were sent to Prentice Hall?

d. What is the price of *A Guide to SQL*? Who is the author? Who is the publisher? How many copies of this book have been ordered?

Which table (or tables) have to be modified to accommodate the following changes in the Bookstore database?

e. The phone number for Sams Publishing is changed to (800) 526-1000.

f. The price of *Exploring Windows* is increased to $25.95.

g. Order number O3 was modified to include 500 copies of *Exploring Windows 3.1* rather than the original 200.

h. Order number O9 was placed on June 6, 1994. The order is for 1,000 copies of *Exploring Windows, Exploring Word for Windows, Exploring Excel,* and *Exploring Access.*

i. The book, *Looking Good in Print,* is no longer carried by the bookstore.

j. Order number O7 is cancelled. Which record(s) have to be deleted from which table(s)?

k. What problems, if any, would be caused by deleting the record for Osborne McGraw-Hill from the Publishers table?

7. The EMPLOYEE.MDB database: The table in Figure 1.15 exists within the EMPLOYEE.MDB database on the data disk. Open the table and do the following:

a. Add a new record for yourself. You have been hired as a trainee earning $20,000 in Boston.

b. Delete the record for Kelly Marder.

c. Change Pamela Milgrom's salary to $59,500.

d. Use the Replace command to change all occurrences of "Manager" to "Supervisor".

e. Print the table after making the changes in parts a through d.

f. Print the All Employees Report after making the changes in parts a through d.

g. Print the Location Report after making the changes in parts a through d.

h. Create a cover page, then submit the output from parts e, f, and g to your instructor.

SocialSecurityNumber	LastName	FirstName	Location	Title	Salary	Sex
255-09-4456	Johnson	James	Chicago	Account Rep	$47500	M
255-69-7854	Marlin	Billy	Miami	Manager	$125000	M
265-30-9876	Manin	Ann	Boston	Account Rep	$49500	F
267-44-9850	Frank	Vernon	Miami	Manager	$75000	M
269-57-4322	Charles	Kenneth	Boston	Account Rep	$40000	M
279-85-2345	Adamson	David	Chicago	Manager	$52000	M
279-85-7644	Marder	Kelly	Chicago	Account Rep	$38500	F
388-56-3443	Brown	Marietta	Atlanta	Trainee	$18500	F
565-87-9002	Adams	Jennifer	Atlanta	Trainee	$19500	F
595-34-0289	Milgrom	Pamela	Boston	Manager	$57500	F
596-84-3222	Rubin	Patricia	Boston	Account Rep	$45000	F
598-65-8994	Coulter	Tracey	Atlanta	Manager	$100000	F
800-39-8764	Smith	Frank	Atlanta	Account Rep	$65000	M
800-56-8944	James	Mary	Chicago	Account Rep	$42500	F

Table: EMPLOYEE

Record: 1 of 14

FIGURE 1.15 Screen for Problem 7

8. Exploring Cue Cards: The best way to learn about Cue Cards is to use them.

a. What are Cue Cards supposed to do?

b. Which command, in which menu, will produce the opening Cue Card?

c. What is the corresponding toolbar icon?

d. Use either the Menu command (in part b) or the corresponding toolbar icon (in part c) to produce the opening Cue Card in Figure 1.16a.

e. Click the arrow next to "See a quick overview" to access the Cue Card in Figure 1.16b.

f. Click the arrow next to "Tables" to learn about this feature in Access. Follow the on-screen instructions to review the material that was presented in the chapter.

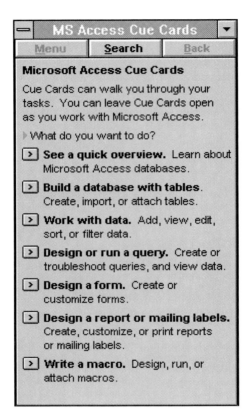

(a)

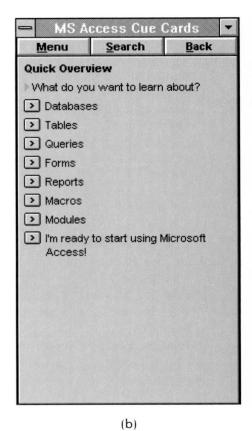

(b)

FIGURE 1.16 Cue Cards for Problem 8

 Case Studies

Planning for Disaster

This case has nothing to do with a database per se, but it is perhaps the most important case of all, as it deals with the question of backup. Do you have a backup strategy? Do you even know what a backup strategy is? You should learn, because sooner or later you will wish you had one. You will erase a file, be unable to read from a floppy disk, or worse yet, suffer a hardware failure in which you are unable to access the hard drive. The problem always seems to occur the night before an assignment is due. The ultimate disaster is the disappearance of your computer, by theft or natural disaster (e.g., Hurricane Andrew, the floods in the Midwest, or the Los Angeles earthquake). Describe in 250 words or less the backup strategy you plan to implement in conjunction with your work in this class.

Your Own Reference Manual

The clipboard is a temporary storage area available to all Windows applications. Selected text is cut or copied from one document into the clipboard from where it can be pasted into another document altogether. Use on-line help to obtain detailed information on several topics in Microsoft Access, copy the information to the clipboard, then paste it into a Word for Windows document, which will become your personal reference manual. To really do an outstanding job, you will have to format the reference manual after the information has been copied from the clipboard. Be sure to include a title page.

The Common User Interface

One of the most significant benefits of the Windows environment is the common user interface, which provides a sense of familiarity when you go from one application to another—for example, when you go from Excel to Access. How many similarities can you find between these two applications? Which menus are common to both? Which keyboard shortcuts? Which formatting conventions? Which toolbar icons? Which shortcut menus?

The Database Consultant

The university's bookstore manager has gone to your instructor and asked for help in improving the existing database. The manager needs to know which books are used in which courses. One course may require several books, and the same book is often used in many courses. A book may be required in one course and merely recommended in a different course. The manager also needs to be able to contact the faculty coordinator in charge of each course. Which additional table(s) should be added to the database in Figure 1.10 to provide this information? Which fields should be present in those tables?

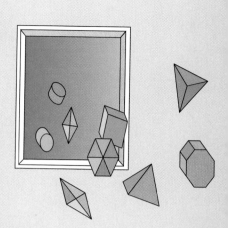

2

Tables and Forms: Design, Properties, Views, and Wizards

After reading this chapter you will be able to:

1. Describe in general terms how to design a table; discuss three guidelines you can use in the design process.
2. Describe the field types and properties available within Access and the purpose of each; set the primary key for a table.
3. Use the Table Wizard to create a table; add and delete fields in an existing table.
4. Discuss the importance of data validation and how it is implemented in Access.
5. Use the Form Wizard to create one of several predefined forms.
6. Distinguish between a bound control, an unbound control, and a calculated control; explain how each type of control is entered on a form.
7. Modify an existing form to include a combo box, command buttons, and color.
8. Switch between the Form view, Design view, and Datasheet view; use a form to add, edit, and delete records in a table.

OVERVIEW

This chapter introduces a new case study, that of a student database, which we use to present the basic principles of tables and forms. The database has only a single table and is the focus of all examples in Chapters 2 and 3. Databases with multiple tables are covered in Chapters 4 and 5.

The first half of the chapter shows you how to create a table using the Table Wizard, then shows you how to modify the table by changing the properties of fields within the table. It stresses the importance of data validation during data entry. The second half of the chapter introduces forms as a more convenient way to enter and display data. You use the Form Wizard to create a basic form, then modify that form to include command buttons, a combo list box, color, and formatting.

The success of any database depends heavily upon the design of the underlying table(s). Thus, you should pay close attention to the conceptual discussion following the case study.

CASE STUDY: A STUDENT DATABASE

As a student you are well aware that your school maintains all types of data about you. They have your social security number. They have your name and address and phone number. They know whether or not you are receiving financial aid. They know your major and the number of credits you have completed.

Think for a moment, then write down all of the fields that might be stored in a student table. Try to include all of the data that is necessary for the school to produce the information it needs. Think how you should characterize each field according to the type of data it contains, such as text, numbers, or dates.

Our solution is shown in Figure 2.1, which may or may not correspond with what you have written. (The order of the fields within the table is not significant.) Whether or not your list of field names is the same as ours is not really important, because there are many acceptable solutions. What is important is that the table contain all necessary fields so that the system can perform as intended.

Figure 2.1 may seem obvious upon presentation, but it does reflect the results of a careful design process based on three essential guidelines:

1. Include the necessary data
2. Store data in its smallest parts
3. Avoid calculated fields

Each guideline is discussed in turn. As you proceed through the text, you will be exposed to many different applications that help you develop the experience necessary to design your own systems.

Field Name	Type
SocialSecurityNumber	Text
FirstName	Text
MiddleName	Text
LastName	Text
Address	Text
City	Text
State	Text
PostalCode	Text
PhoneNumber	Text
Major	Text
BirthDate	Date/Time
FinancialAid	Yes/No
Sex	Text
Credits	Number
QualityPoints	Number

No spaces are used in the field names

FIGURE 2.1 The Student Table

Include the Necessary Data

How do you determine the necessary data? The best way is to create a rough draft of the reports you will need, then check the table to be sure it contains the fields necessary to produce those reports. In other words, ask yourself what information will be expected from the system, then determine the data required to produce that information. Put another way, determine the input needed to produce the required output.

Consider, for example, the type of information that can and cannot be produced from the table in Figure 2.1:

➤ You can contact a student by mail or by telephone. You cannot contact the student's parents if the student lives on campus and thus has an address different from his or her parents' address.

➤ You can calculate a student's grade point average (GPA) by dividing the quality points by the number of credits. You cannot produce a transcript listing the courses a student has taken.

➤ You can calculate a student's age from his or her date of birth. You cannot determine how long the student has been at the university because the date of admission is not in the table.

Whether or not these omissions are important depends on the objectives of the system. Suffice it to say that you must design a table carefully, so that you are not disappointed when it is implemented. *You must be absolutely certain that the data entered into a system is sufficient to provide all necessary information;* otherwise the system is almost guaranteed to fail.

Store Data in Its Smallest Parts

Figure 2.1 divides a student's name into three fields (first, middle, and last) to reference each field individually. You might think it easier to use a single field consisting of the entire name, but that approach is inadequate. Consider the consequences of a single field with respect to the following names:

Allison Foster
Brit Reback
Carrie Graber
Danielle Ferrarro

Whether you realize it or not, the names are listed in alphabetical order (according to the design criteria of a single field). This is because the records are sorted according to the leftmost position in the designated field. Thus the "A" in Allison comes before the "B" in Brit, and so on. The proper way to sort is on last name, which can be done only if last name is stored as a separate field. At other times you may want to reference just the first name, perhaps to send informal letters with a salutation of the form, "Dear Allison" or "Dear Brit".

CITY, STATE, AND ZIP CODE—ONE FIELD OR THREE?

The city, state, and zip code should always be stored as separate fields. Any type of mass mailing requires you to sort on zip code to take advantage of bulk mail. Other applications may require you to select records in a particular state (or combination of states). The guideline is simple: store data in its smallest parts.

Avoid Calculated Fields

A *calculated field* is a field whose value is derived from an existing field or combination of fields. Calculated fields should not be stored in a table because they are subject to change, waste space, and are otherwise redundant.

Grade Point Average (GPA) is an example of a calculated field because it is computed by dividing the number of quality points by the number of credits. It is unnecessary, however, to store the GPA in the Student table since we store the fields on which it is based, and thus can instruct Access to calculate the GPA when it is needed.

BIRTH DATE VERSUS AGE

A person's age and date of birth provide equivalent information as one is calculated from the other. It might seem easier, therefore, to store the age rather than the birth date, and thus avoid the calculation. That would be a mistake because age changes continually, whereas the date of birth remains constant. Similar reasoning applies to an employee's length of service versus the date of hire.

CREATING A TABLE

There are two ways to create a table. The easiest way is to use the *Table Wizard*, an interactive coach that lets you choose from several predefined tables. The Table Wizard asks you questions about the fields you want to include in your table, then creates the table for you. Alternatively, you can create a table yourself by defining every field in the table. Regardless of how a table was created, you can modify it to include a new field or to delete an existing field.

Every field in a table has a field name and a data type. The *field name* should be descriptive of the data that will be entered into the field. It can be up to 64 characters, including letters, numbers, and spaces. We do not use spaces in our field names, which is consistent with the default names provided by Access in its predefined tables. LastName, BirthDate, and Credits are examples of field names in Figure 2.1.

Data Types

The *data type* indicates the nature of the data in the field and determines how Access processes that data. Text, Date/Time, and Number are examples of data types used in Figure 2.1.

The data type determines the values allowed in a field. It controls the amount of space allocated to a field and the types of operations that can be performed. There are eight different data types: Number, Text, Memo, Date/Time, Currency, Counter, Yes/No, and OLE Object.

A *number field* contains a value that can be used in a calculation such as the number of quality points or credits a student has earned. The contents of a number field are restricted to numbers, a decimal point, and a plus or minus sign.

A *text field* stores alphanumeric data such as a student's name or address. It can contain alphabetic characters, numbers, and/or special characters (e.g., an apostrophe in O'Malley). Fields that contain only numbers, but which are not used in a calculation (e.g., social security number, telephone number, or zip code), should be designated as text fields for efficiency purposes. A text field can hold up to 255 characters.

A *memo field* can be up to 64,000 characters long. Memo fields are used to hold descriptive data (several sentences or paragraphs).

A *Date/Time field* holds formatted dates or times (e.g., mm/dd/yy) and allows the values to be used in date or time arithmetic.

A *currency field* can also be used in a calculation and is used for fields that contain monetary values.

A *counter field* is a special data type that causes Access to assign the next consecutive number each time you add a record. By definition, the value of a counter field is unique for each record in the file, and thus counter fields are frequently used as the primary key.

A *Yes/No field* (also known as a Boolean or Logical field) assumes one of two values such as Yes or No, or True or False. A Yes/No field is preferable to one-position text fields because it is more efficient.

An *OLE field* contains an object created by another application. OLE objects include pictures, sounds, or graphics.

Primary Key

The *primary key* is a field (or combination of fields) that uniquely identifies a record. Every table must have a primary key, and there can be only one primary key per table.

A person's name is not used as the primary key because names are not unique. A social security number, on the other hand, is unique and is a frequent choice for the primary key. Social security number is the primary key in the Student table. The primary key emerges naturally in many applications such as a part number in an inventory system, or the ISBN number in the book table of Chapter 1.

Views

A table has two views—the Datasheet view and the Design view. The *Datasheet view* is the view you used in Chapter 1 to add, edit, and delete records. The *Design view* is the view you will use in this chapter to create a table.

Figure 2.2a shows the Datasheet view corresponding to the table in Figure 2.1. (Not all of the fields are visible.) The Datasheet view displays the record selector symbol for the current record (a pencil or a triangle). It also displays an asterisk as the record selector symbol next to the blank record at the end of the table.

Figure 2.2b shows the Design view of the same table. The Design view displays the field names in the table, the data type of each field, and the properties of the selected field. The Design view also displays a key indicator next to the field (or combination of fields) designated as the primary key.

Current record (has been saved)

SocialSecurityN	First Name	Middle Name	Last Name	Address	City	State	Postal Code	Phone Number
111-11-1111	Benjamin	David	Harrison	1718 Rodeo Drive	Coral Springs	FL	33071-8346	(305) 753-1098
222-22-2222	Juliette	Laura	Masters	8900 Main Highway	Chicago	IL	60620-4565	(312) 455-6521
333-33-3333	Patricia	Renee	Jones	500 Park Avenue	New York	NY	10020-0300	(212) 667-4848
444-44-4444	Matthew	James	Baldwin	3433 College Terrace	Baltimore	MD	21224-3443	(410) 444-8712
555-55-5555	Jessica	Lewis	Warner	426 Hardee Avenue	San Francisco	CA	94114-0876	(415) 677-4545
666-66-6666	Karen	Anne	Cutler	13601 S.W. 92 Avenue	Miami	FL	33176-6235	(305) 233-2020
777-77-7777	Kenneth	Neil	Irwin	900 Alamo Drive	Houston	TX	77090-0475	(713) 757-8400

Table: All Students

Record: 1 of 7

Blank record at end of table

(a) Datasheet View

FIGURE 2.2 The Views of a Table

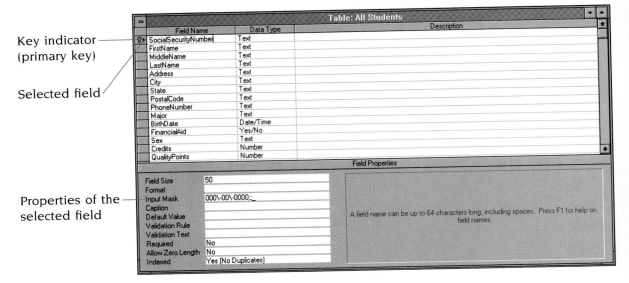

Key indicator (primary key)

Selected field

Properties of the selected field

(b) Design View

FIGURE 2.2   The Views of a Table (continued)

Property	Description
Field Size	Adjusts the size of a text field or limits the allowable value in a number field. Microsoft Access uses only the amount of space it needs even if the field size allows a greater number.
Format	Changes the appearance of number and date fields but does not affect the stored value.
Decimal Places	Controls the number of places after the decimal point for a Number or Currency field.
Input Mask	Displays formatting characters, such as hyphens in a social security number, so that the formatting characters do not have to be entered; imposes data validation by ensuring that the data fits in the mask size.
Caption	Specifies a label other than the field name for forms and reports.
Default Value	Automatically assigns a designated (default) value for the field in each record that is added to the table.
Validation Rule	Rejects any record where the data does not conform to the specified validation rule.
Validation Text	Specifies the error message that is displayed when the validation rule is violated.
Required	Rejects any record that does not have a value entered for this field.
Allow Zero Length	Allows text or memo strings of zero length.
Indexed	Increases the efficiency of a search on the designated field; the primary key is always indexed.

FIGURE 2.3   Field Properties

Field Properties

A *property* is a characteristic of an object that determines how the object appears or works. All Access objects (tables, forms, queries, and reports) have properties that control their behavior.

Each field also has a set of field properties that determine how the data in the field is stored and displayed. The properties are set to *default values* according to the data type but can be modified as necessary. The properties for each field are displayed in the Design view as shown in Figure 2.2b. The properties are described briefly in Figure 2.3 and illustrated in the hands-on exercise that follows.

HANDS-ON EXERCISE 1:

Creating a Table

Objective Use the Table Wizard to create a table; add and delete fields in an existing table; change the primary key of an existing table; establish an input mask and validation rule for fields within a table; switch between the design and datasheet views of a table. Use Figure 2.4 as a guide in the exercise.

Step 1: Create a new database

➤ Pull down the **File menu** and click **New Database** (or click the **New Database icon** on the toolbar). The New Database dialog box will appear as shown in Figure 2.4a.

➤ Click the Drives drop-down list box to specify the appropriate drive, drive C or drive A, depending on whether or not you installed the data disk in Chapter 1.

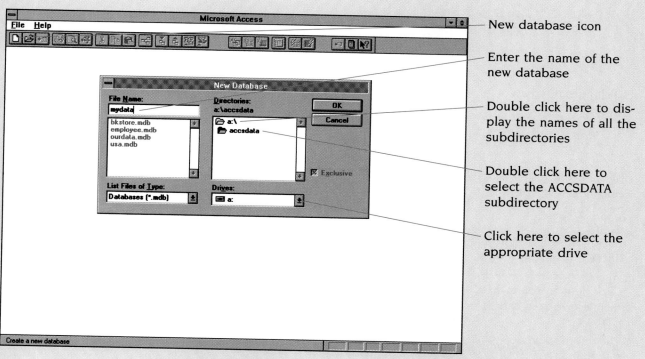

New database icon

Enter the name of the new database

Double click here to display the names of all the subdirectories

Double click here to select the ACCSDATA subdirectory

Click here to select the appropriate drive

(a) Create a New Database (step 1)

FIGURE 2.4 Hands-on Exercise 1

- ➤ Double click the root directory (a:\ or c:\) to display the subdirectories on the selected drive. Use the **working disk** created in Chapter 1 (page 14) if you are not using the hard drive.
- ➤ Scroll through the Directories list box until you come to the **ACCSDATA** directory. Double click this directory to make it the active directory.
- ➤ Click in the **File Name text box** and drag to select **db1.mdb.** Type **MYDATA** as the name of the database you will create. (The MDB extension is added automatically.) Press **enter** or click **OK.**

CHANGE THE DEFAULT DIRECTORY

The default directory is the directory Access uses to retrieve (and save) a database unless it is otherwise instructed. To change the default directory, pull down the View menu, click Options, and select the General category. Click the down arrow in the Items list box and scroll to Default Database Directory. Enter the new directory (e.g., C:\ACCSDATA) and click OK. The next time you access the File menu the default directory will reflect the change.

Step 2: Create the table
- ➤ The Database window for the database MYDATA should appear on your monitor as shown in Figure 2.4b. (The table button is selected by default.)

Click here to create a new table

Table object is selected

Click here to enter selected field in the new table

Click here to scroll through available tables

Click here to select business-related tables

Click here to select a field

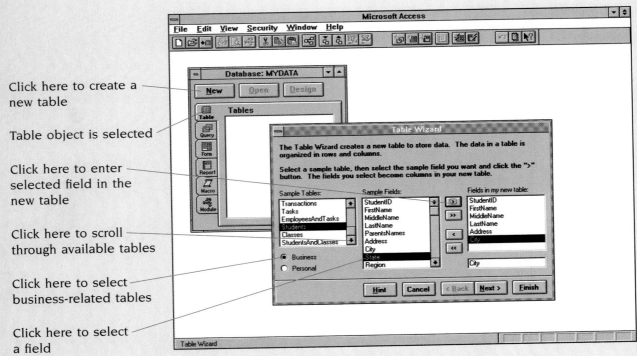

(b) The Table Wizard (step 3)

FIGURE 2.4 Hands-on Exercise 1 (continued)

➤ Click the **New command button** to create a table within the MYDATA database. Click the **Table Wizards button** in the New Table Dialog box to use the Table Wizard. You should see a dialog box similar to Figure 2.4b.

Step 3: The Table Wizard

➤ If necessary, click the **Business option** button. Click the **down arrow** on the Sample Table list box to scroll through the available business tables. (The tables are not in alphabetical order.) Double click the **Students table.**

➤ Click the **StudentID field** in the Sample Fields list box, then click the **>** button to enter this field in the new table list as shown in Figure 2.4b.

➤ Enter the remaining fields: **FirstName, MiddleName, LastName, Address, City, State, PostalCode, PhoneNumber,** and **Major.** Click the **Next command button** when you have entered all the fields.

WIZARDS AND BUTTONS

Many Wizards present you with two open list boxes and expect you to copy some or all fields from the list box on the left to the list box on the right. The **>** and **>>** buttons work from left to right. The **<** and **<<** buttons work in the opposite direction. The **>** button copies the *selected* field from the list box on the left to the box on the right. The **>>** button copies *all* of the fields. The **<** button removes the *selected* field from the list box on the right. The **<<** removes *all* of the fields.

Step 4: The Table Wizard (continued)

➤ The next screen in the Table Wizard asks you to name the table and determine the primary key.
— The Table Wizard suggests Students as the name of the table. Change the name to **All Students.**
— Make sure that the option button **Let Microsoft Access set a primary key for me** is selected.
— Click the **Next command button** to accept both of these options.

➤ The final screen in the Table Wizard asks what you want to do next.
— Click the option button to **Modify the table design.**
— Click the **Finish command button.** The All Students table appears.

➤ Pull down the **File menu** and click **Save** (or click the **Save icon** on the Table Design toolbar) to save the table.

Step 5: Add the additional fields

➤ Click the **maximize button** to give yourself more room to work.

➤ Click the cell immediately below the last field in the table. Type **BirthDate** as shown in Figure 2.4c.

➤ Press the **Tab key** to move to the Data Type column. Click the **down arrow** on the drop-down list box. Click **Date/Time** as the field type for the Birth-Date field.

➤ Add the remaining fields with the indicated field types to the Students table:
— Add **FinancialAid** as a Yes/No field. (There is no space in the field name.)
— Add **Sex** as a Text field.
— Add **Credits** as a Number field.

Table Design toolbar —

Primary key —

Click here to display — available field types

Click here to select — Date/Time field type

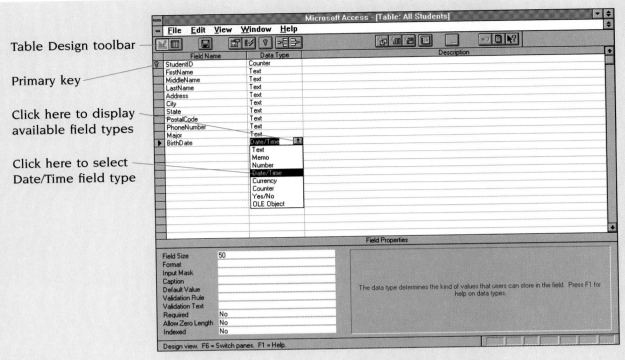

(c) Add the Additional Fields (step 5)

FIGURE 2.4 Hands-on Exercise 1 (continued)

— Add **QualityPoints** as a Number field. (There is no space in the field name.)

➤ Save the table.

CHOOSING A FIELD TYPE

The fastest way to specify the *field type* is to type the first letter; type T for text, D for date, N for Number, and Y for Yes/No. Text is the default data type.

Step 6: Change the primary key

➤ Point to the first row of the table and click the **right mouse button** to produce the shortcut menu in Figure 2.4d. Click **Insert Row** to insert a row.

➤ Click the **Field Name column** in the new row. Type **SocialSecurityNumber** (without spaces) as the name of the new field. Press **enter.** The data type will be set to Text by default.

➤ Click the **Set Primary Key icon** on the toolbar to change the primary key to social security number. The primary key symbol has moved from the StudentID field to the SocialSecurityNumber field.

➤ Point to the **StudentID field** in the second row. Click the **right mouse button** to display the shortcut menu. Click **Delete Row** to remove this field from the table definition.

➤ Save the table.

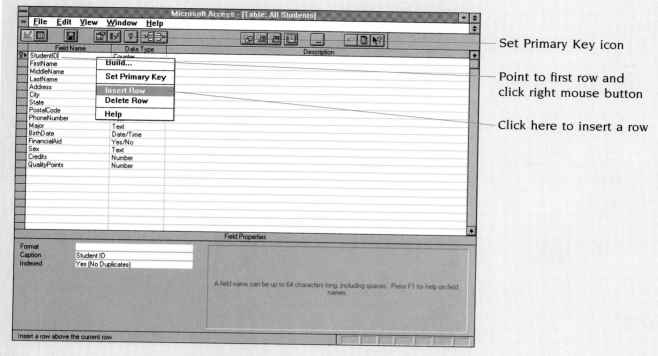

Set Primary Key icon

Point to first row and click right mouse button

Click here to insert a row

(d) Change the Primary Key (step 6)

FIGURE 2.4   Hands-on Exercise 1 (continued)

INSERTING OR DELETING FIELDS

Point to an existing field, then click the right mouse button to produce a shortcut menu. Click Insert Row or Delete Row to add or remove a field as appropriate. To insert (or delete) multiple fields, point to the field selector to the left of the field name, click and drag the mouse over multiple rows to extend the selection, then click the right mouse button to produce a shortcut menu.

Step 7: Add an input mask

➤ Click the field selector column for **SocialSecurityNumber.** Click the **Input Mask** box in the Properties Area. (The box is currently empty.)

➤ Click the **Build button** to display the ***Input Mask Wizard*** as shown in Figure 2.4e. (You may see an informational message telling you to save the table. Click **Yes.**)

➤ Click **Social Security Number** in the Input Mask dialog box. Click the **Try It** text box to see how the mask works. If necessary, press the **left arrow key** until you are at the beginning of the text box, then enter a social security number (digits only). Click the **Finish command button** to accept the default choices associated with establishing an ***input mask.***

➤ Click the field selector column for **BirthDate,** then follow the steps detailed above to add an input mask. (Choose the **Short Date** format.) Click **Yes** if asked whether to save the table.

➤ Save the table.

Click here to select — field

Click to select Social — Security Number

Click here to see how — the mask works

Build button —

Click here to select — Input Mask property

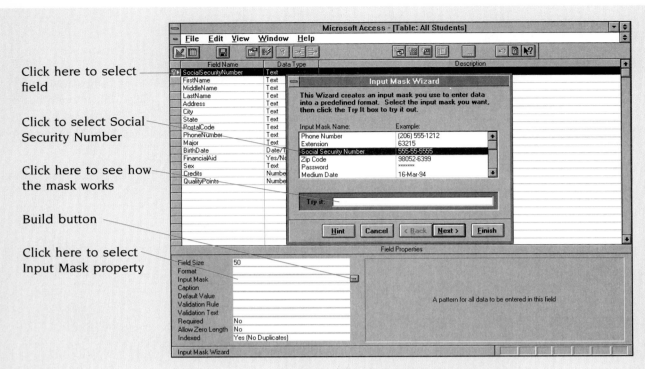

(e) Create an Input Mask (step 7)

FIGURE 2.4   Hands-on Exercise 1 (continued)

KEYBOARD SHORTCUTS

The keyboard is faster than the mouse if your hands are already on the keyboard. Press the Alt key plus the underlined letter to pull down the menu—for example, Alt+F to pull down the File menu—then type the underlined letter in the desired command—for example, S for Save. In other words, Alt+F, then the letter S, executes the File Save command.

Step 8: Add a Validation Rule
➤ Click the field selector column for the **Sex** field. Click the **Field Size box** and change the *field size* to **1** as shown in Figure 2.4f.
➤ Click the **Format box** in the Properties Area. Type a **>** sign to convert the data to uppercase.
➤ Click the **Validation Rule box.** Type **="M" or "F"** to accept only these values on data entry.
➤ Click the **Validation Text box.** Type **Specify M for Male or F for Female.**
➤ Save the table.

Step 9: Specify the required fields
➤ Click the field selector column for the **FirstName** field. Click the **Required box** in the Properties Area. Click the **down arrow** and select **Yes.**
➤ Repeat these steps to require the LastName and PhoneNumber.
➤ Save the table.

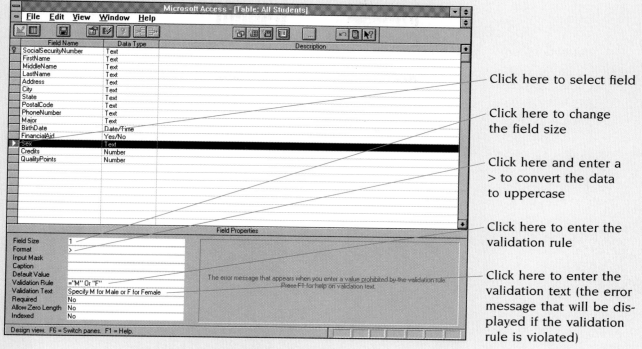

(f) Add a Validation Rule (step 8)

FIGURE 2.4 Hands-on Exercise 1 (continued)

Step 10: Change the field size
- ➤ Click the field selector column for the **State** field. Click the **Field Size box** in the Properties Area. Select **50** and enter **2** to limit the field to two characters corresponding to the accepted abbreviation for a state.
- ➤ Click the **Format box** in the Properties Area. Type a **>** sign to convert the data to uppercase.
- ➤ Change the field size for the **Credits** and **QualityPoints** fields to **Integer.**
- ➤ Save the table.

Step 11: The Datasheet view
- ➤ Pull down the **View menu** and click **Datasheet** (or click the **Datasheet icon** on the toolbar) to change to the Datasheet view as shown in Figure 2.4g.
- ➤ The insertion point (a flashing vertical line indicating the position where data will be entered) is automatically set to the first field of the first record.
- ➤ Type **111111111** to enter the social security number for the first record. (The mask will appear as soon as you enter the first digit.)

CHANGE THE FIELD WIDTH

Drag the border between field names to change the displayed width of a field. Double click the right boundary of a field name to change the width to accommodate the widest entry in that field.

Printer icon

Datasheet icon

Current record has not been saved

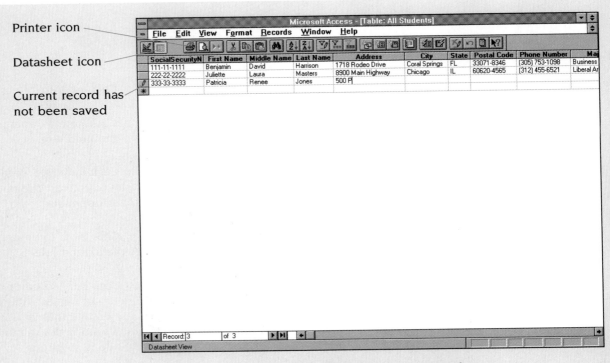

(g) Datasheet View (steps 11 and 12)

FIGURE 2.4 Hands-on Exercise 1 (continued)

➤ Press the **Tab key,** the **right arrow key,** or the **enter key** to move to the First-Name field. Enter the data for Benjamin Harrison as shown in Figure 2.4g. (Use any values you like for additional fields.)

➤ Scrolling takes place automatically as you move within the record.

Step 12: Enter additional data

➤ Enter data for the two additional students shown in the figure, but enter deliberately invalid data to experiment with the validation capabilities built into Access. Some of the errors you may encounter:

— The message, *The value you entered isn't appropriate for this field,* implies that the data type is wrong—for example, alphabetic characters in a numeric field such as Credits or something other than Yes or No for FinancialAid.

UNDO COMMAND

Access remembers the most recent change you made and enables you to undo that change. The Edit menu contains different Undo commands, depending on the nature of that change. The Undo Typing command lets you cancel your most recent change. The Undo Current Field command and Undo Current Record command cancel all changes to the current field or record, respectively. Even after the changes have been saved, the Undo Saved Record command undoes the changes to the previously edited record.

— The message, *Specify M for male or F for female,* means you entered a letter other than an "M" or an "F" in the Sex field (or you didn't enter a value at all).
— The message, *Duplicate value in index, primary key, or relationship,* indicates that the value of the primary key is not unique.
— The message, *Field 'All Students.LastName' can't contain a null value,* implies that you left a required field blank.
— If you encounter a data validation error, Press **Esc** (or click **OK**), then reenter the data.

Step 13: Print the student table

➤ Pull down the **File menu** and click **Print** (or click the **Print icon** on the tool-bar).

➤ Click the **All option button** to print the entire table. Click the **OK** command button to begin printing. Do not be concerned if the table prints on multiple pages.

➤ Pull down the **File menu.** Click **Close** to close the Students table.

➤ Pull down the **File menu.** Click **Exit** if you want to leave Access.

THE PRINT SETUP COMMAND

The Print Setup command lets you change the margins and/or orientation and is helpful in printing tables with many fields. Pull down the File menu, click Print Setup, then click the Landscape option button. Change the left and right margins to .5 inch each to lengthen the print line. Click OK to exit the Print Setup dialog box.

FORMS

A **form** is an object in an Access database that provides an easy way to enter and display the data stored in a table. You type data into a form such as the one in Figure 2.5, and Access stores the data in the underlying table in the database. One advantage of using a form (as opposed to entering records in the Datasheet view) is that you can see all of the fields in a single record without scrolling. A second advantage is that a form can be designed to resemble a paper form, and thus provide a sense of familiarity for the individuals who actually enter the data.

A form may have different views, as does a table. The **Form view** in Figure 2.5a displays the completed form and is used to enter or modify data in the underlying table. The **Form Design view** in Figure 2.5b is used to create or modify the form.

A form is made up of objects called **controls.** Controls are bound, unbound, or calculated. A **bound control** (such as the **text boxes** in Figure 2.5a) has a data source (a field in the underlying table) and is used to enter or modify the data in that table. An **unbound control** has no data source. Unbound controls are used to display titles, labels, lines, or rectangles.

A **calculated control** has as its data source an expression rather than a field. An **expression** is a combination of operators (e.g., +, −, *, and /), field names, constants, and functions. A student's Grade Point Average is an example of a calculated control since it is computed by dividing the number of quality points by the number of credits.

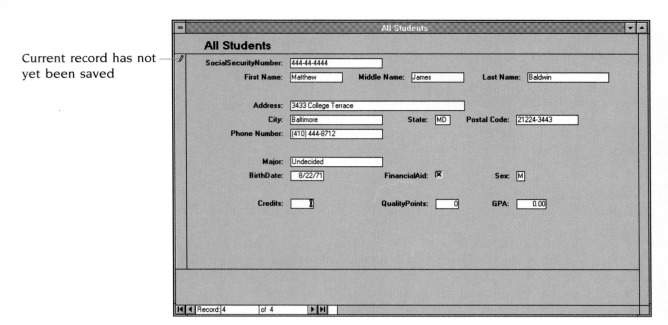

Current record has not yet been saved

(a) Form View

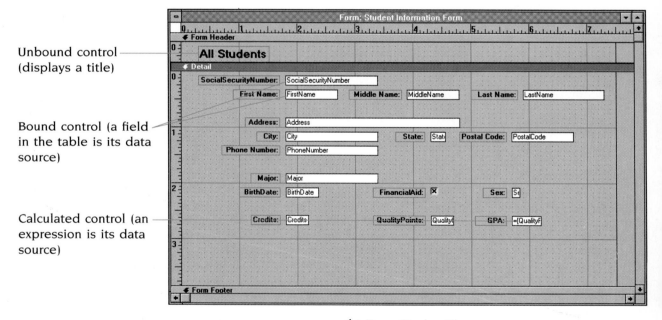

Unbound control (displays a title)

Bound control (a field in the table is its data source)

Calculated control (an expression is its data source)

(b) Form Design View

FIGURE 2.5 Forms

Form Wizard

The easiest way to create a form is with the ***Form Wizard.*** The Form Wizard asks questions about the form you want, then builds the form for you. You can accept the form as it was created, or you can customize it to better suit your needs.

The controls in Figure 2.5 (except for the calculated control for GPA) were created automatically by the Form Wizard, as you will see in the hands-on exercise that follows shortly. It is up to you, however, to select, then move and/or size the controls to customize the form. Controls are treated just as any other Windows object. Thus:

To select a control—	Click anywhere on a control.
To size a control—	Click the control to select it, then drag the sizing handles. Drag the handles on the top or bottom to size the box vertically. Drag the handles on the left or right side to size the box horizontally. Drag the handles in the corner to size both horizontally and vertically.
To move a control—	Point to any border, but *not* to a sizing handle (the mouse pointer changes to a hand), then click the mouse and drag the control to its new position.

The following exercise creates a form based on the Student table from the first hands-on exercise. The Form Wizard is used to create the form initially, after which you will modify the form so that it matches the one in Figure 2.5.

INHERITANCE

A bound control inherits the same properties as the associated field in the underlying table. Due to this **inheritance** feature, changing a property setting of a field *after* the form has been created does *not* change the property of the control. Note, too, that changing the property setting of a control does *not* change the property setting of the field in the table.

HANDS-ON EXERCISE 2:

Creating a Form

Objective Use the Form Wizard to create a form; move and size controls within a form; use the completed form to enter data into the associated table. Use Figure 2.6 as a guide in the exercise.

THE TOOLBARS ARE DIFFERENT

The toolbars displayed by Access change automatically according to the view you are in. The Form Design toolbar contains icons to create or modify a form. The Form View toolbar contains icons used during data entry. Both toolbars contain icons to switch to the other view, to switch to the Datasheet view, and to display Cue Cards.

Step 1: Open the MYDATA database
➤ Load Microsoft Access. Pull down the **File menu** and click **Open Database** to display the Open Database dialog box (or click the **Open Database icon** on the toolbar).

➤ If you haven't changed the default directory:
  — Click the arrow on the Drives list box to select the appropriate drive—for example, drive C or drive A, depending on whether or not you installed the data disk.
  — Double click the root directory (a:\ or c:\) in the Directories list box to display the subdirectories on the selected drive.
  — Double click the **ACCSDATA** directory to make it the active directory.
➤ Double click **MYDATA.MDB** to open the database created in the first exercise.

Step 2: Create a new form
➤ Click the **Form button.** Click **New** to produce the New Form dialog box in Figure 2.6a.
➤ Click the **arrow** in the Select a Table/Query text box. Click **All Students** to select the All Students table created in the previous exercise.
➤ Click the **Form Wizards button** to use the Form Wizard. The first Form Wizards screen appears.

Step 3: The Form Wizard
➤ Click **Single-Column** as the type of form. Click **OK.**
➤ Click the **>> button** as shown in Figure 2.6b to enter all fields in the table on the form. Click the **Next command button.**
➤ Click the **Standard option button** to specify the style of your form. Click the **Next command button.**
➤ The next screen in the Form Wizard asks you for the title of the form and what you want to do next.

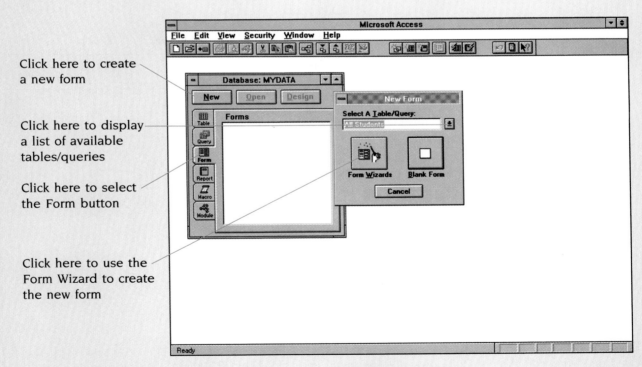

Click here to create a new form

Click here to display a list of available tables/queries

Click here to select the Form button

Click here to use the Form Wizard to create the new form

(a) Add a Form (step 2)

FIGURE 2.6 Hands-on Exercise 2

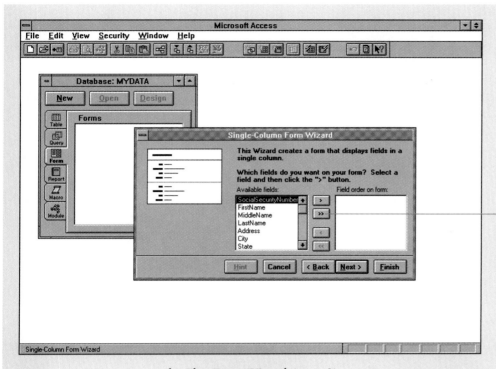

Click here to select all of the fields and enter them on the form in their current order

(b) The Form Wizard (step 3)

FIGURE 2.6 Hands-on Exercise 2 (continued)

— The Form Wizard suggests **All Students** as the title of the form. Keep this entry.

— Click the option button to **Modify the form's design.**

➤ Click the **Finish command button** to display the form in Design view. The Form Design toolbar appears automatically at the top of the window under the menu bar as shown in Figure 2.6c.

➤ The Toolbox toolbar may or may not be displayed. Click the **Toolbox icon** on the Form Design toolbar to toggle the display of the toolbox on and off. End with the toolbox hidden so you have more room to work in the next several steps.

Step 4: The Save command

➤ Click the **Maximize button** so that the form takes the entire screen.

➤ Pull down the **File menu** and click **Save** (or click the **Save icon** on the Form Design toolbar).

➤ Type **Student Information Form** in the Form Name text box as shown in Figure 2.6c. Click **OK.**

THE UNDO COMMAND

The Undo command is invaluable at any time, and is especially useful when moving and sizing controls. Pull down the Edit menu and click Undo (or click the Undo icon on the toolbar) immediately after making a mistake.

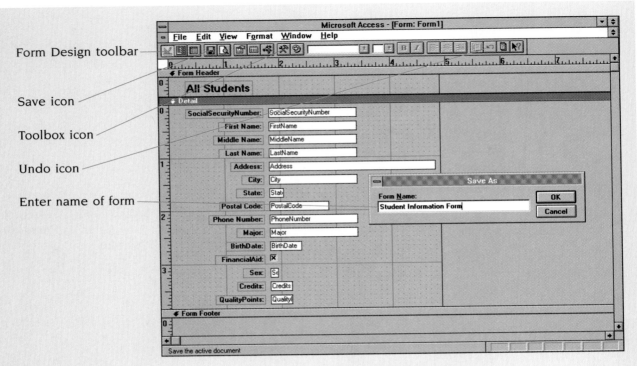

Form Design toolbar

Save icon

Toolbox icon

Undo icon

Enter name of form

(c) The Save Command (step 4)

Click here to select the control for FirstName, then
drag the sizing handle to shorten the text box

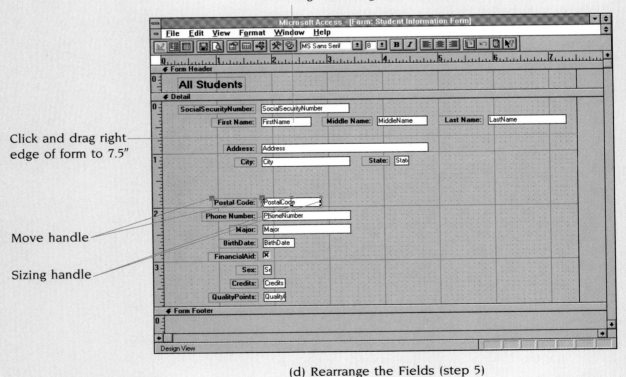

Click and drag right
edge of form to 7.5″

Move handle

Sizing handle

(d) Rearrange the Fields (step 5)

FIGURE 2.6 Hands-on Exercise 2 (continued)

Step 5: Move and size the controls

➤ Drag the right edge of the form so that the form is **7.5** inches wide.

➤ Click the control for **FirstName** to select the control and display the sizing handles. Be sure to click the text box and *not* the attached label. Drag the sizing handle to shorten the text box.

➤ Click the control for **MiddleName** and shorten its text box. Click and drag the border of the control (the pointer changes to a hand) to position the MiddleName field next to the FirstName field. Use the grid to space and align the controls.

➤ Size the control for **LastName,** then move it next to the MiddleName control as shown in Figure 2.6d. Be sure that the text box for LastName does not extend beyond the 7.5-inch border.

➤ Click and drag the other controls to complete the form:
  — Place the controls for City, State, and PostalCode on the same line.
  — Move the control for PhoneNumber up so that it is close to the address.
  — Place the controls for BirthDate, FinancialAid, and Sex on the same line.
  — Place Credits and QualityPoints on the same line.

➤ Do not be concerned if the size and/or placement of your text boxes differ from ours. (See tip box in the middle of page 64 to align the controls.)

➤ Save the form.

Step 6: Add a calculated control (GPA)

➤ Click the **Toolbox icon** on the toolbar to display the toolbox as shown in Figure 2.6e.

➤ Click the **Textbox tool** in the toolbox. The mouse pointer changes to a tiny cross with a text box attached.

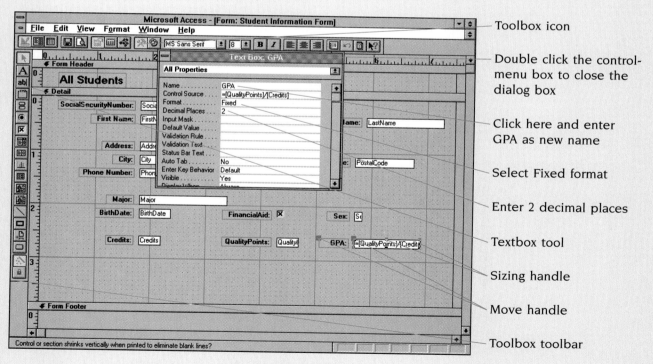

(e) Add a Calculated Control (step 6)

FIGURE 2.6   Hands-on Exercise 2 (continued)

➤ Click and drag in the form where you want the text box (the GPA control) to go, and release the mouse. You will see an Unbound control and an attached label containing a field number (e.g., Field42).

➤ Click in the text box of the control (Unbound will disappear). Type **=[QualityPoints]/[Credits]** to calculate a student's GPA. You must enter the field names *exactly* as they were defined in the table. (Do not include a space between Quality and Points.)

➤ Size the text box appropriately for GPA.

➤ Click and drag to select the text in the attached label (Field42), then type **GPA:** as the label for this control.

ALIGN THE CONTROLS

To align controls in a straight line (horizontally or vertically), press and hold the Shift key and click the labels of the controls to be aligned. Pull down the Format menu and select the edge to align (Left, Right, Top, and Bottom). Click the Undo command if you are not satisfied with the result.

SELECT THE CONTROL OR THE ATTACHED LABEL

A bound control is created with an attached label. Click the control, and the control has sizing handles and a move handle, but the label has only a move handle. Click the label (instead of the control), and the opposite occurs; the control has only a move handle, but the label will have both sizing handles and a move handle.

Step 7: Properties

➤ Point to the text box containing the expression =[QualityPoints]/[Credits] and click the **right mouse button** to display a shortcut menu. Click **Properties** to display the Properties dialog box in Figure 2.6e.

➤ Click the **Name** box. Replace the original name (Field42) with **GPA.**

➤ Click the **Format box.** Click the **down arrow** and select **Fixed.**

➤ Click the box for **Decimal places.** Enter **2** as the number of decimal places.

➤ Double click the **control-menu box** to close the Properties dialog box.

➤ Click the **Save icon** on the toolbar.

THE BORDER VERSUS THE MOVE HANDLE

You can move a control and its label together, or you can move them separately. Click and drag the border of either the control or the label to move them together. Click and drag the move handle (a tiny square in the upper-left corner) of either object to move them separately.

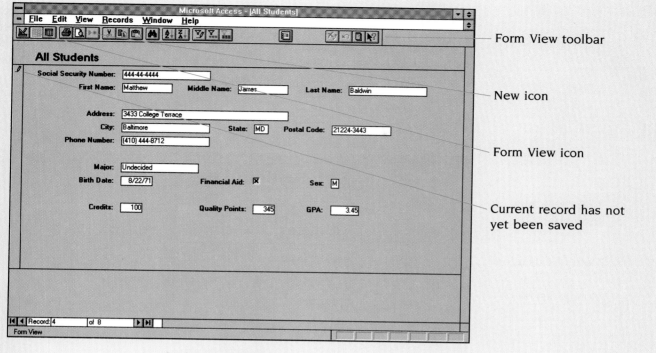

Form View toolbar

New icon

Form View icon

Current record has not yet been saved

(f) The Form View (step 8)

FIGURE 2.6   Hands-on Exercise 2 (continued)

Step 8: The Form View

➤ Click the **Form view icon** to switch to the Form view and the Form view toolbar. You will see the first record in the table (Benjamin Harrison).

➤ Click the **New icon** on the Form View toolbar to move to the end of the table and enter a new record.

➤ Enter data as shown in Figure 2.6f. The record selector symbol changes to a pencil as you begin to enter data.
  — Press the **Tab key** to move from one field to the next within the form.
  — Press the **space bar** or click the *check box* to toggle FinancialAid (a Yes/No field) on or off.
  — All properties (masks and data validation) have been inherited from the All Students table created in the first exercise.

➤ Pull down the **File menu.** Click **Close** when you have completed the record. Click **Yes** if asked to save the changes.

➤ Pull down the **File menu.** Click **Exit** if you want to leave Access.

COMMAND BUTTONS AND COMBO BOXES

The Form Wizard provides an excellent starting point but stops short of creating the form you really want. Once you have mastered the basic operations to move and size controls, you will be looking for other ways to customize the form.

Figure 2.7a shows the Student Information Form at the end of the next hands-on exercise, which represents a marked improvement over its predecessor in Figure 2.5a. The date of execution appears near the top of the form. A combo box has been added to aid in entering a student's major. (A combo box is a combination of a list box and a table box.) Four command buttons appear at the bottom of the screen and correspond to common menu operations. The user's entries appear in blue to stand out from the rest of the form.

Figure 2.7b shows the Form Design view underlying the form in Figure 2.7a. Two additional toolbars are displayed, the **Toolbox** and the **Palette,** both of which are used to customize the form. The icons in the Toolbox enable you to add controls such as list boxes and command buttons. The Palette enables you to change the foreground or background color of text within a textbox and/or the line enclosing the textbox.

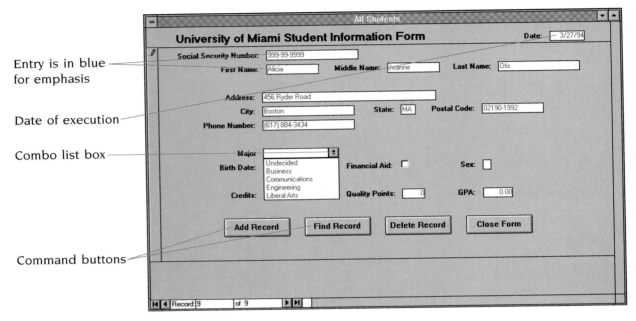

Entry is in blue for emphasis

Date of execution

Combo list box

Command buttons

(a) The Form View

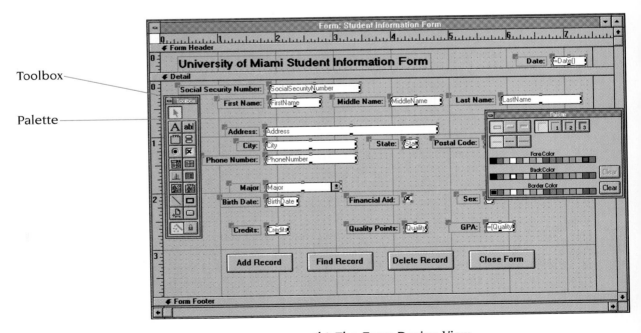

Toolbox

Palette

(b) The Form Design View

FIGURE 2.7 Command Buttons and Combo Buttons

HANDS-ON EXERCISE 3:

Customizing a Form

Objective Add and align command buttons in an existing form; add a combo box to facilitate data entry; use color to highlight selected controls. Use Figure 2.8 as a guide in the exercise.

Step 1: Open an existing form
➤ Open the **MYDATA** database we have been using throughout the chapter.
➤ Click the **Form button** in the Database window. The Student Information Form is already highlighted since there is only one form in the database. Click the **Design command button** to open the form from the previous exercise.
➤ If necessary:
— Click the **Maximize button** so that the form takes the entire window.
— Click the **Toolbox icon** to display the Toolbox toolbar.

FLOATING TOOLBARS

A toolbar can be docked (fixed) along the edge of the application window, or it can be displayed as a floating toolbar within the application window. To move a docked toolbar, drag the toolbar background. To move a floating toolbar, drag its title bar. To size a floating toolbar, drag any border in the direction you want to go. Double click the background of any toolbar to toggle between a floating toolbar and a docked (fixed) toolbar.

Step 2: Unbound controls
➤ Click the control in the Form Header, then click and drag to select the words **All Students.** Type **University of Miami Student Information Form** to change the text as shown in Figure 2.8a.
➤ Select the attached labels (*not* the text boxes) one at a time, to add spaces in the labels for **SocialSecurityNumber, BirthDate, FinancialAid,** and **QualityPoints** as shown in Figure 2.8a.
➤ Click the **Text box tool** in the toolbox.
➤ Click and drag in the form where you want the text box for the date. You will see an Unbound control and an attached label containing a field number (e.g., Field44).
➤ Click in the text box of the control (Unbound will disappear). Type **=Date().**
➤ Click the attached label, then click and drag to select the label. Type **Date:.**
➤ Save the form.

Step 3: Add a command button
➤ Click the **Command Button tool.** The mouse pointer changes to a tiny cross attached to a command button when you point anywhere in the form.
➤ Click and drag in the form where you want the button, then release the mouse. This draws a button and simultaneously opens the Command Button Wizard as shown in Figure 2.8b. (The number in your button may be different from ours.)

Change the text
of the title

Text box tool

Add spaces between
words in the label

Click and drag here (after
selecting the Text box
tool) to create a control
for the date

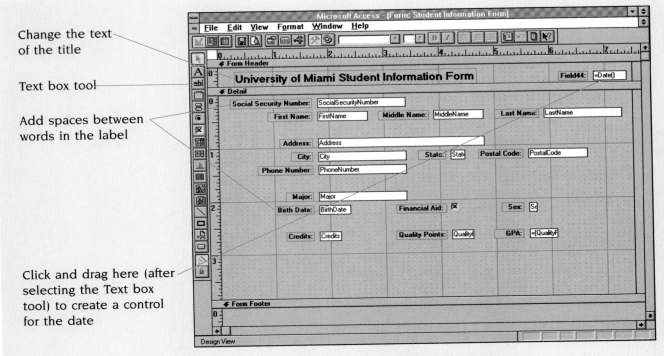

(a) Unbound Controls (step 2)

Categories list box

Click to select operation to
be assigned to the button

Command Button tool

Click and drag to create
the command button

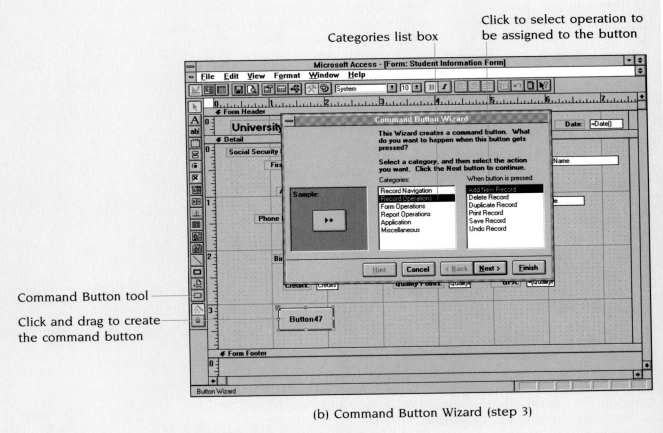

(b) Command Button Wizard (step 3)

FIGURE 2.8 Hands-on Exercise 3

➤ Click **Record Operations** in the Categories list box. Choose **Add New Record** as the operation. Click the **Next command button.**

➤ Click the **Text option button.** Click the **Next command button.**

➤ Type **Add Record** as the name of the button, then click the **Finish command button.** The completed command button should appear on your form.

➤ Save the form.

CUE CARDS

Cue Cards are always accessible and will coach you through a process as you work on your own database. Pull down the Help menu and click Cue Cards, or click the Cue Cards button on the toolbar. Follow the on-screen instructions to select the topic you need.

Step 4: Create the additional command buttons

➤ Click the **Command Button tool.** Click and drag on the form where you want the second button to go.

➤ Click **Record Navigation** in the Categories list box. Choose **Find Record** as the operation. Click the **Next command button.**

➤ Click the **Text option button.** Click the **Next command button.**

➤ Type **Find Record** as the name of the button, then click the **Finish command button.** The completed command button should appear on the monitor.

➤ Repeat these steps to add the command buttons to delete a record (Record Operations) and close the form (Form Operations).

➤ Save the form.

Step 5: Align the command buttons

➤ Select the four command buttons by pressing and holding the **Shift key** as you click each button. Release the Shift key when all of the buttons are selected.

➤ Pull down the **Format menu.** Click **Size** to display the cascade menu shown in Figure 2.8c. Click **to Widest** to set a uniform width for the selected buttons.

➤ Pull down the **Format menu** a second time, click **Horizontal Spacing,** then click **Make Equal.**

➤ Pull down the **Format menu** a third time, click **Align,** then click **Bottom** to complete the alignment.

➤ Save the form.

CHECK YOUR NUMBERS

The width of the form, plus the left and right margins, cannot exceed the width of the page. Thus increasing the the width of a form may require a corresponding decrease in the left and right margins or a change to landscape (rather than portrait) orientation. Pull down the File menu and choose the Print Setup command to modify the dimensions of the form prior to printing.

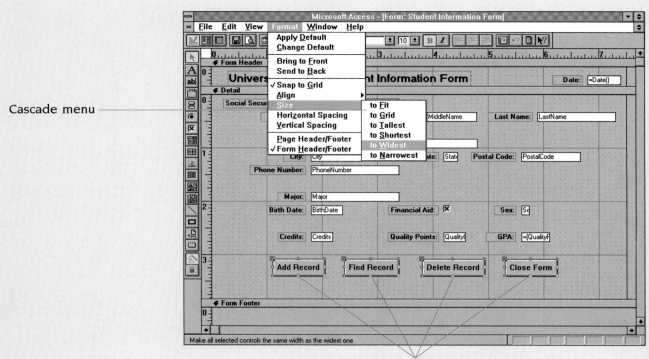

Cascade menu

Make all selected controls the same width as the widest one

Select multiple command buttons at one time by
pressing Shift as you click the additional buttons

(c) Align the Buttons (step 5)

FIGURE 2.8   Hands-on Exercise 3 (continued)

Step 6: Add a Combo box
➤ The Combo box that you create in this step will replace the existing text
  box. Accordingly, click the text box for **Major,** then press the **Del key.** The
  label and text box are deleted.
➤ Click the **Combo Box tool.** The mouse pointer changes to a tiny cross
  attached to the image of a list box. Click and drag in the form where you
  want the combo box, then release the mouse to open the Combo Box
  Wizard.
➤ Click the **option button** indicating that you will type the values you want.
  Click the **Next command button.**
➤ The **Number of Columns** box is selected as shown in Figure 2.8d. Type **1.**

Step 7: The Combo Box Wizard (continued)
➤ Click the first row under Col 1 heading (the second column will disappear).
  Type **Undecided** as shown in Figure 2.8d. Press the **enter key** to move to the
  row for the next major.
➤ Continue to enter majors as shown in Figure 2.8d. The Combo Box Wizard
  follows the same convention with the record selector as with an ordinary
  table.
➤ Click the **Next command button** when you have entered all the majors.
➤ Click the **option button** to store the selected value in a field as shown in Figure 2.8e. Click the arrow on the drop-down list box and select **Major.** Click
  the **Next command button.**

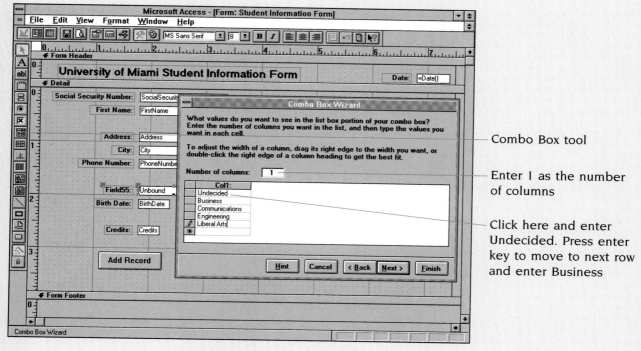

Combo Box tool

Enter 1 as the number of columns

Click here and enter Undecided. Press enter key to move to next row and enter Business

(d) The Combo Box Wizard (steps 6 and 7)

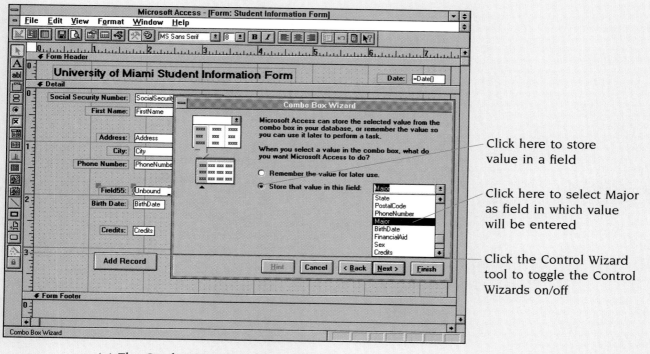

Click here to store value in a field

Click here to select Major as field in which value will be entered

Click the Control Wizard tool to toggle the Control Wizards on/off

(e) The Combo Box Wizard continued (step 7)

FIGURE 2.8   Hands-on Exercise 3 (continued)

➤ Type **Major** when asked for the label of the combo box and press **enter.** Click the **Finish command button.** Size and/or move the control so that it aligns properly on the form.

➤ Save the form.

LIST BOX VERSUS COMBO BOX

The toolbox enables you to create a list box or a **combo box,** both of which let you select a value from a displayed list. The difference is that a combo box lets you enter a value that is not on the list, whereas a list box does not. A combo box takes less room on the form as only the current selection is displayed; a list box displays all available choices.

Step 8: Change the Tab Order
➤ Point to the control for **Major,** click the **right mouse button** to display a short-cut menu, then click **Properties.** Click the drop-down list box and select **All Properties.**

➤ The property box for **Name,** which currently contains a field number, is selected. Type **Major.**

➤ Double click the **control-menu box** to close the dialog box.

➤ Pull down the **Edit menu.** Click **Tab Order** to display the dialog box in Figure 2.8f.

Drag Major to new position below Phone Number in the Custom Order list

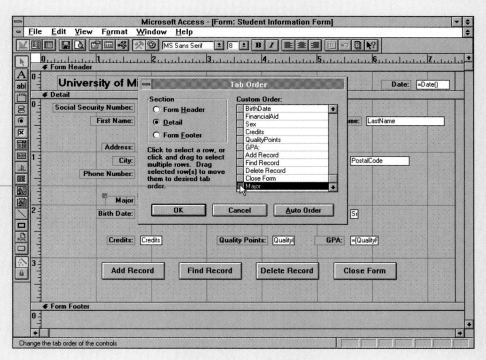

(f) Change the Tab Order (step 8)

FIGURE 2.8 Hands-on Exercise 3 (continued)

➤ Click the **down arrow** in the Custom Order list box to scroll to Major, the last control in the form.

➤ Click the row selector for **Major.** Move the pointer so that it changes to a white arrow, then drag until Major is immediately under PhoneNumber. Click **OK.**

➤ Save the form.

Step 9: Add color

➤ Click the **Palette icon** on the toolbar to display the Palette toolbar as shown in Figure 2.8g.

➤ Select all of the text boxes by pressing and holding the **Shift key** as you click each text box. Release the Shift key when all of the text boxes are selected.

➤ Click **Dark Blue** as the foreground color. The text changes to dark blue in the selected text boxes.

➤ Click in the form to deselect the text boxes.

➤ Save the form.

MORE IS NOT BETTER

More is not better, especially in the case of too many colors that detract from a form rather than enhance it. Access makes it almost too easy to switch foreground, background, and border colors and/or to change fonts and styles. Use restraint. A simple form is far more effective than one that uses too many fonts and colors simply because they are there.

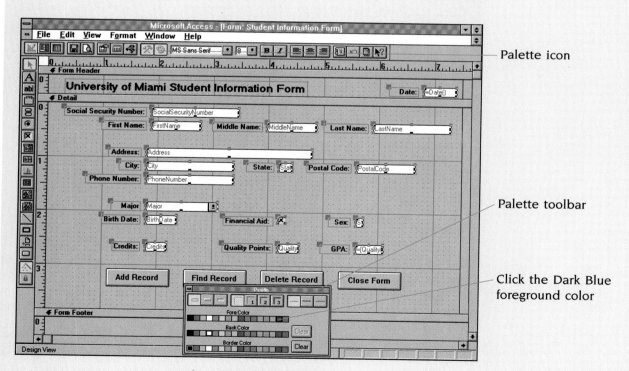

(g) Changing Colors (step 9)

FIGURE 2.8 Hands-on Exercise 3 (continued)

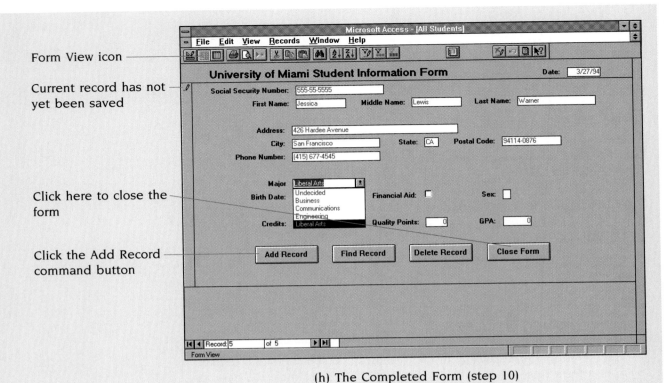

Form View icon

Current record has not yet been saved

Click here to close the form

Click the Add Record command button

(h) The Completed Form (step 10)

FIGURE 2.8 Hands-on Exercise 3 (continued)

Step 10: The completed form

> Click the **Form view icon** to switch to the form view. You will see the first record in the table.
> Click the **Add Record command button.** Click the text box for Social Security Number, then begin to add the record as shown in Figure 2.8h. The record selector changes to a pencil to indicate the record has not been saved.
> Press the **Tab key** or the **enter key** to move from field to field within the record.
> Click the **arrow** on the drop-down list box to display the list of majors.
> Click the **Close Form command button** when you have completed the record.
> Pull down the **File menu.** Click **Exit** to leave Access.

SUMMARY

Data should be stored in its smallest parts and should be sufficient to produce all required information. Calculated fields should not be stored in a table.

The Table Wizard is the easiest way to create a table. It lets you choose from a series of business or personal tables, asks you questions about the fields you want in the selected table, then creates the table for you.

A table has two views—the Design view and the Datasheet view. The Design view is used to create the table and display the fields within the table, as well as the data type and properties of each field. The Datasheet view is used after the table has been created to add, edit, and delete records.

A form provides an easy way to enter and display data in that it can be made to resemble the paper form on which a table is based. The Form Wizard is the easiest way to create a form. The Form Design view enables you to modify a form after it has been created.

A form consists of objects called controls. A bound control has a data source such as a field in the underlying table. An unbound control has no data source. A calculated control contains an expression. Controls are selected, moved, and sized the same way as any other Windows object. Forms may be further customized through the Toolbox and Palette.

Key Words and Concepts

Bound control	Field	Memo field
Calculated control	Field name	Number field
Calculated field	Field property	OLE field
Check box	Field size	Palette toolbar
Combo box	Field type	Primary key
Control	Form	Table Wizard
Counter field	Form Design View	Text box
Cue Cards	Form View	Text field
Currency field	Form Wizard	Toolbox toolbar
Data type	Format property	Unbound control
Datasheet view	Index	Validation rule
Date/Time field	Inheritance	Validation text
Default value	Input mask	Yes/No field
Design view	Input mask wizard	
Expression	Label	

Multiple Choice

1. Which of the following is true?
   (a) The Table Wizard must be used to create a table
   (b) The Form Wizard must be used to create a form
   (c) Both (a) and (b)
   (d) Neither (a) nor (b)

2. Which of the following validation checks is implemented automatically by Access?
   (a) Rejection of a record with a duplicate value of the primary key
   (b) Rejection of numbers in a text field
   (c) Both (a) and (b)
   (d) Neither (a) nor (b)

3. Social security number, phone number, and zip code should be designated as:
   (a) Number fields
   (b) Text fields
   (c) Yes/No fields
   (d) Any of the above, depending on the application

4. Which of the following is true of the primary key?

(a) Its values must be unique

(b) It must be defined as a text field

(c) It must be the first field in a table

(d) It can never be changed

5. Social security number is used as a primary key rather than name because:

(a) The social security number is numeric, whereas the name is not

(b) The social security number is unique, whereas the name is not

(c) The social security number is a shorter field

(d) All of the above

6. Which of the following is true regarding buttons within the Form Wizard?

(a) The > button copies a selected field from a table onto a form

(b) The < button removes a selected field from a form

(c) Both (a) and (b)

(d) Neither (a) nor (b)

7. Which of the following was *not* a suggested guideline for designing a table?

(a) Include all necessary data

(b) Store data in its smallest parts

(c) Avoid calculated fields

(d) Designate at least two primary keys

8. Which of the following are valid parameters for use with a form?

(a) Portrait orientation, a form width of 6 inches, left and right margins of 1¼ inch

(b) Landscape orientation, a form width of 9 inches, left and right margins of 1 inch

(c) Both (a) and (b)

(d) Neither (a) nor (b)

9. Which view is used to add, edit, or delete records in a table?

(a) The Datasheet view

(b) The Form view

(c) Both (a) and (b)

(d) Neither (a) nor (b)

10. Which of the following is true regarding toolbars in the Form view and Form Design view?

(a) The toolbars are identical

(b) The icon to add a new record is on the Form Design toolbar

(c) The icon to display the Palette toolbar is on the Form View toolbar

(d) Both toolbars contain the icon to switch to the Datasheet view

11. In which view will you see the record selector symbols of a pencil and a triangle?

(a) Only the Datasheet view

(b) Only the Form view

(c) The Datasheet view and the Form view

(d) The Form view, the Form Design view, and the Datasheet view

12. To move a control (in the Form Design view), you select the control, then:
    (a) Point to a border (the pointer changes to an arrow) and click and drag the border to the new position
    (b) Point to a border (the pointer changes to a hand) and click and drag the border to the new position
    (c) Point to a sizing handle (the pointer changes to an arrow) and click and drag the sizing handle to the new position
    (d) Point to a sizing handle (the pointer changes to a hand) and click and drag the sizing handle to the new position

13. Which fields are commonly defined with an input mask?
    (a) Social security number and phone number
    (b) First name, middle name, and last name
    (c) City, state, and zip code
    (d) All of the above

14. Which field type appears as a check box in a form?
    (a) Text field
    (b) Number field
    (c) Yes/No field
    (d) All of the above

15. Which properties would you use to limit a user's response to two characters, and automatically convert the response to uppercase?
    (a) Field Size and Format
    (b) Input Mask, Validation Rule, and Default Value
    (c) Input Mask and Required
    (d) Field Size, Validation Rule, Validation Text, and Required

ANSWERS

1. d	**6.** c	**11.** c
2. a	**7.** d	**12.** b
3. b	**8.** c	**13.** a
4. a	**9.** c	**14.** c
5. b	**10.** d	**15.** a

EXPLORING ACCESS

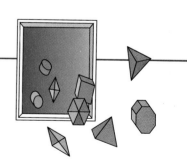

1. Use Figure 2.9 to match each action with its result. A given action may be used more than once or not at all.

Action	Result
a. Click at 1	____ Create a command button
b. Click at 2	____ Move the selected control
c. Click at 3	____ Save the form design
d. Click at 4	____ Create an unbound control
e. Click at 5	____ Suppress the display of the toolbox

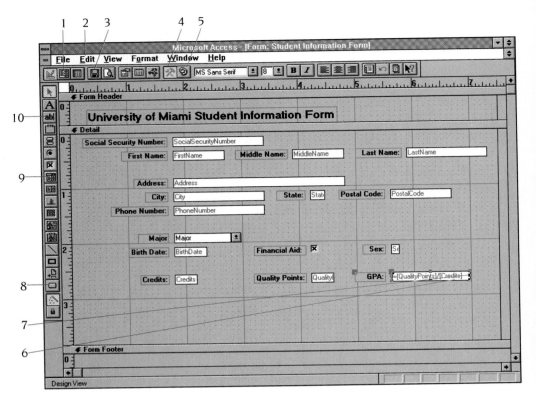

FIGURE 2.9 Screen for Problem 1

Action	Result
f. Click and drag at 6	___ Size the selected control
g. Click and drag at 7	___ Change to the Form view
h. Click at 8, click in the form, and drag to size control	___ Create a combo box
	___ Change the tab order
i. Click at 9, click in the form, and drag to size control	___ Display the palette
j. Click at 10, click in the form, and drag to size control	

2. Careful attention must be given to designing a table or else the resulting system will not perform as desired. Consider the following:

   a. An individual's age may be calculated from his or her birth date, which in turn can be stored as a field within a record. An alternate technique would be to store age directly in the record and thereby avoid the calculation. Which field, age or birth date, would you use? Why?

   b. Social security number is typically chosen as the primary key instead of a person's name. What attribute does the social security number possess that makes it the superior choice?

   c. Zip code is normally stored as a separate field to save money at the post office in connection with a mass mailing. Why?

   d. An individual's name is normally divided into two (or three) fields corresponding to the last name and first name (and middle initial). Why is this done; that is, what would be wrong with using a single field consisting of the first name, middle initial, and last name, in that order?

3. The error messages in Figure 2.10 appeared or could have appeared in conjunction with the hands-on exercises in the chapter. Indicate a potential cause of each error and a suggested course of action to correct the problem.

(a) Error Message 1

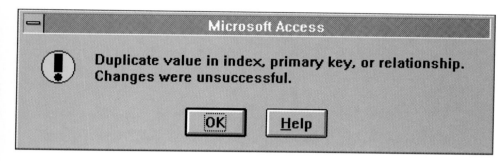

(b) Error Message 2

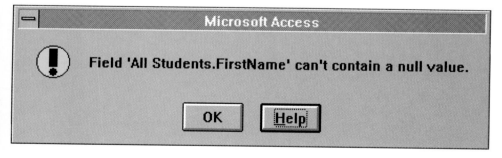

(c) Error Message 3

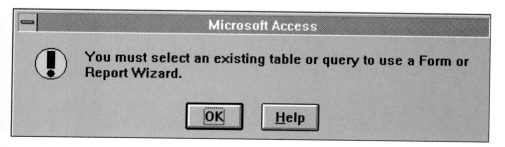

(d) Error Message 4

FIGURE 2.10 Error Messages for Problem 3

4. Field Properties: The Help screen in Figure 2.11 was produced by searching on *Field Size*.
   a. What is the default setting of the Field Size property for a text field? What is the maximum field size for a text field?
   b. What is the default setting of the Field Size property for a number field? Which setting should be used for fields such as QualityPoints or Credits in the Student table that was developed in the chapter?
   c. What is the difference between the Byte, Integer, and Long Integer field sizes?
   d. What is to be gained (or lost) by changing the Field Size property in an existing table from Double to Integer?
   e. What is to be gained (or lost) by changing the Field Size property in an existing table from Integer to Long Integer?

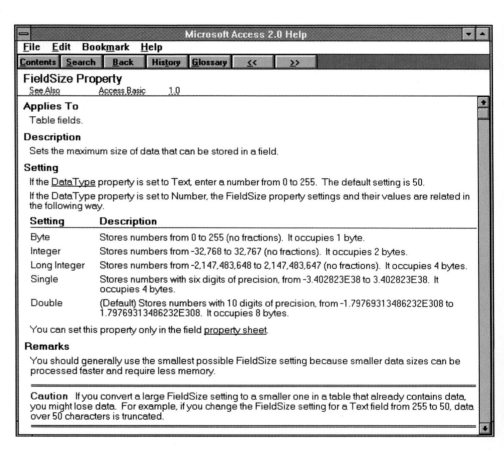

FIGURE 2.11 Screen for Problem 4

5. The Table Wizard: The Table Wizard anticipates several applications you might find useful on a personal basis and includes several tables to get you started. Select one of the personal tables of interest to you such as the Music Collection, Video Collection, or Exercise Log. Create the table and corresponding form, then enter at least 10 records. Use data validation as appropriate.

6. Open the EMPLOYEE.MDB database found on the data disk to create a form similar to the one in Figure 2.12.

   a. The form was created by using the Form Wizard and the Embossed style. The various controls were then moved and sized to match the arrangement in the figure.

   b. The date of execution, combo boxes, and command buttons were added after the form was created, using the techniques in the third hands-on exercise.

   c. To add lines to the form, click the Line tool in the toolbox, then click and drag on the form to draw the line. To draw a straight line, press and hold the Shift key as you draw the line.

   d. You need not match our form exactly, and we encourage you to experiment with a different design.

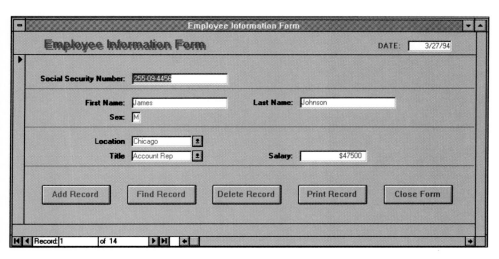

FIGURE 2.12 Screen for Problem 6

7. Open the USA.MDB database found on the data disk to create a form similar to the one in Figure 2.13.

   a. The form was created by using the Form Wizard and Standard style. The various controls were then moved and sized to match the arrangement in the figure.

   b. Population density is a calculated control and is computed by dividing the population by the area.

   c. You need not match our form exactly, and we encourage you to experiment with different designs.

   d. The Find command can be used after the form has been created to search through the table and answer questions about the United States, such as "Which state is nicknamed the Empire State?"

8. Modify the Student Information Form created in the hands-on exercises to match the form in Figure 2.14. (The form contains three additional controls that must be added to the All Students table.)

   a. Add DateAdmitted and EmailAddress as text fields in the All Students table. Add a Yes/No field to indicate whether or not the student is an International student.

   b. Add controls for the Date Admitted and Email address as shown in Figure 2.14. (Pull down the View menu, click Field list, then drag the fields from the Field list to the form.) Be sure to change the tab order after you

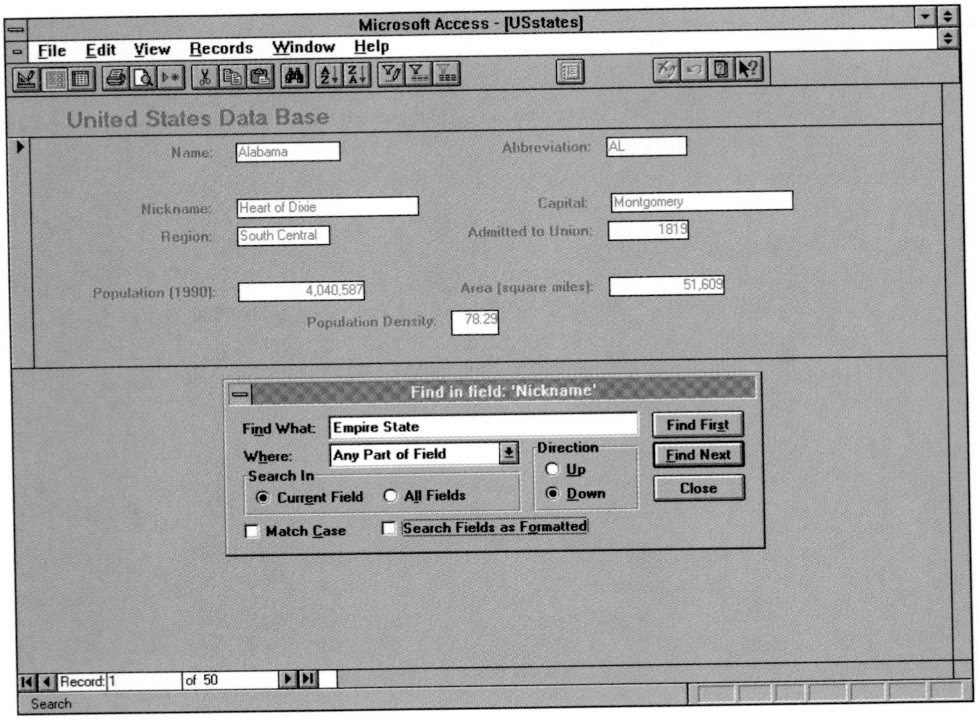

FIGURE 2.13 Screen for Problem 7

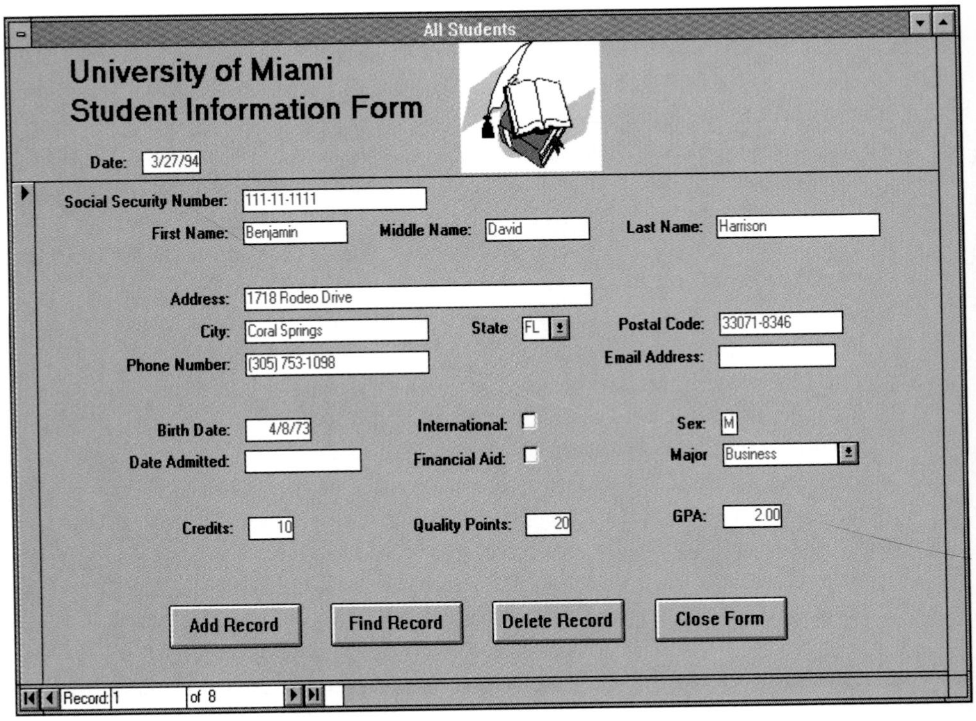

FIGURE 2.14 Screeen for Problems 8 and 9

have added the controls so that the user moves easily from one field to the next when entering data.

c. Create a check box for the International field. (Click the Check box tool in the toolbox, then click and drag the International field from the field list to the form. You may have to pull down the View menu and click Field List to display the field list.)

d. Delete the existing control for State and substitute a combo box instead. Use CA, FL, NJ, and NY as these are the most common states in the Student body. Modify the tab order to accommodate the new control.

e. Resize the control in the Form Header so that *University of Miami Student Information Form* takes two lines. Press Ctrl+Enter to force a line break within the control.

f. Add the graphic as described in problem 9.

9. Object Linking and Embedding: This exercise continues problem 8 (or it can be done immediately after the third hands-on exercise). The steps below describe how to insert a graphic created by another application as an object on an Access form. The exercise works as described, but you will be frustrated unless you have a fast 486 machine.

a. Click the Object Frame tool on the toolbox. (If you are unsure as to which tool to click, just point to the tool to display the name of the tool.)

b. Click and drag in the Form Header to size the frame, then release the mouse to display an Insert Object dialog box.

c. Click the New option button. Scroll through the list box until you can select Microsoft Word 6.0 Picture, then click OK.

d. Word for Windows will be opened automatically and a document window will be displayed with the insertion point in a rectangular frame. (The title bar of the Word document will reflect the Access Form.)

e. Pull down the Insert menu, click Picture, then double click the graphic you want. (We chose BOOKS.WMF). Size the picture in Word so that it is the size you want on the Access form. Click the Close Picture command button.

f. The status bar will display a message indicating that Word is updating the picture, after which you will be returned to Access. The graphic (from Word) appears on the form.

g. You can move the frame containing the graphic in Access. You can also size the frame to display more (or less) of the picture but you *cannot* change its scale unless you double click the graphic and return to Word.

Case Studies

Personnel Management

You have been hired as the Personnel Director for a medium-sized firm (500 employees) and are expected to implement a system to track employee compensation. You want to be able to calculate the age of every employee as well as the length of service. You want to know each employee's most recent performance evaluation. You want to be able to calculate the amount of the most recent salary increase, in dollars as well as a percentage of the previous salary. You also want to know how long the employee had to wait for that increase—that is, how much time elapsed between the present and previous salary. Design a table capable of providing this information.

The Stock Broker

A good friend has come to you for help. He is a new stock broker whose firm provides computer support for existing clients, but does nothing in the way of data management for prospective clients. Your friend is determined to succeed and wants to use a PC to track the clients he is pursuing by telephone and through the mail. He wants to keep track of when he last contacted a person, how the contact was made (by phone or through the mail), and how interested the person was. He also wants to store the investment goals of each prospect, such as growth or income and whether a person is interested in stocks, bonds, and/or a retirement account. And finally, he wants to record the amount of money they have to invest. Design a table suitable for the information requirements of your friend.

Metro Zoo

Your job as Director of Special Programs at the Metro Zoo has put you in charge of this year's fund-raising effort. You have decided to run an "Adopt an Animal" campaign and are looking for contributions on three levels: $25 for a reptile, $50 for a bird, and $100 for a mammal. Adopting "parents" will receive a personalized adoption certificate, a picture of their animal, and educational information about the zoo. You already have a great mailing list—the guest book that is maintained at the zoo entrance. Your main job is to computerize that information and to store additional information about contributions that are received. Design a table that will be suitable for this project.

Form Design

Collect several examples of real forms such as a magazine subscription, auto registration, or employment application. Choose the form you like best and implement the system in Access. Start by creating the underlying table (with some degree of validation), then use the Form Wizard to create the form. How closely does the form you created resemble the paper form with which you began?

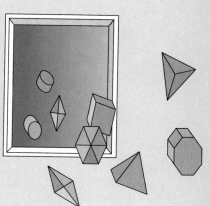

3

Information from the Database: Reports and Queries

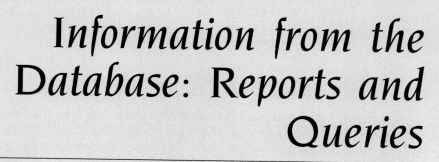

CHAPTER OBJECTIVES

After reading this chapter you will be able to:

1. Describe the different types of reports available through the Report Wizard.
2. Describe the different views in the Report Window and the purpose of each.
3. Describe the similarities between forms and reports with respect to bound, unbound, and calculated controls.
4. List the sections that may be present in a report and explain the purpose of each.
5. Differentiate between a query and a table; explain how the objects in an Access database (tables, forms, queries, and reports) interact with one another.
6. Use the Query By Example (QBE) grid to create and modify a select query.
7. Explain the use of multiple criteria rows within the QBE grid to implement And and Or conditions in a query.
8. Describe the different views in the Query window and the purpose of each.

OVERVIEW

Data and information are not synonymous. Data refers to a fact or facts about a specific record, such as a student's name, major, quality points, or number of completed credits. Information is data that has been rearranged into a more useful format. The fields within an individual student record are considered data. A list of students on the Dean's List is information produced from the data about individual students.

Chapters 1 and 2 described how to enter and maintain data through the use of tables and forms. This chapter shows how to convert the data to information through queries and reports. Queries enable you to ask questions about the database. Reports provide presentation quality output and display summary information about groups of records.

As you read the chapter, you will see that the objects in an Access database (tables, forms, reports, and queries) have many similar characteristics. We use these similarities to build on what you already know. You understand the concept of inheritance and recognize how fields in a form inherit their properties from the corresponding fields in a table. The same applies to the fields in a report. You have worked with the Design views of a table and a form, so you already appreciate the Design views for reports and queries. In similar fashion, since you already know how to move and size controls within a form, you also know how to move and size them in a report.

The chapter contains three hands-on exercises that give you the opportunity to practice what you have learned. All of the examples use an expanded version of the All Students table from Chapter 2.

REPORTS

A *report* is a printed document that displays information from a database. Figure 3.1 shows several sample reports. The reports were created with the Report Wizard and are based on the All Students table that was presented in Chapter 2. (The table has been expanded to 24 records and will be used in the hands-on exercises.) As you view each report, ask yourself how the data in the table was rearranged to produce the information in the report.

The *AutoReport* in Figure 3.1a is the simplest type of report. It lists every field for every record in a single column and typically runs for many pages.

The *Tabular report* in Figure 3.1b displays fields for a given record in a row rather than in a column. Each record in the underlying table is printed on its own row. Only selected fields are displayed, so the tabular report is more concise than the columnar report of Figure 3.1a. The records in Figure 3.1b are listed in alphabetical order by last name.

The report in Figure 3.1c is also a tabular report, but it contains very different information from the first two reports. It displays only the students with a GPA of 3.50 or higher. The Dean's List contains *selected records* from the All Students table, as opposed to the other two reports, which displayed every record.

The *Group/Total report* in Figure 3.1d displays summary calculations for groups of students. It groups students according to their major, then lists them alphabetically within each major. The report displays summary information for each group of students (the number of students in that major). It also contains summary information (not visible in Figure 3.1d) for the report as a whole, which shows the total number of students.

The letters in Figure 3.1e illustrate a *mail merge* in which the same letter is sent to many different people. (See problem 8 at the end of the chapter.) The mail merge uses selected fields (a student's name and address) for selected students (those who qualify for the Dean's List). The form letter is written in Word for Windows (or another word processor), but the data is taken from Access. The *mailing labels* in Figure 3.1f were created in support of the mail merge.

DATA VERSUS INFORMATION

Data and information are not synonymous although the terms are often interchanged. **Data** is the raw material and consists of the table (or tables) that constitutes a database. **Information** is the finished product. Data is converted to information by selecting records, performing calculations on those records, and/or changing the sequence in which the records are displayed. Decisions in an organization are made on the basis of information rather than raw data.

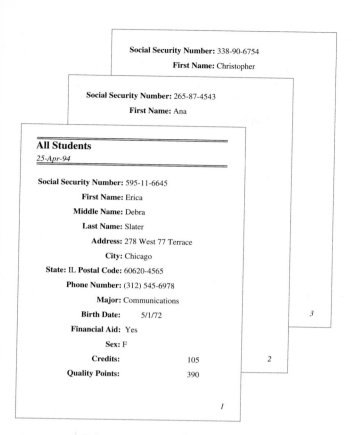

(a) AutoReport (columnar report)

Student Master List

24-Apr-94

Last Name	First Name	Phone Number	Major	Credits
Adili	Ronnie	(612) 445-7654	Business	60
Berlin	Jared	(803) 223-7868	Engineering	100
Camejo	Oscar	(716) 433-3321	Liberal Arts	100
Coe	Bradley	(415) 235-6543	Undecided	52
Cornell	Ryan	(404) 755-4490	Undecided	45
DiGiacomo	Kevin	(305) 531-7652	Business	105
Faulkner	Eileen	(305) 489-8876	Communications	30
Frazier	Steven	(410) 995-8755	Undecided	35
Gibson	Christopher	(305) 235-4563	Business	35
Heltzer	Peter	(305) 753-4533	Engineering	25
Huerta	Carlos	(212) 344-5654	Undecided	15
Joseph	Cedric	(404) 667-8955	Communications	45
Korba	Nickolas	(415) 664-0900	Engineering	100
Ortiz	Frances	(303) 575-3211	Communications	28
Parulis	Christa	(410) 877-6565	Liberal Arts	50
Price	Lori	(310) 961-2323	Communications	24
Ramsay	Robert	(212) 223-9889	Business	50
Slater	Erica	(312) 545-6978	Communications	105
Solomon	Wendy	(305) 666-4532	Engineering	50
Watson	Ana	(305) 595-7877	Liberal Arts	70
Watson	Ana	(305) 561-2334	Business	30
Weissman	Kimberly	(904) 388-8605	Liberal Arts	63
Zacco	Michelle	(617) 884-3434	Undecided	21
Zimmerman	Kimberly	(713) 225-3434	Business	120

Prepared by: Marita Morales

1

(b) Tabular Report

Dean's List

24-Apr-94

First Name	Last Name	Major	Credits	Quality Points	GPA
Peter	Heltzer	Engineering	25	100	4.00
Cedric	Joseph	Communications	45	170	3.78
Erica	Slater	Communications	105	390	3.71
Kevin	DiGiacomo	Business	105	375	3.57
Wendy	Solomon	Engineering	50	175	3.50

1

(c) The Dean's List

Major	Last Name	First Name	GPA
Liberal Arts			
	Camejo	Oscar	2.80
			1.80
			2.79
			2.63
			4

GPA by Major

25-Apr-94

Major	Last Name	First Name	GPA
Business			
	Adili	Ronnie	2.58
	DiGiacomo	Kevin	3.57
	Gibson	Christopher	1.71
	Ramsay	Robert	3.24
	Watson	Ana	2.50
	Zimmerman	Kimberly	3.29
	Total Students in Major:		**6**
Communications			
	Faulkner	Eileen	2.67
	Joseph	Cedric	3.78
	Ortiz	Frances	2.14
	Price	Lori	1.75
	Slater	Erica	3.71
	Total Students in Major:		**5**
Engineering			
	Berlin	Jared	2.50
	Heltzer	Peter	4.00
	Korba	Nickolas	1.66
	Soomon	Wendy	3.50
	Total Students in Major:		**4**

1

(to the right: 2.75, 1.78, 1.29, 2.67, 3.24, **5**, **24**, **2**)

(d) Group/Total Report

FIGURE 3.1 Report Types

(e) Mail Merge

(f) Mailing Labels

FIGURE 3.1   Report Types (continued)

Anatomy of a Report

The ***Report Wizard*** is the easiest way to create a report, just as the Form Wizard is the easiest way to create a form. The Report Wizard asks you questions about the report you want, then builds the report for you. You can accept the report as it is created, or you can customize it to better suit your needs.

The best way to understand the structure of a report is to compare the printed version to the underlying design. Accordingly, Figure 3.2 shows the Design view of the tabular report from Figure 3.1b. (This is the report you will create in the first hands-on exercise.)

Every report is divided into sections, which appear at designated places when the report is printed. There are seven different sections, but a report need not contain all seven.

The ***report header*** appears once at the beginning of a report. It contains information describing the report, such as its title and the date the report was printed. (The report header appears before the page header on the first page of the report.) The ***report footer*** appears before the page footer on the last page of the report and displays summary information.

The ***page header*** appears at the top of every page in a report and can be used to display page numbers, column headings, and other descriptive information. The ***page footer*** appears at the bottom of every page and may contain page numbers (when they are not in the page header) or other descriptive information.

A ***group header*** appears at the beginning of a group of records and usually displays the name of the group. A ***group footer*** appears after the last record in a group and normally shows the group totals. (These sections appear only in a

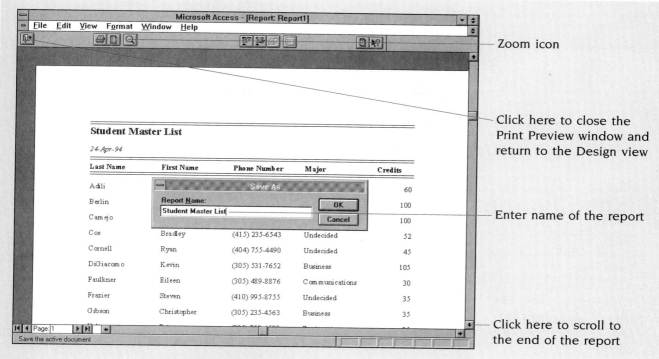

Zoom icon

Click here to close the Print Preview window and return to the Design view

Enter name of the report

Click here to scroll to the end of the report

(c) Save the Report (step 5)

FIGURE 3.3   Hands-on Exercise I (continued)

Step 6: The Design view

➤ Click the **Close Window icon** to close the Print Preview window and display the report in the Design view.

➤ Click the control in the Report Footer, which sums the Credits field. (You may not see the entire entry.) The field is selected as indicated by the sizing handles in Figure 3.3d. Press the **Del key** to delete the control.

➤ Click (select) the line immediately above the summation (the control you just deleted). Press and hold the **Shift key** to select the second line. Press the **Del key** to delete both lines.

➤ Pull down the **File menu** and click **Save** (or click the **Save icon**) to save the report.

ADDING AND REMOVING SECTIONS

Headers and footers, whether for the report as a whole, a page, or a group, are added and removed as a pair. To add or remove a section pair, pull down the Format menu and select (deselect) the desired Header/Footer combination. To suppress a section footer (while displaying the header), delete all of the controls in the footer, then set its height to zero by dragging the bottom edge of the section to meet the top.

Save icon

Click here to select the line

Press Shift as you click to select this line at the same time

Click here to select the control, then press the Del key to delete the control

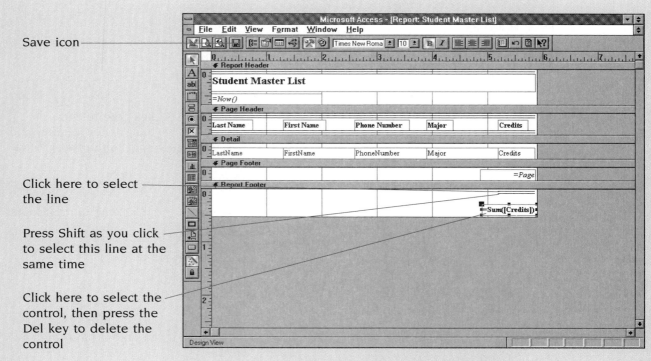

(d) The Design View (step 6)

FIGURE 3.3 Hands-on Exercise I (continued)

Step 7: Control Properties
➤ Click the control for the Report Title in the Report Header. The title of the report (Student Master List) is selected as shown by the sizing handles in Figure 3.3e.
➤ Pull down the **View menu** (or click the **right mouse button** to produce a shortcut menu). Click **Properties** to display the Properties box in Figure 3.3e.
➤ Scroll through the properties until you can click the **Font Size property.** Click the **arrow** to display the point sizes. Click **20.** Double click the **control-menu box** to close the Properties dialog box.
➤ Save the report.

SECTION PROPERTIES

Each section in a report has properties that control its appearance and behavior. Double click the section header (or double click the section background area) to display the property sheet and set the properties. You can hide the section by changing the Visible property to No. You can also change the Special Effect property to Raised or Sunken.

Step 8: Add an unbound control
➤ The Report Design toolbar is displayed immediately under the menu bar.
➤ If necessary click the **Toolbox icon** to display the Toolbox as shown in Figure 3.3f. The Toolbox may be fixed or floating according to its position the last time it was used.

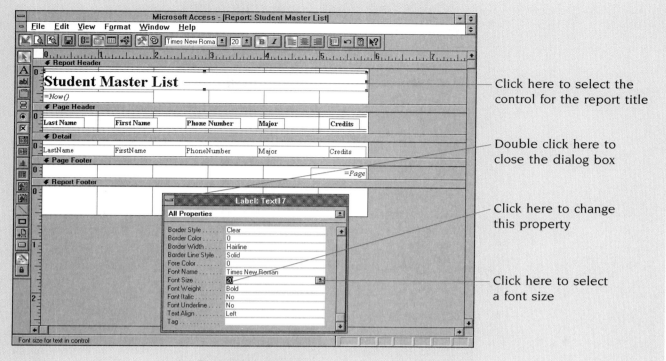

Click here to select the control for the report title

Double click here to close the dialog box

Click here to change this property

Click here to select a font size

(e) Properties (step 7)

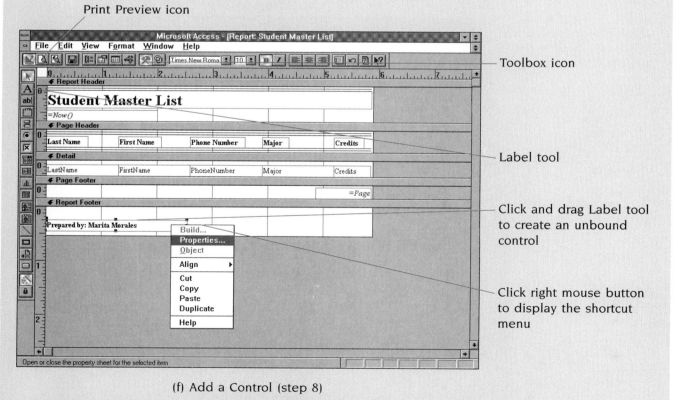

Print Preview icon

Toolbox icon

Label tool

Click and drag Label tool to create an unbound control

Click right mouse button to display the shortcut menu

(f) Add a Control (step 8)

FIGURE 3.3   Hands-on Exercise 1 (continued)

➤ Click the **Label tool,** then click and drag in the Report Footer where you want the label to go, and release the mouse. You should see a flashing insertion point inside the label control. (If you see the word *Unbound* instead of the insertion point, it means you selected the Text box tool rather than the Label tool; delete the text box and begin again.)

➤ Type **Prepared By** followed by your name as shown in Figure 3.3f. Press **enter** to complete the entry and also select the control. Point to the control and click the **right mouse button** to produce the shortcut menu shown in Figure 3.3f. Click **Properties** to display the Properties dialog box.

➤ Click the **down arrow** on the scroll box until you see the Font Name property. Click the box for the **Font Name property,** then click the **arrow** to display available fonts. Click **Arial.**

➤ Double click the **control-menu box** to close the Properties dialog box. Save the report.

Step 9: Print the completed report
➤ Click the **Print Preview icon** to exit the Design view. Click the **Zoom icon** to see the whole page as shown in Figure 3.3g.

➤ Click the **Print icon** to produce the Print dialog box. Click **OK** to print the report.

➤ Pull down the **File menu** and click **Close** (or double click the **control-menu box**) to close the report and return to the Database window.

➤ Close the **OURDATA** database and exit Access if you do not wish to continue with the next hands-on exercise.

Double click the control-menu box to close the Print Preview window

Print icon

Zoom icon

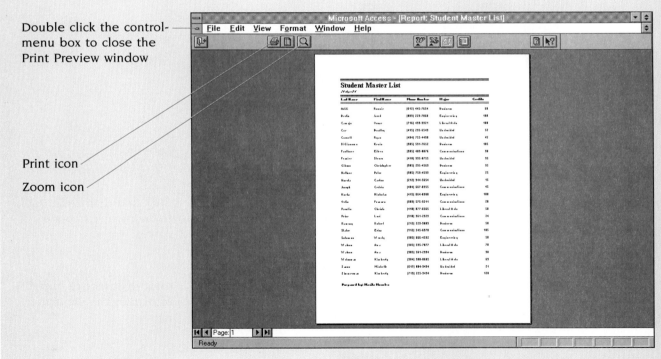

(g) Print Preview (step 9)

FIGURE 3.3 Hands-on Exercise 1 (continued)

INTRODUCTION TO QUERIES

The report you just created displayed every student in the underlying table. What if, however, we wanted to see just the students who are majoring in Business? Or the students who are receiving financial aid? Or the students who are majoring in Business *and* receiving financial aid? The ability to ask questions such as these, and to see the answers to those questions, is provided through a query. Queries represent the real power of a database.

A *query* lets you see the data you want in the order you want it. It lets you select records from a table (or from several tables) and show some or all of the fields for the selected records. It also lets you perform calculations and display fields that are not present in the underlying table(s) such as a student's GPA.

A query represents a question and an answer. The question is developed by using a graphical tool known as the ***Query By Example (QBE) grid.*** The answer is displayed in a ***dynaset,*** which contains the records that satisfy the criteria specified in the query.

A dynaset looks and acts like a table, but it isn't a table; it is a *dyna*mic sub*set* of a table that selects and sorts records as specified in the query. A dynaset is like a table in that you can enter a new record or modify an existing record. It is dynamic because the changes made to the dynaset are automatically reflected in the underlying table.

Figure 3.4a displays the All Students table we have been using throughout the chapter. (For ease of illustration, we do not show all of the fields.) Figure 3.4b contains the ***QBE grid*** used to select students whose major is "Undecided" and further, to list those students in alphabetical order. (The QBE grid is explained in the next section.) Figure 3.4c displays the answer to the query in a dynaset.

The table in Figure 3.4a contains 24 records. The dynaset in Figure 3.4c has only five records, corresponding to the students who are undecided about their major. The table in Figure 3.4a has 15 fields for each record (some of the fields are hidden). The dynaset in Figure 3.4c has only four fields. The records in the table are in social security order, whereas the records in the dynaset are in alphabetical order by last name.

The query in Figure 3.4 is an example of a ***select query,*** which is the most common type of query. A select query searches the underlying table (Figure 3.4a in the example) to retrieve the data that satisfies the query. The data is displayed in a dynaset (Figure 3.4c), which you can change to update the data in the underlying table(s). The specifications for selecting records, determining which fields to display for the selected records, and the sequence of the selected records are contained within the QBE grid of Figure 3.4b.

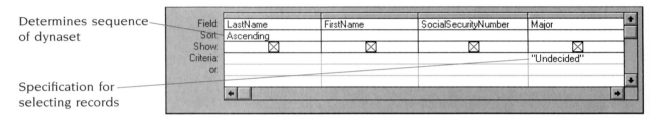

Records in order by
SocialSecurityNumber

(a) All Students Table

Determines sequence
of dynaset

Specification for
selecting records

(b) Query By Example (QBE) Grid

Records in order
by Last Name

(c) Dynaset

FIGURE 3.4   Queries

REPORTS, QUERIES, AND TABLES

Every report is based on a table or a query. The design of the report may be
the same with respect to the fields that are included, but the actual reports
will be very different. A report based on a table contains every record in the
table. A report based on a query contains only the records that satisfy the criteria in the query.

Query Window

The **Query window** has four views. The **Design view** is displayed by default and is shown in Figure 3.5. The Design view is used to create (or modify) a select query. The Datasheet view displays the resulting dynaset. The **Print Preview** shows how the dynaset will appear on the printed page. The **SQL view** enables you to use SQL statements to modify the query and is beyond the scope of the present discussion. The Query Design toolbar contains the icons to display all the views.

A select query is created in the Design view *without* the aid of a wizard. The Design view contains the **field list** for the table(s) on which the query is based (the All Students table in this example). It also displays the QBE grid, which is the essence of a select query.

The QBE grid consists of columns and rows. Each field in the query has its own column. A field is added to the query by dragging it from the field list to the QBE grid. There are several rows for each field. The **Field row** displays the field name. The **Sort row** enables you to sort in ascending or descending sequence. The **Show row** controls whether or not the field will be displayed in the dynaset. The **Criteria row(s)** determine the records that will be selected—for example, students with an undecided major as in Figure 3.5.

Data Type

The data type determines the way in which criteria appear in the QBE grid. A text field is enclosed in quotation marks. Number, currency, and counter fields are shown as digits with or without a decimal point. (Commas and dollar signs are not allowed.) Dates are enclosed in pound signs and are entered in the mm/dd/yy format. A Yes/No field is entered as Yes (or True) or No (or False).

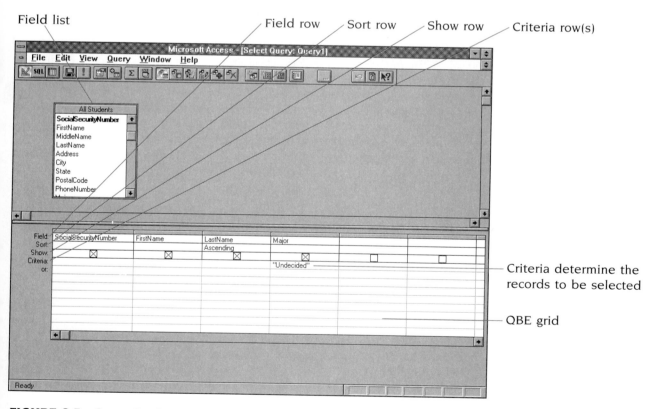

FIGURE 3.5 Query Design View

CONVERSION TO STANDARD FORMAT

Access accepts values for text and date fields in the QBE grid in multiple formats. The value for a text field can be entered with or without quotation marks (Undecided or "Undecided"). A date can be entered with or without pound signs (1/1/94 or #1/1/94#). Access converts your entries to standard format as soon as you move to the next cell in the QBE grid. Thus, text entries are always shown in quotation marks, and dates are enclosed in pound signs.

Selection Criteria

To specify selection criteria in the QBE grid, enter a value or expression in the Criteria row of the appropriate column. Figure 3.6 contains several examples of simple criteria and provides a basic introduction to select queries. Additional and more complex expressions are developed in Chapters 4 and 5.

The criteria in Figure 3.6a select the students majoring in Business. The criteria for text fields are case insensitive. Thus, *"Business"* is the same as *"business"* or *"BUSINESS"*.

Values entered in multiple columns of the same criteria row implement an **AND** condition in which the selected records must meet *all* of the specified criteria. The criteria in Figure 3.6b select students who are majoring in Business *and* who are from the state of Florida. The criteria in Figure 3.4c select Communications majors who are receiving financial aid. (The criterion for a Yes/No field is entered without quotation marks.)

Values entered in different criteria rows are connected by an **OR** condition in which the selected records satisfy *any* of the indicated criteria. The OR criteria in Figure 3.6d select students who are majoring in Business *or* who are from Florida.

Relational operators ($>$, $<$, $>=$, $<=$, $=$, and $<>$) are used with date or number fields to return records within a designated range. The criteria in Figure 3.6e select Engineering majors with less than 60 credits. The criteria in Figure 3.6f select Communications majors who were born after April 1, 1974.

Criteria can grow more complex by combining multiple And and Or conditions. The criteria in Figure 3.6g select Engineering majors with less than 60 credits *or* Communications majors who were born after April 1, 1974.

Other functions enable you to impose still other criteria. The **Between function** selects records that fall within a range of values. The criteria in Figure 3.6h select students who have between 60 and 90 credits. The Not function selects records that do not have the designated value. The criteria in Figure 3.6i select students with majors other than Liberal Arts.

Queries are discussed again in Chapters 4 and 5 where we show you how to develop more complex criteria.

WILD CARDS

Select queries recognize the question mark and asterisk **wild cards** that enable you to search for a pattern within a text field. A question mark stands for a single character in the same position as the question mark; thus H?ll will return Hall, Hill, and Hull. An **asterisk** stands for any number of characters in the same position as the asterisk; for example, S*nd will return Sand, Stand, and Strand.

(a) Business Majors

Field:	LastName	State	Major	BirthDate	FinancialAid	Credits
Sort:						
Show:	⊠	⊠	⊠	⊠	⊠	⊠
Criteria:			"Business"			
or:						

(b) Business Majors from Florida

Field:	LastName	State	Major	BirthDate	FinancialAid	Credits
Sort:						
Show:	⊠	⊠	⊠	⊠	⊠	⊠
Criteria:		"FL"	"Business"			
or:						

(c) Communications Majors Receiving Financial Aid

Field:	LastName	State	Major	BirthDate	FinancialAid	Credits
Sort:						
Show:	⊠	⊠	⊠	⊠	⊠	⊠
Criteria:			"Communications"		Yes	
or:						

(d) Business Majors or Students from Florida

Field:	LastName	State	Major	BirthDate	FinancialAid	Credits
Sort:						
Show:	⊠	⊠	⊠	⊠	⊠	⊠
Criteria:		"FL"				
or:			"Business"			

(e) Engineering Majors with Less than 60 Credits

Field:	LastName	State	Major	BirthDate	FinancialAid	Credits
Sort:						
Show:	⊠	⊠	⊠	⊠	⊠	⊠
Criteria:			"Engineering"			<60
or:						

(f) Communications Majors Born after April 1, 1974

Field:	LastName	State	Major	BirthDate	FinancialAid	Credits
Sort:						
Show:	⊠	⊠	⊠	⊠	⊠	⊠
Criteria:			"Communications"	>#4/1/74#		
or:						

FIGURE 3.6 Criteria

Field:	LastName	State	Major	BirthDate	FinancialAid	Credits
Sort:						
Show:	☒	☒	☒	☒	☒	☒
Criteria:			"Engineering"	<60		
or:			"Communications"	>#4/1/74#		

(g) Engineering Majors with Less than 60 Credits or
Communications Majors Born after April 1, 1974

Field:	LastName	State	Major	BirthDate	FinancialAid	Credits
Sort:						
Show:	☒	☒	☒	☒	☒	☒
Criteria:						Between 60 And 90
or:						

(h) Students with between 60 and 90 Credits (juniors)

Field:	LastName	State	Major	BirthDate	FinancialAid	Credits
Sort:						
Show:	☒	☒	☒	☒	☒	☒
Criteria:			Not "Liberal Arts"			
or:						

(i) Students with Majors other than Liberal Arts

FIGURE 3.6 Criteria (continued)

HANDS-ON EXERCISE 2:

Creating a Select Query

Objective To create a select query using the Query By Example (QBE) grid; to show how changing values in a dynaset changes the values in the underlying table; to create a report based on a query. Use Figure 3.7 as a guide in the exercise.

Step 1: Open the Student Database
➤ Load Access. Open the **OURDATA** database from the first exercise.
➤ Click the **Query button** in the Database window.
➤ Click the **New command button** to produce the New Query dialog box shown in Figure 3.7a. You are going to create a select query and *cannot* use the *Query Wizard.* Click the **New Query button.**

Step 2: Add the All Students table
➤ An open list box will appear within the query windows as shown in Figure 3.7b. The All Students table is the only table in the OURDATA database and is already selected. Click the **Add command button** to add this table to the query.
➤ Click the **Close command button** to close the Add Table dialog box.
➤ Click the **maximize button** to begin working in the query.

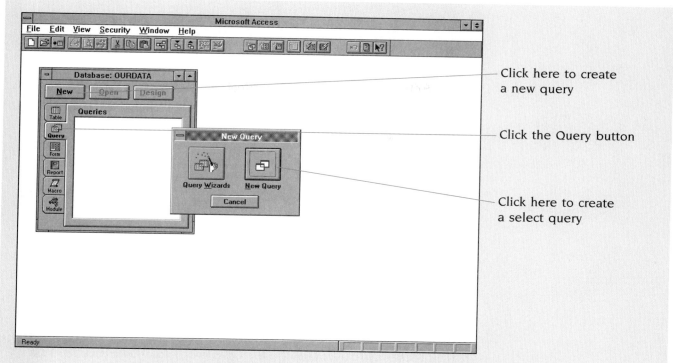

Click here to create
a new query

Click the Query button

Click here to create
a select query

(a) Open the OURDATA Database (step 1)

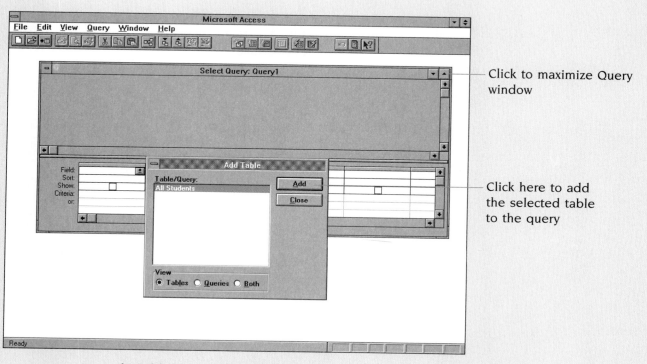

Click to maximize Query
window

Click here to add
the selected table
to the query

(b) Add the All Students Table (step 2)

FIGURE 3.7 Hands-on Exercise 2

CUSTOMIZE THE QUERY WINDOW

The Query window displays the field list and QBE grid in its upper and lower halves, respectively. To increase (decrease) the size of either portion of the window, drag the line dividing the upper and lower sections. Drag the title bar to move a field list. You can also size a field list by dragging a border just as you would size any other window.

Step 3: Create the query

- Click and drag the **LastName** field from the All Students field list to the Field row in the first column of the QBE grid in Figure 3.7c.
- Click and drag the **FirstName, PhoneNumber, Major,** and **Credits** fields in similar fashion, dragging each field to the next available column in the Field row. An X appears in the Show row under each field name to indicate the field will be displayed in the dynaset.

ADDING AND DELETING FIELDS

The fastest way to add a field to the QBE grid is to double click the field name in the field list. To add more than one field at a time, press and hold the Ctrl key as you click the fields within the field list, then drag the group to a cell in the Field row. To delete a field, click the column selector above the field name to select the column, then press the Del key.

Step 4: Specify the criteria

- Click the **Criteria row** for Major. Type **Undecided.**
- Click the **Sort row** under the LastName field. Click the **arrow** to open the drop-down list box. Click **Ascending.**
- Pull down the **File menu** and click **Save** to produce the dialog box in Figure 3.7c.
- Type **Undecided Major** as the Query Name. Click **OK.**

FLEXIBLE CRITERIA

Access offers a great deal of flexibility in the way you enter the criteria for a text field. You may or may not include quotation marks, and you may or may not precede the entry with an equal sign. "Undecided", Undecided, =Undecided, or ="Undecided" are all valid entries. Access converts your entry to standard format ("Undecided" in this example) after you have moved to the next cell.

Step 5: Run the query

- Pull down the **Query menu** and click **Run** (or click the **Run icon**) to run the query and change to the Datasheet view.
- You should see the five records in the dynaset of Figure 3.7d.
- Change Ryan Cornell's major to Business.
- Click the **Design view icon** to change the query.

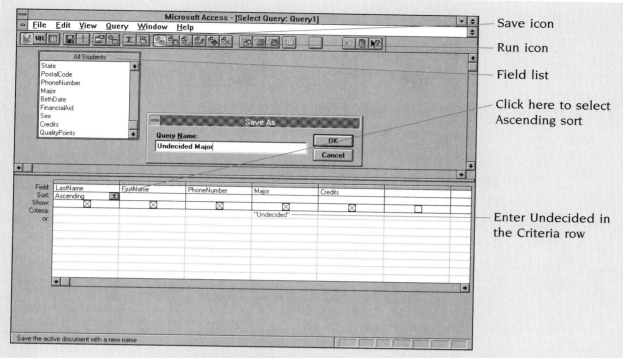

Save icon

Run icon

Field list

Click here to select
Ascending sort

Enter Undecided in
the Criteria row

(c) Create the Query (steps 3 and 4)

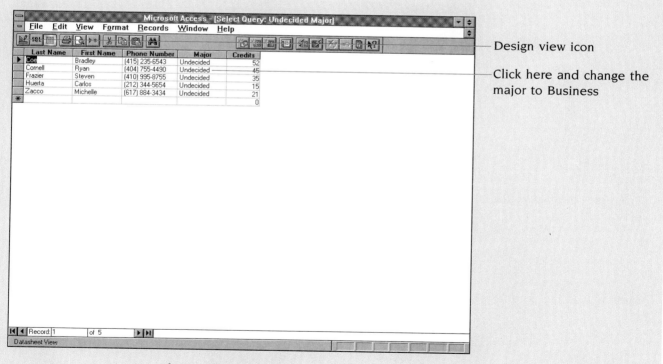

Design view icon

Click here and change the
major to Business

(d) Run the Query (step 5)

FIGURE 3.7   Hands-on Exercise 2 (continued)

Step 6: Modify the query

➤ Click the **Show check box** in the Major field to remove the X as shown in Figure 3.7e.

➤ Click the **Criteria row** under credits. Type **>30** to select only the Undecided majors with more than 30 credits.

➤ Click the **Save icon** to save the revised query.

➤ Click the **Run icon** to run the revised query. This time there are only two records in the dynaset, and the Major field does not appear.
   — Ryan Cornell does not appear because he has changed his major.
   — Carlos Huerta and Michelle Zacco do not appear because they do not have more than 30 credits.

Step 7: Create a report

➤ Pull down the **Window menu** and click **1 Database: OURDATA** (or click the **Database window icon** on the toolbar). You will see the Database window in Figure 3.7f.

➤ Click the **Report button.** Click the **New command button** to create a report based on the query you just created. Select **Undecided Major** from the Select a Table/Query drop-down list as shown in Figure 3.7f.

➤ Click the **Report Wizards command button** to use the Report Wizard to create the report.

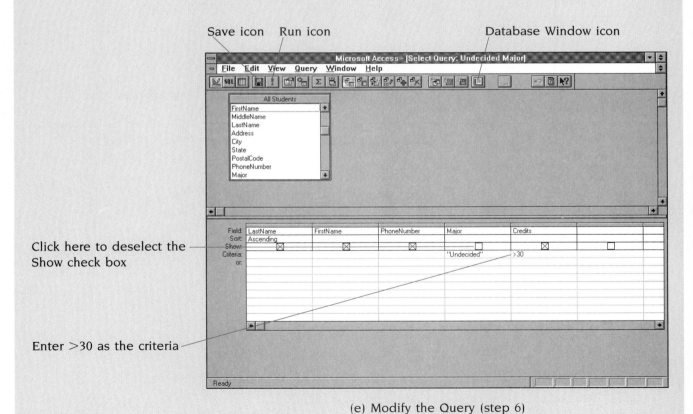

Save icon Run icon   Database Window icon

Click here to deselect the Show check box

Enter >30 as the criteria

(e) Modify the Query (step 6)

FIGURE 3.7 Hands-on Exercise 2 (continued)

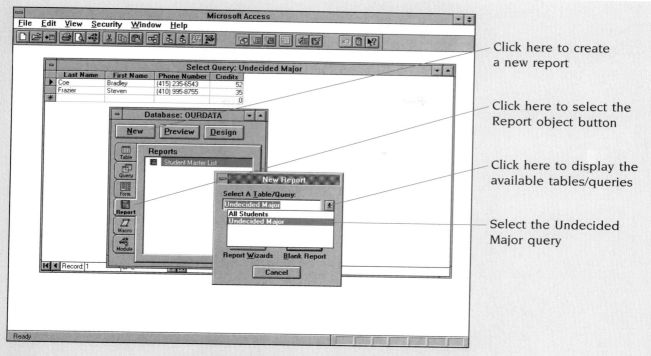

Click here to create a new report

Click here to select the Report object button

Click here to display the available tables/queries

Select the Undecided Major query

(f) Create a Report (step 7)

FIGURE 3.7   Hands-on Exercise 2 (continued)

Step 8: The Report Wizard

➤ Select **AutoReport** in the Report Wizard dialog box and click **OK.** You will see the message, Creating Report, on the status bar as the report is created.

➤ Click the **maximize button** to see the completed report as shown in Figure 3.7g. Click the **Zoom icon** to see the full page.

➤ Pull down the **File menu** and click **Save.** Type **Undecided Major** as the name of the report. Click **OK.**

➤ Click the **Close Window icon** to close the report.

Step 9: The Database Window

➤ If necessary click the **Database Window icon** on the toolbar to return to the Database window. Click the **maximize button.**

   — Click the **Query button** to display the names of the queries in the OUR-DATA database. You should see the *Undecided Major* query created in this exercise.

   — Click the **Report button.** You should see two reports: *Student Master List* (created in the previous exercise) and *Undecided Major* (created in this exercise).

   — Click the **Form button.** You should see the *Student Information Form* corresponding to the form you created in Chapter 2.

   — Click the **Table button.** You should see the *All Students table*, which is the basis of all other objects in the database.

➤ Close the **OURDATA** database and exit Access if you do not wish to continue with the next hands-on exercise.

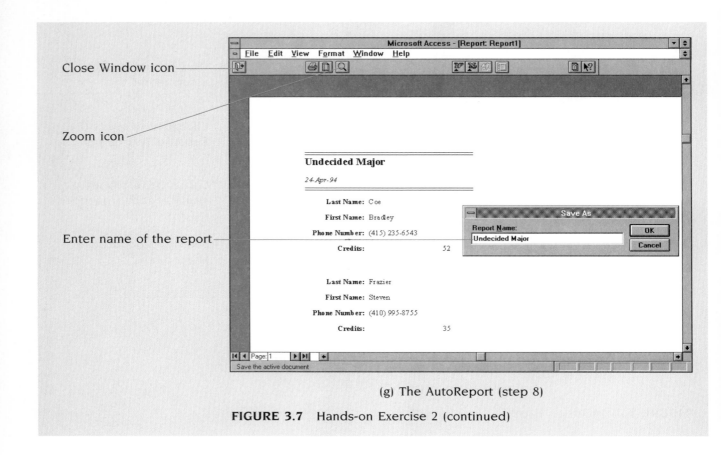

Close Window icon

Zoom icon

Enter name of the report

(g) The AutoReport (step 8)

FIGURE 3.7 Hands-on Exercise 2 (continued)

GROUP/TOTAL REPORTS

A Group/Total report displays summary information about groups of records. It is one of the most frequently used reports and the type you will create in the next exercise. Figure 3.8a shows the first page of the printed report. Figure 3.8b displays the corresponding Design view.

The report in Figure 3.8 groups students by major and then lists them alphabetically within major. A group header appears before each group of students to identify the group and display the major. A group footer appears at the end of each group and displays the average GPA for students in that major.

The report in Figure 3.8 uses the Avg function, but other types of summary calculations are possible:

Sum— The total of all values in a specified field
Avg— The average of values in a field
Min— The minimum value in a field
Max— The maximum value in a field
Count—The number of records with an entry in the specified field

A Group/Total report (like any other report) is based on either a table or a query. We chose to base the report on a query to give you additional practice in creating a select query. The query you will create contains a calculated control, GPA, which is computed by dividing the QualityPoints field by the Credits field. The Criteria row is left empty since the Group/Total report is to contain every record in the All Students table.

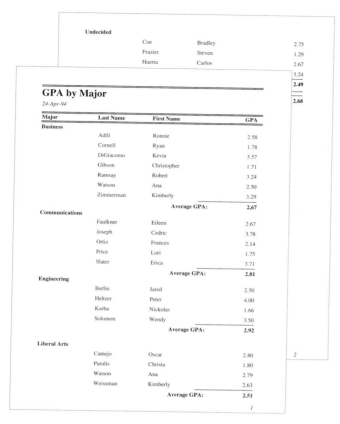

(a) Printed Report

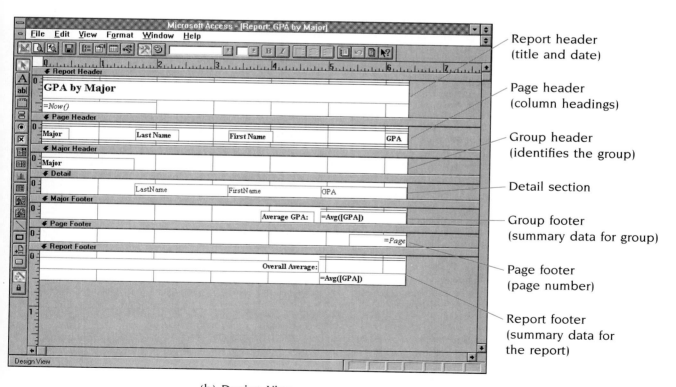

Report header
(title and date)

Page header
(column headings)

Group header
(identifies the group)

Detail section

Group footer
(summary data for group)

Page footer
(page number)

Report footer
(summary data for
the report)

(b) Design View

FIGURE 3.8 Group/Total Report

Creating a Group/Total Report

Objective Create a query containing a calculated field, then use the Report Wizard to create a Group/Totals report based on that query. Use Figure 3.9 as a guide in the exercise.

Step 1: Create the GPA Query

➤ Load Access. Open the **OURDATA** database.

➤ Click the **Query button** in the Database window. Click the **New command** button. Click the **New Query command button** as opposed to the Query Wizard button.

➤ The Add Table dialog box appears with the All Students table already selected. Click the **Add command button** to add this table to the query. Click the **Close command button** to close the Add Table dialog box.

➤ Click the **maximize button** to begin working on the query as shown in Figure 3.9a.

➤ Click and drag the **Major field** from the All Students field list to the query. Click and drag the **LastName, FirstName, QualityPoints,** and **Credits** fields in similar fashion.

➤ Click the **Sort row** for the Major field. Click the **arrow** to open the drop-down list box. Click **Ascending.**

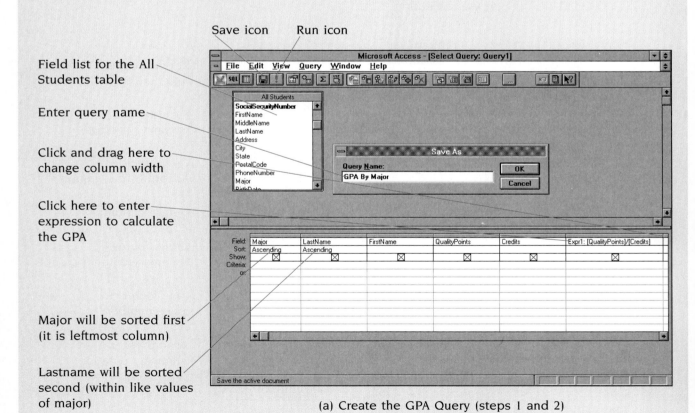

(a) Create the GPA Query (steps 1 and 2)

FIGURE 3.9 Hands-on Exercise 3

➤ Click the **Sort row** for the LastName field. Click the **arrow** to open the drop-down list box. Click **Ascending.**

SORTING ON MULTIPLE FIELDS

You can sort a query on more than one field, but you must be certain that the fields are in the proper order within the QBE grid. Access sorts from left to right (the leftmost field is the *primary key*), so the fields must be arranged in the desired sort sequence. To move a field within the QBE grid, click the column selector above the field name to select the column, then drag the column to its new position.

Step 2: Add a Calculated control

➤ Click the first empty cell in the Field row. Type **=[QualityPoints]/[Credits].** Do not be concerned if you cannot see the entire expression, but be sure you put **square brackets** around both field names.

➤ Press **enter.** Access has substituted Expr1: for the equal sign you typed initially. Drag the column boundary so that the entire expression is visible as in Figure 3.9a. (You may have to make some of the columns narrower to see all of the fields in the QBE grid.)

➤ Pull down the **File menu** and click **Save** (or click the **Save icon**) to produce the dialog box in Figure 3.9a.

➤ Type **GPA By Major** for the Query Name as shown in Figure 3.9a. Click **OK.**

USE DESCRIPTIVE NAMES

An Access database contains multiple objects—tables, forms, queries, and reports. It is important, therefore, that the name assigned to each object be descriptive of its function so that you can select the proper object from the Database window. The name of an object can contain up to 64 characters (letters and numbers) and may include spaces.

Step 3: Run the Query

➤ Pull down the **Query menu** and click **Run** (or click the **Run icon** on the Query Design toolbar). You will see the dynaset in Figure 3.9b:
— Students are listed by major and alphabetically by last name within major.
— The GPA is calculated to several places and appears in the Expr1 field.

➤ Click the **QualityPoints** field for Christopher Gibson. Replace 60 with **70.** Press **enter.** The GPA changes automatically to 2.

➤ Pull down the **Edit menu** and click **Undo Current Record** (or click the **Undo Current Field/Record icon** on the Query toolbar). The GPA returns to its previous value.

➤ Click the **Expr1 (GPA) field** for Christopher Gibson. Type **2.** Access will beep and prevent you from changing the GPA because it is a calculated field.

➤ Click the **Design view icon** to change the query.

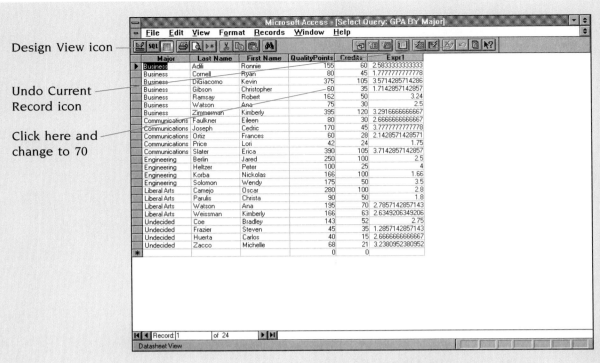

Design View icon

Undo Current
Record icon

Click here and
change to 70

Major	Last Name	First Name	QualityPoints	Credits	Expr1
Business	Adili	Ronnie	155	60	2.5833333333333
Business	Cornell	Ryan	80	45	1.7777777777778
Business	DiGiacomo	Kevin	375	105	3.5714285714286
Business	Gibson	Christopher	60	35	1.7142857142857
Business	Ramsay	Robert	162	50	3.24
Business	Watson	Ana	75	30	2.5
Business	Zimmerman	Kimberly	395	120	3.2916666666667
Communications	Faulkner	Eileen	80	30	2.6666666666667
Communications	Joseph	Cedric	170	45	3.7777777777778
Communications	Ortiz	Frances	60	28	2.1428571428571
Communications	Price	Lori	42	24	1.75
Communications	Slater	Erica	390	105	3.7142857142857
Engineering	Berlin	Jared	250	100	2.5
Engineering	Heltzer	Peter	100	25	4
Engineering	Korba	Nickolas	166	100	1.66
Engineering	Solomon	Wendy	175	50	3.5
Liberal Arts	Camejo	Oscar	280	100	2.8
Liberal Arts	Parulis	Christa	90	50	1.8
Liberal Arts	Watson	Ana	195	70	2.7857142857143
Liberal Arts	Weissman	Kimberly	166	63	2.6349206349206
Undecided	Coe	Bradley	143	52	2.75
Undecided	Frazier	Steven	45	35	1.2857142857143
Undecided	Huerta	Carlos	40	15	2.6666666666667
Undecided	Zacco	Michelle	68	21	3.2380952380952
			0	0	

Record: 1 of 24

Datasheet View

(b) Run the Query (step 3)

FIGURE 3.9 Hands-on Exercise 3 (continued)

ADJUST THE COLUMN WIDTH

Point to the right edge of the column you want to resize, then drag the mouse in the direction you want to go. Alternatively, you can double click the column selector line to fit the longest entry in that column. Adjusting the column width in the Design view does not affect the column width in the Datasheet view, but you can use the same technique in both views.

Step 4: Modify the Query

➤ Click and drag to select **Expr1** in the Field row for the calculated field. (Do not select the colon.) Type **GPA** to substitute a more meaningful field name.

➤ Point to the GPA and click the **right mouse button** to display a shortcut menu. Click **Properties** to display the dialog box in Figure 3.9c.

➤ Click the box for the **Format property.** Click the **down arrow** to display the available formats. Click **Fixed.** Double click the **control-menu box** to close the Field Properties dialog box. Save the query.

Step 5: Rerun the query

➤ Pull down the **Query menu** and click **Run** (or click the **Run icon** on the Query Design toolbar). You will see a new dynaset corresponding to the modified query as shown in Figure 3.9d.

   — Students are still listed by major and alphabetically within major.

   — The GPA is calculated to two places and appears under the GPA field.

➤ Click the **Database window icon.**

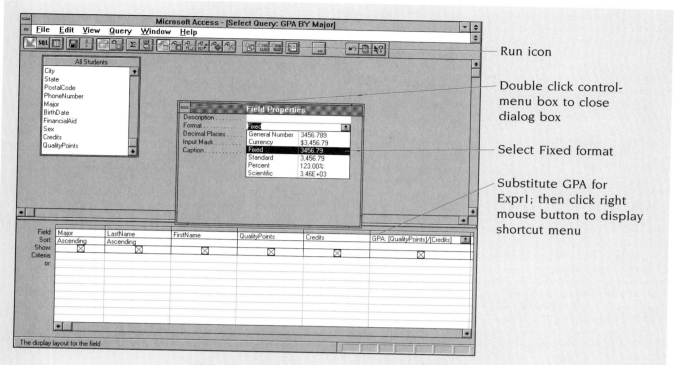

Run icon

Double click control-
menu box to close
dialog box

Select Fixed format

Substitute GPA for
Expr1; then click right
mouse button to display
shortcut menu

(c) Modify the Query (step 4)

Click New to create
a new report

Click the Report
object button

Database Window icon

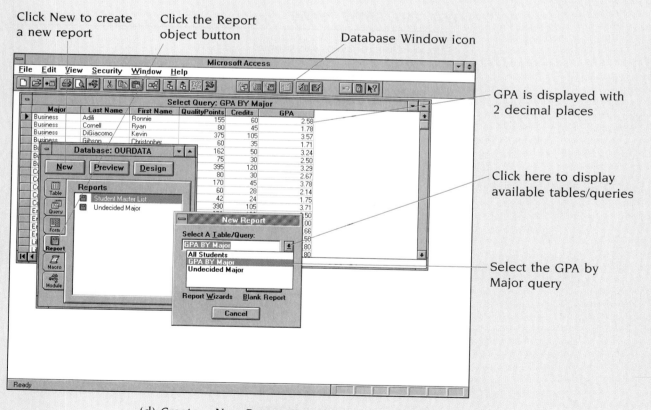

GPA is displayed with
2 decimal places

Click here to display
available tables/queries

Select the GPA by
Major query

(d) Create a New Report (step 6)

FIGURE 3.9   Hands-on Exercise 3 (continued)

THE TOP VALUES PROPERTY

Can you create a query that lists only the five students with the highest GPA? It's easy, if you know about the *Top Values property* to limit the number of displayed records. Click the Sort row in the QBE grid for the GPA field and choose *descending* as the sort *sequence.* Click the right mouse button *outside* the QBE grid to display a shortcut menu, click Properties, then click the box for Top Values. Enter the number of records, then double click the control-menu box to close the Properties dialog box. When you run the query, you will see only the top five students. (You can see the bottom five instead if you specify *ascending sequence* rather than descending as the sort sequence.)

Step 6: Create the report
➤ Click the **Report button.** Click the **New command button.** Select **GPA by Major** from the Select a Table/Query list as the query on which to base the report.
➤ Click the **Report Wizards button** to begin creating the report. Click **Group/Totals.** Click **OK.**

USE THE SAME NAME

Help yourself to select the proper object from the Database window by using the same name for a report and its underlying query. You can also use the same name for a form and its underlying table. A query cannot, however, have the same name as a table. If, when naming a query, you choose the name of an existing table, Access displays a warning message asking whether you want to replace the table. If you respond yes, Access replaces the table with the query and the data in the table is lost!

Step 7: The Report Wizard
➤ Click the **Major field** in the Available fields list box. Click the **> button** to include this field in the report.
➤ Add the **LastName, FirstName,** and **GPA** fields one at a time. Do not include the QualityPoints or Credits fields. Click the **Next command button.**
➤ Select **Major** as the field to group records by and click the **> button.** Click the **Next command button.**
➤ The next dialog box prompts you about how to group the data. Normal is already selected. Click the **Next command button.**
➤ Select **LastName** as the field to sort by and click the **> button.** Click the **Next command button.**
➤ Click the option buttons for the **Executive style** and **Portrait orientation.** Click the **Next command button.**
➤ Check the box to **See all the fields on one page.** Remove the check from the box to calculate percentages.

- ➤ Click the option button to **Modify the report's design.** Click the **Finish command button.** You should see the Report Design view as shown in Figure 3.9e. Maximize the Report window.
- ➤ Save the report as **GPA By Major.**

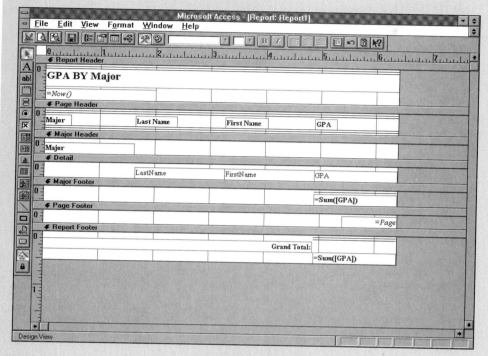

(e) The Report Design View (step 7)

FIGURE 3.9 Hands-on Exercise 3 (continued)

Step 8: Modify the Report

- ➤ Click the control in the Major footer, which displays sizing handles to indicate the control has been selected as shown in Figure 3.9f.
- ➤ Click immediately to the left of the word Sum. Type **Avg,** then press the Del key **three times** to delete the word **Sum.**
- ➤ Click the **Label tool** on the Toolbox to select the tool, then click and drag to the left of the =Avg([GPA]) control in the Major footer to enter a label.
- ➤ You should see a flashing insertion point inside the label control. (If you see the word Unbound instead of the insertion point, it means you selected the Text box tool rather than the Label tool; delete the text box and begin again.)
- ➤ Type **Average GPA:** as shown in Figure 3.9f. Click the control to select it and click the **right justification icon** on the Report Design toolbar.
- ➤ Press and hold the **Shift key** as you click the Average GPA control. Pull down the **Format menu.** Click **Align.** Click **Bottom.**
- ➤ Change the Sum function in the Report Footer to the Average function. Change the label Grand Total to **Overall Average.**
- ➤ Save the report.

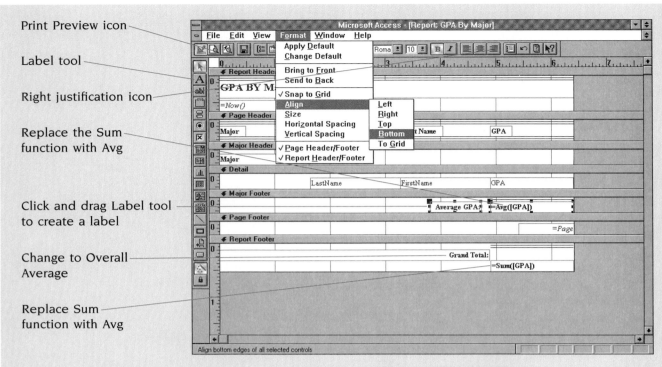

Print Preview icon

Label tool

Right justification icon

Replace the Sum function with Avg

Click and drag Label tool to create a label

Change to Overall Average

Replace Sum function with Avg

(f) Modify the Report (step 8)

FIGURE 3.9 Hands-on Exercise 3 (continued)

Step 9: View and print the report

➤ Click the **Print Preview icon** to view the completed report as shown in Figure 3.9g. The Status Bar shows you are on page 1 of the report.

➤ Click the **Zoom icon** to see the entire page. Click the **Zoom icon** a second time to return to the higher magnification that lets you read the report.

➤ Click the **Navigation button** to move to the next page (page 2). (If you do not move to the next page, it is because you selected Sample Preview instead of Print Preview. Click the icon to close the window and return to the Design view, then click the Print Preview icon.)

➤ Click the **Navigation button** to move back to page 1.

➤ Pull down the **File menu** and click **Print** (or click the **Printer icon**) to display the Print dialog box. The All option button is already selected under Print Range. Click **OK** to print the report.

PRINT PREVIEW VERSUS SAMPLE PREVIEW

Access provides two different ways to preview a report, each with its own icon on the Report Design toolbar. The *Sample Preview* displays every section in a report but contains only a few detail records; it is used to take a quick look at a report to check its overall layout and appearance. Note, too, that while the Sample Preview sorts and groups the data, it ignores any criteria in the underlying query and thus may contain records that do not appear in the actual report. *Print Preview,* on the other hand, displays the entire report exactly as it will be printed and thus can extend to several pages.

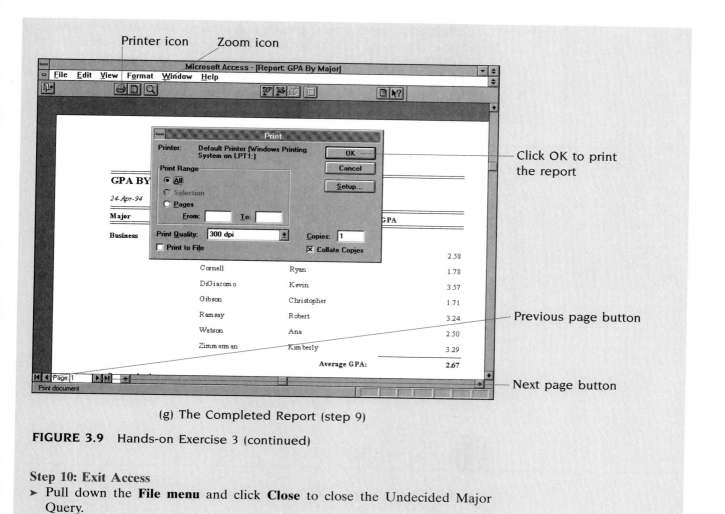

(g) The Completed Report (step 9)

FIGURE 3.9   Hands-on Exercise 3 (continued)

Step 10: Exit Access
➤ Pull down the **File menu** and click **Close** to close the Undecided Major Query.
➤ Close the OURDATA database and exit Access.

SUMMARY

Data and information are not synonymous. Data refers to a fact or facts about a specific record. Information is data that has been rearranged into a more useful format. Data may be viewed as the raw material, whereas information is the finished product.

A report is a printed document that displays information from the database. Reports are created through the Report Wizard, then modified as necessary in the Design view of the Report window. A report is made up of sections. Every section contains controls that are bound, unbound, or calculated, according to their data source.

Every report is based on either a table or a query. A report based on a table contains every record in that table. A report based on a query will contain only the records satisfying the criteria in the query.

A query enables you to select records from a table (or from several tables), display the selected records in any order, and perform calculations on fields within the query. A select query is the most common type of query and is created by using the Query By Example grid. A select query displays its output in a dynaset, which can be used to update the data in the underlying table(s).

All objects (tables, forms, queries, and reports) in an Access database are named according to the same rules. The name can contain up to 64 characters (letters or numbers) and can include spaces. A report can have the same name as the table or query on which it is based to emphasize the relationship between the two.

 Key Words and Concepts

AND criteria	Group footer	Query Wizard
Ascending sequence	Group header	Relational operators
Asterisk	Group/Total report	Report
AutoReport	Information	Report footer
Bound control	Inheritance	Report header
Calculated control	OR criteria	Report Wizard
Criteria row	Page footer	Sample Preview
Data	Page header	Select query
Datasheet view	Primary key	Sort row
Descending sequence	Print Preview	Show row
Design view	QBE grid	Tabular report
Detail section	Query	Top Values property
Dynaset	Query By Example	Unbound control
Field row	Query window	Wild card

 Multiple Choice

1. Which of the following is a reason for basing a report on a query rather than a table?
  (a) To limit the report to selected records
  (b) To include a calculated field in the report
  (c) Both (a) and (b)
  (d) Neither (a) nor (b)

2. An Access database may contain:
  (a) One or more tables
  (b) One or more queries
  (c) One or more reports
  (d) All of the above

3. Which of the following is true regarding the names of objects within an Access database?
  (a) A query and a table may have the same name
  (b) A query and a report may have the same name
  (c) Both (a) and (b)
  (d) Neither (a) nor (b)

4. The dynaset created by a query may contain:
  (a) A subset of records from the associated table but must contain all of the fields for the selected records
  (b) A subset of fields from the associated table but must contain all of the records

(c) Both (a) and (b)

(d) Neither (a) nor (b)

5. Which toolbar contains an icon to display the properties of a selected object?

(a) The Query Design toolbar

(b) The Report Design toolbar

(c) Both (a) and (b)

(d) Neither (a) nor (b)

6. Which of the following does *not* have both a Design view and a Datasheet view?

(a) Tables

(b) Forms

(c) Queries

(d) Reports

7. Which of the following is true regarding the wild card character within Access?

(a) A question mark stands for a single character in the same position as the question mark

(b) An asterisk stands for any number of characters in the same position as the asterisk

(c) Both (a) and (b)

(d) Neither (a) nor (b)

8. Which of the following will print at the top of every page?

(a) Report header

(b) Control header

(c) Both (a) and (b)

(d) Neither (a) nor (b)

9. A query, based on the OURDATA.MDB database within the chapter, contains two fields from the Student table (QualityPoints and Credits) as well as a calculated field (GPA). Which of the following is true?

(a) Changing the value of Credits or QualityPoints in the query's dynaset automatically changes these values in the underlying table

(b) Changing the value of GPA automatically changes its value in the underlying table

(c) Both (a) and (b)

(d) Neither (a) nor (b)

10. Which of the following must be present in every report?

(a) A report header and a report footer

(b) A page header and a page footer

(c) Both (a) and (b)

(d) Neither (a) nor (b)

11. Which of the following may be included in a report as well as a form?

(a) Bound control

(b) Unbound control

(c) Calculated control

(d) All of the above

12. The navigation buttons ▶ and ◀ will:
   (a) Move to the next or previous record in a table
   (b) Move to the next or previous page in a report
   (c) Both (a) and (b)
   (d) Neither (a) nor (b)

13. Assume that you are creating a query based on an Employee table, and that the query contains fields for Location and Title. Assume further that there is a single criteria row and that New York and Manager have been entered under the Location and Title fields, respectively. The dynaset will contain:
   (a) All employees in New York
   (b) All managers
   (c) Only the managers in New York
   (d) All employees in New York and all managers

14. You have decided to modify the query from the previous question to include a second criteria row. The Location and Title fields are still in the query, but this time New York and Manager appear in *different* criteria rows. The dynaset will contain:
   (a) All employees in New York
   (b) All managers
   (c) Only the managers in New York
   (d) All employees in New York and all managers

15. Which of the following is true about a query that lists employees by city and alphabetically within city?
   (a) The QBE grid should specify a descending sort on both city and employee name
   (b) The City field should appear to the left of the employee name in the QBE grid
   (c) Both (a) and (b)
   (d) Neither (a) nor (b)

ANSWERS

1. c	**6.** d	**11.** d
2. d	**7.** c	**12.** c
3. b	**8.** d	**13.** c
4. d	**9.** a	**14.** d
5. d	**10.** d	**15.** b

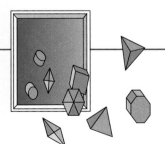

EXPLORING ACCESS

1. Use Figure 3.10 to match each action with its result. A given action may be used more than once or not at all.

b. Select MS PowerPoint 4.0 Slide from the resulting dialog box. Click OK.

c. PowerPoint is now the active application. Pull down the Format menu and select Slide Layout. Choose a blank page as the layout. Click Apply. Click the Insert Clip Art icon on the PowerPoint toolbar.

d. Choose the desired clip art, then double click the control-menu box to return to Access. Respond Yes when asked if you want to Update.

e. You can move the embedded object (the PowerPoint clip art) just as you would any other Windows object. Double click the object to return to PowerPoint if you want to size it, change its position within the frame, or choose a different clip art image.

f. Add your name to the report header and submit the completed report to your instructor.

8. Exploring Mail Merge: A mail merge takes the tedium out of sending form letters, as it creates the same letter many times, changing the name, address, and other information as appropriate from letter to letter. The form letter is created in Word for Windows, but the data file is taken from an Access table or query.

Figure 3.14 shows how Word for Windows is used to create a series of form lettters that will be sent to students on the Dean's List. Proceed as follows:

a. Open the OURDATA.MDB database used in the chapter. Modify the query created in problem 5 to contain the student's address, city, state, and postal code.

b. Click the Report button in the Database window. Click New. Choose the query from part (a) containing the students on the Dean's List as the Table/Query on which to base the report.

c. Click the Report Wizard button. Scroll to MS Word Mail Merge and select it as the Wizard you want. Click OK.

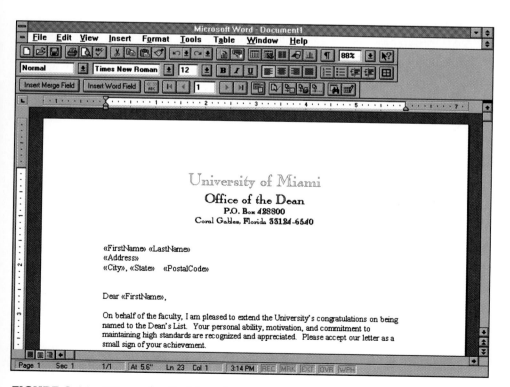

FIGURE 3.14 Screen for Problem 8

d. You should see a dialog box for the Mail Merge Wizard. Click the option button to Create a new document and link the data. Word opens automatically. (Check the box to open Microsoft Word Help if you want to display the Help information.)

e. Create the letter shown in Figure 3.14. To enter a merge field (an entry in angled brackets) click the Insert Merge Field button and choose the appropriate field. Click the Merge to New Document icon (use Tool Tips to identify the icon), then print the letters and submit them to your instructor.

f. Additional information on how to create a mail merge can be obtained by searching on *Mail Merge* in the Word Help menu. You can also refer to *Exploring Word for Windows,* Grauer and Barber, Prentice Hall, 1994, pages 118–128.

 Case Studies

The Fortune 500

Research the Fortune 500 (or a similar list) to obtain the gross revenue and net income for the present and previous year for the twenty largest corporations. Create an Access database to hold a table for this data and an associated form to enter the data. Validate your data carefully, then produce at least three reports based on the data.

The United States of America

What is the total population of the United States? What is its area? Can you name the 13 original states or the last five states admitted to the Union? Do you know the 10 states with the highest population or the five largest states in terms of area? Which states have the highest population density (people per square mile)?

The answers to these and other questions can be obtained from the USA.MDB database that is available on the data disk. The key to the assignment is to use the Top Values property within a query that limits the number of records returned in the dynaset. Use the database to create several reports that you think will be of interest to the class.

The Super Bowl

How many times has the NFC won the Super Bowl? When was the last time the AFC won? What was the largest margin of victory? What was the closest game? What is the most points scored by two teams in one game? How many times have the Miami Dolphins appeared? How many times did they win? Use the data in the SUPERBWL.MDB database to create a trivia sheet on the Super Bowl, then incorporate your analysis into a letter addressed to NBC Sports. Convince them you are a super fan and that you merit two tickets to next year's game.

Version 4.0

EXPLORING MICROSOFT® POWERPOINT®

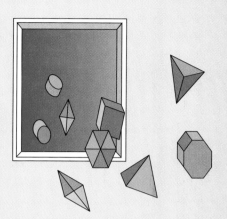

Introduction to PowerPoint: Presentations Made Easy

CHAPTER OBJECTIVES

After reading this chapter you will be able to:

1. Load PowerPoint; open, modify, and view an existing presentation.
2. Describe the elements of the PowerPoint window; discuss how PowerPoint follows the same conventions as other Microsoft applications.
3. Describe the different ways to print a presentation.
4. List the different views in PowerPoint and the purpose of each.
5. Use the Outline view to add and/or modify text in a presentation.
6. Use the AutoLayout feature to add a slide containing clip art.
7. Describe the different types of help available; use Cue Cards to guide yourself through rehearsing and timing a presentation.

OVERVIEW

This chapter introduces you to PowerPoint, one of four applications in the Microsoft Office Professional. (Word for Windows, Microsoft Excel, and Microsoft Access are the other three.) PowerPoint helps you create a professional-looking presentation without relying on anyone else. It enables you to deliver a presentation on the computer (or via 35mm slides or overhead transparencies) and to print that presentation in a variety of formats.

PowerPoint is easy to learn because it is a Windows application and follows all of the conventions associated with the common user interface. This means that if you already know one Windows application, it is that much easier to learn PowerPoint because you can apply what you know. It's even easier if you use Microsoft Word or Excel since there are over 100 commands that are common to all three applications.

The chapter begins with a rapid introduction to PowerPoint in which we describe the presentation window used to create and/or run a presentation. We move almost immediately to a hands-on exercise in which you retrieve an existing presentation in order to appreciate what can be done in PowerPoint. (We show you how to create your own presentation in Chapter 2.)

The chapter also describes the five different views in PowerPoint and the unique capabilities of each. We show you how to add and delete slides in a presentation and how to reorder the slides. We provide a second exercise for you to practice these skills. We also describe the on-line help facility and show you how to rehearse a presentation prior to its delivery.

One final point before we begin is that while PowerPoint can help you create attractive presentations, the content is still up to you. It is important that you deliver the presentation effectively, and the chapter ends with several suggestions to help you in this regard.

INTRODUCTION TO POWERPOINT

A PowerPoint presentation consists of a series of slides such as those in Figure 1.1. Each slide contains different elements including text, clip art, and/or a chart. Nevertheless the presentation has a consistent look from slide to slide with respect to its overall design and color scheme.

You might think that creating a presentation such as Figure 1.1 is difficult, but it isn't. It is remarkably easy and that is the beauty of PowerPoint. In essence PowerPoint allows you to concentrate on the content of a presentation without worrying about its appearance. You supply the text and supporting elements and leave the formatting to PowerPoint.

In addition to helping you create the presentation, PowerPoint provides a variety of ways to deliver it. You can show the presentation on a computer with animated transition effects from one slide to the next. You can include sound in the presentation provided your system has a sound board and speakers. You can also create an automated presentation and distribute it on a disk for display at a convention booth or kiosk. If you cannot show the presentation on a computer, you can convert it to 35-mm slides or overhead transparencies.

PowerPoint enables you to print miniature versions of each slide in the form of audience handouts. This enables the audience to follow the presentation more easily and to take it home after the presentation is over. You can also prepare speaker notes for yourself, consisting of a picture of each slide together with notes for its delivery. All of this is accomplished within the Windows environment and the PowerPoint presentation window as described in the next section.

THE PRESENTATION WINDOW

The PowerPoint window in Figure 1.2 should look somewhat familiar even if you have never worked with PowerPoint. This is because PowerPoint employs the common user interface followed by every Windows application, and thus contains the same basic elements. These include a control-menu box, a title bar, a minimize button, a maximize-or-restore button, a menu bar, and a vertical scroll bar.

The *title bar* displays the name of a window (e.g., Microsoft PowerPoint in Figure 1.2). A presentation window is open within PowerPoint and it, too, has a title bar (INTRO.PPT), which is the name of the current presentation. The *control-menu box* in either window accesses a pull-down menu that contains operations relevant to the window. The *menu bar* provides access to pull-down menus containing commands to create or modify a PowerPoint presentation. The *vertical scroll bar* enables you to display other slides in the presentation.

The PowerPoint window also contains the Standard and Formatting toolbars common to other applications in the Microsoft Office. The *Standard toolbar* appears immediately below the menu bar and contains buttons for the most basic commands in PowerPoint—for example, opening, saving, and printing a

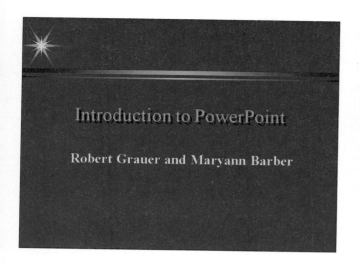

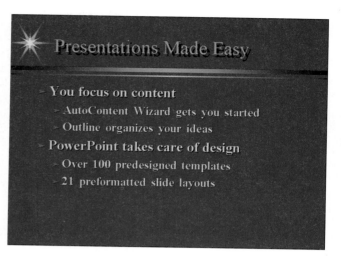

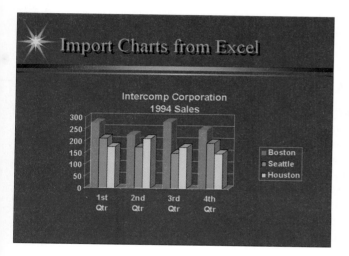

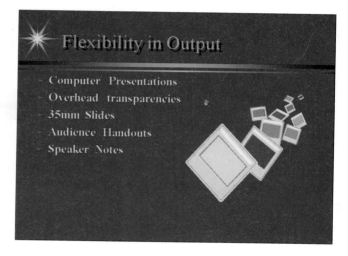

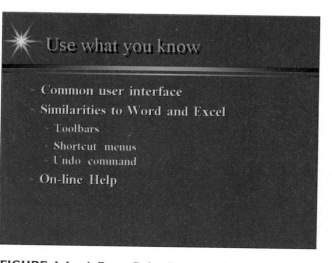

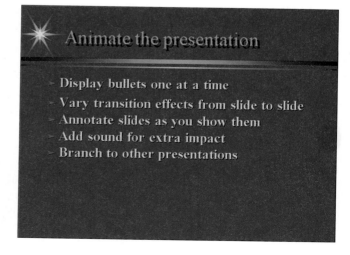

FIGURE 1.1 A PowerPoint Presentation

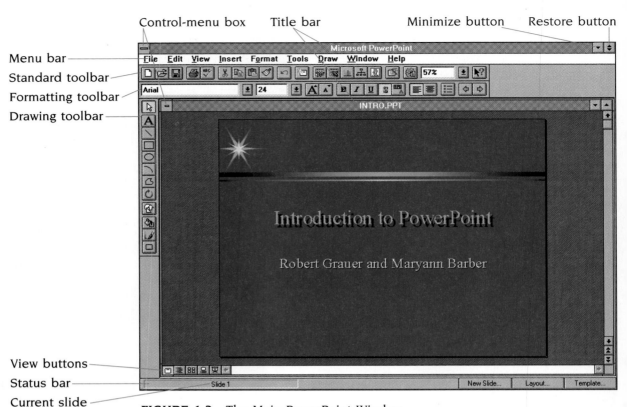

Control-menu box   Title bar   Minimize button   Restore button

Menu bar
Standard toolbar
Formatting toolbar
Drawing toolbar

Introduction to PowerPoint

Robert Grauer and Maryann Barber

View buttons
Status bar
Current slide

FIGURE 1.2   The Main PowerPoint Window

presentation. The ***Formatting toolbar,*** under the Standard toolbar, provides access to formatting operations such as boldface, italics, and underlining.

The ***status bar*** at the bottom of the window displays messages about what you are seeing and doing as you work on a presentation. It will tell you the slide you are working on (Slide 1 in Figure 1.2), or it will provide a message about a command you have selected. The shortcut buttons on the right of the status bar provide immediate access to three additional commands. The ***New Slide button*** is used to add a slide to the presentation. The ***Layout button*** changes the layout of the current slide. The ***Template button*** allows you to choose a different design for your presentation. (Templates are discussed in Chapter 2.)

The ***view buttons*** are located above the status bar and are used to switch among the five different views of a presentation. The Slide view is displayed in Figure 1.2. (The ***Drawing toolbar*** appears by default in the Slide view.) Each view offers a different way of looking at a presentation and has unique capabilities. PowerPoint views are discussed later in the chapter, beginning on page 13.

THE COMMON USER INTERFACE

One of the most significant benefits of the Windows environment is the ***common user interface,*** which provides a sense of familiarity when you begin to learn a new application. In other words, once you know one Windows application, it will be that much easier for you to learn PowerPoint, because all applications work basically the same way. The benefits are magnified if you use other applications in the Microsoft Office; indeed, if you use either Word or Excel, you already know more than 100 commands in PowerPoint.

Toolbars

The Standard and Formatting toolbars are similar to those in Word or Excel and you may recognize several icons from those applications. As with all other Microsoft applications, you can point to any icon on any toolbar, and PowerPoint will display the name of the icon that indicates its function. You can also gain an overall appreciation for the toolbars by considering the icons in groups as shown in Figure 1.3.

Remember, too, that while PowerPoint is designed for a mouse, it provides keyboard equivalents for almost every command. The shortcut buttons on the status bar offer still other ways to accomplish the most frequent operations. You may at first wonder why there are so many different ways to do the same thing, but you will come to recognize the many options as part of PowerPoint's charm. The most appropriate technique depends on personal preference, as well as the specific situation.

If, for example, your hands are already on the keyboard, it is faster to use the keyboard equivalent. Other times, your hand will be on the mouse and that will be the fastest way. It is not necessary to memorize anything, nor should you even try; just be flexible and willing to experiment. The more you do, the easier it will be!

 Starts a new document, opens an existing document, or saves the document in memory

 Prints the document or checks spelling

 Cuts, copies, or pastes the selected text/object; copies format for selected text

 Undoes the previously executed command

 Inserts a new slide

 Inserts a Microsoft Word table, Excel worksheet, graph, organizational chart, or clip art

 Initiates the Pick a Look Wizard

 Exports a PowerPoint outline to Microsoft Word

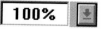 Changes the zoom percentage

 Starts Help

(a) Standard Toolbar

FIGURE 1.3   Toolbars

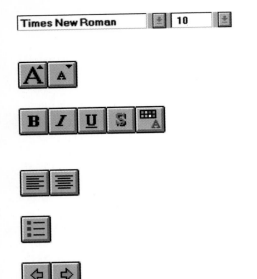

Changes the font and point size for the selected text

Increases or decreases the font size

Toggles boldface, italics, underline, or shadow on and off; changes the color of the selected text

Aligns text left or center

Toggles bullets on and off

Promotes or demotes text

(b) Formatting Toolbar

FIGURE 1.3   Toolbars (continued)

CHANGING TOOLBARS

You can display (hide) toolbars with the right mouse button provided at least one toolbar is visible. Point to any toolbar, then click the right mouse button to display a shortcut menu listing the available toolbars. Click the individual toolbars on or off as appropriate.

LEARNING BY DOING

We believe strongly in learning by doing, and thus there comes a point where you must use the computer if this discussion is to have real meaning. The first exercise introduces you to the *data disk* that is available from your instructor. The data disk contains a variety of presentations referenced in the hands-on exercises throughout the text and can also be used to store the presentations you create. (Alternatively, you can store the presentations on a hard disk if you have access to your own computer.)

The exercise that follows has you retrieve the presentation of Figure 1.1 from the data disk. The exercise has you change the title slide to include your name, then directs you to view the presentation on the computer and to print the corresponding audience handouts.

HANDS-ON EXERCISE 1:

Introduction to PowerPoint

Objective To load PowerPoint, open an existing presentation, and modify the text on an existing slide. To show an existing presentation and print handouts of its slides. Use Figure 1.4 as a guide in doing the exercise.

Step 1: Load Windows

➤ Type **WIN** and press **enter** to load Windows if it is not already loaded. The appearance of your desktop will be different from ours, but it should resemble Figure 1.4a.

➤ You should see an open window containing Program Manager as in Figure 1.4a; if not, you should see an icon titled Program Manager near the bottom of the screen. Double click this icon to open the Program Manager window.

MASTER THE MOUSE

A mouse is essential to the operation of PowerPoint as it is to all other Windows applications, and it is important that you master its operation. The easiest way to practice is to use the mouse tutorial found in the Help menu of Windows itself. Pull down the Help menu, click Windows Tutorial, type M to begin, then follow the on-screen instructions. Exit the tutorial when you are finished to return to Program Manager.

Step 2: Install the data disk

➤ Do this step *only* if you have your own computer and want to copy the files from the data disk to the hard drive. Place the data disk in drive A (or whatever drive is appropriate).

➤ Pull down the **File menu.** Click **Run.** Type **A:INSTALL C** in the text box. Click **OK.** (The drive letters in the command, A and C, are both variable.

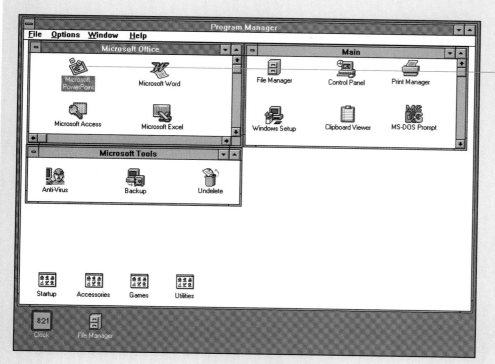

Double click to load PowerPoint

(a) Load Windows (step 1)

FIGURE 1.4   Hands-on Exercise 1

If, for example, the data disk were in drive B and you wanted to copy its files to drive D, you would type the command **B:INSTALL D.**)

➤ Follow the on-screen instructions to install the data disk.

Step 3: Tip of the Day

➤ Double click the icon for the group containing PowerPoint—for example, Microsoft Office, if that group is not already open. Double click the program icon for **Microsoft PowerPoint.**

➤ PowerPoint displays a Tip of the Day every time it is loaded as shown in Figure 1.4b. If you do not see a tip, pull down the **Help menu** and click **Tip of the Day.**
   — To cancel the tips when you start PowerPoint, **clear** the box to **Show Tips at Startup.**
   — To see a tip when you start PowerPoint, **check** the box to **Show Tips at Startup.**

➤ Click **OK** to begin working in PowerPoint.

➤ Click the **maximize button** (if necessary) so that PowerPoint takes the entire screen as shown in Figure 1.4b.

DOUBLE CLICKING FOR BEGINNERS

If you are having trouble double clicking, it is because you are not clicking quickly enough, or more likely, because you are moving the mouse (however slightly) between clicks. Relax, hold the mouse firmly in place, and try again.

Clear the box to suppress the Tip of the Day at startup

(b) Load PowerPoint (step 3)

FIGURE 1.4   Hands-on Exercise 1 (continued)

Step 4: Open an existing presentation

➤ You should see the PowerPoint dialog box in Figure 1.4c. Click the option button to **Open an Existing Presentation.** Click the **OK command button.** (If you do *not* see the PowerPoint dialog box, pull down the **File menu** and click **Open** or click the **Open icon** on the Standard toolbar.)

➤ You should see the Open dialog box in Figure 1.4d. Click the arrow on the Drives drop-down list box to select the appropriate drive—drive A or drive C, depending on whether or not you installed the data disk.

➤ Double click the **root directory** (a:\ or c:\) in the Directories list box to display the subdirectories on the selected drive.

➤ Double click the **PPTDATA** directory to make it the active directory.

➤ Click **INTRO.PPT** to select the presentation and preview the first slide in the dialog box. Click the **OK command button** to open the presentation.

IT'S ALL IN ONE FILE

Everything in a PowerPoint presentation—the slides, handouts, speaker notes, and outline—is stored in a single file (e.g, INTRO.PPT). The file name (INTRO) consists of one to eight characters in accordance with the rules for file names followed by all Windows applications. The PPT extension appears after the file name to indicate a PowerPoint presentation.

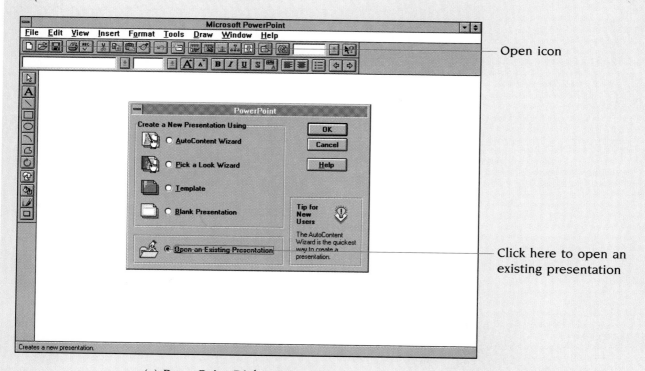

(c) PowerPoint Dialog Box (step 4)

FIGURE 1.4 Hands-on Exercise 1 (continued)

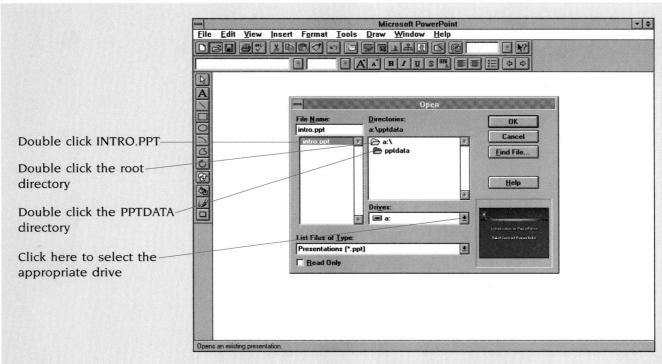

Double click INTRO.PPT

Double click the root directory

Double click the PPTDATA directory

Click here to select the appropriate drive

(d) Open an Existing Presentation (step 4)

FIGURE 1.4 Hands-on Exercise I (continued)

Step 5: Modify a slide
➤ You should be positioned on the first slide as shown in Figure 1.4e.
➤ Press and hold the left mouse button as you drag the mouse over the presenters' names (Robert Grauer and Maryann Barber). Release the mouse.
➤ The names should be highlighted (selected) as shown in Figure 1.4e. The selected text is the text that will be affected by the next command.
➤ Type your name, which automatically replaces the selected text.
➤ Pull down the **File menu** and click **Save** (or click the **Save icon** on the Standard toolbar).

Step 6: Show the presentation
➤ Pull down the **View menu** and click **Slide Show** to produce the Slide Show dialog box.
➤ The **All option button** should be selected under Slides. The **Manual Advance option button** should be selected under Advance. Click the **Show command button** to begin the presentation.
➤ The presentation will begin with the first slide as shown in Figure 1.4f. You should see your name on the slide because of the modification you made in the previous step.
➤ Click the mouse to move to the next slide. Click the mouse again to move to the next (third) slide. (You can press the Esc key at any time to cancel the show and return to the PowerPoint window.)
➤ Continue to view the show until you come to the end of the presentation and are returned to the regular PowerPoint window.

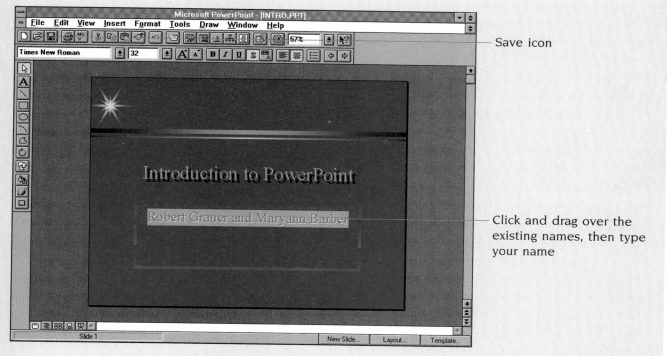

Save icon

Click and drag over the
existing names, then type
your name

(e) Modify a Slide (step 5)

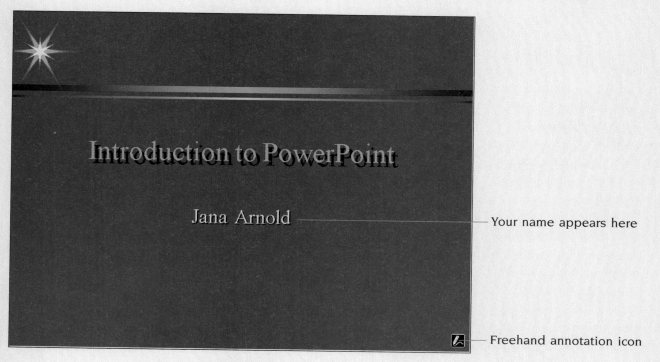

Your name appears here

Freehand annotation icon

(f) View the Presentation (step 6)

FIGURE 1.4 Hands-on Exercise 1 (continued)

THE JOHN MADDEN TOOL

The *Freehand annotation tool* (or the John Madden tool as we like to call it) enables you to add emphasis to a slide as you present the show. (Type the letter A if you do not see the icon.) Click the icon to turn the annotation feature on; click it a second time to turn the feature off. Turn the animation on, then move the mouse pointer (now in the shape of a pencil) over the part of the slide you want to emphasize. Press and hold the mouse to draw on the slide during the show. The marking will disappear when you go to the next slide. You can also press the letter E to erase the marking on the current slide.

Step 7: Print the presentation
➤ Pull down the **File menu.** Click **Print** to produce the Print dialog box in Figure 1.4g.
➤ Click the arrow in the **Print What** drop-down list box. Click **Handouts (6 slides per page)** as shown in Figure 1.4g.
➤ Check that the **All option button** is selected under Slide Range. Click the **OK command button** to print the handouts for the presentation.

Step 8: Exit PowerPoint
➤ There are two ways to exit PowerPoint:
— Pull down the **File menu** and click **Exit.**
— Double click the **control-menu box** at the left of the title bar.
➤ Exit PowerPoint and return to Program Manager.

Double click here to exit PowerPoint

Click here to display options

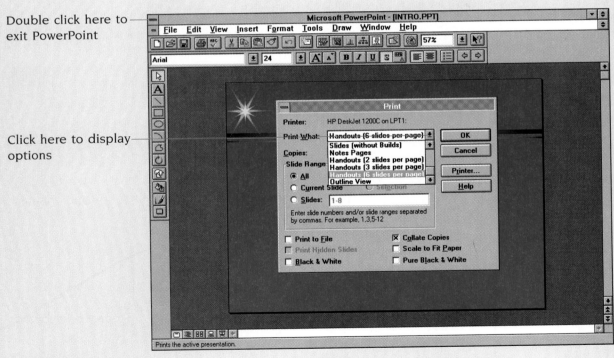

(g) Print the Presentation (step 7)

FIGURE 1.4 Hands-on Exercise 1 (continued)

FIVE DIFFERENT VIEWS

PowerPoint offers five different views in which to create, modify, and show a presentation. Figure 1.5 shows the five views for the introductory presentation from the first exercise. Each view represents a different way of looking at the presentation, and each view has unique capabilities. Some views display only a single slide whereas others show multiple slides, making it easy to organize the presentation. You can switch back and forth between the views by clicking the appropriate view button at the bottom of the presentation window.

The *Slide view* in Figure 1.5a displays one slide at a time and enables all operations for that slide. You can enter, delete, or format text. You can draw or add graphics such as a graph, clip art, or an organization chart. The Drawing Toolbar is displayed by default and is discussed in Chapter 3.

The *Slide Sorter view* in Figure 1.5b displays multiple slides on one screen (each slide is in miniature) and lets you see the overall flow of the presentation. You can change the order of a presentation by clicking and dragging a slide from one position to another. You can delete a slide by clicking the slide and pressing the Del key. You can also set transition (animation) effects from slide to slide to add interest to the presentation. The Slide Sorter view has its own toolbar, which is discussed in Chapter 2 in conjunction with creating transition effects.

The *Outline view* in Figure 1.5c shows the presentation in outline form. You can see all of the text on every slide, but you cannot see the graphic elements that may be present on the individual slides. (A different icon appears next to the slides containing a graphic element.) The Outline view is the fastest way to enter or edit text in that you type directly into the outline. You can drag-and-drop text from one slide to another. You can also rearrange the order of the slides within the presentation. The Outline view has its own toolbar and is discussed more fully in Chapter 2.

The *Notes Pages view* in Figure 1.5d lets you create speaker's notes for some or all of the slides in a presentation. These notes do not appear when you show the presentation, but can be printed for use during the presentation to help you remember what you want to say about each slide.

The *Slide Show view* displays the slides one at a time as an electronic presentation on the computer. The slide show may contain transition effects from one slide to the next as was demonstrated in the first hands-on exercise.

POWERPOINT VIEWS

PowerPoint has five different views of a presentation, each with unique capabilities. Anything you do in one view is automatically reflected in the other views. If, for example, you rearrange the slides in the Slide Sorter view, the new arrangement is reflected in the Outline view. In similar fashion, if you add or format text in the Outline view, the changes are also made in the Slide view.

Adding and Deleting Slides

Slides are added to a presentation by using one of 21 predefined slide formats known as *AutoLayouts.* Click the New Slide button on the status bar to produce the dialog box in Figure 1.6a, then choose the type of slide you want. (The slide will be added to the presentation immediately after the current slide.)

Figure 1.6a depicts the addition of a bulleted slide with clip art. The user chooses the desired layout, then clicks the OK command button to switch to the

Drawing toolbar

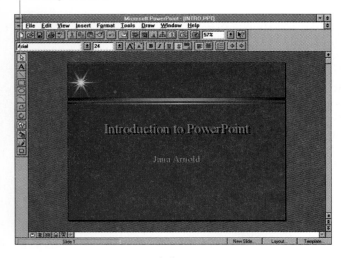

(a) Slide View

Slide Sorter toolbar

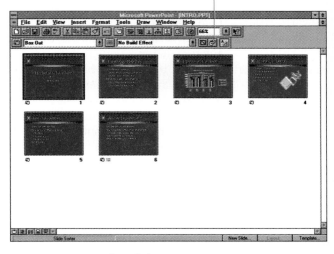

(b) Slide Sorter View

Outline toolbar

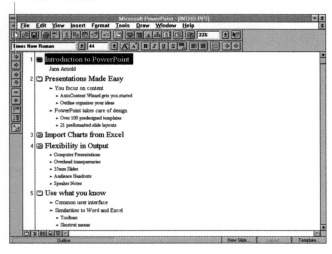

(c) Outline View

Speaker notes associated with current slide can be pri▶

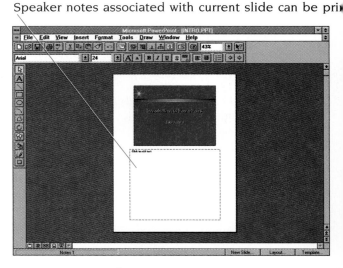

(d) Notes Pages View

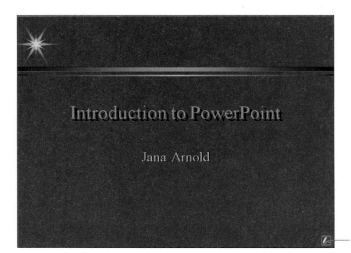

Freehand annotation tool

(e) Slide Show View

FIGURE 1.5   PowerPoint Views

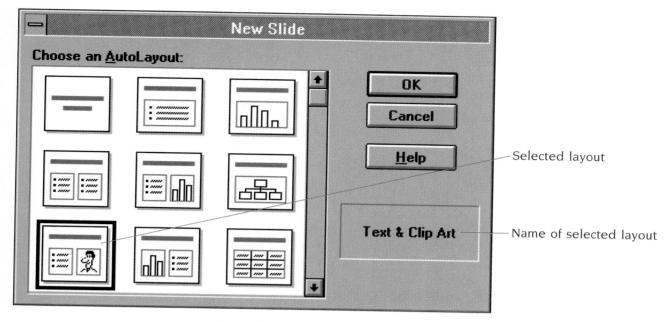

(a) AutoLayout

Selected layout

Name of selected layout

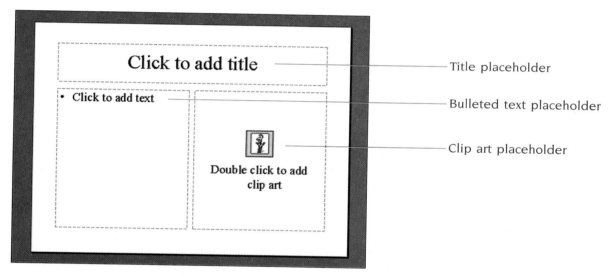

Title placeholder

Bulleted text placeholder

Clip art placeholder

(b) Placeholders

FIGURE 1.6 Adding a Slide

slide view in Figure 1.6b. The AutoLayout contains *placeholders* for the various objects on the slide such as the slide title, bulleted text, and clip art.

Three placeholders are shown in Figure 1.6: one for the title, one for the bulleted text, and one for the clip art. Just follow the directions on the slide by clicking the appropriate place to add the title or text, or double clicking to add the clip art. It's that easy, as you will see in the next exercise.

You can delete a slide from any view except the Slide Show view. To delete a slide from the Slide or Notes Pages views, select the slide by making it the current slide, pull down the Edit menu, and choose the Delete Slide command. To delete a slide from the Slide Sorter or Outline views, select the slide, then press the Del key.

PowerPoint Views

Objective To switch between the different views while modifying a presentation; to use the Clip Art gallery and add clip art to a slide; to add a slide to an existing presentation. Use Figure 1.7 as a guide in the exercise.

Step 1: Add a new slide
➤ Load PowerPoint. Follow the instructions from step 4 in the previous exercise to open the **INTRO.PPT** presentation from the first exercise.
➤ Pull down the **Insert menu** and click **New slide** (or click the **New Slide command button**) on the status bar. You will see the New Slide dialog box in Figure 1.7a.
➤ Click the **down arrow** on the vertical scroll bar to scroll through AutoLayouts within PowerPoint.
➤ Select (click) the **Text and Clip Art layout** as shown in the figure. (The name of the selected Layout appears in the lower-right corner of the dialog box.) Click the **OK command button.**

Step 2: Click here
➤ Click the placeholder where it says **Click to add title** in Figure 1.7b. Type **The Clip Art Gallery** as the title of the slide.
➤ Click the placeholder where it indicates **Click to add text.** Type **Contains more than 1,000 images** as the first bullet. Press **enter** to move to the next bullet.

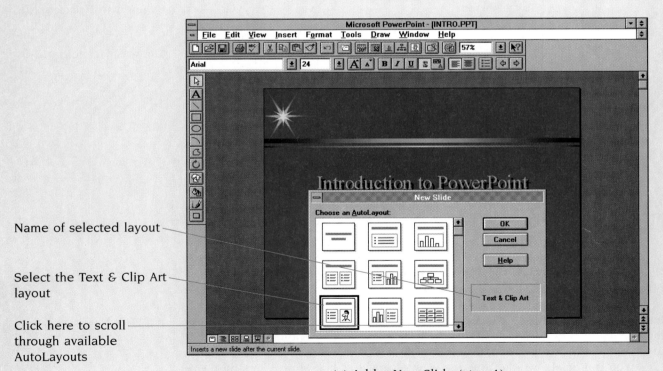

Name of selected layout

Select the Text & Clip Art layout

Click here to scroll through available AutoLayouts

(a) Add a New Slide (step 1)

FIGURE 1.7 Hands-on Exercise 2

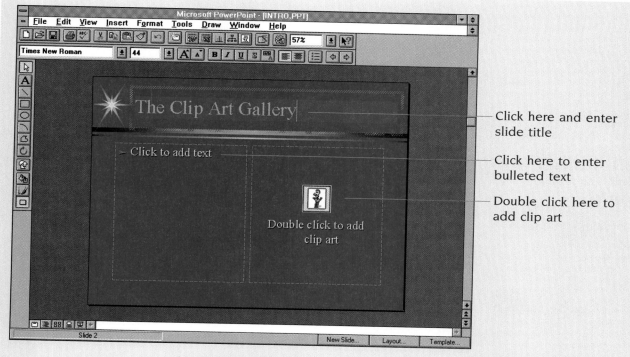

Click here and enter slide title

Click here to enter bulleted text

Double click here to add clip art

(b) Click Here (step 2)

FIGURE 1.7   Hands-on Exercise 2 (continued)

— Press **Tab** to indent the next bullet one additional level. Type **Cartoons.** Press **enter** to move to the next bullet.

— You do *not* have to press the Tab key because PowerPoint automatically aligns each succeeding bullet under the previous bullet. Type **Maps.** Press **enter** to move to the next bullet.

— Type **People.** Press **enter** to move to the next bullet.

➤ Press **Shift+Tab** to move the new bullet to the left. Type **Move and size just like any other Windows object** as the final bullet. Do *not* press the enter key or else you will create another bullet.

BULLETS AND THE TAB (SHIFT+TAB) KEY

Bullets are entered one after another simply by typing the text of a bullet and pressing the enter key. A new bullet appears automatically under the previous bullet. Press the Tab key to indent the new bullet or press Shift+Tab to move the bullet back to the left.

Step 3: Add clip art

➤ Double click the placeholder for the clip art. (Click Yes if you see a box asking if you want to add clip art from the PowerPoint Clip Art Gallery.) You will see the Clip Art Gallery dialog box shown in Figure 1.7c (although you may not see all of the categories listed in the figure).

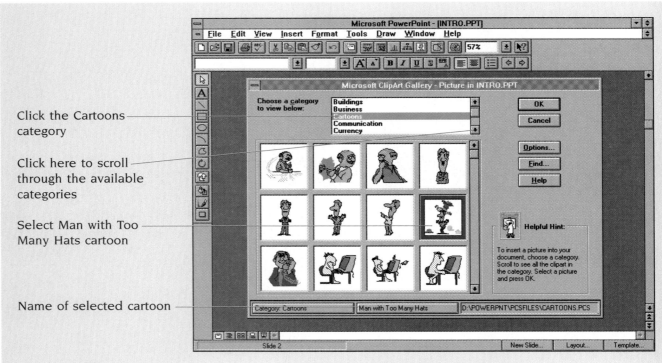

Click the Cartoons category

Click here to scroll through the available categories

Select Man with Too Many Hats cartoon

Name of selected cartoon

(c) The Clip Art Gallery (step 3)

FIGURE 1.7 Hands-on Exercise 2 (continued)

➤ Click the **Cartoons category.** If necessary, click the **down arrow** on the scroll bar to scroll through the available cartoons until you see the image you want.

➤ Click the **Man with Too Many Hats** cartoon as shown in Figure 1.7c. Click the **OK command button** to insert the clip art onto the slide.

Step 4: Select-then-do

➤ You should see the completed slide in Figure 1.7d. Click and drag to select the number 1,000.
   — Click the **Bold icon** on the Formatting toolbar to boldface the selected text.
   — Click the **Italics icon** on the Formatting toolbar to italicize the selected text.

SELECT-THEN-DO

All editing and formatting operations take place within the context of select-then-do; that is, you select a block of text, then you execute the command to operate on that text. Selected text is affected by any subsequent operation; for example, clicking the Boldface or Italics icon changes the selected text to boldface or italics, respectively. In similar fashion, pressing the Del key deletes the selected text. And finally, the fastest way to replace existing text is to select the text, then type a new entry while the text is still selected. Selected text remains highlighted until you click elsewhere on the slide.

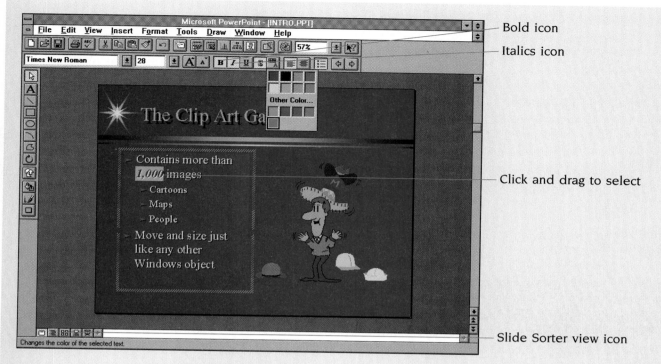

Bold icon

Italics icon

Click and drag to select

Slide Sorter view icon

(d) Select-then-do (step 4)

FIGURE 1.7 Hands-on Exercise 2 (continued)

— Click the **Text color icon** on the Formatting toolbar to display the available text colors. Click **Red.** (You may need to select Other Colors in order to find Red.)

➤ Click outside the text area to deselect the text to see the results.

➤ Save the presentation.

Step 5: The Slide Sorter view

➤ Pull down the **View menu** and click **Slide Sorter** (or click the **Slide Sorter view icon**) on the status bar. This changes to the Slide Sorter view in Figure 1.7e.

➤ Slide 2 (the slide you just created) is already selected as indicated by the heavy border around the slide. Click and drag slide 2 and move it to the end of the presentation (after slide 7). The existing slides are automatically renumbered.

➤ Pull down the **Edit menu** and click **Undo** (or click the Undo icon on the Standard toolbar). The slide containing the clip art goes back to its original position.

➤ Click and drag slide 2 and move it to the end of the presentation.

➤ Save the presentation.

Step 6: The Outline view

➤ Click the **Outline view icon** on the status bar to change to the Outline view in Figure 1.7f. Press **Ctrl+End** to move to the end of the outline where you will enter the next slide:

— Type **Five Different Views** (the title of the slide). Press **enter.**

Undo icon

Slide 2 is selected

Drag slide 2 to end
of presentation

Outline view icon

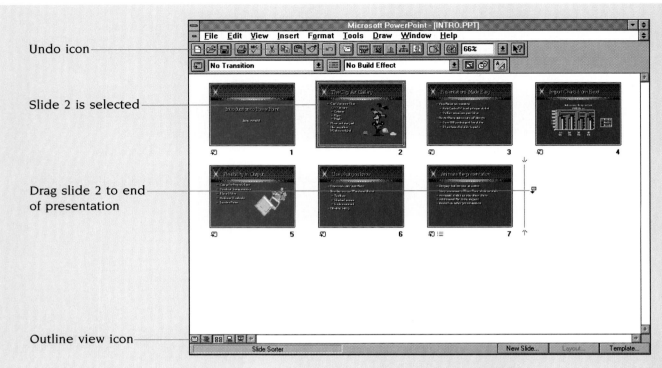

(e) Slide Sorter View (step 5)

Save icon

Slide elevator

The Clip Art Gallery is
slide 7

Enter text for new slide

Slide View icon

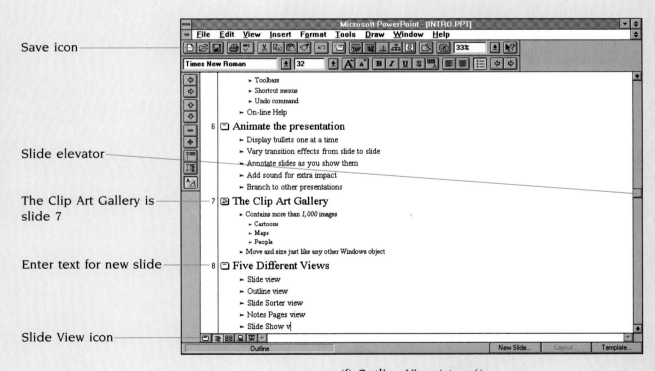

(f) Outline View (step 6)

FIGURE 1.7 Hands-on Exercise 2 (continued)

THE UNDO COMMAND

The **Undo command** reverses the effect of the most recent command. It is executed from within the Edit menu or by clicking the Undo button on the Standard toolbar. You can use the command whenever something happens that is different from what you intended, but you must use the command before any other commands are executed. Some commands, however, cannot be undone; for example, you cannot undo a Save command.

— Press the **Tab key** to indent one level. Type **Slide view** as shown in Figure 1.7f. Press **enter** to move to the next bullet.
— Type **Outline view.** Press **enter.**
— Type **Slide Sorter view.** Press **enter.**
— Type **Notes Pages view.** Press **enter.**
— Type **Slide Show view.**
➤ The slide is complete. Click the **Save icon** on the Standard toolbar.

MOVING WITHIN THE PRESENTATION

Ctrl+Home and Ctrl+End are universal Windows shortcuts that move to the beginning or end of a document, respectively. Not only do the techniques work in PowerPoint, but they work in all views of PowerPoint. Thus you can press Ctrl+Home to move to the first slide in the Slide, Slide Sorter, or Outline view, and press Ctrl+End to move to the last slide.

Step 7: The Slide view
➤ Click the **Slide view icon** to change to the Slide view as shown in Figure 1.7g. You should see the Slide view of the slide created in the Outline view of the previous step.
➤ Click the **Previous slide button** on the vertical scroll bar (or press the **PgUp key**) to move to the previous slide (slide 7) in the presentation.
➤ Click the **Next slide button** on the vertical scroll bar (or press the **PgDn key**) to move to the next slide (slide 8).

THE SLIDE ELEVATOR

PowerPoint uses the **scroll box** (common to all Windows applications) in the vertical scroll bar as an **elevator** to move up and down within the presentation. Click and drag the elevator to go to a specific slide; as you drag, you will see an indicator showing the slide you are about to display. Release the mouse when you see the number of the slide you want.

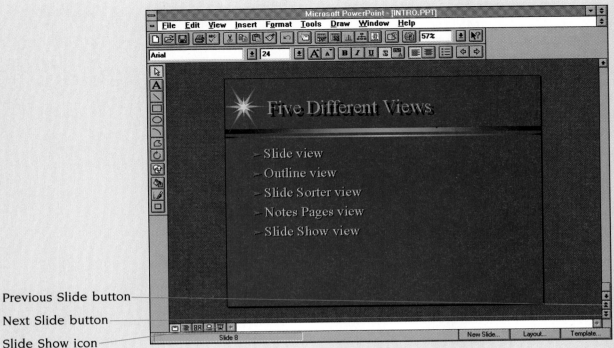

Previous Slide button

Next Slide button

Slide Show icon

(g) Slide View (step 7)

FIGURE 1.7 Hands-on Exercise 2 (continued)

Step 8: The Slide Show view

➤ Press **Ctrl+Home** to move to the beginning of the presentation. Click the **Slide Show icon** to view the presentation from beginning to end:

— Click the **left mouse button** or press the **PgDn key** to move forward in the presentation.

— Click the **right mouse button** or press the **PgUp key** to move backward in the presentation.

— Press the **Esc key** at any time to quit the presentation and return to PowerPoint.

TRANSITIONS AND BUILDS

Transitions add interest and variety to a presentation by changing the way in which you progress from one slide to the next. Slides may move onto the screen from the left or right, be uncovered by horizontal or vertical blinds, fade, dissolve, etc. Transitions may also be applied to individual bullets to display the bullets one at a time. Transitions and builds are further described in Chapter 2.

Step 9: The Notes Pages view

➤ Press **Ctrl+Home** to move to the beginning of the presentation. Click the **Notes Pages View icon** to change to this view as shown in Figure 1.7h. (If necessary, click the **Zoom control icon** to change the magnification to see more of the slide.)

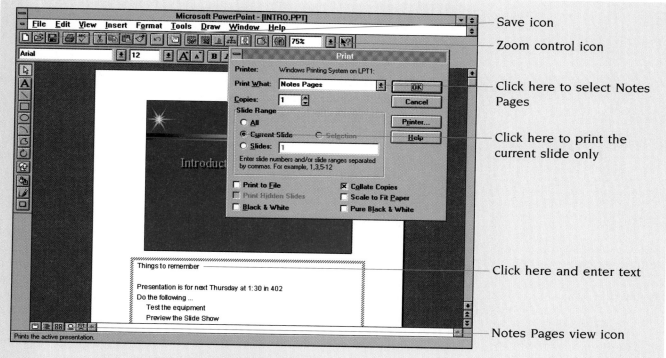

Save icon

Zoom control icon

Click here to select Notes Pages

Click here to print the current slide only

Click here and enter text

Notes Pages view icon

(h) Notes Pages View (step 9)

FIGURE 1.7   Hands-on Exercise 2 (continued)

➤ Click in the notes area, then enter the text in Figure 1.7h. Click the **Save icon** to save the presentation a final time.

➤ Pull down the **File menu.** Click **Print** to produce the Print dialog box.

➤ Click the **down arrow** in the **Print What** drop-down list box. Click **Notes Pages.** Click the **Current Slide option button** to print just this slide. Click the **OK command button.**

➤ Exit PowerPoint and return to Program Manager.

ON-LINE HELP

PowerPoint includes extensive *on-line help,* which is accessed by pulling down the *Help menu.* The commands in the Help menu are similar to those in Word or Excel and are described briefly below:

Contents	Displays a list of help topics
Search for Help on . . .	Searches for help on a specific subject
Index	Displays an alphabetical index of all Help topics
Quick Preview	Provides a demonstration of PowerPoint
Tip of the Day . . .	Accesses the Tip of the Day dialog box
Cue Cards	Provides step-by-step help while you work on your presentation
Technical Support	Describes the different types of technical support available

About Microsoft PowerPoint . . .	Displays the specific release of PowerPoint and contains information about the system you are using

The **Search command** is especially important and is illustrated in Figure 1.8. Execution of the command produces the Search dialog box in Figure 1.8a, which allows you to look for information on a specific topic. Type a key word in the text box (you don't have to complete the word), and the corresponding term is selected in the open list box. Double click the highlighted item (e.g., Help in Figure 1.8a) to produce the list of available topics on that subject in the lower list box. Double click the topic you want (e.g., Online Help) or select the topic and click the Go To command button to see the actual help text, such as the screen shown in Figure 1.8b.

The Help window contains all of the elements found in any other application window: a title bar, minimize and maximize-or-restore buttons, a control-menu box, and a vertical and/or horizontal scroll bar. There is also a menu bar. You can print the contents of the Help window by pulling down the File menu and executing the Print command. You can copy the contents of the Help window to the Windows clipboard by pulling down the Edit menu and clicking the Copy command, then paste the contents into a word processing document to create your own reference manual.

The buttons near the top of the Help window enable you to move around more easily within the on-line Help facility. The Contents button displays the list of available topics. The Back button returns directly to the previous help topic. The History button displays a list of all topics selected within the current session and makes it easy to return to any of the previous topics. The Index button produces a window containing an alphabetical index of the topics in the Help facility.

THE HELP BUTTON

Click the **Help button** on the Standard toolbar (the mouse pointer changes to include a large question mark), then click any other toolbar icon to display a help screen with information about that button. Double click the control-menu box to close the help screen and return to the presentation.

PRESENTATION HINTS

PowerPoint can help you create an attractive presentation, but you are the most important part of any presentation. The audience must buy you before it will be receptive to your message. A poor delivery will kill even the best presentation. Good speakers have adequate volume, vary their delivery, articulate clearly, and pause to emphasize key points while maintaining eye contact with the audience. Poor speakers speak too softly, slur their speech, have a monotonous pitch, and read from their notes.

The exercise that begins on page 26 uses **Cue Cards** to rehearse a PowerPoint presentation. Interspersed in the exercise are additional tips for delivering a successful presentation.

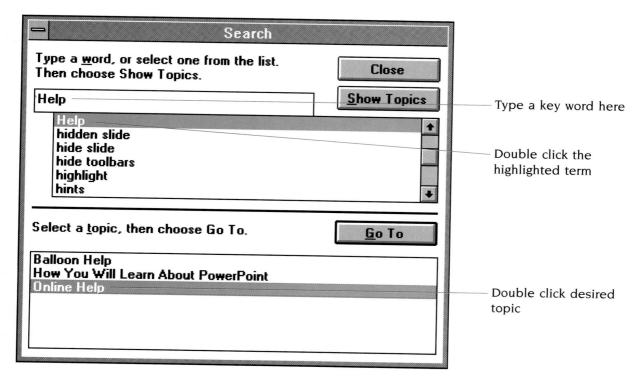

(a) Search Command

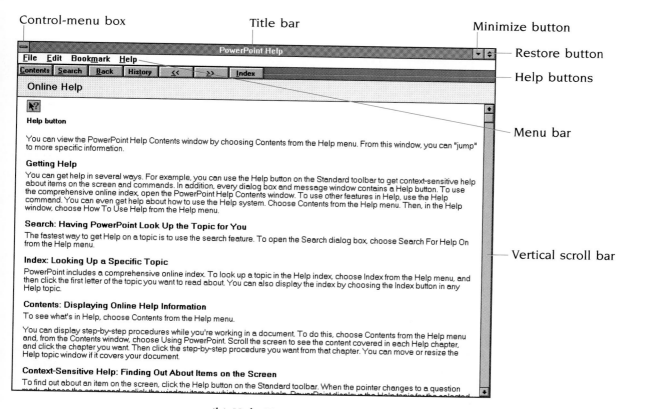

(b) Help Text

FIGURE 1.8 On-line Help

Rehearsing the Presentation

Objective Use Cue Cards to learn how to time and rehearse a presentation. Use Figure 1.9 as a guide in the exercise.

Step 1: Open the existing presentation
➤ Load PowerPoint. Open the **INTRO.PPT** presentation from the previous exercise. Select the Slide view.
➤ Pull down the **Help menu.** Click **Cue Cards** to produce the Cue Cards window in Figure 1.9a.
➤ Click **Rehearse your presentation** to learn how PowerPoint can help you practice your presentation.

ARRIVE EARLY

You will need plenty of time to gather your thoughts and set up the presentation. Load PowerPoint and open the presentation prior to beginning. Be sure your notes are with you or on the podium. Check that water is available for you during the presentation. Try to relax. Greet the audience as they come in.

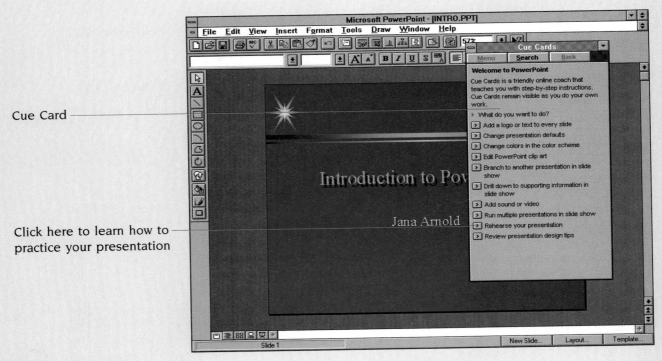

Cue Card

Click here to learn how to practice your presentation

(a) Cue Cards (step 1)

FIGURE 1.9 Hands-on Exercise 3

Step 2: Cue Cards

➤ You should see the first Cue Card on rehearsing a presentation as shown in Figure 1.9b. Just follow the directions on the card.

➤ Pull down the **View menu** and choose **Slide Show.** The Slide Show dialog box appears as in Figure 1.9b. (If necessary, click and drag the title bar of the dialog box to move the box so that it is fully visible.)

➤ Click the **Rehearse New Timings** option. Click the **Show button.**

MAINTAIN EYE CONTACT

Looking at the audience helps you to open communication and gain credibility. Don't read from a prepared text. Speak from memory, using the slides in the presentation as a reminder of what to say. If you use notes, be sure the notes are easily read so that you can look up at the audience during the presentation.

Step 3: Rehearse the presentation

➤ The first slide appears in the Slide Show view as shown in Figure 1.9c. A timer is displayed in the lower-left corner of the screen, and the Cue Card remains on the screen for easy reference. (You can move the Cue Card by clicking and dragging its title bar.)

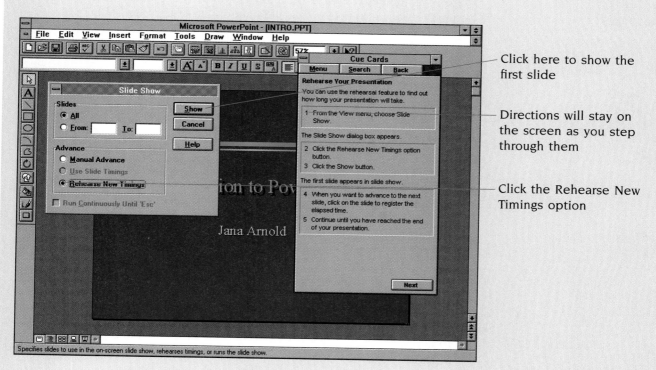

(b) Cue Cards Continued (steps 1 and 2)

FIGURE 1.9   Hands-on Exercise 3 (continued)

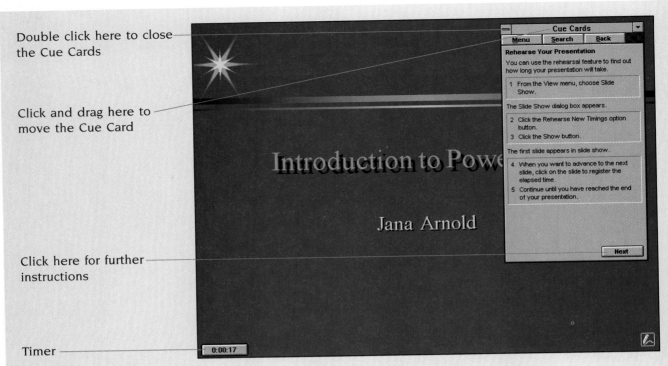

Double click here to close
the Cue Cards

Click and drag here to
move the Cue Card

Click here for further
instructions

Timer

(c) Rehearse the Presentation (step 3)

FIGURE 1.9   Hands-on Exercise 3 (continued)

➤ Speak as though you were presenting the slide, then click the mouse to register the elapsed time for that slide and move to the next slide.

➤ The second slide in your presentation should appear. Once again, speak as though you were presenting the slide, then click the mouse to register the elapsed time and move to the next slide.

➤ Continue rehearsing the show until you reach the end of the presentation.

PRACTICE MAKES PERFECT

You have worked hard to gain the opportunity to present your ideas. Be prepared! You cannot bluff your way through a presentation. Practice aloud several times, preferably under the same conditions as the actual presentation. Everyone is nervous, but the more you practice, the more confident you will be.

Step 4: Slide Sorter view

➤ Click the **Next command button** on the Cue Card for further instructions. The last Cue Card states that you will see a dialog box at the end of the rehearsal, containing the total time of your presentation.

➤ Click **Yes** to record the slide timings in the Slide Sorter view. PowerPoint pauses as it records the timings and switches to the Slide Sorter view.

➤ Double click the Cue Card's **control-menu box** to close the Cue Cards and view your presentation as shown in Figure 1.9d. The elapsed time for each slide appears directly under the slide.

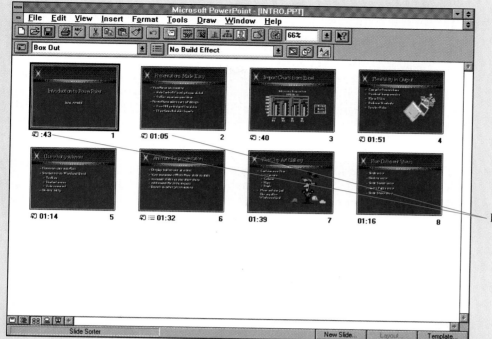

Elapsed time for the slide

(d) Slide Sorter View (step 4)

FIGURE 1.9 Hands-on Exercise 3 (continued)

QUESTIONS AND ANSWERS (Q & A)

Indicate at the beginning of your talk whether you will take questions during the presentation or collectively at the end. Announce the length of time that will be allocated to questions. Rephrase all questions so the audience can hear. Rephrase hostile questions in a neutral way and try to disarm the challenger by paying a compliment. If you don't know the answer, say so.

Step 5: Exit PowerPoint

➤ Double click the control-menu box to close the presentation and exit PowerPoint. Click **Yes** when asked whether to save the changes in your presentation.

QUICK PREVIEW

Quick Preview provides an overview of the main features in PowerPoint. It is an ideal place to review what you have learned and to preview what is coming next. Pull down the Help menu, click Quick Preview, then use the command buttons at the bottom of the screen to move forward or backward in the demonstration. You can watch the entire demonstration or press the Esc key at any time to return to PowerPoint.

SUMMARY

A PowerPoint presentation consists of a series of slides with a consistent design and color scheme. A PowerPoint presentation may be delivered on a computer, via overhead transparencies or 35mm slides, and/or printed in a variety of formats.

The PowerPoint window contains the basic elements of any Windows application. The benefits of the common user interface are magnified further if you are familiar with other applications in the Microsoft Office such as Word or Excel. PowerPoint is designed for a mouse, but it provides keyboard equivalents for almost every command. Toolbars provide still another way to execute the most frequent operations.

PowerPoint has five different views, each with unique capabilities. The Slide view displays one slide at a time and enables all operations on that slide. The Slide Sorter view displays multiple slides on one screen (each slide is in miniature) and lets you see the overall flow of the presentation. The Outline view shows the presentation text in outline form and is the fastest way to enter or edit text. The Notes Pages view enables you to create speaker's notes for use in giving the presentation. The Slide Show view displays the slides one at a time with transition effects for added interest.

Slides are added to a presentation by using one of 21 predefined slide formats known as AutoLayouts. Each AutoLayout contains placeholders for the different objects on the slide. A slide may be deleted from a presentation in any view except the Slide Show view.

PowerPoint provides extensive on-line help, which is accessed by pressing the F1 function key or by pulling down the Help menu. The Search command enables you to look for information on a specific topic. Cue Cards provide step-by-step help while you work in a presentation.

Although PowerPoint helps to create attractive presentations, you are still the most important element in delivering the presentation. The chapter ended with several hints on how to rehearse and present presentations effectively.

Key Words and Concepts

AutoLayout	Layout button	Slide Sorter view
Clip art	Menu bar	Slide view
Common user interface	New Slide button	Standard toolbar
Control-menu box	Notes Pages view	Status bar
Cue Cards	On-line Help	Template button
Drawing toolbar	Outline view	Tip of the Day
Elevator	Quick Preview	Title bar
Formatting toolbar	Placeholders	Transition effects
Freehand annotation tool	Search command	Undo command
Help button	Scroll box	Vertical scroll bar
Help menu	Slide Show view	View button

Multiple Choice

1. How do you save changes to a PowerPoint presentation?
   (a) Pull down the File menu and click the Save command
   (b) Click the Save icon on the Standard toolbar

(c) Either (a) and (b)

(d) Neither (a) nor (b)

2. Which toolbars are displayed by default in all views?

(a) The Standard toolbar

(b) The Formatting toolbar

(c) Both (a) and (b)

(d) Neither (a) nor (b)

3. Which view displays multiple slides on a single screen?

(a) Outline view

(b) Slide Sorter view

(c) Both (a) and (b)

(d) Neither (a) nor (b)

4. Which view displays multiple slides and also shows the graphical elements in each slide?

(a) Outline view

(b) Slide Sorter view

(c) Both (a) and (b)

(d) Neither (a) nor (b)

5. Which view lets you delete a slide?

(a) Outline view

(b) Slide Sorter view

(c) Both (a) and (b)

(d) Neither (a) nor (b)

6. Which of the following can be printed in support of a presentation?

(a) Audience handouts

(b) Speaker's notes

(c) An outline

(d) All of the above

7. Which menu contains the Undo command?

(a) File menu

(b) Edit menu

(c) Tools menu

(d) Format menu

8. Ctrl+Home and Ctrl+End are keyboard shortcuts that move to the beginning or end of the presentation in the:

(a) Outline view

(b) Slide Sorter view

(c) Slide view

(d) All of the above

9. Which of the following will exit PowerPoint and return to Windows?

(a) Double clicking the control-menu box in the title bar for PowerPoint

(b) Pulling down the File menu and clicking Exit

(c) Both (a) and (b)

(d) Neither (a) nor (b)

10. The predefined slide formats in PowerPoint are known as:

(a) View

(b) AutoLayouts

(c) Audience handouts

(d) Speaker notes

ANSWERS

1. c	**6.** d
2. c	**7.** b
3. c	**8.** d
4. b	**9.** c
5. c	**10.** b

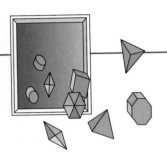

EXPLORING POWERPOINT

1. Use Figure 1.10 to match each action with its result. A given action may be used more than once or not at all.

Action	Result
a. Double click at 1	___ Open an existing presentation
b. Click at 2	___ Save the current presentation
c. Click at 3	___ Change to the Outline view
d. Click at 4	___ Change to the Slide Sorter view
e. Click at 5	___ Insert a new slide
f. Click at 6	___ Move to slide 2
g. Click at 7	___ Print the current presentation
h. Click at 8	___ Run (show) the current presentation
i. Click at 9	___ Exit PowerPoint
j. Click at 10	___ Access on-line help

2. PowerPoint uses the same commands and follows the same conventions as other applications in the Microsoft Office. This means that you can apply what you already know about basic operations in Word or Excel to Power-Point. Answer the questions below, realizing that in every instance the answer is the same for PowerPoint, Word, and Excel.

a. Which icon on which toolbar saves a PowerPoint presentation? a Word document? an Excel spreadsheet?

b. How do you print a PowerPoint presentation? a Word document? an Excel spreadsheet?

c. Which toolbars are displayed by default? How do you display (hide) additional toolbars?

d. How do you boldface or italicize existing text?

e. Which keystroke combination moves immediately to the beginning (end) of a PowerPoint presentation? a Word document? an Excel spreadsheet?

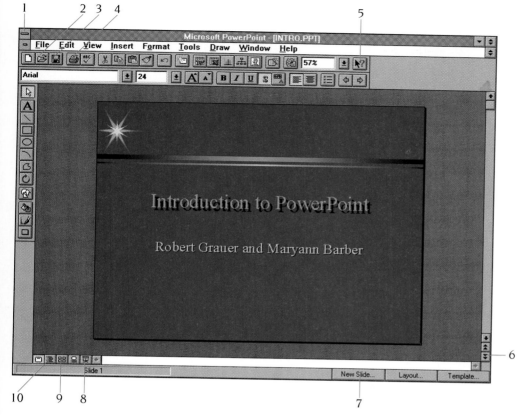

Numbers labeling the figure: 1, 2, 3, 4, 5, 6, 7, 8, 9, 10

Screen text: Microsoft PowerPoint - [INTRO.PPT]

File Edit View Insert Format Tools Draw Window Help

Arial   24

Introduction to PowerPoint

Robert Grauer and Maryann Barber

Slide 1   New Slide...   Layout...   Template...

FIGURE 1.10 Screen for Problem 1

   f. How do you access on-line help?

   g. What happens if you point to a button on a toolbar? What happens if you click the Help button, then point to a different toolbar icon?

3. Answer the following with respect to the presentation shown in Figure 1.11:

   a. What is the name of the presentation as it exists on disk?

   b. Are the Standard and Formatting toolbars both visible? How would you display the missing toolbar?

   c. What would be the effect of typing *Quotations,* given the selected text shown on the screen?

   d. How would you save the presentation after making the change in part c?

   e. In which view is the slide displayed? How would you change to the Outline view? to the Slide Sorter view?

   f. Which slide is selected? How would you move to the first slide in the presentation? to the last slide?

   g. How would you add a new slide at the end of the presentation?

4. Using on-line help: Figure 1.12 displays the Help window that describes how to create a build slide.

   a. Open the INTRO.PPT presentation as it exists at the end of the chapter.

   b. Pull down the Help menu. Click the Search for Help command to produce the Search dialog box.

   c. Type Build in the text box, double click Build Slide when it appears in the open list box, then double click Creating Build Slides for a slide show. You should see the Help window in Figure 1.12.

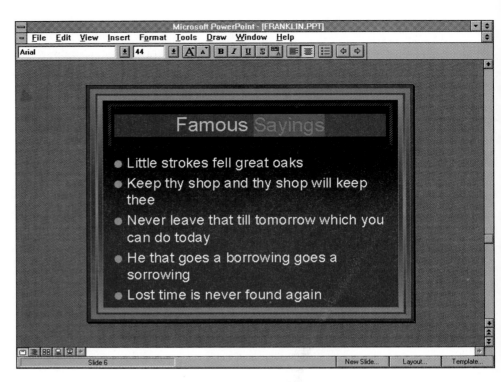

FIGURE 1.11   Screen for Problem 3

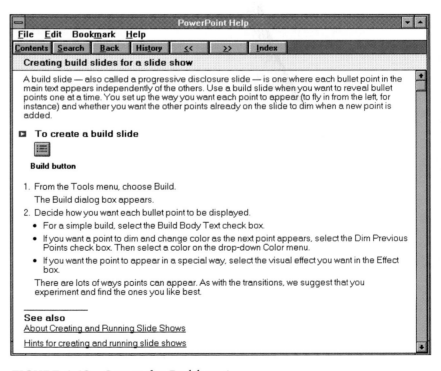

FIGURE 1.12   Screen for Problem 4

d. Pull down the File menu and click Print topic to obtain written documentation.

e. Double click the control-menu box to close the Help window and return to the INTRO.PPT presentation.

f. Change to the Slide view. Press Ctrl+End to move to the last slide in the presentation, which lists the five different views.

g. Follow the instructions in the Help window to create a build slide. Pull down the Tools menu and choose Build to display the Build dialog box.

h. Click the Build Body Text check box, then choose any other effects you want.

i. Click the icon on the status bar to change to the Slide Show view, then click the mouse to display each bullet in turn.

5. Figure 1.13 displays the Outline view of a presentation that explains Object Linking and Embedding. (See Grauer and Barber, *Exploring Microsoft Word for Windows,* pages 215–228, for additional information.)

a. What is the name of the presentation as it exists on disk?

b. Which slide(s) contain clip art or other objects that are not visible in the outline view?

c. Which slide is currently selected?

d. What would happen if you were to press the Del key?

e. How could you reverse the action in part (d)?

f. How do you move to the last slide in the presentation?

g. How do you change to the Slide Sorter view?

h. Retrieve the presentation from the data disk and add your name to the title slide.

i. Move slide 4 (Embedding) after slide 5 (Linking).

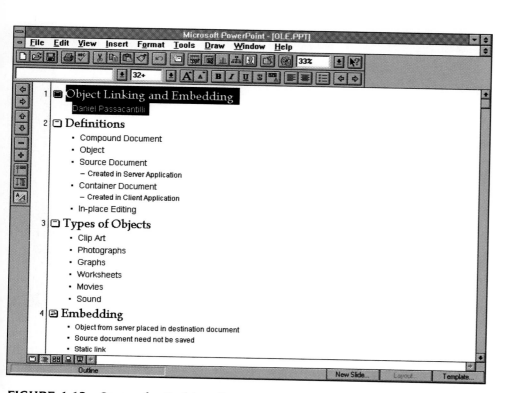

FIGURE 1.13 Screen for Problem 5

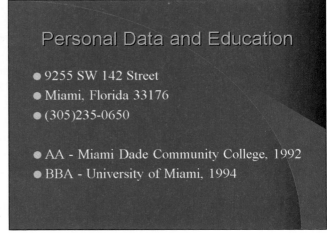

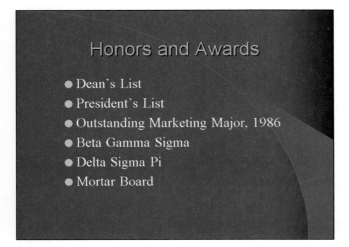

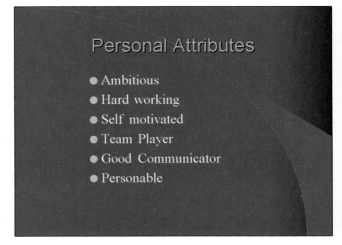

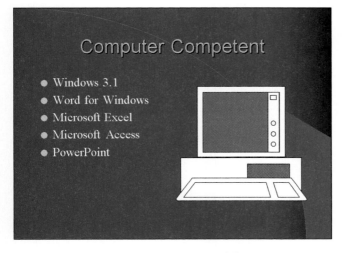

FIGURE 1.14   Presentation for Problem 6

j. Press Ctrl+End to move to the last slide. Edit the slide so that all bullets begin with an uppercase letter.

k. Print the Audience Handouts (six per page) and submit them to your instructor.

6. Figure 1.14 displays Audience Handouts that were printed from the RESUME.PPT presentation on the data disk. (The presentation was created by one of our students and used in a successful search to find a job.) Open the presentation and modify it as necessary so that it reflects your personal data. Print the revised Audience Handouts (six per page) and submit them to your instructor.

Creating a Presentation: Wizards, Templates, and Masters

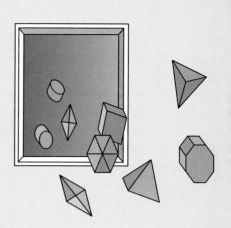

CHAPTER OBJECTIVES

After reading this chapter you will be able to:

1. Use the Outline view to create and edit a presentation; display and hide text within the Outline view.
2. Use the AutoContent Wizard as the basis for developing an initial outline.
3. Check the spelling in a presentation.
4. Use the Pick a Look Wizard to apply a template; change the existing template and/or modify its color scheme.
5. Add transition effects to the slides in a presentation; apply build effects to the bullets in a specific slide.
6. Explain the role of masters in formatting a presentation; modify the Slide Master to include a company name.

OVERVIEW

There are in essence two independent steps to creating a PowerPoint presentation. You must develop the content and you must format the presentation. PowerPoint lets you do the steps in either order, but we suggest you start with the content. Both steps are iterative in nature, and you are likely to go back and forth many times before you are finished.

We begin the chapter by showing you how to enter the content of a presentation in the Outline view. The Outline view is ideal for this purpose since it enables you to view and edit the text in several slides at the same time. We show you how to move and copy text within a slide and how to rearrange the order of the slides within the presentation. We also describe the AutoContent Wizard as a means of creating an initial outline.

The chapter also shows you how to format a presentation by using one of more than 100 professionally designed templates that are supplied with Power-Point. The templates control every aspect of a presentation from the specifications for the text to the color scheme of the slides. You can pick a template yourself, or you can use the Pick a Look Wizard to choose a template for you.

The second half of the chapter shows you how to modify a presentation after it has been created. It describes how to change the template and/or how to vary a color scheme. It also shows you how to add transition effects to individual slides to enhance a presentation as it is given on a computer. And finally, it shows you how to modify the Slide Master to include a corporate logo or other text on every slide.

The chapter contains three hands-on exercises that are essential to the learn-by-doing approach we follow throughout the text.

CRYSTALLIZE YOUR MESSAGE

Every presentation exists to deliver a message, whether it's to sell a product, present an idea, or provide instruction. Decide on the message you want to deliver, then write the text for the presentation. Edit the text to be sure it is consistent with your objective. Then, and only then, should you think about formatting, but always keep the message foremost in your mind.

CREATING A PRESENTATION

The text of a presentation can be developed from the Slide view or the Outline view or a combination of the two. You can begin in the Outline view, switch to the Slide view to see how a particular slide will look, return to the Outline view to enter the text for additional slides, and so on. We prefer the *Outline view* because it displays the text for many slides at once. It also enables you to rearrange the order of slides in a presentation, and to move and copy text from one slide to another.

The Outline View

Figure 2.1 displays the outline of the presentation we will develop in this chapter. The outline shows the title of each slide followed by the text on that slide. (Graphic elements such as clip art and charts are not visible in the Outline view.) Each slide is numbered, and the numbers adjust automatically for the insertion or deletion of slides as you edit the presentation.

A *slide icon* appears between the number and title of each slide. The icon is subtly different depending on the slide layout. In Figure 2.1, for example, the same icon appears next to slides 1 through 5 and indicates that the slides contain only text. A different icon appears next to slide 6 and indicates a graphic element such as clip art.

Each slide begins with a title, followed by bullets, which are indented from one to five levels corresponding to the importance of the item. The main points appear on level one. Subsidiary items are indented on lower levels. Any text can be promoted to a higher level or demoted to a lower level, either before or after it is entered.

Consider, for example, slide 3 in Figure 2.1a. The title of the slide, *Create the Presentation,* appears immediately after the slide number and icon. The first bullet, *Develop the content,* is indented one level under the title, and it in turn has two subsidiary bullets. The next main bullet, *Format the presentation,* is moved back to level one, and it too, has two subsidiary bullets.

Figure 2.1b displays a collapsed view of the outline, which lists only the title of each slide. The advantage to this view is that you see more slides on the screen

1 A Guide to Successful Presentations
   Robert Grauer and Maryann Barber
2 Define the Audience
   • Who is in the audience
      – Managers
      – Coworkers
      – Clients
   • What are their expectations
   • How large is the audience
3 Create the Presentation
   • Develop the content
      – Use the AutoContent Wizard
      – Use the Blank Presentation option
   • Format the presentation
      – Use the Pick a Look Wizard
      – Select a template
4 Develop the Content
   • Use the Outline View
      – Demote items (Tab)
      – Promote items (Shift+Tab)
   • Review the flow of ideas
      – Rearrange the order
      – Cut, Copy, and Paste text
5 Format the Presentation
   • Change the AutoLayout
   • Format the text
   • Modify the color scheme
   • Apply background shading
   • Modify the Slide Master
6 View the Presentation
   • Add transition effects
   • Create builds
   • Rehearse timings

(a) The Expanded Outline

1 A Guide to Successful Presentations
2 Define the Audience
3 Create the Presentation
4 Develop the Content
5 Format the Presentation
6 View the Presentation

(b) The Collapsed Outline

FIGURE 2.1   The Outline View

at the same time, making it easier to move slides within the presentation. Text is expanded or collapsed through the appropriate tool on the Outline toolbar shown in Figure 2.2.

The *Outline toolbar* appears automatically when you switch to the Outline view. The tools are grouped in pairs according to their function, but there is no need to memorize this information. As with the Standard and Formatting toolbars described in Chapter 1, a *ToolTip* will appear when you point to an icon to describe its function.

The outline is (to us) the ideal way to create and edit the presentation. The *insertion point* marks the place where new text is entered and is established by clicking anywhere in the outline. (The insertion point is set automatically to the title of the first slide in a new presentation.) To enter text into an outline, click in the outline to establish the insertion point, then start typing. Press enter after typing the title of a slide or after entering a bullet, which starts a new slide or bullet, respectively. The new item may then be promoted or demoted as necessary.

Editing is accomplished through the same techniques used in other Windows applications. For example, you can use the Cut, Copy, and Paste commands in the Edit menu (or the corresponding icons on the Standard toolbar) to move and copy selected text, or you can simply drag-and-drop text from one place to another.

Text is formatted by using the *select-then-do* approach common to Word and Excel; that is, you select the text, then you execute the appropriate command or click the appropriate icon. The selected text remains highlighted and is affected by all subsequent commands until you click elsewhere in the outline.

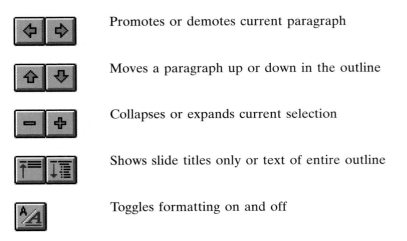

Promotes or demotes current paragraph

Moves a paragraph up or down in the outline

Collapses or expands current selection

Shows slide titles only or text of entire outline

Toggles formatting on and off

FIGURE 2.2 The Outline Toolbar

AutoContent Wizard

Outline or not, one of the hardest things about writing a presentation is getting started. You have a general idea of what you want to say, but are not quite sure where to begin. The *AutoContent Wizard* helps you to get started.

The AutoContent Wizard begins by asking you for your name, topic, and company or organization, and uses this information to create a title slide. The real benefit, however, is in the six predefined outlines, two of which are shown in Figure 2.3. The wizard asks you the type of presentation you are planning to give, then displays the appropriate outline, including suggested text for each slide. You can choose from six different outlines as shown below:

➤ Recommending a strategy
➤ Selling a product, service, or idea
➤ Training
➤ Reporting progress
➤ Communicating bad news
➤ General

Figure 2.3a displays the outline provided by the wizard for selling a product, service, or idea. Figure 2.3b shows the outline suggested to communicate bad news. Both are general outlines (as they must be), but both provide the essential topics to include in a presentation of either type.

You work with the outline provided by the AutoContent Wizard just as you would with any other outline. You can type over existing text, add or delete slides,

---

PRINT THE OUTLINE

You can print the outline of a presentation and distribute it to the audience in the form of a handout. This enables the audience to follow the presentation as it is delivered and gives them an ideal vehicle on which to take notes. Pull down the File menu, click Print, then choose Outline view from the Print What list box.

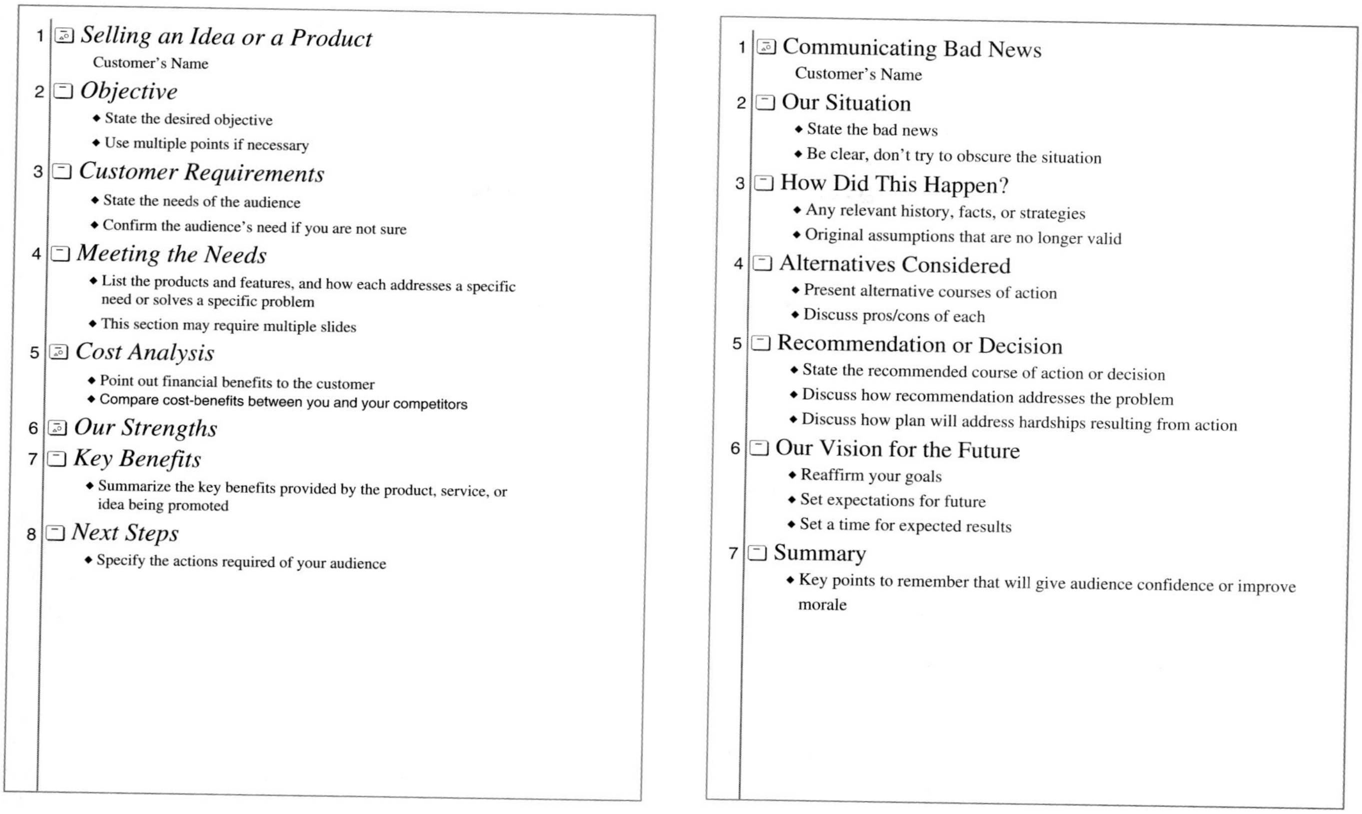

(a) Outline for Selling a Product, Service, or Idea

1 Selling an Idea or a Product
Customer's Name
2 Objective
- State the desired objective
- Use multiple points if necessary
3 Customer Requirements
- State the needs of the audience
- Confirm the audience's need if you are not sure
4 Meeting the Needs
- List the products and features, and how each addresses a specific need or solves a specific problem
- This section may require multiple slides
5 Cost Analysis
- Point out financial benefits to the customer
- Compare cost-benefits between you and your competitors
6 Our Strengths
7 Key Benefits
- Summarize the key benefits provided by the product, service, or idea being promoted
8 Next Steps
- Specify the actions required of your audience

(b) Outline for Communicating Bad News

1 Communicating Bad News
Customer's Name
2 Our Situation
- State the bad news
- Be clear, don't try to obscure the situation
3 How Did This Happen?
- Any relevant history, facts, or strategies
- Original assumptions that are no longer valid
4 Alternatives Considered
- Present alternative courses of action
- Discuss pros/cons of each
5 Recommendation or Decision
- State the recommended course of action or decision
- Discuss how recommendation addresses the problem
- Discuss how plan will address hardships resulting from action
6 Our Vision for the Future
- Reaffirm your goals
- Set expectations for future
- Set a time for expected results
7 Summary
- Key points to remember that will give audience confidence or improve morale

FIGURE 2.3 AutoContent Wizard

move slides around, promote or demote items, and so on. In short, you don't have to use the AutoContent outline exactly as it is presented. Use the outline as a starting point, then modify the outline to make it your own.

Pick a Look Wizard

After you have created the text of a presentation, you can begin to think about its appearance. The *Pick a Look Wizard* is the easiest way to format a presentation and can be invoked at any time. The wizard asks you questions about how you want the presentation to look, then creates the presentation according to the answers you supply.

CHOOSE AN APPROPRIATE TEMPLATE

A template should enhance a presentation without calling attention to itself. It should be consistent with your message, and as authoritative or informal as the situation demands. Choosing the right template requires common sense and good taste. What works in one instance will not necessarily work in another. You wouldn't, for example, use the same template to proclaim a year-end bonus as you would to announce a fourth-quarter loss and impending layoffs.

The wizard helps you choose a template from the more than 100 that are supplied with PowerPoint. A *template* is a design specification that controls every element in a presentation. It specifies the color scheme for the slides and the arrangement of the different elements (placeholders) on each slide. It determines the formatting of the text, the fonts that are used, and the design, size, and placement of the bullets.

Figure 2.4 displays the title slide of a presentation according to four different templates suggested by the Pick a Look Wizard. Just pick the one you like, and PowerPoint will format the entire presentation according to the template you choose. And don't be afraid to change your mind. You can invoke the Pick a Look Wizard at any time (or click the Template button on the status bar) and choose an entirely different template.

(a) Blue Diagonal Template

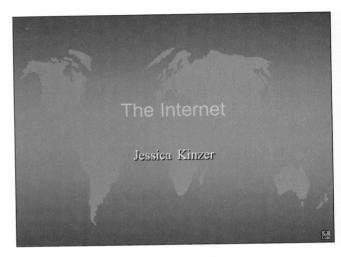

(b) World Template

(c) Double Lines Template

(d) Multiple Bars Template

FIGURE 2.4   Pick a Look Wizard

Creating a Presentation

Objective To create a presentation from the Outline view; to spell check a presentation; to use the Pick a Look Wizard to choose a template. Use Figure 2.5 as a guide in the exercise.

Step 1: Create a new presentation
➤ Load PowerPoint as you did in Chapter 1. If necessary, click the **maximize button** so that PowerPoint takes the entire desktop.
➤ Click the option button to Create a New Presentation Using a **Blank Presentation** as shown in Figure 2.5a. Click the **OK command button.**

CONTENT, CONTENT, AND CONTENT

It is much more important to focus on the content of the presentation than to worry about how it will look. Start with the AutoContent Wizard or with a blank presentation to create your own outline. Save the formatting for last. Otherwise you will spend too much time changing templates and too little time developing the text.

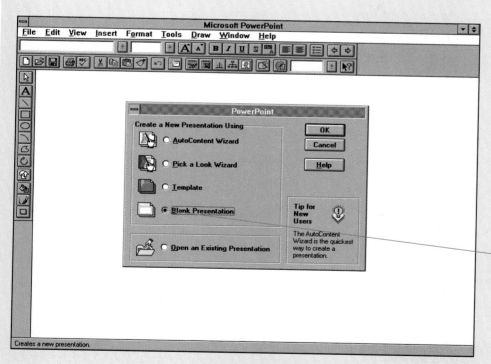

Click here to create a blank presentation

(a) Create a New Presentation (step 1)

FIGURE 2.5 Hands-on Exercise 1

Step 2: Create the title slide

➤ You should see the New Slide dialog box with the AutoLayout for the title slide already selected. Click OK to create the title slide.

➤ Click anywhere in the placeholder containing **Click to add title,** then type the title **A Guide to Successful Presentations** as shown in Figure 2.5b.

➤ Click anywhere in the placeholder containing **Click to add sub-title** and enter your name.

➤ Click the **Outline view icon** on the status bar to change to the Outline view.

THE DEFAULT PRESENTATION

PowerPoint supplies a default presentation containing the specifications for color, text formatting, and AutoLayouts. The default presentation is selected automatically when you work on a blank presentation, and it remains in effect until you choose a different template.

Step 3: The Save command

➤ Pull down the **File menu** and click **Save** (or click the **Save icon** on the Standard toolbar). You will the see the Save As dialog box in Figure 2.5c.

➤ Double click c:\ or a:\ to select the root directory, then scroll through the directory list box until you come to the **PPTDATA** directory. Double click this directory to make it the active directory.

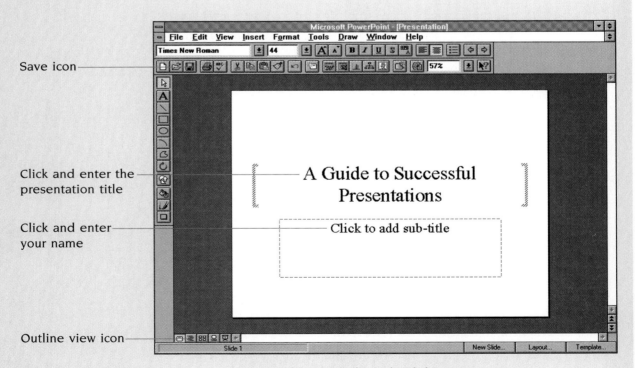

Save icon

Click and enter the presentation title

Click and enter your name

Outline view icon

(b) Create the Title Slide (step 2)

FIGURE 2.5 Hands-on Exercise 1 (continued)

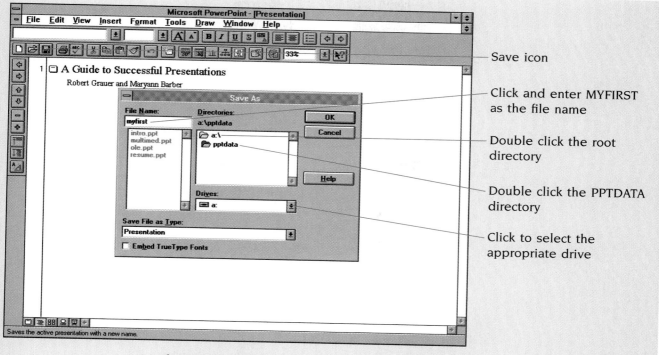

Save icon

Click and enter MYFIRST
as the file name

Double click the root
directory

Double click the PPTDATA
directory

Click to select the
appropriate drive

(c) The Save Command (step 3)

FIGURE 2.5   Hands-on Exercise 1 (continued)

➤ Click in the text box for File Name. Type **MYFIRST** as the name of the presentation, then click the **OK command button** or press the **enter key.**
➤ Click the **Cancel command button** or Press **Esc** if you see a Summary Information dialog box.

SUMMARY INFORMATION

The **Summary Info** dialog box stores information about a presentation that enables you to search for it later, using the Find File command in the File menu. The information includes the title, subject, and author of a presentation, as well as key words that can be used in a subsequent search. The Summary Info dialog box appears by default whenever a presentation is saved for the first time. You can, however, prevent the box from appearing by pulling down the Tools menu, clicking Options, then clearing the Prompt for Summary Info check box.

Step 4: Create the presentation
➤ Click the **New Slide button** on the status bar. The icon for slide 2 will appear in the outline.
➤ Type **Define the Audience** as the title of the slide and press **enter.**
➤ Press the **Tab key** (or click the **Demote icon** on the Outline toolbar) to enter the first bullet. Type **Who is in the audience** and press **enter.**

➤ Press the **Tab key** (or click the **Demote icon** on the Outline toolbar) to enter the second-level bullets.
— Type **Managers.** Press **enter.**
— Type **Coworkers.** Press **enter.**
— Type **Clients.** Press **enter.**
➤ Press **Shift+Tab** (or click the **Promote icon** on the Outline toolbar) to return to the first-level bullets.
— Type **What are their expectations.** Press **enter.**
— Type **How large is the audience.** Press **enter.**
➤ Your screen should now contain the first two slides in Figure 2.5d.
➤ Press **Shift+Tab** to enter the title of the third slide. Type **Create the Presentation.** Add the remaining text for this slide and the remaining slides as shown earlier in Figure 2.1a on page 41. Do *not* press enter after entering the last bullet on the last slide.

JUST KEEP TYPING

The easiest way to enter the text for a presentation is to type continually in the Outline view. Just type an item, then press enter to move to the next item. You will be automatically positioned at the next item on the same level where you can type the next entry. In addition, you can press the Tab key to *demote* an item (move it to the next lower level), or you can press Shift+Tab to *promote* an item (move it to the next higher level).

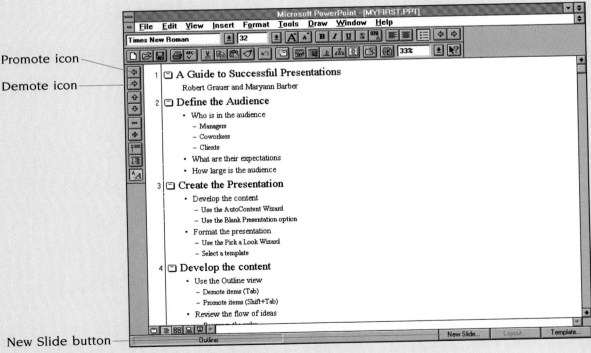

(d) Enter the Presentation (step 4)

FIGURE 2.5 Hands-on Exercise I (continued)

Step 5: Drag and drop

➤ Click the icon for **slide 2** (Define the Audience). The entire slide (the title and its associated bullets) is selected.

➤ Point to the slide icon (the mouse pointer changes to a 4-headed arrow), then click and drag to move the slide to the end of the presentation. Release the mouse.

➤ Click anywhere in the outline to deselect the slide. Notice how all of the other slides have been renumbered automatically as shown in Figure 2.5e.

➤ Click the **Show Titles icon** on the Outline toolbar to collapse all of the slides and display only the titles. (You can drag-and-drop titles just as you can drag-and-drop an entire slide.) Click the **Show All icon** to display the content of each slide.

➤ Click the icon for **slide 6** (Define the Audience) to again select the slide, then drag it back to its original position as slide 2. Click elsewhere in the outline to deselect the slide.

➤ Click the **Save icon** on the Standard toolbar to save the presentation.

SELECTING SLIDES IN THE OUTLINE VIEW

Click the slide icon or the slide number next to the slide title to select the slide. PowerPoint will select the entire slide (its title, text, and any other objects that are not visible in Outline view). Press and hold the Shift key, then click the beginning and ending slides to select a group of sequential slides. Press Ctrl+A to select the entire outline.

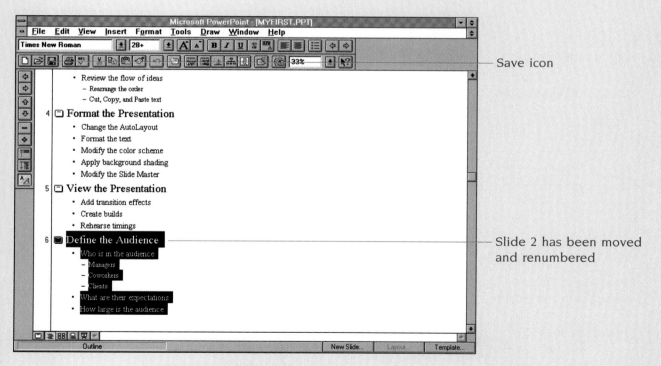

(e) Drag and Drop (step 5)

FIGURE 2.5 Hands-on Exercise 1 (continued).

Step 6: The Spell Check

➤ Click the **Spell Check icon** on the Standard toolbar to check the presentation for spelling. Each word is checked against a built-in dictionary, with any mismatch (a word found in the presentation but not the dictionary) flagged as an error. The result of the spell check will depend on how accurately you entered the text of the presentation.

➤ Click **OK** when PowerPoint indicates it has checked the entire presentation. Save the presentation.

SPELLING COUNTS

You are in the midst of giving your presentation when all of a sudden someone in the audience points out a misspelling in the title of a crucial slide. Take it from us, nothing takes more away from a presentation than a misspelled word. You've lost your audience and it didn't have to happen. PowerPoint provides a full-featured *spelling checker.* Use it!

Step 7: The Pick a Look Wizard

➤ Click the **Pick a Look Wizard icon** on the Standard toolbar to display the dialog box in Figure 2.5f. Click the **Next command button** to begin working in the Wizard.

➤ Click the option button for **On-Screen Presentations.** Click the **Next command button.**

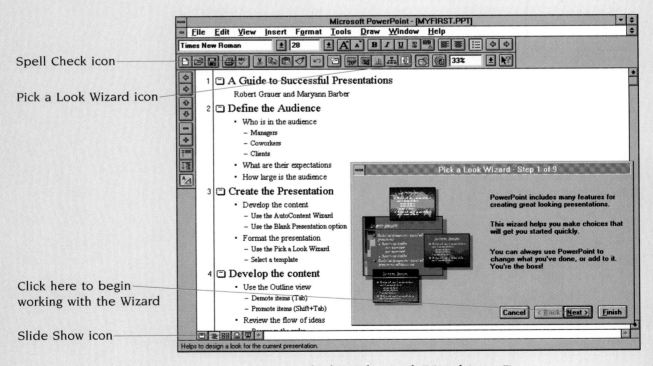

(f) The Pick a Look Wizard (step 7)

FIGURE 2.5   Hands-on Exercise 1 (continued)

➤ Click the option buttons to view each of the four designs in turn, then make a decision. (You can change your mind later, so make a decision quickly.) We chose **Double Lines.** Click the **Next command button.**

➤ Clear the boxes for the Full Page Slides, Speaker's Notes, and Audience Handout Pages; in other words, you will print just the **Outline Pages.** (You can change your mind later.) Click the **Next command button.**

➤ Check the box for **Name, company, or other text,** then click in the associated text box and add your name and school. Check the boxes for the **Date** and **Page Number.** This establishes the options for the Outline Pages. Click the **Next command button.**

➤ Click the **Finish command button.**

➤ Save the presentation.

Step 8: View the presentation

➤ Press **Ctrl+Home** to move to the beginning of the presentation, then click the **Slide Show icon** on the status bar to view the presentation.

➤ You should see the opening slide as shown in Figure 2.5g. (Type the letter **A** if you do not see the Freehand annotation icon and you want to annotate the presentation.)

➤ View the presentation by clicking the **left mouse button** or pressing the **PgDn key** to move from one slide to the next. (You can return to the previous slide by clicking the **right mouse button** or pressing the **PgUp key.**)

➤ Continue to view the presentation until you are returned to the Outline view. (You can press the **Esc key** at any time to cancel the show.)

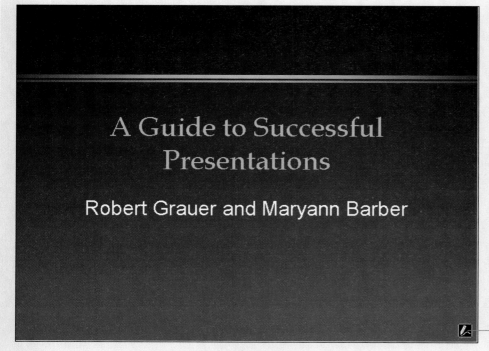

Freehand annotation tool

(g) View the Presentation (step 8)

FIGURE 2.5 Hands-on Exercise 1 (continued)

Step 9: Print the outline

➤ Pull down the **File menu** and click **Slide Setup** to display the dialog box in Figure 2.5h.

➤ If necessary, click the **Portrait option button** under **Notes, Handouts, Outline** as shown in the figure. Click **OK.**

➤ Pull down the **File menu** a second time and click **Print** to display the Print dialog box. Click the arrow in the **Print What list box** and select **Outline View.**

➤ Be sure that the **All option button** is selected under **Slide Range.** Click the **OK command button** to print the Outline pages for your presentation.

➤ Pull down the **File menu** and click **Exit** if you do not want to continue with the next exercise at this time.

KNOW YOUR AUDIENCE

Know your audience and gear your presentation accordingly. The presentation you deliver to your peers will be different from one to your superiors, which is different from a presentation to prospects or to the general public. Try to determine what the audience already knows about the subject and what they expect to learn from your presentation. Know the expected size of your audience and be sure to have an adequate number of handouts.

Click here to select Portrait orientation for the Outline

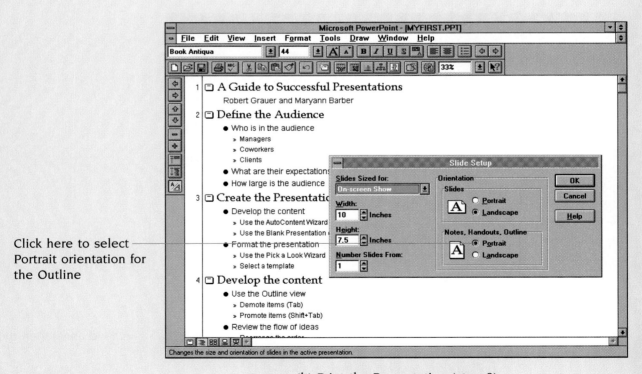

(h) Print the Presentation (step 9)

FIGURE 2.5 Hands-on Exercise 1 (continued)

As indicated at the beginning of the chapter, creating a presentation is an iterative process in which the content or design elements can be changed as often as necessary. You can add, edit, or delete individual slides. You can add interest to individual slides by changing the AutoLayout to include clip art and other objects. (We show you how to add graphs and organization charts in Chapter 3.) You can change the order of slides within the presentation in the Slide Sorter or Outline view.

The Pick a Look Wizard can be used at any time to select a template or to change an existing template. You can also change the template through the Presentation Template command in the Format menu or by clicking the Template button on the status bar. In short, PowerPoint gives you complete control over every aspect of a presentation. Not only can you change the content or the template, but you can change the color scheme within a template and/or the shading in the background.

ADDING CLIP ART

The easiest way to add clip art to a bullet slide is to change to the Slide view, then change the AutoLayout of the slide. Click the Layout button on the status bar, choose the AutoLayout with Text and Clip Art, and click the Apply command button. Double click the clip art placeholder in the slide view, then select the desired image from the Clip Art gallery in the usual fashion.

Changing the Color Scheme

A *color scheme* is a set of eight balanced colors that is associated with a template. It consists of a *background color,* a color for the title of each slide, a color for lines and text, and five additional colors to provide accents to different elements such as shadows and fill colors. Each template has its own color scheme.

Figure 2.6 shows how a color scheme may be modified. Figure 2.6a contains the title slide of the presentation from the preceding hands-on exercise. Figure 2.6b displays the Slide Color Scheme dialog box, which defines the color scheme in effect. Note that there are eight colors in the color scheme and observe how these colors are used in the slide in Figure 2.6a. You can change the color scheme itself (by selecting the Choose Scheme command button), or you can change one or more individual colors (by choosing the Change Color command button).

Figure 2.6c displays the Background Color dialog box, which appears when you select the background color and click the Change Color command button in Figure 2.6b. Choose the color you like (or click the More Colors button to see even more colors), then click the OK command button. Figure 2.6d shows the title slide with a new background color.

SLIDES VERSUS TRANSPARENCIES

The background and shading you select should be consistent with the means of delivering your presentation. Light backgrounds work best for overhead transparencies. Dark backgrounds are preferable for computer presentations and 35mm slides.

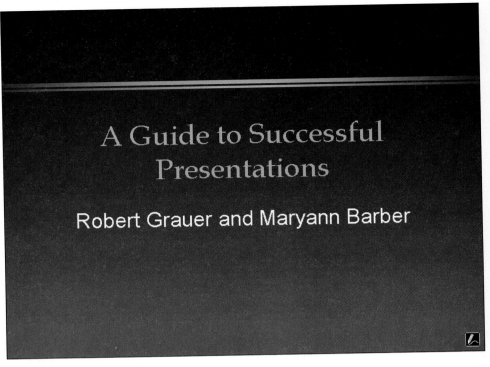

(a) Original Title Slide

Eight colors in the currently selected color scheme

Click here to change one or more colors in the current color scheme

Click here to change the color scheme

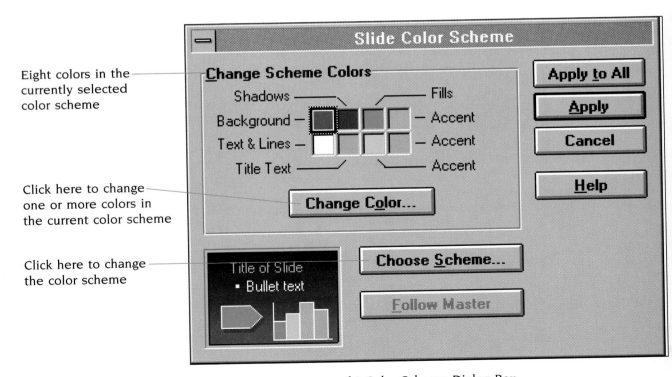

(b) Color Scheme Dialog Box

FIGURE 2.6   Changing the Color Scheme

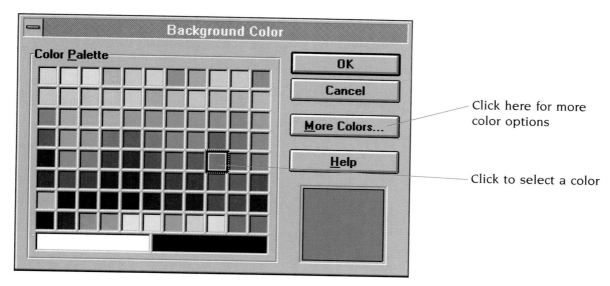

Click here for more color options

Click to select a color

(c) Background Color Dialog Box

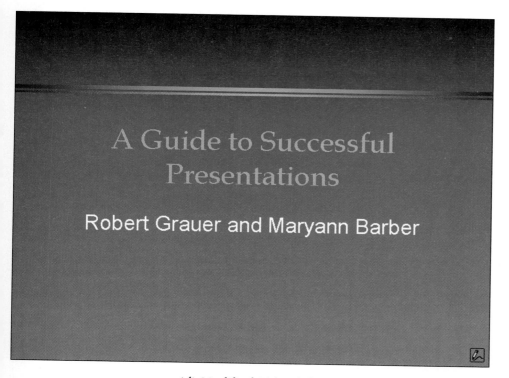

(d) Modified Title Slide

FIGURE 2.6 Changing the Color Scheme (continued)

Changing the Background Shading

You can change the ***background shading*** of a slide in addition to changing any of the colors in its color scheme. This provides the ultimate finishing touch as it enables you to truly fine tune a presentation.

Figure 2.7a displays the Slide Background dialog box in which you choose from several different types of shading. Vertical shading is selected in the figure. Within each type of shading are four variants that further customize the slide. And

Click to apply the background shade to all slides in the presentation

Click to apply the background shade to the current slide

Variants for selected shade style

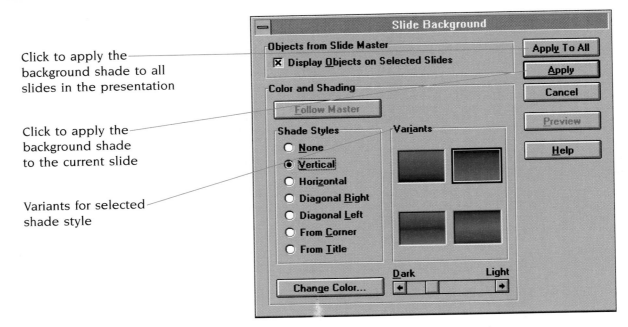

(a) Slide Background Dialog Box

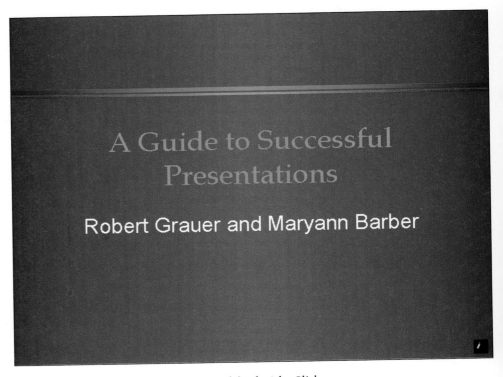

(b) Modified Title Slide

FIGURE 2.7   Changing the Background

finally, you can go from dark to light by dragging the scroll box at the bottom of the window. Figure 2.7b shows the modified title slide after the background has been changed. The background can be applied to the current slide only (Apply) or to all slides in the presentation (Apply to All).

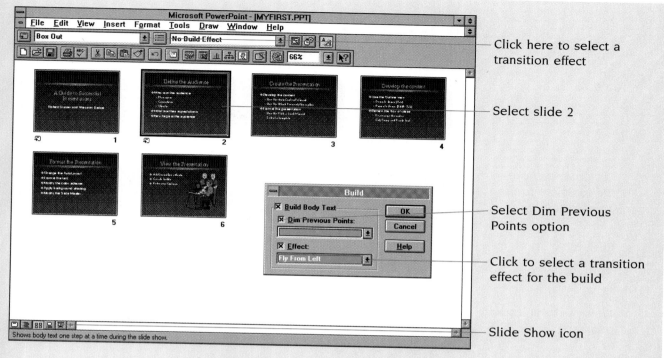

Click here to select a transition effect

Select slide 2

Select Dim Previous Points option

Click to select a transition effect for the build

Slide Show icon

(d) Build (step 4)

FIGURE 2.9 Hands-on Exercise 2 (continued)

➤ Click the **Slide Show icon.** You will see the current slide appear from the center out according to the (Box Out) transition effect you selected.
➤ Click the **left mouse button** to display the first bullet, which flies in from the left.
➤ Click the **left mouse button** a second time. The first bullet dims as the second bullet flies in from the left.
➤ Click the **left mouse button** to display the third and last bullet.
➤ Press the **Esc key** to return to the Slide Sorter view. Add transitions and builds to other slides as desired.

SELECTING MULTIPLE SLIDES

You can apply the same transition or build effect to multiple slides with a single command. Change to the Slide Sorter view, then press and hold the Shift key as you click multiple slides to select the slides. Use the Tools menu or the Slide Sorter toolbar to execute the desired transition or build command when all the slides have been selected. (You can select every slide by choosing the Select All command in the Edit menu.) Click anywhere in the Slide Sorter view to deselect the slides and continue working.

Step 5: Change the template
➤ Pull down the **Format menu** and click **Presentation Template** or click the **Template button** on the status bar. You should see the Presentation Template dialog box in Figure 2.9e.

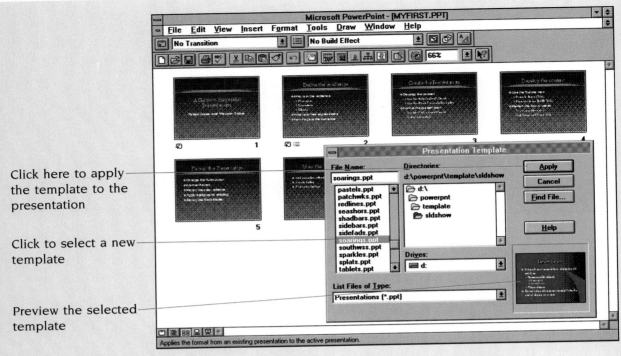

Click here to apply the template to the presentation

Click to select a new template

Preview the selected template

(e) Change the Template (step 5)

FIGURE 2.9 Hands-on Exercise 2 (continued)

➤ If necessary, select the drive and directory (d:\powerpnt\template\sldshow in Figure 2.9e). Click any template in the **File Name** list box, which displays a preview of the template within the dialog box.

➤ Scroll through the File Name until you can select the **SOARINGS.PPT** template, then click the **Apply command button** to use this template in your presentation.

➤ Save the presentation.

Step 6: Change the color scheme

➤ Pull down the **Format menu.** Click **Slide Color Scheme** to display the first dialog box in Figure 2.9f.

➤ Click the box for the **background color,** then click the **Change Color command button** to display the Background Color dialog box in Figure 2.9f.

➤ Choose a lighter shade of blue as shown in the figure. Click the **OK command button** to close the Background Color dialog box.

THE UNDO COMMAND

The Undo command reverses the effect of the most recent operation and is invaluable. Pull down the Edit menu and click Undo (or click the Undo button on the Standard toolbar) whenever something happens that is different from what you expected or intended.

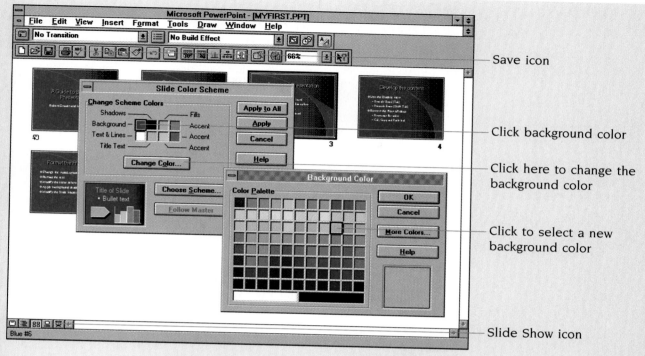

Save icon

Click background color

Click here to change the background color

Click to select a new background color

Slide Show icon

(f) Change the Color Scheme (step 6)

FIGURE 2.9 Hands-on Exercise 2 (continued)

➤ Click the **Apply to All command button** to change the background color of every slide.
➤ Save the presentation.

Step 7: Show the presentation
➤ Click the first slide, then click the **Slide Show button** to view the presentation as shown in Figure 2.9g.
➤ Click the **left mouse button** to move to the next slide (or to the next bullet on the current slide when a build is in effect).
➤ Click the **right mouse button** to return to the previous slide (or to the previous bullet on the current slide when a build is in effect).
➤ Press the **Esc key** at any time to quit the presentation and return to Power-Point.

ANIMATE THE SHOW

Click the Freehand annotation tool (type the letter A if you do not see the tool), then click and drag the mouse to annotate a slide as you deliver the presentation. The annotation disappears automatically when you move to the next slide. You can also press the letter E to erase the marking on the current slide.

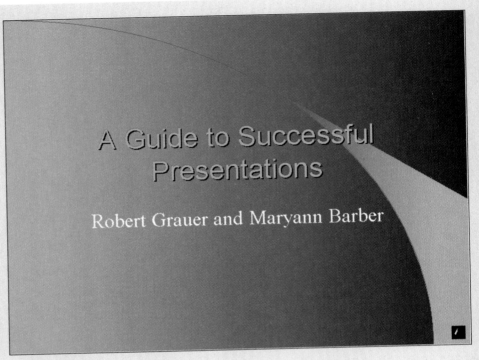

(g) The Completed Presentation (step 7)

FIGURE 2.9 Hands-on Exercise 2 (continued)

Step 7: Exit PowerPoint
➤ Save the presentation. Exit PowerPoint if you do not want to continue with the next exercise at this time.

POWERPOINT MASTERS

Each PowerPoint view (except for the Slide Show) has a corresponding master. The Slide view has a Slide Master, the Outline view has an *Outline Master,* the Slide Sorter View has an Audience Handouts Master, and the Notes Pages View has a *Notes Pages Master.* Each master determines the appearance of the corresponding view. Thus, changing the Slide Master automatically changes the appearance of every slide in a presentation. In similar fashion, changing the Outline Master changes every page of the outline.

The *Slide Master* in Figure 2.10 contains a placeholder for the title of the slide and a second placeholder for the bulleted text. The formatting of the text within each placeholder determines the formatting for that entry in the actual slides. Any change to the font, point size, alignment, and so on would carry through to all of the individual slides.

The most common modification to a Slide Master is the addition of a corporate name or logo. In Figure 2.10, for example, a text box (The University of Miami) has been added to the Slide Master and will appear on every slide in the presentation. The text was added by using the *Text tool* on the Drawing toolbar as will be described in the next hands-on exercise.

Any of the masters may be modified by choosing the appropriate master from the View menu or through the Pick a Look Wizard. The Wizard asks questions about the elements you want to see and modifies the appropriate master

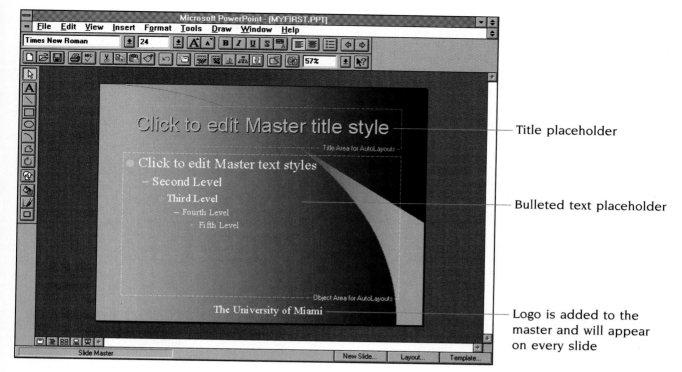

FIGURE 2.10 The Slide Master

accordingly. (See step 7 in the first exercise in this chapter on pages 50–51.) You can also make the changes yourself (without the Pick a Look Wizard) by switching to the Master view and using the appropriate tools to add text or clip art for a corporate logo. The following exercise reviews the use of Cue Cards to step you through the process of modifying the Slide Master.

THE DATE, TIME, AND PAGE NUMBER

You can further customize a presentation by inserting the date, time, and/or page number into any of the masters. Pull down the View menu and select the desired master. Pull down the Insert menu, click the item (the date, time, or page number) to insert, then drag the object to the desired position on the master. PowerPoint inserts a code rather than a specific value on the master. The date appears as //, the time as ::, and the page number as ##. The codes in the Slide Master are updated when you switch to the Slide Show or when you print the Outline or Notes pages.

HANDS-ON EXERCISE 3:

Masters and Cue Cards

Objective Use Cue Cards to modify the Slide Master. Use Figure 2.11 as a guide in the exercise.

Step 1: Open the existing presentation

➤ Load PowerPoint. Open the **MYFIRST** presentation from the previous exercise. Press **Ctrl+Home** to move to the first slide. Click the **Slide view icon.**

➤ Pull down the **Help menu.** Click **Cue Cards** to open the Cue Cards window shown in Figure 2.11a.

➤ Click the option to **Add a logo or text to every slide.**

Select Add a logo ⎯⎯

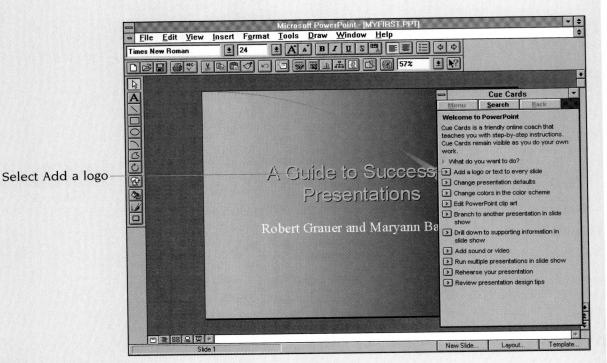

(a) Cue Cards (step 1)

FIGURE 2.11 Hands-on Exercise 3

Step 2: The View menu

➤ You should see the Cue Card shown in Figure 2.11b. Follow the directions on the Cue Card:
— Pull down the **View menu.** Click **Master** to display the cascade menu.
— Choose **Slide Master** from the cascaded menu as shown in Figure 2.11b.

➤ Click **To add text** on the current Cue Card to bring up the next Cue Card.

THE MASTER VIEW

The fastest way to display the Slide Master is to press and hold the Shift key as you click the Slide view icon on the status bar. Use the same technique to change to the Outline or Audience Handouts Master.

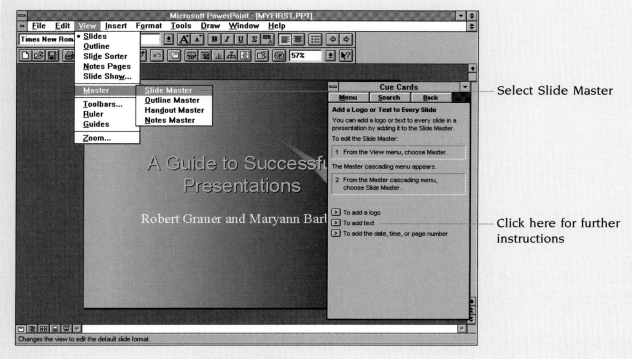

(b) The View Menu (step 2)

FIGURE 2.11 Hands-on Exercise 3 (continued)

Step 3: The Text tool

➤ You should see the Cue Card in Figure 2.11c. Follow the directions:
  — Click the **Text tool** on the Drawing toolbar.
  — Click and drag *outside* the placeholders where you want the text to appear.

➤ Type the name of your school (The University of Miami in our presentation) as shown in Figure 2.11c. Select and format the text as necessary. You can change the font and/or type size, add boldface or italics, or change the color.

THE FORMATTING TOOLBAR

The Formatting Toolbar contains icons for the most common formatting operations such as boldface, italics, or underline. It also contains icons to change the color or justification of selected text, toggle bullets on or off, and promote or demote the selected item. The toolbar also contains two drop-down list boxes that enable you to change the font and/or point size. If you are unsure of the function of a particular icon, just point to an icon, and the resulting ToolTip will display the name of the icon, which is indicative of its function.

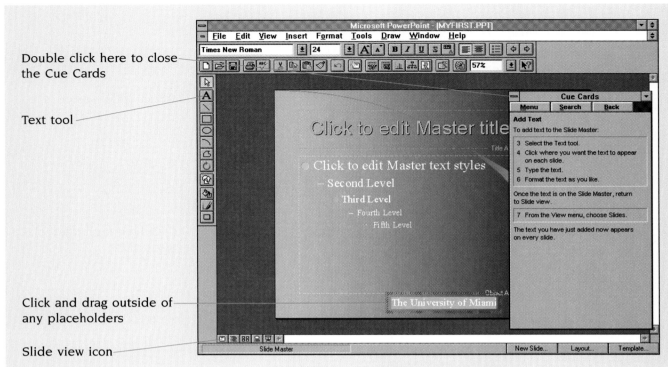

Double click here to close the Cue Cards

Text tool

Click and drag outside of any placeholders

Slide view icon

(c) Add the Text (step 3)

FIGURE 2.11 Hands-on Exercise 3 (continued)

Step 4: The modified slides

➤ Pull down the **View menu** and click **Slides** (or click the **Slide View icon** on the status bar). You should see the text you entered in the previous step appear in the Slide view as shown in Figure 2.11d.

➤ Press the **PgDn key** to move forward in the presentation to the next slide. You should see the identical text as on the first slide in the same position on this slide.

➤ Double click the **control-menu box** in the Cue Cards window to close the Cue Cards.

➤ Save the presentation. Run the show.

➤ Exit PowerPoint.

HIDING OBJECTS

On occasion, you may want to prevent the objects on the master slide from appearing on a specific slide. Select the slide (or slides) on which you want to suppress the objects, pull down the Format menu, click Slide Background, and clear the Display Objects on This Slide check box. Click the Apply command button to hide the object on the current slide and return to PowerPoint.

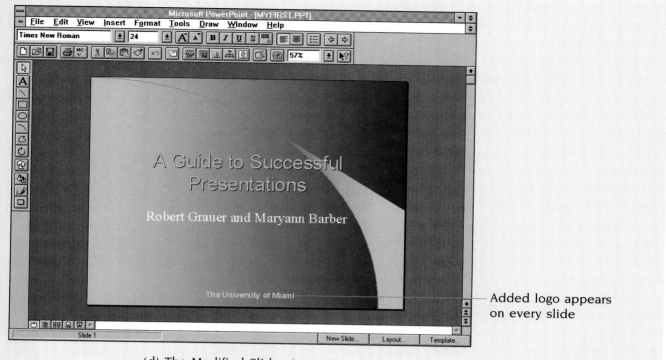

Added logo appears on every slide

(d) The Modified Slides (step 4)

FIGURE 2.11 Hands-on Exercise 3 (continued)

SUMMARY

There are in essence two independent steps to creating a PowerPoint presentation. You must develop the content and you must format the presentation. Both steps are iterative in nature, and you are likely to go back and forth many times before you are finished.

The text of a presentation can be developed from the Slide view or the Outline view or a combination of the two. The Outline view is preferable because it displays the contents of many slides at once, enabling you to see the overall flow of your ideas. You can change the order of the slides and/or move text from one slide to another as necessary. Text can be entered continually in an outline, then promoted or demoted so that it appears on the proper level in the slide.

The AutoContent Wizard asks you questions about the type of presentation you are planning to give, then creates an outline for you. The outline is based on one of six predefined outlines and is a good starting point.

The Pick a Look Wizard is the easiest way to format a presentation and can be executed at any time. The wizard helps you to choose a template (design specification) from the more than 100 supplied with PowerPoint. It also helps you to format the supplements, such as Speaker Notes or Audience Handouts that can be printed to accompany a presentation.

A color scheme is a set of eight balanced colors that is defined with a template. It consists of a background color, a color for the title of each slide, a color for lines and text, and five different accent colors.

Transition effects can be added to individual slides and add interest to a slide show. A build slide is one where the bullets appear one at a time with each successive mouse click.

Four of the five PowerPoint views have a corresponding master that determines the appearance of the view. The masters are modified implicitly through responses to the Pick a Look Wizard or explicitly through the View menu.

Key Words and Concepts

AutoContent Wizard	Outline Master	Slide Sorter toolbar
Background color	Outline toolbar	Spelling checker
Background shading	Outline view	Summary Info
Build slide	Pick a Look Wizard	Template
Color scheme	Promote	Text tool
Demote	Select-then-do	ToolTip
Handouts Master	Slide icon	Transition effect
Insertion point	Slide Master	
Notes Pages Master	Slide show	

Multiple Choice

1. Which view displays multiple slides while letting you change the text in a slide?
   (a) Outline view
   (b) Slide Sorter view
   (c) Both (a) and (b)
   (d) Neither (a) nor (b)

2. Where will the insertion point be after you complete the text for a bullet in the Outline view and press the enter key?
   (a) On the next bullet at the same level of indentation
   (b) On the next bullet at a higher level of indentation
   (c) On the next bullet at a lower level of indentation
   (d) Impossible to determine

3. Which of the following is true?
   (a) Shift+Tab promotes an item to the next highest level
   (b) Tab demotes an item to the next lowest level
   (c) Both (a) and (b)
   (d) Neither (a) nor (b)

4. How can you select (or change) the template used in a presentation?
   (a) With the Pick a Look Wizard
   (b) Using the template button on the status bar or the Presentation Template command in the Format menu
   (c) Both (a) and (b)
   (d) Neither (a) nor (b)

5. Which of the following is true regarding transition and build effects?
   (a) Every slide must have the same transition effect
   (b) Every bullet must have the same build effect

(c) Both (a) and (b)

(d) Neither (a) nor (b)

6. Which of the following *must* be used to create a presentation?

(a) The AutoContent Wizard

(b) The Pick a Look Wizard

(c) Both (a) and (b)

(d) Neither (a) nor (b)

7. Which of the following is true?

(a) Slides can be added to a presentation after a template has been chosen

(b) The template can be changed after all of the slides have been created

(c) Both (a) and (b)

(d) Neither (a) nor (b)

8. Which of the following has a master?

(a) The Slide view

(b) The Outline view

(c) Both (a) and (b)

(d) Neither (a) nor (b)

9. Which of the following can be changed after a slide has been created?

(a) Its layout and transition effect

(b) Its position within the presentation

(c) Both (a) and (b)

(d) Neither (a) nor (b)

10. Which view enables you to select multiple slides?

(a) Outline view

(b) Slide Sorter view

(c) Both (a) and (b)

(d) Neither (a) nor (b)

ANSWERS

1. a   **6.** d

2. a   **7.** c

3. c   **8.** c

4. c   **9.** c

5. d   **10.** c

EXPLORING POWERPOINT

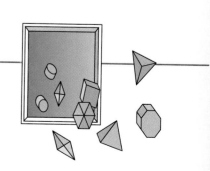

1. Use Figure 2.12 to match each action with its result. A given action may be used more than once or not at all.

Appendix A:
Object Linking and
Embedding 2.0: Sharing
Data Among Programs

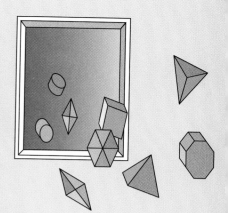

One of the primary advantages of Windows is the ability to create a **compound document**—that is, a document containing data from multiple applications. There are three different ways this can be accomplished: pasting, linking, and embedding.

Pasting is the simplest operation and is done with the cut, copy, and paste commands present in all Windows applications. You cut or copy data onto the **clipboard,** then paste it elsewhere into the same application, or into a different application to produce a compound document. There are two disadvantages to the simple paste operation. First, it is a static connection meaning that if the data is subsequently changed in the original document, the change is not reflected in the compound document. Second, once data has been pasted into a compound document, it can no longer be edited using the original application.

Object Linking and Embedding (OLE) offers a superior way to share data between documents. In actuality, there are two separate techniques, linking and embedding, and each will be illustrated in its own exercise. The following terminology is essential to the discussion:

➤ An **object** is any piece of data created by a Windows application, such as a spreadsheet created in Excel or a document created in Word.

➤ The **source document** is the place where the object originates. The source document—for example, an Excel spreadsheet—is created by the **server application,** Excel 5.0.

➤ The **destination document** is the file into which the object is placed. The destination document (for example, a Word document) is created by the **client application,** Word for Windows.

Figure A.1 displays the compound document that will be created in the first hands-on exercise, in which an Excel spreadsheet is **embedded** into a Word document. Excel is the server application and Word is the client application. The exercise uses the **Insert Object command** in Word to place a copy of the spreadsheet into the Word document, then modifies the (copy of the) spreadsheet through *in-place editing.* In-place editing requires the application to support the Microsoft specification for Object Linking and Embedding 2.0. Both Excel 5.0 and Word for Windows 6.0 support this standard.

In-place editing enables you to double click an embedded object (the spreadsheet) and change it, using the tools of the server application (Excel). In other words, you remain in the client application (Word for Windows in this example) but you have access to the Excel toolbar and pull-down menus. In-place editing modifies the copy of the embedded object in the destination document. It does *not* change the original object because there is no connection between the source and destination documents.

Lionel Douglas

402 Mahoney Hall • Coral Gables, Florida 33124

May 10, 1994

Dear Folks,

I heard from Mr. Black, the manager at University Commons, and the apartment is a definite for the Fall. Manny and I are very excited, and can't wait to get out of the dorm. The food is poison, not that either of us are cooks, but anything will be better than this! I have been checking into car prices (we are definitely too far away from campus to walk!), and have done some estimating on what it will cost. The figures below are for a Jeep Wrangler, the car of my dreams:

Price of car	$11,995			
Manufacturer's rebate	$1,000			
Down payment	$3,000		**My assumptions**	
Amount to be financed	$7,995		Interest rate	7.90%
Monthly payment	$195		Term (years)	4
Gas	$40			
Maintenance	$50			
Insurance	$100			
Total per month	$385			

My initial estimate was $471 based on a $2,000 down payment and a three-year loan at 7.9%. I know this is too much so I plan on earning an additional $1,000 and extending the loan to four years. If that won't do it, I'll look at other cars.

Lionel

FIGURE A.1 A Compound Document

HANDS-ON EXERCISE 1:

Embedding

Objective To embed an Excel spreadsheet into a Word document; to use in-place editing to modify the spreadsheet. The exercise requires both Word 6.0 and Excel 5.0; the faster your computer, the better.

Step 1: Open the Word document

➤ Pull down the **File menu** and click **Open** (or click the **File Open button** on the toolbar).

➤ If you have not yet changed the default directory:
  — Click the **drop-down list box** to specify the appropriate drive, which is the same drive you have been using throughout the text.
  — Scroll through the directory list box until you come to the **WORDDATA** directory. Double click this directory to make it the active directory.

➤ Double click **CAR.DOC** to open the document.

➤ Pull down the **File menu.** Click the **Save As** command to save the document as **MYCAR.DOC.**

➤ The title bar reflects **MYCAR.DOC,** but you can always return to the original document if you edit the duplicated file beyond redemption.

➤ If necessary, change to the **Page Layout view** at **Page Width.**

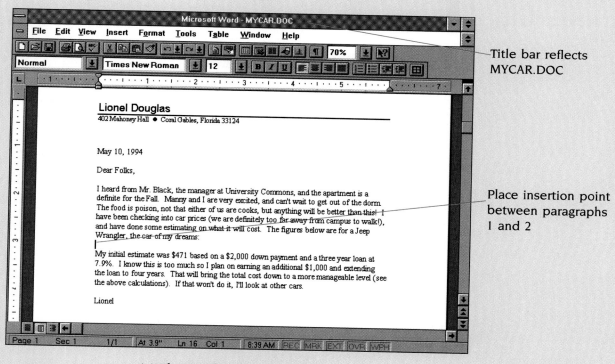

(a) The Word Document (step 1)

FIGURE A.2 Hands-on Exercise 1

Step 2: Embed the Excel spreadsheet

➤ Click the blank line between paragraphs one and two, the place in the document where the spreadsheet is to go.

➤ Pull down the **Insert menu,** click **Object,** then click the **Create from File** tab as shown in Figure A.2b.
  — Click the **drop-down list box** to specify the appropriate drive, which is the same drive you are using for the Word for Windows files.
  — Scroll through the directory list box until you come to the **EXCLDATA** directory. Double click this directory to make it the active directory.
➤ Click **CAR.XLS,** then click the **OK** command button to bring the spread-sheet into the document.

Click Create from File tab

Select CAR.XLS

Double click EXCLDATA
directory

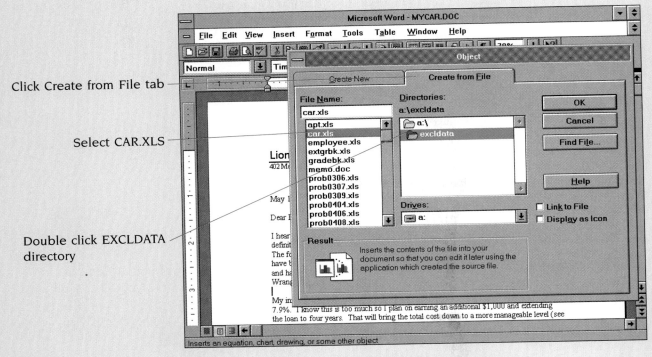

(b) Insert Object Command (step 2)

FIGURE A.2   Hands-on Exercise 1 (continued)

Step 3: Frame the spreadsheet
➤ Point to the spreadsheet, then click the **right mouse button** to produce a Shortcut menu.
➤ Click **Frame Picture** to frame the spreadsheet in order to position it more easily within the document.
➤ Drag the spreadsheet so that it is centered within the memo as shown in Figure A.2c. You may want to enter a blank line(s) between the paragraphs to give the spreadsheet more room.

Step 4: In-place editing
➤ Double click the spreadsheet in order to edit it in place as shown in Figure A.2d. Be patient as this step takes a while, even on a fast machine. Soon the Excel grid, the row and column labels, will appear around the spreadsheet as shown in Figure A.2d.
➤ You are still in Word as indicated by the title bar (Microsoft Word - MYCAR.DOC), but the Excel 5.0 toolbars are displayed in the document window.

- ➤ Click in cell **B3** and change the down payment to **$3,000.**
- ➤ Click in cell **E5** and change the years to **4.** The Monthly payment and Total per month drop to $195 and $385, respectively.

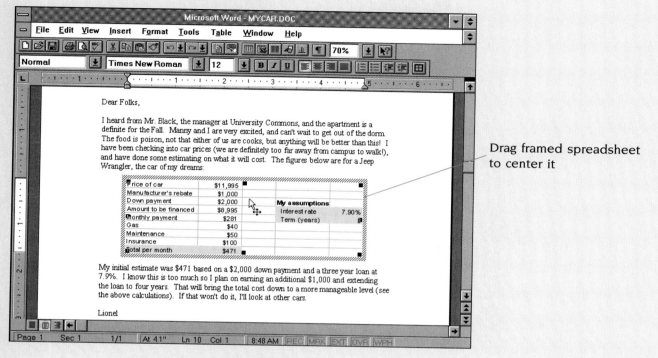

(c) Moving the Spreadsheet (step 3)

Drag framed spreadsheet to center it

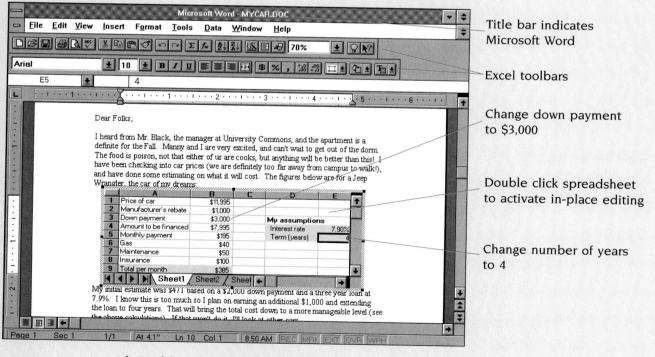

Title bar indicates Microsoft Word

Excel toolbars

Change down payment to $3,000

Double click spreadsheet to activate in-place editing

Change number of years to 4

(d) Modifying the Spreadsheet (step 4)

FIGURE A.2 Hands-on Exercise 1 (continued)

IN-PLACE EDITING

In-place editing is implemented in Microsoft's Object Linking and Embedding 2.0 specification and provides access to the toolbar and pull-down menus of the server application. Thus when editing an Excel spreadsheet embedded into a Word document, the title bar is that of the client application (Word for Windows), but the toolbar and pull-down menus reflect the server application (Excel). There are, however, two exceptions; the File and Window menus are those of the client application (Word) so that you can save the compound document and/or arrange multiple documents within the client application.

Step 5: Save the Word document
➤ Click anywhere outside the spreadsheet to deselect it and view the completed Word document as shown in Figure A.2e.
➤ Pull down the **File menu** and click **Save** (or click the **Save button** on the Standard toolbar).
➤ Exit Word, which returns you to Program Manager.

Step 6: View the original object
➤ If necessary, open the group window that contains Excel 5.0, then double click the **Excel 5.0 program icon** to load Excel.
➤ The *common user interface* imposed on all Windows applications implies

Monthly Payment and Total per month reflect changes made

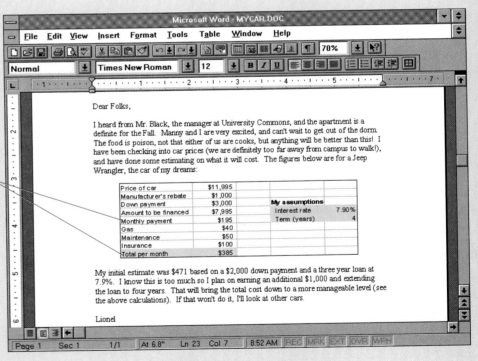

(e) Completed Word Document (step 5)

FIGURE A.2 Hands-on Exercise 1 (continued)

that the procedure to open a file in Excel will be similar (virtually identical) to the procedure in Word:

— Pull down the **File menu** and click **Open** (or click the **File Open button** on the toolbar).

— Click the **drop-down list box** to specify the appropriate drive, which is the same drive you have been using throughout the text.

— Scroll through the directory list box until you come to the **EXCLDATA** directory. Double click this directory to make it the active directory.

— Double click **CAR.XLS** to open the spreadsheet shown in Figure A.2f; this is the original (unmodified) spreadsheet, with a down payment of $2,000 and a three-year loan, that was first inserted into the Word document. The Monthly payment and Total per month are $281 and $471, respectively.

➤ Pull down the **File menu.** Click **Exit,** which returns you to Program Manager.

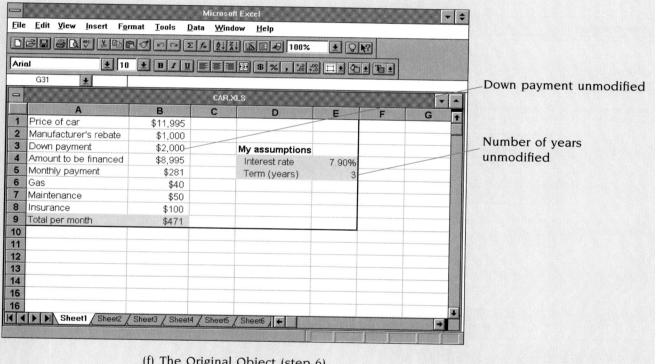

(f) The Original Object (step 6)

FIGURE A.2 Hands-on Exercise 1 (continued)

Linking

Linking is very different from embedding. Linking provides a dynamic connection between the source and destination documents; embedding does not. With linking, the source document (e.g., an Excel spreadsheet) is tied to the destination document (e.g., a Word document) in such a way that any changes in the Excel spreadsheet are automatically reflected in the Word document. The destination document contains a representation of the spreadsheet, as well as a pointer (that is, a link) to the file containing the spreadsheet.

Linking requires that the object be saved to disk prior to establishing the link. Embedding, on the other hand, lets you embed an object *without* saving it as a separate file. (The embedded object simply becomes part of the compound document.)

Consider now Figure A.3, in which the same spreadsheet is linked to two different documents. Both documents contain a pointer to the spreadsheet. In-place editing is not used as in the first exercise, which focused on an embedded object. Instead changes to the spreadsheet are made directly in the source document in Excel so that every document linked to the spreadsheet will reflect these changes.

The following exercise links a single Excel spreadsheet to two different Word documents. During the course of the exercise both applications (client and server) will be explicitly open, and it will be necessary to switch back and forth between the two. Thus the exercise also demonstrates the *multitasking* capability within Windows and the use of the *task list* to display the open applications. (See pages 53-75 in Grauer and Barber, *Exploring Windows,* Prentice Hall, 1994, for additional information on object linking and embedding, multitasking, and the common user interface.)

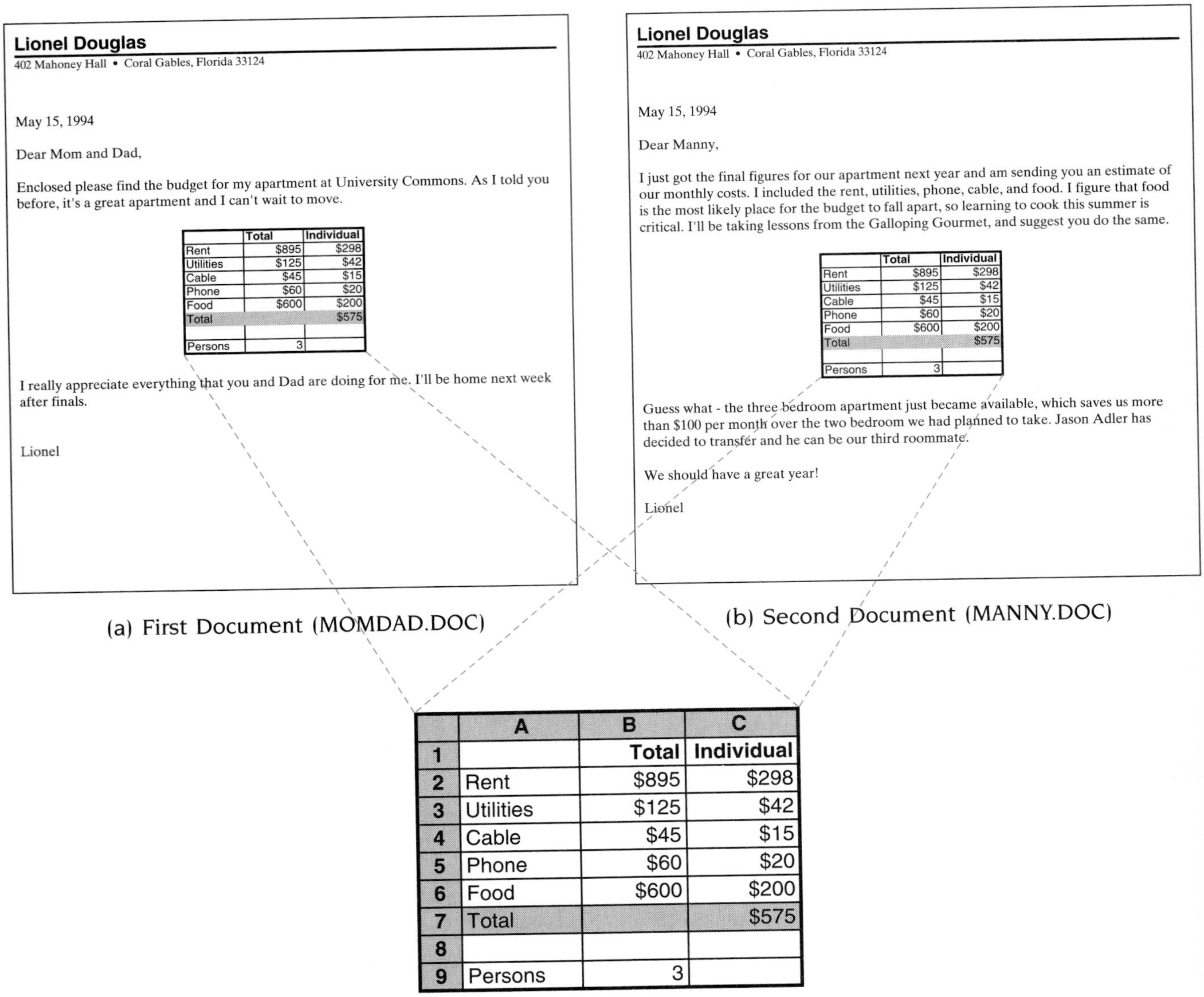

Lionel Douglas
402 Mahoney Hall • Coral Gables, Florida 33124

May 15, 1994

Dear Mom and Dad,

Enclosed please find the budget for my apartment at University Commons. As I told you before, it's a great apartment and I can't wait to move.

	Total	Individual
Rent	$895	$298
Utilities	$125	$42
Cable	$45	$15
Phone	$60	$20
Food	$600	$200
Total		$575
Persons	3	

I really appreciate everything that you and Dad are doing for me. I'll be home next week after finals.

Lionel

(a) First Document (MOMDAD.DOC)

Lionel Douglas
402 Mahoney Hall • Coral Gables, Florida 33124

May 15, 1994

Dear Manny,

I just got the final figures for our apartment next year and am sending you an estimate of our monthly costs. I included the rent, utilities, phone, cable, and food. I figure that food is the most likely place for the budget to fall apart, so learning to cook this summer is critical. I'll be taking lessons from the Galloping Gourmet, and suggest you do the same.

	Total	Individual
Rent	$895	$298
Utilities	$125	$42
Cable	$45	$15
Phone	$60	$20
Food	$600	$200
Total		$575
Persons	3	

Guess what - the three bedroom apartment just became available, which saves us more than $100 per month over the two bedroom we had planned to take. Jason Adler has decided to transfer and he can be our third roommate.

We should have a great year!

Lionel

(b) Second Document (MANNY.DOC)

	A	B	C
1		Total	Individual
2	Rent	$895	$298
3	Utilities	$125	$42
4	Cable	$45	$15
5	Phone	$60	$20
6	Food	$600	$200
7	Total		$575
8			
9	Persons	3	

(c) Spreadsheet (APT.XLS)

FIGURE A.3   Linking

HANDS-ON EXERCISE 2:

Linking

Objective To demonstrate multitasking and the ability to switch between applications; to link an Excel spreadsheet to multiple Word documents. The exercise requires both Word 6.0 and Excel 5.0.

Step 1: Open the Word document
➤ Load Word. Pull down the **File menu** and click **Open** (or click the **File Open button** on the toolbar).
➤ If you have not yet changed the default directory:
— Click the **drop-down list box** to specify the appropriate drive, which is the same drive you have been using throughout the text.
— Scroll through the directory list box until you come to the **WORDDATA** directory. Double click this directory to make it the active directory.
➤ Double click **MOMDAD.DOC** to open this document.
➤ If necessary, change to the **Page Layout view** at **Page Width.**

Step 2: Load Excel
➤ Press **Ctrl+Esc** to display the task list as in Figure A.4a. The contents of the task list depend on the applications open on your system, but you should see Microsoft Word and Program Manager.
➤ Double click **Program Manager** to switch to Program Manager.
➤ If necessary, open the group window that contains Excel 5.0 (for example, Microsoft Office), then double click the **Excel 5.0 program icon** to load Excel.

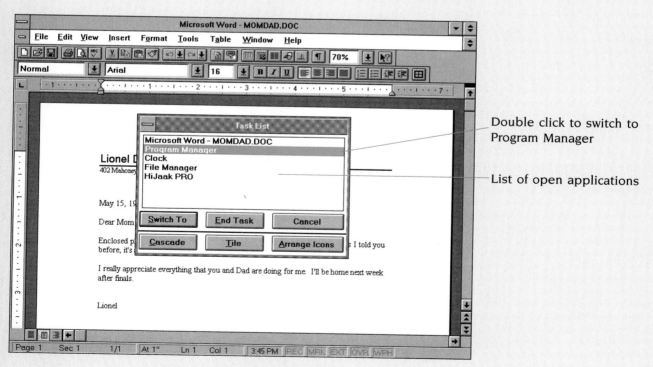

Double click to switch to Program Manager

List of open applications

(a) Display the Task List (step 2)

FIGURE A.4 Hands-on Exercise 2

USE ALT+TAB TO SWITCH BETWEEN APPLICATIONS

Press and hold the Alt key while you press and release the Tab key repeatedly to cycle through the open applications. Release the Alt key when you see the title bar of the application you want.

Step 3: Open the APT.XLS spreadsheet
➤ Pull down the **File menu** and click **Open** (or click the **File Open button** on the toolbar).
➤ Click the **drop-down list box** to specify the appropriate drive.
➤ Scroll through the directory list box until you come to the **EXCLDATA** directory. Double click this directory to make it the active directory.
➤ Double click **APT.XLS** to open the spreadsheet.

Step 4: Copy the spreadsheet to the clipboard
➤ Click in cell **A1.** Drag the mouse over cells **A1 through C9** so that the entire spreadsheet is selected as shown in Figure A.4b.
➤ Point to the selected area, then press the **right mouse button** to display a Shortcut menu as shown in the figure. Click **Copy.** A flashing dashed line (known as a marquee) appears around the entire spreadsheet, indicating that the spreadsheet has been copied to the clipboard.
➤ Press **Ctrl+Esc** to display the task list. Double click **Microsoft Word - MOM-DAD.DOC** to return to the Word document.

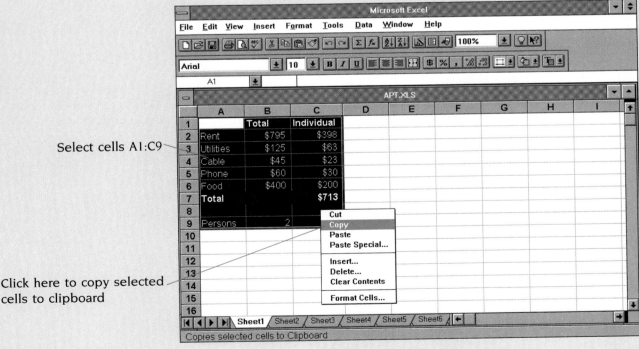

Select cells A1:C9

Click here to copy selected cells to clipboard

(b) Copying to the Clipboard (step 4)

FIGURE A.4   Hands-on Exercise 2 (continued)

Step 5: Create the Link

➤ Click in the document where you want the spreadsheet.

➤ Pull down the **Edit menu.** Click **Paste Special** to produce the dialog box in Figure A.4c.

➤ Click the **Paste Link** option button. Click **Microsoft Excel 5.0 Worksheet Object.** Click **OK** to insert the spreadsheet into the document as shown in Figure A.4d. You may want to insert a blank line before and after the spreadsheet to make it easier to read.

➤ Save the document containing the letter to Mom and Dad.

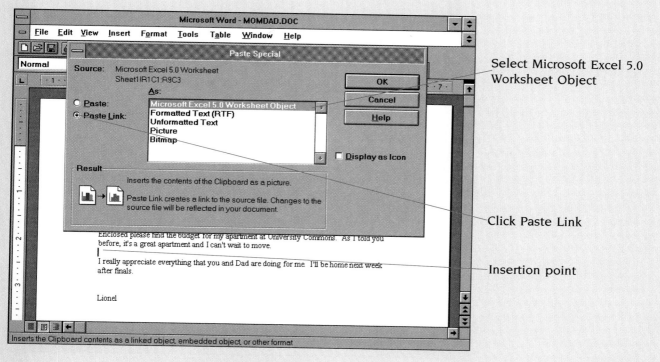

(c) Create the Link (step 5)

FIGURE A.4 Hands-on Exercise 2 (continued)

Step 6: Open the second Word document.

➤ Pull down the **File menu** and click **Open** (or click the **File Open button** on the toolbar).

➤ Double click **MANNY.DOC** to open the *second* document as shown in Figure A.4e, but without the spreadsheet.

➤ The spreadsheet is still in the clipboard. Click in the document where you want the spreadsheet to go.

➤ Pull down the **Edit menu.** Click **Paste Special.** Click the **Paste Link** option button. Click **Microsoft Excel 5.0 Worksheet Object.** Click **OK** to insert the spreadsheet into the document.

➤ Save the document containing the letter to Manny.

Step 7: Modify the spreadsheet

➤ Double click the spreadsheet in order to change it; the system pauses as it switches to Excel and returns to the source document APT.XLS, as shown in Figure A.4f.

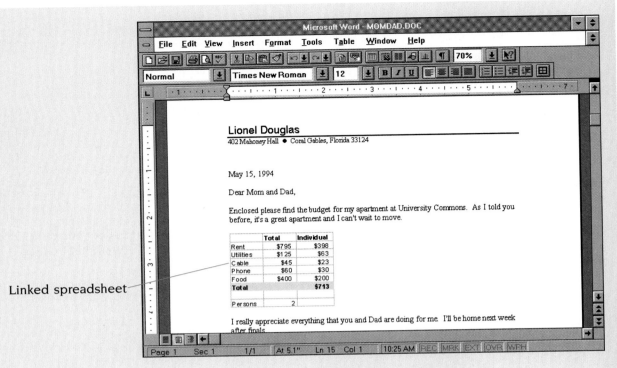

Linked spreadsheet

(d) Create the Link (step 5)

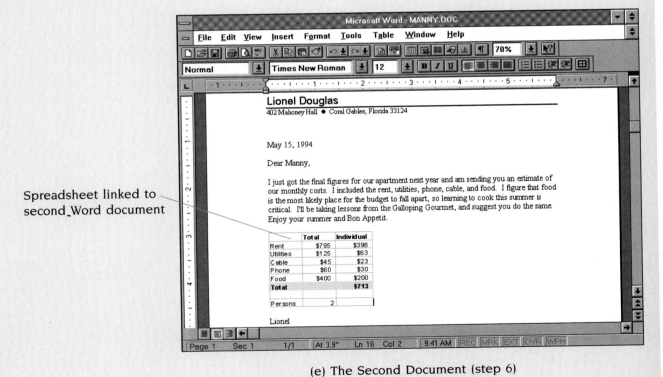

Spreadsheet linked to second Word document

(e) The Second Document (step 6)

FIGURE A.4 Hands-on Exercise 2 (continued)

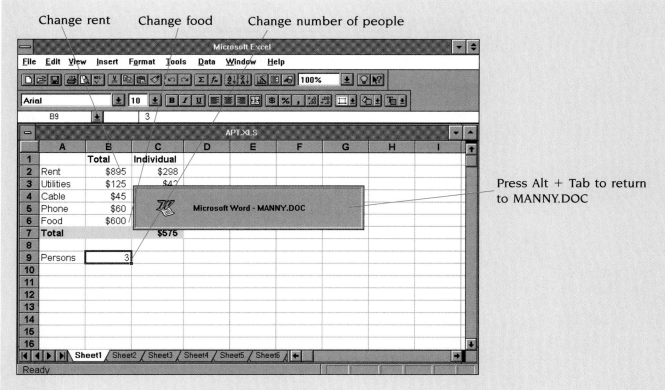

Change rent   **Change food**   **Change number of people**

Press Alt + Tab to return to MANNY.DOC

(f) Modify the Spreadsheet (step 7)

FIGURE A.4 Hands-on Exercise 2 (continued)

➤ Cells **A1 through C9** are still selected from step 4. Click outside the selected range to deselect the spreadsheet.

➤ Click in cell **B2.** Type **$895,** the rent for a three-bedroom apartment.

➤ Click in cell **B6.** Type **$600,** the increased amount for food.

➤ Click in cell **B9.** Type **3** to change the number of people sharing the apartment.

➤ Pull down the **File menu** and click **Save** (or click the **Save icon**) to save the modified spreadsheet.

Step 8: The modified documents

➤ Press and hold the **Alt key** while you press and release the **Tab key** repeatedly to cycle through the open applications. Release the Alt key when you see **Microsoft Word - MANNY.DOC** in a box in the middle of the screen as in Figure A.4f.

➤ The active application changes to Word and you should see the letter to Manny as shown in Figure A.4g; the document displays the modified spreadsheet because of the link established in step 5. Modify the text as shown to let Manny know about the new apartment. Save the document.

➤ Pull down the **Window menu.** Click **MOMDAD.DOC** to switch to the letter to your parents. The note to your parents also contains the updated spreadsheet (with three roommates) because of the link created in step 5.

➤ Exit Word.

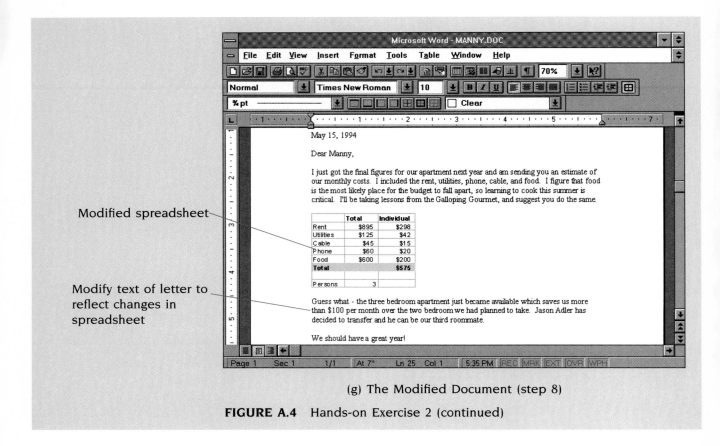

Modified spreadsheet

Modify text of letter to reflect changes in spreadsheet

(g) The Modified Document (step 8)

FIGURE A.4 Hands-on Exercise 2 (continued)

SUMMARY

Linking requires that the source document be saved as a separate file, and further that the link between the source and destination document be maintained. The link will be broken if you give a colleague a copy of the compound document without including the source document. Linking is useful when the same object is present in multiple destination documents. Any subsequent change to the object is made in only one place (the source document), and is automatically reflected in the multiple destination documents.

Embedding does not require a separate source document because the object is contained within the destination document. Embedding lets you give your colleague a copy of the compound document, without the source document, and indeed, there need not be a source document. You would not, however, want to embed the same object into multiple destination documents because any subsequent change to the object would have to be made in every destination document.

Key Words and Concepts

Client application	Embedded object	Object Linking and Embedding (OLE)
Clipboard	In-place editing	Server application
Common user interface	Insert Object command	Source document
Compound document	Linking	Static connection
Destination document	Multitasking	Task list
Dynamic connection	Object	

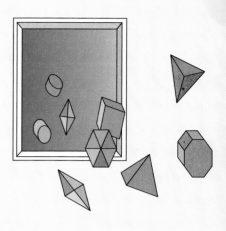

Index

Note: Letters preceding page references refer to the following parts of the text:
W = *Word for Windows* E = *Microsoft Excel*
A = *Microsoft Access* P = *Microsoft PowerPoint*
OLE = *OLE Appendix*

Absolute reference, E44
  shortcut for, E108
Accounting format, E54
Active cell, E15
Agenda Wizard, W111,
  W113–W116
Aggregate functions, A108
Alignment, E56, W67–W68
AND condition, A100
Annotation tool. *See* Freehand
  annotation tool
Antivirus, in Microsoft Tools, A3,
  E3, W3
Antonym, W95
Application window, A3, E3, W3
Arguments, E84
Arial, W56–W57
Arithmetic precedence, E14
Arrow tool, E136, E143
Assumptions, isolation of, E84
AutoContent Wizard, P42–P43
AutoCorrect, W12, W92,
  W94–W95, W103–W104
Autofill, E104–E105
Autofit selection, E92
AutoFormat, with charts, E150
AutoLayout, P13, P15
Automatic replacement, W43
AutoReport, A86
AVERAGE function, E97
Avg function, A108
Award Wizard, W111, W117

Background color, P53
Background shading, P55–P56

Backup, W43–W45, W49–W50
  in Microsoft Tools, A3, E3, W3
BAK extension, W45, W49–W50
Bar chart, E129–E131
Best fit, E94
Between function, A100
Boolean field. *See* Yes/No field
Borders and Shading command,
  W72, W73, W78
Borders button, W78
Border tab, E57, E66
Bound control, A57
Break point, E100
Build slide, P34, P57, P60–P61
Bullets, indentation of, P17
Business writing, W98

Calculated control, A57, A63
Calculated field, A46
Calendar wizard, W111
Cascade menu, E7
Case conversion, W10
Case-insensitive replacement,
  W42–W43
Case-sensitive replacement,
  W42–W43
Casual writing, W98
Category label, E132
Cell, E13
Cell contents, E14
  changing of, E49
Cell formulas, E42
  shortcut for, E69
Cell range, E43, E52
Cell reference, E13

Center across columns, E63, E94
Center tab. *See* Tabs
Character formatting, W61–W67
Chart, E126–E166
  abuse of, E164–E165
  default, E149
  deleting, E132
  enhancing, E135–E136, E143
  moving, E132
  sizing, E132
  types of, E163–E164
Chart sheet, E131
  copying, E149
Chart toolbar, E135
ChartWizard, E133–E135,
  E137–E139
Check box, E7, W10
Clear command, E28
Click, E5, W7
  with right mouse button, E28
Client application, E155, OLE215
Clip art, P17–P18, P58–P59
Clipboard, E44, E80, E155, W41,
  W52, OLE215
Clock, adjusting of, E102
Collapsed outline, P41
Color, E67
Color scheme, P53–P55, P62–P63
Column chart, E129–E131
Column command, E22
Column heading, E13
  printing of, E61
Column width, E54–E55
  adjustment of, A112
  best fit, E94

Combination chart, E164–E165
Combo box, adding to a form,
  A70–A72
Command button, E9, W10
  adding to a form, A65–A69
Common user interface, A3, A18,
  E3–E5, E158, P4, P32, W3–W5
Compound document, E155,
  OLE215
Constant, E14
Control, A57–A58
  aligning of, A64
  moving of, A59, A63
  properties of, A94
  sizing of, A59, A63
Control-menu box, A3, E3, P2, W3
Copy command, E43–E44,
  E49–E50, W41. *See also* Drag
  and drop
  shortcut for, W54
COUNTA function, E97
Counter field, A47
Count function, A108
COUNT function, E97
Criteria row, A99
Crossword, help with, W94
Cue cards, A8, A39, A69, P24,
  P26–P29, P65–P69
Currency field, A47
Currency format, E55
Current record, A12
Custom dictionary, W92, W105
Custom series, creation of, E106
Cut command, E46, E51, W41
  shortcut for, W54

Data, versus information, A85, A86
Database, creation of, A49
Database management system, A10
Database window, A10–A11
Data disk, installation of, P7, W17
Data point, E126
Data series, E126
  multiple, E145–E147
Datasheet view, A12–A13, A17,
  A47
Data source, W118
Data type. *See* Field type
Data validation, A20, A25–A26.
  See also Validation rule
Date, adding to a master, P65
Date arithmetic, E101–E102
Date field, A47, W101
  in select query, A99–A100
  updating of, W103, W104
Date format, E54

DATE function, E101–E102
Date text, W101
DBMS, A10
Decimal places property, A48
Decimal tab. *See* Tabs
Default chart, E149
Default directory, A50, E48,
  W50
Default presentation, P46
Default value property, A48
Delete command, A25, E22, E25
  versus Edit Clear command, E28
Deleting text, W14, W26
Demote, P48
Design view
  forms, A57–A58
  queries, A99–A102
  reports, A88–A89, A108–A109
  tables, A11, A17, A47
Desktop, E2–E3, W2
Destination document, E155,
  OLE215
Destination range, E43
Detail section, A89, A109
Dialog box, A5–A7, E7–E9,
  W9–W10
  shortcuts for, A23, W64
Dimmed command, E7, W9
DOC extension, W43
Docked toolbar, E136
Document window, A3, E3, W3
Double click, E5, W7
  problems with, E16, P8
Drag, E6, W7
Drag and drop, P49, W55
Drawing toolbar, E136, E143
Drop-down list box, A6, E9, W10
Drop shadow, W72
Dynaset, A97

Edit Clear command, E91
  shortcut for, E92
Editing (changing cell contents),
  E49
Elevator, P20, P21
Ellipsis, E7, W9
Embedded chart, E131–E132
Embedding, OLE217–221
End of file marker, W13
Enter mode, E88
Envelopes and Labels command,
  W102, W108
Expanded outline, P41
Exploded pie chart, E127–E129

Fax wizard, W111, W112–W113

Field, A11
  inserting or deleting, A53
  properties of, A48–A49
Field code, W103
Field name, rules for, A46
Field property, A48–A49
Field result, W103
Field row, A99
Field size property, A48, A55
Field type, A46–A47, A52
Fill handle, E87–E88
Find and Replace command, E97
Find command, A20, W42–W43,
  W52
First-line indent. *See* Indents
Floating toolbar, A67, E136
Font, E56–E57, W57
Footer, A89, A109, E59
  adding and removing, A93
Form, A10, A57–A74
  Design View, A57–A58
  Form View, A57–A58
Format Cells command, E54–E57
Format Font command, W59
Format Object command, E140
Format painter, E66, W59, W64
Format Paragraph command,
  W71–W73
Format property, A48
Formatting, E52–E57
  automatic, E64
Formatting toolbar, E5, E22–E23,
  E53, P5–P6, P67, W5–W6
Formula, E14
  adjustment in, E21
Formula bar, E15
Form Wizard, A58, A60–A61
Fraction format, E55
Freehand annotation tool, P12,
  P51, P63
Freezing panes, E103–E104
Function, E14
  adjustment in, E21
  versus formula, E97–E98
Function Wizard, E88–E89, E92,
  E93

GIGO (garbage in, garbage out),
  A20
Global replacement, W43
Grammar checker, W96–W98,
  W106–W107
Gridlines, E57
  suppression of, E61
Group footer, A89, A109
Group header, A89, A109

Group/Total Report, A86, A108–A117

Handouts Master, P64
Hanging indent, W70
Hard page break, W60, W66
Hard return, W16
Header, A89, A109, E59
  adding and removing, A93
Help, A7–A9
Help button, P24–P25, W27, W73, W78–W79
  on Standard toolbar, E28
Help menu, E9–E11, E30, P23, W10
Horizontal ruler, W7

I-beam, versus insertion point, W25
IF function, E98–E100, E107
Illegal cell reference, E98
Indent button, W79
Indents, W69–W70, W76–W77
Indexed property, A48
Information, versus data, A85, A86
Inheritance, A59, A90
In-place editing, E155, OLE216, OLE218–220
Input mask, A48, A53–A54
Insert Columns command, E28
Insert Date command, W101
Insertion mode, W13–W14, W51–W52
Insertion point, A6, A13, P41, W13
  movement of, W35, W51
  with paragraph formatting, W75
Insert menu, E22
Insert Object command, OLE215, OLE218
Insert Rows command, E27
Insert Symbol command, W102, W107–W108

Justification. See Alignment

Label tool, A95, A96
Landscape orientation, E58, W60
Layout button, P4
Leader character, W68
Left indent. See Indents
Left tab. See Tabs
Legend, E148
Line chart, E163–E164
Line spacing, W71
Linking, E155–E163, OLE221–228
List box, E9, W10
Logical field. See Yes/No field

Logical test, E99
Lotus 1-2-3, conversion from, E9

Macro, A10
Mailing labels, A86, A88
Mail merge, A86, W118–W129
  exercise on, A125–A126
  help with, W122
Main document, W118
Margins, W60, W64
  changing of, A57
  versus indents, W70
Marquee, E49, E88
Masters, P64–P68
Max function, A108
MAX function, E96
Maximize button, A3, E3, W3
MDB extension, A16
Memo field, A47
Menu bar, A3, E3, P2, W3
Merge code, W120
Microsoft Tools, A3, E3, W3
Min function, A108
MIN function, E96
Minimize button, A3, E3, W3
Mixed reference, E44
Module, A10
Monospaced font, W59
Mouse
  for left-handed persons, E6, W8
  operations with, A3–A4, E5–E6, W7–W8
  practice with, A14, P7
  tutorial, E16, W17
Mouse pointer, E6, W7
Move command, E44–E46
Moving text, W41. See also Drag and drop
Multiple documents, working with, W117–W118
Multitasking, E155, OLE222
  switching applications, E159

Name box, E15
Navigation buttons, A18
New Slide button, P4
Noncontiguous range, E64, E67
Normal template, W110
Normal view, W22, W24, W46–W47
  icon for, W49
Notes Master, P64
Notes Pages view, P13–P14, P22–P23
NOW function, E105

Number field, A46
  in select query, A99
Number format, E54–E55

Object, E155
  naming of, A111
  types of, A10
Object Linking and Embedding (OLE), A83, E155–E163, OLE215–218
  embedding clip art, A124–A125
OLE field, A47
On-line help, P23–P29, W10, W27–W28. See also Help; Help menu
Open command, E22, E25, W23
Open Database command, A15–A16
Open list box, E17, W10
Option button, A6, E7, E8, W10–W12
OR condition, A100
Orientation, changing of, A57
Outline toolbar, P41–P42
Outline view, P13–P14, P19–P20, P40–P42
  moving text in, P49
  selecting slides in, P49
Overtype mode, W13–W14, W51–W52

Page break, W60, W71–W72
Page footer, A89, A109
Page header, A89, A109
Page Layout view, W22, W24, W46–W47
  icon for, W49
Page number, adding to a master, P65
Page Setup command, E58–61, E95, W60
Palette toolbar, A66
Paragraph formatting, W67–W80
Paragraph mark, effect on formatting, W72
Paste command, E44, E46, E55, E155, W41
  shortcut for, W54
Paste Link command, OLE225
Paste Special command, E159, E160, OLE225
Patterns tab, E57
Percent format, E55
Pick a Look Wizard, P43–P44, P50–P51
Pie chart, E127–E129

Placeholder, P15
PMT function, E82, E84–E87
Point, E5, W7
Pointing, E88, E92–E94
Point mode, E88
Point size, E56. *See also* Type size
Portrait orientation, E58, W60
PowerPoint, loading of, P7–P8
PPT extension, P9
Presentation
 annotation, P12
 creating, P45–P52
 opening, P9
 printing, P12
 rehearsing, P26–P29
 showing, P10, P24, P26–P29
 views in, P13–P14
Presley, Elvis, W99
Primary key, A47
 changing of, A52
Print command, A19, E19, W20
 options in, E58–E61
 selected pages, W109
Printing
 handouts, P12
 note pages, P23
 outline, P52
Print preview, versus sample pre-
  view, A116
Print Preview command, E59, E68
Print Setup command, A57
Program Manager, A2–A3, E3, W3
Promote, P48
Proportional font, W59
Pull-down menu, A5, E6–E7, E20,
  W8–W9

QBE grid, A97
Query, A10, A97–A107
 select query, A97, A102–A108
 updating of, A97
Query window, A99
 views in, A99
Quick Preview, P29
Quit, without saving, W43

Radio button, W10
Range, E43, E52
Record, A11, W118
 adding, A18–A19
 deleting, A25
 editing, A23–A24
 saving, A12
Record selector symbol, A12, A47
Redo command, W41, W54
Reference manual, creation of, E80

Relational database, A29–A31
Relational operator, A100, E99
Relative reference, E44
Repeat command, W41
Replace command, A28,
  W42–W43, W52
Report, A10
 design of, A86–A89
 types of, A86
Report footer, A89, A109
Report header, A89, A109
Report Wizard, A90–A96
Required property, A48, A54
Restore button, A3, E3, W3
Résumé Wizard, W110
Right indent. *See* Indents
Right tab. *See* Tabs
Row command, E22
Row heading, E13
 printing of, E61
Row height, E55
Row selector, A25
Ruler
 setting indents, W77
 setting tabs, W76

Sample preview, versus print pre-
  view, A116
Sans serif typeface, W57
Save As command, E22, E25, W43,
  W50
Save command, E18, E19, E22,
  P46, W19, W43
Scaling, in printing, E59
Scientific format, E55
Scroll bar, E3, W3
 missing, E105
Scroll box, A3, E3, W3. *See also*
  Elevator
Scrolling, E102–E103, W45–W47,
  W51
 keyboard shortcuts for, W51
Search command, P24–P25
Selecting text, W40
 with F8 key, W74
 with selection bar, W62
Selective replacement, W43
Select query, A97, A102–A108
Select-then-do, P18–P19, P41, W40
Serial date, E101
Serif typeface, W57
Server application, E155, OLE215
Shortcut menu, E28, E59, E143,
  W40, W62, W104
Show/Hide button, W19, W25
Show row, A99

Side-by-side column chart, E146
Sizing handles, E132
Slide master, P64–P65
Slide show, P57
Slide Show view, P13–P14
Slide Sorter toolbar, P57, P60
 selecting slides in, P61
Slide Sorter view, P13–P14,
  P19–P20
Slide view, P13–P14
Soft page break, W60, W65
Soft return, W16
Sort, in mail merge, W129
Sort row, A99
 with multiple fields, A111
Sounds like, in Find command,
  W43
Source document, E155, OLE215
Source range, E43
Spell check, E87, E90
Spelling checker, P50, W92–W94,
  W104–W105
 icon for, W114
Spreadsheet
 introduction to, E11–E14
 versus worksheet, E15
SQL view, A99
Stacked columns, E146
Standard toolbar, E5, E22–E23,
  E29, P5, W5–W6
Statistical functions, E96–E97
Status bar, E16, P4, W7
Sum function, A108
Summary information, E25, P47
Summary statistics, W28
Symbols font, W102
Synonym, W95

Tabbed dialog box, E7
Table
 creation of, A46
 design of, A44–A46
 moving in, A17–A18
 saving, A12
 views of, A11–A12, A17, A47
Table lookup, E100
Table Wizard, A46, A51
Tab order, changing of, A72
Tabs, W68, W75–W76
Tabular report, A86
Task list, E155, E157, E158,
  OLE222
Technical support, E9, W10
Template, E82, E84, P44, W110
 changing of, P53, P61–P62
Template button, P4, P44

Text box, E9, W10
  on charts, E136, E143
Text field, A46
  in select query, A99–A100, A104
Text format, E55
Text tool, P67, P68
Thesaurus, W95–W96, W106
Time
  adding to a master, P65
  insertion of, W101
  setting internal clock, W102
Time format, E54
Times New Roman, W56–W57
Tip of the Day, P8, W11
  display of, W18
TipWizard, E22, E24
  resetting of, E47
Title bar, A3, E3, P2, W3
TODAY function, E101, E105,
  E106
Toggle switch, W13
Toolbar, E5, E22–E23, P5–P6
  changing of, E24, W24
  chart, E135
  customizing, W108
  display of, W23
  docked, E136
  drawing, E136, E143
  floating, A67, E136
  formatting, E5, E22–E23, E53,
    P5–P6, P67, W5–W6
  help with, A29, E27
  outline, P41–P42
  palette, A66
  slide sorter, P57, P60
  standard, E5, E22–E23, E29, P5,
    W5–W6
  toolbox, A66

Toolbox toolbar, A66
ToolTips, E7
Top Value property, A114
  with USA database, A126
Transition effect, P57, P59–P61
Troubleshooting, W22–W23
TrueType, E56, W58–W59
Typeface, W56–W57
Type size, W57–W58
Typography, W56–W59

Unbound control, A57
  adding of, A94–A96
Undelete command, in Microsoft
  Tools, A3, E3, W3
Undo command, A20, A24, A56,
  E11, E19, E25, P21, P62, W15,
  W27–W28, W41, W54
Undo Current Field command, A20
Undo Current Record command,
  A20
Undo Saved Record command,
  A20
Undo Typing command, A20
Unindent button, W79

Validation rule property, A48, A54
Validation text property, A48
Value, E54
Vertical ruler, W7, W80
View button, P4
View menu, W23, W24, W46–W48,
  W49
VLOOKUP function, E100–E101,
  E109

What-If analysis, E82, E83
Whole word replacement, W42

Widows and orphans, W72
Wildcard
  in Find command, W43
  in select query, A100
  with spell checker, W94
Windows
  loading of, E16, P7, W17
  tutorial, A14
Wingdings font, W102
Wizards, W110–W118
Word for Windows, common user
  interface, E4–E5
WordPerfect, conversion from,
  W10, W23
Word processing, basics of,
  W13–W16
Word wrap, W15–W16
Workbook, E5, E15
Worksheet
  copying, E151, E153
  renaming, E151

X axis, E129
XLS extension, E22

Y axis, E129
Yes/No field, A47

Zoom command, W47–W48
  many pages, W79–W80